This extremely perceptive study of late twentieth-century Russian Baptist theology and practice, which analyzes a wide range of periodical and oral evidence, is very welcome. Whilst common perception, with much good reason, distances the life and thought of the Baptist and Orthodox denominations in Russia from each other, Constantine Prokhorov helpfully identifies, in a period of political conflict between East and West, much common ground in piety, liturgy and thought. This work also indicates how both denominations are situated within developing and changing Russian culture.

Dr John Briggs
Research Professor
International Baptist Theological Seminary, Prague

This is an outstanding work of historical research, which probes in detail the relationship between Russian Baptist communities and the Russian Orthodox Church in the period 1960-1990. Constantine Prokhorov draws from a very wide range of Russian primary sources and personal interviews to show that in this period Russian Baptist life reflected Orthodox thinking and practice in a number of crucial areas. His argument, which is presented in an appealing and a compelling way, has profound implications for an understanding of evangelical-Orthodox relationships in Russia and also elsewhere.

Dr Ian Randall
Senior Research Fellow
Spurgeon's College, London

D1562836

Russian Baptists and Orthodoxy, 1960-1990: A Comparative Study of Theology, Liturgy, and Traditions

Constantine Prokhorov

Langham

MONOGRAPHS

Published 2013 by Langham Monographs.
an imprint of Langham Creative Projects

Langham Partnership
PO Box 296, Carlisle, Cumbria CA3 9WZ, UK
www.langham.org

ISBNs:
978-1-783689-90-3 Print
978-1-783689-89-7 Mobi
978-1-783689-88-0 ePub

British Library Cataloguing in Publication Data
Prokhorov, Constantine, author.
  Russian baptists and orthodoxy : 1960-1990 : a comparative
study of theology, liturgy, and traditions.
  1. Baptists--Soviet Union--History--20th century.
  2. Russkaia pravoslavnaia tserkov--History--20th century.
  3. Baptists--Relations--Russkaia pravoslavnaia tserkov.
  4. Russkaia pravoslavnaia tserkov--Relations--Baptists.
  5. Baptists--Soviet Union--Doctrines--History--20th
century. 6. Russkaia pravoslavnaia tserkov--Doctrines--
History--20th century. 7. Baptists--Soviet Union--
Liturgy. 8. Russkaia pravoslavnaia tserkov--Liturgy.
  9. Baptists--Soviet Union--Customs and practices.
  10. Russkaia pravoslavnaia tserkov--Customs and practices.
  I. Title
  280'.042'0947'09045-dc23

  ISBN-13: 9781783689903

Cover & Book Design: projectluz.com

To Dr. Ian and Janice Randall with my heartfelt gratitude

Contents

Abstract

Russian Baptists and the Orthodox Church have had a difficult and, at times, dramatic relationship over the past century and a half. However, the purpose of this thesis is to examine certain internal connections between these two Christian bodies. Despite the evident dissimilarity in theology, church practice and traditions, there is common ground which has been largely unexplored. A number of features inevitably brought them together, such as living in the same country over a long period of time, sharing a history and national roots, responding to the same civic concerns, and finally, until recently, using the same Russian ("Synodal") translation of the Bible.

This study explores, first of all, the roots of the issue of Orthodox-Baptist similarities and dissimilarities in the nineteenth century. The remainder of the work focuses on 1960 to 1990. There is a chapter analyzing the way in which, in significant areas, Russian Baptist theology resembled Orthodox thinking. This is followed by a study of church and sacraments, which again shows that Russian Baptist approaches had echoes of Orthodoxy. The study then explores Baptist liturgy, showing the Orthodox elements that were present. The same connections are then explored in the area of Russian Baptist communal spiritual traditions. The examination of the Bible, beliefs and behavior also indicates the extent to which Russian Baptists mirrored Orthodoxy. Finally there is an analysis of the popular piety of the Russian Baptists and the way in which they constructed an alternative culture.

The basic views of Russian Baptists between the 1960s and 1990 have been drawn from periodicals of the Russian Baptist communities and from interviews with pastors (presbyters) and church members who were part of these communities. This often yields insights into "primary theology", which in relation to many issues differs from official Baptist declarations that tend to stress the more Protestant aspects of Russian Baptist life.

The aim of the study is to show that in a period in the history of the USSR when the division between the Western world and the Soviet bloc was marked, there was a strong Eastern orientation among Russian Baptists. This changed when the USSR came to an end. Over a number of years there was mass emigration of Russian Baptists and, in addition, pro-Western thinking gained considerable ground within the Russian Baptist community. During the period examined here, however, it is possible to uncover a great deal of evidence of Russian Baptists participating in Orthodox theology, spiritual mentality and culture.

Abbreviations

Anon	Anonym, anonymous
ARSECB	*Arkhiv Rossiyskogo Soyuza Evangel'skikh Khristian-Baptistov, Arkhiv AUCECB* [The Archives of the Russian Union of the Evangelical Christians-Baptists, the AUCECB Archives, Moscow]
AUCECB	The All-Union Council of Evangelical Christians–Baptists
Bapt.	*Baptist* (periodical)
BV	*Bratsky Vestnik* [Fraternal Bulletin]
BL	*Bratsky Listok* [Fraternal Leaflet]
BSRUECB	*Byulleten' Soveta Rodstvennikov Uznikov Evangel'skikh Khristian-Baptistov v SSSR* [Bulletin of the Council of Prisoners' Relatives of the Evangelical Christians-Baptists of the USSR]
CCECB	The Council of Churches of Evangelical Christians–Baptists
ECB	Evangelical Christians–Baptists
IEDE-2	*Istoriya evangel'skogo dvizheniya v Evrazii* [History of the Evangelical Movement in Eurasia] 2.0 (Windows CD-ROM)
IEDE-4	*Istoriya evangel'skogo dvizheniya v Evrazii* [History of the Evangelical Movement in Eurasia] 4.0 (Windows CD-ROM)
INT	Interview
M.	Moscow
Prep.	*Prepodobny* [Saint]
PV	*Pesn' Vozrozhdeniya* [Song of Revival]
Sv.	*Svyatoy* [Saint]
SV	*Slovo Very* [Word of Faith]

SDP   *Sbornik Dukhovnykh Pesen Evangel'skikh Khristian Baptistov* [The Songbook of the Evangelical Christians-Baptists]

SPb.   St. Petersburg

VestI   *Vestnik Istiny* [Bulletin of the Truth]

VS   *Vestnik Spaseniya* [Bulletin of Salvation]

ZhMP   *Zhurnal Moskovskoy Patriarkhii* [Journal of the Moscow Patriarchate]

ZhSDR   *Zhitiya Svyatykh, Na Russkom Yazyke Izlozhennye po Rukovodstvu Chet'ikh-Miney Sv. Dimitriya Rostovskogo* [Lives of Saints, in the Russian Language, Retold According to the Menology by St. Dimitry Rostovsky], 12 vols. (Moscow: Sinodal'naya Tipografiya, 1903-1911).

Transliteration

In this study, the established English spellings of common Russian names and terms, as found in common dictionaries, will be used. Other Cyrillic words will be transliterated by the following system:

А	–	*A*
Б	–	*B*
В	–	*V*
Г	–	*G*
Д	–	*D*
Е	–	*E*
Ё	–	*YE*
Ж	–	*ZH*
З	–	*Z*
И	–	*I*
Й	–	*Y*
К	–	*K*
Л	–	*L*
М	–	*M*
Н	–	*N*
О	–	*O*
П	–	*P*
Р	–	*R*
С	–	*S*
Т	–	*T*
У	–	*U*

Ф	–	*F*
Х	–	*KH*
Ц	–	*TS*
Ч	–	*CH*
Ш	–	*SH*
Щ	–	*SHCH*
Ъ	–	"
Ы	–	*Y*
Ь	–	'
Э	–	*E*
Ю	–	*YU*
Я	–	*YA.*

Preface and Acknowledgements

This study examines recent history: the period 1960 to 1990 in the USSR. In looking at Soviet Baptists in this period, I am drawing mainly from primary sources. My aim is to seek to show how the Soviet Baptists, who have been considered as part of the worldwide Protestant movement, displayed many features that were similar to Russian Orthodoxy. In pursuing this line of enquiry, I have made a comparative analysis of many Orthodox and Russian Baptist sources and sought to engage in critical judgment during the analysis. This work is cross-disciplinary in character, looking at aspects of history, sociology, theology, culture, and the study of folklore. The study aims to add to academic discourse but it is also my hope that the evidence presented here of deep internal affinities between Orthodoxy and Russian Baptist life could help to reduce the level of historic conflict that has existed between the two communities. As a member of the Russian Baptist community, my desire is to promote better awareness by Baptists and by the Russian Orthodox of each other's history within the Christian tradition of Russia.

This research has been possible thanks to the help of a variety of organizations and individuals. First of all, I want to express my gratitude to the International Baptist Theological Seminary in Prague and the research support programme of John Stott Ministries (USA) for the outstanding all-round support I have received from them during the period of working on this study for my PhD thesis. I wish to express my gratitude also to the staff of Langham Monographs for their considerable assistance in preparation of the manuscript for publishing. Among the individuals who have helped me, I want to mention first of all the sustained academic and personal support of my excellent primary supervisor, Dr Ian Randall, and also of Dr Toivo Pilli (Tartu, Estonia), my second supervisor. I want also to express special gratitude to Dr Keith Jones, the Rector of IBTS, Dr Parush Parushev, the Academic Dean of IBTS, and to others on the faculty of IBTS or associated with the seminary: Dr Peter Penner, Dr James Purves and Dr Derek Murray. Other scholars who have assisted me, and whom I thank, have included Dr Sharyl Corrado (USA), Professor John Briggs (UK) and researcher Mary Raber (Ukraine).

In my search for primary sources a great deal of help was provided by: the Director of the Archives of the Russian Union of the Evangelical Christian-Baptists, A. Sinichkin (Moscow); the Director of the Southern Baptist Historical Library and Archives, B. Sumners, and the archivist, T. Hall (Nashville, USA); the former President of the Southern Baptist Historical Society, Dr Albert Wardin (Nashville, USA); the Director of the Institute of Theology and History at Bibelseminar Bonn, J. Dyck (Oerlinghausen, Germany); and the historians V. Fast (Frankenthal, Germany), V. Getman (Seattle, USA) and others.

I have interviewed more than one hundred ministers and church members within the Soviet Baptist community who have emigrated from the USSR to the USA since the beginning of *perestroika*. Great assistance in this extensive project was rendered by Pacific Coast Slavic Baptist Association (Sacramento, California) and especially the executives of the Association, V.M. Tsvirinko and V.A. Sheremet. I am also very grateful to the presbyters and members of churches of the Evangelical Christians-Baptists (ECB) still in former USSR, who at various times shared with me especially valuable testimonies and materials, particularly N.A. Kolesnikov (Moscow, Russia), S.V. Sannikov (Odessa, Ukraine), L.A. Golodetsky (Odessa), V.N. Khot'ko (Petropavlovsk, Kazakhstan), I.P. Fast (Shchuchinsk, Kazakhstan), Ya.A. Meleshkevich (Bishkul, Kazakhstan), P.K. Sedletsky, D.G. Savchenko, and G.E. Kuchma (Omsk, Russia).

Some unique written sources of the evangelical movement in Russia were found in: the V.A. Pashkov Papers (University of Birmingham, UK – the copies of this Archive are in the library of the International Baptist Theological Seminary, Prague, Czech Republic); the V.I. Lenin State Library (Moscow); the libraries of Wheaton College (Wheaton, Illinois) and Pepperdine University (Malibu, California); as well as in several public libraries in Siberia and Central Asia.

I am grateful to the Archpriest Vyacheslav Rubsky and the Orthodox theologian D.V. Arabadzhi (Odessa, Ukraine) for valuable consultations concerning ongoing Orthodox-Protestant dialogue.

Finally, I want to express my heartfelt appreciation and gratitude for the most touching care that I have received from my wife Galina, who during what has been long years in which I have been engaged in research not only assumed the greater part of the domestic chores and troubles, but also suggested some significant ideas which have been used in this research.

CHAPTER 1

Introduction

The aim of this study is to analyze the experience of the Evangelical Christians-Baptists (ECB) in the USSR in the period 1960 to 1990, with the particular focus being on the way Russian Orthodox thinking and practice was mirrored in the Russian Baptist movement. In 1944 the All-Union Council of Evangelical Christians-Baptists (AUCECB) was formed, but the emergence of Russian Baptist and (what would become) "Evangelical Christian" communities began in the 1860s and 1870s. The process of formation and of re-formation which led to them uniting eventually as the AUCECB went on through the later nineteenth century and the early decades of the twentieth century. Recent PhD theses have been shedding new light on these significant developments.[1] However, no academic study to date has specifically examined the question of ways in which Orthodoxy might have helped to shape Russian Baptist life. Both Russian Orthodoxy and the Russian Baptist movement have forged their own identities. Much has been written about the centuries-old isolation of the Eastern Church

---

1. A. Puzynin, "The Tradition of the Gospel Christians: A Study of their Identity and Theology during the Russian, Soviet, and Post-Soviet Periods" (PhD thesis, University of Wales, 2008); M. Kuznetsova, "Early Russian Evangelicals (1874-1929): Historical Background and Hermeneutical Tendencies Based on I.V. Kargel's Written Heritage" (PhD thesis, University of Pretoria, 2009); G.L. Nichols, "Ivan V. Kargel (1849-1937) and the Development of Russian Evangelical Spirituality" (PhD thesis, International Baptist Theological Seminary, University of Wales, 2010); Alexander Popov, "The Evangelical Christians-Baptists in the Soviet Union as a hermeneutical community: Examining the identity of the All-Union Council of the ECB (AUCECB) through the way the Bible was used in its publications" (PhD thesis, International Baptist Theological Seminary, University of Wales, 2010). Some of the theses have been published – see the Bibliography. I will be referring to these later.

from Western Christendom,[2] and more generally the way in which a society creates its own unique traditions and culture, is well known to historians and ethnographers.[3] In the case of Russia, the isolation of the USSR from the West in the period of the "Iron Curtain" accentuated the pre-existent distinctiveness of Russian culture, a culture which had a profound impact on the religious movements in the period of the Russian Empire and then in the Soviet era.[4] Under the Communist government, there were determined attempts to separate Russian Orthodox Christians and Russian Baptists from their co-religionists elsewhere. One crucial consequence of this was that these two Christian confessions in Russia drew closer together. Aspects of this phenomenon are analyzed in this study.

Russian Baptists and their interpreters

The AUCECB, formed in 1944, was a product of expressions of Baptist and evangelical life that emerged and developed in various parts of what became the USSR. This work will concentrate on the Russian dimension of ECB life, rather than seeking to deal with what happened in all the Soviet Republics.[5] The Russian scholar A.I. Klibanov, Professor at the Institute of History of the Academy of Sciences of the USSR, wrote an influential work in 1965 suggesting that the Russian evangelical movement took root and spread out from the following areas in the 1860s and 1870s: southern Russia

---

2. See, for instance, V. Rozanov, *"Russkaya Tserkov'"* [The Russian Church], *Polyarnaya Zvezda*, vol. 8 (1906), pp. 524-40; A. Schmemann, "Moment of Truth for Orthodoxy", in K. Bridston and W. Wagoner, eds., *Unity in Mid-Career: an Ecumenical Critique* (N.Y.: Macmillan, 1963), pp. 47-56; T. Masaryk, *Rossiya i Evropa* [Russia and Europe: Essays on Spiritual Currents in Russia], 3 vols. (SPb.: RHGI, 2004), vol. II, pp. 512-15.

3. Among studies in the Russian language see, for instance, A. Zhukov, ed., *Istoriya Yaponii* [The History of Japan], 2 vols. (M.: Institut vostokovedeniya RAN, 1998), vol. I, pp. 338-400.

4. It can be noted that according to modern geneticists, one of the most important conditions for the formation of large ethnic groups has been isolation. See, for instance, F. Vogel and A. Motulsky, *Human Genetics: Problems and Approaches* (Heidelberg, Germany: Springer, 1997), p. 617.

5. Thus there will be many references to Russian Baptists – as a shortened form of Evangelical Christians-Baptists.

and Right-bank Ukraine, Transcaucasia, and St. Petersburg.[6] Although this is an over-simplification, since the movements were pluriform, it is helpful as a working framework.[7] The spiritual awakenings of the period involved very different groups of people. In the Ukraine, awakening began among Ukrainian peasants (who were mainly Orthodox); in Transcaucasia the evangelical movement flourished among the Molokans (a major group within traditional Russian sectarianism), and in St. Petersburg it spread among members of the aristocracy, who were all Orthodox by affiliation. These first groups of evangelical believers in the Russian Empire were given different designations. Those in Ukraine were often termed "Stundists", a reference to the German Lutherans and Mennonites in the Ukraine who practiced their "*Bibelstunden*" – Bible studies or Bible hours. The first congregations in the Caucasus were usually described as Baptists, as they had links with Germans Baptists. In St. Petersburg the common appellations were "Radstockists" or "Pashkovites", after the names of two leaders: the Englishman, Lord Radstock, and the Russian Colonel, Vasily A. Pashkov. A significant event in the early period was in 1867 when a Russian Molokan leader, Nikita Voronin, was baptized "as a believer" in the Kura River. He then founded a Russian Baptist community in Tiflis.[8]

There is no doubt that the influence of wider evangelical life outside Russia was felt within the developing Russian evangelical movements in the later nineteenth century and the beginning of the twentieth century. Two recent theses have contributed in important ways to this discussion. A. Puzynin has stressed especially the role and influence of English evangelicals such as Radstock.[9] However, his thesis does not present the full picture

6. A. Klibanov, *Istoriya religioznogo sektantstva v Rossii (60-e gody XIX v. – 1917 g.)* [History of Religious Sectarianism in Russia (from the 1860s to 1917)] (M.: Nauka, 1965), pp. 189-90.

7. In chapter 2 I will probe the relationship of the evangelical movements to Orthodoxy and Russian sectarianism.

8. See, for instance, S. Durasoff, *The Russian Protestants, Evangelicals in the Soviet Union* (Rutherford: Farleigh Dickinson University Press, 1969), pp. 35-49.

9. See Puzynin, "The Tradition of the Gospel Christians". This has been published in Russian and English: A. Puzynin, *Traditsiya Evangel'skikh Khristian* [The Tradition of the Gospel Christians] (M.: BBI, 2010). A.P. Puzynin, *The Tradition of the Gospel Christians: A Study of Their Identity and Theology during the Russian, Soviet, and Post-Soviet Periods* (Eugene, Oregon: Wipf and Stock, 2011).

of other influences on Russian evangelicals. G.L. Nichols has examined
the impact of the holiness spirituality of the Keswick Convention (named
after the town of Keswick in the English Lake District) on a significant figure within Russian Baptist life, Ivan Kargel.[10] Nichols establishes the way
nineteenth-century Keswick themes are to be found in Russian evangelical
spirituality. His work is also valuable for the way it investigates Kargel's
relationships both with the Russian Baptist Union, whose founding is
usually traced back to a conference in 1884 in Novo-Vasilievka (Taurida
province), and the Union of Evangelical Christians. The latter body was
led by Ivan S. Prokhanov, who announced its formation in 1905.[11] The
British Baptist and evangelical connections of Prokhanov included studies
at Bristol Baptist College[12] and his involvement in the British Evangelical
Alliance, to which he reported on the persecution of evangelicals in the
Russian Empire.[13] German pietism and Mennonite tradition also fed
into Russian evangelical thinking and practice. In this respect, Sergei I.
Zhuk has offered illuminating perspectives on the period 1830 to 1917.[14]
However, the question of how the Orthodox milieu had an impact on the
Russian Baptists has not been examined in these recent works.

---

10. Nichols, "Ivan V. Kargel (1849-1937) and the Development of Russian Evangelical
Spirituality"; see also G.L. Nichols, "Ivan Kargel and the Pietistic Community of Late
Imperial Russia", in S. Corrado and T. Pilli, eds., *Eastern European Baptist History:
New Perspectives* (Prague: IBTS, 2007), pp. 71-87. Also, M. Kuznetsova has analyzed
the important role of Kargel's hermeneutics in the Russian evangelical movement and
its theology in "Early Russian Evangelicals (1874-1929): Historical Background and
Hermeneutical Tendencies Based on I.V. Kargel's Written Heritage".

11. *Istoriya Evangel'skikh Khristian-Baptistov v SSSR* [History of the Evangelical Christians-
Baptists in the USSR] (M: VSECB, 1989), pp. 150-1. See also I.S. Prokhanoff, *In the
Cauldron of Russia, 1869-1933* (New York: All Russian Evangelical Christian Union,
1933), p. 131.

12. The studies at Bristol College came about through Friedrich Baedeker, who was an
associate of Radstock, Pashkov and Kargel. See Prokhanoff, *In the Cauldron of Russia*,
p. 97.

13. *Jubilee of the Evangelical Alliance: Proceedings of the Tenth International Conference Held
in London, June-July, 1896* (London: J.F. Shaw, 1897), pp. 307-13. Cited in I.M. Randall,
'Eastern European Baptists and the Evangelical Alliance', in Corrado and Pilli, eds.,
Eastern European Baptist History, p. 32.

14. S. Zhuk, *Russia's Lost Reformation: Peasants, Millennialism, and Radical Sects in
Southern Russia and Ukraine, 1830-1917* (Washington, D.C.: Woodrow Wilson Center
Press, 2004).

Nonetheless, there is extensive literature which has a bearing on the subject. Various influences from outside and inside Russia on the Russian Evangelical-Baptist movement have been investigated by historians. O.V. Beznosova has focused on Ukraine in the period 1850 to 1905.[15] Yu. Reshetnikov has also studied the genesis of the early national evangelical movement in the Ukraine, as well as the legal position of the first evangelicals in the Russian Empire.[16] Among the most influential German works are those by P.M. Friesen, W. Gutsche, W. Kahle, and J. Pritzkau.[17] Aspects of the story in the twentieth century have been examined in the groundbreaking work of Heather Coleman on Baptists in the period 1905 to 1929.[18] Paul Steeves picks up the Russian Baptist story at 1917 (while also looking at the previous history) and shows the developments in the Russian Baptist Union up to 1935.[19] The post-WWII era up to the end of the 1970s, is covered by Walter Sawatsky in his widely read *Soviet Evangelicals since World War II*.[20] Post-war developments among Baptists have also been of particular interest to Michael Bourdeaux, who has written more broadly

---

15. O.V. Beznosova, "Pozdnee Protestantskoe Sektantstvo Yuga Ukrainy, 1850-1905" [Late Protestant Sectarianism in the South of Ukraine, 1850-1905] (PhD thesis, Dnepropetrovsk State University, 1997).

16. Yu. Reshetnikov, "Stanovlennya ta Diferentsiatsiya Evangel'skogo Rukhu v Ukraini" [Formation and Differentiation of the Evangelical Movement in the Ukraine] (Candidate of Philosophy degree thesis, G.S. Skovoroda Philosophy Institute of National Academy of Sciences of Ukraine, 2000).

17. P.M. Friesen, *Die Alt-Evangelische Mennonitische Bruderschaft in Russland (1789-1910) im Rahmen der Mennonitischen Gesamtgeschichte* (Halbstadt, Taurien: Raduga, 1911) [English translation: P.M. Friesen, *The Mennonite Brotherhood in Russia (1789-1910)* (Fresno, CA: General Conference of Mennonite Brethren Churches, 1978)]; W. Gutsche, *Westliche Quellen des russischen Stundismus: Anfänge der evangelischen Bewegung in Rußland* [Western Sources of Russian Stundism], 2nd ed. (Kassel: J.G. Oncken, 1957); W. Kahle, *Evangelische Christen in Russland und der Sovetunion* [Evangelical Christians in Russia under the Soviet Union] (Wuppertal und Kassel: Onken Verlag, 1978); J. Pritzkau, *Geschichte der Baptisten in Sudrussland* [History of the Baptists in South Russia] (Lage: Logos Verlag, 1999).

18. H.J. Coleman, "The Most Dangerous Sect: Baptists in Tsarist and Soviet Russia, 1905-1929" (PhD thesis, University of Illinois, 1998); H.J. Coleman, *Russian Baptists and Spiritual Revolution, 1905-1929* (Bloomington, IN: Indiana University Press, 2005).

19. P. Steeves, "The Russian Baptist Union, 1917-1935: Evangelical Awakening in Russia" (PhD thesis, University of Kansas, 1976).

20. W. Sawatsky, *Soviet Evangelicals since World War II* (Kitchener, Ontario: Herald Press, 1981).

on religion in the USSR.[21] The most detailed examination to date of the AUCECB is the work by Alexander Popov on the identity of the ECB in the Soviet Union as "a hermeneutical community". Popov suggests that up to 70-80% of all publications about Evangelical Christians and Baptists written in the Russian language are devoted to the pre-AUCECB period.[22]

Among these publications are many which attempt to show the distinctive character of the Evangelical-Baptist tradition in Russia and the Ukraine. Often these link the emergence of the Baptists in this region with progressive religious advance and specifically with positive spiritual developments taking place within existing sectarian groups and communities in the Russian empire. The volume produced by S.N. Savinsky (1999-2001) on the history of the Evangelical Christians–Baptists of the Ukraine, Russia, and Belorussia is a standard text.[23] Another respected historian writing from within the ECB tradition is Marina Sergeevna Karetnikova.[24] Yu. Reshetnikov and Sergei Sannikov have traced the Baptist story in the Ukraine.[25] Other Russian authors such as V. Lyubashchenko,[26] V. Bachinin,[27] and T. Nikolskaya,[28] writing from similar perspectives, have

---

21. From many books by this author, I would single out here: M. Bourdeaux, *Opium of the People: The Christian Religion in the USSR* (Indianapolis: The Bobbs-Merrill Company, 1966).

22. Popov, "The Evangelical Christians-Baptists in the Soviet Union as a hermeneutical community", p. 3.

23. S. Savinsky, *Istoriya evangel'skikh khristian-baptistov Ukraini, Rossii, Belorussii* [History of the Evangelical Christians-Baptists of the Ukraine, Russia, and Belorussia] (1867-1917) (SPb.: Biblia dlya Vsekh, 1999); *Istoriya evangel'skikh khristian–baptistov Ukraini, Rossii, Belorussii* [History of the Evangelical Christians–Baptists of the Ukraine, Russia, and Belorussia) (1917-1967)] (SPb.: Biblia dlya Vsekh, 2001).

24. See, for example, M. Karetnikova, "*Russkoe Bogoiskatel'stvo*" [Russian God-seeking], in M. Karetnikova, ed., *Al'manakh po Istorii Russkogo Baptizma* [Almanac of the History of Russian Baptists] (SPb.: Bibliya Dlya Vsekh, 1999), pp. 3-84.

25. Yu. Reshetnikov, S. Sannikov, *Obzor Istorii Evangel'sko-Baptistskogo Btatstva na Ukraine* [A Review of the History of the Evangelical–Baptist Brotherhood in the Ukraine] (Odessa: Bogomyslie, 2000). See also S. Sannikov, *Dvadtsat' Vekov Khristianstva* [Twenty Centuries of Christianity], 2 vols. (Odessa: Bogomyslie, 2001), vol. II.

26. V. Lyubashchenko, *Istoriya Protestantizmu v Ukraini: Kurs Lektsiy* [History of Protestantism in the Ukraine: A Course of Lectures], 2nd ed. (Kyiv: Polis, 1995).

27. V. Bachinin, *Vizantizm i Evangelizm: Genealogiya Russkogo Protestantizma* [Byzantinism and Evangelism: The Genealogy of Russian Protestantism] (SPb.: Izd-vo S.-Peterburgskogo Universiteta, 2003).

28. T. Nikolskaya, *Russky Protestantizm i Gosudarstvennaya Vlast' v 1905-1991 Godakh*

in some measure sought to protect the Russian Baptist movement from accusations that it is a foreign import. Nor is this perspective only to be found among Russian writers who have a definite apologetic intent. Samuel John Nesdoly, in his 1971 study of the Stundists, Baptists, Pashkovites, and Evangelical Christians, 1855-1917, while aware of the complexity of the arguments about Russian Baptist origins, tends to stress the impact of Russian rather than foreign factors.[29] Trevor Beeson's approach in *Discretion and Valour* (1974) is similar. He places Baptists under "Sects of Soviet Origin".[30] J.A. Hebly also supports the concept of the Russian evangelical movement as an indigenous movement.[31]

A number of Russian authors who do not belong to (or even oppose) the Evangelical Christians-Baptists have also written on the movement. Among these were notable Orthodox "anti-sectarian" authors in the decades from the 1880s onwards, such as A. Rozdestvensky, A. Ushinsky, Bishop Alexis and V. Val'kevich.[32] Writings by Orthodox apologists in relation to sectarians convey a kind of "confessional haughtiness". In the early twentieth century a number of Russian liberal-democratic figures such as A. Bobrishchev-Pushkin, A. Prugavin, S. Melgunov, and V. Yasevich-

---

[Russian Protestantism and State Authority, 1905-1991] (SPb.: Izd-vo Evropeyskogo Universiteta, 2009).

29. See S. Nesdoly, "Evangelical Sectarianism in Russia: A Study of the Stundists, Baptists, Pashkovites, and Evangelical Christians, 1855-1917" (PhD thesis, Queen's University, 1971), pp. 135-202.

30. See T. Beeson, *Discretion and Valour: Religious Conditions in Russia and Eastern Europe* (Philadelphia: Fortress Press, 1982), pp. 98-101.

31. See, for instance, his comments on the self-dependent Russian "sectarian" tradition: J. Hebly, *Protestants in Russia* (Belfast: Christian Journals Ltd, 1976), pp. 74-83. He links the Baptists with the Molokans.

32. See A. Rozhdestvensky, *Yuzhnorussky Shtundism* [South-Russian Stundism] (SPb.: Tipografiya Departamenta Udelov, 1889); A. Ushinsky, *O Prichinakh Poyavleniya Ratsionalisticheskikh Ucheniy Shtundy i Nekotorykh Drugikh Podobnykh Sekt v Sel'skom Pravoslavnom Naselenii* [On the Causes of the Appearance of the Rationalistic Teachings of the Stunda and some other Similar Sects in the Rural Orthodox Population] (Kiev, 1884); Bishop Alexis, *Materialy Dlya Istorii Religiozno-Ratsionalisticheskogo Dvizheniya na Yuge Rossii vo Vtoroy Polovine XIX Stoletiya* [Materials for the History of the Religious-Rationalistic Movement in the South of Russia in the Second Half of the 19th Century] (Kazan: Tsentral'naya Tipografiya, 1908); V. Val'kevich, *Zapiska o Propagande Protestantskikh Sekt v Rossii i v Osobennosti na Kavkaze* [A Report on the Propaganda of Protestant Sects in Russia and in Particular in the Caucasus] (Tiflis: Tipografiya Kants. Glavnonachal'stvueshchego Grazhd. ch. na Kavkaze, 1900).

Borodaevskaya, wrote on Russian sectarianism and the issue of freedom of conscience.[33] Many of these writings are marked by "anti-ecclesiasticism", and in some respects they are at the opposite end of the spectrum to pro-Orthodox polemic. Finally, some works by Soviet scholars were influential, notably V. Bonch-Bruevich, L. Mitrokhin, whose book on the Baptists (1966) was especially influential, A. Klibanov, and G. Lyalina.[34] Mitrokhin's work was ideologically driven and Lyalina, by comparison with Klibanov, was more dogmatic in her Marxist interpretations. But all of these writers – Orthodox, liberal and socialist – have material which is of value. For example, the extensive factual material about the initial stage of the evangelical movement in Russia that was scrupulously collected by Orthodox contemporaries counterbalances the writings of Russian evangelical authors today who want to dissociate their history from any Western influences. The pre-revolutionary liberal-democratic authors, by contrast with their Orthodox counterparts, investigated the national roots of Russian sectarianism, demonstrating its "Russianness". Finally, the best Soviet authors helped to collect data on the social and economic aspects of Baptist believers' life in the Soviet Union, which were difficult for Baptists themselves to obtain. Indeed, "scientific" approaches were often ignored by Baptist communities.

Despite this range of secondary commentary on the genesis and development of the Russian Evangelical-Baptist movement written from a wide variety of perspectives, the question of the role of Russian Orthodoxy in the shaping of Russian Baptist life, especially in the Soviet period, has not

33. See, for instance, A. Bobrishchev-Pushkin, *Sud i Raskol'niki-Sektanty* [The Court and Dissenters-Sectarians] (SPb.: Senatskaya Tipografiya, 1902); A. Prugavin, *Raskol i Sektantstvo v Russkoy Narodnoy Zhizni* [Schism and Sectarianism in Russian National Life] (M.: T-vo I.D. Sytina, 1905); S. Melgunov, *Tserkov' i Gosudarstvo v Rossii: K Voprosy o Svobode Sovesti* [Church and State in Russia: On the Issue of Freedom of Conscience] (M.: T-vo I.D. Sytina, 1907); V. Yasevich-Borodaevskaya, *Bor'ba za Veru: Istoriko-Bytovye Ocherki i Obzor Zakonodatel'stva po Staroobryadchestvu i Sektantstvu* [Struggle for the Faith: Historical and Every-Day Essays and Legislation Review of Old Belief and Sectarianism] (SPb.: Gosudarstvennaya Tipografiya, 1912).
34. See, for instance: V. Bonch-Bruevich, *Izbrannye Sochineniya* [Selected Works], 3 vols. (M.: Izd-vo AN SSSR, 1959), v. I; L. Mitrokhin, *Baptizm* [The Baptists] (M.: Politizdat, 1966); A. Klibanov, *Religioznoe Sektantstvo i Sovremennost'* [Religious Sectarianism Today] (M.: Nauka, 1969); G. Lyalina, *Baptizm: Illyuzii i Real'nost'* [Baptists: Illusions and Reality] (M.: Politizdat, 1977).

been addressed in any depth. A short article by Mark Elliott in 1995 on the subject did little more than pose the question, and a Master's dissertation by L. Greenfeld in 2002, which looked at Orthodox influence, focused mainly on some ecclesiological aspects of the issue.[35] Yet connections were clear: many known pioneers of the Russian evangelical movement had left the Orthodox Church and were critical of Orthodoxy. At the end of the nineteenth century and in the early twentieth century the predominant attitude to be found among Russian Baptists and evangelicals towards Orthodoxy was a negative one. Negativity was mutual: for Orthodox leaders, Baptists had abandoned the true faith. This did not encourage specialists to look for possible Orthodox-Baptist commonalties. Such a connection seemed too improbable: the two traditions appeared to be implacably opposed to one another. However, in the post-war USSR there was a very different religious situation, not marked by such mutual antipathy, and this study examines the ways in which Russian Orthodox tendencies began to be more evident in Russian Baptist life.

Religion in the USSR: the 1950s to the 1980s

In order to place in context the experience of Baptists in the period 1960-1990, an understanding of the wider setting – especially in relation to religion in the USSR – of that period is necessary. The 1920s can be seen as a relative "golden age" for evangelicals in the Soviet Union.[36] But the period of freedom was followed by one in which there was an attempt to destroy completely all religious confessions in the USSR, an attempt based on the essentially atheistic roots of Communist ideology. The Law on Religious Associations of 8 April 1929 forbade religious communities to undertake any social, charitable, missionary or educational activity. As a result, the

---

35. See M. Elliott, "Eastern Orthodox and Slavic Evangelicals: What Sets Them Both Apart From Western Evangelicals?" East-West Church & Ministry Report, nos. 3-4 (1995), pp. 15-16; L. Greenfeld, "Eastern Orthodox Influence on Russian Evangelical Ecclesiology" (MTh Dissertation, University of South Africa, 2002).

36. See C. Prokhorov, "The 'Golden Age' of the Soviet Baptists in the 1920s", in Corrado and Pilli, eds., *Eastern European Baptist History: New Perspectives*, pp. 88-101.

majority of Orthodox churches and almost all Protestant churches in the Soviet Union were closed in the 1930s.[37] This move had devastating effects internally and also cut off Russian evangelicals from outside contacts. In 1943 there was a partial restoration of religious freedom by Joseph Stalin, a situation which lasted until his death in 1953.[38] Some writers have connected Stalin's change of religious policy with patriotic support given to the Soviet authorities by Russian believers and with the need for united effort to address the burdens of the war period.[39] Freedom was tenuous: there was no change in the law. Apart from Stalin, all members of the governing body and the Communist Party leaders – V.M. Molotov, G.M. Malenkov, K.E. Voroshilov, L.P. Beriya and Nikita S. Khrushchev – were strict atheists who opposed the restitution of rights to churches in the Soviet Union. During the first half of the period of leadership by Nikita Khrushchev, who followed Stalin, the personality cult of Stalin was denounced and there was a general liberalization of Soviet society. But Khrushchev's criticism of Stalin's crimes included a reversal of the latter's policy on religious freedoms. The widespread popularity of Khrushchev's reforms, both within the country and abroad (the famous "Khrushchev Thaw"), masked his determined struggle against all Soviet believers (the new *Zamorozki* – "Late Frosts").[40] Both Orthodox and Baptist believers suffered in this struggle.

In 1954 two decrees by the Central Committee of the Communist Party were issued. The titles were: "On the Grave Shortcomings of

---

37. This law was abrogated in full only in 1990. See A. Nikolin, *Tserkov' i Gosudarstvo* [Church and State] (M.: Izd-vo Sretenskogo monastyrya, 1997), pp. 182, 382-93.

38. In September 1943 Stalin suddenly invited Metropolitan Sergy (Stragorodsky) to the Kremlin, told him about the new policy on religion, and demanded that he summon the Episcopal Council of the Russian Orthodox Church in order to normalize Church life as soon as possible. The funds needed were given from the state budget. See, for instance: M. Odintsov, *Put' Dlinoyu v Sem' Desyatilety* [The Way lasted Seventy Years], in *Na Puti k Svobode Sovesti* [On the Way to Liberty of Conscience], ed. by D. Furman (M.: Progress, 1989), p. 60; D. Pospielovsky, *Pravoslavnaya Tserkov' v Istorii Rusi, Rossii i SSSR* [The Orthodox Church in the History of Old Russia, Russia and the USSR] (M.: BBI, 1996), p. 298.

39. See, for instance: Sawatsky, *Soviet Evangelicals Since World War II*, pp. 48-9; D. Pospielovsky, *Russkaya Pravoslavnaya Tserkov' v 20 veke* [The Russian Orthodox Church in the 20th Century] (M.: Respublika, 1995), pp. 186-8.

40. M. Shkarovsky, *Russkaya Pravoslavnaya Tserkov' pri Staline i Khrushcheve* [The Russian Orthodox Church under Stalin and Khrushchev] (M.: Krutitskoe Patriarshee Podvor'e, 1999), pp. 359-60, 389.

Scientific-Atheistic Propaganda and Measures for its Improvement" (7 July) and "On the Errors in the Realization of Scientific-Atheistic Propaganda among the Population" (10 November). L.N. Mitrokhin spoke of the resultant renewed demand for anti-Christian propagandists to take up the cudgels: "The decree directed them to fight against religion, in the form of the scientific and materialistic outlook struggling with anti-scientific religious notions. It was interesting to watch as former investigators and 'red professors' assumed the delicate work of spreading all kinds of knowledge."[41] The first decree was aimed at maximizing the quantity and raising the quality of atheistic lectures, articles, books, films and broadcasts.[42] The second enunciated a quite specific interpretation of the separation of church and state:

> Though religion is a private affair in relation to the State, and the church is disestablished, the Communist Party, which is based on the only true scientific outlook – Marxism-Leninism and its theoretical basis, dialectical materialism – cannot be indifferent to religion as an ideology which has nothing in common with science... The Party considers it necessary to conduct deep, systematic, scientific and atheistic propaganda, though not permitting insults to the religious feelings of believers and ministers.[43]

A decade later the General Secretary of the AUCECB, Alexander V. Karev, commented: "The church is separated from the state, but the state is not separated from the church!"[44]

There was increased pressure on religious believers within the USSR – Orthodox, Baptist and other confessions – from the end of the 1950s. The second half of the period of Khrushchev's leadership was directed, as

---

41. L. Mitrokhin, *Baptizm: Istoriya i Sovremennost'* [The Baptists: The History and the Present] (SPb.: Russky Khristiansky Gumanitarny Institut, 1997), p. 56. The translation into English here and everywhere, if not stated otherwise, is mine. – C.P.
42. See *O Religii i Tserkvi: Sbornik Dokumentov* [On Religion and Church: Collected Documents] (M.: Politizdat, 1965), pp. 71-7.
43. Ibid., pp. 80-1.
44. ARSECB, F. 1, op. 32.1, d. 32.1-23, l. 8. [1966].

the 21st Congress of the Communist Party in 1959 declared, to "large-scale building of the Communist society".[45] The reasonable rate of economic growth in the USSR led Khrushchev's government to announce that in seven years "the socialist countries will produce more than half of the entire world's industrial production".[46] In 1961, the 22nd Congress of the Communist Party echoed these political themes: "We are guided by strict scientific calculations, and the calculations show that we will build the core of Communist society in 20 years";[47] and "the Party solemnly declares: the present generation of Soviet people will live in Communism!"[48] Besides the political and economic aims, there was what might be termed a moral agenda, with a vision – intended to compete with and eliminate the Christian vision – of "the rise of the new man", who would be "the active builder of Communism".[49] The Communist goal was in a sense "religious". Popular Soviet songs said, for example, "Lenin is always alive; Lenin is always with you... Lenin is in you and in me."[50] The style of many of the Communist messages was "sermonic", for example, the famous "Moral Code of the Builder of Communism", approved by the 22nd Congress.[51]

Khrushchev's call at the end of the 1950s for a resolute struggle against religion led to new penal legislation. Article 70 of the Russian Soviet Federated Socialist Republic (RSFSR) criminal code, "anti-Soviet propaganda", was enacted as the successor to article 58 of Stalin's code.[52] Other new articles included article 142 (1960), "Violation of the Laws on the Separation of Church from State and School from Church", with viola-

---

45. *Materialy Vneocherednogo XXI S"ezda Kommunisticheskoy Partii Sovetskogo Soyuza* [The Materials of the Extraordinary 21st Congress of the Communist Party of the Soviet Union] (M.: Gospolitizdat, 1959), p. 11.

46. Ibid., p. 59.

47. *Materialy XXII S"ezda Kommunisticheskoy Partii Sovetskogo Soyuza* [The Materials of the 22nd Congress of the Communist Party of the Soviet Union] (M.: Gospolitizdat, 1961), p. 140.

48. Ibid., pp. 319, 428.

49. Ibid., pp. 86, 111.

50. J. Dunstan, "Soviet Schools, Atheism and Religion", in S. Ramet, ed., *Religious Policy in the Soviet Union* (Cambridge, UK: Cambridge University Press, 1993), pp. 166-7.

51. *Materialy XXII S"ezda Kommunisticheskoy Partii Sovetskogo Soyuza*, pp. 410-11.

52. *Podrazhayte Vere Ikh: 40 Let Probuzhdennomu Bratstvu* [Imitate their Faith: The 40th Anniversary of the Revival Brotherhood] (M.: Sovet Tserkvey ECB, 2001), p. 173.

tion entailing up to three years of imprisonment, and article 227 (1962), "Encroachment of the Personality and Rights of Citizens under the Pretence of the Discharge of Religious Rites", which meant five years of imprisonment.[53] These RSFSR articles had their equivalents in the other Soviet Republics, and there were additional laws in Central Asian Soviet Republics (Kirghiz SSR, Tajik SSR, Turkmen SSR, and Uzbek SSR) that allowed imprisonment for up to three years for "deception" through "religious superstitions".[54] The RSFSR penal code article 143 also stipulated up to six months of community work (or a public reprimand) for "hindering the discharge of [legal] religious rites",[55] but this was not a severe punishment and, in addition, it was never known to have been applied. Many Baptist believers spoke of the intimidations of ministers, the beatings of preachers and choir members, and the breaking of prayer house windows with stones, all of which went unpunished.[56]

Despite all of this effort by Khrushchev, religion did not wither away. In addition to the permanent religious resistance within the country, there was the strong external pressure of Western public opinion, with constant accusations about the USSR's disregard of human rights in general, and liberty of conscience in particular, as well as non-observance of many international commitments in the humanitarian sphere.[57] Leonid Brezhnev, who followed Khrushchev and was Soviet leader from 1964 to 1982, sought religious compromise. In January 1965, the decree "On Some Facts regarding the Infringement of Socialist Legality Concerning Believers" was

---

53. *O Religii i Tserkvi: Sbornik Dokumentov* [On Religion and Church: Collected Documents] (M.: Politizdat, 1981), pp. 161-3. On the application of these articles to Baptists see, for example: *"Spisok Uznikov, Osuzhdennykh za Slovo Bozh'e v SSSR"* [The List of the Prisoners for the Word of God in the USSR], *VestI*, no. 2 (2001), pp. 22-3.

54. *O Religii i Tserkvi* (1981), p. 165.

55. Ibid., p. 162.

56. As one example, a Baptist community was forced to hold their church services with the wooden shutters of their prayer house closed because some unpunished hooligans, with the connivance of the militia, regularly broke the windows with stones. See Savinsky, *Istoriya (1917-1967)*, p. 317.

57. Starting in the second half of the 1950s, the USSR signed some important international pacts and conventions on human rights, but their implementation in the country was always a problem. See *Prava Cheloveka: Osnovnye Mezhdunarodnye Dokumenty* [Human Rights: the Fundamental International Documents] (M.: Mezhdunarodnye Otnosheniya, 1989), pp. 4-5, 20, 35, 151.

enacted, one consequence of which was the large-scale discharge of prisoners of conscience in the USSR, first of all the Orthodox and Baptists.[58] This
period also saw the emergence of the Soviet dissident movement, which
had a strong moral vision. Philip Boobbyer writes: "Dissident intellectuals
believed that the Soviet system they lived in was founded on lies, and that
moral opposition was therefore imperative."[59] Further political changes took
place. In August 1974 the Council for Religious Affairs issued a decree "On
the Measures for the Regulation of the Network of Religious Communities
Consisting of Citizens of German Nationality and Strengthening of the
Control of its Activities". As a result of this document, soon many underground Lutheran, Catholic, Mennonite, and German Baptist communities
in the USSR were registered and gained official rights.[60] But attempts at
the normalization of these relationships were too late. In the second half of
the 1970s demands for emigration were common among Soviet evangelicals of different nationalities: Germans generally asked to be allowed to go
to Western Germany;[61] Russians mainly preferred the USA;[62] Ukrainians
tended to prefer Canada;[63] and some groups even asked to be allowed to
go "to any foreign country outside the USSR".[64] The authorities were not
expecting such a widespread "anti-Soviet" mood.

---

58. M. Shkarovsky, *Poslednyaya Ataka na Russkuyu Pravoslavnuyu Tserkov'* [The Last Attack
against the Russian Orthodox Church], in Yu. Afanasiev, ed., *Sovetskoe Obshchestvo:
Vozniknovenie, Razvitie, Istorichesky Final* [Soviet Society: Origins, Development, and
Historical Finale] 2 vols. (M.: RGGU, 1997), vol. II, pp. 328-99; *Podrazhayte Vere Ikh*,
pp. 84, 173.

59. P. Boobbyer, "Religious Experience of the Soviet Dissidents", *Religion, State and
Society*, vol. 27, nos. 3/4 (1999), p. 373.

60. See, for instance, A. Fast, ed., *Sovetskoe Gosudarstvo, Religiya i Tserkov', 1917-1990.
Dokumenty i Materialy* [Soviet State, Religion and Church, 1917-1990. Documents and
Materials] (Barnaul: IPP "Altai", 2009), pp. 191-2, 201-4. See also P. Vibe, L. Sennikova,
"*Postradavshie za Veru: O Sud'be Nemetskikh Religioznykh Obshchin Omskoy Oblasti v
1950 – 1980 gg.*" [Aggrieved People: Their Faith: On the Life of German Religious
Communities of the Omsk Region, 1950-1980], *Kul'tura dlya Rossiyskikh Nemtsev Omskoy
Oblasti*, no. 4 (2003), pp. 10-15.

61. See, for instance, *BSRUECB*, no. 23 (1975), p. 7.

62. See, for instance: Yu. Kuksenko, *Nashi Besedy* [Our Conversations], Kazakhstan's
Baptist Union Archives (2002), pp. 150-1.

63. See, for instance, *BSRUECB*, no. 24 (1975), pp. 1-2.

64. *BSRUECB*, no. 21 (1975), p. 20.

The Law on Religious Associations of 1929 was redefined by some important changes in June 1975. Some articles were completely removed. Religious communities obtained the status of "juridical person".[65] The 1975 law said: "Religious communities have the right to purchase church plates, religious items, means of transport, as well as to rent, build and buy buildings for their needs according to that established by the legal order."[66] At the same time, many restrictions on the religious activity of communities of believers were retained, especially articles 17-20.[67] In August 1975, the Soviet Union, following the lead of the democratic countries, signed the Helsinki Final Act, which dealt with human rights.[68] According to the Helsinki agreements, independent committees were established in different countries for monitoring the implementation of citizen's rights. In the USSR, however, such committees were soon dispersed; some of its activists were even imprisoned.[69] Soviet society was, nonetheless, moving step by step towards more liberalization. The decade of the 1970s was a time of political détente. The USSR and the USA signed important treaties on the restriction of the production of weapons of mass destruction; the frontiers of post-war Europe were recognized as inviolable; and trade relations between the "capitalist West" and the "socialist East" increased greatly.[70] Public opinion polls indicated a change in the religious mood in the 1970s. In 1970 workers in Leningrad, the "model proletariat" from the "cradle of the Bolshevik revolution", thought of religion in the following way: nega-

---

65. This status had been forfeited as far back as 1918, according to Lenin's decree "On the Separation of Church from State and School from Church". Article 12 of the 1918 decree said, "No church or religious community has the right to possess property. They do not have the status of a juridical person." See the text of the 1918 decree in *O Religii i Tserkvi* (1965), p. 96. Article 3 of the law of 1929 stated: "Religious communities and groups of believers do not have the status of a juridical person". See the text of the 1929 law in Nikolin, *Tserkov' i Gosudarstvo*, p. 382.

66. See the text of the 1975 law in *O Religii i Tserkvi* (1981), p. 126.

67. Ibid., p. 130.

68. See *Prava Cheloveka*, p. 66; P. Walters, "A Survey of Soviet Religious Policy", in Ramet, ed., *Religious Policy in the Soviet Union*, p. 27.

69. Sawatsky, *Soviet Evangelicals since World War II*, pp. 410-1; *Amnesty International Report 1980* (London: Amnesty International Publications, 1980), 302.

70. A. Prokhorov, ed., *Sovetsky Entsiklopedichesky Slovar'* [The Soviet Encyclopedia] (M.: Sovetskaya Entsiklopediya, 1982), p. 1095; J. Suri, *Power and Protest: Global Revolution and the Rise of Détente* (Cambridge, MA: Harvard University Press, 2003).

tively, 44%; positively, 11%; uncertain, 7.4%. The rest did not answer the question. By 1979, the workers' opinions had changed appreciably: only 14% of responses were negative towards religion; 19% were positive; and 8.8% were uncertain. The rest did not respond.[71] Such a large percentage of "abstentions" did not testify to strong atheism.

Probably the climax of the liberalization of Russian religious life in the 1970s was the new Constitution of the USSR of 1977. The 52nd article of that Constitution proclaimed guarantees of "liberty of conscience". In Soviet understanding this was "the right to confess any religion or to confess none, to conduct religious worship or to carry on atheistic propaganda".[72] There was no real equality while religious "propaganda" was not permitted, but Russian Orthodox and Baptist Christians were happy to have even this measure of official confirmation of their right to exist. A final wave of repression against believers in the USSR started, however, in 1979, when all "East–West" policies of détente were renounced and the decree "On the Further Improvement of Ideological and Political-Educational Works" was issued. This again called on members of the Communist Party and *Komsomol* (the Communist Union of Youth) to struggle against "religious prejudices" in Soviet society.[73] Hundreds of religious activists, the majority Baptists, were imprisoned in Brezhnev's last years and during the periods of leadership of Yu.V. Andropov (1982-1984) and K.U. Chernenko (1984-1985).[74] The repression ceased in 1985-1986 when the new Soviet leader, Mikhail Gorbachev, started his policies of *Glasnost'* and *Perestroika*.[75] In 1988, the Soviet government welcomed the celebration of 1,000 years of Christianity in Russia, an event that signalled the end of the period of State militant atheism. In February 1990 the Central Committee of the Soviet

71. See Pospielovsky, *Pravoslavnaya Tserkov' v Istorii Rusi, Rossii i SSSR*, p. 341.

72. *Konstitutsiya (Osnovnoy Zakon) Soyuza Sovetskikh Sotsialisticheskikh Respublik* [The Constitution of the USSR] (M.: Politizdat, 1978), p. 24.

73. See, for instance S. Skazkin, ed., *Nastol'naya Kniga Ateista* [The Handbook of Atheists] (M.: Politizdat, 1983), p. 433.

74. See *Amnesty International Report 1982* (London: Amnesty International Publications, 1982), p. 298; Walters, *A Survey of Soviet Religious Policy*, p. 27.

75. Gorbachev spoke of this at the 27th Congress of the Communist Party: *Materialy XXVII S"ezda KPSS* [Materials of the 27th Congress of the CPSU] (Moscow: Politizdat, 1986), p. 25.

Communist Party agreed to give up its monopoly on power and the disintegration of the USSR followed.

Baptist life: a brotherhood and sisterhood

This study has as its focus the period 1960-1990. Different dates could have been chosen because the religious tendencies, which will be examined in this study, were of a long-term nature. However, the period 1960 to 1990 has particular significance. As noted below, there was a serious split in the AUCECB as a result of new directives in 1960, and this study examines the publications of the AUCECB and also the group that split from the main body. In addition, the period is important because Khrushchev's antireligious campaign started at the end of 1950s and gathered pace. In the Khrushchev and Brezhnev periods, features of the Russian Orthodox impact on Soviet Baptist life, which had been present before, were especially clear. During Gorbachev's period, with *perestroika*, the culmination of these specific religious tendencies can be observed. But from 1990 the situation changed.

The AUCECB was formed in 1944, and the formation of this new body took place under government pressure – a single Evangelical Christian-Baptist body was easier to control. But the new Union leadership affirmed it as their own decision at that time "to create from two Unions one: the Union of Evangelical Christians and Baptists under the authority of the All-Union Council which will reside in the city of Moscow."[76] Unions with their own national traditions, such as those in the Baltic countries, became part of the AUCECB.[77] In 1945 the Pentecostals joined,[78] and Mennonite communities followed in the 1960s.[79] The two major Russian Unions, al-

---

76. *Sovmestnaya rezolyutsiya evangel'skikh khristian i baptistov po voprosu sliyaniya v odin soyuz* [The Joint Resolution of Evangelical Christians and Baptists on the Question of Amalgamation into the One Union], *BV*, no. 1 (1945), p. 33.

77. See T. Pilli, *Dance or Die: The Shaping of Estonian Baptist Identity under Communism* (Milton Keynes: Paternoster, 2008).

78. A. Karev, '*Eshche odin shag v dele edinstva*' [One more Step to Unity], *BV*, no. 3 (1945), pp. 7-8.

79. In the mid-1960s, a considerable part of the Mennonite Brethren communities in the

though differing historically in some areas of ecclesiology, shared many basic convictions. However, the AUCECB was an unstable coalition, and a serious split occurred in the 1960s.[80] In 1960 the AUCECB produced *New Statutes* and a *Letter of Instructions for the Senior Presbyters*, with the latter incorporating instructions "to reduce the number of baptisms among the 18-30 age group as much as possible" and to ensure that "children, both under school age and school age, should, as a rule, not be allowed attend services".[81] The pressure for this came from the State and in 1961 Russian Orthodox clergy received a similar letter, using Orthodox language.[82] An Initiative Group (the *Initsiativniki* – also known as Reformed Baptists or "underground congregations", and later as the CCECB, the Council of Churches of Evangelical Christians-Baptists) left the AUCECB in 1961, refusing to accept the new restrictions.[83] Gennady K. Kryuchkov, the major leader of the *Initsiativniki*, later recalled how he and others appealed to the leaders of the AUCECB: "We tried to convince them of the necessity to change their attitude toward God. The AUCECB did not answer us."[84] The majority of the AUCECB communities decided to back a moderate line in which they accepted the laws of the State.[85]

The Russian Baptists, in this period of strain and tension, were not operating from a position of numerical weakness. At their lowest point after Stalin's "great terror" in the 1930s, the Evangelical Christians and the

USSR affiliated with the AUCECB. See *Istoriya Evangel'skikh Khristian-Baptistov v SSSR*, pp. 430-1; *Sobesedovanie VSECB s Predstavitelyami Bratskikh Mennonitov* [Negotiations of the AUCECB with Representatives of the Mennonite Brethren] (editorial article), *BV*, no. 3 (1976), pp. 67-74.

80. This split in the Union has been the subject of considerable comment: see descriptions, for example, in M. Bourdeaux, *Religious ferment in Russia: Protestant opposition to Soviet religious policy* (London: MacMillan, 1968), and J.A. Hebly, *Protestants in Russia* (Belfast: Christian Journals Limited, 1976).

81. *Instruktivnoe Pis'mo Starshim Presviteram VSECB* [Letter of Instructions for the Senior Presbyters of the AUCECB], Novosibirsk Baptist Church Archives, pp. 7, 9.

82. Shkarovsky, *Poslednyaya Ataka na Russkuyu Pravoslavnuyu Tserkov'*, p. 375.

83. It was in 1965 that this group became the Council of Churches of Evangelical Christians-Baptists – CCECB.

84. G. Kryuchkov, "*Ya s Vami, Govorit Gospod*" [The Lord says, "I am with you"], *Vestl*, nos. 3-4 (1991), p. 13.

85. C. Prokhorov, "The State and the Baptist Churches in the USSR (1960-1980)", in K.G. Jones and I.M. Randall, eds., *Counter-Cultural Communities. Baptist Life in Twentieth-Century Europe* (Milton Keynes, UK: Paternoster, 2008), pp. 1-62.

Baptists had only four official churches,[86] but by 1948, with new freedoms, they numbered approximately 4,000 congregations with about 400,000 people,[87] and according to some officials in the AUCECB the figure by the mid-1950s was about 5,400 congregations and a community of more than half a million.[88] However, in the 1959 archival document "Statistical data of the AUCECB" two sets of figures were included. One set showed actual members, while another showed the figures given to foreign countries. In this "cold war" period Russian Baptists' international links were seriously restricted, but nonetheless some information was sent abroad.

1. Real figures: communities registered, 2,093; communities unregistered, 1,000. Members of registered communities, 202,006; members of unregistered communities, 100,000.

2. Figures for distribution to foreign countries: communities, 5,450; church members, 540,000.[89]

Many official Soviet statistics, not only church records, were unreliable.[90] The number of unregistered evangelical communities (1,000) and their members (100,000) appears to be an estimate. There was no doubt a lack of exact information about these communities among the leaders of the AUCECB. Also, although the inflation of the figures for foreign consumption appears to be designed to deceive, it could be argued that data in the internal report did not take into account any children from believing fami-

---

86. See S. Savinsky, *Istoriya (1917-1967)*, p. 355.

87. S. Bolshakoff, *Russian Nonconformity* (Philadelphia: The Westminster Press, 1950), p. 128. Such growth had deep historical roots. In 1928, before Stalin's terror, the Evangelical Christians and Baptists already had nearly 4,000 congregations with approximately 800,000 members in the USSR: Sawatsky, *Soviet Evangelicals since World War II*, p. 42; Savinsky, *Istoriya (1917- 1967)*, p. 12.

88. See Savinsky, *Istoriya (1917- 1967)*, p. 195.

89. Statisticheskie Svedeniya po VSECB (Statistical data of the AUCECB) [1959], ARSECB, F. 1, op. 2pd, d. 06, l. 1. Cf. data on registered churches of the AUCECB on 1.1.1958, signed by A.V. Karev: communities – 2,111; church members – 196,550. (ARSECB, F. 1, op. 2pd, d. 08, l. 2). Also in 1958 the leaders of the AUCECB, Ya.I. Zhidkov and A.V. Karev, suggested to the Council for Religious Affairs that they inform the countries of the West that 3,638 AUCECB communities were in the European Region of the country and 1,762 communities in the Asian Region (in total: 5,400 communities of ECB in the USSR). – ARSECB, F. 1, op. 2pd, d. 15, l. 1.

90. See, for instance, research by M. Voslensky, *Nomenklatura: Gospodstvuyushchy Klass Sovetskogo Soyuza* ["Nomenklatura": The Soviet Ruling Class] (M.: Sovetskaya Rossiya, 1991), pp. 202-15.

lies, who regularly attended church services but were not members. Soviet Baptist churches, as a rule, did not baptize people younger than age 18.[91] Often those baptized were older than that.[92] It is likely, therefore, that the statistical data for foreign readers was a reasonable indicator of the total size of the community.

Although a Baptist community of over half a million is substantial and significant (for comparison, the population of the USSR in the period was over 200 million, and growing), there were nonetheless serious internal weaknesses. Gennady Kryuchkov, the leader of the CCECB and admittedly a severe critic of the AUCECB, said about the demographic situation in the Soviet Baptist communities at the beginning of the 1960s, at the time of the split:

> Our brotherhood was ageing and dying out. Look at the former membership of our communities. They were 80 percent sisters, mainly old women! They were a grey-haired and wrinkled church. We might rather be called a sisterhood than a brotherhood...[93]

Undoubtedly Kryuchkov knew the situation in the Baptist communities well enough to describe the main tendencies. He did not mention the (unbaptized) Christian young people in the communities; he was concerned to paint a bleak picture of the "compromised" AUCECB. However, young people were certainly present in considerable numbers: it is well known that an average Baptist family in that period had 4-5 children. The "Statistical

---

91. See, for instance: *Ustav Soyuza ECB v SSSR* [The Regulations of the Union of the ECB in the USSR], *BV*, no. 6 (1966), p. 52; *Ustav Soyuza ECB v SSSR* [The Regulations of the Union of the ECB in the USSR], *BV*, nos. 1-2 (1980), p. 64.

92. M. Orlov, A. Karpov, *"Vodnye Kreshcheniya po Vere"* [Water Baptism by Faith], *BV*, no. 1 (1953), IEDE-2. There are also testimonies of the Baptists from Donetsk Region, church minister M.M. Kolivayko and church member V.Ya. Sedykh (INT, Sacramento, California, USA, 2006). I use the abbreviation "INT" when I officially interviewed someone and so I have an audio file recording of the main points of the conversation. When I use the word "testimony" without the abbreviation "INT", this means I did not interview the people officially but made a record of their words in my notebook after day-to-day contact with them.

93. G. Kryuchkov, *20 Let po Puti Vozrozhdeniya* [20 Years on the Way of Revival], *BL*, no. 4 (1981), p. 1.

data of the AUCECB" of 1959 has the following: "Men are 20%, women 80%, youth (under 30 years of age) 20%; church members in towns, 45%, and in villages, 55%. The social composition of believers is: industrial workers 20%, peasants 30%, and office workers 15%."[94] Soviet sociological studies in the mid-1960s confirmed the gender ratio in the AUCECB. The age range was reported as follows: up to 30, 3%; from 31-40, 10%; from 41-50, 11%; from 51-60, 16%, and over 60, 60%. Employees were 37%, pensioners 29%, and housewives 32%. The rest were dependants. Their educational level was as follows: higher education, 0.5%; secondary, 2.3%; incomplete secondary, 12.1%; primary, 43.1%, and semi-literate, 42%.[95]

In Russian Orthodox parishes, according to Soviet sociological research in the 1960s and 1970s, there was an equally high percentage of women (75-85%) among those attending, the majority of whom (about 70%) were elderly and had low educational levels. The age and education profiles for men were similar to that of the women.[96] The gender proportion of the congregations of the Council of Churches of the ECB (CCECB) itself was probably similar. Nikolai P. Khrapov, one of the most respected leaders of the CCECB, wrote: "In our brotherhood, there are many communities and groups where only sisters preach, lead meetings, and are included in the church councils."[97] Secular social scientists were inclined to

---

94. ARSECB, F. 1, op. 2pd, d. 06, l. 1. The rest, 35% of the church members by social composition, included groups such as housewives and students.

95. G. Lyalina, *Baptizm: Illyuzii i Real'nost'* [Baptists: Illusions and Reality] (M.: Politizdat, 1977), p. 13; L. Mitrokhin, *Baptizm* [The Baptists] (M.: Politizdat, 1966), pp. 252-3; A. Klibanov, *Religioznoe Sektantstvo i Sovremennost'* [Religious Sectarianism Today] (M.: Nauka, 1969), pp. 73-6.

96. See, for instance: M. Teplyakov, *Sostoyanie Religioznosti Naseleniya i Otkhod Veruyushchikh ot Religii v Voronezhskoy Oblasti, 1961-1964* [The State of Religiosity of the Population and the Break of Believers with Religion in the Voronezh Region, 1961-1964], in N. Krasnikov, ed., *Voprosy Preodoleniya Religioznykh Perezhitkov v SSSR* [The Issues of Overcoming Religious Carry-overs in the USSR] (M.: Nauka, 1966), pp. 31-52; *Nastol'naya Kniga Ateista*, pp. 434-5. Sociologists estimated the number of "convinced believers" among Russian Orthodox people as being not more than 10% of the total number of self-reported Orthodox in the Khrushchev and Brezhnev periods. See, for instance: C. Lane, "Russian Piety among Contemporary Russian Orthodox", *Journal for Scientific Study of Religion*, vol. 14 (1975), p. 156; I. Yablokov, *Sotsiologiya Religii* [Sociology of Religion] (M.: Mysl', 1979), p. 157.

97. N.P. Khrapov, ed., *Dom Bozhy i Sluzhenie v Nem (Sovet Tserkvey Evangel'skikh Khristian-Baptistov)* [God's House and its Service (The Council of Churches of the Evangelical Christians–Baptists)] (1972-1974), <http://www.blagovestnik.org/

connect the religiosity of women with the fact that they had not achieved complete equality in society. This continuing inequality was seen as a vestige of imperial Russia. Women, to compensate for their position, often as unskilled labourers, found refuge in religion.[98] A very different point of view was to be heard within religious communities: the predominance of women in church was because "they suffer more than men and that is why God is so merciful to them".[99] Lack of education among Baptists, as well as among the Orthodox, was due in large part to the policy of the authorities. Believers were not allowed to study at universities and technical colleges.[100] In turn this meant that a believer had great difficulty finding a well-paid job. Russian Baptists were often dismissed by their employers, and many had trouble finding any work, despite labor shortages in the USSR.[101] Nonetheless, 15% of the members of Baptist communities were office workers who would have had advanced training. The impression given by the Soviet data that Baptists had extremely low educational levels was to some extent a misrepresentation for ideological reasons. There is a wide discrepancy also between the social studies figure for church youth – 3% of the membership – and the AUCECB figure of 20%. Even after taking into account the atheistic influence in Soviet schools and the restrictions on young people attending church meetings, Baptist youth undoubtedly made up much more than 3% of the evangelical communities. The CCECB churches generally had a higher percentage of Christian youth

books/00280.htm#40> accessed 20 November 2009.

98. See I. Pantskhava, ed., *Konkretno-Sotsiologicheskoe Izuchenie Sostoyaniya Religioznosti i Opyta Ateisticheskogo Vospitaniya* [Specific-Sociological Study of the State of Religiosity and the Experience of Atheistic Education] (M.: Izd-vo Moskovskogo Universiteta, 1969), pp. 214-8; *Nastol'naya Kniga Ateista*, p. 435; N. Gordienko, *Osnovy Nauchnogo Ateizma* [Principles of Scientific Atheism] (M.: Prosveshchenie, 1988), pp. 131-8.

99. For instance, the testimony of a Baptist evangelist from Dushanbe, P.A. Semeryuk (INT, Sacramento, California, USA, 2006).

100. See, for instance: *"Soobshchenie o Khodataystvakh Soveta Tserkvey ECB"* [A Report on the Petitions of the CCECB], *BL*, no. 3 (1968), p. 3; I. Bondarenko, *Tri Prigovora* [Three Verdicts] (Odessa: n.p., 2006), pp. 54-7; K.S. Sedletsky, "Vospominaniya" [Memoirs], personal files of P.K. Sedletsky (Omsk, Russia, 2007), pp. 57-67.

101. See, for instance: L. Kovalenko, *Oblako Svideteley Khristovykh* [Cloud of Witnesses for Christ] (Kiev: Tsentr Khristianskogo Sotrudnichestva, 1997), p. 209; BSRUECB, no. 24 (1975), p. 13.

than those of the AUCECB, in part because of the attraction to young people of the radicalism of the "underground" movement.[102]

What is more striking, however, than the differences between Orthodox, AUCECB and CCECB communities was the degree of commonality in terms of their make-up. Nor was this restricted to issues of social composition. There was also an awareness, especially as the AUCECB engaged with the Orthodox Church, of a common Christian faith that was being expressed in Russia within a fiercely hostile environment. This dimension of Christian commonality is of crucial importance to this study. Thus in 1958, Yakov I. Zhidkov and A.V. Karev, as leaders of the AUCECB, sent this fulsome message, printed in the official AUCECB magazine, *Bratsky Vestnik* [Fraternal Bulletin], to the Russian Orthodox Patriarch, Patriarch Alexius, who had been elected in 1945.

> The All-Union Council of Evangelical Christians–Baptists sends warmest greetings to the Russian Orthodox Church on the occasion of the 40th anniversary of the restoration of Patriachate in Russia... We wish His Holiness Alexius, the Patriarch of Moscow and All Russia, as well as all the episcopacy and priesthood of the Russian Orthodox Church, great divine blessings in their ministry, that it might be full of grace... [signed]
>
> President of the AUCECB, Ya.I. Zhidkov, and Secretary-General, A.V. Karev.[103]

The title given to Patriarch Alexius by Zhidkov and Karev is significant. They did not use the common language employed by ministers of the AUCECB, which was "brother in Christ", nor did they place emphasis on hierarchy by using, for example, an allowable but more modest Orthodox appellation "*vladyko*".[104] Rather, they deliberately chose what the Orthodox themselves used as their ecclesiastical title – "His Holiness Alexius, the

---

102. See, for instance: Reshetnikov, Sannikov, *Obsor Istorii Evangel'sko-Baptistskogo Bratstva na Ukraine*, p. 199; *VS*, no. 3 (1965), p. 2.

103. *BV*, no. 4 (1958), p. 5.

104. This Russian word means a sovereign.

Patriarch of...". In this period it is possible to observe a growing affirmation by Russian Baptist leaders of the role of the leadership of the Russian
Orthodox Church and a growing warmth in the character of their mutual
relationships.[105]

The willingness of the AUECB leadership not only to affirm but also
to learn from Russian Orthodoxy was even more evident a decade later. In
1971 Alexei Bychkov, who became General Secretary of the AUCECB in
that year, wrote an article in *Bratsky Vestnik* on the recent "Local Council
of the Russian Orthodox Church". In his article, Bychkov wrote particularly about the Local Council's lifting of the anathemas that had been
pronounced on the schismatic Old Believers in Russia in 1667. Bychkov
noted that the Council's decision did away with the "formidable obstacles"
to unity within Russian Orthodoxy.[106] The Soviet Baptists had not been
able to achieve reconciliation following the serious split of the 1960s and
there had been "anathemas" pronounced within Baptist ranks. In the light
of this, the AUCECB was seeking any help that might be available from
the example of the Orthodox Church's experience in healing the scars of
schisms. In addition, as Beeson notes, on "more than one occasion" in this
period "the influence of the Patriarchate secured some amelioration of conditions for a heavily pressed national church".[107] It was helpful for Baptists
if they could be associated with the Patriarch. In the issue of *Bratsky Vestnik*
containing the report of the Local Council there was the following significant statement: "Our Holy Russian Orthodox Church, like other local
Orthodox churches, holds as her basis the creed of the One Church of the
seven Ecumenical Councils and is not only the keeper but also the dis-
penser of great spiritual treasures."[108] This warmth was reciprocated, as can
be seen from these greetings in the 1970s.

---

105. See also, for this, the warmth of the article in memory of Patriarch Alexius published
in *BV*, no. 5 (1970), pp. 58-60.
106. See *BV*, no. 4 (1971), pp. 11-12. The move was taken at face value by some, but can
also be seen as suspiciously benevolent. See *Pomestny Sobor Russkoy Pravoslavnoy Tserkvi*
[Local Council of the Russian Orthodox Church], *ZhMP*, no. 7 (1971), pp. 63-73.
107. Beeson, *Discretion and Valour*, p. 70.
108. *BV*, no. 4 (1971), p. 13.

To the president of the AUCECB, A.E. Klimenko, 'Dear brother in the Lord! We greet you with a holy kiss and compliment you on the high grand feast of Christmas… With unfailing brotherly love, in Christ's love – Pimen, the Patriarch of Moscow and All Russia.'[109]

To the president of the AUCECB, A.E. Klimenko, 'Dear brother in the Lord! … Greeting you with an Easter kiss, we stand in the unfailing love of the Risen Christ. Pimen, the Patriarch of Moscow and All Russia.'[110]

The Patriarch's Christmas and Easter greetings to Klimenko, who was President of the AUCECB from 1974 to 1985, are significant for the reiteration of the "holy kiss". This Orthodox language (and practice) was found among Russian Baptists.[111] The Soviet Baptists normally reserved the "holy kiss" for those within their communities, and the publication of these letters in *Bratsky Vestnik* in the 1970s, and the implied acceptance of the "holy kiss", showed that the "brotherhood" was opening itself up to Orthodoxy in a new way. The period from 1960 to 1990, which is analyzed in this study, offers important material regarding Russian Orthodox tendencies within the Russian Baptist brotherhood.

The approach of the study

Much of the material analyzed in this study is primary source material. I have read and evaluated many authoritative Orthodox and Russian Baptist sources in order to probe the way in which mutual critical judgments were expressed and also to seek to demonstrate the numerous points of

---

109. *BV*, no. 2 (1975), p. 13.

110. *BV*, no. 3 (1979), p. 40.

111. On the Orthodox custom of "holy kissing" see, for instance: Archbishop Veniamin, *Novaya Skrizhal', ili Ob"yasnenie o Tserkvi i Vsekh Sluzhbakh i Utvaryakh Tserkovnykh* [The New Tablet, or an Explanation of the Church, Liturgy and all Church Services and Utensils] [1908] (M.: Izd-vo Pravoslavnogo Bratstva Sv. Filareta, 1999), p. 120.

typological affinity and cross-denominational features. Other non-confessional Russian primary sources are also used. A major source for the thinking of the AUCECB is *Bratsky Vestnik*, but I have also drawn from many publications of the CCECB. The historiography of the Russian Evangelical-Baptist movement is extensive, and I have used the work of a wide range of researchers, both those who are well known and those often overlooked. In addition I have carried out extensive oral interviews and have drawn from them at many points in the study.[112] Although the overwhelming majority of my sources are in Russian, and I have translated them as necessary into English, I have also used secondary works written in English. These contribute to the wider picture of evangelical and Baptist life as it relates to Russian Baptists. To a lesser degree I have used German and Ukrainian material. My purpose has been to portray Russian Baptist life up to 1990, but not beyond. I have usually used the past tense in referring to the period being examined. There is good reason for this. Since 1990, the overwhelming majority of the members of the traditional evangelical communities have left Russia, and new mission agencies in the country have contributed to marked changes taking place in much Russian Baptist thinking and practice.[113]

The academic historical study of the evangelical movement from the eighteenth century onwards was advanced considerably by the publication in 1989 of David Bebbington's *Evangelicalism in Modern Britain: A History from the 1730s to the 1980s*. In this seminal work, Bebbington argues that evangelicalism has been and is a movement comprising all those who stress the Bible, the cross, conversion and activism.[114] The investigation of evangelical movements in the Anglo-Saxon world has been proceeding,

---

112. The names of those interviewed are in the bibliography. All those named agreed to have their names being published. Some parts of these interviews have been transcribed and have been compiled in a 400-page publication: C. Prokhorov, ed., *Podvig Very: Unikal'nye Svidetel'stva o Zhizni Khristian v SSSR* [Fight of Faith: Unique Testimonies about the Life of Christians in the USSR] (n.p.: Pacific Coast Slavic Baptist Association, 2009).

113. See, for example, M. Elliott, A. Deyneka, "Protestant Missionaries in the former Soviet Union", in J. Witte and M. Bordeaux, eds., *Proselytism and Orthodoxy in Russia: The New War for Souls* (Maryknoll, N.Y.: Orbis Books, 1999), pp. 197-220.

114. D.W. Bebbington, *Evangelicalism in Modern Britain: A History from the 1730s to the 1980s* (London: Unwin Hyman, 1989), pp. 2-17.

but much remains to be done on Eastern European developments. In particular, there is a need to place the shaping and re-shaping of evangelical identity within the changing contexts of Eastern Europe, not least in the Communist period. Toivo Pilli broke new ground with his study, *Dance or Die: The Shaping of Estonian Baptist Identity under Communism* (2008), and in introducing that study he argued that just as scholarly attention had been given to evangelicals in Western Europe, so Eastern European church life merited such attention.[115] Bebbington's work showed that evangelicalism adapted over time as it found itself in different cultural contexts, such as the Enlightenment and the Romantic movement. Pilli has looked at the Communist context and its effect on Baptists and other evangelicals in Estonia. This study seeks to add to these studies by probing the Orthodox context of Baptist life in Russia.

In particular, this work seeks to challenge the common perception that Russian Evangelical-Baptists and the Russian Orthodox Church had little in common. The attempt to explore this issue more deeply has involved looking not only at "words" spoken at an official level but also at what is said in local settings and also at "deeds", that is at practices. The research is historical, while engaging with, for example, theology, spirituality, sociology, culture and the study of folklore. The exploration of areas of internal kinship between Orthodox Christianity and Russian evangelicals is not only of scholarly significance, but has the potential, I would argue, to reduce the conflicts between the two confessions and the, often unfounded, mutual recriminations that have characterized the relationship. The evidence I have uncovered leads me to emphasize shared roots, opening up the possibility that Orthodoxy has been a much more powerful presence in much of Russian Baptist life generally than has usually been thought.[116]

Chapter 2, which follows this introduction, prepares the ground for a detailed analysis of the period 1960-1990. The Orthodox influence on the Evangelical Christians-Baptists in the USSR did not start from scratch in the post-WWII era. An understanding of issues such as the historical

---

115. Pilli, *Dance or Die: The Shaping of Estonian Baptist Identity under Communism*, p. 12.
116. See C. Prokhorov, "On the Shared Roots of Russian Baptist and Russian Orthodox Spirituality", *Baptistic Theologies*, vol. 2 (2010), pp. 82-94.

Russian "choice of faith" and the long relationship of the Russian Orthodox Church to sectarian movements in Russia are crucial in evaluating later developments.[117] Chapter 3 takes up major theological themes, with the aim of clarifying possible Baptist indebtedness to Orthodoxy. The main themes are the nature of God, soteriology, anthropology, scripture and tradition, and eschatology and the interpretation of eternity.[118] In the next chapter the topic is ecclesiology, and in particular the sacraments of Russian Baptists. I look at water baptism, the Lord's Supper, and what I see as the "seven sacraments" of the Russian Baptists.[119] Chapter 5 examines Russian Orthodoxy and Baptists in the area of liturgy: the liturgical year, the rite of Divine Service, and ceremonial acts. In chapter 6, I explore "spiritual traditions", which include the "Monastic Way" of Russian Baptists, saints and fools for Christ's sake, and the Eastern Christian self-consciousness of Soviet Baptists.[120] In chapters 7 and 8 the intention is to probe some of the beliefs, behavior and popular piety in the Russian Baptist communities more deeply. The concluding chapter seeks to bring together the threads of the argument.

Conclusion

There is no doubt that the emergence and the shaping of early evangelical and Baptist life in Russia was indebted to the work of evangelicals

---

117. I have also examined aspects of this in C. Prokhorov, "Orthodoxy and Baptists in Russia: The Early Period", in I.M. Randall, ed., *Baptists and the Orthodox Church: On the Way to Understanding* (Prague: IBTS, 2003), pp. 98-112.

118. I have published some work related to these topics: C. Prokhorov, *Tayna Predopredeleniya* [The Mystery of Predestination] (Idar-Oberstein, Germany: Titel Verlag, 2003); *Opyt Otechestvennogo Evangel'skogo Bogosloviya* [An Introduction to Russian Evangelical Theology] (SPb.: Mezhdunarodnoe Khristianskoe Izdatel'stvo "Titul", 2009); "Apophaticism and Cataphaticism in Protestantism", *Theological Reflections*, vol. 6 (2006), pp. 58-68.

119. On this see also C. Prokhorov, "On Several Peculiarities of the Understanding of Baptism in the Russian Baptist Church", *Theological Reflections*, vol. 8 (2007), pp. 89-105.

120. Some of this material has appeared recently in C. Prokhorov, "'Living as Monks' and Fools for Christ's Sake in the Russian Baptist Brotherhood", *Theological Reflections*, vol. 11 (2010), pp. 155-74.

and Baptists from outside Russia.[121] However, the Orthodox context in which the growth of these movements took place cannot be neglected if the specific character of the movements is to be understood. The historical developments also included isolation from Western influences. This was especially true after Stalin's accession to power, and again in the post-WWII years, in the period of the cold war. As the Christian confessions in the USSR came under pressure from the atheistic Soviet state, and wider Western contacts were curtailed, one result was that the Orthodox Church and Russian Baptists came into a closer relationship. From the creation of the AUCECB in 1944, and particularly from 1960 onwards, the conditions that prevailed contributed to the strengthening of Russian Orthodox tendencies within the communities of Evangelical Christians-Baptists.

The details of how this took place in Khrushchev's and Brezhnev's periods of leadership of the USSR are examined in detail in this study. Thus this study is not a narrowly Baptist denominational history, but an account that places Soviet Baptists in the wider religious, political and cultural context of Soviet life. The religious context was of a country where the most important religious role was that played by Russian Orthodoxy. But neither is this study an examination of the social and political context of the USSR as such. Philip Boobbyer notes the way in which social and political perspectives have been employed to understand the developments in the later period of the Soviet Union. His focus, in his outstanding study, *Conscience, Dissent and Reform in Soviet Russia* (2005), is on 'conscience'. He writes: 'In the last decades of Soviet rule there emerged an alternative moral and spiritual culture that undermined the Soviet system and ideology.'[122] As with Boobbyer's work on the moral dimension, this work has a quite specific focus – a religious focus. It argues that as neighbors living at the same country, suffering together under the atheistic Communist regime, Baptist believers were close to Orthodoxy in their mentality, and drew from Orthodoxy aspects of their theology, ecclesiology, liturgy, way

---

121. The most recent study which examines this in detail is Nichols: Gregory L. Nichols, *The Development of Russian Evangelical Spirituality: A Study of Ivan V. Kargel (1849-1937)*, (Eugene, OR: Wipf and Stock, 2011).
122. Philip Boobbyer, *Conscience, Dissent and Reform in Soviet Russia* (Abingdon: Routledge, 2005), p. 2.

of living and customs. To put it another way, Orthodoxy offered the "kiss of peace",[123] and many Russian Baptists, whether or not they realized fully what was happening, responded to the Orthodox embrace.

---

123. In 1964, J. Pollock cited the words of an Orthodox Archbishop that the times of persecution of Russian Baptists by the Orthodox Church had changed into their "kiss of peace". See J. Pollock, *The Faith of the Russian Evangelicals* (N.Y.: McGraw-Hill Book Company, 1964), p. 99.

CHAPTER 2

Roots of the Issue

The issue being addressed in this study has to be understood in the broader context of the position of Orthodoxy as the faith of the Russian people. This means exploring aspects of the long history of Russian Orthodoxy. However, such an examination must be linked with the complex history of deviations from the teaching and practice of the Orthodox Church, of which there have been many. The evangelicals and Baptists are examples of the diverse religious protest groups which have abounded in Russia. Orthodoxy was the chosen faith of the Russian nation as a whole (or at least its leaders) in the tenth century, but other choices have subsequently been made. These choices have certainly involved commitments to new religious ideas, as these have emerged from time to time, but they have also been shaped by the questioning that has taken place of inherited Russian traditions of faith. The emergence of the Baptist and evangelical movements in Russia in the second half of the nineteenth century, and the developments that took place over the course of the remainder of that century and the first half of the twentieth century, are crucial in providing a context for the argument of this study regarding Orthodoxy and the shape of Baptist life in Russia from 1960 to 1990. This chapter seeks to analyze the roots of the issues that have shaped both Orthodoxy and Baptist developments, and explores the understanding of these developments in the two traditions.

The Russian "choice of faith"

The ancient *Povest' vremennykh let* or "Russian Primary Chronicle" (translated as "The Tale of Bygone Years"), records that "Rus" was established after the Eastern Slavs called on foreigners ("Varangians") to reign over them. The motivation for this was that "our land is great and rich, but there is no order in it".[1] In this way, according to the Chronicle, the foundation of Russian statehood was laid, probably in the ninth century. Later the chronicler speaks about a "choice of faith" made by the Slavs: in 987 the Grand Duke Vladimir, of Kiev, having heard foreign ambassadors praising their own beliefs, sent his envoys to several countries to become better acquainted with their faiths. He heard accounts from them about the Muslims, who were reported as having no "gladness"; about the Roman Catholics in Germany, where his messengers stated no "beauty" was seen; and about the Byzantine Orthodox worship in Constantinople.[2] The prince's servants, in their report of the Byzantine Divine Service, said: "We cannot forget that beauty. Every man, after tasting something sweet, is afterwards unwilling to accept that which is bitter…"[3] Vladimir was baptized into the Orthodox faith in 988.[4]

The reliability of these accounts has been questioned.[5] But even if the chronicler's "apocryphal" details are discounted in the light of known events

---

1. L. Dmitriev and D. Likhachev, eds., *Pamyatniki Literatury Drevney Rusi, XI – Nachalo XII Veka* [Literary Monuments of the Early Rus, the 11th – the Beginning of the 12th Centuries] (M.: Khudozhestvennaya Literatura, 1978), p. 36.

2. In the case of Judaism, Vladimir confined himself to a conversation with Khazaria envoys. Ibid., p. 100.

3. Ibid., p. 124.

4. It is not that Western Christianity played no role in Russian Orthodoxy. A number of Western Christians were even canonized in Russia, for instance: St. Anthony the Roman (who was born in Rome, and worked in Novgorod), St. Procopius of Ustyug (a German), and St. Isidore of Rostov (born in Germany). See V. Toporov, *Svyatost' i Svyatye v Russkoy Dukhovnoy Kul'ture* [Holiness and the Saints in the Russian Spiritual Culture] 2 vols. (M.: Yazyki Russkoy Kul'tury, 1998), vol. II, pp. 17-45; G. Fedotov, *Svyatye Drevney Rusi* [The Saints of Old Russia] (M.: Moskovsky Rabochy, 1990), pp. 202-5.

5. For example, the famous Orthodox historian E.E. Golubinsky considered the chronicler's story about the "choice of faith" to be not simply a fabrication, but a *Greek fabrication*. See E. Golubinsky, *Istoriya Russkoy Tserkvi* [The History of the Russian Church], 2 vols. (M.: Universitetskaya Tipografiya, 1901-1911), vol. I, part 1, pp. 105, 135.

in Russian history, it seems clear that there was active participation by foreigners in a number of the important developments in the Slavic people's life.[6] If stories of such involvement did not reflect the actual state of affairs, it would be difficult to explain why the Chronicle was kept and copied. If the "calling of the Varangians" and the choice of a "non-Russian faith" were simply inventions of ancient authors, the likelihood is that they would subsequently have been "corrected" by the "true patriots of the Motherland", who could easily have composed alternative narratives that did not wound Russian national pride. This nationalist tendency was clearly displayed in the work written in 1510 by the monastic elder Philotheus of Pskov, *Povest' o Novgorodskom Belom Klobuke* [The Legend of the Novgorodian White Cowl], which recorded the passage of this important relic from Rome to Constantinople and then to Novgorod.[7] In similar vein, in the 1520s Philotheus reinforced the view of Moscow as the Third (and, of course, the final) Rome.[8] It should be noted that the chronicler did not suggest (for example) that the Varangians were able to impose their reign on Russia: they were invited. Nor did the Greeks bring Orthodoxy to Kiev on the edges of their spears and swords. Rather, in the case of the religious choice, the Slavs themselves decided to accept forms of spiritual life that were "non-Russian", but which they found attractive.

The determination of the Russians not to be seen as religiously subservient was evident in the way in which Grand Duke Vladimir, even when he had already made the decision to be baptized according to the Eastern Christian rite, attacked the strong Greek town Korsun' (Chersonese) in the Crimea, and conquered it. He did not want to be viewed as a weak

---

6. For the role of foreigners in the early history of Russia, see, for example, V. Klyuchevsky, "*Kurs Russkoy Istorii*" [A Course in Russian History], in V. Klyuchevsky, *Sochineniya* [Works], 9 vols. (M.: Mysl, 1989), vol. I, pp. 144-56.

7. See *Povest' o Novgorodskom Belom Klobuke* [The Legend of the Novgorodian White Cowl], in *Pamyatniki Literatury Drevney Rusi, Seredina XVI Veka* (M.: Khudozhestvennaya Literatura, 1985), pp. 198-233.

8. See Philotheus, *Poslanie o Neblagopriyatnykh Dnyakh I Chasakh* [The Letter about Adverse Days and Hours], in E. Vasiliev, ed., *Russkaya Ideya* [The Russian Idea] (M.: Ayris Press, 2004), pp. 25-31. The Russian historian A.V. Kartashev expressed it in the following way: "The dream of the Third Rome, of the final Orthodoxy on earth, is the first and last love of the Russian soul": A. Kartashev, "Spirit of the Old Believers' Schism", *St. Vladimir's Theological Quarterly*, vol. 2-3 (1974), p. 144.

proselyte. He then made his famous call to the residents of Kiev to be baptized, announcing rather ominously that "if any inhabitant, rich or poor,
did not betake himself to the river, he would risk the Prince's displeasure".[9]
Rather than seeing Vladimir as "won over" to the Eastern Christian faith,
it is perhaps better to follow the Russian historian N.M. Karamzin who
astutely commented that Vladimir "took into his head, so to say, to *win*
the Christian faith" and to accept the faith as a victor.[10] Yet at the same
time, almost all the first Christian clergy in Kievan Russia were Greeks,
the decoration of churches copied the Byzantine pattern, doctrinal points
were interpreted according to Greek Christian tradition, and the huge
Russian metropolitan district became only one of sixty (most of them
rather small) Byzantine districts.[11] This is not to belittle the importance
of the subsequent development of the Russian Church independent from
Constantinople, and the gradual formation of the characteristic national
features of Russian Orthodoxy, but nonetheless it is significant that all of
this took place through development over time. The ecclesiastical situation
was not static.

This analysis has relevance to the question of the distinguishing
"Eurasian" features of the Russian Evangelical-Baptist movement. I understand the Russian Evangelical-Baptist movement to be part of a large-scale
nineteenth-century "spiritual awakening" which was given added strength
at the turn of the nineteenth and twentieth centuries. Research is continuing into the ways in which Russian Baptists (by comparison for example
with Baptists in Western Europe and America), display features that can
be properly described as indigenous.[12] The attempt by some historians to

---

9. *Pamyatniki Literatury Drevney Rusi, XI – Nachalo XII Veka*, p. 133.

10. N. Karamzin, *Istoriya Gosudarstva Rossiyskogo* [History of the Russian Empire] (M.: Eksmo, 2009), p. 77.

11. See P. Smirnov, *Istoriya Khristianskoy Pravoslavnoy Tserkvi* [History of the Christian Orthodox Church] (M.: Krutitskoe Patriarshee Podvorie, 1998), pp. 139-40; A. Klibanov, ed., *Russkoe Pravoslavie: Vekhi Istorii* [Russian Orthodoxy: Milestones of the History] (M.: Politizdat, 1989), pp. 55-6.

12. See, for instance: I. Podberezsky, *Protestanty i Drugie* [Protestants and Others] (SPb.: Mirt, 2000), p. 325; A. Wardin, "How Indigenous was the Baptist Movement in the Russian Empire?" *Journal of European Baptist Studies*, vol. IX, no. 2 (2009), p. 30. They doubt the possibility of much originality in the expression of Christianity in any country since early Christianity, strictly speaking, penetrated to other countries from Judea and

highlight the originality of Russian Protestantism is still being undertaken, although the way this is presented is, I will argue, unconvincing.[13] Proper weight should certainly be given to the role of German colonies in Little Russia, where Lutheran pietism,[14] the teachings of the Mennonites,[15] and the influence of German Baptists[16] as well as of some other confessions, were mixed. All of this affected the formation of Ukrainian Stundism, and the emergence of Baptist congregations in the context of the numerous reforms under Tsar Alexander II in the 1860s and 1870s. Also, colonists contributed to rapid capitalist development in the later nineteenth century. Among individuals from a non-Slavic background who helped to shape evangelical movement in Russia were Johann Oncken,[17] Johann Wieler,[18]

---

consequently it can be considered (to some extent) unique perhaps only within the limits of the Jewish Christian tradition.

13. For this, see, for instance: G. Emel'yanov, *"Ratsionalizm na Yuge Rossii"* [Rationalism in South Russia], *Otechestvennye Zapiski* [Notes of the Fatherland], nos. 3, 5 (1878); I. Yuzov, *Russkie Dissidenty: Starovery i Dukhovnye Khristiane* [Russian Dissidents: the Old Believers and Spiritual Christians] (SPb.: Tipografiya A.M. Kotomina, 1881); A. Bobrishchev-Pushkin, *Sud i Raskol'niki-Sektanty.* See also modern works, mentioned in chapter 1: Karetnikova, *Russkoe Bogoiskatel'stvo;* Savinsky, *Istoriya evangel'skikh khristian-baptistov Ukraini, Rossii, Belorussii* (2 vols.); Bachinin, *Vizantizm i Evangelizm;* and Sannikov, *Dvadtsat' Vekov Khristianstva,* vol. II.

14. See, for instance: J. Pritzkau, *Geschichte der Baptisten in Sudrussland* [History of the Baptists in South Russia] (Lage: Logos Verlag, 1999), pp. 18-25; P. Friesen, *The Mennonite Brotherhood in Russia (1789-1910)* (Fresno, CA: General Conference of Mennonite Brethren Churches, 1978), pp. 205-27.

15. See, for instance: Friesen, *The Mennonite Brotherhood in Russia,* pp. 230-2; W. Kahle, *Evangelische Christen in Russland und der Sovetunion* [Evangelical Christians in Russia under the Soviet Union] (Wuppertal und Kassel: Onken Verlag, 1978), 51-64.

16. See, for instance: W. Gutsche, *Westliche Quellen des Russischen Stundismus* [Western Sources of Russian Stundism] (Kassel: J.G. Oncken, 1957), 31-42; Kahle, *Evangelische Christen in Russland und der Sovetunion,* 65-77.

17. The "Father of German Baptists", who visited Russia in the 1860s. Later one of the leaders of the Russian Baptists, V.G. Pavlov, studied under Oncken in Hamburg and was ordained by Oncken. See I.M. Randall, *Communities of Conviction: Baptist Beginnings in Europe* (Prague: EBF, 2009), pp. 87-91.

18. A Mennonite Brethren minister and the first president of the Russian Baptist Union in 1884. See L. Klippenstein, "Johann Wieler (1839-1889) Among Russian Evangelicals: A New Source of Mennonites and Evangelicalism in Imperial Russia", *Journal of Mennonite Studies,* no. 5 (1987), pp. 44-60.

Lord Radstock (Granville Waldegrave),[19] Friedrich Baedeker,[20] Abraham Unger,[21] John Melville,[22] and Kascha Jagub (Jacob Delyakov).[23]

An example of how German Protestant influence was brought to bear on Russians is illustrated in the experience in the 1850s of Mikhail Ratushny, who became one of the best-known Ukrainian Stundist leaders. In 1893 he wrote a letter recalling his youth and his evangelical conversion. Writing to a leading member of the Mennonite Brethren Church, G.I. Fast, in St. Petersburg, Ratushny recalled that, as a member of the Orthodox Church, on Sunday mornings he prayed using the church calendar, sanctified candles, and burnt incense. He loved Orthodox worship. But he continued:

> After my prayer I always visited a tavern where there were drunkards and debauchery; and I liked that too… I had started to ask the Germans (because I knew that the Russian people do not know about God and his law)… how I might be saved… I met an old man, a German who was repentant, and he said to me: 'Buy a Bible and read it; those who will tell you what is written in the Bible, welcome those.' At that time

---

19. An English preacher, associated with the Plymouth Brethren, who gave impetus to the evangelical awakening in St. Petersburg in the 1870s. See J.A. Hebly, *Protestants in Russia* (Belfast: Christian Journals Ltd, 1976), pp. 63-6. A. Puzynin states that Lord Radstock remained an Anglican throughout his life. See Puzynin, *Traditsiya Evangel'skikh Khristian*, pp. 77-80. Puzynin does not give proper weight to Radstock's Brethren links.

20. An evangelical preacher from England, of German origin. At the end of the 19th century, he made two long trips through Russia, from Petersburg to Sakhalin, preaching and distributing literature to prisoners. See R.S. Latimer, *Dr. Baedeker and His Apostolic Work in Russia* (London: Morgan & Scott, 1908); J. Pollock, *The Faith of the Russian Evangelicals* (N.Y.: McGray - Hill Book Company, 1964), pp. 71-2.

21. A Mennonite Brethren minister, who in 1869 baptized E. Tsimbal, one of the founders of the evangelical movement in the Ukraine. See A. Brubacher, "Abraham Unger", in *Mennonite Encyclopaedia*, 4 vols. (Scottdale, PA: Mennonite Publishing House, 1959), vol. IV, p. 773.

22. A Scotsman, a British and Foreign Bible Society representative, who distributed Bibles in Russia in the years 1837 to 1875. See W. Kolarz, *Religion in the Soviet Union* (London: Macmillan & Co Ltd, 1961), pp. 284-5; J. Urry, "John Melville and the Mennonites: A British Evangelist in South Russia, 1837 – ca. 1875", *Mennonite Quarterly Review*, vol. 54 (1980), pp. 305-22.

23. A Nestorian from Persia, who began his missionary work in Russia after being influenced by American Presbyterian missionaries in Urmia (Persia). See H. Brandenburg, *The Meek and the Mighty. The Emergence of the Evangelical Movement in Russia* (London: Mowbrays, 1976), pp. 61-3.

I had such a hope: I would buy a Bible and would be saved.
In 1857, I bought a Bible and began to read it, but of what I
read I understood nothing. I applied to the old man who had
advised me to buy the Bible, and he instructed me.[24]

I would argue that this testimony by Ratushny, which was quite typical for
Ukrainian Stundists, has parallels with the "calling of the Varangians" or
the seeking for true faith found in the "Russian Primary Chronicle". There
was admission of areas of inadequacy: "after my prayer I always visited a
tavern", and "the Russian people do not know about God and his law".
As a result there was a voluntary choice of the Protestant, "German" faith.
In Ratushny's case (as in the case of many others) the famous principle
of the Protestant Reformation, *Sola Scriptura* (Scripture alone), turned
out to be ineffective, and he soon needed interpretation of the Bible ("of
what I read I understood nothing", "and he instructed me.").[25] But what
the Ukrainian Stundists – and later Baptists – accepted from the Germans
was a Protestant rather than an Orthodox perception of the place of Holy
Scriptures. It is important to emphasize that this was their own choice; the
new beliefs were not imposed on them. The initiative proceeded, as a rule,
from the Russians themselves.[26]

Some Mennonite historians hold the viewpoint that in the second
half of the nineteenth century some Mennonite colonists in the South of
Russia who actively preached to Russians and Ukrainians (in practice few
did so) persuaded those who were spiritually "awakened" to form Baptist
churches (instead of accepting them into Mennonite communities). The
purpose of such a policy was to protect the Mennonites from accusations

---

24. Val'kevich, *Zapiska o Propagande Protestantskikh Sekt v Rossii*, Supplement no. 5,
pp. 133-4.

25. Scripture and tradition in Russian Evangelical-Baptist history will be examined in
more detail in chapter 3.

26. Sometimes writers are surprisingly insensitive to the question: who were the initiators
of events? They interpret rather simplistically the influence of European Protestantism on
Russians. See, for instance: M. Bourdeaux, *Opium of the People: The Christian Religion in
the USSR* (Indianapolis: The Bobbs-Merrill Company, 1966), pp. 151-2; H.L. McBeth,
The Baptist Heritage (Nashville, TN: Broadman Press, 1987), pp. 810-1; E. Hulse, *An
Introduction to the Baptists* (Haywards Heath, UK: Carey Publications Ltd., 1973),
pp. 72-3.

of infringement of existing State laws, and to ensure that they retained their long-established privileges in Russia.[27] But if the Russians and Ukrainians had wanted to join the Mennonite rather than the Baptist communities, but were prevented by the conditions pertaining before the Bolshevik revolution,[28] why did they not join the Mennonites in the 1920s, at a time of relative freedom for the evangelicals in the USSR, when the former religious prohibitions and the privileges of imperial Russia's legislation had ceased to operate?[29] There are Russian Baptist historians who, for their part, assert that the Russian Stundists themselves did not wish to accept the "German faith", either the confessional statements of Lutheranism or certain Mennonite practices,[30] though this interpretation does not explain clearly why the Slavs did not reject Baptist beliefs as something "German".

It does seem that considerable numbers of Russians in the later nineteenth century found in Baptist life an opportunity to develop their own

27. This opinion is stated, for example, by the historian V. Fast (INT, Frankenthal, Germany, 2008). See also: V. Fast, *Ya s Vami vo Vse Dni do Skonchaniya Veka* [I Am with You Always to the End of the Age] (Karaganda – Steinhagen: Aquila, 2001), p. 19; P. Epp, *100 Let pod Krovom Vsevyshnego* [100 Years in the Shelter of the Most High] (Omsk – Steinhagen: Samenkorn, 2007), p. 52; O. Besnosova, *Die Mission der Mennonitenbruder unter Orthodoxen Sud-Ukrainas 1860-1890* [The Mission of the Mennonite Brethren among Orthodox People in the South of Ukraine in 1860-1890], *Aquila*, no. 3 (1999), S. 18-23; O. Besnosova, *Deutsche Siedler und Mennoniten und die Verbreitung der evangelistischen Bewegung in der Ukraine im 19. Jh* [German Settlers and Mennonites and the Spread of the Evangelistic Movement in the Ukraine in the 19th C.], *Aquila*, no. 4 (1999), S. 16-19. The Russian empire's laws contained strict punishments for the "seduction" of Orthodox people to other beliefs. The Mennonites, for example, might have lost historical privileges in Russia if they had been convicted. See *Istoriya Evangel'skikh Khristian-Baptistov v SSSR*, pp. 62-6; Reshetnikov, Sannikov, *Obzor Istorii Evangel'sko-Baptistskogo Btatstva na Ukraine*, pp. 71-4.

28. On the excessive isolation of the Mennonite communities in Russia, partly encouraged by the Russian authorities, see, for example: J. Urry, "The Mennonite Commonwealth in Imperial Russia Revisited", *The Mennonite Quarterly Review*, no. 2 (2010), pp. 229-47; G. Lohrenz, "The Mennonites of Russia and the Great Commision", in C.J. Dyck, ed., *A Legacy of Faith: The Heritage of Menno Simons* (Newton, Kans.: Faith and Life Press, 1962), pp. 178-9; A. Wardin, "Mennonite Brethren and German Baptists: Affinities and Dissimilarities", in P. Toews, ed., *Mennonites and Baptists, A Continuing Conversation* (Winnipeg: Kindred Press, 1993), pp. 97-112.

29. See, for instance: L. Klippenstein, "Mennonite Pacifism and State Service in Russia: A Case Study in Church–State Relations, 1789-1936" (PhD thesis, University of Minnesota, 1984), pp. 283-322; 341-6.

30. This point of view is held, for instance, by S.N. Savinsky, M.S. Karetnikova, and S.V. Sannikov.

Russian rather than imported spirituality. Although the expressly nationalistic (*pochvennichesky*) approach of a considerable number of Russian Baptist writers to these historical developments has been too narrow, it is an understandable reaction to the imbalance in the writings of the "Russian Orthodox missionary" school at the end of the nineteenth century and in the early twentieth century. These Orthodox writers promoted biased views of Protestantism as absolutely "alien" to Russia, and saw only foreign ("German", "Anglo-Saxon") influence as responsible for the formation of Russian Protestantism.[31] Undoubtedly there was foreign influence, but there were also deep preconditions in the national history, not least in the many internal sectarian currents, that caused the streams of the Russian evangelical movement to emerge. According to J. Dyck, "Stundism owed its spread, first of all, to unknown ordinary participants of the movement."[32] The way in which Russian evangelical movements took root reflected the diverse and age-old spiritual seeking of Russian people. They were prepared to make choices. If Russian Protestantism had been only an alien import, it would have withered.

Russian sectarians and evangelicals

Russian sectarians through the centuries sought spiritual renewal within an Orthodox context. There was the mass movement of the Strigolniks

31. See the reviews of the theme and the voluminous collections of primary sources: V. Val'kevich, *Zapiska o Propagande Protestantskikh Sekt v Rossii i v Osobennosti na Kavkaze*; Bishop Alexis, *Materialy Dlya Istorii Religiozno-Ratsionalisticheskogo Dvizheniya na Yuge Rossii vo Vtoroy Polovine XIX Stoletiya*; O. Beznosova, ed., *Evangel'skoe Dvizhenie v Rossiyskoy Imperii, 1850-1917: Ekaterinoslavskaya Guberniya, Sbornik Dokumentov i Materialov* [The Evangelical Movement in the Russian Empire, 1850-1917: The Ekaterinoslav Province, Collection of Documents and Materials], (Dnepropetrovsk: Samencorn, 2006). For the most detailed thematic bibliography: A.W. Wardin, Jr. *Evangelical Sectarianism in the Russian Empire and the USSR*. ATLA Bibliography Series, 36 (Lanham, MD: Scarecrow, 1995).

32. J. Dyck, "Sut' Glavnykh Religioznykh Konfliktov v Rossii vo Vtoroy Polovine XIX Veka: Vzglyad Iznutri" [The Essence of the Main Religious Conflicts in Russia in the Second Half of the 19th C.: An Internal Assessment], in S. Bobyleva, ed., *Nemtsy Ukrainy i Rossii v Konfliktakh i Kompromissakh XIX – XX Stoletiy* [The Germans of the Ukraine and Russia in the Conflicts and Compromises in the 19th-20th Centuries] (Dnepropetrovsk: RVV DNU, 2007), p. 113.

(in the 14th and 15th centuries) in Pskov and Novgorod. They rejected Orthodox priests who were appointed *na mzde* (for a bribe) or who did not show exemplary Christian conduct.[33] Thus long before the Reformation in Europe, a kind of "Protestant spirit" arose in Russia.[34] The Strigolniks were formally charged with being "self-righteous", "schismatics", "stubborn and hardhearted" and "imprudent".[35] However, inherently this movement was a purifying movement, which played a considerable role in the difficult process of sustaining living Russian Christianity. The Strigolniks, for their part, suffered imprisonments and executions.[36] In the seventeenth century the Old Believers' Schism took place. The Old Believers wanted to preserve "ancient and true" Orthodoxy, reacting against the reforms of Patriarch Nikon, yet among the Old Believers there were *bespopovtsy* ("priestless" groups) with some characteristically "Protestant" features. For example, the principle of "teaching equality" meant that community decisions were made not only by spiritual leaders but also by rank-and-file members. In some groups there was free interpretation of the Holy Scriptures and the advocacy of the superiority of personal faith over the ceremonial side of Christian life. Divine worship could be simple and there was encourage-ment of individual prayer.[37]

Such beliefs, stressing the idea that the church was essentially about faith and life, were enthusiastically welcomed by many ordinary Russians and they contributed to classical Russian sectarianism.[38] The connections of Russian sectarianism with some Old Believers' "priestless" trends, were explored by a number of researchers in the pre-revolutionary period in Russia. For example, O. Novitsky noted the place of the Doukhobors (also

---

33. See, for instance, B. Rybakov, *Strigol'niki* [The Strigolniks] (M.: Nauka, 1993), pp. 14-15.

34. To include the Strigolniks in the annals of the Russian "antiquities of the Baptists" is already the generally accepted practice in the ECB. See more below.

35. See Metropolitan Makary (Bulgakov), *Istoriya Russkoy Tserkvi* [History of the Russian Church] (M.: Izd-vo Spaso-Preobrazhenskogo Valaamskogo Monastyrya, 1995), vol. III, pp. 93-100.

36. See Ibid., pp. 93; 98-9.

37. See, for instance, S. Zenkovsky, *Russkoe Staroobryadchestvo* [The Russian Old Believers] (Minsk: Belorussky Ekzarkhat, 2007), pp. 464-8; 492-3; 501-5.

38. Ibid., pp. 359; 492-3. Representatives of the "classical" Russian sectarians were, for instance, the Molokans.

known as the "Spiritual Christians") who were mentioned officially (under this name) for the first time in a State decree of 1799. The accusation was made that they had corrupted minds and hearts in Russia "from time immemorial" – *izdavna* – which might be hyperbole but might suggest earlier Doukhobor roots.[39] The brilliant representative of the liberal-populist trend in Russian social and political life in the second half of the nineteenth century, I. Yuzov, also wrote on the issue. To some extent he categorized the "Spiritual Christians" with Old Believers and also with evangelicals. He wrote:

> 'Spiritual Christians' are divided into: the Doukhobors, the Molokans… and the evangelicals [the Stundists]. The extreme Old Believers' priestless trends, the Wanderers and especially the Nemolyaks, hold [beliefs] closely in common with the 'Spiritual Christians' and are even called by their name.[40]

A.S. Prugavin's works echo this theme: "It is possible to find quite a number of common principles, and common viewpoints, which are believed equally by both a Filippovets and a Stundist, both a Molokan and a Nemolyak."[41]

A.P. Shchapov, in his work *Zemstvo and the Schism* (first published in 1862), was probably one of the first scholars who claimed to have found in Russian Old Belief elements that were creative and constructive, although he also spoke of its superstitious ("dark") sides. The positive features, for example, included: the so-called *narodnoe uchitel'stvo* ("popular education"),

---

39. O. Novitsky, *Dukhobortsy: Ikh Istoriya i Verouchenie* [The Doukhobors: Their History and Beliefs] (Kiev: Universitetskaya Tipografiya, 1882), pp. 2-3.

40. I. Yuzov, *Russkie Dissidenty: Starovery i Dukhovnye Khristiane* [The Russian Dissidents: The Old Believers and the Spiritual Christians] (SPb.: Tipografiya A.M. Kotomina, 1881), pp. 6-7. The name Molokan, or milk-drinkers, may derive from drinking milk during the Orthodox fasts. Many Molokans became the first Russian Baptists. The Wanderers and Nemolyaks are representatives of the Old Believers' trends – the priestless movement.

41. A. Prugavin, A., *Raskol i Sektantstvo v Russkoy Narodnoy Zhizni* [Schism and Sectarianism in Russian National Life] (M.: T-vo I.D. Sytina, 1905), pp. 77-80. The *Filippovtsy* were also representatives of the Old Believers' the priestless trend. See also T. Mamsik, "Sibirskie Raskol'niki-Nemolyaki: Radikal'ny Protestantizm na Vostoke Rossii" [Siberian Dissenters, the Nemolyaks: The Radical Protestantism in the East of Russia], in L. Dmitrieva, *et al.*, eds., *Protestantizm v Sibiri: Istoriya i Sovremennost'* [Protestantism in Siberia: The History and the Present] (Omsk: TOO "Poligraf", 1998), pp. 76-81.

carried out by many wandering preachers; the gradual spread of religious literacy among the common people; the interpretation of sacred books, which for all the "simplicity" of the approach nonetheless strengthened society's moral principles; and respect for personal liberty, including the rights of women. All this was to be found at a time when Russia still had legal serf slavery, with peasants reduced to the level of dumb brutes, and landowners dividing peasant families on a whim.[42] The pre-revolutionary researcher of schism and religious sectarianism, V.I. Yasevich-Borodaevskaya, cited the words of an Orthodox priest, words which seem to confirm the force of Shchapov's argument:

> What are they? And what is the source of their unusual preaching power?... Some sort of a tailor or a shoemaker goes from door to door with the customary bag on his shoulders and the New Testament in his pocket... He is able to direct any talk to a religious theme; he talks with reluctance on other subjects, but as soon as he finds a matter concerned with religion, here he is always inexhaustible. He is ready to talk with you day and night, forgetting about sleep and food. He entirely burns with the desire to preach, and he himself is inspired by what he is preaching. His sincerity and goodwill to you are unquestionable. You feel this and involuntarily come under his influence, the more so because the firm knowledge of the Holy Scriptures and deep religious inspiration turn his words into smooth and orderly speech, full of substance. And the most important thing is that the words of the preacher are entirely in character with his actions.'[43]

---

42. See A. Shchapov, *Sochineniya* [Works], 3 vols. (SPb.: Izdanie M.V. Pirozhkova, 1906), vol. I, pp. 451-579.

43. V. Yasevich-Borodaevskaya, *Bor'ba za Veru: Istoriko-Bytovye Ocherki i Obzor Zakonodatel'stva po Staroobryadchestvu i Sektantstvu* [Struggle for the Faith: Historical and Every-Day Essays and a Legislative Review of Old Belief and Sectarianism] (SPb.: Gosudarstvennaya Tipografiya, 1912), p. 348.

In spite of a certain idealization of the image of a wandering sectarian preacher, which sounds odd coming from a priest,[44] not least given the Orthodox tendency to persecute schismatics,[45] this passage sums up the feelings which for centuries inspired the many "God-seekers" among the simple Russian people. Those who were not satisfied with the official church life only, chose to join Russian sectarian communities.

A strongly spiritual dimension was a central feature of the schismatic and sectarian movements in Orthodoxy. The influential Orthodox historian, A.V. Kartashev, wrote:

> The Orthodox Russian soul thirsts not merely for salvation…
> but also for the ordering even here on earth of all life 'in God's
> way'… The Old Believers and the Dukhobors, having demon-
> strated both in their fatherland and in emigration the union
> of faith and a prosperous and productive way of life, manifest
> precisely the potential and the practical metaphysics, so to
> speak, of Russian Orthodoxy.[46]

According to another Orthodox historian, E.E. Golubinsky, the theme of morality and spiritual education in Russian Orthodoxy was, for many centuries, "the subject not so much of laudatory odes as of mournful elegies".[47] Many shortcomings were noted in the life of Orthodox parishes in the nineteenth century and the beginning of the twentieth century. Regrettably low moral standards and educational levels characterized many ordinary (in particular rural) priests. Many "anticlerical" Russian popular proverbs and sayings have this as their theme.[48] The well-known writer and expert

---

44. Yasevich-Borodaevskaya refers to an Orthodox source which is now inaccessible.

45. For example, according to St. Joseph of Volotsk's teaching, since criminals are executed for the murder of the body, it is all the more necessary to execute heretics, who are "killing the soul". See D. Pospielovsky, *Totalitarizm i Veroispovedanie* [Totalitarianism and Confession] (M.: BBI, 2003), pp. 377, 646-7.

46. A. Kartashev, "Spirit of the Old Believers' Schism", *St. Vladimir's Theological Quarterly*, no. 2-3 (1974), pp. 144-5.

47. Golubinsky, *Istoriya Russkoy Tserkvi*, vol. I, part 2, p. 830.

48. See, for instance: Z. Zosimovsky, *Est' li u Russkikh Religiya?* [Do the Russians have a Religion?] (SPb.: "Stroitel", 1911), pp. 9-22.

on national spiritual life, P.I. Melnikov (Pechersky), complained in a report in 1860: "Is it possible for people to respect priests who spend their time in the gin mills, write defamatory petitions, fight with the cross in their hands, and abuse each other in bad language at the altar?"[49] Coupled with this was the problem of very long church services in the Church Slavonic language, which the majority of parishioners found hard to understand. Nikolay S. Leskov, the Russian story-teller, novelist and journalist, said in the 1870s: "Our ladies do not understand at all many church prayers and canons... Even the men... who studied the Church Slavonic language and maybe even wrote about its special beauty, do not understand them."[50]

Although these were the primary issues that produced schismatic and sectarian tendencies, the phenomenon of widespread "ordinary priestless life" in Russian Orthodoxy should also be noted, since this disconnected people from priestly ceremonies. The severe Russian climate, the long distances between settlements, and the bad conditions of roads, inevitably led to "non-canonical divine services", which were not conducted by ordained priests. Any bans issued against such services were not effective.[51] In addition, many priests were not inclined to settle in very remote parts of Russia, and this contributed to a permanent lack of priests in certain provinces.[52] All of these factors contributed to the situation in which millions of Russian people were accustomed to living their Christian lives without the aid of the priests of the Orthodox Church and were willing to use "simplified" divine services. In such soil, both the Old Believers' communities and sectarian communities with anticlerical views took root.[53] Yet this was not a stable spiritual situation. Many Orthodox writers wrote about the

---

49. P. Melnikov, "Zapiska o Russkom Raskole" [A Report on the Russian Schism], in V. Kelsiev, ed., *Shornik Pravitel'stvennykh Svedeny o Raskol'nikakh* [Collection of Government Data on Schismatics], Part 1 (London: Trubner & Co., Paternoster Row, 1860), pp. 188-9.

50. N.S. Leskov, "*Velikosvetsky Raskol*" [Schism in High Society] [1876-7], in N. Leskov, *Zerkalo Zhizni* [The Mirror of Life] (SPb.: Biblia dlya Vsekh, 1999), p. 57.

51. See Zenkovsky, *Russkoe Staroobryadchestvo*, p. 525.

52. See, for instance, the works by S.I. Gusev-Orenburgsky, which realistically described Christian life in pre-revolutionary Russian rural districts: S. Gusev-Orenburgsky, *Glukhoy Prikhod, i Drugie Rasskazy* [A Remote Parish and Other Stories] (N.Y.: Izd-vo im. Chekhova, 1952).

53. Zenkovsky, *Russkoe Staroobryadchestvo*, p. 526.

deepening all-Russian spiritual crisis of the later nineteenth and early twen-teth century era, with the most terrible consequences being the Bolshevik Revolution of 1917 and fratricidal civil war.[54]

Analyzing the history of Russian sectarianism, there is credible evidence that Russian Evangelical-Baptist communities belong to a freedom-loving religious tradition. It is not that there is a literal succession from the Old Believers through the Doukhobors, the Molokans and/or the Stundists to the evangelicals, but rather there is a continuation of the same spirit, in its own way a "Protestant spirit". There were always many Russians who were morally opposed to any violence from State-linked Orthodoxy, but who did not oppose "true Orthodoxy". Although the radical movements varied greatly, in certain areas they were surprisingly consonant with each other. "The Russian Evangelical Christians-Baptists… are rooted in the [Orthodox] schism", writes M.S. Karetnikova, the prominent historian of the brotherhood of the ECB. She sees continuity rather than disconti-nuity, noting that the Doukhobors themselves related their origins to the Schism.[55] This idea of continuity is to be found, in one form or another, in other Russian evangelical authors' works.[56]

These are not simply romantic notions or attempts by Russian evangeli-cals to distance themselves from the charge of being "Western", although these dimensions are present. It is significant for the purpose of this study to see that the unwillingness of numerous sectarians to submit to official Orthodoxy in Russia was historically connected, as a rule, not with any

---

54. See, for instance, D. Pospielovsky, *Russkaya Pravoslavnaya Tserkov v 20 veke*, pp. 17-8. V.F. Martsinkovsky cites the distressing words of an Orthodox bishop in 1917: "We actually do not have any Church; there is only a crowd, where people are pushing one another during the great feasts. There is less pushing during the smaller feasts, and there is nobody on weekdays." – V. Martsinkovsky, "Kreshchenie Vzroslykh i Pravoslavie" [Adult Baptism and Orthodoxy] [1920], in V. Martsinkovsky, *Smysl Zhizni: Sbornik Statey* [Meaning of Life: Collected Articles] (Novosibirsk: Posokh, 1996), p. 244.

55. Karetnikova, *Russkoe Bogoiskatel'stvo*, pp. 45-6. The further steps in the succession are from the Doukhobors through the Molokans to the Baptists in Russia.

56. See, for instance M. Ivanov and A. Sinichkin, eds., *Evangel'skie Khristiane-Baptisty: 140 Let v Rossii* [The Evangelical Christians-Baptists: During 140 Years in Russia] (M.: RS ECB, 2007), p. 6; Savinsky, *Istoriya (1867-1917)*, p. 44; V. Trubchik, *Vera i Traditsiya* [Faith and Tradition] (Kobrin: Soyuz ECB v Resp. Belarus, 2007), p. 271; V. Franchuk, *Prosila Rossiya Dozhdya u Gospoda* [Russia has asked the Lord for Rain], [Windows CD-ROM] *Istoriya evangel'skogo dvizheniya v Evrazii* [History of the Evangelical Movement in Eurasia] 2.0 (Odessa, Ukraine: EAAA, 2002).

insidious anti-Orthodox or even anti-Christian purposes. On the contrary, the main motivation that drove them was a sincere search for "God's truth". This same zeal and commitment, sometimes termed the *muzhitskaya vera* (Russian peasants' beliefs), can be seen in the early evangelical communities of the nineteenth century. Thus, the Ukrainian Efim Tsimbal asked the German Abraham Unger, a Mennonite Brethren minister, about baptism "by faith" – the baptism of believers – in 1869: the impetus did not come from the German side. Indeed Ungar, well aware of the penalties that could be meted out under Russian law if a Russian converted from Orthodoxy, tried to avoid conducting such a baptism. Only in the light of the persistence of Tsimbal, and his (possibly legendary) words that Unger would "answer before God for the refusal to baptize", was the baptism performed.[57] This incident, like the conversion of Ratushny, provides a picture of the tumultuous events of those days. The idea that these early Russian evangelicals were in continuity with Russian peasant spiritual movements is confirmed through the biographical data on leaders of the Stundo-Baptist movement such as F. Onishchenko, M. Ratushny, G. Balaban and I. Ryaboshapka.[58] It is noteworthy that Tsimbal himself did not finally become a member of any German church, but, in spite of persecutions from the authorities, founded a number of independent Ukrainian Stundo-Baptist congregations.[59] The spirit of Russian sectarianism can be clearly observed.

Baptist growth in the Orthodox setting

At the end of the nineteenth and the beginning of the twentieth centuries, it is reckoned that evangelicals and Baptists in the Russian empire, as a result of an interweaving of "internal" (national) and "external" (foreign) factors, could be numbered in hundreds of thousands.[60] The convictions

57. See, for instance, Savinsky, *Istoriya (1867-1917)*, pp. 111-2.
58. See L. Kovalenko, *Oblako Svideteley Khristovykh*, pp. 57-61, 65-8; Savinsky, *Istoriya (1867-1917)*, pp. 95-104.
59. See *Istoriya Evangel'skikh Khristian-Baptistov v SSSR* [History of the Evangelical Christians-Baptists in the USSR) (M.: AUCECB, 1989], pp. 63, 552.
60. See, for instance, S. Savinsky, *Istoriya (1917-1967)*, p. 12.

that led to the growth were strong, and the growth itself gave the movements confidence. This is well illustrated by the following statement from the very first issue of the periodical *Baptist* (1907). It is highly probable that the author was D.I. Mazaev, the editor and the publisher of this periodical as well as the chairman of the Union of Russian Baptists. Mazaev was also a distinguished sheep-breeder, and belonged to one of the most successful and wealthy families in the South of Russia. The article stated:

> Many of our brothers are confused by this non-Russian name… Our present name – 'the Baptists' – as well as the name of the first disciples of the Lord – 'the Christians': these are equally non-Russian… What do we, the Russians, have to do with, or in general may have to do with those people who once and somewhere abroad accepted this name?… If we nowadays, as our Russian Prince Vladimir once did, sent our observers to seek the 'righteous faith' we are sure that our observers would decide in favor of neither the Catholics, nor the Lutherans, nor any other evangelical community, but they would decide in favor of the Baptists alone, and only because Baptists, as well as the Apostles, have the same one Lord, the same one faith and the same one baptism – which you will not find anywhere, in any other Christian community.[61]

Behind this striking degree of confidence, which was also found in the writings of other evangelicals,[62] it is significant that appeal was made to the example of Prince Vladimir. The connections being made here are often missed. There is an awareness that just as Vladimir and a part of the

---

61. [Anon], *"Nazvanie 'Baptisty"* [The Name 'the Baptists'], *Bapt.*, no. 1 (June 1907), pp. 2-3.

62. The Evangelical Christians (I.S. Prokhanov's followers), whose doctrines were very close to those of the Baptists, sometimes defended the name of their communities even more passionately: "The Baptist movement in Russia is in the same relation to the Evangelical one as John the Baptist was to Christ… The Baptists must decrease, but the Evangelical-Christian movement must increase (John 3:30)." – *Pis'ma k Brat'yam Evangel'skim Khristianam – Baptistam* [Letters to the Brothers, the Evangelical Christians–Baptists] (Tiflis: 'Trud' F.E. Machkovskoy, 1916), p. 36. See also Val'kevich, *Zapiska o Propagande Protestantskikh Sekt v Rossii*, Supplement no. 3, pp. 41-2.

Slavs represented by the princes and boyars voluntarily chose Orthodoxy (although for the majority of the people later the "choice" was "compulsory"), so in Russian pre-revolutionary society people (both poor and rich) by their own free will were favoring the "Baptist faith".

There are certainly legitimate parallels. For example, the Greeks in the tenth century did not impose on the Russians their form of Christian belief, and neither did the Germans in the nineteenth century impose Protestantism on Russians. After the first Russians became evangelicals, it was mainly the Russians and the Ukrainians themselves who disseminated Evangelical-Baptist views within the Russian empire. Many Germans, though living in the empire, did not know the Russian language well and they were for the most part law-abiding citizens who did not want to break Russian laws about the conversion to other Christian traditions of Orthodox people. L.E. Kovalenko in his collection of 52 biographies of the best known and most influential pioneers of the Evangelical-Baptist brotherhood in Russia, pays attention to their national identity: Russian – 23 people, Ukrainian – 12, German – 7, Byelorussian – 3, Jewish – 2, Latvian – 1, Moldavian – 1, Armenian – 1, English – 1, Persian – 1.[63] It is hard to argue from this that the movement was foreign-led. From the very beginning, the Stundist and Baptist movements in Russia were "international". They included representatives of many nationalities, as opposed, for example, to mono-ethnic Mennonite and Lutheran churches (the main German denominations in the Russian territory). But to be international is different from being foreign. An artificial "planting from outside" would have found it hard to take root among Russians, especially given the severe persecutions which the Russian Baptists endured.[64]

---

63. Kovalenko, *Oblako Svideteley Khristovykh*, p. 35.

64. See, for instance: M. Kalnev, "*Pochemu Pravoslavnye Otpadayut v Sektantstvo?*" [Why do Orthodox People go over to Sectarianism?], *Missionerskoe Obozrenie*, nos. 7-8 (1906), pp. 62-73; B. Bonch-Bruevich, *Presledovanie Baptistov* [The Persecution of Baptists] (Izdanie "Svobodnogo Slova", 1902). For a detailed review of the pre-revolutionary laws and police circulars directed against Russian sectarians, see, for instance, Savinsky, *Istoriya (1867-1917)*, pp. 169-89; 217-38; A. Blane, "The Relations between the Russian Protestant Sects and the State, 1900-1921" (PhD thesis, Duke University, 1964), pp. 26-97.

Although there are parallels between the choices made by Russians who accepted Orthodoxy in the tenth and eleventh centuries and Russians who accepted the Baptist faith in the nineteenth and twentieth centuries, there are also differences. It is significant that while the decisive factor for the choice of the observers of Prince Vladimir, according to the Chronicle, was the aesthetic value ("beauty") of the Byzantine divine service, the Russian Baptists emphasized the conformity of Baptist beliefs with the Gospel ("the true doctrine"), or, to be more precise, with their (the Russian sectarians') own understanding of the Christian faith. Thus, the success of evangelical missionary work in Russia as well as the emergence and growth of Baptist life took place not because of a certain, amazingly effective "contextualization" practiced by Western evangelical preachers in Russia,[65] but because in most cases the Russian Christians wished themselves to adopt something which from their point of view was useful. In some cases what was particularly attractive was the way Baptists and Mennonites successfully organized their communities.[66] In other cases written doctrinal statements, notably of the German Baptists, were accepted.[67] One factor in this process was that Russian sectarians always lacked members who were well-educated in the area of theology.

However, it is crucial to note that Russian Baptists and other Russian evangelicals very quickly filled the aforementioned foreign *form* of the faith with their own, "very Russian" *content*, i.e. with views which in practice diverged from those that had been promulgated by non-Russian evangelicals. For example, they filled what some Russian Baptists later saw as a rather dry and rationalistic (even if evangelical) "German jar" with their own "elixir of life", a phrase which was primarily a reference to age-old semi-Orthodox and in many cases semi-Molokan enigmatic opinions and theological predilections. For example, although they translated the German Baptist

---

65. The very problematic character of the foreign missionaries' work in Russia at that time is well known. See, for instance: Wardin, "How Indigenous was the Baptist Movement in the Russian Empire?", pp. 29-37.

66. See, for instance: J. Dyck, "Fresh Skins for New Wine", *Theological Reflections*, vol. 6 (2006), pp. 104-6; G. Ellis, L. Jones, *Russian Evangelical Awakenings* (Abilene, TX: ACU Press, 1996), pp. 72-3.

67. See *Istoriya Evangel'skikh Khristian-Baptistov v SSSR*, pp. 438-9; S. Sannikov, ed., *Istoriya Baptizma* [History of the Baptists] (Odessa: OBS, 1996), p. 421.

Confession into Russian and distributed it among their communities, the Russian Baptists at the same time disagreed with some of the major statements in that Confession. The Calvinistic orientation of German Baptist belief was never advocated by Russian Baptist leaders, probably because of the strength within Russian Baptist life of Orthodox and Molokan roots.[68] Russian evangelicals never accepted the view that their faith was a "German faith". If borrowing from others negated "Russian-ness" then it would follow that Peter the Great was not Russian (because of his "European" reforms), and Tsar Alexis (Mikhaylovich) and other famous Russians were foreigners in their own country.

A striking example of Russian Baptist divergence from wider Baptist views in the pre-revolutionary period has to do with the respectful attitude that the Russians adopted towards the Apocrypha. Thus in the early issues of the periodical the *Baptist*, for example in issues produced in 1910 and 1914, the following books were repeatedly mentioned in the most positive way: Judith, Tobit, The Wisdom of Jesus (Son of Sirach), and the books of the Maccabees.[69] The Baptists also derived from Molokan tradition the deliberate wearing of formal ("semi-monastic") clothes, an absolute prohibition on the use of alcohol and tobacco,[70] and strict fasts ("[they] tasted neither bread nor water"), with the *Baptist* publishing in 1910 a homily by Vasily V. Ivanov – of the Baptist congregation in Baku – on the proper observance of fasts in the spirit of the Molokan traditions that were common among early Russian Baptists.[71] Unconditional obedience to the elders was also a Molokan feature adopted by many Baptists. Thus the academician L.N. Mitrokhin remarks that "the Baptists of Mazaev's pattern in many

68. See, for instance: A. Sinichkin, "*Osobennosti Vozniknoveniya i Formirovaniya Rossiyskogo Baptizma*" [The Peculiarities of the Origin and Formation of the Russian Baptist Movement], in E. Mel'nikova, M. Odintsov, eds., *Svoboda Sovesti v Rossii: Istorichesky i Sovremenny Aspekty* [Freedom of Conscience in Russia: Historical and Modern Aspects] (M.: Rossiyskoe Ob"edinenie Issledovateley Religii, 2007), pp. 11-12; A. Klibanov, *History of Religious Sectarianism in Russia (1860s-1917)* (Oxford: Pergamon Press, 1982), p. 223.

69. See for example *Bapt.*, no. 27 (1910), p. 4; nos. 21-24 (1914), p. 20.

70. See, for instance: Sinichkin, *Osobennosti Vozniknoveniya i Formirovaniya Rossiyskogo Baptizma*, pp. 9-12.

71. V. Ivanov, "*O Postakh*" [On Fasts], *Bapt.*, no. 14 (1910), pp. 5-6.

respects kept the succession from the Molokan 'eldership'".[72] At the same time, the majority of the Molokans interpreted the main church ordinances – Baptism and Holy Communion – in a "spiritual" way (not literally), a viewpoint which the Russian Baptists rejected from the beginning.[73]

As the causes of the rapid spread of the evangelical views throughout the Russian empire in the last third of the nineteenth century were analyzed, the most acute Orthodox authors-contemporaries noted not so much "the German factor" as certain important political events, as well as features of Russian sectarian communities. Thus the resolute reforming of Russian society by Tsar Alexander II, including the abolition of serfdom in 1861, caused a marked growth of free self-consciousness among the peasants and their increased questioning of the Orthodox priests. For instance, N.S. Leskov wrote in 1871: "In former times our people, being serfs, suffered in their constant poverty and sorrows, and so resorted to the Lord; but... if you wish to see what happens now, a peasant goes to church only when he wants to."[74] The gradual spread of literacy and the mass publications of the Holy Scriptures in the Russian language were also of great significance. A Russian Bible Society was active.[75] In addition, there was the desire of the peasants to free themselves from the excessive burden of "paid services" in the Orthodox Church, to emulate the positive and sober nature of sectarian life, and to embrace the attractive message of salvation by faith alone.[76]

Orthodox anti-sectarian pamphlets often expressed the thought that Orthodoxy, as the true church, showed Christian love to her children, while the Russian Baptist communities were based on hatred for the priesthood

---

72. See Mitrokhin, *Baptizm: Istoriya i Sovremennost'*, p. 378.

73. See, for instance: Savinsky, *Istoriya (1867-1917)*, pp. 49, 67-8.

74. N. Leskov, *Sobranie Sochineniy* [Collected Works], 12 vols. (M.: Pravda, 1989), vol. V, p. 84.

75. See, for instance, J.C. Zacek, "The Russian Bible Society and the Russian Orthodox Church", *Church History*, vol. 35 (1966), pp. 411-37.

76. See, for instance, such important sources as: A. Rozhdestvensky, *Yuzhnorussky Shtundism* [South-Russian Stundism] (SPb.: Tipografiya Departamenta Udelov, 1889), pp. 19-21; Bishop Alexis, *Materialy Dlya Istorii*, pp. 228-9; 430-1; A. Ushinsky, *O Prichinakh Poyavleniya Ratsionalisticheskikh Ucheniy Shtundy i Nekotorykh Drugikh Podobnykh Sekt v Sel'skom Pravoslavnom Naselenii* [On the Causes of the Appearance of the Rationalistic Teachings of the Stunda and Some Other Similar Sects in the Rural Orthodox Population] (Kiev, 1884), pp. 42-62.

and the church.[77] But the history of the church is more complex than these commentators were willing to recognize. The dissociation of the Eastern Church from the Western (Roman) Church in the eleventh century (and, practically, even earlier), with the accompanying mutual offences and ex-communications, hardly exemplifies Christian charity. It is not surprising that the ordinary Russian believers, who constituted the overwhelming majority of those within the Russian Baptist movement, made some harsh statements about what they saw as Orthodox deficiencies. If the Baptists and other evangelicals were motivated, as was often alleged, by "fierce pride" or "hatred", then the most likely outcome as time passed would have been that they would have split up further and degenerated. This was in fact predicted by the far-seeing – certainly in his other prophecies – F.M. Dostoevsky.[78] However, what actually happened was almost exactly the opposite: despite many internal disagreements, the majority of the Russian sectarians at the end of the nineteenth and the beginning of the twentieth centuries coalesced and founded the first large Russian Protestant denominations ("brotherhoods") – the Russian Baptist Union and the Russian Union of Evangelical Christians.[79]

Causes of conversion

More analysis needs to be made, however, of the possible causes of the wide-spread conversions that took place from Orthodoxy in this period and the consequences of these conversions for later Baptist and Orthodox perspectives. There was considerable debate about the role of the Orthodox priests. Some Orthodox observers noted that peasants "fell away into

---

77. See, for instance: *Razgovor Pravoslavnogo i Pashkovtsa o Svyashchennom Pisanii i Predaniyakh Tserkovnykh* [The Conversation of an Orthodox and a Pashkovite about Scripture and Church Tradition]. – The copies of V.A. Pashkov Papers, 1/9, The Library of the International Baptist Theological Seminary, Prague, Czech Republic.

78. See F. Dostoevsky, "Mirages: Stundism and Radstockists", in F. Dostoevsky, *A Writer's Diary*, Vol. 2, 1877-1881, trans. by K. Lantz (Evanston, IL: Northwestern University Press, 1994), pp. 816-20.

79. See, for instance: *Istoriya Evangel'skikh Khristian-Baptistov v SSSR*, pp. 98-159; L. Shenderovsky, *Evangel'skie Khristiane* [The Evangelical Christians] (Toronto: Izdanie Kanadskogo Soyuza Evangel'skikh Khristian, 1980), pp. 81-115.

sectarianism" to a greater extent in those areas where local priests did not display even minimal care for their flock and thought mainly about their own ("worldly") problems and about the ceremonial part of religious life.[80] There was also considerable discussion and widely divergent views about whether financial incentives to convert were being offered by German Baptists and others from outside Russia. In August 1886, *Ekaterinoslavskie Eparkhial'nye Vedomosti* (The Ekaterinoslav Diocesan Bulletin), somewhat unusually for an Orthodox publication, pointed out the tendentiousness of correlating the peasants' secession from Orthodoxy with material assistance "from the Germans", stating: "But the German Baptists do not shower the peasants of Sofievka with gold!" The article argued that there was material help available in all communities, Protestant and Orthodox, and expressed the wish that "any small help and small deed would be done with loving care".[81] It is at this point that an aspect of the root of the issue, and a certain moral justification for the "falling away" (from Orthodoxy) of simple Russian people, can be seen. Many of them did not receive any Christian love in pre-revolutionary Russian Orthodoxy, and if they seemed inclined towards a questioning of Orthodoxy they knew that they faced the possibility, indeed probability, of all kinds of threats, beatings, imprisonments and exile.[82]

A certain strand of argument within the traditional criticism from Orthodox authors of the Baptist movement arguably reveals their own inadequate spiritual perspectives. To assert that the material factor -- money or other "tangible" help from the sectarians -- was crucial in conversion, as some authors do,[83] is to follow the line of interpretation used by

---

80. For a large collection of typical documents and testimonies of that epoch see O. Beznosova, ed., *Evangel'skoe Dvizhenie v Rossiyskoy Imperii, 1850-1917: Ekaterinoslavskaya Guberniya, Sbornik Dokumentov i Materialov*.

81. Ibid., p. 55.

82. To feel the severe spirit of the epoch it is sufficient to read the well-known Russian writer S.M. Stepnyak-Kravchinsky's book *Stundist Pavel Rudenko* (1894). See also V. Bonch-Bruevich, ed., *Materialy k Istorii i Izucheniyu Russkogo Sektantstva i Raskola* [Materials for the History and Study of Russian Sectarianism and Old Believers], Part 1 (SPb.: Tip. B.M. Vol'fa, 1908); and V. Pavlov, *"Vospominaniya Ssyl'nogo"* [Memoirs of an Exile] [1899], *Al'manakh po Istorii Russkogo Baptizma*, vol. I (1999), pp. 194-219.

83. See the theme review, for instance, in *Evangel'skoe Dvizhenie v Rossiyskoy Imperii, 1850-1917: Ekaterinoslavskaya Guberniya*, pp. 104-5, 207-8, 217-8, 262; G. Emel'yanov,

some Marxist historians to explain the Reformation in Europe simply as a German rejection of the way German money was flowing to Rome.[84] No doubt at times material reasons have driven apparently spiritual conversions in Russia and elsewhere. N.S. Leskov speaks in one of his documentary stories about a successful Orthodox missionary who in a remarkably short time baptized a great number of non-Russians in Siberia, but the secret of his success was that he distributed free vodka among the candidates for baptism.[85] There are also some reports about official offers of exemption from taxes for three years for heathens baptized into the Orthodox Church in Russia in the nineteenth century.[86] However, just as it would be unfair to assert that the missionary work of the Orthodox Church as a whole was based on such principles, so similar accounts of the conversion of evangelicals are inadequate.

Studying the documents of the period, it becomes clear that many Russians who became sectarians in the nineteenth century, as they considered their situation within Orthodoxy and made new choices, were guided by deep religious and moral motives. Perhaps they did fail to appreciate properly Russian Orthodoxy's undoubted spiritual achievements in the nineteenth century, for example: new translations of the Bible, selfless missionary work in the outlying districts of the Empire, and the development of the living tradition of *starchestvo* – the monastic eldership.[87] Yet what the individuals who began to question Orthodox practice often experienced was the hostile side of the church. Before the Revolution of 1905,

---

"*Ratsionalizm na Yuge Rossii*" [Rationalism in South Russia], *Otechestvennye Zapiski*, no. 5 (1878), pp. 206-7; Bishop Alexis, *Materialy Dlya Istorii*, pp. 282, 293.

84. See the theme reviewed, for instance, in E. Cairns, *Christianity through the Centuries: A History of the Christian Church*, 3rd ed. (Grand Rapids: Zondervan, 1996), pp. 271-77.

85. N. Leskov, *Na Krayu Sveta* [At the Edge of the World] [1876], in N. Leskov, *Sobranie Sochineniy*, 12 vols., vol. I, pp. 392-3.

86. See A. Znamenski, "Shamanism and Christianity on the Russian Siberian Borderland: Altaian Responses to Russian Orthodox Missionaries (1830-1917)", *Itinerario*, no. 1 (1998), pp. 113-6. Also some Baptist ministers of the end of the 19th century spoke about attempts at bribery: "When their words do not work, the Orthodox missionaries often promise their opponents [Baptists and Old Believers] a vacant post as a priest with a good salary": Pavlov, *Vospominaniya Ssyl'nogo*, p. 217.

87. See, for instance, the detailed review in N. Talberg, *Istoriya Russkoy Tserkvi* [The History of the Russian Church] (M.: Izd-vo Sretenskogo Monastyrya, 2004), pp. 724-924. See also N. Zernov, *Moscow the Third Rome* (N.Y.: AMS Press, 1971), pp. 77-94.

the major part of the legislation enacted in the Russian Empire concerning the Old Believers' and sectarian communities had a strongly repressive character.[88] Inevitably there was a response from those who were being attacked in this way. "The Stundists are always ready for debates", wrote one of the Orthodox researchers of sectarianism, "and not only the laity, but also the priests have difficulties in arguing against them… Even such a skilful warrior for the Orthodox faith as the most eminent Leontius, in his archiepiscopate days in Odessa, during the struggle with the Stundists *felt exhaustion*."[89] At the same time, the questioning that took place was not generally of a theological nature. Early Baptists and evangelicals did not usually have the theological or indeed intellectual tools with which to engage in sophisticated discussions with defenders of Orthodoxy. Rather, the points they made had to do with how faith worked out in daily life, "Formerly when I was a drunkard and debauchee, I was still considered an Orthodox member, but now, when I believe in Christ, my life has completely changed."[90] The sectarians repeated such statements over and over again, and not infrequently confirmed their words by living a new kind of life. Zhuk argues that the change of life of the newly converted, their abandonment of drunkenness, the change from a violent to a peaceful way of living, and their commitment to marital fidelity, popularized Stundism especially in the eyes of the female peasant population.[91]

---

88. See, for instance, *Zakony o Raskol'nikakh i Sektantakh* [The Laws on the Old Believers and Sectarians] (M.: Izdanie A. Skorova, 1903), pp. 92-193.

89. G. Emel'yanov, "Ratsionalizm na Yuge Rossii", *Otechestvennye Zapiski*, no. 3 (1878), p. 207. [Italics in the original]. Probably Emel'yanov is referring to Archbishop Leontius Lebedinsky (1822-93). Some modern writers continue to put questions "in the Stundist spirit" to the Orthodox hierarchy: see, for example: M. Gorokhov, *Kniga Nasushchnykh Voprosov o Pravoslavnoy Vere* [Book of Vital Issues concerning the Orthodox Faith] (M.: Arbor, 1998).

90. See such motifs, for instance, in A. Karev, "*Russkoe Evangel'sko-Baptistskoe Dvizhenie*" [The Russian Evangelical-Baptist Movement], *BV*, no. 3 (1957), pp. 24-6; A. Vvedensky, *Bor'ba s Sektantstvom* [Struggle against Sectarianism] (Odessa: Tipografiya Eparkhial'nogo Doma, 1914), pp. 198-9; G. Emel'yanov, "*Ratsionalizm na Yuge Rossii*", *Otechestvennye Zapiski*, no. 5 (1878), pp. 210-11; H. Coleman, "Becoming a Russian Baptist: Conversion Narratives and Social Experience", *Russian Review*, vol. 61, no. 1 (2002), pp. 94-112.

91. S.I. Zhuk, *Russia's Lost Reformation: Peasants, Millennialism, and Radical Sects in Southern Russia and Ukraine, 1830-1917* (Washington, D.C.: Woodrow Wilson Center Press, 2004), pp. 221-2; 304.

Given the way in which discussions focused on the apparent failure of Orthodoxy to deliver changed lives rather than on issues of theology, it might be thought that the evangelical movement was to be found only among those who were ignorant regarding the deeper spirituality of Orthodoxy. However, at the same time as the Baptist movement was growing among the peasants, dissatisfaction with the purely "ceremonial" form of Russian Orthodoxy, a form of Orthodoxy that was dominant, was growing among a section of the St Petersburg aristocracy and intelligentsia.[92] Clearly for them no desire for material gain through conversion was involved. The deep and growing desire was for personal spiritual experience. In the 1870s (as noted in chapter 1), a significant boost was given to the embryonic evangelical movement in the metropolis by the British aristocrat and lay preacher, Lord Radstock. The sermons preached by Radstock were outwardly simple, but were well received because of their spiritual depth and sincerity. Radstock had been influenced by the spirit of the interdenominational and international Keswick holiness movement.[93] His message inflamed the hearts of a considerable number of well-known and wealthy people in Russia and aroused a zeal for practical Christian activity among them. This new group of aristocratic evangelicals included retired Colonel Vasily A. Pashkov, Count M.M. Korf, Count A.P. Bobrinsky, Princess N.F. Lieven, Princess V.F. Gagarina, and others.[94]

As with the question of the conversion of Russian peasants who had contact with Germans, the question has inevitably been raised as to whether

---

92. See, for instance: E. Heier, *Religious Schism in the Russian Aristocracy, 1860-1900. Radstockism and Pashkovism* (The Hague: Martinus Nijhoff, 1970), pp. 30-56.

93. On the involvement of Lord Radstock with the annual meetings held in Keswick (in the north of England) see, for example, G.N. Nichols, "Ivan Kargel and the Pietistic Community of Late Imperial Russia", in S. Corrado and T. Pilli, eds. *Eastern European Baptist History: New Perspectives* (Prague: IBTS, 2007), pp. 78-9; For a comprehensive treatment of the influence of Keswick spirituality in Russia, principally channeled through Ivan Kargel, see G.L. Nichols, "Ivan V. Kargel (1849-1937) and the Development of Russian Evangelical Spirituality" (PhD thesis, International Baptist Theological Seminary, University of Wales, 2010). See also M. Kuznetsova, "Early Russian Evangelicals (1874-1929): Historical Background and Hermeneutical Tendencies: Based on I.V. Kargel's Written Heritage" (PhD thesis, University of Pretoria, 2009), pp. 101-4.

94. See, for instance: Shenderovsky, *Evangel'skie Khristiane*, pp. 89-91; M. Rowe, *Russian Resurrection: Strength in Suffering. A History of Russia's Evangelical Church* (London: Marshall Pickering, 1994), pp. 22-5.

the conversion of these aristocrats was something in which they took the initiative or where it was primarily an English import. The argument of this chapter has been that Russian-Ukrainian sectarians, peasants by birth, still *chose* the "Baptist faith", rather than having it imposed, and I would argue that something similar happened to the Russian aristocrats who heard Radstock. It was not that Radstock arrived in St. Petersburg to undertake preaching there on his own initiative. He had an invitation from a person belonging (according to Princess S.P. Lieven) "to one of the branches of the Russian Imperial House", Countess E.I. Chertkova, who had made the acquaintance of the English preacher in Europe.[95] From a Russian Orthodox standpoint, N.S. Leskov, who might have been expected to see Radstock as coming into Russia as an alien figure, also saw the initiative as lying with Chertkova. He remarks: "She found Radstock in England and gave him a start in Petersburg."[96] It is unlikely that the meeting took place in England. It is more probable that it was when Radstock was in Paris (in 1868) and was preaching in French at meetings which several members of the Russian aristocracy who were in Paris attended.[97] Leskov continued: "she ordered [*vypisala*] him to Russia",[98] and Leskov saw the whole enterprise as being under Chertkova's direction: "It all went, of course, under her guidance... she was so mother-like, so pleased with his success."[99] Leskov also asserts that the movement in the aristocrat circle in St. Petersburg (*"velikosvetskaya bespopovshchina"* – high society priestless sect) took shape as far back as the beginning of the 1860s, since the time of Alexander II's reforms, and that the invitation of Radstock to Russia was one of the stages of development of this spiritual process.[100]

---

95. S. Lieven, *Dukhovnoe Probuzhdenie v Rossii* [The Spiritual Awakening in Russia] (Korntal, Germany: Svet na Vostoke, 1990), pp. 10-11.

96. Leskov, *Velikosvetsky Raskol* [Schism in High Society], p. 113.

97. A. Trotter, *Lord Radstock: An Interpretation and a Record* (London: Hodder and Stoughton, 1914), pp. 187-8. However, according to Robert Sloan Latimer, meetings with Russians present took place in Switzerland. See Robert Sloan Latimer, *Under Three Tsars: Liberty of Conscience in Russia* (New York: F. H. Revell, 1909), p. 73.

98. Leskov, *Velikosvetsky Raskol*, p. 117.

99. Ibid., p. 118.

100. Ibid., pp. 113-8. On the earlier period see, for example: W. Sawatsky, "Prince Alexander N. Golitsyn (1773-1844): Tsarist Minister of Piety" (PhD thesis, University of Minnesota, 1976).

The interpretation offered by Leskov probably places too much emphasis on the role of Chertkova. However, the AUCECB official history of the Evangelical Christians-Baptists notes (somewhat enigmatically) that E.I. Chertkova and also N.F. Lieven "were born again before Lord Radstock's arrival in Petersburg from England".[101] If such a view of events in the metropolis in the 1870s is accepted, it helps to explain why the British preacher was so well accepted by his Russian audiences (large aristocratic homes were opened to him to hold meetings) when many of the features of his theological views and his practice of Divine Service – a term he did not use – were strange to Russians. The main message brought by Radstock was of salvation by faith, together with exhortations to the newly converted to live a holy life. This was enthusiastically accepted by people who were then termed "Radstockists". However, some of Radstock's beliefs could not but cause tension among the Russian aristocrats: for instance, his neglect of any sacraments and church organizations, his ignoring of the church fathers' authority, and his rejection for religious reasons of music, literature, and medicine.[102] Vasily Pashkov, who became the leader of the group in St. Petersburg, came from one of the wealthiest families in Russia and had been a Colonel of the Imperial Guard. Although initially he was reluctant to listen to what Radstock had to say, a prayer made by Radstock changed Pashkov's life. Pashkov's influence was such that it led to those in the new movement later becoming known as Pashkovites. The core of Radstock's evangelical thinking was continued by Pashkov, but the latter was aware of the Orthodox tradition of the sacraments in a way that was not true of Radstock.[103] In all these cases of conversion, from whatever rank in society, what can be observed is a desire for spiritual reality. There was an awareness among these converts to the evangelical movement that

---

101. *Istoriya Evangel'skikh Khristian-Baptistov v SSSR*, p. 14. This idea was strengthened by S.N. Savinsky, who saw E.I. Chertkova and N.F. Lieven as the proper sources of the Petersburg revival. See Savinsky, *Istoriya (1867 – 1917)*, p. 92. Savinsky does not deny the influence of English evangelicals on Russian high-society ladies, but sees, as primary, their own "spiritual seeking". – Ibid., p. 142.

102. See Leskov, *Velikosvetsky Raskol*, pp. 42-87; Trotter *Lord Radstock: An Interpretation and A Record*, pp. 134-5. See also Puzynin, *Traditsiya Evangel'skikh Khristian*, pp. 106-20.

103. See S. Corrado, *Filosofiya Sluzheniya Polkovnika Pashkova* [The Philosophy of Ministry of Colonel Vasily Pashkov] (SPb.: Bibliya Dlya Vsekh, 2005), pp. 66-9.

this spiritual reality was something which they found lacking in the offices of the Orthodox Church. It was this that meant they looked elsewhere for satisfaction. However, the overall evidence is that the conversions did not take primarily place as a consequence of – or even in the context of – explicit, sustained expressions of dissatisfaction with the Orthodox Church or Orthodox Christianity.

Molokans and Baptists

Russian Baptist continuity with the past, rather than any radical discontinuity, can also be seen in the emergence of Baptists in Tiflis, in the Caucasus. The influence of the Molokans is noteworthy in the developments in this region. The first person to request "baptism as a believer" among the Russians there – in the summer of 1867 – was probably Nikita Isaevich Voronin, who had previously established himself as a Molokan leader. He was a prosperous person, who had an independent approach to his spiritual pathway. Voronin made his request for believer's baptism to a German Baptist, Martin Kalweit.[104] According to P.V. Ivanov-Klyshnikov (one of the key leaders of the Russian Baptist Union in the 1920s): "Voronin… got to know that Kalweit had been professing exactly such [Baptist] convictions, which he had reached after his own difficult inward struggle and careful examination of the Word of God… Immediately Voronin desired to be baptized."[105] Kalweit had shortly before moved to Tiflis from Lithuania and was a tinsmith,[106] or according to other information, a tailor.[107] The

104. M. Kalweit in his memoirs defined N.I. Voronin as "the first of the Molokans who carefully studied the Scripture and wished to be baptized". – *Avtobiografiya M.K. Kalweita* [The Autobiography of M.K. Kalweit] [1913], ARSECB, F. 1, op. 5-8, d. 20, l. 2.

105. P. Ivanov-Klyshnikov, "*Shestidesyatiletie: 1867-1927*" [The Sixty Years: 1867-1927], *Bapt.*, no. 5 (1927), p. 14.

106. See "The Autobiography of Jacob Delakoff, Independent Missionary in Russia", *The European Harvest Field*, September 1935, p. 11.

107. See A. Karev, "*Yubileyny Doklad v Svyazi so 100-letney Godovshchinoy Bratstva ECB v SSSR*" [The Jubilee Report on the Occasion of the 100th Anniversary of the Brotherhood of the ECB in the USSR], *BV*, no. 4 (1967), p. 13. V.V. Ivanov, who was closely associated with the early Tiflis congregation, called M. Kalweit a "simple artisan". See V. Ivanov, "*Kniga Episkopa Alekseya*" [The Book by Bishop Alexis], *Bapt.*, no. 9 (1908), p. 24.

fact that Kalweit was apparently a person of lower social position, indicates that Voronin could not have any other interest except a spiritual one in fostering their relationship.[108] Kalweit at that time, by his own account, led German meetings in the narrow family circle and by no means proselytized his Baptist beliefs.[109]

Some researchers point to the significant influence exerted on Voronin by Jacob Delyakov, who was a missionary in Russia on his own initiative and mainly at his own expense.[110] At that time Delyakov was, strictly speaking, a deacon of the Nestorian Church,[111] though he had Presbyterian connections.[112] From the Baptist point of view he was a believer in infant baptism and so was hardly able to assist with the matter of "believer's baptism".[113] Nonetheless, Delyakov was not rigid in his beliefs, and he would later (in 1886) become a Baptist.[114] In 1867, when Delyakov understood more fully the developing convictions of Voronin, he advised him to accept baptism from Kalweit.[115] The whole episode testifies to conversations going on which were characterized by a certain independence of

---

108. On the poverty of M. Kalweit, see also A. Wardin, "Penetration of the Baptists into the Russian Empire in the Nineteenth Century", *Journal of European Baptist Studies*, no. 3 (2007), pp. 45-6. Thus, in the case of Voronin, to link his new faith with the hope of material assistance "from the Germans" has no credibility.

109. *Avtobiografiya M.K. Kalweita*, ll. 1-2. For some extracts from the reminiscences of M. Kalweit see also: *BV*, no. 5 (1947), pp. 36-7; Savinsky, *Istoriya (1867-1917)*, pp. 132-3.

110. See "The Autobiography of Jacob Delakoff", *The European Harvest Field*, May 1935, p. 15.

111. Delyakov in his memoirs mentions several times that before joining the Baptist church in Russia he was a Nestorian, who was ordained a deacon according to the Nestorian rites in Urmia (Persia) in 1862. See "The Autobiography of Jacob Delakoff", *The European Harvest Field*, March 1935, p. 5; April 1935, p. 6; May 1935, p. 15. At a later stage, after Voronin's baptism, Delyakov was ordained a presbyter by the Nestorian bishop in Urmia. See Ibid., September 1935, p. 12.

112. Delyakov graduated in 1858 from a seminary founded by American Presbyterians in Persia. See Ibid., April 1935, p. 5.

113. See Karev, *Yubileyny Doklad v Svyazi so 100-letney Godovshchinoy Bratstva ECB v SSSR*, pp. 12-13; Kovalenko, *Oblako Svideteley Khristovykh*, pp. 43-4.

114. *Istoriya Evangel'skikh Khristian-Baptistov v SSSR*, p. 524.

115. Later, when Delyakov explained why he did not baptize Voronin, he used the following enigmatic phrase: "in order not to be disdained by the Molokans". – Delyakov's Letter to V.A. Pashkov, November 2, 1884 (Copies of Pashkov Papers, 2/8/39). This seems strange, because Voronin himself wished to be baptized secretly. See "The Autobiography of Jacob Delakoff", September 1935, p. 11. It is noteworthy also that Voronin did not follow Delyakov's Nestorian (or Presbyterian) views.

religious beliefs. In this context, one influence on Voronin was the "water" Molokans, who diverged from the main body of Molokans in teaching "water" rather than purely "spiritual" baptism.[116] At first Voronin rejected the advice from Delyakov to be baptized "by faith" (as a believer) by the German Baptist, Kalweit. The principal reason for this was the hostility of the Molokans towards the Germans, motivated in particular by the fact that the Germans (unlike the Molokans) ate pork.[117] Only after Delyakov vigorously emphasized the international character of the Christian faith did Voronin finally agree to be baptized by Kalweit.[118]

It is significant also that the majority of the members of the Tiflis Baptist Church, established at that time (in 1869-1871), were former Molokans, and it was N.I. Voronin who became the pastor there, while Martin Kalweit became a deacon. Kalweit was not elected a deacon until 1879.[119] It is clear that the Tiflis Baptist congregation, which became the "mother church" for many communities in the Caucasus, experienced some friction between "pro-Molokan" and "pro-German" ways of conducting church life and ministry, to the extent that two somewhat separate congregations functioned. Voronin himself was, in a measure, a representative of the first tradition.[120] In a letter to A.M. Mazaev in 1889, Voronin mentioned some charges made against him personally regarding his alleged aversion to the customs of the German brethren.[121] It was the Russian group that Kalweit ultimately joined. "Our… German meetings", wrote

---

116. See the letter, N.I. Voronin to A.M. Mazaev (1889). Voronin says he first started to think about the necessity of baptism in 1863, after a conversation with "water" Molokans, N.I. Severov and Ya.I. Tanasov. See Val'kevich, *Zapiska o Propagande Protestantskikh Sekt v Rossii*, Supplement no. 5, p. 27. See also: *Istoriya Evangel'skikh Khristian-Baptistov v SSSR*, pp. 42-3. Also V.V. Ivanov: *Bapt.*, no. 9 (1908), p. 24. In these sources, the point made is about "internal", i.e. Molokan, influence, not an "external" influence on Voronin.

117. See "The Autobiography of Jacob Delakoff", September 1935, p. 11. According to this source, N.I. Voronin could not be "the first Russian Baptist" because he did not follow the Molokans in their attitude to "pig's meat". Thus the official date of the beginning of the Russian-Ukrainian brotherhood of ECB (usually taken as August 20, 1867, the day of Voronin's baptism) would be questionable.

118. Ibid.

119. *Istoriya Evangel'skikh Khristian-Baptistov v SSSR*, p. 78; Kovalenko, *Oblako Svideteley Khristovykh*, p. 37.

120. See Val'kevich, *Zapiska o Propagande Protestantskikh Sekt v Rossii*, pp. 108-9.

121. Ibid., Supplement no. 5, pp. 25-6.

Kalweit in his memoirs, "were disrupted at that time, because many had left. Then I told my wife: 'Let us go and look at what our Russian brothers do!' We went, and immediately joined them."[122] Among the fragments of the reminiscences of Kalweit, later published in *Bratsky Vestnik*, there are the following words about the Russian meeting, mostly composed of former Molokans: "My wife and I also joined them. And we served them… by singing… Then we worked all together; I served as a deacon and Voronin was the presbyter."[123]

The second, more "pro-German" line was represented by Vasily Gur'evich Pavlov, a Russian who would become a highly influential leader in the Russian Baptist Union. Pavlov received his theological education in Hamburg, translated the Confession of the German Baptists into Russian, and, according to some reports, orientated Russian sectarian communities, in the organizational and "liturgical" sense, towards the German Baptist model.[124] Although Pavlov's approach became influential among many Baptists, with those who did not follow Pavlov's way being put under pressure to conform,[125] an alternative approach was promoted by another very authoritative figure among the early Russian Baptists, the evangelist and presbyter, Vasily V. Ivanov (the father of P.V. Ivanov-Klyshnikov).[126] In 1895, V.V. Ivanov, in the underground periodical *Beseda* [Conversation] expressed his sharp criticism of the "overseas'" Baptists and Russian-German Baptists, even to some extent doubting the purity of their motives for spiritual work in Russia.[127] In 1899, he wrote in a very forthright way to D.I. Mazaev that it would be wrong for Russians to follow Western

122. *Avtobiografiya M.K. Kalweita*, l. 2.

123. *BV*, no. 5 (1947), p. 37.

124. See V. Pavlov, "Pravda o Baptistakh" [The Truth about the Baptists] [1911], *Al'manakh po Istorii Russkogo Baptizma*, vol. I (1999), pp. 244-5; Coleman, *Russian Baptists and Spiritual Revolution*, pp. 96-7.

125. N.I. Voronin was even excommunicated for a time and lost his presbyter's position. See Val'kevich, *Zapiska o Propagande Protestantskikh Sekt v Rossii*, Supplement no. 1, pp. 40-1.

126. On V.V. Ivanov's encouragement of N.I. Voronin's group (a move that was contrary to Ivanov's financial interests), see Bishop Alexis, *Materialy Dlya Istorii*, pp. 631, 636; Val'kevich, *Zapiska o Propagande Protestantskikh Sekt v Rossii*, pp. 81, 113.

127. See this letter in Val'kevich, *Zapiska o Propagande Protestantskikh Sekt v Rossii*, Supplement no. 3, pp. 26-8.

Christianity, because it was in large measure based on material values, and there was "nothing to learn" from its representatives regarding spiritual life.[128] In 1908, in the periodical the *Baptist*, Ivanov published an article which became famous, entitled "The Book by Bishop Alexis", in which he tried to give proofs for the idea of the absolute originality and independence of the Russian Baptists "from the Germans".[129]

In 1913-1914, shortly before his death, V.V. Ivanov became the editor-in-chief of the *Baptist*, an appointment which testified to the support he was accorded from the Russian Baptist brotherhood. In articles in that period he again wrote critically about Western spiritual culture, mentioning with disdain "the foreign articles, short reports, and unsubstantial stories" which were being translated and through which, according to him, Russian Baptists were being carried away.[130] He also disapproved of the spread among the churches of the practice of choir singing, at the same time nostalgically recalling the "common" (probably Molokan[131]) singing, with all the community joining in together. He compared the old ways to the new: the old were like joyful sunbeams, while the new he described as like lifeless electric light.[132] But the future lay neither with a dogmatically

---

128. See this letter of V.V. Ivanov in H. Coleman, "The Most Dangerous Sect: Baptists in Tsarist and Soviet Russia, 1905-1929" (PhD thesis, University of Illinois, 1998), p. 52. See also analysis of the letter in Coleman, *Russian Baptists and Spiritual Revolution*, pp. 97-8.

129. V. Ivanov, "*Kniga Episkopa Alekseya*" [The Book by Bishop Alexis], *Bapt.*, no. 9 (1908), pp. 23-7. See some criticism of this position, for instance, in A. Wardin, "Baptist Immersions in the Russian Empire: Difficult Beginnings", *Journal of European Baptist Studies*, no. 3 (2010), pp. 37-44.

130. V. Ivanov, "*Obshchiny i Presvitery*" [Communities and Presbyters], *Bapt.*, nos. 21-24 (1914), p. 8.

131. Old Molokan practices included many things that were alien to Baptist tradition, for example, prayers for the dead, which connected Molokans with the Orthodox. See, for instance, "*Iz Veroucheniya Molokan Tambovskogo 1-go i 2-go Sobraniya i Vladimirskogo [1896]*" [From the Creed of the Molokans of the 1st and 2nd Tambov's Gatherings and of Vladimir's (1896)], in S. Golovashchenko, ed., *Istoriya Evangel'sko-Baptistskogo Dvizheniya v Ukraine: Materialy i Dokumenty* [History of the Evangelical-Baptist Movement in the Ukraine: Materials and Documents] (Odessa: Bogomyslie, 1998), pp. 230-1. There is also some information about the closeness of Don Molokans to Orthodoxy (eg. recognition of sacraments, baptism of infants). See *Istoriya Evangel'skikh Khristian-Baptistov v SSSR*, p. 32; Mitrokhin, *Baptizm: Istoriya i Sovremennost'*, pp. 202-3. On prayers for the dead, reference was made by Molokans to the apocryphal books 2 Maccabees 12:42 and Baruch 3:4. See more in chapter 3.

132. *Bapt.*, nos. 21-24 (1914), pp. 21-2.

pro-Western nor anti-Western form of Baptist life. In 1923 P.V. Pavlov, who came from a Molokan background and called himself "a seventh generation sectarian",[133] reported to the Baptist World Congress in Stockholm:

> The Baptist movement in Russia came from the depths of Russian sectarianism, whose roots are in the distant past of Russian history... The Molokans, who were the ground whence the Russian Baptists appeared, accepted from foreign Baptists their organizational forms, which give the strength and stability that was not sufficiently present among the former Molokans.[134]

This shows that among the first Russian Evangelical-Baptist communities and their leaders there was heterogeneity. The movement included both Western-looking and nationalistic spiritual tendencies. The direct or the mediated adoption of European Protestant (specifically, evangelical) ideas was tempered by the self-dependence of the Russian sectarians. Russians, if they experienced evangelical conversion, made a "choice of faith". This faith was not only for "the Germans"; it was for the representatives of any of the other nationalities in Russia, but most of all it was to be a "Russian" faith. In terms of "choice", Kalweit also made a choice when he and his wife "joined" a Russian Baptist congregation, leaving the German one. This open situation at the end of the nineteenth century and the beginning of the twentieth century provided significant religious possibilities and created the conditions for the unprecedented success of the multi-ethnic evangelical movement in Orthodox Russia.

Evangelicals in Russian literature

The crowded meetings of the Pashkovites in St. Petersburg and also the spread of the "Stundo-Baptist" communities in the Ukraine did not go

---

133. *Bapt.*, no. 3 (1925), p. 6.
134. Ibid.

unnoticed in Russian society. The new developments were reported on in classical Russian literature. Thus, for example, N.S. Leskov published his story *Two Swineherds* in 1884, in which, basing his work on real events, he highlighted some differences between the views of the St Petersburg high society evangelicals and the Russian peasant Stundists, especially in relation to church discipline. In St Petersburg, he recounted, a cadet shot a girl who refused to marry him, and then mutilated her. He was imprisoned. The cadet repented when some members of the Radstock/Pashkov group visited the prison and spoke to him, and their connections led to the very early release of their "new brother". Soon he began to be a "model member" of the evangelical community. Leskov, wrote ironically of this, while also seriously questioning why the former cadet, taught by the evangelicals about salvation by faith *only*, did not feel any necessity to suffer because of his terrible sin and had no more interest in the crippled girl. Leskov's second story demonstrated that he felt certain sympathies for the Stundists' strictness in matters of faith and piety.[135] This story was about a Stundist community in the south of Russia. A young peasant Stundist was unfaithful to his wife and became the father of an illegitimate child. The Stundists decided that the man must take responsibility for the child and the mother, must divide his land into two parts, and must pay enough money for their needs. If he refused, he would "go to feed swine" (Luke 15:13-15), a euphemism for excommunication. The man repented publicly and agreed with the penalty. Leskov wrote, in conclusion:

> These two incidents of the punishments of sinners, [seen] in contrasting ways, probably help in understanding the differences between the customs and directions of the 'high life' sectarians and the customs of the peasants holding the teaching named the 'Stunda'. Obviously, these are not people of a similar kind: the Petersburg's cadet, who shot the girl, would

---

135. On Leskov's sympathies for the search for God among Russian people (and not only the Orthodox), see, for instance: T. Il'inskaya, "*Fenomen 'Raznoveriya' v Tvorchestve N.S. Leskova*" [The Phenomenon of 'Raznoverie' in N.S. Leskov's Writings] (Doctor of Philology degree thesis, St. Petersburg State University, 2010).

not sing, accompanied by the organ, among the Stundists, but... would go to feed the swine.[136]

But not all the leading writers were as critical as Leskov of the St Petersburg evangelical community. For example, F.M. Dostoevsky, although clearly opposed to the growth of Protestantism in Russia, certainly did not unequivocally condemn Radstock's preaching. This is how he described his experience:

> At that time I happened to hear him [Radstock] preaching in a certain 'hall', and, I recall, I didn't find anything special in him: he did not speak particularly well, nor particularly badly. Yet he works miracles over human hearts; people flock to hear him; many are deeply moved: they seek out the poor so as to do good deeds for them and almost reach the point of giving away their possessions. However, this may be happening only among us in Russia; it seems he [Radstock] is not so prominent abroad... Nevertheless, he produces remarkable conversions and arouses magnanimous feelings in the hearts of his followers. However, that is as it should be: if he is indeed sincere and is preaching a new faith, then, of course, he is possessed by all the spirit and fervour of the founder of a sect.[137]

Dostoevsky recognized that the conversions which were taking place were having a concrete effect: that the newly converted were motivated to "seek out the poor so as to do good deeds for them". At the same time Dostoevsky was perplexed, wondering why Russian people needed a kind of Protestantism. Dostoevsky (wrongly) saw Radstock as the founder of a new sect, but he knew the German Protestant tradition, and asked: "In fact, what kind of Protestants, what kind of Germans are our people anyway? And why should they learn German in order to sing psalms? Isn't

---

136. Leskov, *Zerkalo Zhizni*, pp. 467-8.
137. F. Dostoevsky, *A Writer's Diary*, Vol. 1, 1873-1876, trans. by K. Lantz (Evanston, IL: Northwestern University Press, 1994), pp. 419-20.

everything, everything that they are seeking, to be found in Orthodoxy? Does not Orthodoxy, and Orthodoxy alone, contain the truth and the salvation of the Russian People, and in ages yet to come the salvation of the whole of humanity?"[138] That was the theory, but Dostoevsky partly answered his own question about the growth of Protestantism when he admitted: "Our church has been in a state of paralysis since Peter the Great; it's a terrible time..."[139]

An interesting and psychologically very exact description of the inconsistencies and ambiguities present in the reception of Protestant ideas in Russia was given by L.N. Tolstoy in his novel *Resurrection* (1899):

> The Countess Katerina Ivanovna, however strange it may seem, and however little it seems to be in keeping with the rest of her character, was a staunch adherent to that teaching which holds that the essence of Christianity lies in belief in redemption. She went to meetings where this teaching, then in fashion, was being preached, and assembled the 'faithful' in her own house. Though this teaching repudiated all ceremonies, icons, and sacraments, Katerina Ivanovna had icons in every room, and one on the wall above her bed, and she kept all that the church prescribed without noticing any contradiction in that.[140]

An anonymous author, in the magazine edited by F.M. Dostoevsky, wrote ironically about women such as Countess Katerina Ivanovna, commenting on: "The *religious* mood of ladies of the Petersburg high life... Ball dresses are packed up in chests for a while, and all have begun to love Christ in honor of the new apostle of Christianity, who has arrived to Petersburg, the Englishman Lord Radstock!"[141] At a later date it was not unknown for

---

138. Ibid., p. 192.
139. F.M. Dostoevsky, *Polnoe Sobranie Sochineniy* [The Complete Works], 30 vols. (Leningrad: Nauka, 1984), v. XXVII, p. 49.
140. L. Tolstoy, *Resurrection* (Charleston, SC: Forgotten Books, 2008), p. 305.
141. *"Novy Apostol v Peterburgskom Svete"* [The New Apostle in Petersburg High Life], *Grazhdanin*, no. 8 (1874).

some Russian Baptists (and especially Baptist women), to set aside (*pribra-li*) Orthodox icons temporarily – "until better times", as one lady expressed herself.[142] Those Russians who rejected Orthodoxy in favor of the evangelical faith could still retain a form of Orthodox mentality.

As Russian writers wrote about Protestantism, they generally saw it as acceptable if it was "in the right place", i.e. in Europe. If it entered Russia, it should remain among the "Germans" who had moved there. Many Russians sympathized with the "brave Protestants" who had risen against the "Latin heresy". Orthodoxy historically directed hostility more towards Catholicism than towards Protestantism.[143] For example, N.M. Karamzin wrote: "The poor monk Martin Luther came, took off his monastic clothes, and holding in his hand the Gospel, dared to name the Pope Antichrist, exposing his [the Pope's] lies, self-interest, distortion of the holy."[144] However, if Protestantism crossed the "sacred borders" of "Mother Russia" and affected Orthodox society, the response was, as A. Khomyakov put it: "Protestantism can't happen here… we stand on completely different soil."[145] For some Russians in the nineteenth century, little had changed since Ivan the Terrible wrote in 1570 to Jan Rokita, a pastor of the Moravian Brethren, and said: "You are not only a heretic, but a servant of the antichrist and the devil's council; maybe, a bigger servant than Luther was. *Henceforth, do not bring your teaching in our land!* We pray to our Lord Jesus Christ, the Savior, to protect our Russian nation from the darkness of your disbelief."[146]

---

142. For instance, I once heard an emotional testimony on the subject from Baptist presbyter V.N. Khot'ko (Petropavlovsk, Kazakhstan, 2001), mentioning several such "strange events".

143. See, for instance: D. Tsvetaev, *Protestantstvo i Protestanty v Rossii do Epokhi Preobrazovany* [Protestantism and Protestants in Russia before the Age of the Reforms] (M.: Universitetskaya Tipografiya, 1890), pp. 4-7. The Orthodox theologian N.M. Zernov, for instance, wrote that even the devastating Tartars' invasion was not so dangerous to Russia as the invasion of "Latin Christianity". See N. Zernov, *The Russians and Their Church* (Crestwood, NY: St. Vladimir's Seminary Press, 1978), p. 22.

144. Karamzin, *Istoriya Gosudarstva Rossiyskogo*, p. 588.

145. A. Khomyakov, "*Neskol'ko Slov Pravoslavnogo Khristianina o Zapadnykh Veroispovedaniyakh*" [Some Notes of an Orthodox Christian on the Western Denominations], in A. Khomyakov, *Tserkov' Odna* [The Church is One] (M.: Dar", 2005), p. 97.

146. Ivan Grozny, *Sochineniya* [Works] (SPb.: Asbuka, 2000), p. 115.

Yet Protestantism did have an appeal to the Russian soul. One of the greatest Russian poets, F.I. Tyutchev, wrote his famous lines:

I love the services of Lutherans,
Their rite so stern, so weighty, so simple.
I understand the sacred teaching
Of these naked walls, this empty temple.[147]

Tyutchev was uncompromising in his defence of Orthodoxy, even echoing at times the radical views of Slavophiles and Pan-Slavists.[148] For example, he dreamed about winning back Constantinople from the Turks: "Is it not already time to cross yourself, to strike the bell in Tsargrad? ...O, Russia, how great is the coming day – the universal, Orthodox day!"[149] But, simultaneously, there were some "European" features in Tyutchev's Slavophilism.[150] Against the background of the deep crisis in the Orthodox Church at the end of the nineteenth century and the beginning of the twentieth, the best representatives of Russian society raised their voices in defence of freedom, including the freedom of the "sectarians", especially during the periods of their severest persecutions. For example, Leo Tolstoy's articles and his active participation on behalf of the needs of the Doukhobors are well-known.[151] In one of his works, Tolstoy prophetically noted:

---

147. *Poems and Political Letters of F.I. Tyutchev*, trans. by J. Zeldin (Knoxville: University of Tennessee Press, 1973), p. 45.

148. Slavophiles: the name given to a part of the Russian intelligentsia who, from the 19th century onwards, advocated the supremacy of Slavic culture and religion, and resisted Western influences on Russia. The Pan-Slavists were followers of a movement (from the mid-19th C.) which aimed at the unity of all Slavic peoples. The ideas of the latter were especially popular during the Russo-Turkish War of 1877-8.

149. F. Tyutchev, *Stikhotvoreniya* [Poetry] (M.: Pravda, 1978), p. 168; R. Conant, *The Political Poetry and Ideology of F.I. Tiutchev* (Ann Arbor, MI: Ardis, 1983), p. 36.

150. See, for instance, a remarkable work: B. Bukhshtab, *Russkie Poety* [Russian Poets] (Leningrad: Khudozhestvennaya Literatura, 1970), pp. 9-75.

151. See, for instance, "*Posleslovie k Stat'e P.I. Biryukova 'Gonenie na Khristian v Rossii v 1895 g.*" [Afterword to the Article 'The Persecution of Christians in Russia in 1895' by P.I. Biryukov], and "*Pis'mo v Inostrannye Gazety po Povodu Goneniy na Kavkazskikh Dukhoborov*" [Letter to Foreign Newspapers about Persecutions of the Caucasian Dukhobors]. – L. Tolstoy, *Polnoe Sobranie Sochineniy* [The Complete Works], 90 vols. (M.: GIHL, 1956), vol. XXXIX, pp. 99-105, 209-15.

The half-savage Cossacks who beat the Dukhobors by order of
the officers, 'very soon began to be tired of it'... That means,
conscience began to agitate them; and the authorities, fear-
ing the influence of the Dukhobors upon them, hastened to
withdraw them. Never was there a persecution of innocent
people which has not ended in the persecutors receiving the
principles of the persecuted.[152]

The democratic opposition to absolutism within the Empire, coupled
with pressure exerted on Russia by public opinion in Western Protestant
countries, meant that sectarians were not completely deprived of their
civil rights. According to one of the testimonies of that time, the Ober-
Procurator of the Orthodox Holy Synod, Konstantin P. Pobedonostsev,
railed that the sectarians were "filling Europe with their complaints".[153]

For the severely uncompromising Pobedonostsev, such complaints were
a potentially serious threat to the freedom of the Orthodox Church. But
others saw the Orthodox Church as itself a threat to freedom. For example,
philosopher Vladimir Soloviev wrote to Pobedonostsev in 1892:

The politics of religious persecution and the violent spread
of official Orthodoxy have clearly exhausted the Divine patience... Meanwhile, from right and left, from Eastern Siberia
to the western border of European Russia, reports are coming
that this situation is not becoming milder, but is even getting worse. The missionary congress in Moscow, with unprecedented cynicism, has proclaimed the powerlessness of spiritual means of struggle against schism and sectarianism, as well
as the necessity of the secular sword.[154]

---

152. Ibid., p. 103; L. Tolstoi, *The Novels and Other Works of Lyof N. Tolstoi*, 24 vols. (N.Y.:
Charles Scribner's Sons, 1911), vol. XXI, p. 301.

153. See Savinsky, *Istoriya (1867-1917)*, p. 171.

154. *K.P. Pobedonostsev i Ego Korrespondenty: Pis'ma i Zapiski* [K.P. Pobedonostsev and his
Correspondents: Letters and Memoranda] (Moscow – Petrograd: Gos. Izd-vo, 1923), vol.
I, part 2, p. 969.

In his work "On Spiritual Authority in Russia", V.S. Soloviev spoke bitterly about the Russian Church as represented by some of its ecclesiastical
leaders: "At first, during the time of Nikon, it reached for the *crown of the
State*, then it grappled persistently for the *sword of the State*, and finally
it was forced to don the *uniform of the State*."[155] Many Russian writers
and public figures, impelled by an individual rather than a "state" understanding of Orthodoxy, and influenced by general democratic values, selflessly defended the freedom of conscience of the first Russian evangelicals.
Among those who were prominent in their civic stand were Soloviev,[156]
A.M. Bobrishchev-Pushkin,[157] A.S. Prugavin,[158] A.F. Koni,[159] and S.P.
Melgunov.[160] The last-named, a famous historian, argued: "The issues of
freedom of conscience and freedom of belief... cannot be under the authority of executive police power..."[161] Orthodoxy was defended by adminis-
trative and bureaucratic means, including brutal compulsion of sectarians,
but this policy diminished rather than enhanced the church. According to
Russian writer P.I. Melnikov (Pechersky), "Our people do not respect the
clergy because the clergy themselves continually present examples of lack

---

155. V. Soloviev, *Freedom, Faith, and Dogma: Essays by V.S. Soloviev on Christianity and
Judaism*, trans. by V. Wozniuk (Albany, NY: State University of New York Press, 2008), p.
25. [Italics in the original].

156. See also: V. Soloviev, "*O Dukhovnoy Vlasti v Rossii*" [On Spiritual Authority in
Russia], in V. Soloviev, *Sobranie Sochineniy* [The Collected Works], 9 vols. (SPb.:
Obshchestvennaya Pol'za, 1901), vol. III, pp. 206-20.

157. See A. Bobrishchev-Pushkin, *Sud i Raskol'niki-Sektanty*.

158. See A. Prugavin, *Monastyrskie Tyur'my v Bor'be s Sektantstvom: K Voprosu o
Veroterpimosti* [Monastery Prisons in the Struggle against Sectarianism: On the Issue of
Toleration] (M.: Posrednik, 1905).

159. See A.F. Koni, "*Shtundisty*" [The Stundists], in A.F. Koni, *Na Zhiznennom Puti: Iz
Zapisok Sudebnogo Deyatelya* [On Life's Path: From the Notes of a Lawyer], 2 vols. (M.:
T-vo I.D. Sytina, 1914), vol. I, pp. 600-32.

160. See S. Melgunov, *Tserkov' i Gosudarstvo v Rossii: K Voprosy o Svobode Sovesti*
[Church and State in Russia: On the Issue of Freedom of Conscience] (M.: T-vo I.D.
Sytina, 1907).

161. S. Melgunov, "*Shtundisty ili Baptisty? Po Povodu Sudebnogo Presledovaniya Sektantov
po 29 st. Ustava o Nakazaniyakh*" [Stundists or Baptists? On the Subject of Prosecution
of Sectarians According to Article 29 of the Penal Code], *Russkaya Mysl'*, vol. XI (1903),
p. 166.

of respect for the faith."[162] In Russian literary circles, the sectarians could sometimes receive more favorable evaluation than the Orthodox Church.

Orthodox-Baptist commonalities

Although there were considerable differences between Orthodoxy and the emerging Baptist and evangelical movements in the nineteenth century, this study seeks to explore ways in which connections and commonalities existed, persisted and increased. Some within the Orthodox Church were seeking to find an authentic new way to live out a Christian witness in Russian society. This was also a profound concern of the evangelicals. In the second half of the nineteenth century, the Byzantine symphony of empire and church still dominated in Russia. There was an excessive idealization of the "old times". The Russian philosopher V.V. Rozanov once expressed this using the picture of a "decaying and dying" old woman (Byzantium) whispering to a young girl (Russia) that the "church statute" and "statutory practice" constituted "the most essential thing of religion, the main point of the faith". Russia, said Rozanov, "in a frightened manner accepted this incomprehensible, but for her holy idea", and consequently exerted every effort to fulfil the commission to keep the old forms and rites.[163] Though somewhat extreme, this picture reflects the spirit of the age, when Orthodoxy in Russia was, at least in its traditional form, in danger of appearing to be played out. This fuelled a growing desire for reform. The idea of a great Church Council, unprecedented in the history of Russia up to that time, was in the air.[164]

At the same time as some within Orthodoxy were seeking to respond positively to the challenges of the times, Russian evangelical movements were developing their own life within the Empire. In part a natural

---

162. P. Melnikov, *Zapiska o Russkom Raskole*, p. 189.

163. Rozanov, *Russkaya Tserkov'*, p. 525.

164. See, for instance: S. Rimsky, *Rossiyskaya Tserkov' v Epokhu Velikikh Reform* [The Russian Church in the Age of the Great Reforms] (M.: Krutitskoe Patriarshee Podvor'e, 1999), pp. 190-214; M. Shkarovsky, *Russkaya Pravoslavnaya Tserkov pri Staline i Khrushcheve*, pp. 68-71.

reaction to the evident problems of Orthodoxy, they were also one of the responses to the new historical developments within Russian society. The eminent Ukrainian poet, T.G. Shevchenko, who looked quite objectively at Orthodox–Protestant issues (certainly by comparison with Orthodox priests on the one hand and sectarian preachers on the other), powerfully expressed the religious feelings of the ordinary people in one of his later poems, composed on the eve of the widespread evangelical awakening in the Ukraine. What he wrote, with its criticism of popular Orthodoxy, breathes something of the spirit of Stundism:

> They know no faith without a cross,
> They know no faith without a priest…
> …………………The people lie
> And the Byzantine Lord Sabaoth
> Deceives! But God does not…
> He will help us bear our grief,
> And bury our sorrows by dark of night
> In a quiet and joyful hut.[165]

The focus needed to be on God, in a time of deep spiritual anxiety.

Yet there was also a focus, among both the Orthodox and the evangelicals, on past events in Russian religious history. In the case of the Orthodox, this valuing of the past is not surprising. But Russian Baptist communities, in a paradoxical way, showed a similar "extremely conservative", national-religious spirit. Both Orthodox and evangelical took the view that God had given to Christianity in Russia a unique identity and a worldwide importance. In 1907, A. Kartashev, in an article "Did the Apostle Andrew Visit Russia?", quoted Tsar Ivan the Terrible, who wanted to by-pass the Greeks

---

165. T. Shevchenko, "*Likere*" [To Likera] [1860], in T. Shevchenko, *Zibrannya Tvoriv* [Collected Works] (Kyiv: Naukova Dumka, 2003), vol. II, p. 351. Among those who may be regarded as Ukrainian forerunners of Russian Protestantism was the philosopher G.S. Skovoroda, who sympathized with the "Spiritual Christians", having very simple ceremonials, and was known for his remarkable sayings, such as: "He who has no needs is near to heaven." On the close relations of Skovoroda with the Doukhobors, see Karetnikova, *Russkoe Bogoiskatel'stvo*, pp. 60-6; Reshetnikov, Sannikov, *Obzor Istorii Evangel'sko-Baptistskogo Btatstva na Ukraine*, pp. 62-3.

and to trace Russian Christianity back to the apostles: "The Greeks are no Gospel to us. We believe not in the Greeks but in Christ. We received the Christian faith at the birth of the Christian church."[166] There was a tradition which said: "At the time when St. Apostle Andrew was in Tsargrad, he traveled across the Black Sea to us, and then we accepted baptism from him, not from the Greeks";[167] or in another source, "truly Russia is not any less than any other Eastern nation, because the Apostle enlightened it too".[168] The "Debate on the Faith" (1650) spoke in similar tones and was reprinted many times. The author, Russian thinker A. Sukhanov, asserted: "Listen, you Greeks, and heed this. Do not boast, and do not call yourselves the source, because today the words of the Lord have been fulfilled in you: you were first, and now you are last; whereas we were last, but now we are first."[169] This tradition was continued by Archpriest Avvakum in his famous speech to Greek Patriarchs (1667) when he stated, "Your Orthodoxy became motley because of the violence of the Turkish Mahommed… You became frail. So in the future come and learn from us."[170] It was a tradition that was alive in the thinking of N.S. Leskov, who questioned, "Whether or not we are obligated to the Greeks because we know of God through them – you can't demonstrate or prove that the Greeks revealed him to us. We found him neither in the magnificence of Byzantium nor in the smoke of the censer, but he is simply our known co-sufferer, walking everywhere with us."[171] But whereas Leskov saw God as "co-sufferer", Avvakum was

166. Cited in A. Kartashev, *"Byl li Apostol Andrey na Rusi?"* [Did the Apostle Andrew Visit Russia?], *Khristianskoe Chtenie*, no. 7 (1907), p. 93. See also Golubinsky, *Istoriya Russkoy Tserkvi*, vol. I, part 1, p. 27.

167. Cited in A. Kartashev, *Ocherki po Istorii Russkoy Tserkvi* [Essays on the History of the Russian Church], 2 vols. (Paris: YMCA-PRESS, 1991), vol. II, pp. 126-7. See also D. Shubin, *A History of Russian Christianity*, 4 vols. (N.Y.: Algora Publishing, 2005), vol. I, pp. 9-10.

168. Cited in S. Soloviev, *Sochineniya* [Works], 18 vols., part 5: *Istoriya Rossii s Drevneyshikh Vremen* [The History of Russia since Earliest Times], vol. IX-X (M.: Mysl', 1990), p. 414.

169. A. Sukhanov, *"Preniya o Vere"* [Debate on the Faith], *Chteniya v Obshchestve Istorii i Drevnostey Rossiyskikh*, no. 2 (1894), p. 101.

170. *Zhitie Avvakuma i Drugie Ego Sochineniya* [The Life of Avvakum and his other Writings] (M.: Sovetskaya Rossiya, 1991), p. 60.

171. Leskov, *Na Krayu Sveta*, p. 348.

impressed by Russian power: "By the grace of God we have autocracy."[172] And he admonished Tsar Alexis Mikhaylovich: "Say in Russian: 'Lord, forgive me, a sinner!' Be done with the *Kyrie-eleison* – this is what the Greeks say – spit on them! For thou art the son of Mikhail: a Russian, not a Greek. Speak thy native tongue... We ought to speak as Christ taught us."[173] Even Christ, it seems, spoke Russian.

What is more remarkable is that somewhat similar ideas were to be found among Russian evangelical writers. For many of them, it was intolerable to suggest that Russian Protestants had simply adopted religious beliefs "from the Germans". Probably one of the first Russian Baptists who exemplified in his writings a nationalist Baptist approach to this issue was the powerful figure of V.V. Ivanov. He wrote in the *Baptist* in 1908:

> Baptist beliefs in Russia... are much more unique and national than Byzantine Orthodoxy, and even more so: they are *absolutely unique*, i.e. they arose without the slightest influence from German Baptists.[174]

> While the secular scholars, the researchers of Russian sectarianism, almost unanimously affirm its originality and proudly point to the sectarians as the proof of the creativity of the Russian nation, the spiritual 'writers' [i.e. Orthodox authors] are excessively desirous to prove that ... our Baptist doctrines are 'German' beliefs.[175]

Later in the same article, and flying in the face of historical evidence (but without any embarrassment), Ivanov again asserted: "The Baptists in Russia... arose without any participation of the Germans."[176] It is significant

---

172. *Zhitie Avvakuma i Drugie Ego Sochineniya*, p. 60.

173. *Zhitie Avvakuma i Drugie Ego Sochineniya*, p. 273. *Kyrie-eleison*: Lord, have mercy! (Greek)

174. V. Ivanov, *Kniga Episkopa Alekseya* [The Book by Bishop Alexis], *Bapt.*, no. 9 (1908), p. 24. [Italics in the original].

175. Ibid.

176. Ibid.

that this highly polemical article by Ivanov in the *Baptist* was accompanied by a comment explaining that the author, "at the request of the editorial board", had written in response to a new book published in that year by the Orthodox Bishop Alexis, who, among other things, emphasized the "German faith" of Russian Baptists.[177] The mention of the editorial board indicates that these "apologetic" ideas were not only Ivanov's private opinion, but were at least to some extent the official Russian Baptist line. The periodical *Baptist* was the main press organ of the Russian Baptist Union.[178]

S.N. Savinsky, as a leading historian of the ECB looking at the reasons for the beginnings of evangelical communities in Russia in the nineteenth century, put direct divine action in the first place. Referring to the early colporteurs distributing the Holy Scriptures in Russia he says: "None other than the Holy Spirit inspired those who were insignificant in the eyes of the world, modest people, but men of spirit." He goes on to speak of the "spontaneous" beginnings of the Society for the distribution of the Scriptures in Russia and, in the same period, the "unique evangelical awakening among the Molokans of Transcaucasia" and among peasants in the South of Ukraine (where Germans, of course, were clearly involved). According to Savinsky, the fact that these events were simultaneous is "wrapt in mystery" and "can be explained only by the action of the Holy Spirit."[179] M.S. Karetnikova continues this interpretative approach: "The Ukrainian peasants did not adopt any 'German faith'! None of them became Lutheran, Reformed, or Mennonite... While terrible religious ignorance and superstitions dominated among the people, Stundism should be considered as a miracle and God's favor with us."[180] S.V. Sannikov also denies much German influence: "This ideological point of view is not supported by

177. See Bishop Alexis, *Vnutrennyaya Organizatsiya Obshchin Yuzno-Russkikh Neobaptistov* [Internal Structure of Communities of the South-Russian neo-Baptists] (Kazan: Tsentral'naya Tipografiya, 1908), pp. 7-8.

178. See Ivanov, *Kniga Episkopa Alekseya*, p. 23. In the second half of the 1880s, sceptical attitudes to German Baptists were also expressed by V.A. Pashkov, who wrote not so much in a nationalistic vein but in the spirit of European "open-mindedness". See the analysis of some "anti-German" letters of Pashkov in Puzynin, *Traditsiya Evangel'skikh Khristian*, pp. 195-7.

179. Savinsky, *Istoriya (1867-1917)*, p. 162.

180. Karetnikova, *Russkoe Bogoiskatel'stvo*, p. 77.

historical facts."[181] Savinsky concludes in nationalist-theological vein: "The historical truth reveals itself: the Russian-Ukrainian Baptist beliefs were not an outside implanting… but were the result of seeking for fellowship with the living God, and issued from the depths of the national spirit, awakened by the Holy Spirit and by God's Word."[182]

Where evangelicals with this viewpoint make a connection between Russian Baptist life and earlier movements of renewal and reform in the church they were less likely to make links with the European Protestant Reformation and more likely to talk about the Novgorod Strigolniks (mentioned earlier), who lived one and a half centuries before Martin Luther. From this perspective Russia, not Germany, saw the first Protestant Reformation. Politely mentioning German Baptist sensibilities, "May German brothers not be offended at us",[183] such researchers then start their original interpretations of Old Russian history. Here are some examples from respected authors, to a significant degree expressing widespread opinions held within the ECB community. The first quotation is as recent as 2007, which suggests that this is not a view that has died away:

> In the 14th century, uncoordinated outbreaks of religious protest were poured out in the large *Protestant* movement known under the name of the Strigolniks. The modern Russian Baptists consider the Strigolniks as their remote predecessors, seeing in their doctrinal statements and practice of life many kindred elements.[184] [Italics mine. – C.P.].

> There is a strong resemblance between the teachings of the Strigolniks, these evangelical Christians of the 14th-15th centuries, and the believers of the evangelical awakening in Russia

181. Sannikov, *Dvadtsat' Vekov Khristianstva*, vol. II, pp. 511-12.
182. S. Savinsky, "Baptisty v Rossii v XIX Veke" [The Baptists in Russia in the 19th Century], in *Istoriya Baptizma*, p. 343.
183. I have often heard this phrase used by some Russian Baptists.
184. V. Popov, "*Protestanty Zemli Russkoy*" [The Protestants of the Russian Land], *NG–Religii*, 19 September 2007.

in the 19th century… The movement of the Strigolniks… was the 'native product of the Russian mind'.[185]

The forerunners of the evangelical movement in Russia were… the Strigolniks (14th C), the Old Believers' priestless bodies (17th C), the Dukhobors and the Molokans (18th C), and the Stundists (19th C).[186]

The point to be noted here is not so much the extent to which the statements are (or are not) drawn from serious historical research. There are others within the Russian Baptist tradition who have seen the story in a different way. An example is the work of I.P. Plett, who does not discount the role of foreigners – for example, German settlers as well as Protestant missionaries from other countries – but does justice to their evangelical ministry in Russia.[187] The significance of the perspectives offered by Ivanov and later by Savinsky and others is the degree to which, in their determination to play down German influence on Russian Baptists, they are in keeping with the *apologia* of Russian Orthodoxy, with its tendency to distance itself from the Greek influence. Both Orthodox and Baptist authors in Russia readily admit the adoption by their traditions of external aspects of the religious life that they saw elsewhere (the formal creeds, ceremonies, organizational structure and hierarchy). However, they did not usually go beyond that. The majority of them object to any talk of a "foreign faith". In both cases there is a desire to "prolong" the history of the churches into the distant past, and in the course of doing this statements are made which

---

185. S. Savinsky, *Strigol'niki* [The Strigolniks], *Al'manakh "Bogomyslie"*, vol. 1 (1990), p. 188.

186. Trubchik, *Vera i Traditsiya*, p. 271. See also an extensive historical review of the origins of Russian Protestantism in the work of a Pentecostal author: Franchuk, *Prosila Rossiya Dozhdya u Gospoda*, [Windows CD-ROM] *Istoriya evangel'skogo dvizheniya v Evrazii 2.0*.

187. See I. Plett, *Zarozhdenie Tserkvey ECB* [The Origin of Churches of the ECB] (Izd-vo CCECB "Khristianin", 1994). Among early valuable testimonies on the theme see, for instance, Johann Wieler's memoirs *Some Brief Comments on the Origin of the Stundists and Baptists and the Baptist Movement Among the Russian People of South of Russia* (1884), published a century later by L. Klippenstein: *Johann Wieler (1839-1889) "Among Russian Evangelicals: A New Source of Mennonites and Evangelicalism in Imperial Russia"*, *Journal of Mennonite Studies*, no. 5 (1987), pp. 44-60.

cannot seriously be substantiated. On the one hand both the Orthodox and the Baptists are adopting the same methods to defend their traditions, while on the other hand, in a paradoxical way, the attempt by each to show that their own tradition is unique at times has pushed both Orthodox people and Baptists towards apparently irreconcilable opposition to each other.

Many Russian Orthodox authors are so focused on Orthodoxy as the true faith that they can see no room for any other confession. Extreme apologists of Orthodoxy would rather affirm the role of atheism than of any form of Protestantism, asserting that the Communists "providentially protected" Russia for the future triumph of Orthodoxy.[188] This perspective cannot entertain the possibility that Russian evangelicals had and have living roots in the Orthodox tradition. At the same time, many Russian Baptists reject their obvious historical and the spiritual-kindred bonds with Orthodoxy.[189] Yet in the period of the formation of the first Stundist and Baptist communities in the 1860s and 1870s, by no means all sectarians sought to separate themselves from Orthodoxy. There is evidence that many of them continued for years to visit Orthodox churches, to sing Orthodox hymns, and to turn to parish priests with requests for weddings, burials, and other ceremonies. This happened despite their engagement in their own meetings.[190] The process of separation from the official church was considerably speeded up by the persecutions which Russian sectarians suffered on a massive scale. The key to the problem of why Orthodox connections are so rarely recognized in the writing of the history of Russian Baptists is, I would argue, that those who might be termed "Westernizers" within the ECB have been more ready to recognize the foreign influences on the origins of the Russian Baptists and have not given attention to Orthodoxy, while the "Slavophile" wing is more open to the possibility of the influence of Orthodoxy (to avoid any suggestion of "German" influence), but many on this wing are more likely to say something that

---

188. See Podberezsky, *Protestanty i Drugie*, pp. 66-7.

189. "It was not our Mother but a wicked stepmother!" they say, remembering their old grievances and oppressions. For instance, testimony of presbyter V.N. Khot'ko (Petropavlovsk, Kazakhstan, 1999).

190. See, for instance: A. Borozdin, *"Shtundizm"* [Stundism], in S. Averintsev, ed., *Khristianstvo: Entsiklopedichesky Slovar'* [Christianity: Encyclopedia] 3 vols. (M.: Bolshaya Rossiyskaya Entsiklopediya, 1995), vol. III, p. 247.

echoes A. Sukhanov's words: "Our faith is from God, period!"[191] More work remains to be done to show that behind the surface level conflicts between the Orthodox and the Baptists in Russia in the formative Baptist period, in many areas the ideas that were held within their traditions were very similar.

Conclusion

The "choice" of faith, I have argued in this chapter, is important in Russian history. There is no doubt that in the history of Russia a choice was made in favor of Orthodoxy. Later Baptist ideas came into Russia, brought by foreign migrants and missionaries. At this stage another "choice of faith" was made by many Russians. It is true that there was strong internal influence, principally from Russian sectarianism. However, specifically Baptist beliefs, though they were formerly foreign to Russia, became acceptable and were *chosen* by the Russians in a similar way to that in which Orthodoxy had been chosen centuries before. Baptists grew in the Orthodox setting. From the very beginning the Baptist movement was "nondiscriminatory", containing many nationalities, as opposed, for example, to the Lutheran and Mennonite churches, which had strong features of ethnic religion in Russia.[192] A critical attitude to the "beliefs of the Reformers" prevailed in Russian classical literature. Thus Pushkin famously wrote: "What doth he act? ...Childe Harold, Quaker, devotee, or other mask donned playfully?"[193] In the light of this, Baptists, especially those from a Molokan background, were keen to stress that they were not simply "German Baptists". To a considerable extent this was true. Germans were extremely limited in their influence on the Russian-Ukrainian population, due to their ignorance of the national languages, Russian nationalism, strict laws concerning religious

---

191. Some Russian Baptist confessional historians come close to making to such a statement.

192. See, for instance: *Istoriya Evangel'skikh Khristian-Baptistov v SSSR*, pp. 409-10; Friesen, *The Mennonite Brotherhood in Russia*, pp. 87-92; A. Wardin, "Mennonite Brethren and German Baptists: Affinities and Dissimilarities", pp. 108-12.

193. A. Pushkin, *Eugene Oneguine*, VIII, 8. – trans. by H. Spalding (Charleston, SC: BiblioLife, 2009), p. 225.

conversion, and the immense territory of the Empire. The major impact made by missionaries was on German settlers in Russia, not on Russians and Ukrainians.[194] When Russians and Ukrainians accepted some of the Baptist ideas, what they accepted and absorbed was what corresponded to their own spiritual needs and understanding of the "true faith". Thus the fully-formed Russian Baptist phenomenon proper was unique and deeply national. This is crucial in thinking about Baptist roots in relation to Orthodoxy. In being national, Russian Baptists also exhibited certain Russian Orthodox elements, for example a view of the tradition to which they belonged as having "divine origin". This study explores the way in which that process was happening in the period 1960 to 1990, a period in which pressures on the religious associations within the USSR created conditions for closer relations between Orthodoxy and the Russian Baptists, and in which many aspects of Orthodox thinking and practice appear to have been evident in the churches of the ECB.

---

194. See, for instance: Beznosova, *Pozdnee Protestantskoe Sektantstvo Yuga Ukrainy, 1850-1905*, pp. 152-5.

CHAPTER 3

Russian Orthodoxy
and Baptist Theology

In the period being examined in this study, Russian Baptists did not have theological seminaries and were not able to write and publish serious theological books, although they did begin to produce material for the Bible correspondence courses which began in 1968. Despite these severe limitations, Russian Baptists nevertheless had their own theology and gradually developed it.[1] It is important to observe, however, that there was often a divergence between certain official declarations of ministers within the Evangelical Christians-Baptists communities and common Baptist church practice. Nor do Russian Baptist Confessions of Faith necessarily reflect the actual theological convictions held in the churches. It is now possible to reconstruct these theological beliefs through a variety of means: by analyzing Russian Baptist periodicals and other published materials (hymnals, collections of sermons, devotions, etc.), by interviews with older pastors (usually known as presbyters) and church members,[2] and by examining evangelical traditions in the Russian provinces. These methods of examination uncover so-called "everyday" or "primary" theology.[3] This chapter

---

1. One of few attempts in this period to understand Soviet Baptist theology was made by A. de Chalandeau but his perspective was limited. See A. de Chalandeau, "The Theology of the Evangelical Christians-Baptists in the USSR, as Reflected in the Bratskii Vestnik" (PhD thesis, Strasbourg: Universite des Sciences Humaines, 1978).

2. Since many of the authoritative Russian Baptist ministers emigrated to the USA after *perestroika*, I mainly interviewed them there.

3. See P.R. Parushev, 'Towards Convictional Theological Education: Facing challenges of contextualisation, credibility and relevance', in Peter F. Penner, ed., *Theological Education*

contains a comparative study of commonalities between Soviet Baptist and Orthodox on theological themes. A certain gap can be seen between public statements and beliefs "on the ground", in that it was commonplace among many Russian Baptist writers to condemn Orthodox doctrines and traditions,[4] with numerous Orthodox "deviations" from the beliefs of the Apostolic Church being emphasized.[5] In reality, however, as will be seen, in a number of areas Russian Baptist beliefs mirrored Orthodox beliefs. This chapter considers this phenomenon by looking at five areas of theology: the nature of God, soteriology, anthropology, scripture and tradition, and eschatology. Other areas could be added, but these show Russian Baptist theological distinctives most clearly.

The Nature of God

A major point of disagreement between the Eastern and Western churches in their teaching on the Triune God has been and is the *filioque* clause, which was added by the Western church to the 8th article of the Niceno-Constantinopolitan Creed: the wording stating that the Holy Spirit proceeded "from the Father" was changed to "from the Father and the Son". Western Protestants, across the various Protestant confessional bodies, have generally followed the Catholic wording.[6] Orthodox theologians have always held to the original, traditional formula, "from the Father". They have also emphasized the important personal distinctions within the Holy

---

as Mission (Erlangen, Germany: Neufeld Verlag Schwartzenfeld, 2005), pp. 185-208.

4. See, for instance, the following popular Russian Baptist books, either expressly or by implication related to the theme, reprinted many times: P. Rogozin, *Otkuda vse eto poyavilos'?* [From whence do all these come?] [1955] (Rostov-na-Donu: Missiya "Probuzhdenie, 1993); S.P. Liven, *Dukhovnoe probuzhdenie v Rossii* [Spiritual Revival in Russia] (Korntal: Svet na Vostoke, 1967), P. Savchenko, *Sravnitel'noe Bogoslovie* [Comparative Theology] [1974] (M.: AUCECB, 1991). The last of these was study material for the Bible correspondence courses.

5. See, for example: A. Karev, K. Somov, *Istoriya Khristianstva* [History of Christianity] (M.: AUCECB, 1990), pp. 113-7, 215; *Istoriya Evangel'skikh Khristian-Baptistov v SSSR*, p. 73.

6. See, for instance, D. Hilborn, ed., *Evangelicalism and the Orthodox Church* (London: ACUTE, 2001), pp. 70-2. For a basic introduction from a Reformed perspective, L. Berkhof, *Systematic Theology* (Grand Rapids: Eerdmans Publishing Co., 1981), p. 97.

Trinity: the Father is unbegotten; the Son is begotten of the Father; the Son is derived from the Father, but the Father is not derived from the Son; the Spirit proceeds from the Father. In their view, just as it is wrong to say that the Father suffered on the Cross so it is wrong to say that the Holy Spirit proceeds from the Son.[7] The only concession acceptable for the Christian East is to discuss the possibility of the formula "from the Father *through* the Son".[8] This theological approach to Trinitarian doctrine has found its way into the Russian Baptist and Russian evangelical traditions. It is significant that the founder of the Union of the Russian Evangelical Christians, Ivan S. Prokhanov, in a statement of faith in 1910, wrote, "The Holy Spirit proceeds from the Father, and is sent by the Father and the Son."[9]

In 1966 *Bratsky Vestnik* republished the Russian evangelical Confession of 1913 (which had been compiled by Ivan Kargel) and in doing so mentioned that the AUCECB was working on a renewed, broadened basis of belief. In the document of 1913 there had been no *filioque* clause. It read: "We believe… in God the Holy Spirit, the Paraclete, proceeding from the Father, glorifying the Son…"[10] However, A.V. Karev, General Secretary of the AUCECB from 1944 to 1971 and the editor of *Bratsky Vestnik*,[11] seems to have wanted to include the addition *and the Son* in a new Russian Baptist credo. In a crucial *Bratsky Vestnik* article, "*Mysli o Dukhe Svyatom*" [Reflections on the Holy Spirit] (1968), Karev, citing John 20:19-22 and Luke 11:13, wrote:

7. See, for instance, Metropolitan Makary, *Pravoslavno-dogmaticheskoe bogoslovie* [Orthodox-Dogmatic Theology] [1883], 2 vols. (M.: Palomnik, 1999), vol. I, pp. 270-5; T. Ware (Bishop Kallistos of Diokleia), *The Orthodox Church* (London: Penguin Books, 1997), pp. 212-17.

8. See, for instance Archbishop Filaret, "*O Filiokve*" [On Filioque], *ZhMP*, no. 1 (1972), pp. 66-73.

9. *Izlozhenie evangel'skoy very* [Statement of the Evangelical Faith] in *Istoriya Baptizma*, p. 435. In 1911, commenting upon this confession of Evangelical Christians, Prokhanov said that it "was written by *the Russian side without assistance…* [italics in the original] and so it has some peculiarities". – ARSECB, F. 1, op. 11de, d. 25, l. 19.

10. *Verouchenie Evangel'skikh Khristian-Baptistov* [The Creed of the Evangelical Christians–Baptists], *BV*, no. 4 (1966), p. 15.

11. A.V. Karev was the chief editor of *Bratsky Vestnik* from 1944 to 1971 and was followed by V.G. Kulikov from 1972 to 1993. See "A. Popov, The Evangelical Christians-Baptists in the Soviet Union as a Hermeneutical Community" (PhD thesis, International Baptist Theological Seminary, Prague, 2010), pp. 63, 92.

Christ says very clearly that both the Heavenly Father and he himself are giving the Holy Spirit. Meantime, the theologians continue their several centuries old controversies... "He breathed on them, and said to them, 'Receive the Holy Spirit'." There is conclusive evidence: Christ gives the Holy Spirit![12]

If the evidence was so conclusive, the disagreement between the Western and Eastern churches would have been readily resolved. However, disagreements continued, and even persisted among Russian Baptists. Karev died in 1971,[13] and 1980 saw proposed new wording for a Russian Baptist Confession being published in *Bratsky Vestnik*. The wording on the Spirit followed Western terminology: "We believe that the Holy Spirit... was sent by the Father and the Son from heaven to earth on the Day of Pentecost."[14] However, in the final text, approved by the 43rd Council of the Russian Baptists in Moscow in 1985,[15] there was no *filioque* clause.[16] The Orthodox version of the Creed was the one that was known by Russian Baptists: this creed was sung in Russian Baptist church services, and it was this creed which became the accepted version in Russian Baptist theological textbooks.[17]

Another area in which Russian Baptists tended to follow the Orthodox approach concerns the question of the ways by which Christians know God. St. Dionysius the Areopagite, the sixth-century Syrian theologian, in his classic treatise *Mystical Theology*, discussed two ways to think about the Christian knowledge of God.[18] The first way is termed "cataphatic"

---

12. *BV*, no. 4 (1968), p. 47.

13. See Savinsky, *Istoriya (1917-1967)*, p. 379.

14. *BV*, no. 4 (1980), p. 37.

15. See *Istoriya Evangel'skikh Khristian-Baptistov v SSSR*, p. 254.

16. See *BV*, no. 4 (1985), pp. 37-8.

17. See in any edition of the hymnbook *Pesn' Vozrozhdeniya* (complemented), hymn no. 1109. See also the Orthodox version of the Creed in the Russian Baptist textbook: Savchenko, *Sravnitel'noe Bogoslovie*, p. 39.

18. See also his other treatises, especially *Bozhestvennye Imena* [Divine Names] in the selection *Mysticheskoe Bogoslovie* [Mystical Theology] (Kiev: Put' k Istine, 1991). I am using the prefix St., here and elsewhere, not because Russian Baptists used it (they did not), but as a way of highlighting the extent to which Baptist authors drew from

(καταφατικός), consisting of positive statements (for example, "God is light," 1 John 1:5), and the second is termed "apophatic" (ἀποφατικός), based on complete negation (for example, continuing the thought in 1 John 1:5, "There is no darkness in him"). Eastern theologians gradually moved to the apophatic way, and even proclaimed the superiority of a person's *ignorance*.[19] As one Russian Orthodox poet said:

> ... I pity people who do not know God,
> I pity people who know all about him.[20]

Mystical theology, based on the apophatic approach, gradually received affirmation in the whole Christian world, both West and East,[21] although the Orthodox Church embraced it most fully.[22] Western Protestant theology has given relatively little attention to apophaticism.[23]

Russian Baptists were not generally familiar with the term "apophatic", but their writings, especially in the period being studied here, conveyed this perspective. The following are typical quotations from issues of *Bratsky Vestnik* and from *Vestnik Istiny* [Bulletin of the Truth], which was a periodical of the "underground" Council of Churches of the ECB. Thus I.I. Motorin, a frequent contributor to *Bratsky Vestnik*, wrote in 1962:

> We do not understand... the inner mystery of Divinity but
> believe in him according to the Word of God... God's nature

Orthodox Saints.

19. See, for instance: V. Lossky, *The Mystical Theology of the Eastern Church* (Crestwood, NY: St. Vladimir's Seminary Press, 1976), pp. 23-36.

20. Hieromonk Roman, *Stikhi* [Poems], <http://tropinka.orthodoxy.ru/zal/poezija/roman/index.htm> accessed 18 December 2009.

21. See Lossky, *The Mystical Theology of the Eastern Church*, pp. 23-4.

22. See, for instance J. Meyendorff, *Byzantine Theology: Historical Trends and Doctrinal Themes* (N.Y.: Fordham University Press, 1983), pp. 11-14; V. Lossky, *Orthodox Theology: An Introduction* (Crestwood, NY: St. Vladimir's Seminary Press, 1978), pp. 31-5.

23. It is significant that widely-used Protestant theological dictionaries such as *The Encyclopedia of Protestantism*, 4 vols., ed. by H. Hillerbrand (New York: Routledge, 2004), *Evangelical Dictionary of Theology*, ed. by W. Elwell (Grand Rapids: Baker Book House, 1991), *Encyclopedia of Protestantism*, ed. by J. Melton (New York: Facts On File, 2005), and *The Oxford Encyclopedia of the Reformation*, 4 vols., ed. by H. Hillerbrand (New York: Oxford University Press, 1996), do not include articles on apophaticism.

is above all understanding, not only of men, but also of angels; because God dwells in unapproachable light, and nobody has seen or can see him (1 Tim 6:16).[24]

In 1982 and 1992 *Vestnik Istiny* carried articles with these striking statements about God:

> Our human mind is simply unable to penetrate into the divine mystery… Christ… is unapproachable, inexplicable, and unfathomable for our mind - the Light - as well as [being] unfathomably and inexplicably God himself. What are we able to know about the essence of the true heavenly Light?[25]

> The impossible task fell on me to speak… about the Lord Jesus Christ himself. I tremble at the thought because I am not capable of this… There are so many great and deep truths here that it is impossible to retell them in my whole life… God! This name is unfathomable… The limited human mind cannot comprehend it… Heaven is the place where God dwells in unapproachable light.[26]

These expressions of utter human inability to understand the essence of heavenly mysteries are in marked contrast to the theological atmosphere that characterized early "Stundist" and Baptist communities at the end of the nineteenth and the beginning of the twentieth centuries, when evangelical preachers in Russia confidently entered into theological debates with educated Orthodox priests and, allegedly, "routed" them.[27]

---

24. I. Motorin, "*Uchenie Biblii o Boge*" [The Biblical Doctrine of God], *BV*, no. 1 (1960), IEDE-2.

25. B. Shmidt, "*Khristos – Istinny Bog*" [Christ is the True God], *VestI*, no. 1 (1982), p. 11.

26. N. Baturin, "*Da Budet Svet…*" ["Let There Be Light…"], *VestI*, no. 2 (1992), p. 4.

27. See, for example G. Mazaev, *Vospominaniya* [Memories] (Korntal: Svet na Vostoke, 1992), pp. 35-66; V. Popov, *Stopy Blagovestnika* [The Feet of the Evangelist] (M.: Blagovestnik, 1996), pp. 60-6.

Although the periods in which changes in theological outlook took place among Russian Baptists cannot be pinpointed with precision, after World War II the desire to appear theologically superior to Orthodoxy was much less evident. By the 1960s and 1970s, Russian Baptists were much more aware of a shared Eastern Christian "community spirit". The common suffering of the Orthodox and Baptists for the faith under Communism was also a cause of their sense of mutual sympathy. In 1975, in *Bratsky Vestnik*, this profound theological statement by Orthodox Metropolitan Iliya was quoted.

> We find difficulty in understanding the mystery of the Atonement in its inward depths, as well as other mysteries of our faith, but we are able to see the evidence of the gracious fruits. When the human mind is powerless to understand eternal truths, symbols come to the rescue. So, the mystery of the Atonement, in its interpretation for weak human language, is explained as the following. Sin as breach of the moral law is inseparable from suffering... But such punishment cannot free man from his feeling of guilt before the judgment of the holy God's truth. So, the Son of God became Man, assuming all human sufferings for Adam's sin... all human guilt before the judgment of the holy God's truth, and by His love enfolded in His divine-human heart people of all times, who lived both before and after His incarnation. With humankind held in the heart, our Savior made His sacrifice on Calvary for all people. So, all people became like an organic whole, with Christ and each other, redeemed and renewed through the sacrificial act of His love.[28]

This extensive passage undoubtedly expresses traditional Orthodox views. The apophatic and "communal" approach to the theme of Christ's work is typical of the sentiments of Orthodox theologians and monks. It is

---

28. "*Vstrecha v Leningrade*" [Meeting in Leningrad] (editorial article), *BV*, no. 4 (1975), pp. 25-6.

notable that such sentences were published by the main Russian Baptist periodical with evident approval. Not that every aspect of the Orthodox approach to God was embraced by Russian Baptists. Among Orthodox theologians, from St. Gregory Palamas (14th century) and his followers on-wards, a distinction was made between God's essence, which cannot be comprehended and portrayed, and his "energies", which are displayed in any theophany and even by means of material objects, for instance, icons.[29] Russian Baptists did not make this distinction, and it could be argued that by concentrating on God's mystery, Russian Baptists were actually more consistently apophatic than some Orthodox. The veneration of icons can be seen as an expression of cataphatic thinking. For Russian Baptists, how-ever, God was seen as inexpressible in his majesty and unfathomable in his being – as one who cannot be portrayed.[30]

This apophaticism was present in the worship of Russian Baptist com-munities. This is evident in a number of widely-sung hymns. The lyrics in Hymn 455 from the selection *Sbornik Dukhovnykh Pesen* (*SDP*), for a number of years the main hymn book of the Russian Baptists, contain these words:

> Oh, immeasurable love,
> indeed wonderful and holy,
> unfathomable goodness,
> my mind cannot comprehend.
> Lamb, offered as a sacrifice!
>
> How can I repay you
> for this unspeakable gift?[31]

---

29. See, for instance: Archpriest J. Meyendorff, *Pravoslavie i sovremenny mir* [Orthodoxy and the Contemporary World] (Minsk: Luchi Sofii, 1995), pp. 87-92.

30. The same opposition to "images" has been present in Protestantism, but I am seeking to examine Russian Baptist views in their specific context.

31. *Sbornik Dukhovnykh Pesen Evangel'skikh Khristian Baptistov* [The Songbook of the Evangelical Christians–Baptists] (M.: AUCECB, 1968), p. 303.

Such apophatic expressions and ideas are present in many other hymns in this hymnbook. For instance, as early as the first hymn in the book there is an address to God who has "founded a kingdom" for himself "in my poor heart", and the hymn then continues, "My mind falls silent." (*SDP*, no. 1). The second hymn has these words: "Thy love is beyond my mind, Lord... above all words... I know nothing." (*SDP*, no. 2). Apophaticism is perhaps particularly evident in lyrics associated with worship addressed directly to God, since worshippers seek a spiritual ascension into the presence of the Lord through such the singing. Yet human language itself is seen, for example in Hymn 50, as powerless to express the inexpressible.[32] Primacy is given to prayerful-mystical fellowship in worship with the invisible, incomprehensible God, who cannot be depicted or seen, yet who loves humanity with an infinite love and whose presence is real. This reality is perceived by faith. The lyrics in a hymn (no. 114) from another widely-used Russian Baptist selection *Pesn' Vozrozhdeniya*, the main hymnbook of the CCECB, take up these themes:

> To behold You with our eyes
> is not granted to us, sinners,
> but we can embrace You by faith,
> with love.
> Although invisible
> You give inexpressible
> delight to the soul.[33]

There are a number of classic hymns sung by Western Christians (including Baptists), such as "Immortal, invisible, God only wise", which contain similar sentiments.[34] However, the "apophatic" hymns used in Russian Baptist

---

32. "I talk with God often, but His lovely words cannot be conveyed..." (*SDP*, no. 50, p. 40).

33. *Pesn' Vozrozhdeniya* [Song of Revival] (Izdanie CCECB, 1978), p. 74. In this hymnbook see also: nos. 66, 91, 189.

34. See, for example, hymns 6 and 47 in the American *The Baptist Hymnal* (Nashville, TN: Convention Press, 1991), pp. 6, 47: "Immortal, invisible, God only wise, unresting, unhasting and silent..."; "God... infinite in time and place... wielding unimagined power..."; and other well-known hymns, which speak of the "Traveller unknown"

churches are Russian creations, not translations, and many of them echo
Orthodox language about God. The sense of mystery in Russian Baptist
writings and in worship is ubiquitous.[35] "The characteristic feature of our
brotherhood", writes one of the most influential contemporary Russian
Baptist theologians, S.V. Sannikov, "was its penetration into mystical
knowledge of God, reflections about God's Word and profound medita-
tion on God."[36] The evidence suggests that Russian Baptist theology reflected something of the Eastern apophatic tradition.

Soteriology: the possibility of salvation

A book on the Orthodox doctrine of salvation by Archbishop Sergy
Stragorodsky, published in 1898, argued that the Orthodox soteriological
tradition was marked by a belief in the synergy of divine grace and free
will. The theological storms in the West over this issue largely bypassed
the Eastern Church.[37] According to the Russian philosopher, L.A. Zander,
writing in 1952, Eastern Christian theology differed from Western for-
mulations because it did not experience the influence of the anthropology
of Augustine, Anselm's teaching on redemption, or the Scholastic meth-
odology of Thomas Aquinas.[38] In Orthodox soteriology, God wishes the
salvation of all people, and the predestination of anyone to eternal death
is unthinkable. Human beings possess real free will, which was seriously
damaged but not lost through original sin. The process of salvation includes both what God does and what is done by human beings. Salvation
is possible only by the working of grace, but this does not violate the moral
freedom of an individual. God's fore-knowledge of human choice has been

---

(Charles Wesley) or the "hidden love of God".

35. See more details in C. Prokhorov, "Apophaticism and Cataphaticism in
Protestantism", *Theological Reflections*, vol. 6 (2006), pp. 58-68.

36. S. Sannikov, "*Razmyshleniya Redaktora*" [Editor's Thoughts], *Almanach 'Bogomyslie'*,
vol. 1 (1990), p. 3.

37. See Archbishop Sergy (Stragorodsky), *Pravoslavnoe uchenie o spasenii* [The Orthodox
Doctrine of Salvation] [1898] (M.: Izdatel'sky otdel Moskovskogo Patriarkhata, 1991),
pp. 55, 159-60.

38. See L. Zander, *Vision and Action* (London: Gollancz, 1952), p. 59.

emphasized.[39] God sees beforehand the choices of those individuals, inclined by grace, who respond to him with sincere repentance, and they are those who are predestined to God's Kingdom. Those who reject God's grace deprive themselves of salvation.[40]

John of Damascus, recognized by the East and West as a Saint, wrote in the eighth century in his *Exact Exposition of the Orthodox Faith*:

> We ought to understand that while God knows all things beforehand, yet he does not predetermine all things... For it is not his will that there should be wickedness nor does he choose to compel virtue. So that predetermination is the work of the divine command based on foreknowledge.[41]

Archbishop Sergy Stragorodsky summarizes Orthodox soteriology in this way:

> Salvation cannot be some outwardly-judicial or physical event, but is necessarily a moral action; and, as such, it surely supposes, as an inevitable condition and law, that man accomplishes this action himself, though with the help of grace. Grace, though it operates, though it accomplishes everything, necessarily does so within freedom and consciousness.[42]

Orthodox authors relish repeating: although God created human beings without our permission, to save anyone in that way is not pleasing to him. One illustration used was of a drowning man. If a rope is thrown to a

39. See, for instance, Makary, *Pravoslavno-dogmaticheskoe bogoslovie*, vol. II, pp. 280-6.
40. A. Lopukhin, ed., *Tolkovaya Bibliya* [Study Bible], 12 vols. (SPb.: Strannik, 1912), vol. X, p. 476; Meyendorff, *Byzantine Theology*, pp. 143-6; P. Leporsky, "*Blagodat*" [Grace], in *Khristianstvo: Entsiklopedichesky Slovar'*, vol. III, pp. 333-6; N. Berdyaev, *Tsarstvo Dukha i Tsarstvo Kesarya* [The Kingdom of the Spirit and the Kingdom of Caesar] [1949] (M.: Respublika, 1995), pp. 324-7; Archbishop Sergy (Stragorodsky), *Pravoslavnoe uchenie o spasenii*, p. 203.
41. St. John of Damascus, *Tochnoe izlozhenie pravoslavnoy very* [Exact Exposition of the Orthodox Faith] (M.: Lod'ya, 1998), p. 187.
42. Archbishop Sergy (Stragorodsky), *Pravoslavnoe uchenie o spasenii*, pp. 161-2.

drowning man and he does not grab it, he will inevitably sink.[43] The human being is free to receive or not to receive salvation.

The acceptance by Russian Baptists of Orthodox thinking in this crucial area of theology was evident in the publication in *Bratsky Vestnik* of sizeable articles in 1974 by two well-known figures of the Russian Orthodox Church, Metropolitans Nikodim and Iliya. These articles reflected Eastern understandings of Christian piety and of the way of salvation.[44] A year later the editorial board of *Bratsky Vestnik* quoted with favor Patriarch Pimen of Moscow and All Russia (elected in 1971) on salvation, and also the words of the Orthodox theologian, N. Zabolotsky. The quotations were from *Zhurnal Moskovskoy Patriarkhii* [Journal of the Moscow Patriarchate], a journal which never carried Baptist material. Christians, it was argued in this journal, were not to isolate themselves from the society around them through "pride and self-righteousness". While this was in tune with Russian Baptist piety, the Orthodox articles also connected "self-righteous" people with those who were "allegedly justified by faith".[45] This seems to have been a criticism of Protestant soteriological teaching, but it was one that *Bratsky Vestnik* was apparently willing to echo. The Russian Baptists feared that teaching "justification by faith" without an equal emphasis on how a person lived, could lead to spiritual complacency and carelessness. Thus the *Bratsky Vestnik* editors were prepared to publish an article by Patriarch Pimen in 1982 in which the Patriarch quoted in part the famous words of St. Seraphim of Sarov, "Acquire the spirit of the peaceful and thousands around you will be saved."[46] This did not necessarily imply that to have "the spirit of the peaceful" was a more important factor in seeing others brought to salvation than teaching about Christ's salvific work. However,

---

43. See Archpriest A. Belotsvetov, "*Usloviya spaseniya s nashey storony*" [The Conditions of Salvation from our Side], in P. Dudarev, ed., *Sbornik propovednicheskikh obraztsov* [Collection of Preaching Samples] (SPb.: Izdanie I. Tuzova, 1912), p. 474.

44. See Metropolitan Nikodim, "*Iisus Khristos Osvobozhdaet i Ob"edinyaet*" [Jesus Christ Makes Free and Joins Together], *BV*, no. 6 (1974), pp. 16-19; Metropolitan Iliya, "*Doklad na Obshchuyu Temu*" [Report on General Theme], *BV*, no. 6 (1974), pp. 24-5.

45. *BV*, no. 1 (1975), pp. 25, 54.

46. Patriarch Pimen, "*Spasenie Svyashchennogo Dara Zhizni*" [Saving the Sacred Gift of Life], *BV*, no. 4 (1982), pp. 43-4.

it did indicate that Orthodox thinking was making significant inroads into Russian Baptist life.

Russian Orthodoxy did not engage with the issues of predestination and free will to anything like the extent that major Western theologians did, and similarly Russian Baptists gave relatively little attention to traditional Protestant debates about Calvinism and Arminianism. In 1966 *Bratsky Vestnik* went as far as to say that Soviet Baptists knew nothing about theological discussions between Western Calvinists and Arminians.[47] This was probably the first mention of "Arminianism" in a Soviet Baptist publication. No definition of the terms used was offered, however, which suggests that some prior understanding of their meaning was present. There was a tradition of Orthodox critique of Reformed soteriology. For Orthodoxy, traditional Reformed theological thought in this area was dominated by ideas of "legal relationships".[48] God threatens to punish those who fail to keep his law. Only those will be saved who are predestined for salvation. In Orthodox thinking this Reformed framework – "crime leading to punishment" – is grounded in scripture, but by no means reflects all its fullness.[49] Rather, as Metropolitan Makary put it in 1883, only those who reject the great mercy of God, following many opportunities for reconciliation, will perish.[50] For Orthodoxy, God wants to be seen through the prism of his love and mercy. His relationships with human beings are on a gracious basis.[51] In similar vein, A.V. Karev argued that God "did not predestine sin and did not intend it... But salvation from sin was predestined, was intended by God before the creation of the world in the person of the Lamb of God without blemish and without spot."[52] Karev followed Orthodox

47. See "*Doklad General'nogo Sekretarya VSECB A.V. Kareva*" [Report of the General Secretary of AUCECB, A.V. Karev], *BV*, no. 6 (1966), p. 17.

48. See Lossky, *Orthodox Theology*, p. 111.

49. See, Ibid.; Archbishop Sergy (Stragorodsky), *Pravoslavnoe uchenie o spasenii*, p. 83.

50. See Makary, *Pravoslavno-dogmaticheskoe bogoslovie*, vol. II, pp. 587-8.

51. See V. Lossky, *In the Image and Likeness of God* (Crestwood, NY: St. Vladimir's Seminary Press, 1974), pp. 97-110.

52. A.V. Karev, *Dukhovnye stat'i* [Theological Articles] (Korntal: Svet na Vostoke, 1974), p. 56.

teaching, too, in seeing sin as a spiritual illness rather than a crime against the Lord.[53] Implicitly, if not explicitly, Reformed theology was rejected.

In making a case for human free will in respect of salvation, Orthodox theologians like Metropolitan Makary argued that just as God has freedom, so humanity, created in his image and likeness, also has real freedom.[54] This sense of being free could lead to moral pride, but such a tendency was to be counteracted by the Orthodox teaching on humility as the main Christian virtue.[55] Russian Baptists taught the same: human beings, as those made in God's image, have free will. They have the opportunity to participate in salvation, and this participation must be entered into with humility of heart. Every human being is fully responsible before God for all their actions. True faith is the driving force for good works. In several articles in *Bratsky Vestnik* from the 1960s to the 1980s authors insisted that "saving faith is unthinkable without works".[56] Chapter 6 of the draft Russian Baptist Confession (published, as noted above, as a proposal in 1980) included human free will as a basic belief, and while declaring salvation by faith, added, "Good works also testify about true faith".[57] Chapter 6 of the approved Russian Baptist Confession (1985) speaks about the synergy of divine grace and human free will, and then repeats the words of the 1980 statement on the importance of good works.[58] The emphasis on good works connected with the traditional piety found in the Russian Baptist communities: regular reading of scripture, strict fasting, kneeling to pray,

---

53. See, for instance, A. Karev, "*Grekh i Pobeda nad Nim*" [Victory over Sin], *BV*, no. 1 (1972), p. 18.

54. See Makary, *Pravoslavno-dogmaticheskoe bogoslovie*, vol. I, pp. 454-7.

55. See G. Fedotov, *The Russian Religious Mind* (N.Y.: Harper & Row, 1965), p. 224.

56. See A. Mitskevich, "*Iz Evangel'sko-Baptistskoy Dogmatiki*" [Extracts from Evangelical-Baptist Theology], *BV*, no. 5 (1956), IEDE-2; [Anon], "*Chto Takoe Blagodat'?*" [What does Grace Mean?], *BV*, nos. 5-6 (1960), pp. 114-16; K. Somov, "*Vera i Dela*" [Faith and Works], *BV*, no. 2 (1963), pp. 53-5; *Dogmatika: Zaochnye Bibleyskie Kursy* [Dogmatics: Bible Correspondence Courses] (M.: AUCECB, 1970), pp. 90-1; S. Nikolaev, *Reformatskaya Tserkov'* [The Reformed Church], *BV*, no. 1 (1984), pp. 48-9. Sometimes the Russian Baptist stress on good works meant that Luther's teaching on justification by faith was transformed beyond recognition, "We should show not a 'straw' faith, as Luther says, but faith with good works.": I. Tatarchenko, "*Dukhovnaya Lestnitsa*" [Spiritual Ladder], *BV*, no. 6 (1969), p. 47.

57. *BV*, no. 4 (1980), pp. 39-41.

58. See *BV*, no. 4 (1985), pp. 38-40.

night vigils, giving alms, and suffering for Christ's sake.[59] In 1985, *Bratsky Vestnik* tried to find a "faith and good works" balance in the following way: "Good works confirm our faith… If we want to be sure of our salvation let us look at our life."[60]

Although *Bratsky Vestnik* asserted in 1966 that Soviet Baptists knew nothing about discussions between Western Calvinists and Arminians, there were some Russian Baptists who explicitly supported Calvinistic ideas. There was a Russian Baptist Calvinist Confession of Faith produced in 1906 by Vasily Pavlov.[61] This was a translated and edited version of the German Baptist Confession of 1847. The translation was not, however, widely used in Russia.[62] There was some Calvinistic teaching present in the 1920s, when there were stronger contacts with European and American Baptists, and it seems that there was a small Calvinistic Baptist group in Stavropol Territory in the 1950s-1960s.[63] Senior presbyter S. Fadyukhin expressed his concern in the 1970s about a form of Calvinistic influence on some Baptist congregations.[64] A decade later Alexei Bychkov,

---

59. These issues will be dealt with at length in chapters 7 and 8.

60. [Anon], *"My Sozdany vo Khriste Iisuse na Dobrye Dela"* [We are Created in Christ Jesus for Good Works], *BV*, no. 1 (1985), pp. 15-16. This view of good works can be seen as paralleling the Calvinistic thinking of some seventeenth-century English Puritans: someone's good works were seen as a proof of being elect. But Russian Baptists did not favor this Calvinistic standpoint. They were closer to an Arminian Puritan, John Goodwin, who argued that Calvinism fostered presumption. For Goodwin, those presuming they were elect "needed to be taught that good works mattered". See J. Coffey, *John Goodwin and the Puritan Revolution: Religion and Intellectual Change in Seventeenth-Century England* (Woodbridge: The Boydell Press, 2006), p. 209.

61. *Verouchenie Russkikh Evangel'skikh Khristian-Baptistov* [The Creed of the Russian Evangelical Christians-Baptists] (Rostov na Donu: Tipografiya F.P. Pavlova, 1906). Later it was republished in Moscow: *Ispovedanie Very Khristian-Baptistov* [The Creed of the Christians–Baptists] (M.: Izdanie N.V. Odintsova, 1928).

62. See Savinsky, *Istoriya (1867-1917)*, p. 314. The authoritative early Russian confessions by I.S. Prokhanov (1910) and I.V. Kargel (1913) included declarations about the joint work of God and of human beings in the process of salvation. See *Izlozhenie evangel'skoy very* [Statement of the Evangelical Faith], pp. 444-5; *Verouchenie Evangel'skikh Khristian-Baptistov* [The Creed of the Evangelical Christians–Baptists], *BV*, no. 4 (1966), p. 16.

63. The majority of the older Russian Baptists I interviewed (who ministered after World War II) say they did not hear about Calvinist ideas before *perestroika*. The rare testimonies about elements of Calvinist teaching among Russian Baptists are from S.G. Odaryuk (Everett, Washington, USA, 2006) and V.N. Savinsky (Spokane, Washington, USA, 2006) who mentioned the small Calvinistic Baptist group in Stavropol Territory.

64. See S. Fadyukhin, *"Ob Osoboy Bozh'ey Lyubvi k Izbrannym"* [On God's Special Love

AUCECB General Secretary, categorically declared: "We... do not preach the principle 'once saved, always saved' and do not take away from the merit of the fight of faith. We are consistent, on the basis of the Word of God, in this theme."[65] Soviet Baptists taught, by contrast with Calvinists, that a Christian, under certain conditions, could reject the Lord and his salvation,[66] could fall away from grace,[67] and could be blotted out from the book of life in heaven.[68]

It is not surprising, given these beliefs, that Russian Baptists have been seen as holding to Arminian theology.[69] But this classification fails to take account of the Orthodox context. Because they opposed Calvinist teaching, they were not necessarily Arminian. What was said by them about falling away from salvation, for example, might sound Arminian, but its roots were in another historical and theological tradition. Russian Baptist authors such as A.V. Karev, in teaching about predestination and free will and criticizing Calvinism, usually made no mention of Arminianism as a theological alternative.[70] Thus the teaching about the possibility of a be-

for the Elect], *BV*, no. 5 (1978), p. 17.

65. A. Bychkov, "*Iisus Khristos – Spasitel*" [Jesus Christ is the Saviour], *BV*, no. 1 (1986), p. 16. Cf. the words of another leading Baptist minister of that period, A.K. Sipko: "Russian Baptists, keeping the simple Gospel, with fasting and praying, remained faithful to their Lord and His Word without any doctrine of predestination". – A. Sipko, *Derzhis' Obraztsa Zdravogo Ucheniya: Sbornik Statey* [Keep the Pattern of Sound Teaching: Collection of Articles] (Spokane, WA: NCG Inc., 2010), p. 138.

66. See, for instance: A. Karev, "*Chto Govorit Bibliya ob Otstuplenii*" [What does the Bible say on Apostasy?], *BV*, no. 1 (1964), pp. 57-9.

67. See, for instance, V. Meshcheryakov, "*Spasenie Po Blagodati*" [Salvation by Grace], *BV*, no. 6 (1977), pp. 39-41.

68. See, for instance, V. Kulikov, "*Raduytes', Chto Imena Vashi v Knige Zhizni*" [Rejoice that your Names are in the Book of Life], *BV*, no. 2 (1991), p. 13. Russian Baptist belief about the book of life was that when a person starts to believe in Jesus Christ, his or her name is recorded in heaven, but if a Christian falls away from God, he or she is blotted out from the book of life. Those who do not believe in Christ are never put down in this heavenly book. See also S. Fadyukhin, "*Ispovedanie Nashey Very*" [Our Creed], *BV*, no. 5 (1970), p. 50.

69. See, for instance: H.L. McBeth, *The Baptist Heritage*, p. 817; M. Sidwell, *The Russian Baptists*, <http://www.bju.edu/library/collections/fund_file/russianbap.html#russ65> accessed 7 January 2010.

70. See, for instance, A. Karev, "*Chto Govorit Bibliya o Predopredelenii*" [What does the Bible say on Predestination?], *BV*, no. 1 (1964), pp. 55-7. No doubt Karev was aware of Mennonite teaching, which favored free will, but although Mennonites did influence some early Russian Baptist life he did not mention them.

liever losing his or her salvation was drawn from a theology of human freedom (mirroring God's freedom) which, as has been seen, was of great importance in Orthodoxy. The common Russian explanation of this belief was the following: for believers to lose their salvation by some accidental misdeed is impossible, since God is faithful to his promises and saves his children. But a person is able to *refuse* salvation (by a conscious and volitional decision), and so can perish.[71] A.V. Karev, answering queries in *Bratsky Vestnik*, used the illustration of people who are out in the cold and become frozen. It is possible to bring people inside and warm them up, so that they revive. But some believers stay in those circumstances and freeze to death. In spiritual terms these people are apostates.[72] In the Communist era, this was a very sensitive question, not only in theory but in practice. By the middle of 1960s, about 200 Orthodox priests had left their calling, openly collaborating with Soviet atheists.[73] There was also apostasy among Soviet Baptists. For example, a book was published in 1960, *My Byli Baptistami* [We were Baptists]. A.V. Karev, commenting on this book, noted that it contained "28 Baptist denials of the faith".[74]

In his compilation of traditional Russian Baptist theological views, S.V. Sannikov includes a formulation to be found in Odessa (Ukraine), and perhaps elsewhere. Local Baptists constructed what appears to have been their own way of interpreting and explaining the correlation between actions of

---

71. See, for instance: V. Slobodyanik, "*Voprosy Dukhovnoy Zhizni*" [The Issues of Spiritual Life], *BV*, no. 4 (1965), pp. 29-31. See also a historical review of the theme in the Russian Baptist context: C. Prokhorov, *Opyt Otechestvennogo Evangel'skogo Bogosloviya* [An Introduction to Russian Evangelical Theology] (SPb.: Mezhdunarodnoe Khristianskoe Izdatel'stvo "Titul", 2009), pp. 160-6.

72. See A.V. Karev, "*Voprosy Veruyushchikh*" [Believers' Queries], *BV*, no. 3 (1966), p. 21.

73. See Shkarovsky, *Russkaya Pravoslavnaya Tserkov' pri Staline i Khrushcheve*, p. 370. This reliable author, making reference to some archival documents of the 1960s, says that many of those who rejected their priesthood "became hard drinkers, or committed suicide; some asked their superiors for forgiveness". All of the clerical apostates were excommunicated from the Church. See also: *ZhMP*, no. 2 (1960), p. 27; Archpriest V. Tsypin, *Istoriya Russkoy Pravoslavnoy Tserkvi, 1917-1990* [History of the Russian Orthodox Church, 1917-1990] (M.: Izdatel'sky Dom "Khronika", 1994), pp. 155-7.

74. V. Golubovich, ed., *My Byli Baptistami* [We were Baptists] (M.: Gospolitizdat, 1960). A.V. Karev, "*Dnevnik A.V. Kareva*" [A.V. Karev's Diary], *BV*, no. 1 (1999), p. 47. On this there are also the testimonies: of deacon Ya.S. Shevchuk (INT, Los Angeles, California, USA, 2006), presbyter A.T. Evstratenko (INT, San Diego, California, USA, 2006); and presbyter M.P. Zakharov (INT, Sacramento, California, USA, 2006).

divine grace and human free will. The picture used was of the balancing of scales. People in the condition described by Paul in Romans 7:15-25, these Baptists said, are unable to make a free choice to follow Christ, because "the weight of sin" pulls them down to eternal death. In this picture the error of predestinarian thinking is that it understands grace as – relatively speaking – a heavier "weight" which overbalances the burden of sin and so "irresistibly" saves a sinner, without that person playing any part in the process. In Russian Baptist thinking the divine grace does not "overbalance", but only "balances" the scales, depriving sin of its force, even if for a short time, and giving the individual the opportunity for self-determination: for exercising a truly free choice. Human self-determination is seen as logically grounded in the fact that men and women were created in the image of God, and the Lord gave them freedom, which meant that they were fully responsible for their actions.[75] Though these kinds of illustration were very simple, and often other theological views were misunderstood, they do reflect a robust Russian Baptist "primary theology" which has affinities with Orthodox conceptions.

The aforementioned ideas also have some parallels with John Wesley's concept of "prevenient" (preparatory) grace.[76] However, this does not necessarily prove a direct Wesleyan influence. Contemporary scholars point to the influence of Eastern theology on Wesley's soteriological views.[77] This could account for the similarity of some ideas. However, it is certainly the case that there are clear Protestant elements within Russian Baptist soteriology. In contrast to Orthodox believers, Russian Baptists usually stressed salvation by faith and saw the role of good works as accompanying faith. Russian Baptists also wrote about salvation coming through the grace of God. Their statements about grace mirrored traditional Protestant

---

75. See S. Sannikov, ed., *Podgotovka k kreshcheniyu* [Preparation for Baptism] (Odessa: OBS, 2005), p. 122. See also an early attempt to comprehend this issue in the Russian Evangelical brotherhood: [Anon], *"Predvaryayushchaya Blagodat"* [Prevenient Grace], *Khristianin*, no. 10 (1926), pp. 17-8. See also A. Mitskevich, *Iz Evangel'sko-Baptistskoy Dogmatiki* [Extracts from Evangelical-Baptist Theology], *BV*, no. 5 (1956), IEDE-2.

76. See, for instance: H.R. Dunning, *Grace, Faith and Holiness. A Wesleyan Systematic Theology* (Kansas City: Beacon Hill Press, 1988), pp. 338-9.

77. See the bibliography on the subject in R. Maddox, *Responsible Grace: John Wesley's Practical Theology* (Nashville, TN: Kingswood Books, 1994).

theology, although they always added that God's grace does not save anyone by force.[78] Another area in which Russian Baptists can be seen to di-
verge from Orthodox tradition is on the issue of assurance of believers
about their salvation.[79] David Bebbington has shown the centrality of
assurance of salvation in the eighteenth-century Evangelical Revival, especially among evangelical Arminians. John Wesley claimed in 1740 that
he had never known one person saved without "the faith of assurance".[80]
Many Soviet Baptists testified about their assurance of salvation,[81] quoting
favorite hymns such as, "Yes, I am saved! That is not a word of pride."[82] But
some traditional, popular Russian Baptist hymns conveyed a somewhat
different message:

> Please, tell me, my God!
> Whether I have been counted in,
> On the shining pages
> of the eternal book of the saved?
> …Whether I am counted in there,
> In the book of the eternal Kingdom?
> …Where the angels glorify You,
> Whether I am counted in there?[83]

A similar uncertainty can be also found in the following hymns: in no. 85
in *Sbornik Dukhovnykh Pesen*, which has the line "Disperse my doubts";

---

78. See, for instance, E. Mad'yugin, "*Blagodat' Bozhiya*" [The Grace of God], *BV*, no. 1
(1989), pp. 22-3.

79. See *Dogmatika: Zaochnye Bibleyskie Kursy*, p. 138; [Anon], *Uverennost' v Spasenii*
[Assurance of Salvation], *BV*, no. 4 (1972), pp. 56-9; I. Sergey, "*Uverennost' v Spasenii*"
[Assurance of Salvation], *BV*, no. 4 (1991), p. 16.

80. N. Curnock, ed., *The Journal of the Rev. John Wesley, A.M.*, vol. 2 (London: Epworth
Press, 1911), pp. 333f., cited in Bebbington, *Evangelicalism in Modern Britain: A History
from the 1730s to the 1980s*, pp. 6-7; cf. pp. 42-50.

81. For instance, the testimonies of Baptist ministers V.M. Tsvirin'ko and N.N. Tsvirin'ko,
who lived and worked in Latvia (INT, Fresno, California, USA, 2006), a minister from
Alma-Ata, V.V. Zinchenko (INT, Sacramento, California, USA, 2006), and others.

82. *SDP*, no. 310, pp. 209-10. See similar sentiments in *SDP*, no. 15, p. 17; no. 160, pp.
112-3; no. 244, p. 169; no. 262, p. 180; *PV*, nos. 166, 169.

83. *SDP*, no. 566, p. 377.

and in no. 744 of *Pesn' Vozrozhdeniya*, "Can I really be without fruit?", which also expresses the desire to be counted "in the Book of Life". Also, a hymn in *SDP* (no. 170), while written as if to proclaim assurance, says that Christ "will give me salvation on the day when he comes again", perhaps suggesting that certainty will come only then.

There was a deep concern among Russian Baptists to avoid any idea that salvation was "easy". Russian Baptists asked themselves, for example, the following anxious questions: "Were there not ten virgins who went out to meet the Bridegroom? But only five of them were worthy to come to the marriage"; or "Are you saying that you are saved?... But why then does the Lord ask whether he will find faith on the earth at his second coming?"; or "We all, Christians of the last time, have to watch, because it is written: two people will be in one bed, or grinding together, or working together in the field, but only one of them will be taken to the Lord."[84] There are echoes here of Orthodox teaching. Russian Orthodox authors often quote the words of St. Elder Agatho, "I am a man, and I do not know whether my works will be pleasing to God... I do not presume when I come before God: for the judgments of God are not the judgments of men."[85] The widespread Orthodox teaching that Christians, while living on the earth, are on the way to eternal salvation, could probably help to explain the specific Russian Baptist views of assurance of salvation.[86] Russian Baptists appear to have absorbed Orthodox as well as evangelical views of assurance.

When the USSR came to an end, Russian Baptists were able to set out their soteriology in a considered fashion. In "The Creed of Odessa Theological Seminary" (a seminary which was a pioneering theological institution in the former USSR), S.V. Sannikov wrote about salvation and

---

84. These questions are found in the testimonies of experienced presbyters of the brotherhood of the ECB such as V.N. Khot'ko (Petropavlovsk, Kazakhstan, 2000), and I.A. Kabluchkin (Omsk, Russia, 2009). The texts cited are Matt 25:1-13, Luke 18:8-9 and Luke 17:30-36.

85. *Dostopamyatnye Skazaniya o Podvizhnichestve Svyatykh i Blazhennykh Ottsov* [Memorable Stories about the Asceticism of the Holy and Blessed Fathers] (M.: Pravilo Very, 1999), pp. 67-8.

86. See, for instance, A. Lopukhin, ed., *Tolkovaya Bibliya*, vol. X, p. 474. V.E. Logvinenko, the former president of the AUCECB, explained this in the following way: yes, we are saved – like a drowning man taken out of the water into a boat. But while we are alive this boat does not reach land (Odessa, Ukraine, 1995).

in doing so expressed ideas that were in accordance with the spirit of the Eastern Christian tradition:

> The idea of sovereign, but not arbitrary Divine election under-lines the justice of God who owed it to nobody to save all, but by virtue of his love he places all people in an equal position, even those about whom he knew before that they would not accept salvation. Thus, he gave the possibility to everyone to be saved... Submitting himself to God's will, a believer has the joy of salvation and assurance of eternal security, which means that nobody and nothing from outside can separate him from grace... However, deliberate sin and conscious disobedience to God's will, permanent ignoring of the divine warnings and reluctance to abide in Christ, compels God, who respects the freedom of human persons, after frequent reminders, to re-move from himself the one who so acts.[87]

Thus, in Russian Baptist soteriology, as analyzed here, there was a unique synthesis of some Eastern and Western theological ideas.

Russian Baptist anthropology: seeking holiness

In the period examined here, Russian Baptists displayed two apparently opposing tendencies in relation to the spheres of Christian anthropology and hamartiology. The first tendency was strict perfectionism, which was in part indebted to the Mennonite Brethren tradition in Russia[88] (itself a

---

87. S. Sannikov, ed., *Nashe kredo: Odesskaya bogoslovskaya seminariya ECB* [Our Creed: Odessa Baptist Theological Seminary] (Odessa: Bogomyslie, 1993), pp. 11-12.

88. See *Istoriya Evangel'skikh Khristian-Baptistov v SSSR*, pp. 420-31. For the influence of the Mennonite Brethren doctrine of holiness on the first Russian Evangelicals see J. Dyck, "Moulding the Brotherhood: Johann Wieler (1839-1889) and the Communities of the Early Evangelicals in Russia" (MTh Dissertation, IBTS, University of Wales, 2007), pp. 29-32, 51-2. On "Anabaptist perfectionism" in general see, for instance, K. Davis, *Anabaptism and Asceticism: A Study in Intellectual Origins* (Kitchener, Ontario: Herald Press, 1974).

product of an Anabaptist tradition stretching back to the sixteenth century[89]), and was also indebted to works on the subject of sanctification
by Ivan Kargel, who was influenced by Keswick holiness teaching.[90] The
Council of Churches of the ECB, which in the later 1960s and early 1970s
claimed the allegiance of around 10% of the Soviet Baptists, in line with
their separatist outlook often emphasized the necessity of absolute holiness
among "genuine believers".[91] According to D.I. Chueshkov, one of the former leaders of the CCECB, "personal holiness was always the main issue
for us".[92] The second tendency mirrored the Russian Orthodox tradition
of openly confessing self-imperfection and "shedding tears" over personal
sins. The main Russian Orthodox Prayer Book says, "Now I, a burdened
sinner, approach Thee, my Lord and God. But I dare not raise my eyes to
Heaven. I only pray, saying: Give me, O Lord, the sense to weep bitterly
over my deeds."[93] Such an attitude was found more often in the AUCECB.
But *Bratsky Vestnik* articles, as well as echoing such sentiments, also called
for holiness:

---

89. See A. Snyder, *Anabaptist History and Theology: An Introduction* (Kitchener, Ontario:
Pandora Press, 1995), p. 362. In 1526 Balthasar Hubmaier defined the Church as "a
community of saints, a brotherhood of many pious and believing men… They are called
together, regulated and ruled here on earth through the only and living Word of God.
This church is beautiful, without spot, unerring, pure, without wrinkle". See W. Claassen,
ed., *Anabaptism in Outline (Selected Primary Sources)* (Kitchener: Herald Press, 1981),
p. 102.

90. In this connection, his book *Khristos – Osvyashchenie Nashe* [Christ our Sanctification]
[1912] should be specially mentioned. The impact of the British Keswick movement
on the holiness teaching of Kargel has been noted. See, for instance, G. Nichols, "Ivan
V. Kargel (1849-1937) and the Development of Russian Evangelical Spirituality" (PhD
thesis, International Baptist Theological Seminary, University of Wales, 2009), pp. 123-7,
231; Puzynin, *Traditsiya Evangel'skikh Khristian*, pp. 211, 237. Keswick meetings were
mentioned in early Russian evangelical periodicals: see, for instance: *Konferentsii Kezikskie*
[Keswick Conferences], BL, *Prilozhenie k Zhurnalu "Khristianin"*, no. 8 (1906), p. 8.

91. See, for instance: *Ob Osvyashchenii* [On Sanctification] [1964] (Sovet Tserkvey ECB,
1990); *Osvyatis'!* [Be Holy!] [From *Vestnik Spaseniya*, 1973], ARSECB, F. 1, op. 28d, d.
18, ll. 1-3. It was estimated that there were 250,000-350,000 Soviet Baptist members in
this period, between 30,000 and 40,000 of them in the CCECB: see *BL*, no. 3 (1968),
pp. 7-8; no. 1 (1973), p. 2. No firm figures on membership exist.

92. D.I. Chueshkov (INT, Seattle, Washington, USA, 2006).

93. The Prayer Book continues: "Have mercy on me, O God, have mercy on me. O woe
is me, a sinner! Wretched am I above all men. There is no penitence in me. Give me, O
Lord, tears to weep bitterly over my deeds." *Canon of Repentance, To our Lord Jesus Christ,
Song 1, Tone 6* in *Pravoslavny Molitvoslov i Psaltyr'* [Orthodox Prayer Book and Psalmbook]
(Omsk: Omsko-Tarskaya Eparkhiya, 1995), p. 24.

> Every bride prepares for her wedding. She usually purchases a
> white dress for this event. The Holy Scripture speaks about a
> similar preparation of the church… Every believer should care
> about his/her clothes to prevent them being dirty…[94]

This picture was a favorite one of some Soviet Baptist preachers, illustrating
as it did the idea of the full separation of believers from all worldly things,
for the preservation of their own purity. Christ would not take a bride with
terrible dirty spots on her dress; she (the church or the believer) should
keep herself in all purity and holiness.

Here are some typical statements on the subject of holiness in the
CCECB's *Vestnik Spaseniya* [Bulletin of Salvation] and in its *Vestnik Istiny*,
in the period 1960s–1980s:

> Some brief advice to the youth: …avoid even the smallest sins,
> do not give scandal by your behavior towards anybody… do
> not miss even one church service… bring sinners to Christ.[95]

> If a man has committed even a small sin, and reaches his hand
> to take the broken Body and Blood of Christ… this is a ter-
> rible situation: such a man becomes guilty of [profaning] God
> himself.[96]

> Even a small insincerity that we often think to be of little ac-
> count … an impure thought… can end badly. Many people
> can lose the Kingdom of Heaven because of this.[97]

Such extreme perfectionist attitudes ("even one church service" missed,
or "has committed even a small sin", or "a small insincerity") within the

---

94. "*Tserkov' – Nevesta Khrista*" [The Church is the Bride of Christ] (editorial article), *BV*,
no. 4 (1974), pp. 42-3.
95. "*Kratkie Sovety Molodezhi*" [Short Advice to the Youth], *VS*, no. 3 (1965), p. 32;
ARSECB, F. 1, op. 28d5, d. 2, l. 32.
96. D. Minyakov, "*O Vechere Gospodney*" [On the Lord's Supper], *VestI*, no. 1 (1983), p. 9.
97. S. Germanyuk, "*Pribliz'tes' k Bogu*" [Draw near to God], *VestI*, no. 1 (1984), p. 19.

CCECB were connected with stories designed to act as "pious deterrents", and also, for those who failed to live up to this rigorous standard, church discipline. Many "instructive", at times "gruesome" stories were told, for example: about a Baptist girl who, after apostasy, died instantly;[98] or about a "prodigal" son of pious Christian parents who lost his eyes and legs, after which he returned to God.[99] Linked with this were stories of God judging those who mocked true believers: about a Soviet school teacher who died during her lesson because she made fun of the faith of a boy in the class who was a believer from a Baptist family;[100] or about local Soviet authorities (Religious Affairs officers, school principals, KGB agents, or policemen) who threatened to close Baptist churches and then suddenly, somehow perished.[101] Holy people suffered, but their enemies could experience divine retribution.

Along with these "negative" stories, there were also "positive" narratives, designed to train young people to be true and honest in all they said and did. For instance: a pious believer bought ten buns, traveled a dozen miles, and then found that there were actually eleven buns in his bag. To maintain his honesty, he decided he needed to return the unpaid-for roll (or take extra money) to the baker. He immediately returned to the shop.[102] Another well-known story (in the form of a poem) of the Russian brotherhood of the ECB has the following remarkable plot: a group of robbers stopped an elderly Baptist presbyter on the road, and he told them that he "had not a penny". He was allowed to go. The elder came to his home, began to undress before going to bed, and suddenly a small coin ("a penny") fell out of his pocket. He exclaimed: "I deceived them!" The man was terrified and left the house again, found the robbers, and, apologizing for his previous lie, gave them the coin. The robbers were moved and ultimately repented of

---

98. See "*Kak Bog Razgovarivaet s Lyud'mi*" [How God Speaks with People] (editorial article), *VestI*, no. 2 (1980), pp. 17-8.

99. Ibid., pp. 18-9. There are a number of these kinds of stories, for instance, in A. Redin, "*Rodilis' li Vy Svyshe?*" [Are You Born Again?], *VestI*, nos. 2-3 (1984), pp. 26-8.

100. *Kak Bog Razgovarivaet s Lyud'mi*, p. 17.

101. For instance, the testimony of church members from Belorussia, M.I. Petrenko and I.E. Petrenko (INT, Fresno, California, USA, 2006). See more in chpayer 8.

102. I heard this sermon illustration at a Baptist church in North Kazakhstan in the early 1990s.

their sins.[103] These narratives were not original to the Baptist community. Although they show some distinctively "perfectionist" Russian Baptist elements, such stories resemble some traditional Orthodox hagiographies.[104] Also, these "holy" plots are quite traditional for Slavic culture and often appear in Russian literature, for example in *The Idiot* by Fyodor Dostoevsky, *The Little Fool* by Nikolay Leskov, as well as in some stories by Leo Tolstoy. The plot of the meeting of a holy man and robbers (with their subsequent repentance) is common in traditional hagiographical stories.[105] Although Orthodoxy did not teach perfectionism, an Orthodox understanding of particularly holy people was widespread.

In the hostile Soviet atheistic context, the logical development of the Baptist perfectionist position became the wish for suffering for Christ. *Vestnik Istiny* articles in the 1980s stated:

'I want to be bound'... These words are of importance, especially at the present time. If we do not want this, we never will be prisoners and, consequently, will never be bearers of the glory of God...[106]

---

103. See the poem "The Penny" in Appendix III. To all appearances, this is a version, with only minor changes, of the work "An Old Legend" by Cloistress Valeriya (Makeeva). In the ECB version, some words pointing to the Orthodox source of the poem ("priest", "cassock", etc.) were changed to neutral ones, but the essence of the story was conveyed correctly and even with extra details. It is also notable that Baptist editor accepted such expressions as: "I pledged myself to poverty", "grace-filled miracle", and "they bowed before the elder".

104. See, for instance: "*Drevny Paterik*" [The Ancient Paterikon], XVI, 20, in *Drevny Paterik ili Dostopamyatnye Skazaniya o Podvizhnichestve Svyatykh i Blazhennykh Ottsov* [The Ancient Paterikon or Memorable Legends about the Asceticism of the Holy and Blessed Fathers] (M.: Blagovest, 2002), p. 228.

105. See, for instance, the section "Robber" in Hegumen Mark (Lozinsky), *Otechnik Propovednika: 1221 Primer iz Prologa i Paterikov* [Book of the Lives of the Fathers for Preachers: 1221 Illustrations from the Prologue and Paterikons] (Izd-vo Svyato-Troitskoy Sergievoy Lavry, 1997); Toporov, *Svyatost' i Svyatye v Russkoy Dukhovnoy Kul'ture*, vol. I, pp. 727-8.

106. P. Peters, "*Vse Sie Preodolevaem*" [In all these Things we are more than Conquerors], *VestI*, no. 2 (1982), p. 27.

> To be ready to suffer and die for Christ... To die with joy, to
> die willingly! – That is what God wants from us.[107]

Such ideas were very popular among those on the radical wing of the
Russian Baptists in the era of Khrushchev and Brezhnev. There was even
a special Baptist youth slogan, "Are you a believer? Be ready to die!"[108] An
editorial entitled *Luchshaya Uchast'* [The Best Lot] in *Vestnik Istiny* in 1983
was about a minister in the CCECB who in 1972 was looking at a photo
of the racked body of Vanya Moiseev, a young Baptist who had been killed
by atheists in the Soviet Army, and said, "I could not wish a better lot for
my own son."[109] This comment illustrates the strength of the spirit of martyrdom among a part of the Soviet Baptists.

At the same time, those advocating this perfectionist type of theology
tended to censure the majority of the Russian Baptists who tried to live
at peace with the authorities. Those who were "not suffering" (or supposedly were not suffering), were considered by the radicals to be spiritually
dead. For example, a former minister of the Moscow unregistered Baptist
Church, V.P. Zinchenko, said later: "In the Communist times, our senior
brethren explained to us – the youth of the Council of Churches – the
doctrine of salvation in this way: 'This is the reality of life: either you go
for Christ to prison, or you go to hell.'"[110] The problem for those seeking
martyrdom was that the Soviet authorities increasingly listened to world
opinion, and the state's desire to persecute its citizens because of their belief in God gradually lessened. This was seen in the change of approach to
this issue from Khrushchev to Brezhnev. Taking into consideration even
the worst periods for the Baptists, perhaps not more than 0.6-0.8% of the
total number of Soviet Baptists suffered imprisonment in the period from
the early 1960s to the 1980s.[111] This represented great suffering for indi-

---

107. B. Artyushchenko, "*Pobednaya Pesn*" [The Victorious Song], *VestI*, no. 3 (1985),
p. 32.

108. E. Rodoslavov, "*Udivitel'ny Podvig*" [Amazing Exploit], *VestI*, nos. 3-4 (1986), p. 15.

109. *VestI*, no. 2 (1983), p. 38.

110. Testimony of V.P. Zinchenko (INT, Seattle, Washington, USA, 2006).

111. Around 2,000 members of both Baptist unions (mainly from the CCECB) were
imprisoned from 1961 to the middle of the 1980s. See A. Rudenko, "*Evangel'skie
Khristiane-Baptisty i Perestroyka v SSSR*" [The Evangelical Christians–Baptists and

viduals and families, and there were heroic martyrs for Christ in the 1960s and 1970s. But it seems that along with the desire to be faithful, there was an aim, especially among the young, to be provocative. Baptist radicals (mostly in the CCECB) sang evangelical hymns while traveling on Soviet public transportation,[112] stuck Christian placards on to the doors of KGB buildings,[113] wore badges with slogans such as "God is Love" pinned to their shirts,[114] and goaded lecturers in atheism into fury during their public lectures.[115] This kind of behavior was connected with the perfectionist perception of holiness found within a section of Russian Baptist life.

However, the outlook of the mainstream of Soviet Baptists regarding this issue was different, and was much closer to Orthodoxy. This is what A.V. Karev wrote in *Bratsky Vestnik* in 1971:

> The church is called to be the Bride of Christ, 'holy and chaste'... However, what do we see in reality? We see sin already in the first churches of the Apostolic Age... Sin... came and comes into Christian communities on the earth and set its seal even on the best of the righteous... We should follow the practice of excommunication as in the apostolic churches, i.e. mainly for three kinds of sin: 1) immorality; 2) veering towards serious false teachings and preaching them; and 3) denial of Christ. All other kinds of sin should be considered as

Perestroika in the USSR] in D. Furman, ed., *Na Puti k Svobode Sovesti* [On the Way to Liberty of Conscience] (M.: Progress, 1989), p. 353; *VestI*, no. 3 (2001), p. 36.

112. Testimony of V.P. Zinchenko (INT, Seattle, Washington, USA, 2006).

113. One of the founders of the Initiative Group in 1961, Boris M. Zdorovets, told me about some young Baptists in Kharkov (Ukraine) in 1962 who stuck on the local KGB door one night a placard with the text, "Repent and believe in the Gospel! (Mark 1:15)". (INT, Spokane, Washington, USA, 2006).

114. Testimony of V.P. Zinchenko (INT, Seattle, Washington, USA, 2006).

115. For instance, testimonies of presbyters of Baptist churches in the USSR: P.F. Kunda (INT, Sacramento, California, USA, 2006), V.N. Gavelovsky (INT, Sacramento, California, USA, 2006), and others. See also a striking recollection on the subject by B.M. Zdorovets in chapter 7. See more information on Soviet Baptist radicalism in C. Prokhorov, "The State and the Baptist Churches in the USSR (1960-1980)", in K.G. Jones and I.M. Randall, eds., *Counter-Cultural Communities: Baptist Life in Twentieth-Century Europe*, pp. 1-62.

spiritual illnesses and be treated with great Christian love and
long-suffering.[116]

Such an approach to the issue of holiness bears the marks of mature reflec-
tion. It is also highly significant that at the end of 1971, the new General
Secretary of the AUCECB, A.M. Bychkov, quoted with respect in *Bratsky
Vestnik* the following words of the then Patriarch-elect, Pimen.

> Starting this ministry... confessing my infirmity, with all hope
> for divine grace, which accompanied me from the monastery
> cell to this ministry, I ask you – do not forget me in your
> prayers.[117]

The impact of this kind of testimony, in which a notable Orthodox leader
spoke of his "infirmity" and asked for prayer, was considerable. Faced with
the choice of promoting Baptist perfectionist tendencies or confessing their
imperfections in the spirit exemplified in Orthodoxy, AUCECB leaders of
the 1970s and 1980s chose the latter course. This is borne out by statements made in many articles in issues of *Bratsky Vestnik* in this period.[118] In
1985, for example, these words appeared:

> We all are sinners... How many commandments are not kept
> by us and how many commandments we transgress! ... The
> more we depreciate or condemn ourselves before God, the
> greater the love and mercy given to us by the Lord... The
> genuine Christian should weep over the fact that he lost God's
> image and constantly offends God by his sins. He should
> weep over the fact that he is named as Christian but does not
> keep the vows he made when he was baptized; that he holds to

116. A. Karev, "*Zloupotrebleniya Otlucheniyami*" [Abuse of Excommunication], *BV*, no. 1
(1971), pp. 66-9.
117. See A. Bychkov, "*Pomestny Sobor Russkoy Pravoslavnoy Tserkvi*" [The Local Council of
the Russian Orthodox Church], *BV*, no. 4 (1971), p. 12.
118. See, for instance, *BV*, no. 5 (1972), p. 26; no. 6 (1975), pp. 26-35; no. 3 (1976),
p. 28.

transient things and does not think about heaven and eternal life.[119]

The mention of the "image" of God is significant. Some Russian Baptists, following the Orthodox tradition, distinguished between the "image" and "likeness" of God in humanity. "Image", for Orthodoxy, is an entity of humanity created by God, and it is only through a long spiritual process of "theosis" or "divinization", in which the leading role belongs to grace (always operating, however, along with the human will), that the "likeness" of God appears in a human being.[120] Russian Baptists saw the Christian life as one in which a believer came nearer to God, but as this happened the believer would feel a greater sense of imperfection.[121]

Seeing the true holiness of a Christian in terms of his or her permanent repentance before God was a theme widely represented in the main song-books of the Russian Baptists.

> O, I am a poor sinner!
> It is true, I am.[122]

> Give me, O God, holiness…
> Grant me to weep over my sins![123]

> I try to avoid evil…
> But I cannot be pure.[124]

Such deeply-held convictions pervaded Soviet Baptist communities. Soviet Baptists heard preaching on these themes, sang about them and also tried

---

119. [Anon], "*Velika Vasha Nagrada na Nebesakh*" [Your Reward in Heaven is Great], *BV*, no. 5 (1985), pp. 12-13.

120. See Metropolitan Nikodim's article "*Iisus Khristos Osvobozhdaet i Ob"edinyaet*" [Jesus Christ Makes Free and Joins Together], *BV*, 6 (1974), pp. 16-19.

121. See [Anon], "*Velika Vasha Nagrada na Nebesakh*" [Your Reward in Heaven is Great], p. 13.

122. *SDP*, no. 42, p. 35.

123. *SDP*, no. 62, p. 48. See also *SDP*, nos. 36, 43.

124. *PV*, no. 77, p. 51. See also: nos. 7, 86.

to persuade others about them. They insisted to other evangelicals that the confession "I cannot be pure" was the correct spiritual approach. Thus a famous Russian Baptist evangelist, P.A. Semeryuk, recalled a conversation that an old Baptist minister had with a Russian evangelical group in the 1950s who were holding out the possibility of living a life of great spiritual power. The minister said to them: "We Baptists are very imperfect people... In past times, as it is written, the shadow of the apostle Peter healed the sick, but we are still forced to take pills. By the way: how are you getting on with this?"[125] In this case, the Baptist minister convinced his hearers. However, soon after the beginning of *perestroika*, under the influence of some Western evangelists of Methodist and Pentecostal orientation, there was a new emphasis among some Russian evangelicals on "absolute holiness" and also on Pentecostal power. The sermons of John Wesley and Charles Finney were disseminated among Russian Baptists. There were also various attempts to draw parallels between the Pentecostal doctrine of "Christian transformation" and Orthodox teaching on theosis.[126] At the same time, older Russian Baptists looked back to what they believed was a higher spiritual and moral tone that had existed in the past in their communities.[127] For most Soviet Baptists, it was not the church members who considered themselves holy who were to be emulated. Rather, it was Christians who sought holiness but felt their own imperfection, and repented before God for their smallest sins, who had true holiness. The presence among

---

125. The group belonged to an underground movement, "*evangel'skie khristiane sovershennye*" (Evangelical Perfect Christians). The old Baptist minister continued: "In past times, the Holy Scripture says, Christians prayed and the place where they had gathered together was shaken, but we are not able to pray in our churches with such power today. What about you?... we read in Acts, the believers sold their houses and distributed the money to the poor, not claiming that anything on the earth was their own, but we, alas, still live in our own houses. And you?.." Finally, the Baptist minister apparently led the "*sovershenye*" to the idea that they were also "unprofitable servants" rather than "perfect" Christians. – Testimony of P.A. Semeryuk (INT, Sacramento, California, USA, 2006).

126. See E. Rybarczyk, "Beyond Salvation: An Analysis of the Doctrine of Christian Transformation Comparing Eastern Orthodoxy with Classical Pentecostalism" (PhD thesis, Fuller Theological Seminary, 1999); E. Rybarczyk, *Beyond Salvation: Eastern Orthodoxy and Classical Pentecostalism on Becoming Like Christ* (Milton Keynes: Paternoster, 2004).

127. See on the theme, for instance, I. Leshchuk, *Labirinty Dukhovnosti* [Labyrinths of Spirituality] (Odessa: Khristianskoe Prosveshchenie, 2001).

Baptists of this spirit, one which marked the Orthodox tradition, suggests Orthodox influence.

Scripture and tradition

Soviet Baptists were unable because of their circumstances to engage in any serious study of the original biblical languages.[128] The text of the Bible that they knew and used was the Russian Orthodox translation – the famous Synodal Bible of 1876. Russian Baptists considered the Synodal Bible as the best (almost "divinely-inspired") of all Bible translations. The following idea can be found stated repeatedly in *Bratsky Vestnik*, "The language of the Russian Synodal Bible became very dear to each believer... Praise the Lord for all the teachers who worked... on the Russian text of the Holy Scripture."[129] Undoubtedly the Synodal Bible is Orthodox: it was translated in accordance with the Orthodox Holy Tradition.[130] Russian scholar I. Apatova has convincingly shown that several "extreme Protestant" (as they were perceived) passages of the New Testament on salvation by grace alone were moderated in the Russian Synodal Bible, probably in order to uphold the traditional Orthodox understanding of the value of good works for salvation.[131] As Russian Baptists have used the Synodal version, Orthodox tradition has been conveyed to them.

---

128. J. Dyck described an attempt at "underground" learning of New Testament Greek by a group of Baptist young people under the supervision of A. Rudenko, in Russia and Kazakhstan, in 1981-1982. This was a unique event. (INT, Oerlinghausen, Germany, 2007).

129. A. Bychkov, S. Fadyukhin, *"Istoriya Perevoda Biblii na Russky Yazyk"* [The History of Translation of the Bible into Russian], *BV*, no. 3 (1976), pp. 61, 66. See also *BV*, no. 2 (1986), p. 64; no. 1 (1988), p. 63; no. 3 (1988), p. 71.

130. The much-quoted (by Orthodox authors) 19th canon of the Sixth Ecumenical Council in part says, "We declare that the deans of churches... must teach... words of truth out of the Holy Bible, analyzing the meanings and judgments of the truth, and not deviating from the definitions already laid down, or the teaching derived from the God-bearing Fathers; but also, if the discourse is concerning a passage of Scripture, one should not interpret it otherwise than as the luminaries and teachers of the Church in their own written works have presented it." – Bishop Nikodim, ed., *Pravila Pravoslavnoy Tserkvi* [The Canons of the Orthodox Church] 2 vols. [1911] (M.: Otchiy Dom, 2001), vol. I, p. 490.

131. See I. Apatova, *Germenevtika Sinodal'nogo perevoda* [Hermeneutics of the Synodal Translation] (Diploma thesis, Moscow Theological Seminary of ECB, 2006), pp. 109-23.

Officially, the Russian Baptists, like other Baptists, have always declared their allegiance to the *Sola Scriptura* principle.[132] That meant, "denying any human traditions". Thus the Estonian leader O. Tyark, writing in *Bratsky Vestnik* in 1982, mentioned some interpretations by very authoritative authors on a particular biblical text, and then added, "Let us take away all… suppositions and try to understand what Christ himself wanted to say."[133] This is not to argue that Russian Baptists placed tradition on the same level as the Bible. They did not. However, I am arguing that they made quite explicit statements that showed greater respect for tradition than has been true of many evangelicals elsewhere, certainly for much of the twentieth century. A Russian Baptist author such as P. Savchenko, who was involved in the Bible Correspondence Courses in Moscow, was aware that views held in the longer Protestant story could not always accurately be described as adherence to "the Bible alone". He wrote: "The Lutheran Church bases its teachings on the Bible and holds its [the Bible's] interpretation to be given in the theological works by M. Luther and in the Confessions of the Book of Concord."[134] Certainly early Anabaptists, with their desire to restore the New Testament church, tried to hold the *Sola Scriptura* principle consistently,[135] and in line with this approach A.M. Bychkov said to the Council of the AUCECB in 1974: "From the time of the earthly life of Jesus Christ… traditions arose and were established in the church. However, each time accretions and traditions were tested in the light of the Word of God, they were rejected. God's Spirit encouraged the hearts of people to return to the pure spring of the Gospel."[136] Yet later in the same

---

132. See, for instance: "*Verouchenie Evangel'skikh Khristian – Baptistov*" [The Creed of the Evangelical Christians–Baptists], *BV*, no. 4 (1985), pp. 33-4; *Osnovnye Printsipy Very Evangel'skikh Khristian-Baptistov* [The Basic Principles of Belief of the Evangelical Christians–Baptists] (Sbornik Publikatsy) (Odessa: Russian Gospel Ministries, 1992), p. 92.

133. O. Tyark, "*Pritchi Iisusa Khrista*" [Proverbs of Jesus Christ], *BV*, no. 3 (1982), p. 14.

134. P. Savchenko, "*Lyuteranskaya Tserkov*" [The Lutheran Church], *BV*, no. 3 (1987), p. 49.

135. See R. Friedman, *The Theology of Anabaptism* (Eugene, OR: Wipf and Stock Publishers, 1998), pp. 36-7, 149; A. McGrath, *Reformation Thought: An Introduction*, 3rd ed. (Oxford: Blackwell Publishers, 2001), p. 155; Snyder, *Anabaptist History and Theology*, pp. 159-72.

136. *BV*, no. 1 (1975), p. 23.

report, Bychkov (somewhat inconsistently) said this: "Our brotherhood firmly follows the evangelical traditions and principles."[137]

This sense of being part of an ongoing tradition was more fully explicated at an AUCECB Plenum in 1981 by Bychkov and A.E. Klimenko:

> We have instilled in... our children the spirit of faithfulness to the Lord ...to plant the desire to abide by the good traditions of our brotherhood... According to the Statutes of our Union, based on the Holy Scriptures and our practice of service, senior presbyters should bear in mind in preaching the Gospel the beliefs and principles of our brotherhood... Senior presbyters have to prepare sermons... in connection with the beliefs and principles of our brotherhood... to encourage ministers to be faithful to the views and preserve the principles of our multi-national united Evangelical Baptist brotherhood... So as to avoid any violent interpretations [of the Bible], we should use the good heritage of printed matter of the pioneers of the Evangelical Baptist movement in our country... published by the periodicals *Baptist* [The Baptist], *Khristianin* [The Christian] as well as our contemporary *Bratsky Vestnik*... Senior presbyters, as Fathers, should build up truly Christian characters... Senior presbyters, as experienced Fathers, should know their children very well.[138]

There are several very significant phrases here: "good traditions of our brotherhood"; "our practice"; "beliefs and principles of our brotherhood"; "the principles of our multi-national united Evangelical Baptist brotherhood"; and "the good heritage... of the pioneers of the Evangelical-Baptist movement in our country". A.I. Negrov, Rector of St. Petersburg Christian

---

137. *BV*, no. 1 (1975), p. 29.

138. "*Materialy Plenuma AUCECB, Iyun' 1981 Goda*" [Materials of Plenum of the AUCECB, June 1981], *BV*, no. 5 (1981), pp. 54-65. See similar ideas in *Doklad General'nogo Sekretarya VSECB A.V. Kareva* [Report of the General Secretary of AUCECB, A.V. Karev], *BV*, no. 6 (1966), p. 22; A. Mitskevich, "*O Vospitanii Veruyushchikh*" [On the Upbringing of Believers], *BV*, no. 5 (1986), p. 59.

University, writes: "Traditionally, the hermeneutics of Russian evangelicals has mirrored the eastern hermeneutics of Orthodoxy in that the ecclesiastical mind is considered epistemologically superior to individual human reasoning… Bible interpretation cannot be (and should not be) done apart from the church."[139] So the deep and ineradicable link with the Orthodox Church and its exalted view of "Tradition" in a measure created "the Russian Evangelical-Baptist tradition". Certainly Baptists did not give "tradition" the same status as it had in Orthodoxy, but there were echoes of Orthodox thinking among Baptists. The desire in the 1981 Baptist statement to avoid "any violent interpretations of the Bible" was followed by references to the role of senior presbyters as "Fathers",[140] with church members being called "children". This language has definite echoes of Orthodoxy. Eastern Christians quoted St. Barsanophius the Great: "Bind your laden boat to your Fathers' ship, and they [the Fathers] will lead you to Jesus."[141] Following Orthodox practice, some Russian Baptist senior presbyters began to call themselves bishops.[142]

Orthodox authors always taught that the Bible would not exist without the canon of Scripture, but that the canon would not exist without church tradition.[143] Also they insisted that people could not "apprehend Scripture adequately" outside the Holy Tradition.[144] Individual interpretations were too subjective. The necessity of tradition – oral tradition –

---

139. A. Negrov, "Hermeneutics in Tradition", *Theological Reflections*, vol. 4 (2004), p. 46.

140. See also: A. Mitskevich, "*Pastyrskoe Sluzhenie*" [The Shepherd's Ministry], *BV*, no. 2 (1979), p. 27. There was a similar state of affairs in the CCECB. G. Kostyuchenko recalled a Soviet jail where prisoners named him "Father Gregory". See *VestI*, no. 1 (1983), p. 36.

141. Cited in Archpriest A. Soloviev, *Starchestvo po Ucheniyu Svyatykh Ottsov i Asketov* [The Eldership According to the Teaching of the Holy Fathers and Ascetics] (M.: Blagovest, 1995), p. 54.

142. The common argument that the New Testament words "presbyter" and "bishop" are synonyms was not followed. Any "ordinary" (for instance, rural) presbyters among the Russian Baptists were not permitted to name themselves bishops.

143. See, for instance, A.S. Khomyakov, *Neskol'ko Slov Pravoslavnogo Khristianina o Zapadnykh Veroispovedaniyakh*, p. 176.

144. See K. Leontiev, "*O Vsemirnoy Lyubvi*" [On Universal Love] [1885], in *Russkaya Ideya*, p. 208; Metropolitan Nikodim, "*Predanie i Sovremennost*" [Tradition and Modernity], *ZhMP*, no. 12 (1972), pp. 54-6; Archpriest Sergei (Bulgakov), "*Tserkov' kak Predanie*" [The Church as the Tradition], *ZhMP*, no. 12 (1989), pp. 67-73.

was also seen as being related to Christ's oral teaching: he did not write a book.[145] Indeed, in periods when many people in churches could not read, oral tradition was vital. The Russian Baptist approach to tradition contained both affirmations of tradition and questions about its role. When observing Protestant proprieties, *Bratsky Vestnik* from time to time spoke disapprovingly of "deviations from the Apostolic Church". However, such references commonly had to do with Roman Catholicism, rather than Orthodoxy.[146] This was despite there being many more Orthodox parishes than Roman Catholic parishes in the Soviet Union.[147] It is clear that Russian Baptists were very far from agreeing with what was at one time a Roman Catholic maxim, *Biblia est mater haereticorum* ["The Bible is the mother of heretics"].[148] On the other hand, a very strict *Sola Scriptura* approach was not, in practice, how a number of these Baptists seemed to operate. There were appeals to tradition. Thus senior presbyter V. Mitskevich, in an article in *Bratsky Vestnik* in 1985 on the Apostles' Creed, wrote about the close connection of the Holy Scripture and church tradition regarding the formation of Christian doctrines, speaking positively of the ancient Orthodox teaching on Christ's descent into hell.[149] Under the editorship of A.V. Karev and then V.G. Kulikov, articles in *Bratsky Vestnik* frequently quoted with approval certain Eastern (rarely Western) church fathers. Orthodox hymns and poems were published. There was mention of many Christian feasts celebrated by both Russian Orthodox Christians and Russian Baptists, and regular Easter and Christmas greetings from the Orthodox Patriarch and Metropolitans were included.

---

145. See Archimandrite Illarion, *Svyashchennoe Pisanie i Tserkov'* [The Holy Scripture and the Church] (M.: Pechatnya A. Snegirevoy, 1914), pp. 3-17.

146. See, for instance: *BV*, no. 4 (1970), pp. 68-9; no. 1 (1971), pp. 66-7; no. 4 (1988), pp. 64-6.

147. At the beginning of the 1980s, the USSR officially had around 8.5 thousand Russian Orthodox churches and a little more than 1,000 Roman Catholic parishes. See V. Kuroedov, *Religiya i Tserkov' v Sovetskom Obshchestve* [Religion and Church in the Soviet Society] (M.: Politizdat, 1984), p. 108.

148. From a different standpoint, the Doukhobors, seen by some as predecessors of Russian Baptists, saw the Bible as a "great troublemaker". See Karetnikova, *Russkoe Bogoiskatel'stvo*, p. 67; Savinsky, *Istoriya (1867-1917)*, p. 48.

149. V. Mitskevich, *"Apostol'sky Simvol Very"* [The Apostles' Creed], *BV*, no. 5 (1985), pp. 21-31.

As an example of the way the Patristic tradition was used in *Bratsky Vestnik*, one of the AUCECB leaders, I.I. Motorin, made a serious comparison between the number of delegates at the Baptist Council in Moscow in 1963 and the number of the Fathers at the First Ecumenical Council in Nicaea (A.D. 325).[150] The Ecumenical Councils which are so central to Orthodoxy also inspired the respect of the majority of the Russian Baptists. This approach contrasts with early Stundist and Russian Baptist rejection of "all Church Councils".[151] *Bratsky Vestnik* also quite uncritically recounted legendary stories from Orthodox Church tradition, for example about the lives and deaths of the evangelists Luke,[152] Mark,[153] and John;[154] and spoke about the eunuch in Acts chapter 8, who was said to have preached the gospel in Ethiopia and converted his Queen to the Christian faith.[155] One AUCECB theologian respectfully referred to the ancient Christian tradition of weakening the wine at the Eucharist with water,[156] though Russian Baptists, as a rule, used unmingled wine for the Lord's Supper.[157] *Bratsky Vestnik* also, remarkably, often showed sympathy for the Apocryphal books

---

150. See I. Motorin, "*Torzhestvo Edinstva Veruyushchikh*" [Triumph of the Believers' Unity], *BV*, no. 1 (1964), p. 24.

151. See, for instance: S. Stepnyak-Kravchinsky, *Shtundist Pavel Rudenko* [Stundist Pavel Rudenko] [1894] (SPb.: Bibliya dlya Vsekh, 1997), pp. 94-9; Popov, *Stopy Blagovestnika*, p. 61.

152. See N. Mel'nikov, "*Obzor Evangel'skikh Povestvovany*" [Review of the Gospel Stories], *BV*, no. 5 (1973), p. 61.

153. See O. Tyark, "*Evangelie ot Marka*" [The Gospel according to Mark], *BV*, no. 1 (1976), p. 31.

154. See I. Chekalov, "*O Evangelii ot Ioanna*" [On the Gospel according to John], *BV*, no. 2 (1979), p. 49.

155. See P. Shatrov, "*Deyaniya Apostolov*" [The Acts of the Apostles], *BV*, no. 1 (1985), p. 21.

156. O. Tyark, "*Evangelie ot Marka*" [The Gospel according to Mark], *BV*, no. 5 (1980), p. 21. In the Eucharist of the Russian Orthodox Church, wine weakened with water is also used. See, for instance: A. Men', *Tainstvo, Slovo i Obraz: Pravoslavnoe Bogosluzhenie* [Sacrament, Word and Image: The Orthodox Divine Service] (M.: Fond imeni A. Menya, 2001), p. 52.

157. Traditional Russian Baptists, as total abstainers, suggest that Jesus Christ drank grape juice, not wine, but at the same time they use real wine at the Lord's Supper. This is one more enigmatic Russian Baptist tradition. See N. Kolesnikov, *Khristianin, znaesh' li ty, kak dolzhno postupat' v dome Bozh'em?* [Christian, do you know how People ought to Conduct themselves in God's Household?], 3 vols. (M.: Druzhba i Blagaya Vest', 1998), vol. I, p. 51.

of the Old Testament. Soviet Baptists did not consider them as "God-inspired", but recognized them "as ethical and historical books".[158] The stories of Susanna (Dan 13) and the idol Bel (Dan 14) were retold with enthusiasm in *Bratsky Vestnik*.[159] In their view of the Apocrypha, Russian Baptists were closer to Orthodox Tradition than to Western Protestantism, which excluded Apocryphal books from the canonical scriptures.[160]

Of all the church fathers cited in *Bratsky Vestnik*, St. John Chrysostom was the most popular. In the 1970s and 1980s, there were only a few issues of *Bratsky Vestnik* that did not cite Chrysostom. In Issue Number 5 of 1987, an article, "Thoughts on Christian Peacefulness", was published.[161] There were four Patristic quotations, two of which appeared with the author's name: both belonged to John Chrysostom.[162] The other quotations were from St. Gregory of Nyssa,[163] but the article did not name him. Perhaps to recognize more than one church father in a single article was difficult for *Bratsky Vestnik*.[164] In Issue Number 6 of 1987, under the heading "Thoughts on Man" Chrysostom's words were also quoted, with his name.[165] However, a sentence by St. Macarius the Elder was not attributed.[166] In Issue Number 2 of 1989, under the surprising title,[167] "The

---

158. [Anon], "*O Biblii*" [On the Bible], *BV*, no. 4 (1972), p. 73.

159. See [Anon], "*Kniga Proroka Daniila*" [The Book of Daniel], *BV*, no. 2 (1986), pp. 29-30. Though Soviet Baptists published the Bible without the Apocrypha, Russian Orthodox editions of the Scripture, with the Apocrypha, were held in esteem among them. Several Baptist presbyters and preachers at the end of the 1980s, in my experience, preferred to use the "fat" Orthodox Bibles.

160. See, for instance: *The Encyclopedia of Protestantism* (Hillerbrand), vol. III, p. 1415; D. Wallace, "Apocrypha, Old Testament", in *Evangelical Dictionary of Theology*, pp. 66-7.

161. "*Mysli o Khristianskom Mirolyubii*" [Thoughts on Christian Peacefulness], *BV*, no. 5 (1987), p. 47.

162. Ibid.

163. See, for instance: St. Gregory of Nyssa, "*O Blazhenstvakh, Slovo 7*" [On the Beatitudes, the Homily 7], *ZhMP*, no. 7 (1977), pp. 25-6.

164. The author was sometimes disguised. For instance, St. Abba Dorotheos (VII c) was called a certain "A. Dorotheos". See *BV*, no. 6 (1974), p. 25.

165. "*Mysli o Cheloveke*" [Thoughts on Man], *BV*, no. 6 (1987), p. 48.

166. See, for instance: "*Nastavleniya Sv. Makariya Velikogo o Khristianskoy Zhizni*" [The Homilies of St. Macarius the Elder on the Christian Life], in *Dobrotolyubie* [The Philokalia], 5 vols. (M.: Tipo-Litografiya I. Efimova, 1895), vol. I, p. 156.

167. The title was surprising (for a Baptist periodical) because the sentences were actually from Eastern Church Fathers, not from the Gospels.

Gospel's Homilies",[168] Chrysostom was again quoted by name, while a saying by St. Abba Isaiah (4th C) remained anonymous.[169] Chrysostom was also highly regarded by the CCECB. Indeed their periodical *Vestnik Istiny* not only published some of his aphorisms but also whole homilies of Chrysostom, for instance *On Prayer*,[170] and the *Homily on Repentance*.[171] An editorial in *Vestnik Istiny* in 1977 helps in understanding the special sympathy of Soviet Baptists for Chrysostom: the piece noted that he was baptized as an adult believer; that he was strict and intolerant of any sin; that he condemned the rich and the "powers that be"; and that he spoke against women who wore fineries and adornments.[172] His dismissal from his ministry because of his stand "for the truth" particularly impressed the radical wing of the Baptists.[173]

Other church fathers who were popular among and were quoted by Soviet Baptists were Sts. Basil the Great, Gregory Palamas, Gregory of Nyssa, Athanasius of Alexandria, Nilus of Sinai, and Macarius the Elder. Often one article in *Bratsky Vestnik* contained references to several Fathers.[174] The respect for the Eastern church fathers and for certain Orthodox traditions was so profound that, for instance, the senior presbyter of the AUCECB in the Ukraine, Ya. Dukhonchenko spoke quite uncritically in 1986 about an old Orthodox legend regarding the sudden death of Arius (known and

---

168. "*Evangel'skie Poucheniya*" [The Gospel's Homilies], *BV*, no. 2 (1989), p. 33.

169. See, for instance: *St. Abba Isaiah*, in *Nastol'naya Kniga Svyashchennosluzhitelya* [The Handbook for Priests], 7 vols. (M.: Izdanie Moskovskoy Patriarkhii, 1977-1994), vol. VI, p. 731.

170. See John Chrysostom, "*O Molitve*" [On Prayer], *VestI*, no. 2 (1987), pp. 17-20. It seems that the editorial staff of *Vestnik Istiny* used the text of this homily from the following edition: *Tvoreniya Svyatogo Ottsa Nashego Ioanna Zlatousta, Arkhiepiskopa Konstantinopol'skogo, v Russkom Perevode* [The Writings of St. John Chrysostom, Our Father, the Archbishop of Constantinople, a Russian Translation] (SPb.: Izdanie S.-Peterburgskoy Dukhovnoy Akademii, 1906), vol. XII, part. 2, pp. 484-97.

171. See John Chrysostom, "*Slovo o Pokayanii*" [Homily on Repentance], *VestI*, no. 1 (1990), pp. 11-3. Probably this was a compilation from several homilies of St. John.

172. See "*John Chrysostom*" (editorial article), *VestI*, no. 4 (1977), pp. 30-2.

173. Ibid., p. 32.

174. See, for instance: L. Semlek, "*Zhanry Khristianskikh Pesnopeny*" [The Genres of Christian Songs], *BV*, no. 3 (1983), pp. 68-71; [Anon], "*Istoriya Kanona Novogo Zaveta*" [The History of the Canon of the New Testament], *BV*, no. 6 (1983), pp. 32-41; B. Gladkov, "*Podlinnost' Evangely*" [The Authenticity of the Gospels], *BV*, no. 1 (1989), pp. 25-35.

condemned for his heretical teaching in the 4th C.), which supposedly took place after a prayer by a saint.[175] When *Bratsky Vestnik* did not attribute Patristic sayings to the authors this was probably connected with the sensitivities of some Soviet Baptists who spoke against close relationships with Orthodoxy. In 1969 a member of Moscow Central Baptist Church wrote (anonymously) to A.V. Karev denouncing him because "the first Christians separated from idolaters... but you have mingled with them... On Whit Monday, you elevated the [Orthodox] priest with his cross to the pulpit and greeted him saying, 'this is our brother'".[176] However, denunciations of this kind were rare.

In the 1980s *Bratsky Vestnik* published several selections of unattributed Christian aphorisms, but these can now be identified. In Issue Number 6 of 1986, there is a piece, "Thoughts on Prayer".[177] All six quotations cited in it are quotations from Eastern church fathers. Five of them are not named. The six are: 1) St. Basil the Great;[178] 2) St. Gregory Palamas;[179] 3) St. John Chrysostom (the only author named); 4) St. Basil the Great again;[180] 5) St. Nilus of Sinai;[181] 6) and St. Basil the Great once more.[182] Analyzing the Patristic selections in *Bratsky Vestnik*, it is clear that the editorial board used the five-volume *The Dobrotolubie*, the authoritative collection of ascetic writings of classical Orthodox authors.[183] In "Thoughts on Prayer", the

---

175. See Ya. Dukhonchenko, *"Bud' Obraztsom Dlya Vernykh"* [Be a Good Example for the Faithful], *BV*, no. 5 (1986), p. 23.

176. ARSECB, F. 1, op. 28d7a, d. 19, l. 2.

177. *"Mysli o Molitve"* [Thoughts on Prayer], *BV*, no. 6 (1986), pp. 30-1.

178. See, for instance: *Sv. Vasiliya Velikogo Nastavleniya o Molitve i Trezvenii* [St. Basil the Great on Prayer and Abstinence], in *Svyatootecheskie Nastavleniya o Molitve i Trezvenii* [The Patristic Writings on Prayer and Abstinence] (M.: RIPOL klassik, 2008), pp. 7-8. For this quotation, along with the other extracts mentioned here from the patristic works, as represented both in Russian Orthodox sources and *Bratsky Vestnik*, see also the table in Appendix II.

179. See, for instance, *Iz Zhitiya Sv. Grigoriya Palamy, Arhiepiskopa Solunskogo* [From the Life of Saint Gregory Palamas, the Archbishop of Thessalonica], in *Dobrotolyubie*, vol. V, pp. 480-1.

180. See *Sv. Vasiliya Velikogo Nastavleniya o Molitve i Trezvenii*, pp. 16-17.

181. See, for instance: *Asketicheskie Nastavleniya Prepodobnogo Nila Sinayskogo* [The Ascetic Homilies of St. Nilus of Sinai], in *Dobrotolyubie*, vol. II, p. 211.

182. See *Sv. Vasiliya Velikogo Nastavleniya o Molitve i Trezvenii*, p. 17.

183. For example, the second pre-revolutionary edition: *Dobrotolyubie* [The Philokalia – "Love of the Beautiful and Good"], 5 vols. (M.: Tipo-Litografiya I. Efimova, 1895-1900).

words by St. Nilus of Sinai which were quoted are found in the second volume of *The Dobrotolubie*,[184] and the maxim by St. Gregory Palamas is from the fifth volume.[185] In another piece, "Thoughts on Man" (*Bratsky Vestnik*, 1987), the words by St. Macarius the Elder from the first volume of *The Dobrotolubie* were reprinted,[186] and an utterance by St. Abba Isaiah, which was published in *Bratsky Vestnik* under the heading "The Gospel's Homilies" (1989), was probably taken from the same volume.[187] *Bratsky Vestnik* took the sayings of the Eastern Fathers with great seriousness.

Other Orthodox sources from which *Bratsky Vestnik* drew included famous Russian Orthodox figures of the eighteenth century, such as St. Tikhon Zadonsky, who was quoted and named, but without the prefix "St.",[188] and Metropolitan Stefan Yavorsky, whose name appeared in *Bratsky Vestnik* in 1989 without any mention of his position, as if he was a secular person.[189] In the same year *Bratsky Vestnik* included some sentences by Patriarch Pimen.[190] It seems that in this period the number and variety of references to representatives of the Orthodox tradition and the Orthodox Church multiplied. The intuitive inclination towards the Eastern Christian Tradition is also seen in the publication of classical Russian Orthodox poetry by *Bratsky Vestnik*. For instance, a poem by the popular nineteenth-century Russian poet Semen Nadson was published in the late 1980s, and contains the following words:

---

184. See *Asketicheskie Nastavleniya Prepodobnogo Nila Sinayskogo* [The Ascetic Homilies of St. Nilus of Sinai], in *Dobrotolyubie*, vol. II, p. 211. (See also our collation of the quotations from *Dobrotolyubie* and *Bratsky Vestnik* in the Appendix I).

185. See *Iz Zhitiya Sv. Grigoriya Palamy, Arhiepiskopa Solunskogo* [From the Life of Saint Gregory Palamas, the Archbishop of Thessalonica], in *Dobrotolyubie*, vol. V, pp. 480-1. (See also the Appendix I).

186. See *Nastavleniya Sv. Makariya Velikogo o Khristianskoy Zhizni* [The Homilies of St. Macarius the Elder on Christian Life], in *Dobrotolyubie*, vol. I, p. 156. (See also the Appendix I).

187. See *Prepodobny Avva Isaiya o Podvizhnichestve i Bezmolvii* [St. Abba Isaiah on Asceticism and Silence], in *Dobrotolyubie*, vol. I, pp. 464-5. (See also the Appendix I).

188. His saying was quoted alongside words from John Chrysostom. See P. Shatrov, *"Deyaniya Svyatykh Apostolov"* [The Acts of the Saint Apostles], *BV*, no. 5 (1988), p. 42.

189. See *"Evangel'skie Poucheniya"*, *BV*, no. 2 (1989), p. 33.

190. He was also published anonymously as *"The Gospel's Homilies"*. See *BV*, no. 2 (1989), p. 33; *ZhMP*, no. 9 (1985), p. 7. (See also Appendix II).

The common people were able,
Warmly and piously, to encase
In the holy tradition the memory
About faith and love in the olden times.[191]

The image of the Russian "common people" being those who connected with "holy tradition" is significant in this poem. Perhaps there was an idea here of Baptists as those common people who could still be the pious bearers, in their worship, of "memory about faith". Articles in *Bratsky Vestnik* quoted famous Orthodox liturgical songs: for instance in 1971 in a piece by a member of the AUCECB presidium, I.Ya. Tatarchenko; and in 1985 in an article by senior presbyter V.A. Mitskevich.[192] The Russian Christian tradition was affirmed and celebrated in poems and songs as well as through drawing from the writings of the past.

Another facet of Orthodox tradition, which was quoted and retold in *Bratsky Vestnik*, was that connected with the theme of the beginnings of Christianity in Russia. The "Slavophilism" of the Soviet Baptists was evident at this point. In connection with the celebration in 1988 of the baptisms in 988 which established Christianity in Russia, *Bratsky Vestnik* published in its columns old traditions and legends on the theme and bestowed praise on Russian Orthodoxy.[193] The readers of *Bratsky Vestnik* were told in 1988 about the legends of the preaching of the Gospel on the old Slavic territories as far back as the first century A.D. by the Apostle Andrew and Bishop Clement of Rome. Clement was reported as having daily baptized "up to five hundred souls". The responses of several early church fathers to those events were also included.[194] V.G. Kulikov, the *Bratsky Vestnik* editor, writing in the following year, agreed with the tradition that the Apostle Andrew "visited the Southern areas of our country". Kulikov also retold at length the famous Orthodox traditions about Princess Olga and Prince

---

191. S. Nadson, *"Khristianka"* [A Christian], *BV*, no. 5 (1988), p. 63.

192. I. Tatarchenko, *"Sretenie Gospodne"* [The Meeting of the Lord], *BV*, no. 2 (1971), p. 42; V. Mitskevich, *"Apostol'sky Simvol Very"* [The Apostles' Creed], *BV*, no. 5 (1985), p. 31.

193. See, for instance: V. Popov, *"Vozniknovenie Khristianstva na Rusi"* [The Beginnings of Christianity in Russia], *BV*, no. 1 (1988), pp. 46-50.

194. Ibid., pp. 46-7.

Vladimir (in the 10th century) from the "Russian Primary Chronicle" ("The Tale of Bygone Years").[195] In 1989 V.E. Logvinenko, the president of the AUCECB, noted the "good and friendly relationship" between the Orthodox people and Baptists in the USSR, and he also reiterated the Orthodox legends about the early origins of Christianity in Russia, adding that Princess Olga and Prince Vladimir "were baptized as adults" and referring at that point to the baptismal practice of the Baptists.[196]

It is certainly true that Russian Baptists never placed tradition on the same level as the Scriptures, but there was a sense of an older tradition to be appreciated and also a living tradition. A short letter of thanks published in *Bratsky Vestnik* in 1974 illustrates how Baptists saw the living tradition: "I appreciate your periodical… the issues are great aids for me in the understanding of the Bible…". In 1980 there was a similar letter.[197] The sentiments were typical. In 1988 one of the authors in *Bratsky Vestnik*, G. Sergienko, writing against the background of considerable Russian Baptist acknowledgement of Orthodox history in that period, tried to remind the readers of the periodical of the Protestant *Sola Scriptura* principle, saying that "the Gospel only is the basis of our faith, the Gospel determines… the theology… as well as the practice of our worship".[198] But the idea of a single basis for faith among Russian Baptists was an idealistic position. The interrelation between Scripture and tradition within the Soviet Baptist communities was a complex one. Some of the basic tendencies in the Orthodox and Baptist communities were antithetical, but it seems that something of the sense of tradition in Orthodoxy found it way into Russian Baptist life.

---

195. See *"Prazdnovanie Tysyacheletiya Kreshcheniya Rusi v Moskovskoy Tserkvi"* [The Celebration of the Millennium of the Baptism of Russia in the Moscow Church] (editorial article), *BV*, no. 1 (1989), pp. 69-71.

196. See *"Prazdnovanie Tysyacheletiya Kreshcheniya Rusi v Moskve"* [The Celebration of the Millennium of the Baptism of Russia in Moscow] (editorial article), *BV*, no. 2 (1989), p. 62.

197. *BV*, no. 2 (1974), p. 77; *BV*, no. 5 (1980), p. 64.

198. G. Sergienko, *"Edinenie i Preemstvennost' v Sluzhenii"* [Unity and Continuity of Ministry], *BV*, no. 4 (1988), p. 82.

Eschatology and the life to come

Throughout their history, Russian Baptists and evangelicals have held differing views about the coming of Christ. Ivan Prokhanov's *Creed of the Evangelical Christians* suggested that the "second coming of Christ would be preceded by the spreading of the Gospel all over the world." This was a postmillennial vision. Antichrist would appear, but would be overthrown.[199] However, there were other eschatological tendencies. Ivan Kargel, whose contribution to the development of Russian evangelical theology was significant, absorbed and advocated premillennial dispensationalist eschatology, owing to the influence of the (Plymouth) Brethren and the Keswick movement.[200] In the period under review, the main tendency represented in the Soviet Baptist sources was to follow dispensationalist eschatology, a reflection of the continuing influence of the early Brethren and Keswick teaching absorbed by Kargel. This thinking included a belief in the "rapture" of the church (at the time of the second coming), before the great tribulation and appearance of Antichrist and prior to the inauguration of the millennial kingdom of Christ. This was the pre-tribulation variant within premillennialism.[201] In holding these views, Russian Baptists were not drawing from Orthodoxy, which traditionally maintained the

---

199. *"Izlozhenie Evangel'skoy Very"*, in *Istoriya Baptizma*, p. 457.

200. Sawatsky, *Soviet Evangelicals Since World War II*, pp. 340-1; Kuznetsova, "Early Russian Evangelicals", pp. 327-30; Puzynin, *Traditsiya Evangel'skikh Khristian*, pp. 78-9; Nichols, "Ivan V. Kargel (1849-1937) and the Development of Russian Evangelical Spirituality", pp. 218-22. See Kargel: *Se, Gryadu Skoro* [Surely I Come Quickly] and *Tolkovatel' Otkroveniya Svyatogo Ioanna Bogoslova* [Interpretation of the Revelation of Saint John the Evangelist], in I. Kargel, *Sobranie Sochineniy* [Collected Works] (SPb.: Bibliya Dlya Vsekh, 1997), pp. 378-448, 449-670; *Lektsii o Vtorom Prishestvii Gospoda Iisusa Khrista* [Lectures on the Second Coming of the Lord Jesus Christ], <http://www. blagovestnik.org/books/ 00417.htm> accessed 11 November 2010.

201. See *"Verouchenie Evangel'skikh Khristian – Baptistov"*, ch. XII (*BV*, no. 4 (1980), p. 51; no. 4 (1985), p. 48); as well as the articles on eschatology in *Bratsky Vestnik* by A. Karev: no. 5 (1963), pp. 21-3; no. 6 (1963), pp. 56-67; no. 4 (1971), pp. 35-6; no. 3 (1972), pp. 24-6; and A. Mitskevich: no. 5 (1977), pp. 34-43; no. 1 (1978), pp. 45-54. See also: A. de Chalandeau, "The Theology of the Evangelical Christians-Baptists in the USSR", pp. 141-53. For the development of premillennialism in British evangelicalism, which influenced Kargel, see Bebbington, *Evangelicalism in Modern Britain*, pp. 81-8.

amillennial position.[202] There was, however, some diversity of opinion within Russian Baptist circles.

In 1965, *Bratsky Vestnik* published an article on eschatology in which it was said categorically that the second coming of Christ would occur "only after the rapture of the church and the great tribulation".[203] However, an unusual "Note of the Editorial Board" explained: "There are also other opinions on the theme mentioned in this article to be found in our brotherhood."[204] These "other opinions" surfaced in a debate between the AUCECB and the CCECB. At the Moscow Baptist Council of 1969, A. Mitskevich as a representative of the AUCECB, referred to a letter from the former leader of the Initiative Group, A. Prokofiev, which opposed Karev's thinking on this issue. *Bratsky Vestnik* wrote about what Mitskevich said:

> A.I. Mitskevich quoted the following passage from A. Prokofiev's letter, 'All statutes of religious organizations are a kind of adjustment… But what will he [A.V. Karev] teach at the time of the great tribulation when Antichrist… comes? Will he fulfill the requirements of Antichrist's laws?' Commenting on these words, A.I. Mitskevich said, 'I do not know, maybe Prokofiev intends to live at the time of Antichrist, but Brother Karev and I do not intend to live on the earth at the time of Antichrist.'[205]

It is clear from this rather acrimonious debate that not all Soviet Baptists maintained the teaching of the leadership of the AUCECB on the rapture of the church before the great tribulation. The brotherhood of the Council of Churches, suffering most from the Communist persecutions, was nearer to what might be termed a "pessimistic" eschatology, which taught that the church would be on earth during the time of Antichrist and would be

---

202. See, for instance, Makary, *Pravoslavno-dogmaticheskoe bogoslovie*, vol. II. pp. 644-8.
203. A. Mitskevich, *"Vtoroe Prishestvie Khista"* [The Second Coming of Christ], *BV*, no. 5 (1965), p. 53.
204. Ibid.
205. *"Vystupleniya po Voprosu Edinstva"* [Speeches on the Theme of Unity] (Council of ECB, 1969), *BV*, no. 2 (1970), pp. 65-6.

very sorely tried. In the official documents of the Council of Churches, this topic, which was seen as questionable, was usually avoided, but there were references which show the tendency within the leadership at least. Here, for example, is one of the questions which it was recommended should be asked before the ordination of a minister within the CCECB in the early 1970s:

> *The ordaining presbyter:* Hard times may come for the church and grave sorrows may overtake you personally... Do you promise not to give up the church and your ministry at that bad time? *The answer:* Yes, I promise, with God's help...[206]

There was an underlying eschatological meaning to these words. The CCECB community was being severely persecuted in the first half of 1970s and hundreds of its members were imprisoned.[207] Nonetheless, the question is asked here about the "hard times" that "may come", i.e. the most terrible persecutions were obviously expected in the future.

Concerning the position of the AUCECB, even A. Mitskevich was not fully consistent in his pre-tribulationism, perhaps holding to a further variant position. In 1964, he wrote in *Bratsky Vestnik*, "Not all of those atoned for by Christ will go to meet the Lord at the time of the rapture of the church. There are those who will stay on the earth for their further purification."[208] The belief that some but not all believers will stay on earth and will experience the great tribulation might have been a form of what has been termed "partial rapture". The description "great tribulation" could also be used in unusual ways. In 1982, *Bratsky Vestnik* published a telegram sent to the government of the USSR:

---

206. Khrapov, *Dom Bozhy*, <http://www.blagovestnik.org/books/00280.htm#19> accessed 20 November 2009.

207. See *"Spisok Uznikov, Osuzhdennykh za Slovo Bozhie v SSSR"* [A List of the Prisoners for the Word of God in the USSR], *VestI*, no. 2 (2001), pp. 22-3. See also: *VestI*, no. 1 (2001), pp. 18-19.

208. A. Mitskevich, *"O Sudakh Bozh'ikh"* [On God's Judgments], *BV*, no. 6 (1964), p. 25.

On behalf of the believers, Evangelical Christian-Baptists, we pay sincere respects in connection with the death of Leonid Il'ich Brezhnev... We are whole-hearted partakers in this great tribulation of all people and are praying to the Almighty for the peace and prosperity of our fatherland... A.E. Klimenko, President of the AUCECB, and A.M. Bychkov, the Secretary-General of AUCECB.[209]

Using the specific term the "great tribulation" (in Russian here: *velikaya skorb*) in relation to the death of the General Secretary of the Central Committee of the Communist Party of the Soviet Union, L.I. Brezhnev, in the AUCECB's periodical, is striking. It is all the more astonishing because A.M. Bychkov, one of the signatories, was a theologian, the author of a textbook on dogmatics written for the Bible Correspondence Courses of the AUCECB.[210] An alternative expression, for instance "bitter grief", would not have carried any eschatological associations. Therefore, the impression is that the love of the AUCECB to L.I. Brezhnev actually reached biblical proportions.[211]

While the premillennialism of most Russian Baptists was quite distinct from Orthodox thinking about eschatology, ideas about the life to come and about eternity among Soviet Baptists present areas of similarity to (as well as distinction from) Orthodox doctrines. In the numerous obituaries in *Zhurnal Moskovskoy Patriarkhii* and *Bratsky Vestnik*, there is a noticeable

---

209. *"Telegramma Presidiumu Verkhovnogo Soveta SSSR"* [Telegram to the Presidium of the Supreme Soviet of the USSR], *BV*, no. 6 (1982), p. 51.

210. *Dogmatika: Zaochnye Bibleyskie Kursy* [Dogmatics: Bible Correspondence Courses] (M.: AUCECB, 1970). See some details on the making of this book (based on research by W. Evans and I.V. Kargel), for instance in A. Mitskevich, *"Desyatiletie Pervogo Vypuska Uchashchikhsya ZBK VSEKhB"* [The 10th Anniversary of the First Graduates of the Bible Correspondence Courses of the AUCECB], *BV*, no. 4 (1981), p. 61; Popov, "The Evangelical Christians-Baptists in the Soviet Union as a Hermeneutical Community", pp. 152-3, 182.

211. A.M. Bychkov, in his published memoirs, does not distance himself from the Soviet past (by contrast with others writers and writings of the era), and speaks very positively of L.I. Brezhnev, noting his "friendliness" and remembering his gratitude to the leadership of the Russian Orthodox Church and the Baptists, for example when Brezhnev said "thank you, my friends, for praying for peace [around the world]...". See A. Bychkov, *Moy Zhiznenny Put'* [My Life] (M.: Otrazhenie, 2009), p. 128.

difference between the formulae used for announcements about someone's death: while the Orthodox source used a common verb "to die", or spoke of "the deceased",[212] *Bratsky Vestnik* used the euphemistic expression "to go into eternity".[213] What is behind these words? Orthodox theologians speak about the sufferings of souls after death (*mytarstva*) and their long waiting for the resurrection of the body, the Last Judgment, and finally the beginning of a glorious eternity.[214] By contrast Russian Baptists, as well as many other Protestants,[215] believe in the immediate entry of the soul of a person after death into eternal life. *Bratsky Vestnik* can be quoted:

We consider death… as the beginning of eternal life.[216]

Our eternal dwelling is there, where our Lord Jesus Christ is, who… died, was raised, ascended into heaven, opened the door of the Kingdom of Heaven… and waits for us there after the end of our short earthly life… A man going to eternal life waxes strong in thought about the dwelling place where he will enter as soon as his path of life finishes.[217]

…And this meeting with Christ has started for… [our brother]. 'Blessed are those who die in the Lord'.[218]

---

212. See, for instance: *"Vechnaya Pamyat' Pochivshim"* [Imperishable Memory of the Deceased], *ZhMP*, no. 1 (1971), pp. 32-3; no. 2 (1971), pp. 32-5; no. 3 (1971), pp. 19-23; no. 1 (1972), pp. 27-9; no. 3 (1972), pp. 29-32; no. 4 (1972), pp. 29-30.

213. See, for instance: *"Vesti iz Obshchin"* [News of the Congregations], *BV*, no. 4 (1971), p. 80; no. 1 (1973), p. 64; no. 5 (1973), pp. 78-9; no. 4 (1974), pp. 76,78; no. 2 (1979), p. 78. *Vestnik Istiny* (the Council of Churches) says the same: "our dear brother has gone into eternity". – *VestI*, no. 2 (1976), p. 21; no. 4 (1982), pp. 29-30; no. 2 (1983), p. 26.

214. See, for instance: Makary, *Pravoslavno-dogmaticheskoe bogoslovie*, vol. II. pp. 530-46; *Khristianstvo: Entsiklopedichesky Slovar'*, vol. II, pp. 643-4.

215. See, for instance: Berkhof, *Systematic Theology*, p. 679; M. Erickson, *Christian Theology*, 2nd ed. (Grand Rapids: Baker Book House, 1998), pp. 1188-90.

216. Ya. Dukhonchenko, *"Khozhdenie pered Bogom"* [Walking with God], *BV*, no. 4 (1972), p. 50.

217. [Anon], *"Putniki v Nebesny Khanaan"* [Travellers to the Heavenly Canaan], *BV*, no. 6 (1976), pp. 52-3.

218. From an obituary: *BV*, no. 1 (1985), p. 66.

The ideas, about the immediate transition from this temporal world to eternity, are to be found in many articles and sermons of the Soviet Baptists, as well as in obituaries.[219] There is no passage of time in eternity, and where there is no time, there cannot be the chronology of actions and events experienced in this life.[220] B.Ya. Shmidt, a well-known theologian of the brotherhood of the CCECB, spoke of this in the following way: "In eternity, before the beginning of time... Time started with the creation of the world – 'in the beginning God created...'"[221]

Thus, the birth of a human being is an entry into time, and to leave this earth at death is to return to eternity, which has no time present in it. This is why physical death was seen as, precisely, "returning home". A member of presidium of the AUCECB, N.A. Kolesnikov, said, "The earthly paths of life [of our brother]...his detached duty... have ended and he has returned to the heavenly Native Land."[222]

There, in the glorious eternity, a Christian immediately meets all the saints of all times and all nations.[223] One of the hymns of the ECB speaks about this:

> The way of all things will soon be gone,
> The gates of Zion will begin to shine.
> ...All those washed by the Blood of Christ
> Are waiting for me there.
> Burning with love, they will meet me,
> A pilgrim from the weary earth.[224]

---

219. See, for instance: *BV*, no. 2 (1985), p. 64; no. 5 (1985), pp. 70-1; no. 2 (1986), p. 61; no. 1 (1988), p. 9; no. 3 (1988), p. 61.

220. See *Dogmatika: Zaochnye Bibleyskie Kursy*, p. 22.

221. B. Shmidt, *"Khristos – Istinny Bog"* [Christ is the True God], *VestI*, no. 1 (1982), p. 10.

222. From an obituary: *BV*, no. 2 (1985), p. 64. One of the leaders of the CCECB, G.P. Vins, also wrote about this. See G. Vins, *Pora Domoy* [It is Time to Go Home], <http://www.blagovestnik.org/books/00430/db/ v6059350.html> accessed 25 April 2010.

223. "The departed brother is already beholding the Lord and Saviour... Now, the brother has joined the great cloud of witnesses... of Christ". – From an obituary: *BV*, no. 5 (1985), pp. 70-1. See also: *SDP*, no. 554, pp. 369-70.

224. *PV*, no. 540, p. 345.

In an instant, it was believed, the saved person meets all those he or she already knows well. Reference was made to that way in which, on the Mount of Transfiguration, Peter immediately recognized Moses and Elijah (Luke 9:30-33),[225] and also to the rich man in hell who saw not a particular saint, but Abraham himself in paradise (Luke 16:23).[226] In addition, it was taught that nobody needs to "wait" after death until all believers are finally together in this heavenly meeting. As soon as the soul of a Christian leaves the perishable body (and the earth, and time with it) that person enters into the eternal dwelling place.[227] The views of Russian Baptists set out above on eternity are not in full agreement with Orthodox doctrines. However, in other aspects of teaching about life after death it seems that Russian Baptists were more inclined to follow Orthodox teaching. For example, in the period being examined here the AUCECB held to Orthodox teaching on the Descent of Christ into Hell. Articles in *Bratsky Vestnik* in 1964 and 1985 explained:

> 'Having loosed the pains of death' (Acts 2:24), Christ led all Old Testament believers out who were in these pains... having died on the Cross, before his resurrection, Christ in the Spirit descended into the lower parts of the earth... where [the Old Testament righteous] were and... released them... They felt the fullness of joy... on the day of their entry into the heavenly dwelling places.[228]

> The Body of Jesus Christ was in the Sepulchre, but in the Spirit he descended into hell... The entry into the underworld by Jesus Christ is confirmed in the Holy Scripture... [Matt 12:40; Ps 16:10; 1 Pet 3:18-20]... The Savior, in the Spirit,

---

225. See [Anon], *"Ispovedanie Petra i Preobrazhenie Khrista"* [The Confession of Peter and the Transfiguration of Christ], *BV*, no. 4 (1960), p. 48.

226. See [Anon], *"Evangelie ot Luki"* [The Gospel according to Luke], *BV*, no. 6 (1970), p. 46.

227. See V. Slobodyanik, *"Voprosy Dukhovnoy Zhizni"* [The Issues of Spiritual Life], *BV*, no. 5 (1964), pp. 28-9.

228. Ibid.

descended into the realm of the dead for the testimony is that he fully tasted death, 'that through death he might destroy him that had the power of death, that is, the devil' (Heb 2:14). The Redeemer descended into hell to proclaim the good news of the atonement to the realm of the dead... (Eph 4:8-10).[229]

The authoritative authors of *Bratsky Vestnik* held this teaching.[230] According to these Soviet Baptist leaders, who were in this area following the Eastern tradition, to doubt Christ's descent into hell was like not fully believing in the truth of the death of the Savior. As a true Man, Christ died and went in the Spirit to the place where the souls of the dead were imprisoned.[231] There Christ proclaimed his victory over death and led Old Testament saints out.[232] This teaching, to a degree rejected by Russian Baptist writers in the 1990s (under Western influence),[233] had a close connection with some traditional Orthodox perceptions of the afterlife.

Another area in which Soviet Baptists were not typical of Baptists generally, and were close to the practice of Orthodox believers, was in the way obituaries and "memorial services" among the Soviet Baptists frequently contained a direct address to the dead person. Here are examples from obituaries in *Bratsky Vestnik*:

Peace to your ashes, dear brother. See you soon in heaven![234]

229. V. Mitskevich, "*Apostol'sky Simvol Very*" [The Apostles' Creed], *BV*, no. 5 (1985), p. 30.

230. See also: A. Karev, "*Chto Govorit Bibliya*" [The Bible Says], *BV*, no. 1 (1964), pp. 60-1; A. Karev, "*Golgofa*" [Calvary], *BV*, no. 3 (1964), p. 16.

231. See V. Mitskevich, "*Apostol'sky Simvol Very*", p. 30.

232. See V. Slobodyanik, "*Voprosy Dukhovnoy Zhizni*", *BV*, no. 5 (1964), p. 28.

233. Among Western evangelical scholars, a tendency towards the allegorical interpretation of 1 Pet 3:18-20 has been common. See *The Bible Knowledge Commentary: New Testament*, ed. by J. Walvoord and R. Zuck (Wheaton, IL: Victor Books, 1983), pp. 850-2; C. Keener, *The IVP Bible Background Commentary: New Testament* (Downers Grove, IL: IVP, 1993), p. 718; W. MacDonald, *Bibleyskie Kommentarii dlya Khristian, Novy Zavet* [Believer's Bible Commentary, New Testament] (Bielefeld, Germany: CLV, 2000), pp. 653-5.

234. From an obituary: *BV*, no. 4 (1971), p. 80.

See you in heaven, dear brother and friend, before the throne of our Father![235]

See you soon, brother, in the eternal dwelling places![236]

See you, dear brother, in the Kingdom of our Lord Jesus Christ![237]

See you, dear brother, in eternity at the feet… of Jesus Christ![238]

See you, dear brother, at the feet of our Lord…[239]

The candle of his life has burnt down… Farewell, my dear friend! We will see each other again soon…[240]

These statements are short prayers and greetings addressed to the dead believers, assuring them (the dead) that all will soon meet in heaven. There are analogies in ancient Orthodox prayers, "May you receive the Kingdom of Heaven!" The following are some specific examples of statements in Orthodox sources:

May the Kingdom of Heaven be your inheritance, our memorable, ever and dear Most Reverend![241]

Memory Eternal to you, our blessed mother… God rest your soul with the righteous![242]

235. From an obituary: *BV*, no. 1 (1979), p. 69.
236. From an obituary: *BV*, no. 6 (1983), p. 74.
237. From an obituary: *BV*, no. 3 (1985), p. 80.
238. From an obituary: *BV*, no. 5 (1985), p. 71.
239. From an obituary: *BV*, no. 3 (1987), p. 72.
240. From an obituary: *BV*, no. 4 (1990), pp. 59-60.
241. From an obituary: *ZhMP*, no. 4 (1971), p. 24.
242. From an obituary: *ZhMP*, no. 2 (1972), p. 27.

Peace to your ashes, dear Father![243]

Peace to your ashes, dear Most Reverend, of Memory
Eternal![244]

Within standard Protestantism, communication with the dead is forbidden, and is sometimes even equated with spiritism.[245] However, in this
as in other customs the emotional side of Russian Baptist life often prevailed over the dogmatic. An old, popular Russian Baptist hymn has these
words, "Pray when your strength fails you; pray when you become con-
ceited! Pray at the grave of your dear one."[246] Russian Baptist attitudes
towards prayers for the dead were not so definite in practice. This may well
have owed something to Molokan tradition,[247] but also indicates the influence of Orthodoxy with its rich experience of remembrance of the dead in
prayer.[248]

The teaching materials of the Bible Correspondence Courses of the
AUCECB on Moral Theology (compiled in the 1980s and with some official status, since it was republished more than once) stated:

---

243. From an obituary: *ZhMP*, no. 4 (1972), p. 28.

244. From an obituary: *ZhMP*, no. 12 (1972), p. 22.

245. See, for instance: G. Gololob, *Evangel'skie Vozrazheniya Pravoslavnym* [The
Evangelical Answer to Orthodox People], <http://rusbaptist.stunda.org/dop/antipr2.htm>
accessed 16 September 2010.

246. *SDP*, no. 80, p. 59. Probably this is a Russian Orthodox poem. In any case, it is
found under the title *Infallible Healing* in some classical Orthodox collections of poetry.
See, for instance: *Stikhotvoreniya o Molitve* [Poems about Prayer], Vserossiyskoe Ioanno-
Predtechenskoe Pravoslavnoe Bratstvo "Trezvenie", <http://trezvenie.org/dobr/stih/
full/&id=738#_Toc249208258> accessed 28 October 2010.

247. As noted, many early Baptists were Molokans by birth. See, for instance: Ya.
Zhidkov, *Molokane – Nashi Predki* [The Molokans are our Forefathers], *BV*, no. 1
(1953), pp. 50-1. Molokan creeds said: "We commemorate the deceased as well as
pray for them..." See *Istoriya Evangel'sko-Baptistskogo Dvizheniya v Ukraine: Materialy
i Dokumenty*, pp. 230-1. See also: N. Karaev, *"V Trudakh Blagovestiya"* [In Labours in
Evangelism], *Dukhovny Khristianin*, no. 3 (1914), pp. 72-4; A. Sinichkin, *Osobennosti
Vozniknoveniya i Formirovaniya Rossiyskogo Baptizma*, p. 9.

248. See, for instance: Bishop Athanasius (Sakharov), *O Pominovenii Usopshikh po Ustavu
Pravoslavnoy Terkvi* [On Remembrance of the Dead according to the Statutes of the
Orthodox Church] (SPb.: Satis", 1999).

There are some words [to be said] about our attitude towards the dead. Christian love embraces not only the living but also the dead; ... love to them does not stop after their death, though any communication with them has ceased; but nonetheless we are in the same Kingdom of Christ, because Christ reigns over both the living and the dead (Luke 20:37-38).[249]

Although the standard Protestant position – "any communication with them has ceased" – is set out here, this idea is somewhat weakened by the powerful statement about the oneness of the Kingdom of Christ, including both living and dead believers. The reference to the text from the Gospel of Luke 20:37-38, "He calls the Lord the God of Abraham, and the God of Isaac, and the God of Jacob. For he is not a God of the dead, but of the living: for all live unto him", is significant. The Kingdom of Christ is not divided by the border of human death or life. This shows the conditional character (if not the mere formality) of death itself for Christians. Reports in *Bratsky Vestnik* of funeral services conveyed the atmosphere:

Those present paid their last respects to the ministers who had finished their paths of life and entered into the eternal dwelling places. The brethren chanted the hymn *Many Saints Already Passed to the Faraway Coasts...* The Senior Presbyter came to give the last honors to the brother. In his speech, he... read from Luke 20:38, 'For he is not the God of the dead, but of the living: for all live unto him'.[250]

The deacon departed for eternity... Now the children of God consoled themselves by the words of their Savior, who said, 'For he is not the God of the dead, but of the living: for all live unto him' (Luke 20:38). Therefore, they chanted with

---

249. I. Chekalov, *Nravstvennoe Bogoslovie: Khristianskaya Etika* [Moral Theology: Christian Ethics] (M.: FS ECB, 1993), p. 162.
250. *"Iz Zhizni Pomestnykh Tserkvey"* [From the Life of the Local Churches] (editorial article), *BV*, no. 2 (1984), pp. 76, 79.

unquestioning faith in him, 'I belong to you forever, whether I live or die.'[251]

Thus Russian Baptists could feel free to address their dead brothers and sisters in Christ: for all live unto God (Luke 20:38).[252] A famous minister of the CCECB said: "Those faithful to the Lord do not die... The faithful are going to the beauties of heaven."[253] It is logical for Protestants not to pray for the dead if believers who have died are already in a glorious eternity – the "beautiful heaven". Many Russian Baptists held this belief. However, for Orthodox believers, not to pray for the dead family and friends is illogical (and even cruel) if there is a long waiting for God's final Judgment beyond the tomb. Some Soviet Baptist authors involuntarily drifted, in whole or in part, towards the Orthodox belief in the "long waiting".[254] And then Christians needed a bond with those who had died. Soviet Baptists did not have purposeful prayers for the dead, but undoubtedly there was a certain lively unity with those who had died, since "Christian love embraces not only the living but also the dead". That perception of the world could not but be given a shape in words and deeds, as shown, for example, in these words, which are typical of many other instances:

Sleep, dear brother, until the glorious coming of Christ![255]

A solemn divine service, devoted to the memory of NN, took place in the Moscow [Baptist] Church... Brother... started his words citing Psalm 112:6, 'The righteous will be remembered forever'... He was loved while alive, and he is loved

---

251. "Iz Zhizni Pomestnykh Tserkvey", BV, no. 5 (1988), pp. 80-1.

252. We find the same motifs in the periodicals of the CCECB: "If you hear that I have died, do not trust this, since a believer does not die but goes from death into life". – M. Khorev, "Pishu Vam, Deti" [I Write You, My Children], VestI, no. 1 (1983), p. 29.

253. From a poem by E.N. Pushkov. Translating the Russian literally, the expression "beauties of heaven" is "blue sky".

254. See, for instance: S. Fadyukhin, "Dukh Svyatoy" [The Holy Spirit], BV, no. 5 (1974), p. 47; [Anon], "Osen'" [The Autumn], BV, no. 4 (1972), pp. 68-9; K. Somov, "Voprosy Very" [The Issues of Faith], BV, no. 6 (1964), p. 40. Cf.: "Izlozhenie Evangel'skoy Very", in Istoriya Baptizma, p. 457.

255. From an obituary: BV, no. 3 (1984), p. 74.

now. It seems this love is growing... more and more. Truly, our memory of the righteous is forever... A sister, choir singer, read a poem about the paths of life of NN...[256]

The brother was addressed. There was a "solemn divine service, devoted to the memory of ..." The Lives of the Saints of the Baptist community were being written.

Conclusion

This chapter has shown that Russian Baptists in the period from the 1960s to the 1980s had their own distinctive theology. Writers made clear their views about the importance of their distinctive beliefs, sometimes in a way that showed little self-criticism. Thus A.V. Karev wrote: "Our dogmatics are the most pure and beautiful evangelical dogmatics... Our convictions are the most delightful and wonderful".[257] In similar exaggerated vein, but more fully, A.K. Sipko argued for Russian Baptist theology as a superior way of approaching truth, speaking of it as a "theology born in the hearts of holy men, who, suffering torments, in their prayers on bended knees, received revelations from God, like St. John on the island of Patmos".[258] The authors do not explore the way their thinking mirrors Orthodoxy, but Sipko's words point to a mystical form of theology – "born in the hearts of holy men", with "revelations from God" – and this chapter has argued for the presence of Orthodox apophaticism in Russian Baptist understandings of God. For Orthodoxy, "negative" language is better than daring to speculate about heavenly mysteries. Baptists intuitively agreed with this Eastern Christian tradition.[259] In their thinking about salvation, Russian

---

256. *"Bogosluzhenie v MOECB"* [Divine Service at Moscow Church] (editorial article), *BV*, no. 6 (1985), pp. 59-61. I have used NN rather than the name of the person, although the name appeared in *BV*.

257. Cited in *"Bratskomy Vestniky – 40 Let"* ['Bratsky Vestnik' is Aged 40] (editorial article), *BV*, no. 5 (1984), p. 45.

258. A. Sipko, *Derzhis' Obraztsa Zdravogo Ucheniya*, p. 224.

259. See, for instance: S. Sannikov, *Vecherya Gospodnya* [The Lord's Supper] (M.: Protestant, 1990), pp. 12-9; N. Kolesnikov, *V Pomoshch' Propovedniku: Sbornik Konspektov*

Baptists also display affinities with Orthodoxy. Their soteriology has been seen as Arminian, but the first reference to Arminius in *Bratsky Vestnik* was probably in 1984.[260] The soteriological environment was in Russia itself. In the area of holiness, many Russian Baptists followed the Orthodox in seeing their human frailty and weeping over it. In the CCECB there was greater stress on the necessity of living up to the highest standards, but more broadly, in *Vestnik Istiny* "Orthodox" tendencies are also clearly to be found, for instance in accolades to St. John Chrysostom and monasticism.[261] At the same time, the CCECB used slightly more Western Baptist sources than the AUCECB. But the root of Russian Baptist specificity is found in the common history they shared with Orthodoxy, especially as the Communist regime unintentionally contributed to bringing them together. As neighbors living in the same country, Orthodox and Baptist Christians shared a common mentality. In the areas considered in this chapter – God, salvation, holiness, scripture and tradition, and eschatology and life beyond death – Russian Baptists in the former Soviet Union exhibited some Western Protestant views but in certain crucial respects they drew from Eastern Orthodox theological conceptions.

[Assistance to the Preacher: A Collection of Sermons] (M.: Zlatoust, 1995), vol. I, p. 441; V. Popov, *"Isikhazm Kak Chayanie Dukhovnosti: Opyt Istoricheskogo Analiza"* [Hesychasm as Spiritual Aspiration: An Attempt at Historical Analysis], *Al'manakh "Bogomyslie*, vol. 2 (1991), pp. 117-18.

260. See S. Nikolaev, *"Reformatskaya Tserkov"* [The Reformed Church], *BV*, no. 1 (1984), pp. 48-9.

261. *VestI*, no. 4 (1977), pp. 30-2; no. 4 (1979), p. 33. See also the panegyric to Russian religious philosopher Vladimir Soloviev (*VestI*, no. 1 (1979), pp. 34-41; no. 2 (1979), pp. 31-8) and Orthodox Patristic aphorisms on the importance of Scripture (*VestI*, no. 4 (1979), p. 33).

CHAPTER 4

Church and Sacraments

The traditional position of the Evangelical Christians and the Baptists in Russia regarding the sacraments – or ordinances, as they were usually called – was that there were two: baptism and the Lord's Supper. This mirrored standard Protestant and Baptist thinking. Before the 1940s there is no evidence of any departure from this view. All the basic Russian Evangelical Christian and Baptist official documents set out this position.[1] However, in the official AUCECB document *Statutes of the Union of ECB* (1948), the following statement was made: "The presbyter of the congregation performs all church ordinances, namely: baptism, breaking of bread, marriage, praying for infants and for the sick."[2] A further list of church "ordinances" appeared in 1960, in the new *Statutes of the Union*, which stated: "The presbyter of the congregation performs all church ordinances, namely: baptism, breaking of bread, marriage, burial and praying for the sick."[3] At this point burial, which had not been in the *Statutes* of 1948, was included, although praying for infants was not in the list. The aim was probably not to produce a definitive statement about ecclesial ordinances. The *Letter of Instructions for the Senior Presbyters* (of 1960), which was approved by the AUCECB simultaneously with the new *Statutes* of 1960, also mentioned the ordination of church ministers

---

1. See, for instance: *"Izlozhenie Evangel'skoy Very, Verouchenie Evangel'skikh Khristian 1910 g."* [Statement of the Evangelical Faith, The Creed of the Evangelical Christians, 1910], in *Istoriya Baptizma*, pp. 450-2; *Ispovedanie Very Khristian-Baptistov* [The Creed of the Christians-Baptists] (M.: Izdanie N.V. Odintsova, 1928), pp. 30-9.

2. ARSECB, F. 1, op. 1d1, d. 96, l. 4.

3. ARSECB, F. 1, op. 28d, d. 52, l. 7.

and the "celebration of our church feasts".[4] This chapter explores the understanding among Russian Baptists of ecclesiology and especially of the sacraments in the period covered by this study, with the aim of identifying parallels with Orthodoxy.

"Holy water baptism"

Among the written and oral sources of the Russian Baptist movement in the post-World War II period, it is possible to find advocates of both the "symbolic" and the "sacramental" approaches to baptism. The approaches are not mutually exclusive: in the Russian language *svyashchennodeystvie* ('holy ordinance') is the first synonym of *tainstvo* ('sacrament'). Nonetheless, there was and is diversity in Russian Baptist life, which to some extent mirrors the diversity found in the wider evangelical and Baptist world. There are those in the evangelical traditions who speak of baptism as a "symbol" or perhaps a "seal".[5] There are, however, Baptists who have stressed the sacramental aspect of baptism, arguing that it is "more than a symbol".[6] This chapter will focus on the contribution in the Russian setting of those authoritative Russian Baptist authors after World War II, and especially in the period from 1960s to the 1980s, who have spoken in sacramental and also apophatic terms.[7] Clearly there were significant differences between

---

4. See *Instruktivnoe Pis'mo Starshim Presviteram VSECB* [Letter of Instructions for the Senior Presbyters of the AUCECB], ARSECB, F. 1, op. 22d.6, d. 4, ll. 3,8. See also this letter in A. Mitskevich, *Istoriya Evangel'skikh Khristian-Baptistov* [History of the Evangelical Christians-Baptists] [1983] (M.: Rossiysky Soyuz ECB, 2007), pp. 332, 335.

5. "Baptism symbolizes spiritual cleansing or purification": Berkhof, *Systematic Theology*, pp. 628-9. See an overview of the theme in, for example, Erickson, *Christian Theology*, pp. 1098-1114. Baptism is "a sign", "a seal" of God's covenant, or "a token of salvation", Ibid, pp. 1102-3. Another author states that baptism "means identification with the message of the Gospel": C. Ryrie, *Basic Theology* (Wheaton, IL: Victor Books, 1986), p. 422. The stress is on the *external aspect* of baptism.

6. See S. Fowler, *More Than A Symbol: The British Baptist Recovery of Baptismal Sacramentalism* (Carlisle: Paternoster Press, 2002); A.R. Cross and P.E. Thompson, eds., *Baptist Sacramentalism* (Carlisle: Paternoster Press, 2003).

7. All the following are quotations from traditional Russian Baptist sources, such as books and articles written before *perestroika* (even if some of them were published in recent years).

Russian Baptists and the Russian Orthodox Church in the area of baptismal belief and practice. By contrast with the Orthodox, Baptists did
not baptize infants and they did not immerse three times – one act of
immersion took place, in the name of the Father, Son and Holy Spirit. In
looking at baptism, my intention is to seek to show that despite the distinctive Baptist beliefs in relation to believer's baptism, there were nonetheless
Orthodox-like elements that can be traced in the baptismal theology of
some significant Russian Baptists.

One Baptist author, M.Ya. Zhidkov, writing as a leading member of the
AUCECB (more widely, he was the first Russian President of the European
Baptist Federation, in 1966-68[8]), argued that "baptism is closely connected
with the receiving of the Holy Spirit" in the New Testament. He wrote in
Bratsky Vestnik in 1975:

> Searching the Scriptures, we see, in the book of Acts espe-
> cially, that baptism is closely connected with the receiving of
> the Holy Spirit. On the other hand, we cannot restrict God in
> His freedom in pouring out the Holy Spirit. Examining the
> different conditions of the outpouring of the Spirit, we clearly
> see that, although a doctrine can be formulated, life is more
> complicated than any formula.[9]

This contains echoes of Orthodox thinking on the sacraments of baptism
and chrismation.[10] The receiving of the Holy Spirit constitutes a crucial
distinction between the baptism of people in the Jordan River by John the
Baptist (which was a sign of the future sacrament: "I baptize you with water, but…") and a later baptism when Christ comes ("He will baptize you

---

8. See G. Simon, *Church, State and Opposition in the USSR* (London: C. Hurst &
Company, 1974), p. 147.

9. M. Zhidkov, "*Vodnoe kreshchenie i vecherya Gospodnya*" [Water Baptism and the Lord's
Supper], *BV*, no. 2 (1975), p. 57.

10. See, for instance: P. Malkov, *Vvedenie v Liturgicheskoe Predanie* [Introduction to
Liturgical Tradition] (M.: Izd-vo PSTGU, 2006), pp. 57-62; Archpriest A. Schmemann,
Of Water and the Spirit: A Liturgical Study of Baptism (Crestwood, NY: St. Vladimir's
Seminary Press, 1974), pp. 75-81.

with the Holy Spirit").[11] The language of baptism links water baptism with the baptism of the Holy Spirit, although for most Russian Baptists the time of the outpouring of the Holy Spirit could not unequivocally be formulated since, as Zhidkov put it, "life is more complicated than any formula".[12] On the specific question of timing, R.P Vyzu, an Estonian theologian and a senior presbyter of the AUCECB, wrote in *Bratsky Vestnik* in 1985:

> Receiving of the Holy Spirit and baptism are closely connected with each other, though one [single] order cannot be established. It is important that by baptism someone becomes a member of a local church...[13]

An important connection was being made by Vyzu between the "receiving of the Holy Spirit and baptism", and entry into the Body of Christ, the church. This point was made more strongly two years later by V.G. Kulikov, an editor of *Bratsky Vestnik*:

> Immersion of Christ in the baptismal water foreshadowed his immersion in the water of death... He voluntarily took on himself retribution for the sins of all people... It is necessary to note that in baptism we receive special blessings. The Lord

---

11. In relation to the difference between being plunged in water and the powerful work of the Spirit, the following words, as an example, of the Russian Baptist presbyter N.V. Sabursky, from Tatarstan may be noted: "I bathed in the Volga one hundred times, but was baptized once in my lifetime in the same Volga." (INT, Minneapolis, Minnesota, USA, 2006).

12. Russian Baptists usually teach that the Holy Spirit regenerates a person in the moment of repentance, i.e. before baptism as a believer. However, the Spirit comes invisibly, and full assurance of the presence of the Spirit, according to some ECB theologians, comes after sincere repentance and subsequent baptism as a believer. The actual moment of the Spirit's coming usually remains a mystery. See details in C. Prokhorov, "On Several Peculiarities of the Understanding of Baptism in the Russian Baptist Church", *Theological reflections*, vol. 8 (2007), pp. 98-100.

13. R. Vyzu, "*Vy hram Bozhy, i Dukh Bozhy zhivet v vas*" [You are God's Temple and God's Spirit Lives in You], *BV*, no. 2 (1985), p. 21. I am not suggesting that Vyzu was directly influenced by Orthodoxy. He came from Estonia and thus from a Lutheran-inclined context.

grants us the grace of the Holy Spirit and accepts us into the church as His children.[14]

What Kulikov said of baptism ruled out its being seen only as "symbolic". What he stressed was "the grace of the Holy Spirit" in water baptism and he linked that with what appears to be an understanding of a mystical entry of the baptized person into the church. Similarly language about "the grace of His blessing" received in baptism is found in another member of the leadership of the AUCECB, N.A. Kolesnikov. He wrote:

> We realize that behind the visible form of the ministry done is the hidden invisible spiritual meaning in which God himself gives the grace of His blessing... Baptism as external, i.e. a ritual, does not save, but for those who have experienced regeneration it is necessary, because it is really an element of salvation, 'Corresponding to that, baptism now saves you... through the resurrection of Jesus Christ' (1 Pet 3:21)... So, baptism is not a ritual giving the right to participate in the Lord's Supper, but a requirement for communion in the Body of Jesus Christ – the church (1 Cor 12:13).[15]

The use of 1 Peter 3:21 to argue that water baptism "is really an element of salvation" is highly significant.

A similar theology of baptism to that found in the AUCECB was present in the CCECB. N.P. Khrapov, one of the most authoritative leaders of the Council of Churches, stated in the early 1970s that "our salvation" was both "confirmed" and "accomplished" by baptism. Like Kolesnikov, he cited 1 Peter chapter 3.

---

14. V. Kulikov, "*Nadlezhit nam ispolnit' vsyakuyu pravdu*" [It is Proper for us to do this to Fulfill all Righteousness], *BV*, no. 6 (1987), p. 11.

15. N. Kolesnikov, *Khristianin, znaesh' li ty, kak dolzhno postupat' v dome Bozh'em?* [Christian, do you know how People ought to Conduct themselves in God's Household?], 3 vols. (M.: Druzhba i Blagaya Vest', 1998), vol. I, pp. 44, 49.

> Although the means of salvation for sinners is only the Blood
> of Christ cleansing us from sin, nevertheless, our salvation is
> confirmed and accomplished by baptism into the death of the
> Lord. The risen life of Jesus takes effect in us only through
> baptism into His death (1 Pet 3:21; Rom 6:3-4)... A bride-
> groom and a bride... enter married life only after a wedding...
> Baptism is a kind of wedding of a Christian with the Body of
> Christ – the church.[16]

In both Kolesnikov and Khrapov, baptism is connected with the church,
but in the latter's statement it is significant that there is the idea of the
wedding of the individual Christian not so much with Christ (which is
the usual and readily recognizable picture among evangelicals) as with
"the Body of Christ – the church". This points more to the communal,
ecclesiological aspects of the Christian's salvation (through the church)
than to an individualistic soteriology. It is difficult to avoid the conclusion that the Orthodox concept of the church as central to salvation was
an influence. The church was also the arena of the Spirit. In his recollections, a legendary minister of the CCECB, Joseph Bondarenko, spoke
in a poetic way of the time when he was baptized: "On 5 June 1960...
during that incomparable, enchanting and unforgettable night, we experienced the descent of the Holy Spirit in our hearts."[17] The communal
context again echoes Orthodoxy: the language used was not what "I"
experienced, but what "we" (believers) experienced of the Spirit. S.V.
Sannikov summed up generally-held ideas when he spoke of baptism as
having a "profound" meaning but not one that could be "completely explained". Baptism was "a kind of final point in the process of conversion
of a sinner and uniting him with Christ; that is why it is presented as a
necessary element of salvation... Salvation depends not on repentance
itself, but exclusively on a spiritual and physical unity: faith from the
whole heart, expressed in repentance and water baptism."[18] Sannikov's

---

16. Khrapov, *Dom Bozhy*, <http://www.blagovestnik.org/books/00280.htm#5> accessed
20 November 2009.

17. Bondarenko, *Tri Prigovora*, p. 60.

18. Sannikov, *Podgotovka k kreshcheniyu*, pp. 164-5.

emphasis on the soteriological significance of both repentance and water baptism indicated that Russian Baptists had absorbed both Protestant and Orthodox thinking in this area.[19]

This perspective was not only one that was held by major authors representing the AUCECB and the CCECB. It is evident in local church reports included in *Bratsky Vestnik*.[20] These reports appeared in the 1970s: "Odessa Region, the city of Reni: The church held water baptisms. Several souls redeemed by the Blood of Christ joined the church. The children of God sincerely thanked the Lord for His saving grace."[21] Similarly: "Sumy Region, the city of Romny: Souls washed by the Blood of Christ joined with the church through holy water baptism."[22] The wording in the 1980s about baptisms was even more emphatic in the use of the language of "holy water" and of "salvation". A report in 1986 stated: "In July of this year through holy water baptism new souls joined the church in Yaroslavl... Brothers and sisters in faith cordially congratulated those baptized and wished [for] them to grow in the divine grace."[23] There is a remarkable interweaving of the biblical concepts of washing of the believers' souls by the Blood of Christ, immersion of their bodies in water and the operation of saving grace in *holy* baptism. In other reports the themes of the accounts included a saving "covenant" in baptism and being baptized "before the face of the Lord". Thus in 1987 "Children of God in the church of Zhitomir baptized new members. Those who made covenant with the Lord sincerely thanked him for salvation and the gift of eternal life."[24] In Kazakhstan, in the village of Ust'-Kalmanka, there was "holy water baptism". "Believers in turn entered the water of the river in order that before the face of the Lord and the church they might bury their old self

---

19. See also: L. Greenfeld's Master's Dissertation, "Eastern Orthodox Influence on Russian Evangelical Ecclesiology", pp. 69-99. Greenfeld sees baptism as an example of sacramentalism in Russian evangelical churches, and explores the general influence of Russian Orthodox mysticism on the brotherhood of the ECB.

20. These excerpts are from the regular column of news items entitled, "From the life of the local churches".

21. *BV*, no. 5 (1975), p. 77.

22. *BV*, no. 6 (1979), p. 67.

23. *BV*, no. 5 (1986), p. 74.

24. *BV*, no. 5 (1987), p. 68.

in the water and rise to a new life."[25] The emphasis is not on an external form of worship but on the core of the mystery, related to "salvation and the gift of eternal life".

As part of their understanding of the descent of the Holy Spirit on those baptized, in Russian Baptist churches the tradition was to have laying of hands on the newly-baptized as they came out of the water. This was seen as being in line with apostolic practice (Acts. 8:16-17; 19:5-6), although Russian Baptists did not use Acts 19:5-6 to teach speaking in tongues. One example from *Bratsky Vestnik* in 1977, about baptisms in Kirovograd, illustrates the procedure: "The new converts made a covenant with the Lord through the holy water of baptism. This holy ordinance was done in the baptistry of the church building... After reading the words [spoken to Jesus]: 'Come, lay... your hand...' (Matt 9:18) the brothers prayed over the baptized people with the laying on of hands."[26] The text used is about Jesus being asked to lay his hand on the daughter of the ruler of the syna-gogue so that she might be raised from death. Although Russian Baptists did not associate laying on hands with a definite expectation of healing, there are numerous reports of miracles they believed had taken place by the action of divine grace at the moment of baptism. For example: in the 1950s a newly converted Baptist, whose legs were paralyzed, was able to walk again after his baptism, and kept others awake all night showing them how he was walking;[27] a Baptist girl, living near Voronezh, was apparently cured of a serious skin disease when she was baptized;[28] and around 1990, in Karaganda, it was reported that an old woman was cured of long-term asthma after her baptism.[29] Ministers of churches, too, often testified about healings of their own serious illnesses when they baptized others.[30] There

---

25. *BV*, no. 2 (1992), p. 92.

26. *BV*, no. 6 (1977), p. 71. Meanwhile, Baptist presbyters often mentioned also the biblical passage which said that "the Spirit was bestowed through the laying on of the apostles' hands" (Acts 8:17-18).

27. Testimony of presbyter Y.A. Meleshkevich (INT, Bishkul, Kazakhstan, 2003).

28. Testimony of church member L.V. Savinskaya (INT, Salt Lake City, Utah, USA, 2006).

29. Testimony of church member T. Sysoeva (INT, Syracuse, NY, USA, 2007).

30. See, for example, memoirs of Ya. Leven, *"Kreshchenie – Istselenie"* [Baptism as Healing], in *Mezhdunarodnaya Khristianskaya Gazeta* [International Christian

were also signs and visions connected with baptisms: a Baptist presbyter from Kiev, P.F. Kunda, testifies that, when he was baptized near Minsk on a summer night in 1967, he saw a miraculous rainbow reaching from the river's surface to the sky.[31] Russian Baptists did not teach that healings and visions were linked to baptism, but acceptance of these phenomena was congruent with the sacramental attitude to baptism of many of them.

Other aspects of baptismal practice, while not connected with healing, signs or visions, involved a heightened awareness of divine activity at baptisms. Before baptismal services began, presbyters as a rule offered special prayer, stretching their hands out over the water. This was something similar to the Orthodox rite of sanctification of the water. It is also related to the prayer of sanctification of oil (olive oil), which, as noted for example in *Bratsky Vestnik* in 1988, was practiced by Russian Baptist presbyters before anointing the sick.[32] Preparation for baptism also involved fasting on the part of those being baptized, to bring about a specially elevated spiritual condition.[33] Some new Russian Baptist converts wanted to be baptized in cold and even icy water (for example, in winter in a hole cut in the ice), as a mark of their dedication.[34]

Other features can be noted. There was a great desire on the part of some to be baptized as a challenge to the tight restrictions in the USSR, and even contrary to fears by presbyters about the authorities.[35] While immersing someone in water, Russian Baptists considered it important not to leave even the smallest part of the body out of the water. This was connect-

---

Newspaper], no. 8 (2005), p. 2.

31. Testimony of presbyter P.F. Kunda (INT, Sacramento, California, USA, 2006).

32. See, for example: I. Gnida, "*Tserkovnye ustanovleniya*" [The Church Institutions], *BV*, no. 4 (1988), pp. 75, 78.

33. See Khrapov, *Dom Bozhy*, <http://www.blagovestnik.org/books/00280.htm#6>

34. See, for example, interview with A. Galkin in *Khristianskoe Slovo*, no. 3 (2005), pp. 12-13. Presbyter from Tatarstan, N. Sabursky (INT, Minneapolis, Minnesota, USA, 2006) also tells about a similar practice. One of the leaders of the Council of Churches, M. Khorev says that he baptized people twice in winter, in icy water. See *VestI*, no. 1 (1984), p. 44.

35. Testimony of R.F. Vasilieva and V.T. Vasiliev (INT, Sacramento, California, USA, 2006). There was also an uncontrollable desire to return to the place of baptism outside of the city next day, in order to pray, although it was a very long walk. – Testimony of church member from Kazakhstan, N.D. Chumakina (INT, Seattle, Washington, USA, 2006).

ed with the spiritual world, since immersion was viewed as complete death to sin so that the spiritual enemy ("the price of darkness") would not have any opportunity to gain a "foothold" through any part of the body that was not baptized. If an immersion was incomplete, they did not immerse in water again, but a presbyter took a handful of water and "washed" the dry part of the body.[36] Finally, the Russian Baptist tendency to re-baptize those converted from other Christian traditions should be noted. The AUCECB tried to discourage this practice, but it continued in many communities.[37] This also shows lurking sympathies with sacramentalism, since there was a desire to have "true baptism".

In the traditional hymns of Russian Baptists which were being sung in the later Soviet era,[38] the wording used at baptisms often conveyed the idea of an inexpressible sacrament.

> The babbling brook will not tell
> My holy mystery to anyone.
> It will not tell what the waves heard
> My mystery – of a humble soul…
> I accepted holy baptism,
> I made a holy covenant with God…
> Making my soul alive, with peace,
> God sent grace to my heart.

---

36. See a characteristic editorial article, "Our Battle", in *Vestnik Istiny*. This says that "the prince of darkness reigns in the air; and so we should be wary of him during each… 'breathing-in'…" – *VestI*, no. 1 (1977), pp. 8-10.

37. See A. Karev's report to the All-Union Council of 1966, *BV*, no. 6 (1966), p. 21. Rebaptism among the unregistered Baptists could not be controlled. They not only re-baptized other Christians but also re-ordained presbyters from other traditions. – Testimonies of Baptist ministers from the former USSR: M.M. Kolivayko, P.V. Sedykh (Sacramento, California, USA, 2006) and A.I. Kolomiytsev (Vancouver, Washington, USA, 2006).

38. Many early evangelical hymns used in Russia were translated from foreign languages. But then Russian evangelical hymns began to be written. The most prolific Russian author, I.S. Prokhanov, spoke of 413 translated hymns and 624 of his own hymns in a book. See I. Prokhanov, *In the Cauldron of Russia, 1869-1933* (N.Y.: All-Russian Evangelical Christian Union, 1933), pp. 146-7. By the later Soviet period the most often selected hymns in the ECB songbooks, whether translated or not, reflected the "true spirit" of Russian Baptists.

The brook was a silent witness
To my great and holy mystery...[39]

These lines are replete with sacramental terms: "mystery", "holy mystery", "great and holy mystery", "holy baptism", "holy covenant with God", and "God sent grace". The piety of this Russian Baptist hymn can be compared with the most sacramental, traditional liturgical Orthodox chants. A further example is also instructive.

I am on the bank of burial,
In the watery graveyard;
As a sacrifice to God,
Without a single doubt
I give myself wholeheartedly.
Oh, accept me, Savior,
Into your faithful Church...[40]

Again, the phrases "the bank of burial" and "the watery graveyard", in the context of water baptism, indicate sacramental theology. "Oh, accept me, Savior, into your faithful Church" conveys the genuine wish of the Russian Baptists to be part of the mysterious Body of Christ. These hymns, as well as some others, can be described as apophatic, with their inscrutable approach to holy water baptism. In Orthodox infant baptisms the same inscrutability is present, but the infant being baptized is not conscious of the mystery, and arguably there might therefore even be a form of "mystical advantage" for Russian Baptists as they entered into the drama which is the sacrament of baptism.

---

39. *SDP*, no. 312, p. 211.
40. Ibid., no. 306, p. 207.

Acceptance into the Brotherhood

In the Russian Baptist tradition, the importance of baptism has been underlined by the unusually strict probation procedure that Russian Baptists instituted and implemented in their congregations. Although the Orthodox tradition does not have this kind of procedure for families bringing their children for baptism, the preparation for baptism in Russian Baptist communities can be compared with the Orthodox order for monastic profession. I have made an analysis of significant points in the Orthodox monastic probationary procedures and in the Russian Baptist pre-baptismal approach in order to demonstrate the way in which Baptist thinking mirrored the monastic world.

Orthodox Monastery	Baptist Congregation
1) There is a traditional three-year trial period of "obedience" before taking the habit.[41]	1) In the period examined in this study, there was a two or three year trial period before baptism.[42]

In addition, in both cases similar motivations can be identified: adult believers in Orthodox and Baptist communities were preparing for "irrevocable" vows that were going to be made, in which they were dedicating all of their lives to God. This was not a step that was appropriate for those who might later change their minds and abandon the cloister or the church fellowship. Thus, all aspirants should be proved first.

---

41. See M. Kudryavtsev, *Istoriya Pravoslavnogo Monashestva* [History of Orthodox Monasticism] (M.: Krutitskoe patriarshee podvor'e, 1999), p. 72.

42. See "Polozhenie o Soyuze Evangel'skikh Khristian-Baptistov v SSSR" [The Statutes of the Union of Evangelical Christians-Baptists of the USSR] (1960), ARSECB, F. 1, op. 28d, d. 52, l. 6.

2) The work and spiritual obedience of a novice in the monastery is usually supervised by a monastic elder; and novices, as a rule, do the "lowest" or the most menial jobs in the monastery.[43]	2) New Baptist converts were usually tutored by experienced members of the congregation.[44] Physical work at houses of prayer was often an integral part of this period of preparation.

Christian believers in the Soviet Union who wanted to live out their faith were constantly confronted by serious difficulties. Because of this, only those with genuine faith would be likely to visit a church. Yet testing was still required. Those Soviet citizens, who wanted, despite Soviet atheistic propaganda, to enter a monastery, should be ready for hard work. In the case of those seeking to be baptized, it was important to stress the virtue of Christian humility, and in part this was inculcated through working at the prayer house. A new convert also had to realize that there were likely to be economic implications after baptism, for example, believers might lose their jobs.[45]

---

43. Kudryavtsev, *Istoriya pravoslavnogo monashestva*, p. 72; *Monasheskaya Zhizn'*, *Vypusk 1* [Monastic Life, Issue 1] [1885] (Svyato-Uspensky Pskovo-Pechersky monastyr', 1994), pp. 7-25.

44. N. Levindanto, *"Blagochinie Pomestnykh Tserkvey"* [Discipline of Local Churches], in *Nastol'naya Kniga Presvitera* [The Handbook for Presbyters] (M.: AUCECB, 1982), pp. 135-6; Kolesnikov, *Khristianin, znaesh' li ty*, vol. I, pp. 46-7.

45. The Russian monastic literature teaches novices obedience to their elders as to Christ himself. Menial labor helped to deal with any pride. One piece of monastic advice said, "When you see a youth flying [in the air], take his leg and bring him to the ground." – *Monasheskaya Zhizn'*, p. 20. There was the same tendency among Soviet Baptists. Several Baptist presbyters started their Christian work as church janitor, undertaking tasks such as cleaning toilets.

3) Immediately before monastic profession, a long and carefully elaborated procedure of "testing" of a novice takes place. At the beginning of the ritual a novice stands on the porch of the monastery, waiting for permission to enter.[46]	3) Immediately before baptism and acceptance as a member of a Baptist congregation, a new convert went through serious "testing".[47] Before testing, new converts waited outside the sanctuary for their turn to come in, and they came by invitation.

These procedures were largely of a ritual character. The people being tested, whether this was for the monastic life or for baptism, were usually well known to those who were testing them. Thus even in the Baptist case, the testing was usually somewhat ceremonial. The person's character was, however, again subjected to scrutiny.[48]

4) In the monastery, the brothers meet a novice with singing, likening this event to the meeting of the father with the prodigal son in the New Testament parable.[49] The hegumen (the head of the monastery) gives a short exhortation to the novice, reminding him of the importance of his monastic vows.[50]	4) At a membership meeting, hymns are sung, usually about the church, with the theme traditionally being that of joining the church, which was compared to joining a friendly family.[51] A presbyter directed the attention of the new convert to the importance of membership in the church and responsibility before God.

---

46. Kudryavtsev, *Istoriya pravoslavnogo monashestva*, p. 73.

47. Kolesnikov, *Khristianin, znaesh' li ty*, vol. I, pp. 46-7.

48. Ibid.

49. See Kudryavtsev, *Istoriya pravoslavnogo monashestva*, p. 73; *Zakon Bozhy* [God's Law], 5 vols., ed. by M. Dobuzhinsky (M.: Terra, 1991), vol. II, pp. 134-5.

50. Kudryavtsev, *Istoriya pravoslavnogo monashestva*, p. 73.

51. "Church is our spiritual family, so we are named brothers and sisters". – Kolesnikov, *Khristianin, znaesh' li ty*, vol. II, p. 18. See also: *SDP*, no. 293, pp. 198-9; no. 297, pp. 201-2.

In the singing and in the exhortations, there was the idea of the person joining and becoming part of the larger body. This idea is figuratively expressed in the monastic Russian Orthodox song about the prodigal son, as well as in the well-known Baptist hymns about the lost sheep,[52] or the lost piece of silver (Luke 15).[53]

5) The first of the three "irrevocable" vows required at the time of profession by a novice is *virginity* or celibacy; this has often been compared with the vow of marital fidelity, implying here the heavenly Bridegroom – Christ.[54]	5) Although there is no official vow of celibacy among the Russian Baptists, in practice, especially among women, there was a high percentage of singles who, in fact, become nuns, completely dedicating themselves to serving God.

Since about 80% of the membership of Baptist churches in the USSR in the 1960s-1980s consisted of women, it is clear that many of them could not find husbands who were believers. Some of the Baptist women married unbelievers. Those who did were usually excommunicated at that point, but they were often restored to church membership a few years later.[55] The majority of younger women, however, either voluntarily,[56] or

---

52. *SDP,* no. 309, p. 209.

53. *SDP,* no. 149, pp. 105-6.

54. See *O Trekh Obetakh Monashestva* [On the Three Monastic Vows] [1845], <http:// www.wco.ru/biblio/ books/triobeta/Main.htm> accessed 21 April 2010.

55. Many Baptist ministers testify about this as a common situation, such as Ya.D. Shevchuk (INT, Portland, Oregon, USA, 2006); V.Ya. Baranov (INT, Minneapolis, Minnesota, USA, 2006). The latter talks even about the "prearranged tears of repentance" of some young sisters who knew the strict church marriage practice well.

56. I have several testimonies about the unofficial, but genuine vows of chastity of some Soviet Baptist girls in the 1960s. There are testimonies of a presbyter from the Ukraine, M.M. Kolivayko (INT, Sacramento, California, USA, 2006); a church member from Belorussia, N.N. Tsvirin'ko (INT, Fresno, California, USA, 2006); and a presbyter from Tatarstan, N.V. Sabursky (INT, Minneapolis, Minnesota, USA, 2006).

involuntarily,[57] became "nuns". There were some Baptist men who also chose celibacy, but by far the majority of single church members were women.[58] Finally, there is some data about a few younger married couples in Baptist churches who chose to abstain from sexual relationships.[59]

6) The second obligatory life-long vow is *poverty* or "voluntary poverty", the deliberate refusal to own any property and to give personal belongings to the monastery for the benefit of all the brethren.[60]	6) Many Soviet Baptists saw being poor as a virtue. Many, although not all, disapproved of business initiative. Despite most members being poor, regular church offerings created sizeable congregational property.[61]

It was famously argued by Max Weber that in the "Puritan" tradition, economic success was not infrequently considered as an evidence of being chosen and favored by God.[62] The traditional Russian Orthodox mentality usually condemned any display of covetousness or even the desire to make money.[63]

---

57. Often Baptist women, who were involuntarily unmarried, over time became the most zealous church members, helping pastors, and acting as "pillars" of their communities. There is an Orthodox saying from St. John Climacus, "I saw that brethren forced to take the habit became more righteous than free [monks]". Cited in Ivan Grozny, *Sochineniya* [Works] (SPb.: Azbuka, 2000), p. 42. See also: St. John Climacus, *Lestvitsa* [The Ladder of Divine Ascent] (Svyato-Uspensky Pskovsko-Pechersky Monastyr', 1994), Homily 1,18.

58. Testimonies of a church member from Krasnodar Territory, O.E. Avdeeva (INT, Everett, Washington, USA, 2006) and a church member among the "pure" Baptists in Donetsk Region, V.Ya. Sedykh (INT, Sacramento, California, USA, 2006). Groups of so-called "pure" Baptists existed, which were distinct from the CCECB.

59. Ibid.; testimony of N.V. Sabursky (INT, Minneapolis, Minnesota, USA, 2006).

60. *O Trekh Obetakh Monashestva*, <http://www.wco.ru/biblio/books/triobeta/Main.htm>

61. Nikolskaya, *Russky Protestantizm i Gosudarstvennaya Vlast' v 1905-1991 Godakh*, pp. 24-5; Kolesnikov, *Khristianin, znaesh' li ty*, vol. I, pp. 153-6.

62. See, for example, the famous work: M. Weber, *The Protestant Ethic and The Spirit of Capitalism* (1904).

63. See S. Bulgakov, "Pravoslavie i Khozyaystvennaya Zhizn'" [Orthodoxy and Economics], in S. Bulgakov, *Ocherki Ucheniya Pravoslavnoy Tserkvi* [Essays on the Doctrines of the Russian Orthodox Church] (Paris: YMCA-Press, 1989), pp. 345-69. See also A. Makeev, "Analiz Filosofsko-Teologicheskikh Osnov Trudovoy Etiki Anglo-Shotlandskikh Puritan i Rossiyskikh Protestantov: Na Primere Baptistov i Evangel'skikh Khristian" [An Analysis of the Philosophical and Theological Foundations of the Work Ethics of the English-Scottish Puritans and Russian Protestants: By Way of the Baptists' and Evangelical Christians' Example] (Candidate of Philosophy degree thesis, Russian

The Soviet Baptists in general, were very close to the Orthodox monastic outlook on material values. They were also undoubtedly influenced by Socialist ideas.[64]

7) The third and final life-long monastic vow is *obedience*, which involves complete submission to a superior and to spiritual elders and the specific monastic rules. [65]	7) The person on probation was required to agree to accepted rules and discipline; at the heart of these was obedience to the ministers and the decisions of the congregation.[66]

Normally both Russian Orthodox monks and Soviet Baptists have had strict forms of discipline in the monastery and in the church, and have been obedient to their spiritual leaders. Vows in the Orthodox monastery are for life, and similarly Baptist presbyters usually saw their ministry as being life-long. The presbyter was traditionally considered "the Lord's anointed". The members also, as they committed themselves to a congregation, held to the same life-long perspective. For a church to change its presbyter (except in an emergency) was sometimes compared with denial of one's own father or even with "spiritual adultery".[67]

Academy of Public Service under the President of the Russian Federation, 2002).

64. Many Baptist articles spoke of Russian Baptists as Soviet citizens, loving their country and honestly working on Soviet enterprises. There was reference to Jesus Christ being from a poor carpenter family; his disciples were also common fishermen, and they were the first to proclaim the socialist slogan, 'he who does not work shall not eat'. Baptist beliefs were described as similar to the 'Moral Code for the Builders of Communism'. See *BV*, no. 1 (1963), p. 51; nos. 3–4 (1955), p. 64. See also: Mitrokhin, *Baptizm: Istoriya i Sovremennost'*, pp. 392-3.

65. *O Trekh Obetakh Monashestva*, <http://www.wco.ru/biblio/books/triobeta/Main.htm>

66. Kolesnikov, *Khristianin, znaesh' li ty*, vol. II, pp. 135-6.

67. For example, the testimony of Baptist minister V.N. Mokey from Tyumen Region (INT, Minneapolis, Minnesota, USA, 2006).

8) The hegumen traditionally asks before the beginning of profession, "Why did you come, brother, to this holy altar and holy company?" The expected answer is, "I desire a life of penance, honest Father!" Then the hegumen asks many additional questions, for example: Does the novice profess by his own free will? Did he make the choice for his whole life? Will the new monk keep himself in reverence and obedience? Will he suffer for the Lord's sake? The expected answer to all those questions is, "Yes, with God's help."[68]	8) The presbyter traditionally asked at the beginning of the probation, "What brought you here? What do you desire from the church?" The expected answer was, "I desire to be baptized and become a member of the church!" The presbyter and church members asked many other questions in order to make sure of a new convert's sincerity and the firmness of his or her desire to become a church member.[69] The expected answer to all the questions, whether a new convert can live according to Christ's commandments, was, "Yes, with God's help."[70]

The affinity of the spiritual traditions of Orthodoxy and Russian Baptists has undoubtedly not so much to do with the external character as the internal. Therefore, it is important to see the relation of the rites of "testing" (before the monastic profession and the Baptist water baptism) lying behind the similarities in some of the ceremonial words.

---

68. Kudryavtsev, *Istoriya pravoslavnogo monashestva*, pp. 73-4; M. Dobuzhinsky, ed., *Zakon Bozhy*, vol. II, p. 135.

69. Kolesnikov, *Khristianin, znaesh' li ty*, vol. II, p. 20.

70. I experienced this style of reply during the testing ceremony, at least in Kazakhstan's Baptist churches, where I began my evangelical Christian life.

9) The hegumen makes clear what the monk's life is about; he reminds the novice about temptations and Satan's attacks; he gives the example of Christ and the holy men of the past who overcame the evil one. Then he asks, "Will you abide in these vows till the end of your life?" "Yes, with God's help". The hegumen then hands the scissors to be used for the tonsure to the novice and asks him to give him the scissors. This happens three times, thereby underlining the strong commitment of the novice.[71]	9) The presbyter reminded the candidate of the meaning of baptism, saying that after it a young Christian is exposed to especially strong temptations, for it was so with Christ himself: after baptism Satan tempted him. Then often a question was posed, "Do you promise to serve God in good conscience?" "Yes, I do!" (with God's help).[72] The presbyter, after finishing the testing, traditionally asked, as if talking a new convert out of a rash decision, "What if the church refuses to baptize you today? What about being baptized next year?"[73]

In this area, too, there are similarities between Orthodox and Russian Baptist traditions. The rigorous procedures show that the widespread "warnings" in the atheistic propaganda in the USSR that religious organizations supposedly lured Soviet people into their communities in any possible way could hardly be further from reality.[74] To become either a monk or a Russian Baptist was very difficult.

---

71. Kudryavtsev, *Istoriya pravoslavnogo monashestva*, pp. 74-5; *Zakon Bozhy (God's Law) [1957]*, ed. by S. Slobodskoy (Omsk: Omich, 1995), p. 694.

72. "*Verouchenie Evangel'skikh Khristian – Baptistov*", *BV*, no. 4 (1985), p. 46.

73. The questions, aimed at testing the converts' humility, were very popular among Russian Baptists before *perestroika*. I was a witness of such trials at Baptist communities several times at the end of the 1980s – beginning of the 1990s.

74. See, for instance, S. Skazkin, ed., *Nastol'naya Kniga Ateista* [Handbook for Atheists] (M.: Politizdat, 1983), pp. 422-3.

10) The profession is made in the name of the Holy Trinity, after which the novice becomes a monk.[75]	10) Baptism is carried out in the name of the Holy Trinity, after which the candidate becomes a member of the church.[76]

The argument of this section is not that Russian Baptist "testing" before baptism was explicitly modelled on monastic practice, or was influenced only by this historic Orthodox procedure. There was undoubtedly an influence on Russian Baptists from German Baptist and Mennonite procedures.[77] I also recognize that I have used the example of novices becoming monks, rather than looking at nuns, and that could appear to be dissonant, given that most Russian Baptist members were women. However, the testing for nuns was similar to that for monks. Thus: "Hegumene Euphrasia… accepted sisters with caution, strictly *testing* them and *exacting* strict observance of the monastic rules from them… Many sisters were true ascetics."[78] In similar vein, Khrapov speaks of Baptist "sisters" who were *tested* and had to be "known for doing good deeds and leading a life of purity and sanctity… not enslaved by wine, overeating, greedy for money… Our sisters are notable for their exemplary God-fearing life."[79] It might also be objected that Russian Baptists lived their lives "in the world", not in a monastery, but there was also within Russian Orthodoxy the phenomenon of "monasticism in the world".[80] In the light of the similarities outlined, it

---

75. Kudryavtsev, *Istoriya pravoslavnogo monashestva*, p. 75; Dobuzhinsky, ed., *Zakon Bozhy*, vol. II, p. 135.

76. Kolesnikov, *Khristianin, znaesh' li ty*, vol. I, p. 49; "*Verouchenie Evangel'skikh Khristian – Baptistov*", BV, no. 4 (1985), p. 46.

77. See, for instance: *The Autobiography of Jacob Delakoff*, September 1935, p. 11; Friesen, *The Mennonite Brotherhood in Russia*, p. 291.

78. Cloistress Taisiya, *Russkoe Pravoslavnoe Zhenskoe Monashestvo* [Russian Orthodox Women's Monasticism] (Minsk: Izd-vo Belorusskogo ekzarkhata, 2006), p. 32.

79. Khrapov, *Dom Bozhy*, <http://www.blagovestnik.org/books/00280.htm#40>

80. On Orthodox monasticism lived in the world see the following books: Archbishop Ioann (Shakhovskoy), *Beloe inochestvo* [White Monasticism] [1932], in Archbishop Ioann (Shakhovskoy), *Izbrannoe* [Selected Works] (Petrozavodsk: Svyatoy ostrov, 1992), pp. 118-28; Archpriest Valentin (Sventsitsky), *Monastyr' v miru* [Monastery in the World] (M.: Lestvitsa, 1999). It was considered that Christians could live very close to the pure monastic life even in the world.

seems reasonable to suggest that Orthodox ways influenced Baptists living in a predominantly Orthodox country.

For Russian Baptists the ceremony of baptism was not an end in itself. From this point the candidate was part of the *sobornost*, the church community.[81] *Sobornost* is an Orthodox term: nineteenth-century Russian Orthodox theologian A.S. Khomyakov defined *sobornost* as unity in multiplicity, "unity of the grace of God, living in a multitude of rational creatures, submitting themselves willingly to grace".[82] This can be compared and contrasted to the individualism that is demonstrated by many Baptists in the USA, with the strong stress among them on individual relationship with God.[83] In Russian Baptist practice, the stress was on baptism as that which joins a person to the church, the holy assembly. This also reflected the idea of *sobornost*. Here is a very typical Soviet Baptist reflection: "Many tasks of the Kingdom of God cannot be accomplished individually…but only by all the church conjointly. So… we pray with all the church together for the coming of the Kingdom of God, and our active serving in the church helps to fulfill the prayer."[84] It was only after testing and baptism that a new convert became a fully-fledged member of the church, with his or her name written down in the church book.[85] Thereafter the new member participated in the Lord's Supper, was admitted to the members' meeting and was eligible for service in the church. The testing process had far-reaching implications.

---

81. See Levindanto, *Blagochinie Pomestnykh Tserkvey*, pp. 121-2.

82. Khomyakov, *Tserkov' Odna*, p. 3.

83. See, for example, how this question is handled in I.J. Van Ness, W. Nowlin, *The Baptist Spirit and Fundamentals of the Faith* (Whitefish, MT: Kessinger Publishing, 2008), pp. 33-5. See also J.T. Odle, ed., *Why I am a Baptist* (Nashville, TN: Broadman Press, 1972); W.P. Tuck, *Our Baptist Tradition* (Macon, GA: Smyth & Helwys Publishing, Inc., 1993); C.P. Stanton Jr., ed., *Why I am a Baptist: Reflections on Being Baptist in the 21ˢᵗ Century* (Macon, GA: Smyth & Helwys Publishing, Inc., 1999). Eastern European Evangelicals usually incline to a compromise between communal and individualistic approaches – see, for instance: E. Bartos, "Salvation in the Orthodox Church: An Evangelical Perspective", in I. Randall, ed., *Baptists and the Orthodox Church: On the Way to Understanding* (Prague: IBTS, 2003), pp. 59-61.

84. R. Vyzu, "*Nagornaya propoved*" [The Sermon on the Mount], *BV*, no. 2 (1982), p. 13.

85. This book is a list of church members, sometimes not very modestly compared to "the book of life", Phil 4:3 and Heb 12:23.

The Lord's Supper

Although the Lord's Supper in Russian Baptist churches has usually been called an ordinance rather than a sacrament, the way in which it was regarded in the Soviet period was sacramental in spirit. This was seen in the way congregations prepared for the Lord's Supper. There was an all-congregation Friday fast (with full abstention from food and often from water) before the Communion Sunday. There was then a personal fast on the morning of the Sunday of the Lord's Supper.[86] It is almost certainly the case that this was connected with the ancient Orthodox tradition of fasting before the Communion. In the Bible there is no record of fasting before the Lord's Supper. However, Orthodox tradition was insistent: canon 41 of the Carthaginian Council says, "The holy sacrament of the altar should be performed by fasting people."[87] Married people in Russian Baptist churches also abstained from sexual relations in preparation for the Supper.[88] Another feature of preparation had to do with the necessity of asking for forgiveness and being reconciled with all people before participation in the ordinance. At the service itself, as preparation was made and the service began, there was concern to ensure that those present recognized the seriousness of what was being done. An old presbyter in a Baptist church in Omsk typically said to his congregation during his preparatory remarks: "Please be careful, brothers and sisters, not to spill the Blood of Christ!" Any crumb of bread accidentally dropped on the floor was immediately picked up reverently, and the elders and deacons made clear the importance of taking care not to spill from the precious cup.[89] All of this preparation had deeply sacramental overtones.

During the service there were penitential prayers, singing in a minor key, frequently accompanied with tears, and a message about the suffering Christ. As the cover was slowly and solemnly taken off the Bread and

---

86. See Khrapov, *Dom Bozhy*, <http://www.blagovestnik.org/books/00280.htm#10>

87. *Pravila Pravoslavnoy Tserkvi*, vol. II, p. 189.

88. Khrapov, *Dom Bozhy*, <http://www.blagovestnik.org/books/00280.htm#10>

89. It should also be noted that Communion could be served by ordained church ministers only. See Khrapov, *Dom Bozhy*, <http://www.blagovestnik.org/books/00280. htm#11>

Cup, there was special common prayer by the presbyter and all the congregation (as the "royal priesthood"), calling down the divine grace on the
"great holy" Bread and Cup.[90] The bread and wine were always received
standing.[91] Russian Baptists, following the Orthodox Church's practice,
always used leavened, not unleavened bread.[92] A common Russian Baptist
description of the Lord's Supper was the "Breaking of Bread". There was
also, however, stress on the "Cup", and a widespread belief that communi-
cants must drink deeply from the Cup, not just sip from it.[93] The biblical
text "For he who eats and drinks, eats and drinks judgment to himself…
For this reason many among you are weak and sick, and a number sleep"
(1 Cor 11:29-30) was taken literally. In the light of this warning, church
discipline, restricting access to the bread and wine, could be severe.[94] At
the same time, regarding illnesses, it was common to hear something like
the following from church ministers: "It has never happened that anyone
ever became ill because of taking Communion from the common cup (although some say this is unsanitary), and on the contrary, we often hear
about illnesses being healed."[95] Some members were unwell, however, and
when bread and wine was taken to the homes of these sick members, the
view was that it was better to take this from the bread broken and the wine
used at the church.[96]

---

90. See A. Kadaev, *"Vecherya Gospodnya – Khleboprelomlenie"* [The Lord's Supper –
Breaking of Bread], *BV*, no. 3 (1990), pp. 12-3.

91. Ibid., p.13. For standing, as an expression of awe during the Lord's Supper, see
"Polozhenie o Soyuze Evangel'skikh Khristian-Baptistov" [The Statutes of the Union of
Evangelical Christians-Baptists] (1944), ARSECB, F. 1, op. 11da, d. 54, l. 6. This is in
contrast to the argument of C.H. Spurgeon that sitting was closer to the model of the Last
Supper. It should be noted that Spurgeon held to a very "high" view of the Supper. C.H.
Spurgeon, *12 Sermons on the Lord's Supper* (Grand Rapids, MI: Baker Book House, 1994).

92. See Malkov, *Vvedenie v Liturgicheskoe Predanie*, p. 163.

93. I have heard this repeatedly from Russian Baptist ministers in Siberia and Kazakhstan.

94. An active participant of the movement of "pure" Baptists, A.I. Musiets (INT,
Sacramento, California, USA, 2006), spoke about the East Ukrainian "old pious practice"
of even banning a brother or sister from partaking in Communion if the person's
unbelieving spouse was being unfaithful. The argument was that it was necessary to
prevent the "pollution" of all the community by such church members, since "husband
and wife are one flesh".

95. For instance, testimony of presbyter S.Yu. Sipko (Omsk, Russia, 2008).

96. See letter of Baptist church member Yu. Paydich to A.V. Karev (1969), ARSECB, F. 1,
op. 28d7a, d. 13, l. 3.

There was particular joy, as well as the customary reverence in the service if some newly-baptized people were taking the Lord's Supper for the first time. These are typical reports in *Bratsky Vestnik*:

> From the life of the local churches, in the city of Alma-Ata. ...
> At the end of the church feast, the Lord's Supper was served.
> In a solemn atmosphere, with deep awe, the newly baptized
> brothers and sisters participated in the Body and Blood of our
> Lord Jesus Christ for the first time.[97]

> From the life of the local churches, in the city of Yaroslavl. ...
> After the baptism, the Communion was served. With joy and
> reverence the new church members participated in the Body
> and Blood of Christ.[98]

Aspects of the conclusion of the Communion service, and the possible results of the service, were also noteworthy. The "holy kiss" was practiced after the Lord's Supper. The remains of the consecrated bread were eaten by church members or perhaps the ministers at the end of the service.[99] As an example of the high view of the consecrated bread, in 1982 a famous minister of the CCECB, S.N. Misiruk, was arrested during his celebration of the Lord's Supper, and after his (three year) imprisonment ended the brethren apparently "gave him the bread they had been keeping with care for the three years."[100] This was clearly a very touching meeting, reminis-

---

97. *BV*, no. 5 (1985), p. 73.

98. *BV*, no. 5 (1986), p. 74.

99. By members, as in Khrapov, *Dom Bozhy*, or by ministers, as in Gnida, *Tserkovnye ustanovleniya*, p. 73. In addition, Khrapov comments, "It is impossible to use the remains for a normal meal, because there is a blessing upon them". Khrapov, *Dom Bozhy*, <http://www.blagovestnik.org/books/00280.htm#12>

100. *VestI*, no. 2 (1996), supplement, p. 38. As another example of the power of the bread and wine, church members P.D. Karavan and N.O. Sobchenko (INT, Sacramento, California, USA, 2006) testify that a few days before the Chernobyl catastrophe (April 1986) Soviet militiamen brutally dispersed an unregistered Baptist meeting in a forest near Kiev and the consecrated bread and wine were thrown to the ground and trampled underfoot. It was said, "and after that – at once there was the Chernobyl explosion! ... God's endurance came to an end". See a similar report also in *"Kievskoe Ob"edinenie Mezhdunarodnogo CCECB"* [Kiev Association of International CCECB] (editorial article),

cent of the pious tradition of the long-lasting *artos* (the Easter consecrated bread) among Russian Orthodox Christians.[101]

The practices that have been described within the Russian Baptist churches were not entirely shaped by a particular theology of the Lord's Supper, but a theology was developed. A *Bratsky Vestnik* editorial in 1947 suggested that the "peculiarly difficult task" for many Russian Baptist believers was "to reject the idea of transubstantiation, which comes from the so-called historic churches... the idea that visible bread and wine transubstantiate into the Body and Blood of Christ during the sacrament of the Eucharist."[102] The idea that it was "difficult" to reject this theology is in line with the argument of this study regarding the significance for Baptists of Orthodox thinking and practice. Within Orthodoxy generally, there had been a trend (from the Middle Ages), towards transubstantiation, and older, more apophatic understandings of Communion declined.[103] Although among Russian Baptists there was – it is clear – persistent nervousness about transubstantiation, Russian Baptist theological thinking seems to have moved, by the 1970s, in a much more explicitly sacramental direction. In 1979 N.A. Kolesnikov wrote in *Bratsky Vestnik*: "We have received the right to partake in the gracious sacrament of the remembrance of Christ's death, the Lord's Supper, and be named children of God."[104] It is interesting to see here the mixing of the symbolic concept of "remembrance" of Christ's

---

VestI, no. 2 (2009), p. 19.

101. See, for instance: N. Budur, ed., *Pravoslanaya Vera* [The Orthodox Faith] (M.: OLMA-PRESS, 2002), pp. 171-2.

102. *"Vecherya Gospodnya"* [The Lord's Supper] (editorial article), *BV*, no. 3 (1947), IEDE-2.

103. For example, the classical work by Metropolitan Makary, *The Orthodox-Dogmatic Theology*, very frequently quoted by all Russian theologians, explains the sacrament of the Eucharist as transubstantiation or its synonyms, *prelozhenie* and *pretvorenie*. See Makary, *Pravoslavno-dogmaticheskoe bogoslovie*, v. II. pp. 367, 385, 396. In this sense the condemnation of the Orthodox theologian, A.I. Osipov, is remarkable: he dared to speak of the "Chalcedonian" approach to the Eucharist. See A. Osipov, *Evkharistiya i Svyashchenstvo* [The Eucharist and Priesthood], <http://orthtexts.narod.ru/17_Evhar_svyasch.htm> accessed 30 November 2010. For criticism of this work, see, for example: Archimandrite Rafail (Karelin), *Eshche Raz o Ereticheskich Zabluzhdeniyach Professora MDA, A.I. Osipova* [More on the Heretical Errors of Professor MDA, A.I. Osipov] (M.: Krest sv. Niny, 2003).

104. N. Kolesnikov, *"Pospeshim k sovershenstvu"* [Let us go on to Maturity], *BV*, no. 2 (1979), p. 35.

suffering at the Lord's Supper and the Orthodox idea of the "gracious sacrament". Kolesnikov also wrote: "What do the bread and wine mean for
the partakers of the Lord's Supper? Are they just visible signs?" His answer
was that there is "sharing in the Body and Blood of Christ" (1 Cor 10:16-
17) and so a participator "becomes a real communicant of Christ and his
church. The same is true for all the holy ordinances."[105]

When official Baptist statements were made about the Breaking of
Bread it was "remembrance" which was, as a rule, mentioned.[106] The bread
and wine were symbols; but they were not only symbols. When theology was discussed at local level and was related to the practical side of
celebration of the Lord's Supper what was emphasized was the distinctive
sacramental thinking that increasingly prevailed. For instance, a conten-
tious issue was whether it was permissible to mix consecrated wine (during
the Communion) with unconsecrated wine. Some ministers were strictly
against this, whereas others were in favor, giving the following explanation, "When the ministers dilute the consecrated wine with unconsecrated,
the whole of the wine becomes consecrated."[107] D. Minyakov from the
CCECB, writing in 1983 on the Lord's Supper, typically addressed the
problem of sin in the congregation. His view was categorical: "Where sin
arises, there is no Christ, no broken Body and no shed Blood. There is just
bread and wine, to taste which is not to participate in the death and sufferings of Christ and His shed Blood."[108] This well known minister clearly
distinguished between an observance of the Lord's Supper in which there
was something beyond bread and wine – there was broken Body and shed
Blood – and on the other hand an observing in which, because of sin, there
was "just bread and wine".

S.V. Sannikov, summarizing the views of the Russian Baptists on the
meaning of Communion, writes:

---

105. Kolesnikov, *Khristianin, znaesh' li ty*, vol. II, p. 76.
106. See, for instance, *"Verouchenie Evangel'skikh Khristian – Baptistov"*, BV, no. 4 (1985),
pp. 46-7.
107. The first view was held, for example, by a presbyter from Tatarstan, N.V. Sabursky
(INT, Minneapolis, Minnesota, USA, 2006). The opposite opinion was held by the
minister of Omsk Baptist church A.N. Krivorotov (Omsk, Russia, 2008).
108. D. Minyakov, *"O Vechere Gospodney"* [On the Lord's Supper], *VestI*, no. 1 (1983),
p. 8.

In our brotherhood, the following opinion is acknowledged. The bread and wine are tangible objects which are not, in themselves, the Body and Blood of Christ, but in partaking of them people have the opportunity to participate in His Body and Blood... In the moment when we 'all partake of the one bread' (1 Cor 10:17), there is, in a way unknown to us, the 'sharing in the body of Christ' (1 Cor 10:16)... The true Body and Blood of the risen Savior exist, but there is the bread and there is the wine during the Lord's Supper which fully reflect the Truth and are identical with it.[109]

The Bread, even after the united prayer of the presbyter and the congregation, remains, undoubtedly, bread, and yet simultaneously becomes the genuine Body of Christ.[110] This is not something that can be explained; a parallel is the mystery of the two natures of Christ. With the Cup, after the common prayer of the presbyter and the whole congregation at Communion the wine remains wine, and yet, at the same time, becomes the genuine Blood of Christ.[111] Sannikov speaks of this happening "in a way unknown to us", which is a traditional apophatic qualification. A similar view of the Lord's Supper was held by the Eastern Church in earlier times. Russian Orthodox Professor N.D. Uspensky gives a number of citations on the theme from works of the church fathers.[112] The "high" view held by Russian Baptists was summed up by A.K. Sipko, a leading AUCECB minister, who asserted that baptism and the Lord's Supper were both "sacraments". He then went on: "There is the special sharing of divine grace

---

109. S.V. Sannikov, *Vecherya Gospodnya* [The Lord's Supper] (M.: Protestant, 1990), pp. 17-18. See also S.V. Sannikov *"Vecherya Gospodnya"* [The Lord's Supper], in *Almanach 'Bogomyslie'*, vol. 1 (1990), pp. 65-116.

110. "We consider a person guilty of unworthy participation in the Lord's Supper not for failing to discern the bread, but for not discerning the Lord's Body (1 Cor 11:29)". – A. Sipko, *Derzhis' Obraztsa Zdravogo Ucheniya*, p. 247.

111. See details in C. Prokhorov, "Apophaticism and Cataphaticism in Protestantism", pp. 58-68. As the ancients said, "Many things may happen between the cup and the lip..." (Aulus Gellius, *Attic Nights*, XIII, 18,1).

112. See N. Uspensky, *"Anafora, Opyt historiko-liturgicheskogo analisa"* [Anaphora, An Attempt of The Historical-Liturgical Analysis], Bogoslovskie trudy, vol. 13 (1975), pp. 125-47.

by way of the Communion… we hold the opinion that the Lord's Supper, not by the form of its celebration, but in its very essence and purpose, is the greatest sacrament."[113] Sipko wanted to emphasize Baptist freedom in relation to "form", but his view of "divine grace" in relation to the Lord's Supper mirrored Orthodox thinking, and Sipko could not have been more explicitly sacramental. Although the sacramental thinking could have developed within the Russian Baptist movement through other influences apart from Orthodoxy, it does seem reasonable to argue from the evidence that in the Russian context there was indebtedness to Orthodoxy in the period being examined. This sacramental thinking was extended beyond baptism and the Lord's Supper to include a range of Russian Baptist ordinances or sacraments.

Seven Sacraments

Those joining the Evangelical Christians-Baptists communities were baptized, joined formally as members and then participated in the Lord's Supper. Other church "ordinances" then became part of their lives. Links with Orthodox sacramental thinking can be traced in these ordinances. The enumeration of the traditional Orthodox sacraments is the following: baptism, chrismation, communion, confession, holy orders, matrimony, and anointing with oil. A connection is made with the seven gifts of the Spirit from Isaiah 11:2-3, the seven loaves from Matthew 15:36-37, and the seven golden lampstands and the seven stars from Revelation 1:12, 16. This list became firm only in the thirteenth century; before this various options were to be found in the church.[114] As noted in the introduction to this chapter, the Russian Baptist enumerations of the church ordinances in the later Soviet period did not fully agree with each other. In the 1960s the items which appeared were baptism, breaking of bread, marriage, burial, praying for the sick and ordination. The AUCECB's 1960 *Statutes* and the *Letter of Instructions* affirmed these aspects. These documents led

---

113. A. Sipko, *Derzhis' Obraztsa Zdravogo Ucheniya*, pp. 245-6.
114. See, for instance: *Khristianstvo: Entsiklopedichesky Slovar'*, v. III, p. 7.

to the split in the Union and the formation of the Iniative Group, the *Initsiativniki*, later the CCECB, but the serious tension among Baptists was not about the list of ordinances. Rather it concerned other points of the *Statutes* and the *Letter of Instructions*, such as the restrictions regarding children attending services and new rules in relation to baptisms.[115] In 1961, when A.F. Prokofiev and G.K. Kryuchkov, for the Initiative Group, circulated their amendments to the *Statutes of the Union of ECB* (1960), the paragraph on the ordinances was formulated like this: "The presbyter of the congregation... performs all church ordinances, namely: baptism, breaking of bread, marriage, burial, praying for the sick and praying for children."[116] Thus the *Initsiativniki* not only accepted the AUCECB list but even restored praying for children.[117] This list of church ordinances was repeated word for word in the *Regulations of the Council of Churches of ECB* (the versions of 1965 and 1974).[118] Russian Baptists – both the registered and unregistered – were evidently not satisfied by the two Protestant "ordinances"; they were strikingly persistent in this period in approximating to Orthodoxy's "seven sacraments".[119]

From 1963, revisions of the *Regulations of the Union of ECB*, confirmed by several councils of the AUCECB, meant that new versions of Union policies took the place of the discredited *Statutes* of 1960.[120] The paragraph on the ordinances in the versions of the *Regulations* of 1966 and 1979 states: "Local churches of the ECB conduct divine services with preaching of the Gospel, praying and performing baptisms, breaking of bread, marriage, burial and other ordinances."[121] The reference to "other ordinances"

---

115. See details, for instance, in Prokhorov, *The State and the Baptist Churches in the USSR*, pp. 1-62.

116. ARSECB, F. 1, op. 28d.2, d. 5, l. 10.

117. It seems that the leaders of the Initiative Group referred to the *Statutes of the Union of ECB* of 1948 where, for the first time in the history of ECB, "praying for infants" was brought into the list with baptism and breaking of bread.

118. See *BL*, no. 11 (1965), supplement. See also *Ustav Soyuza Tserkvey ECB: Izdanie Soveta Tserkvey ECB* [The Regulations of the Union of the ECB: Publication of the Council of Churches of the ECB], IEDE-4.

119. Though the Roman Catholic Church also has seven sacraments, Catholic teaching had no identifiable impact on the Russian Baptists.

120. See *Istoriya Evangel'skikh Khristian-Baptistov v SSSR*, p. 244.

121. *BV*, no. 6 (1966), p. 52; nos. 1-2 (1980), pp. 63-4.

was somewhat enigmatic. By the time of the version of the *Regulations* produced in 1990, there was some clarification of the situation: "Local churches of the ECB conduct divine services with preaching of the Gospel, study
of the Bible, praying, psalms... with performing water baptism by faith,
breaking of bread, marriage, praying for children, ordination, burial and
other ordinances."[122] But the authors of the AUCECB *Regulations* still used
the wording of "other ordinances", so that in these documents, throughout
this period, the actual number was not defined.

While the official AUCECB documents are not entirely clear regarding the number of recognized ordinances, two very well-known Russian
Baptist ministers and theologians, A.V. Karev and N.A. Kolesnikov, were
willing to specify a number – seven. In 1963 Karev wrote in *Bratsky Vestnik*
on "The Holy Ordinances of the Church". This work was re-published in
1977, which indicates its authoritative nature. Karev stated:

> What are the ordinances of the New Testament church? I
> name the seven ordinances of the church: preaching, [church]
> singing, praying, serving with love to the neighbor, baptism,
> communion, and keeping the peace at the church. Within
> this [list], the preaching is the main ordinance of the New
> Testament Church.[123]

Kolesnikov also raised the question of what to say...

> ...as the holy ordinances of the churches of the Evangelical
> Christians-Baptists are considered: water baptism, the Lord's
> Supper, ordination, marriage, praying for the sick and for
> children, the consecration of houses of prayer, and burial.

---

122. *"Ustav Soyuza ECB"* [The Regulations of the Union of ECB], *BV*, no. 3 (1990),
p. 84.
123. A. Karev, *"Svyashchennodeystviya Tserkvi"* [The Holy Ordinances of the Church], *BV*,
no. 1 (1963), p. 36. See also: A. Karev, *Izbrannye Stat'i* [Selected Articles] (M.: AUCECB,
1977), p. 150.

The administration of these holy ordinances has foundational
meaning in the life of the church.[124]

Both authors used the term "ordinance" or "holy ordinance" rather than
"sacrament", but it is significant that both had the number seven, although
not the same seven. The list of ordinances from N.A. Kolesnikov has more
of a "sacramental" character than the list offered by Karev. The emphasis
by Karev on preaching is typical of many Baptist communities. Kolesnikov
did not actually mention preaching. In Karev's list, the ordinances of baptism and communion were the only two items which coincided with the
Orthodox list of sacraments. Kolesnikov had at least four that were identical with Orthodox belief and practice – water baptism, the Lord's Supper,
ordination, and marriage. The number is five, if Kolesnikov's "praying for
the sick" is identified with Orthodox anointing with oil.[125] Even with Karev,
the enumeration of *seven* ordinances of the Russian Baptists is significant.

To some extent these differences of viewpoint are a mark of the different
traditions present in the AUCECB. A.V. Karev came from the Evangelical
Christians and he had a more international outlook.[126] N.A. Kolesnikov
belonged to the national Russian Baptist tradition.[127] While the differences
over central evangelical teaching between these two traditions were not
significant, the Baptists had traditionally given ordained ministers a role
in their churches in relation to the sacraments which at times was questioned by the Evangelical Christians. Thus A.I. Mitskevich, one of the well-
known leaders of the AUCECB, in his textbook on the history of the ECB,
notes that the Evangelical Christians had made critical remarks about the
ecclesiology of the Baptists, such as the following: "[The Baptists] declare
that only ordained presbyters have the right to perform baptism and the
breaking of bread… However, the same churches freely allow ordinary
church members to preach. Such an approach is based on the assumption
that baptism and the breaking of bread are much more important than

---

124. Kolesnikov, *Khristianin, znaesh' li ty*, v. I, p. 41.
125. See the chapter "Praying for the sick" in Kolesnikov, *Khristianin, znaesh' li ty*, vol. I,
pp. 56-9.
126. See Savinsky, *Istoriya (1917-1967)*, p. 379.
127. See Kolesnikov, *Khristianin, znaesh' li ty*, vol. I, p. 3.

preaching."[128] After taking into account the polemical spirit behind this statement, it does indicate that Baptists such as Kolesnikov were drawing from a sacramental tradition among the Russian Baptists.

It is not my intention to seek to argue that the understanding of the sacraments promoted by Kolesnikov, and by other Russian Baptists with his viewpoint, was in full agreement with classical Russian Orthodox sacramental theology. However, in speaking of seven "holy ordinances" the Russian Baptists were not following traditional Protestant thinking. As noted, in the Russian language the word *svyashchennodeystvie* ('holy ordinance') is the first synonym of the word *tainstvo* ('sacrament'). It is true that there has been a sacramental strain in English Baptist life. Ian Randall has traced how this was expressed at times in the twentieth century, for example in the Cassock Club, a group of Baptist ministers trained at Regent's Park College, Oxford, in the 1950s.[129] In 2005 John Colwell, a British Baptist theologian at Spurgeon's College, London, produced *Promise and Presence: An Exploration of Sacramental Theology*, in which he argued for seven sacraments – baptism, confirmation, the Lord's Supper, cleansing, healing, Christian ministry and marriage.[130] But many other Baptists would even be reluctant to use the term "sacrament", and even if they did, they would have in mind only baptism and the Lord's Supper. Outside of Russian Baptist life it is very rare indeed to find any Baptists (in the 20th century or any other century) thinking in terms of seven "holy ordinances" of the church. Among Russian Baptists, Eastern Orthodox theology was a powerful presence.

The Ordination of Presbyters

In the light of the Orthodox view of ministry, and the stress within Orthodoxy of a tradition going back to the Apostles, it is not surprising

---

128. Mitskevich, *Istoriya Evangel'skikh Khristian-Baptistov*, p. 223.

129. I.M. Randall, *The English Baptists of the Twentieth Century* (Didcot: Baptist Historical Society, 2005), p. 323.

130. J.E. Colwell, *Promise and Presence: An Exploration of Sacramental Theology* (Milton Keynes, UK: Paternoster, 2005).

that the question of "Apostolic succession" was one that was raised among Russian Evangelical Christians-Baptists. P.K. Shatrov, referring (significantly) to St. John Chrysostom, proposed the following argument on the subject, one which he clearly felt could assist the churches to deal with the problem of their lack of "Apostolic succession". The argument was that a little-known disciple of Christ, named Ananias, who was not one of the twelve apostles, laid his hands on Saul (later Paul), and the latter was filled with the Holy Spirit (Acts 9:10-18).[131] The view being promoted was that it was God who chose ministers, drawn from those pleasing to him, and that their ordination need not be restricted to a line drawn from the Twelve. However, despite their objection to literal "Apostolic succession", the Russian Baptists did think in terms of "spiritual succession" of presbyters in the Russian Baptist brotherhood.[132] The word that was sometimes used to describe some of those who helped to found the movement that ultimately became the Evangelical Christians-Baptists is significant. Kryuchkov, the leader of CCECB, spoke about "our *pervozvannye* [those first called] brethren – Ryaboshapka, Ratushny, Onishchenko..."[133] This word – *pervozvannye* – is a specific Orthodox word, referring to the calling by Jesus of the first apostles.[134] Thus what is conveyed is a partly hidden conviction about the apostolic calling of the first Russian Stundists and Baptists (like St Andrew) by the Lord himself.

This authentic succession was also to be found among the Russian Baptists in their keeping of the "true biblical teaching".[135] For Karev, the most important ordinance in the church was preaching. Kolesnikov, with his more sacramental emphasis, included "ordination" to the office of minister among his "holy ordinances", and in this respect it is noteworthy that early Russian Baptists, like Orthodox clergy, kept detailed

---

131. See P. Shatrov, *"Deyaniya Apostolov"* [The Acts of the Apostles], *BV*, no. 2 (1985), pp. 26-7.

132. See Pavlov, *Pravda o Baptistakh*, p. 222; Savinsky, *Istoriya (1867-1917)*, p. 10.

133. See, for instance: G. Kryuchkov, *"Prorochesky Golos"* [The Prophetic Voice], *Vestl*, nos. 4-5 (2007), p. 19.

134. For instance: St. Andrew the first Apostle to be called.

135. Pavlov, *Pravda o Baptistakh*, p. 222; Savinsky, *Istoriya (1867- 1917)*, p. 10.

records of ordinations, with information about who was involved in the ordination.[136] The issue of ordinations that were not properly carried out – perhaps without the correct presbyters present – was always very sensitive among Russian Baptists (i.e. new "Ananiases" were not welcomed), and if queries were raised the ordinations in question normally became the subject of serious investigation.[137] The service of ordination always involved the laying-on of hands. P.K. Shatrov, one of the leaders of the AUCECB, wrote in 1982 in *Bratsky Vestnik* about "The Acts of the Apostles" and said the following:

> Laying-on of hands is not simply a symbolic action accompanying the [ordination] prayer but a very important part of the consecration to the ministry... John Chrysostom wrote about this, 'The ordination has been performed from the days of Moses according to God's determinate order. Though men perform the laying on of hands, God himself does everything... if the ordination is being done properly.' The consecration to the ministry by the laying on of hands is a holy ordinance, where the Lord is actively working - if it is performed according to His will.[138]

There is a strong stress in the quotation here from St. John Chrysostom on the issue of tradition. Here the tradition is not only back to the beginnings of the church in the New Testament, but further back into the Old Testament. The words from Chrysostom also underline that it is "God

136. See *Bapt.*, 1907: no. 1, pp. 20-1; no. 2, p. 10; no. 4, pp. 17-8; no. 5, p. 12. Later such information was not usually entered in the same detail in official sources, but was passed on in oral tradition. See also P. Steeves, "The Russian Baptist Union, 1917-1935: Evangelical Awakening in Russia" (PhD thesis, University of Kansas, 1976), pp. 28-9.

137. For example, the testimony of the ex-president of the AUCECB, V.E. Logvinenko (Odessa, Ukraine, 1995). See also a circular letter of the AUCECB leaders on that subject: ARSECB, F. 1, op. 1d1, d. 1d1-139, l. 1.

138. P. Shatrov, *"Deyaniya Apostolov"* [The Acts of the Apostles], *BV*, no. 4 (1982), p. 17. As noted, *svyashchennodeystvie* is the first synonym of *tainstvo* ('sacrament'). For ordination as *svyashchennodeystvie* see K. Sedletsky, *"Izbranie i Rukopolozhenie Sluzhiteley"* [Election and Ordination of Ministers], *BV*, no. 6 (1988), p. 52; "From the Life of the Local Churches": *BV*, no. 3 (1985), p. 79; no. 2 (1986), p. 74; no. 1 (1987), p. 75.

himself" who does everything in ordination. The sacramental nature of what takes place is clearly in view. This perspective was helpful to the leaders of the AUCECB as they sought to promote their teaching about the special status of the presbyter. At the same time, the human acts done were also important: these had to be "done properly".

Bratsky Vestnik carried further articles on this subject. In 1984 Shatrov followed up on his 1982 article with an even stronger statement:

> Laying-on of hands is a visible sign of God's blessing during the [act of] consecration to the ministry, praying for the sick, and during the receiving of the Holy Spirit... Only the ministers, to whom God gave such a right, can perform this holy ordinance.[139]

Kolesnikov went even further:

> Ordained ministers are considered the Lord's anointed... God performs the sacrament of making presbyters... A non-ordained person has no right to perform any holy ordinances... [otherwise] he just does them as a matter of form, which gives nothing.[140]

The language here could not be more categorical. The view of ministry is "high" – the "Lord's anointed" – and ordination itself is unambiguously termed a "sacrament". There is a clear distinction between the ordained and the "non-ordained", with the latter having no rights in the area of "holy ordinances". It is difficult to see traditional Baptist views of ministry here. Among the range of ecclesial models available in Protestantism, Russian Baptist concepts of ministry appear to have approximated to high Presbyterianism, but, despite the use of the term presbyter, there is no evidence of Presbyterian influence. The Orthodox framework of thought

---

139. P. Shatrov, *"Deyaniya Apostolov"* [The Acts of the Apostles], *BV*, no. 4 (1984), p. 24.
140. Kolesnikov, *Khristianin, znaesh' li ty*, v. II, pp. 48, 57. See also: Kolesnikov, *V Pomoshch' Propovedniku*, v. I, pp. 285-6 (his homily based on 1 Samuel 16:13, "Then Samuel took the horn of oil...").

appears to be much more significant than any Protestant ecclesiology. Any attempt to reconcile such Russian Baptist views with the Protestant concept of the "royal priesthood" of all believers is, at the least, problematic.[141] In fact, what was being espoused was a marked division between Baptist "clergy" and "laity", very similar to the Orthodox Church approach. Such a tendency impelled ministers of the brotherhood of the ECB to lay more and more stress on laying-on of hands.

In 1976 an unusual incident took place which underlined the growing Russian Baptist reverence for laying on of hands. The incident took place in Geneva, during an international and ecumenical Christian Conference. The General Secretary of the AUCECB, A.M. Bychkov, met with the famous Orthodox Archbishop John (Shakhovskoy) of San Francisco.[142] Bychkov had expressed his appreciation and admiration for the Christian radio broadcasts transmitted in "The Voice of America", which Archbishop John led for many years. Then – as Bychkov recorded in his memoirs, which were later published – they talked with enthusiasm for about an hour, in private, on spiritual topics.[143] It was at the end of the meeting that something unexpected and indeed quite amazing happened. Archbishop John said (I quote from Bychkov's memoirs): "'God bless you. Allow me also to bless you.' He put his hand upon my head and prayed. Then he thanked me for the periodical *Bratsky Vestnik*... I wished him God's blessings in his preaching of the Gospel, and then we parted."[144] The authoritative Orthodox Archbishop, who was then in his declining years, of his own accord blessed with prayer and laying on of hands one of the two AUCECB leader,[145] and the Baptist senior presbyter gratefully accepted the blessing. Later the account of the episode was published by Bychkov, showing that he did not want it kept secret. A blessing of this kind cannot be regarded as equivalent to what took place in ordination, but it does illustrate the extent

---

141. See, for instance, R. Beermann, "The Baptists and Soviet Society", *Soviet Studies*, Vol. 20, 1 (1968), p. 77.

142. Archbishop John (Shahovskoy) belonged to the autocephalous Russian Orthodox Church in America.

143. See Bychkov, *Moy Zhiznenny Put'*, pp. 176-8.

144. Ibid., p. 178.

145. At that time, the President of the AUCECB was A.E. Klimenko.

of the spiritual affinity that existed at that time between Orthodoxy and Russian Baptists. It is also significant that in the mystical rite of laying on of hands it was the Orthodox Archbishop who blessed the Baptist.

In Baptist ordinations, however, the laying on of hands was not by a single authoritative figure, but by a group of presbyters. A traditional hymn used among the ECB at services of ordination included the following prayer, invoking God's power as "we" lay on "our" hands:

> We lay our hands on our brother
> And beseech You, 'Bless him!'...
> Come as an invisible guest,
> Lay Your hands on him.[146]

The last line was not, for Russian Baptists, merely pictorial language. The author of the hymn and those who sang it considered God's blessing as something real, as a mystical divine presence – that of the "invisible guest" – in the sacrament, and thus it could properly be said: "Lay Your hands on him…" This can be compared with Metropolitan Makary's words from his textbook of dogmatics, "Man performs the laying on of hands, but God does everything, and His hand touches the head of the person who is being ordained."[147] The Lord's "anointing", or a special spiritual gift, was believed to be given through the laying of hands of other presbyters. Therefore, any election to ministry among Soviet Baptists, for all the formal importance of such a procedure, could not replace the sacrament itself (the ordination). Such views were sung about as well as being affirmed by authoritative teachers.

This approach to ordination and ministry represented a development over time. The tradition of the Evangelical Christians had not seen the ordination of ministers as obligatory (indeed at times had opposed this view), but that perspective gave way to the high view of ministry which was increasingly promoted by the Russian Baptists and which was the dominant position after the two Unions united in 1944.

---

146. *SDP*, no. 337, p. 228.
147. Makary, *Pravoslavno-dogmaticheskoe bogoslovie*, vol. II. p. 492.

The Statutes of 1944 read:

> "All congregations of Evangelical Christians and Baptists, as
> far as possible, ought to have ordained presbyters and deacons,
> in accordance with God's Word."[148]

With the high office of presbyter came serious responsibility. There
could be divine judgment on preachers who were unfaithful to their calling. According to one Russian Baptist account, a preacher in the Soviet
period was punished by instantaneous death for loose behavior in the pulpit.[149] A former minister of the CCECB, L.E. Kovalenko, commented that
the pulpit in prayer houses was always considered "holy ground".[150] The
work of the presbyter was in fact linked with all the "holy ordinances" in
the church, not only with preaching. It was the presbyter who baptized,
who tested people for membership, who presided at the Lord's Supper,
and who led the church in prayer. As one Russian Baptist presbyter put
it, "First of all, let us pray, since there is a house of prayer here, not first
of all the house of sermon."[151] This was arguably a monastic rather than
a classically Protestant view.[152] It placed the ordained presbyter in direct
contact with the divine. This was combined with the idea of "succession"
to create an elevated view of ordained ministry. The following proposition
from Kolesnikov sums of a prevailing view which came to prominence,
appearing more frequently among Russian Baptists in the later 1980s.
Kolesnikov said: "Laying-on of hands is a continuation of the succession
in ministry."[153]

---

148. Clause 7 of the Statutes of the Union of Evangelical Christians-Baptists (1944),
ARSECB, F. 1, op. 11da, d. 54, l. 6.

149. Testimony of Baptist presbyter V.N. Khot'ko (Petropavlovsk, Kazakhstan, 2000).

150. INT, Sacramento, California, USA, 2006.

151. Testimony of presbyter S.Yu. Sipko (Omsk, Russia, 2009).

152. Cf. the traditional monastic approach to the matter: "Prayer is above all... The
significance of prayer... is possibly even higher than preaching." – Cited in N. Pestov,
Sovremennaya Praktika Pravoslavnogo Blagochestiya [The Contemporary Practice of
Orthodox Piety], 4 vols. (SPb.: Satis, 1995), vol. II, p. 288.

153. See, for instance: *BV*, no. 4 (1986), p. 72.

Consecration of a House of Prayer

A further "holy ordinance" in the list offered by Kolesnikov was the consecration (*osvyashchenie*) of houses of prayer. Where Christians assembled, there was "prayer-filled", "holy" ground, conditioned as such by God's presence. *Bratsky Vestnik,* had this typical statement in 1981 from a consecration: "The choir has chanted the hymn 'Here is holy ground', preparing the souls of those present for the moment of consecration... The house where people worship God and where he dwells is holy ground."[154] Russian Baptist church thinking and practice in this area had close connections with the ancient Orthodox idea of *sacred space.*[155] The sanctity of the walls themselves in Baptist prayer houses was emphasized by the reverently written "words of eternal life" on the walls. These were concise but crucially important biblical verses, which fully reflected the spiritual and moral priorities of the brotherhood of the ECB: for example, "God is love", "We preach Christ crucified", or "Go, and sin no more". Such wall tablets, lovingly painted and periodically renewed, can be seen as being, at least to some extent, a substitute for icons. In these texts a vital component of Baptist sacred space was expressed. The Word of God was visible: painted in oil, the words pointed to God the invisible, present in the church by the Spirit. The Russian Baptists' spiritual feelings about their buildings are borne out in reports from the time of the destruction of prayer houses in the period of Khrushchev's attack on religion. The reports spoke of Baptists risking arrest or the possibility of being run over by bulldozers, as they rescued items from their prayer houses, including the tablets with God's words written on them.[156]

---

154. "From the Life of the Local Churches", *BV,* no. 4 (1981), p. 66. Older preachers loved to quote in this connection the text: "How awesome is this place! This is none other than the house of God, ...the gate of heaven" (Gen 28:17). See, for instance: Kolesnikov, *V Pomoshch' Propovedniku,* vol. I, pp. 211, 408-9.

155. See, for instance, A. Lidov, ed., *Ierotopiya: Issledovanie Sakral'nykh Prostranstv* [Hierotopy: Study of Sacral Spaces] (M.: Radunitsa, 2004); D. Arabadzhi, *Ocherki Khristianskogo Simvolizma* [Essays on Christian Symbolism] (Odessa: Druk, 2008).

156. For instance, the testimony of a Baptist evangelist from Dushanbe, P.A. Semeryuk (INT, Sacramento, California, USA, 2006). See also: *Khristova Tserkov' Est' Sobranie Krestom Iskuplennykh Lyudey: 90-letie Petropavlovskoy Tserkvi ECB* [Christ's Church is the Assembly of Atoned-for People: The 90th Anniversary of the Petropavlovsk church of the

Many reports in *Bratsky Vestnik* in the 1980s indicated how the consecration of buildings was seen not as a formal act, but as a sacramental one.[157]

> From the life of the local churches, Bryansk Region, the city of Dyat'kovo. ...Here the consecration of the new house of prayer took place... The choir singers chanted a solemn hymn 'How lovely are Thy dwelling places, O Lord of hosts'. Then the presbyter read Solomon's prayer of dedication of the Temple in Jerusalem (1 Kings 8), and then the church ministers prayed for the consecration.[158]

> The city of Nikolaev. ...The high point of the feast came. The three presbyters, standing near the pulpit, read Solomon's prayer from 2 Chronicles 6:14-42. Then... the presbyters, lifting their hands up, besought the Lord for the consecration of the house of prayer. All the church was also earnestly praying to God.[159]

In the majority of cases, the Russian Baptists' acts of consecration of buildings suggested the "Temple" theme – that here the presence of God was going to be found. The conduct of authentic divine worship was to be done in the awareness of the reality, the internal mystical reality, that God really did dwell in the Russian Baptist houses of prayer. Kolesnikov, elucidating the understanding of this particular "holy ordinance" by Russian Baptists, emphasizes the literal way in which consecration was understood:

> All the newly built... houses of prayer have to be consecrated and dedicated to the Lord... Does the service which we perform really mean *consecration*? Yes, absolutely... We believe,

---

ECB] (Petropavlovsk, 1998), pp. 7-8.

157. For the consecration of houses of prayer as *svyashchennodeystvie*, see, for example, *BV*, no. 2 (1986), p. 74.

158. *BV*, no. 6 (1986), p. 70.

159. *BV*, no. 1 (1987), p. 78.

we humble ourselves, and we are seeking God's favor… to hear His word, 'I have heard your prayer and your supplication… I have consecrated this house…' (1 Kings 9:3).[160]

The well-known minister, M.V. Vanin, who had been a leader of the Union of Evangelical Christians, and was a long-term prisoner for his faith (and was at one time proposed as head of the movement started by the Initiative Group: a position he refused),[161] spoke powerfully about the essence of consecration.

> What is the essence of consecration?.. 'Moses! Put off thy shoes from off thy feet…' It did not come into Moses' mind that the ground on which he stood was sacred. It was no different from the surrounding earth… The sanctity of the ground on which Moses stood was because God set foot on it… Everything the Holy God touches becomes consecrated… Moses was shown the Tabernacle sample… which he had to construct for divine service… The suitable materials (wool, cloth, gold, silver, etc.) …put together in the single whole structure, could not be named holy. Only when the Lord descended in the cloud… from that point the Tabernacle became holy… became His house… The essence of consecration is in the touch of God. Everything God touches becomes consecrated.[162]

It was this sense of the need for the building to be touched by God which was the reason for the action of consecration of the space for divine service. This included all the components of the building itself, as well as the items inside.

---

160. Kolesnikov, *Khristianin, znaesh' li ty*, vol. I, p. 60.

161. See, for instance: Yu. Kryuchkov, *Vnutritserkovnoe Dvizhenie ECB v Byvshem Sovetskom Soyuze* [Within the Church Movement of the ECB in the Former Soviet Union] (Sacramento, CA: n.p., 2001), pp. 43-4. Also testimony of B.M. Zdorovets (INT, Spokane, Washington, USA, 2006).

162. M. Vanin, "*Osvyashchenie*" [Consecration], *BV*, no. 2 (1964), p. 46.

In the light of this understanding of the sanctuary, it is not surprising that the Soviet Baptist view of the prayer house meant that it was not permissible to joke and laugh there.[163] Indeed it was not acceptable to do much talking in the Lord's house, even if no church service was being held. Even if somebody was holding an appropriate spiritual conversation, it should be done quietly, in a low voice. Among other customs and rules, coming into church with any animals was prohibited. It is a highly probable that this custom goes back to old Orthodox tradition based on the 88th canon of the Sixth Ecumenical Council, "Let no one introduce into a sacred temple any beast whatsoever."[164]

It was noticeable that older Baptists, before occupying a seat in the church at the beginning of a service, asked God's blessing on it. Any items belonging to the church – cups, communion table, pews, treasury, etc. – were seen as "holy", and must be used only "according to its intended purpose".[165] It was known that Russian Baptists, in spite of their normal benevolence and readiness to help their neighbors, often refused unbelievers, even those regarded as good neighbors, who asked (for example) to borrow pews from the prayer house for a secular celebration such as of a wedding, or a birthday.[166] They would also refuse to lend church musical instruments for performance of "worldly" songs, stating that "our instruments are devoted to the Lord".[167] The 73rd Apostolic canon and the 10th canon of the Constantinopolitan Council of 861 utterly forbad the use of

---

163. Sports were not allowed. I remember the shock felt by a small Russian evangelical congregation in the *perestroika* period when they saw their guests, young American Baptists, playing ping-pong in the sanctuary.

164. *Pravila Pravoslavnoy Tserkvi*, vol. I, p. 582. Cf. with modern regulations of the Russian Orthodox Church, "One cannot come into a church with animals or birds". – *Povedenie v Khrame* [Church Behaviour], ed. by S. Burenin (Rostov-na-Donu: Feniks, 2007), p. 74.

165. Kolesnikov, *Khristianin, znaesh' li ty*, vol. I, pp. 72-3; *V Pomoshch' Propovedniku*, vol. II, pp. 383-4.

166. Testimony of presbyter L.I. Mikhovich (Minsk, Belarus, 2008).

167. See, for instance, S. Ryzhenko, *Stranniki My Na Zemle. Istoriya Petropavlovskoy Obshchiny ECB, 1908-1988* [We are Strangers on the Earth. Chronicle of the Petropavlovsk Community of the ECB, 1908-1988] (Petropavlovsk – Steinhagen: Samenkorn, 2008), p. 138.

any pieces of church property for personal needs.[168] The reverence for the sanctuary found among Russian Baptists mirrored Orthodox tradition.

Russian Baptists could also consider sacred space much more widely. They were not bounded by the church walls, despite their reverence for their buildings. Thus, when someone was cut off from the congregation and the building in which worship took place, God was nevertheless still to be found. It was possible for persecuted believers to find a place for prayer – "holy ground" – even in a prison cell.[169] However, it was better not to use for the purpose of divine services any clubhouses or cinemas, sometimes referred to as places containing the "devil's playthings".[170] Buildings could be inhabited by God or could be inhabited by evil. In the case of dwelling houses, Russian Baptists (like their Orthodox counterparts) usually invited their presbyters (in the case of the Orthodox, the priest) to pray for a new home, perhaps one which they had moved into, and to pray that there would be no evil spirits present in the home. This was not seen as exorcism, but rather as a prayer for protection. The open space was also seen as God's dwelling. For many Russian Baptist congregations it was better to baptize people in a lake or a river rather than a baptistery, since the setting was the natural world, made by the Creator. The sense of outdoor space as sacred is conveyed in this *Bratsky Vestnik* report in 1988:

> From the life of the local churches, in the city of Petropavlovsk. …G.I. Mazaev lived a distance of 90 kilometers from Petropavlovsk… His workers were mainly believers. The Mazaev farm had a Sunday school and weekly prayer services. The local population said, 'There is holy ground for seven versts in this neighborhood'.[171]

Probably the "local population" mentioned here was Russian Orthodox. So these people freely used the common expressions "holy ground" and

---

168. See *Pravila Pravoslavnoy Tserkvi*, vol. I, p. 154, vol. II, pp. 302-3.

169. See testimony on the subject in Bondarenko, *Tri Prigovora*, p. 167.

170. Though during *perestroika*, the meetings of new Baptist congregations often took place in rented clubhouses and cinemas, older believers usually resisted this practice.

171. *BV*, no. 5 (1988), p. 94. *Versta* is an old Russian unit of distance equal to 0.66 mile.

"for seven versts".[172] A connection can be made with the well-known words by Russian classical writer N.V. Gogol about his journey to the monastery *Optina Pustyn*: "Grace is present there visibly… Several versts away from the monastery, moving towards it, you already feel its fragrance."[173] What is noteworthy in this case is that *Bratsky Vestnik* repeated traditional Orthodox words with pleasure, because they were delighted that they had been said about an eminent leader of the Baptist brotherhood. This is further evidence of the considerable mental similarity between the Russian Baptists and the Orthodox believers.

There were several important facets to the "essence of consecration" of prayer houses in the tradition of the Russian Baptists. As noted, there was the sanctity of the building, of the walls of the prayer house, within which a person should act seriously. The pulpit was "holy ground". Any part of consecrated space was to be seen as "prayer-filled". To be there was to be "blessed" and simultaneously to consider God as "awesome": truly "God dwells" there. Even the most simple items in church inevitably become "holy". The Eastern Christian concept of a literal "touch of God" can be seen in the Russian Baptist approach to consecration. Russian Baptists were in tune with the following words of a famous Orthodox bishop: "All that comes from God, or whatever His grace-filled power touches, becomes sanctified and sacred. That is why the Scripture, which is the Word of God, is sacred; God's churches are sacred, prayers are sacred, as are sacraments and services of the church. Angels, Prophets, Apostles and other bearers of God's grace are holy. People and things… also become sanctified."[174] The Russian Baptist "holy ordinances" fitted in this framework.

---

172. We see here the sacred number "7".

173. Letter to A.P. Tolstoy, in N. Gogol, *Polnoe Sobranie Sochineniy* [Complete Works], 14 vols. (M.: Izd-vo AN SSSR, 1952), vol. XIV, p. 194.

174. Bishop Alexander (Mileant), "Thoughts about the Kingdom of God, or the Church", *Missionary Leaflet*, no. 83 (1999).

The sacraments of human life

"People… also become sanctified." The Russian Baptists thought of the "holy ordinances" as having a crucial part to play at the most important stages in human experience. In Kolesnikov's list of ordinances (quoted above), after water baptism, the Lord's Supper and ordination, Kolesnikov mentioned marriage. He also wrote: "I believe that marriage is a holy ordinance which is identical with baptism, the Lord's Supper, and others."[175] The holy ordinance of *marriage*, in traditional Russian Baptist theology, was an ontological union of two believers transfiguring into "one flesh" (spiritually and physically), to be a "household church". So bridegroom and bride must have the same beliefs,[176] and when they had children their aim was to form their children in the faith. Khrapov, the CCECB leader, wrote: "The marriage of a believer and an unbeliever is sin." He asked how one should proceed when unbelievers asked Baptist presbyters to officiate at a marriage ceremony, and replied that the church's "sacraments are not to be sold".[177] Thus, marriage was unambiguously termed a sacrament. For Russian Baptists a "genuine" wedding could only be at church, and any kind of "worldly" marriage was "sin". A traditional Russian Baptist wedding hymn says,

> O God, here are the groom and bride
> Before You, according to Your will…
> Lay Your hand on them.
> To bless their holy union,
> May You lead them into good ways.[178]

The wedding prayer "Lay Your hands on them", which parallels the ordination prayer, "Lay Your hands on him", is not a literary trope, but a call for God's real presence, to be received by the laying-on of the hands

---

175. Kolesnikov, *Khristianin, znaesh' li ty*, vol. I, p. 55.
176. In practice, this meant being Baptists.
177. Khrapov, *Dom Bozhy*, <http://www.blagovestnik.org/books/00280.htm#81>
178. *SDP*, no. 333, pp. 224-5.

of the presbyters prayerfully performing the holy ordinance. Divorce was unacceptable in traditional Russian Baptist communities. Even in the case of adultery, Soviet Baptists did not usually advocate divorce. The unfaithful partner was seen as a morally sick person who needed recovery. Excommunication of an unfaithful spouse took place, but the couple were encouraged to stay together.[179] Marriage, as a sacrament, was permanent.

Another ordinance or sacrament related to stages in human life was *prayer for the blessing of infants*. The logic of this ordinance in Russian Baptist church life was the following. Jesus Christ himself was circumcised in infancy, which is the traditional analogue of infant baptism in Orthodoxy,[180] but it was as an adult that he was voluntarily baptized. Kolesnikov, typically, pointed out that Christ did not baptize children brought to him, nor did he command his disciples to baptize them, but rather he blessed them (Matt 19:13-15; Mark 10:13-16; Luke 18:15-17). Consequently, Kolesnikov argued, the blessing of children by a minister of God, with the laying on of hands, was a holy ordinance established by our Lord Jesus Christ.[181] Khrapov and others in the CCECB held to similar views. Through prayer, a gracious spiritual seed was planted in the souls of infants, which enabled them to grow in faith in Christ. The sacramental dimension in the Russian Baptist blessing of children drew something from traditional Orthodox thinking about infant baptism. Aspects of Orthodox practice were also followed. Many infants born into Russian Baptist families were solemnly blessed at church on the 40th day after their birth.[182] Although it was not considered that blessing ensured salvation, in the case of early death such infants were believed to be saved.[183] Also, children did not properly become members of Baptist churches through the prayer of

---

179. See, for instance: Khrapov, *Dom Bozhy*, <http://www.blagovestnik.org/books/00280. htm#85>. See also: V. Nemtsev, *Soyuz Lyubvi* [The Love Union] (Minsk: "Probuzhdenie", 2002), pp. 374-9.

180. "...If in the Old Testament God considered infants to be able to make covenant with God, why deprive them of this benefit in the New Testament?" – Makary, *Pravoslavno-dogmaticheskoe bogoslovie*, vol. II, p. 338.

181. Kolesnikov, *Khristianin, znaesh' li ty*, vol. I, pp. 55-6.

182. See, for instance: Khrapov, *Dom Bozhy*, <http://www. blagovestnik.org/books/00280. htm#86>

183. There were also some superstitions relating to this subject. I return to this in chapter 7.

blessing. Later they had to make a deliberate choice: either to remain part of the believing community or to reject the blessing granted in infancy.[184]

Kolesnikov summed up his theology of infant blessing in this way.

> Blessing is asked at the beginning of every deed. So, the blessing of children should be done in their infancy… Infant baptism does not correspond to the Scripture, but children cannot remain outside of spiritual communion, which is the ministry of blessing children that we have. It should be taught and observed so that the people of God would not be deprived of blessing… Christ himself commanded, 'Suffer the little children, and forbid them not, to come unto me' (Matt 19:14).[185]

The reference to children as being brought into "spiritual communion" is significant. What was in view was a life-time of blessing, of which baptism and entry into the local church as a member were part. This blessing was often understood as both spiritual and physical. The following report from a presbyter is typical for Russian Baptists: "Once a baby was brought to me for blessing. They asked, 'Please, bless him!' I answered those parents, 'Who am I to bless him? I can only wish your baby happiness and health, but I cannot give him anything; only God can bless…' And then they exhorted, saying, 'Yes, please, pray that God would bless!'" The presbyter continued his account. He said to the parents: "What is the difference between the church prayers of blessing from our usual prayers for children? Here is a real example: soon the same baby who was blessed fell into an open basement from a high place, and there was not a single bruise or scratch! That is how God protected him, with His grace and blessing."[186] Blessing was a powerful act. In 1988 I. Gnida stated: "Evangelical Christians-Baptists do

---

184. See details in C. Prokhorov, "On Several Peculiarities of the Understanding of Baptism in the Russian Baptist Church", pp. 102-4.

185. Kolesnikov, *Khristianin, znaesh' li ty*, vol. I, p. 56.

186. Testimony of a presbyter from Rostov, M.P. Zakharov (INT, Sacramento, California, USA, 2006).

not baptize infants, but... there is prayer for them and a consecrating of them to the Lord."[187]

However, in Russian Baptist communities the prayer and consecration was followed by many other actions to confirm the direction of the child's life and the way in which he or she developed as a young person. There was a strong church and family environment and atmosphere, in which a child unconsciously or consciously memorized fragments of Christian hymns, sermons and prayers, had a sensation of the solemnity of divine worship, and acquired believing friends in the community. Therefore children quite often felt exhilarated by regular attendance at church, even though there were many things said and done in the services which they did not understand. It was certainly true to say, as Russian Baptist ministers often did, that "Baptists deny infant baptism, professing the *conscious, deliberate* baptism by personal faith [in Christ]."[188] In practice it was the case that only "*adult people, who have experienced the new birth*" were baptized.[189] But this is not the full story. The subconscious emotional impulses that are present in childhood were channelled in certain ways in the Russian Baptist brotherhood. Children in their community became involved in the Christian way of life early. Thus conflict flared up between Russian Baptists and the Soviet State in the early 1960s, when the authorities attempted to restrict (or even forbid) attendance at church services by children. Many parents defied the officials, and some were imprisoned, but finally they succeeded in asserting the right to have their children in church.[190] In Orthodoxy infant baptism was seen as bringing infants into the church; in Baptist life the blessing of infants was a comparable ordinance.

Under the ordinance of praying for children a link was made to another dimension of prayer in human experience – *prayer for the sick*, accompanied

---

187. Gnida, *Tserkovnye ustanovleniya*, p. 76.

188. V. Popov, *Khristiane Baptisty v Rossii: Istoriya i Sovremennost'* [Christians-Baptists in Russia: History and the Present], <http://baptist.org.ru/go/history> accessed 4 September 2009. See also: Rogozin, *Otkuda vse eto poyavilos'*, pp. 70-1; *Osnovnye Printsipy Very Evangel'skikh Khristian – Baptistov*, pp. 112-6.

189. *Evangel'skie Khristiane-Baptisty: 140 Let v Rossii*, p. 7; "Verouchenie Evangel'skikh Khristian – Baptistov", *BV*, no. 4 (1985), p. 46.

190. See, for instance: Savinsky, *Istoriya (1917-1967)*, pp. 204-7; [Anon], *"Poydem s Maloletnimi Nashimi…"* ["We will go with our Young…"], *BV*, no. 1 (2001), pp. 38-40.

by anointing with oil. This was based on the biblical texts James 5:14-15 and Mark 6:12-13,[191] and this rite was often interpreted in a sacramental way. Kolesnikov wrote: "Olive oil, first prayed over by presbyters, can be used for the anointing. The sanctified oil is to be used for the holy ordinances only, that is for the anointing of the sick."[192] The former senior presbyter of Krasnodar Territory, Ya.A. Grinchenko, also spoke about the practice of the sanctification of oil before the ordinance of the anointing of the sick, adding that Baptist presbyters in the USSR used in this ceremony not only olive oil (which was a rarity in the USSR) but also sunflower oil.[193] Kolesnikov mentioned in this connection "any vegetable oil", emphasizing also the part played by the faith of the sick person and of the presbyters who were taking part in what he called the holy ordinance of anointing and prayer for cure.[194] In an interview, one of the former leaders of the CCECB, a presbyter from Sukhumi, D.I. Chueshkov, spoke at length about the efficacy of the ordinance and openly paralleled it with the Orthodox sacrament of anointing with oil.[195] In a series of interviews, all of the long-standing Russian Baptist ministers and church members spoke about the prayers made for the sick, with the anointing of oil, very positively.[196]

The last of the seven sacraments found in Russian Baptist life is *burial*.[197] Life began and ended with sacraments. In the previous chapter of this study the Russian Baptist understanding of the subject of eternity was explored. At the time of what was seen as a gracious and mysterious transition of a Christian from this life to eternity, the ceremony of burial takes place. Why did this act of burial become a distinctive holy ordinance in traditional Russian Baptist churches? It should be noted here that burial was also sometimes considered as a genuine sacrament in the ancient

---

191. See Kolesnikov, *Khristianin, znaesh' li ty*, vol. I, pp. 56-7.

192. Gnida, *Tserkovnye ustanovleniya*, p. 78.

193. Ya.A. Grinchenko (INT, Sacramento, California, USA, 2006).

194. Kolesnikov, *Khristianin, znaesh' li ty*, vol. I, pp. 57-8.

195. D.I. Chueshkov (INT, Seattle, Washington, USA, 2006).

196. For instance, these are also testimonies of: P.A. Chumakin (INT, Kent, Washington, USA, 2006), V.P. Litovchenko (INT, Los Angeles, California, USA, 2006), L.E. Kovalenko (INT, Sacramento, California, USA, 2006), and others.

197. See, for instance, Kolesnikov, *Khristianin, znaesh' li ty*, vol. I, pp. 61-3.

Eastern Christian tradition. For instance, St. Dionysius the Areopagite and St. Theodore the Studite held that opinion.[198]

Kolesnikov wrote about the service appropriate for a believer and stressed the Christian hope of life beyond death:

> ...It is necessary to create an atmosphere of recollection of the life, ministry, good works and deeds of the departed... Even if he was not a church minister... he was a lamp for his family circle... The existence of a man does not cease after death.[199]

Before burial, as a rule, there was a special divine service, in which Russian Baptist preachers spoke about the frailty of human life on earth and about the eternal heavenly dwelling places.[200] An important part of this service was mourning songs, which were usually also influenced by Orthodox traditional melodies (so-called *otpevanie*). One of the most famous Soviet Baptist composers, N.I. Vysotsky wrote in *Bratsky Vestnik*:

> ...We should be cautious in selecting and singing our songs: any lilting tunes... do not fit well with such a time; they are incompatible with our respect for the memory of the deceased... At the same time, the Orthodox songs such as *With the Saints Give Rest* or *Memory Eternal*, and others, fit the situation very well.[201]

Thus, burial in the Russian Baptist tradition was a tranquil event and also a melancholy event, accompanied by inescapable tears, and yet also offering spiritual consolation through the prayers, songs and words of the congregation. There was a strong trust and a firm hope of seeing a departed neighbor in heaven soon. This was marked by the holy ordinance of burial.

---

198. See, for instance, Malkov, *Vvedenie v Liturgicheskoe Predanie*, p. 15.

199. Kolesnikov, *Khristianin, znaesh' li ty*, vol. I, p. 63.

200. See, for instance: Khrapov, *Dom Bozhy*, <http://www.blagovestnik.org/books/00280. htm#88>.

201. N. Vysotsky, *"Znachenie i Sila Dukhovnoy Muzyki"* [The Meaning and Power of Religious Music], *BV*, no. 5 (1978), pp. 61-2.

Conclusion

This chapter has argued that in the period after World War II, and especially from the 1960s to the 1980s, Soviet Baptists were moving by degrees towards a more sacramental theology and to appropriate church practices that expressed this theology. Whereas the traditional Russian Baptist view of the ordinances had been that there were two – baptism and the Lord's Supper – by the 1960s seven ordinances were being listed, and the language of sacrament was being used. This process owed much to the shift of Baptist ecclesial ideas in Russia in this period from the more customary "international" Protestant view to a mainly national, "Russian path". Such tendencies were already there in incipient form because of the historically established great predominance of the Russian Orthodox faith in the country. The links between Orthodoxy and Russian Baptists were especially notable during the extreme Communist pressure against all kind of believers. Russian Baptists found themselves expressing sacramental ideas that were standard within Orthodoxy. Their views of baptism, entry into the church, the Lord's Supper, ministerial ordination, consecration of buildings, marriage, prayers for children and for the sick, and burial, all contain elements found in Orthodox practice. These sacraments were vehicles of divine blessing. Thus baptism, to take a typical example, was viewed as a "necessary element of salvation", i.e. salvation was not only through repentance, but through "faith expressed in repentance and baptism".[202] In the post-WWII decades the influence on Russian Baptists from Baptist life elsewhere lessened, as international contacts were restricted by the government. In this period a distinctive Russian Baptist understanding of the church and of seven sacraments was developed. A high point of "Baptist sacramentalism" appeared to be reached in the 1980s. In the period of

---

202. Modern Russian Baptist followers of the sacramental line explain it in this way, "Just as the two natures of Christ cannot be confounded or separated without detriment to the truth, so salvation is unconfounded and inseparable, and obtains fullness from repentance and baptism. Although outwardly it appears pious to emphasize the deity of Christ, if such emphasis does injustice to Christ's humanity, we immediately do not have piety, but 'blind in one eye' Monophysitism. Likewise, the fullness of salvation is in repentance and baptism, not in repentance only (and not in baptism only)." – See more details in C. Prokhorov, "On Several Peculiarities of the Understanding of Baptism in the Russian Baptist Church", pp. 89-105.

perestroika, a new non-sacramental theological tendency, promoted by numerous American evangelical missionaries and preachers, started to have an appreciable influence in Russia. But in the decades under review a creative spiritual framework, reflecting several crucial themes to be found in Orthodoxy, characterized Russian Baptist ecclesial life.

CHAPTER 5

Orthodoxy and Baptist Liturgy

The liturgical practices of the Russian Orthodox Church and the Soviet Baptist congregations differed significantly from each other in their outward form. On the one hand there is the magnificent and solemn Byzantine divine service (*sluzhba*), which incorporates many ancient liturgical rites and historic sequences of prayers. On the other hand, in a typical Russian Baptist gathering (*sobranie*) there was typically an aesthetically modest form of worship, in which any ceremonialism was rejected in favor of what was seen as a simple, but deep expression of communal spirituality. However, such a perspective does not take account of many areas in which there were Russian Orthodox-Baptist commonalities. As in the case of the theology, the ecclesiology and the sacramental practice that were examined in the previous two chapters, when Orthodox and Baptist liturgies are probed at greater depth, new discoveries are made. This chapter examines liturgical issues through an analysis of the liturgical year, including the basic feasts found in Russian Baptist communities; the liturgical order that was observed in Baptist services; the key prayers and psalms that Soviet Baptists used in their worship; what I would term ceremonial objects and acts; and the use by Russian Baptists of the Bible. In each of these areas, on the basis of the evidence examined, I wish to propose that Soviet Baptist worship exhibited traits found in Orthodoxy to a greater extent than might be supposed.

The Liturgical Year

As a rule, those who write about Orthodox liturgical practice place emphasis on the three chronological cycles: the daily circle (with vespers in the evening, matins in the morning, and the liturgy in the daytime), the weekly circle (every day of the week is connected with a specific liturgical theme), and the yearly circle (the fixed and moveable feasts).[1] This section of the chapter looks at the liturgical year, and in Russian Baptist observance there are remarkable similarities to the Orthodox yearly cycle. The liturgical year of the Soviet Baptists included many Orthodox feasts. A list of the number of special days observed by the Soviet Baptists shows their affinity with the Eastern Christian tradition. It is possible in some Western countries to find Baptist churches in which the only evidence of awareness of the "Christian year" is that Easter and Christmas are celebrated.[2] It is also possible, on the other hand, to find Baptists, for example in Britain, who advocate (and practice) the giving of serious attention to the Christian year.[3] Thus in Baptist communities across the world, and even within communities in a single country, the situation in relation to liturgical awareness in worship is varied.[4] In Russia, however, there was a high degree of liturgical uniformity. Here is the complete list, according to an announcement in *Bratsky Vestnik* in 1975, of the church feasts of the Russian Baptists for the following year.[5]

---

1. See, for instance, M. Krasovitskaya, *Liturgika* [Study of Liturgy] (M.: Izd-vo Pravoslavnogo Svyato-Tikhonovskogo Bogoslovskogo Instituta, 2000), p. 154; *Khristianstvo: Entsiklopedichesky Slovar'*, vol. I, p. 855.

2. Thus Gwyne Milne, as President of the Baptist Union of Australia, stated: "We celebrate Christmas. We celebrate Easter… Baptists tend to reject the church year with all its various celebrations. What is Epiphany Sunday, or Trinity Sunday or many other special holy days (holidays) of the church?" – G. Milne, Australian Baptist Ministries, <http://www.baptist.org.au/index.php?option=com_content& task=view&id=48&Itemid=8> accessed 17 November 2007.

3. J.E. Colwell, *The Rhythm of Doctrine: A Liturgical Sketch of Christian Faith and Faithfulness* (Milton Keynes: Paternoster, 2007). Colwell bases his whole approach to Christian doctrine on the Christian year.

4. For an overview, see C.J. Ellis, *Gathering: A Theology and Spirituality of Worship in the Free Church Tradition* (London: SCM Press, 2004).

5. See *Tserkovnye Prazdniki ECB na 1976 God* [Church Feasts of the ECB for 1976], *BV*, no. 6 (1975), p. 75.

New Year's Day	– January 1
Christmas Eve	– January 6 (December 24)
Christmas Day	– January 7 (December 25)
Second Day of Christmas	– January 8 (December 26)
Third Day of Christmas	– January 9 (December 27)
Baptism of the Lord	– January 19
Meeting of the Lord	– February 15
Annunciation Day	– April 7
Christ's Entry into Jerusalem (Palm Sunday)	– April 18 (11)
Holy Thursday	– April 22 (15)
Easter Day	– April 25 (18)
Second Day of Easter	– April 26 (19)
Third Day of Easter	– April 27 (20)
Ascension of the Lord	– June 3 (May 27)
Trinity Sunday	– June 13 (6)
Whit Monday	– June 14 (7)
Transfiguration of the Lord	– August 19
Harvest Feast	– September 26
Day of Unity	– October 31
New Year's Eve	– December 31

The first dates mentioned in the list (except New Year's Day), correspond to the Julian calendar and the Eastern Orthodox paschal table, which are the calendar and dates commonly used not only in the Russian Orthodox Church but also in the majority of the Russian Baptist congregations. The dates in parentheses are given according to the Gregorian calendar and the Western paschal cycle, which were not so popular among Soviet Baptists. Thus, it can be observed from this calendar that the church year of the Baptists drew from Orthodoxy to a very large extent.[6] Indeed earlier versions of the list of the Soviet Baptist feasts did not even mention dates that accorded with Western dating and Western Christian tradition.[7]

---

6. Russian Baptists usually issued their calendars based on the Russian Orthodox Church calendar, in order "not be confused" about the dates.

7. See, for instance: the feasts of the AUCECB for 1961, in *BV*, nos. 5-6 (1960), p. 124; and for 1968, in *BV*, no. 1 (1968), p. 80.

The liturgical year of the Russian Baptists, in the same way as the Orthodox liturgical year, included both fixed and moveable feasts. The first group relates to Christmas Eve and Christmas Day, the Baptism of the Lord, the Meeting of the Lord, Annunciation Day and the Transfiguration of the Lord. The dates of these feasts did not change from year to year. The second group includes Christ's Entry into Jerusalem (Palm Sunday), Holy Thursday, Easter Day, the Ascension of the Lord, Trinity Sunday and Whit Monday. The dates of such feasts, being closely connected with Easter, changed every year. Lent was not generally observed by Baptists. Looking at the church calendar of the Russian Baptists with a view to finding Baptist distinctives, it is significant that there was a preference for the so-called "feasts of the Lord" (related to the Lord Jesus Christ). Thus Baptists did not celebrate, for instance, the Nativity of the Virgin or the great Orthodox feast, the "Dormition of the Theotokos", which celebrates the death, resurrection and glorification of the Virgin Mary.[8] However, they could not completely avoid the "feasts of the Mother of God". Both the Meeting of the Lord and also Annunciation Day were traditionally days when special attention was paid to the Virgin Mary. Russian Baptists have been embarrassed by the Orthodox tendency towards "deification" of the Lord's Mother, but as a rule Soviet Baptists were respectful towards the Virgin Mary as God's chosen vessel.[9]

It is possible to gain insights into the yearly church cycle as it was observed among Soviet Baptists by looking at the traditional liturgical psalms and hymns sung and the "holiday" sermons preached among the Soviet Baptists. The services on *New Year's Day* were liturgically linked to the theme of the speed with which time passes.[10] The hymns that were used

---

8. The following dictum is popularly ascribed to Yu.K. Sipko, the ex-president of the Russian Baptist Union, "What feasts have the Russian Baptists not celebrated! Here is the Meeting of the Lord, and Palm Sunday, and Whit Monday... It seems the only one we do not observe is The Beheading of St. John the Baptist." This does not, however, tell the full story.

9. See, for example, A. Karev's articles in: *BV*, no. 1 (1960); no. 6 (1978). It was not that Baptists were ignorant of Orthodox theology. But for them worshipping Mary as divine led to (among other things) an imbalance in Christ's two natures. They wanted to stress that his human nature came from Mary.

10. See, for instance, the chapter *Na Novy God* [On the New Year] in *Sbornik Dukhovnykh Pesen*, pp. 283-95; Kolesnikov, *V Pomoshch' Propovedniku*, vol. I, p. 363.

recognized the shortness of human life, lack of knowledge about what the future (on earth) held, and, at the same time, the reality of eternity. These themes were designed to motivate people to repentance, for the first time or at a new point in their lives, and to seek to be reconciled with their Creator and Savior.[11] The first day of January usually inaugurated a week of prayer.[12] Church members would go to the churches every day during this week and pray for blessings in the year that had started. During the New Year's Day and the Christmas holidays, many Evangelical Christians-Baptists churches placed inside their buildings modestly decorated Christmas trees. The Russian Baptist divine service on Christmas Eve (*sochel'nik*) was devoted to the joyful waiting for the birth of the Infant Christ. All believers recollected the biblical magi, who were observing the stars on Christmas night, and the Jewish shepherds keeping watch over their flocks. The people gathered in the church and sang in soft tones the internationally-known hymn *Silent Night, Holy Night* (*Stille Nacht*), a hymn that was written by a Roman Catholic priest but is also associated with Western Protestant tradition.[13] Although there were elements evident on Christmas Eve that Russian Baptists shared with Western Christians, there were also traditional Orthodox customs. Young people would be sure to *kolyadovat'*, to sing Christmas carols near the doors of Christians they knew and to collect gifts in sacks, while many Baptist women, especially in rural areas, cooked *sochivo*[14] – boiled wheat with honey – according to a traditional (Orthodox) custom.

Russian Baptists celebrated the *Christmas* season for several days. The Soviet Baptist communities which observed this holiday on 25 December (the minority) generally continued their celebrations over a period of two

---

11. "How fast our days run by!" (*SDP*, no. 425, p. 283); "How fast our days are flying by in their seamless procession!" (no. 427, pp. 284-5); and "There is quiet holiday time…" (no. 431, p. 287).

12. Many Russian Baptist congregations traditionally had a divine service on the night of December 31–January 1 and welcomed the New Year kneeling in prayer. Then the week of prayer began. See, for instance, Khrapov, *Dom Bozhy*, <http://www.blagovestnik.org/books/00280.htm#73>

13. *SDP*, no. 414, p. 275. On the origin of this hymn see, for instance: R.M. Clancy, *Sacred Christmas Music: The Stories Behind the Most Beloved Songs of Devotion* (N.Y.: Sterling Publishing, 2008), pp. 92-3.

14. This word was the origin of the word *sochel'nik*.

weeks, until the Orthodox Christmas time. The hymns used during this period took up the theme of Christ's humility, the one who as God created the whole world, but as man was born in a poor stable.[15] The hymn "The Holy Angels Sang" focused on Mary, the mother of the Lord Jesus, lovingly taking care of her son.[16] One hymn of Charles Wesley's (*Hark, the Herald Angels Sing*) was often sung. The translation used in the hymnbooks of Russian Baptists is significant. The original words, "Offspring of a Virgin's womb", were translated in a way that reflected more clearly the spirit of the Russian Orthodox tradition in relation to Mary: "He was born of the most pure Virgin" (in Russian: *rozhden ot prechistoy Devy*).[17] The hymns sung also recalled the Angelic hymns and the response of the shepherds near Bethlehem,[18] the Magi from the East,[19] and the terror as King Herod slew the infants.[20] However, the main theme of the period was the eternal salvation achieved for and given to sinful humankind by Christ.[21] The common customs during the Christmas season were to give gifts to children, to act out in bright clothes some episodes of the events in Bethlehem, and to help the needy in the church and the wider community.

During the January celebration of the *Baptism of the Lord*, preachers in Russian Baptist churches usually noted that Christ himself set an example of how biblical baptism was to be conducted, since he did not receive the sacrament of baptism as a child, but was baptized at the age of 30 years.[22] The hymn sung to commemorate this event says that John the Baptist, with

---

15. "Here the Savior descended to us from heaven" (*SDP*, no. 409, p. 272); "Look, here is God's Son in the manger" (no. 410, p. 273); "Birds of the air have nests" (no. 424, pp. 282-3).

16. *SDP*, no. 419, pp. 278-9.

17. "At the end of the ages He was born of the most pure Virgin". – *SDP*, no. 412, p. 274; *PV*, no. 607, p. 388. Cf. M. Marshall, *Common Hymnsense* (Chicago: GIA Publications, Inc., 1995), p. 47.

18. *SDP*, no. 415, p. 276; no. 422, pp. 280-1; Kolesnikov, *V Pomoshch' Propovedniku*, vol. I, pp. 143-4, 356.

19. *SDP*, no. 416, pp. 276-7; no. 421, p. 280; Kolesnikov, *V Pomoshch' Propovedniku*, vol. I, pp. 414-5.

20. *SDP*, no. 407, pp. 270-1.

21. *SDP*, no. 404, p. 269; no. 405, pp. 269-70; no. 408, pp. 271-2; Kolesnikov, *V Pomoshch' Propovedniku*, vol. I, pp. 329-30.

22. See, for instance, Khrapov, *Dom Bozhy*, <http://www.blagovestnik.org/books/00280.htm#64>

a humble spirit, baptized Jesus Christ; the voice of the Father sounded out of heaven by peals of "thunder"; and the Holy Spirit descended upon Jesus as a dove.[23] In this way it was emphasized that the fullness of the Holy Trinity was revealed to people.[24] Following the example of Christ the Redeemer, all Christians should accept New Testament baptism.[25] In February Soviet Baptists celebrated the *Meeting of the Lord*, in memory of the meeting of the righteous Simeon and the prophetess Anna, with the infant Jesus and his parents in the Temple in Jerusalem (Luke 2:22-35).[26] This event was applied in a specific way: to show that "the birth of Christ was a great expectation of righteous Israelites; and that he was to be seen as salvation for all nations, the light of revelation to the Gentiles and the glory of Israel".[27] During the feast of the Meeting of the Lord, Russian Baptists traditionally sang the anthem known in Eastern and Western churches, "Lord, Now lettest Thou Thy Servant Depart in Peace",[28] and their preachers sometimes even quoted words from the Orthodox hymn for this feast, "Rejoice, thou also, O righteous Elder, as thou receivest in thine arms the Redeemer of our souls, Who also granteth unto us the Resurrection!"[29] Preachers also read from Luke 2:34-35 and interpreted the prophetic words to Mary, "A sword will pierce even your own soul", in the light of the future sufferings of Christ on Calvary.[30] Celebration of the *Annunciation Day* was connected with the event described in Luke 1:26-38: the appearance of the Angel Gabriel (often named Archangel) to the Virgin Mary, to announce that she would conceive and give birth to Jesus, the Son of God.[31] Church members

---

23. *SDP*, no. 444, pp. 295-6.

24. See Kolesnikov, *V Pomoshch' Propovedniku*, vol. I, p. 117.

25. *SDP*, no. 304, pp. 205-6; Kolesnikov, *V Pomoshch' Propovedniku*, vol. I, pp. 117-8.

26. See Kolesnikov, *V Pomoshch' Propovedniku*, vol. I, p. 354.

27. Khrapov, *Dom Bozhy*, <http://www.blagovestnik.org/books/00280.htm#65>

28. *SDP*, no. 445, p. 296; *PV*, no. 678, p. 438. I have generally used older English wording in this section.

29. For instance, the member of the AUCECB presidium I.Ya. Tatarchenko cites this, not mentioning the source and introducing it with the following words, "As a Christian song puts it…" – I. Tatarchenko, *"Sretenie Gospodne"* [The Meeting of the Lord], *BV*, no. 2 (1971), p. 42.

30. See, for instance, *"Luchshaya Uchast"* [The Best Lot] (editorial article), *VestI*, no. 2 (1983), p. 38.

31. See, for instance, Khrapov, *Dom Bozhy*, <http://www.blagovestnik.org/books/00280.

sang "My Soul Doth Magnify the Lord" (*The Magnificat*),[32] and heard sermons about the humility and obedience of Mary, who was named "highly
favored", and who became a prototype of the church.[33] Annunciation Day
was invariably celebrated by Russian Baptists, even when this feast fell in
Passion Week.

On Palm Sunday, normally known as *Christ's Entry into Jerusalem*, in
celebrating the triumphal event at the beginning of Passion Week (drawing
from Matt 21; Mark 11; Luke 19; John 12), Russian Baptist congregations joyfully sang the hymns "Hosanna"[34] and "You Bring the Palms".[35]
Preachers traditionally emphasized that Christ entered into Jerusalem sitting on a colt, not as a worldly ruler but as the King of the kingdom of
heaven, one who came to suffer for humanity. There was usually reference
to the people who sang Hosanna to him as being the people who cried out,
"Let him be crucified!" some days later.[36] Hearers were urged to make a
connection: just as Jesus entered into Jerusalem, so, the preachers stressed,
he wants to enter into the heart of everyone listening to his word in Russian
Baptist congregations.[37] Following an old Orthodox tradition, new-blown
branches of pussy willow in glass jars with water in them were placed in
many Russian Baptist churches (some members brought them to church).
The use of pussy willow (in the absence of palms) gave Palm Sunday the
name Pussy Willow Sunday (*Verbnoe*).[38]

On *Holy Thursday*, keeping a strict fast, Russian Baptists gathered together for an evening divine service and had a special Lord's Supper in
memory especially of the Last Supper of Christ with his apostles.[39] It is

htm#62>

32. *SDP*, no. 446, pp. 296-7.

33. See Kolesnikov, *V Pomoshch' Propovedniku*, vol. I, pp. 361-2.

34. *SDP*, no. 447, p. 297; *PV*, no. 674, p. 435.

35. *SDP*, no. 450, p. 299.

36. See, for instance, A. Karev, "*Osanna*" [Hosanna], *BV*, 3 (1965), pp. 18-19.

37. See Kolesnikov, *V Pomoshch' Propovedniku*, vol. I, pp. 87-8.

38. See Krasovitskaya, *Liturgika*, p. 244: "Palm trees do not grow in this country...
At this time of year in Russia, only pussy willow is new-blown, so this Sunday has the
name '*Verbnoe*'."

39. See, for instance. Khrapov, *Dom Bozhy*, <http://www.blagovestnik.org/books/00280.
htm#67>. During the Lord's Supper, Russian Baptists do not "wash the disciples' feet".
See the details in Kolesnikov, *Khristianin, znaesh' li ty*, vol. III, pp. 85-7.

noteworthy that, instead of the traditional "liturgical" text from 1 Cor 11:23-30 normally used at Russian Baptist celebrations of the Lord's Supper, the words of Christ taken directly from the Gospels (Matt 26:26-28; Luke 22:19-20) were usually read during the sacrament on that day. In the sermons and in the hymns the central themes were The Garden of Gethsemane, Judas' betrayal,[40] and the great sufferings of the Lord Jesus.[41] Singing was traditionally in a minor key, using the chants, "Lord, when your Disciples",[42] "Oh, how Sorrowful",[43] and others in similar vein. There were also, as a rule, evening meetings on Good Friday and Holy Saturday. During the Passion Week services in Baptist churches, it was considered appropriate not to use any musical instruments.[44]

On *Easter Day*, there was a very early morning divine service,[45] at dawn, in order to proceed mentally with the myrrh-bearing women to the Holy Sepulchre and to receive the joyful news about the victory of life over death.[46] The service always began with the triple singing of the ancient Orthodox hymn "Christ Risen from the Dead",[47] and the thrice-repeated Easter greeting, "Christ is Risen! – Christ is Risen Indeed!"[48] Then church members sang, "He is Alive",[49] "O Death, Where is Thy Sting?"[50] and other hymns of celebration. Preachers proclaimed the empty Sepulchre, the

---

40. There are, for instance, the following words in a traditional hymn, "Here the betrayer himself // Goes by his unsteady gait… // He betrays with words 'Hail, Rabbi!' and a kiss…" – *SDP*, no. 454, p. 302.

41. See Kolesnikov, *V Pomoshch' Propovedniku*, vol. I, pp. 67-8; "Come and see what death // was prepared for the eternal Son by our sin!" – *SDP*, no. 453, p. 301.

42. *SDP*, no. 322, p. 218.

43. *SDP*, no. 456, pp. 303-4.

44. See Khrapov, *Dom Bozhy*, <http://www.blagovestnik.org/books/00280.htm#67>. This author speaks also about the "blessed custom" of Russian Baptists to gather on the night of Holy Saturday through to Easter Sunday to read the Gospel and pray. (Ibid.)

45. In some places, Baptist Easter services started as early as 4 a.m. – Testimony of former senior presbyter from the South Kazakhstan, P.A. Chumakin (INT, Kent, Washington, USA, 2006).

46. See, for instance, Khrapov, *Dom Bozhy*, <http://www.blagovestnik.org/books/00280.htm#67>

47. *SDP*, no. 473, p. 315; *PV*, no. 623, p. 399.

48. See Khrapov, *Dom Bozhy*, <http://www.blagovestnik.org/books/00280.htm#67>

49. *SDP*, no. 478, p. 319.

50. *SDP*, no. 482, pp. 321-2.

appearances of Christ before the stunned disciples, and the radical change in the apostles' life, as they became evangelists to many nations.[51] Divine services on Easter Sunday always lasted beyond the usual time. On this Sunday, and for several subsequent days, plenty of coloured eggs and Easter cakes were to be found on the tables of Russian Baptists, as was the tradition with Orthodox Christians. Because of Orthodox associations, colouring of eggs was inadmissible for early Russian Baptists,[52] but the much-loved tradition had been restored by the later Soviet period. According to Baptist historian M.S. Karetnikova, some Soviet Baptist presbyters attempted to eradicate this old custom "as an Orthodox one" but failed.[53] Even the strict CCECB members coloured eggs at Easter.[54] In the churches, Russian Baptists celebrated Easter, as the main Christian holiday, at least over the course of three days. The Easter theme itself was present in the worship of the churches until Trinity Sunday.[55]

The *Ascension of the Lord* was celebrated on the 40th day after Easter, with the stress being placed not only on Christ being taken up into heaven but also on his commission to the apostles to go and preach to all nations (Mark 16; Luke 24, Acts 1).[56] Russian Baptists often sang the hymns, "Heaven Glorifies",[57] and "I hope for Christ gone into Heaven".[58] Traditionally the sermons included the idea of the completeness of Christ's ministry in this world, his preparation of heavenly dwelling places for believers, and the

---

51. See A. Karev, "*Voskresenie Iisusa Khrista*" [The Resurrection of Jesus Christ], *BV*, no. 2 (1966), pp. 22-3; Kolesnikov, *V Pomoshch' Propovedniku*, vol. I, pp. 174-5, 283, 401-2, 436-7.

52. See, for instance, G. Emelianov, "*Ratsionalizm na Yuge Rossii*" [Rationalism in the South of Russia], *Otechestvennye Zapiski*, no. 3 (1878), p. 222.

53. Testimony of M.S. Karetnikova (St. Petersburg, Russia, 2004).

54. See, for instance, G. Vins, *Evangelie v Uzakh* [The Gospel in Bonds] (Elkhart, IN: Russian Gospel Ministries, 1991), p. 143.

55. See Khrapov, *Dom Bozhy*, <http://www.blagovestnik.org/books/00280.htm#69>. In line with Orthodox terminology, Russian Baptists often named the first Sunday following Easter Day – *Fomino (the Thomas Sunday)*: on this day they preached about the appearance of the risen Christ to the "unbelieving" apostle Thomas (John 20:24-29). Cf. Krasovitskaya, *Liturgika*, pp. 294-6.

56. See Khrapov, *Dom Bozhy*, <http://www.blagovestnik.org/books/00280.htm#68>

57. *SDP*, no. 451, pp. 299-300.

58. *SDP*, no. 448, pp. 297-8.

necessity of continuing to evangelize all peoples.[59] This last aspect was impossible in Soviet times, but that limitation was not mentioned. *Trinity Sunday* and *Whit Monday* were solemnly observed in commemoration of the Holy Spirit descending on the apostles in Jerusalem and of the foundation of the church.[60] Church members sang "Come, Eternal Spirit",[61] "The Blazing Spirit",[62] and other hymns with similar themes. Preachers spoke about the new birth, the church growing, and ministry in the Holy Spirit.[63] On Whit Monday, as a rule, preachers emphasized the divinity of the Third Person of the Holy Trinity, a divinity shared with the Father and the Son.[64] On these days, many Baptist meeting places were decorated, mirroring Orthodox tradition, with natural flowers and green birch branches, symbolizing the renewal of the whole world by the vivifying Holy Spirit.[65]

The *Transfiguration of the Lord* was observed in memory of the event depicted by the Matthew, Mark and Luke (Matt 17; Mark 9; Luke 9). The date of celebration of the Transfiguration of the Lord was set by an old Russian Orthodox tradition.[66] Following another Orthodox tradition, Russian Baptists usually named the place of the Transfiguration of Christ – Mount Tabor.[67] That was reflected, for example, in the words of a traditional hymn that was sung by Russian Baptists, "We will stay on Tabor and follow the Lord again."[68] On Transfiguration Sunday the hymn "There, at

59. See, for instance: Kolesnikov, *V Pomoshch' Propovedniku*, vol. I, pp. 318-9, 446.

60. See A. Mitskevich, *"Deystviya Svyatogo Dukha"* [Actions of the Holy Spirit], *BV*, no. 3 (1969), p. 36; Khrapov, *Dom Bozhy*, <http://www.blagovestnik.org/books/00280.htm#69>

61. *SDP*, no. 491, pp. 327-8.

62. *SDP*, no. 494, pp. 329-30.

63. See Kolesnikov, *V Pomoshch' Propovedniku*, vol. I, pp. 148-50; I. Ivolin, *"Ogon' Svyatogo Dukha"* [The Fire of the Holy Spirit], *BV*, no. 3 (1969), pp. 45-6.

64. For instance, testimony of the ex-president of the AUCECB, V.E. Logvinenko (Odessa, Ukraine, 1995). Cf. *Khristianstvo: Entsiklopedichesky Slovar'*, vol. I, p. 498.

65. See C. Prokhorov, "Orthodoxy and Baptists in Russia: The Early Period", in I.M. Randall, ed., *Baptists and the Orthodox Church: On the Way to Understanding* (Prague: IBTS, 2003), p. 111.

66. See Krasovitskaya, *Liturgika*, p. 174; Savchenko, *Sravnitel'noe Bogoslovie*, p. 102.

67. See, for instance, S. Fadyukhin, *"O Preobrazhenii Khrista"* [On the Transfiguration of Christ], *BV*, no. 5 (1963), p. 33; Krasovitskaya, *Liturgika*, p. 174.

68. *SDP*, no. 354, p. 240; *PV*, no. 679, p. 439.

the Illuminated Summit"[69] was also sung, as well as other hymns related to the theme. Preachers usually proclaimed that Christ, although on earth, showed his disciples the Kingdom of Heaven on the Day of Transfiguration. Preachers held this out as a great encouragement for all believers.[70] The event of the Transfiguration of Christ was also seen as partly opening the door into eternity, since Moses and Elijah had appeared. As Kolesnikov put it: "God is not the God of the dead; God is not encircled by death; he is alive and there are living beings round him!"[71] Many aspects of this feast were drawn from Russian Orthodoxy.

There were other feasts that did not come from the Orthodox heritage. The *Harvest Feast* was usually observed on the last Sunday of September. This holiday has been compared with Thanksgiving Day in America, but the Russian celebration was drawn from the tradition of German Baptists and Mennonites.[72] The Harvest Feast was the day in which believers expressed gratitude to God for what had come from the fields and from vegetable gardens. However, the idea of "spiritual harvest", or the theme of eternal salvation, usually dominated.[73] One harvest hymn often sung said: "I would not want to come before the Lord's throne fruitless // I want to lead others to Jesus, if only one soul."[74] Congregations also sang: "Sow the Good Seed",[75] "The Fields are White",[76] and other songs. The church pulpit or even the whole of the meeting house was decorated with the best, specially selected fruit and vegetables, usually called "the fruit of the land".[77] In

---

69. *SDP*, no. 452, p. 300.

70. See Ya. Iordansky, "*Na Gore Dukhovnogo Preobrazheniya*" [On the Mount of Spiritual Transfiguration], *BV*, no. 5 (1967), p. 53.

71. Kolesnikov, *V Pomoshch' Propovedniku*, vol. I, pp. 350-1.

72. For instance, German historian P.M. Friesen mentions several times the traditional celebration of the Harvest Feast in the Mennonite settlements in the South of Russia in the second half of the 19th century. See P.M. Friesen, *Die Alt-Evangelische Mennonitische Bruderschaft in Russland (1789-1910) im Rahmen der Mennonitischen Gesamtgeschichte* (Halbstadt, Taurien: Raduga, 1911), S. 422, 561.

73. See Kolesnikov, *V Pomoshch' Propovedniku*, vol. I, pp. 198, 451-2; Khrapov, *Dom Bozhy*, <http://www. blagovestnik.org/books/00280.htm#74>

74. *PV*, no. 656, p. 421; *SDP*, no. 435, p. 290.

75. *SDP*, no. 238, p. 165.

76. *PV*, no. 662, p. 425.

77. See Khrapov, *Dom Bozhy*, <http://www.blagovestnik.org/books/00280.htm#74>

the handling of this "fruit" aspects of Orthodox practice were evident. The fruit was considered (by some church members) to be "blessed".[78] At the conclusion of the celebration congregations ate a common meal and food was given to the poor.

A month later the *Day of Unity* was observed. This Sunday celebration was established in connection with the joining of the Evangelical Christians and Baptists as the AUCECB in 1944.[79] During the service, the believers sang hymns such as "For the Evangelical Faith",[80] and "Endowed with Salvation".[81] Preachers spoke about Christian cohesion and accord, from various biblical texts, for example: "That they all may be one" (John 17:21), and "How good and pleasant it is when brothers live together in unity" (Ps 133.1).[82] After the painful split into two Unions in the 1960s, the theme of unity was especially poignant. The CCECB, as a rule, did not celebrate the Day of Unity.[83] With the clear exception of Harvest and the Day of Unity, all the other feasts among the Russian Baptists, whether intentionally or not, drew from ancient Orthodox traditions. N.P. Khrapov wrote: "Christ and the apostles observed feasts, so let us observe them, too".[84] Orthodox patterns clearly had a major impact on the church year of the Russian Baptists.

The Rite of Divine Service

The Baptist liturgical cycle traditionally connected with Sunday worship went from a Saturday evening service to the Sunday evening, with

---

78. For instance, testimony of Baptist minister M.V. Ivanov (Moscow, 2007). The blessing of fruit and vegetables, by prayer and holy water, was mainly performed in the Russian Orthodox Church during the Day of Transfiguration of the Lord. See, for instance, Bishop Feodosy, "*O Blagoslovenii Plodov*" [On the Blessing of Fruits], *ZhMP*, no. 9 (1971), pp. 41-3.

79. See, for instance, F. Molokanov, "*O Edinstve*" [On Unity], *BV*, nos. 5-6 (1961), p. 78.

80. *SDP*, no. 347, p. 235; *PV*, no. 185, p. 121.

81. *SDP*, no. 342, p. 232.

82. See A. Karev, "*Mysli o Edinstve Tserkvi*" [Thoughts on Church Unity], *BV*, no. 5 (1973), pp. 26-7; Kolesnikov, *V Pomoshch' Propovedniku*, vol. I, pp. 181, 410.

83. See Khrapov, *Dom Bozhy*, <http://www.blagovestnik.org/books/00280.htm#61>

84. Khrapov, *Dom Bozhy*, <http://www.blagovestnik.org/books/00280.htm#74>

services held on Sunday morning and evening. The weekly cycle in large Baptist congregations usually included divine services not only on Saturday and Sunday but also on Wednesday and Friday. The similarity with the Orthodox tradition increases as the whole week is considered. Saturday was associated in Soviet Baptist congregations with a waiting, or anticipation, of the main day, Sunday. Christ was in the realm of the dead before his resurrection.[85] This waiting on the threshold of Sunday was also partly based on the biblical day ("and the evening and the morning were the first day").[86] Sunday was liturgically connected with the theme of Christ's rising from the dead.[87] Wednesday was a prayer meeting, and some Baptists fasted on this day.[88] The Russian Orthodox tradition was of regular fasting on Wednesdays and Fridays.[89] Russian Baptists usually also kept their general church fast every Friday, and Friday also involved a meeting for Bible reading and study, perhaps with an emphasis on Christ's sufferings.[90]

Alongside the Soviet Baptist annual and weekly worship cycle, both of which drew from the Orthodox liturgical cycle, there was also a monthly cycle in Soviet Baptist divine services: whereas the Orthodox Eucharist was celebrated almost every day (except for a few days in the year),[91] among Soviet Baptists the Lord's Supper or Breaking of Bread (the meaning of which for Russian Baptists was explored in the previous chapter) was

---

85. The Orthodox Church has remembrance of the dead on Saturdays (see Krasovitskaya, *Liturgika*, pp. 46, 272). Traditional Russian Baptist churches devoted at least one Saturday a year to the memory of their church members who had "gone into eternity". For example, such a service in Omsk Central ECB Church usually takes place in December. Some Baptist congregations held this service several times a year.

86. Testimony of Baptist minister A.N. Krivorotov (Omsk, Russia, 2008).

87. See, for instance: "*Verouchenie Evangel'skikh Khristian-Baptistov*", *BV*, no. 4 (1985), p. 47; Khrapov, *Dom Bozhy*, <http://www.blagovestnik.org/books/00280.htm#70>

88. On Wednesdays, as a rule, CCECB members fasted for their personal needs. See, for instance, the testimony by a well-known Russian Baptist minister, E. Pushkov, *Ne smushchyaysya!* [Do not be Confused!] (SPb.: Bibliya Dlya Vsekh, 2010), p. 82.

89. See, Men', *Tainstvo, Slovo i Obraz: Pravoslavnoe Bogosluzhenie* [Sacrament, Word and Image: The Orthodox Divine Service] (M.: Fond imeni A. Menya, 2001), p. 247; *Khristianstvo: Entsiklopechesky Slovar'*, vol. II, p. 377.

90. Many aged Baptists, especially from the CCECB, speak about the weekly Friday fast in the Soviet times. Testimonies of: B.M. Zdorovets (INT, Spokane, Washington, USA, 2006), P.D. Karavan (INT, Sacramento, California, USA, 2006), spouses Tsvirin'ko (INT, Fresno, California, USA, 2006), and others.

91. See, for instance, A. Men', *Tainstvo, Slovo i Obraz*, pp. 67, 113.

celebrated on the first Sunday of every month, twelve times a year.[92] In Passion Week, the Holy Thursday Lord's Supper was seen as being able to replace the regular Communion in the current month (if Easter fell at the beginning of the month) or else became the thirteenth Communion of a year (if Easter was celebrated in the second half of the month). The final decision about the precise days on which the Lord's Supper was celebrated rested with the ministers of the local Baptist church.[93]

As the content and style of Russian Baptist divine services during the Soviet period is examined, one striking feature is the desire for a fixed form. There was little or no wish for change. This mirrored the value placed by Orthodoxy on keeping the liturgy unchanged. In the second half of the seventeenth century, Archpriest Avvakum opposed amendments made to the old Orthodox service books by Patriarch Nikon, who wanted to conform to Greek Orthodox standards. Avvakum uttered the legendary words regarding the old ways of worship, "Before we were born, it was set down; let it remain as it is unto the ages of ages!"[94] Russian Baptists retained this kind of outlook on religious life in no small measure. Russian Orthodox Old Believers, who became schismatic rather than accepting change, lamented: "Like cats among earthenware pots, today's editors are maltreating the Books, and, like mice, are gnawing the Sacred Writ."[95] Similarly, new Russian translations of the Bible were unfavorably compared by Russian Baptists to the Synodal Bible. One old Baptist minister pronounced, "All the new translations of the Scriptures were made without the fear of God, by absolutely unbelieving people. You are looking for a famous verse in the Holy Gospel but it is not there."[96] There was strong commitment, too, among Soviet Baptists to the traditional hymn books, *Sbornik Dukhovnykh Pesen* and *Pesn' Vozrozhdeniya* (based on Prokhanov's hymnals). A revised edition of *Pesn' Vozrozhdeniya* was produced, but this

---

92. See, for instance, A. Kadaev, "*Vecherya Gospodnya – Khleboprelomlenie*" [The Lord's Supper – Breaking of Bread], *BV*, no. 3 (1990), p. 12.

93. See, for instance, Sannikov, *Vecherya Gospodnya* [The Lord's Supper] (M.: Protestant, 1990), p. 45.

94. See S. Soloviev, *Istoriya Rossii s Drevneyshikh Vremen*, part 7, vol. XIII-XIV, p. 165.

95. Cited in F. Melnikov, *Kratkaya Istoriya Drevlepravoslavnoy Tserkvi* [A Short History of the Old Orthodox Church] (Barnaul: Izd-vo BGPU, 1999), p. 33.

96. Testimony of presbyter V.N. Khot'ko (Petropavlovsk, Kazakhstan, 2001).

aroused strong hostility. The Old Believers' spirit was felt in the words of one well-known Russian Baptist minister, Ya.G. Skornyakov, about the revised book: "What have you done! There is hardly an unspoiled song left. And these are songs which were not born yesterday... I have no doubt that you did not ask God about this... This songbook of yours has brought so much disturbance, pain, and troubles into our brotherhood... that many brethren have agreed not to use it at all... 'If you lift a word out of a song, you spoil the whole song'..."[97]

This tendency to prefer a fixed tradition was evident not only in what was read from the Bible and in what was sung, but in the whole of the Russian Baptist divine service. Because there was little in the way of written liturgy, it might appear that there was spontaneity and a "free style" in the meetings of Russian Baptists. However, they had their established order, which remained unchanged over decades.[98] The format was governed to a large extent by tradition. Though some Russian Baptist authors asserted that Baptist meetings took place in accordance with Holy Scripture,[99] the majority of them admitted that the structure of worship followed a certain tradition.[100] Thus I.S. Gnida, a member of presidium of the AUCECB, wrote:

> Divine worship... is conducted in accordance with the available directions of the Word of God and the inherited traditions... So long as church members are accustomed to the

97. Ya. Skornyakov, *Slovo k Knizhnikam Poslednego Vremeni* [A Word to the Scribes of the Last Times], <http://www.rushhohol.com/sermons/Book/ Skornyakov/Slovo_knizhnikam. doc> accessed 13 June 2008. And a presbyter from Tatarstan, N.V. Sabursky, categorically said about the old songs of the ECB, "Not poets, but the Holy Spirit himself inspired our hymns!" (INT, Minneapolis, Minnesota, USA, 2006).

98. See, for example, the section "The Rite of Divine Service of the Moscow Congregation", in I. Motorin, "*O Bogosluzhenii*" [On the Divine Service], *BV*, no. 1 (1957), IEDE-2.

99. See, for instance, A. Kadaev, "*Vecherya Gospodnya – Khleboprelomlenie*" [The Lord's Supper – Breaking of Bread], *BV*, no. 3 (1990), pp. 12-13.

100. See, for instance, Khrapov, *Dom Bozhy*, <http://www.blagovestnik.org/books/00280. htm#60>

established order of conducting divine worship and church
ordinances, any deviation can sometimes upset them.[101]

Although Gnida was ready to acknowledge the power of "inherited traditions" and "established order", his words about the effect of "deviation"
do not do justice to the strength of feeling when there were changes to
the form of worship. As an example, a presbyter of a fairly large Russian
Baptist congregation tried to make a small change to the church tradition
regarding giving greetings and prayer requests. He ("only") wanted to move
them from the end of the service to the beginning. However, his words immediately stirred up a storm in the church, and he nearly lost his position
as presbyter. The members announced: "As our forebears gave greetings
at the end of service, so we will do!" It was as if something sacred was to
be violated. Over several weeks, the presbyter mildly tried to persuade his
flock, but faced with such strong adherence to "tradition", he retreated.[102]

The greetings and the prayer requests were one part of a well-established
liturgy. Before the beginning of the divine service, in the "brothers' room",
as it was termed, the presbyter would confirm who were the preachers for
that service and what hymns were chosen for the choir and for congregational singing, following which those present would pray for blessing on
the forthcoming worship.[103] Then the presbyter walked towards the pulpit, while other ministers and preachers occupied their special seats in the
church. These were seats which, as a matter of custom, were never occupied
by "ordinary" church members. The presbyter opened the meeting with
the words, "Peace be unto you!", and a short introductory prayer. At that
point, all those in the congregation rose. The presbyter would announce a
hymn appropriate to the occasion and this was sung. Then the first anthem
from the choir was sung, with church members continuing to stand. It
seems that standing in worship ("before the face of God") was partly influenced by Orthodox liturgy. Orthodox churches usually have only a few

---

101. Gnida, *Tserkovnye ustanovleniya*, p. 72.

102. I witnessed this conflict at a Baptist church in North Kazakhstan in the early 1990s.

103. See, for instance, Khrapov, *Dom Bozhy*, <http://www.blagovestnik.org/books/00280.
htm#60>

pews.[104] After that, the presbyter invited the flock to sit and introduced the first sermon with the phrase "Let us listen to the Word of God!" A short sermon followed, as a rule, with readings from the Psalter. Typically there were three sermons. Each sermon ended with an "Amen", repeated by the whole community.[105]

After the first sermon, the presbyter introduced an extended time of prayer.[106] During that time, the majority of Russian Baptists would kneel; elderly people would pray standing.[107] Several people prayed aloud in turn. Then, the choir sang again, followed by the congregation singing. Some church members would then read poetry, sing solos or sing in groups with musical accompaniment. At the end of each item in this part of this service, all those present exclaimed, "Praise the Lord!" A second, longer-lasting sermon followed, after which the congregation did not usually pray but the choir sang right away. The task of the choir director was to choose a hymn in line with the main subject of the preacher, so that a deeper impression was made.[108] Then the congregation sang once more and a collection was taken.[109] A third sermon followed. The tradition of having three sermons was so strong that sometimes rural congregations, where there was just one preacher, forced their preacher to "proclaim the Word" three times in a meeting on different themes.[110] The third sermon was entrusted to the

---

104. In general, Russian Baptists spend a comparatively long time in church standing - during singing, prayers, greetings and the announcement of prayer requests. Some congregations even listen to any Scripture readings standing. At the same time, the sitting position during services is often justified by Russian Baptists with an Orthodox aphorism, "It is better to sit thinking about God, than to stand thinking about one's legs."

105. See Khrapov, *Dom Bozhy*, <http://www.blagovestnik.org/books/00280.htm#60>

106. See I. Motorin, "*O Bogosluzhenii*" [On the Divine Service], *BV*, no. 1 (1957), IEDE-2.

107. Soviet Baptists did not sit to pray, seeing this as almost blasphemous. A minister of the ECB, L.E. Kovalenko, commented approvingly of Orthodox practice: "Orthodox people sing piously, always standing, but some Baptists actually pray sitting…" (INT, Sacramento, California, USA, 2006).

108. See A. Keshe, "*Iz Praktiki Regentskogo Sluzheniya*" [From Practical Experience of Choir Ministry], *BV*, no. 5 (1981), p. 44.

109. See Gnida, *Tserkovnye ustanovleniya*, pp. 72-3.

110. Testimony of presbyter L.I. Mikhovich (Minsk, Belarus, 2008). The theoretical possibility that "every brother" could speak the word was limited not only by someone's ability to speak and his spiritual level but also by the necessity to conform to "the spirit of the brotherhood". This led in practice to a relatively circumscribed circle of preachers.

most respected or aged brethren. Its duration depended upon the time remaining until the end of the church service. At the end of the sermon, the church members were invited to kneel in prayer once more; and unbelievers were invited to repent. The last part of the meeting was devoted to greetings from other churches, announcements, and reading of written prayer requests. Among Russian Baptists these notes with prayer requests were given to presbyters, which mirrored the way Orthodox members gave notes to the priests.[111] The presbyter pronounced the dismissal, usually including the words, "The grace of the Lord Jesus Christ, and the love of God, and the communion of the Holy Ghost, be with you all. Amen." (2 Cor 13:14).[112] The shorter "Go in the Peace of God!" was also used. In total, these services usually lasted two hours.

It is significant, but not always noted, that well-known Russian Baptist ministers often said, "The rite of divine service can be the following…" Since the phrase used was "can be the following", rather than "should" or "must" be the following, some degree of freedom might have been expected. What followed this statement, however, was often a quite detailed description of the order of worship as found in all the churches.[113] The Russian Baptist tradition was one that had historic links with a "free" approach to worship,[114] although in all churches there is a tendency to adopt a set pattern. In the case of Russian Baptists the liturgy in the Soviet period was a strict one. This is explicitly acknowledged in a book by N.P. Khrapov: "No presbyter has the right… to establish [anything] with the exception of that which the Gospel mentions and *that which was accepted by ministers of our brotherhood through the compulsion of the Holy Spirit*".[115] [my italics]. Soviet Baptist authors certainly spoke in standard evangelical terms about

---

111. See, for instance, *Povedenie v Khrame*, pp. 83-4. In large congregations, few of the church members were confident enough to speak aloud about their needs.

112. See Gnida, *Tserkovnye ustanovleniya*, p. 72.

113. See Gnida, *Tserkovnye ustanovleniya*, p. 72; Kadaev, *Vecherya Gospodnya – Khleboprelomlenie*, p. 12; Khrapov, *Dom Bozhy*, <http://www.blagovestnik.org/ books/00280.htm#60>; Motorin, "*O Bogosluzhenii*", *BV*, 1 (1957), IEDE-2.

114. For German Baptist influence on Russian Baptists in this area, see, for instance: Savinsky, *Istoriya (1867-1917)*, pp. 124-6; J. Dyck, "Fresh Skins for New Wine", pp. 119-21.

115. Khrapov, *Dom Bozhy*, <http://www.blagovestnik.org/books/00280.htm#12>

conforming to the Word of God, and also about praying "from the bottom of one's heart", and "in the Spirit", without a formal prayer book, but in practice there was little improvisation. In the prayers offered in local congregations, Soviet Baptists quite often used archaic Orthodox words and expressions.[116] The AUCECB was also concerned to limit improvisation in worship. In 1981 the AUCECB president, A.E. Klimenko, called on all presbyters to control the Christian poetry read during church services, stopping anything "untried" and "contradicting the spirit of our doctrines". Those poems considered "exemplary" were often those by famous Russian Orthodox authors.[117] The Orthodox presence was pervasive.

Church music and singing

Though the author of the earliest hymnbook used by the Stundists – *Prinoshenie Pravoslavnym Khristianam* [An Offering to Orthodox Christians], published in St. Petersburg in 1864 – is unknown, and some who have written on Russian sectarianism consider it to be a compilation of German Protestant hymns, it is noted that this book includes a hymn written in honor of Mary as "the Mother of God".[118] Russian Baptist authors (probably owing to the ambiguous title of the hymnbook) often connect its usage by the first Stundists and Baptists with their Russian Orthodox roots.[119] Later, the first Russian Baptists borrowed Orthodox hymns for worship; these were present in substantial numbers in their hymn books.[120] This borrowing continued. The founder of the Union of

---

116. For example, *ramena* – shoulders, *lanity Khrista* – cheeks of Christ, *v sretenie Gospodu* – to meet the Lord, *vo imya... Svyatago Dukha* – in the name... of the Holy Ghost. The "free" prayers also included phrases from famous Orthodox prayers, such as "Holy God, Holy and Mighty, Holy and Immortal..."

117. See *Materialy Plenuma AUCECB, Iyun' 1981 Goda* [Materials of a Plenum of the AUCECB, June 1981], *BV*, no. 5 (1981), p. 59. *Bratsky Vestnik* published these "exemplary" poems (which were read during meetings in local churches) by Orthodox authors. I will come back to topic of Orthodox poetry in chapter 6.

118. See Rozhdestvesky, *Yuzhnorussky Shtundizm*, pp. 244-5.

119. See, for instance, I. Timchenko, "*Muzykal'naya Osnova Bogosluzheniya ECB*" [The Musical Basis of Church Service of the ECB], *Put' Bogopoznaniya*, no. 1 (1996), pp. 63-4.

120. See L. Kharlov, "*Iz Istorii Muzykal'no-pevcheskogo Sluzheniya Nashego Bratstva*" [From

Evangelical Christians, I.S. Prokhanov, commented in the preface to the Evangelical Christian Songbook of 1927-1928 (and in his comment he seems to have been voicing a general opinion), on the distinctive nature of Russian singing, which was vividly described as having an "inborn mystical grief".[121] The solemn feelings, expressed in a minor key and conveying a deep fear of God, which are so characteristic of many Russian Orthodox chants, were also present in the traditional church singing of the Russian Evangelical Christians-Baptists.[122]

Orthodox hymns have been an essential part of the Russian Baptist liturgy. Songbooks used by Baptist choirs, with printed music, usually included many classical Orthodox works. There were, for example, compositions by S. Degtyarev, D. Bortnyansky, P. Tchaikovsky, A. Arkhangelsky, and A. Vedel.[123] The majority of Soviet Baptist composers and choir directors expressed high praise for the Orthodox singing tradition. Here are a few typical quotations from *Bratsky Vestnik* in the 1970s and 1980s:

> ...Russian Orthodox singing is notable for the [use of] simple and at the same time beautiful and substantial melodies... They strike one with the awe of the Lord. The tunes, as if they are coming from ancient times, are very impressive.[124]

> Nobody can create from scratch. We have the real treasure of Russian sacred music; and we cannot afford to break with these traditions. We should follow them and learn them...

---

the History of the Musical and Singing Ministry of our Brotherhood], *BV*, no. 6 (1981), p. 47; Savinsky, *Istoriya (1867-1917)*, p. 98.

121. See *Dukhovnye Pesni (s notami)* [Songbook with Printed Music], 3 vols. (Leningrad: Izdanie I.S. Prokhanova i Ya.I. Zhidkova, 1927-1928), vol. I, p. 7.

122. See N. Vysotsky, *"Znachenie i Sila Dukhovnoy Muzyki"* [The Meaning and Power of Religious Music], *BV*, no. 5 (1978), p. 58; S. Kokhanets, *"Khristianskaya Peasn"* [Christian Song], *BV*, no. 2 (1989), p. 52; I. Timchenko, *Muzykal'naya Osnova Bogosluzheniya ECB*, p. 64.

123. See, for instance, *Notny Sbornik Dukhovnykh Pesen ECB* [Musical Songbook of the ECB] (M.: AUCECB, 1988), vol. II, part I, pp. 5-19; E. Goncharenko, ed., *Alliluiya* [Hallelujah] (M.: Kinoob"edinenie "Moskva", 1991), pp. 5-37.

124. N. Vysotsky, *"Znachenie i Sila Dukhovnoy Muzyki"* [The Meaning and Power of Religious Music], *BV*, no. 5 (1978), p. 58.

The [musical] compositions by A. Arkhangelsky... exemplify this very well.[125]

How majestic and wonderful are the old, but not obsolescent, church songs like *Praise the Name of the Lord* (by D. Bortnyansky), and *With My Voice* (by A. Arkhangelsky)...[126]

Such strong words are indicative of the profound relationship of Russian Baptists with the Orthodox musical tradition. In the second quotation, in an article in *Bratsky Vestnik* in 1980, V. Kreyman, who was writing on sacred music, deliberately stated regarding Russian sacred music that "we cannot afford to break with these traditions". Both Kreyman and S. Kokhanets, who wrote in *Bratsky Vestnik* in 1989 on "Christian Song", referred to Alexander Arkhangelsky, a Russian composer of church music and conductor, who was born in 1846 and died (in Prague) in 1924. L. Kharlov, writing in *Bratsky Vestnik* on the history of church music and singing, was enthusiastic about well-known features of Orthodox hymnody: the *contakion* and the *acathistos*. In a *contakion* (which means a pole around which a scroll is wound) a leader reads the stanzas of the hymn and the choir or the whole congregation repeat the refrain. In many Soviet Baptist communities there was a very similar practice: a presbyter or choir director would read a stanza and then the congregation would sing it. The *acathistos* has to do with "not sitting". In this part of Orthodox liturgy, in which praise is sung in honor of Jesus Christ or the saints, everyone stands. Similarly, in Russian Baptist liturgy there were hymns glorifying the Lord that were always sung in a standing position.[127]

There was a desire among some Russian Baptists to make connections with a Christian tradition of singing going back to the early church. Thus V. Volchansky wrote in *Bratsky Vestnik* in 1982 about a musical history

---

125. V. Kreyman, "*Nekotorye Voprosy Dukhovnogo Muzykal'nogo Tvorchestva*" [Some Issues in Sacred Musical Creativity], *BV*, no. 4 (1980), p. 60.

126. S. Kokhanets, "*Khristianskaya Peasn*" [Christian Song], *BV*, no. 2 (1989), p. 52.

127. L. Kharlov, "*Istoriya Tserkovnoy Muzyki i Peniya*" [The History of Church Music and Singing], *BV*, no. 4 (1979), pp. 57-60; L. Kharlov, "*Istoriya Razvitiya Khristianskogo Peniya na Rusi*" [The History of the Development of Christian Singing in Russia], *BV*, no. 6 (1979), pp. 55-6.

of which the AUCECB (despite being a recent Union) was part, which had "deep roots going back to the first Christians and ancient psalms".[128] Almost every author who wrote in this period about singing in Russian Baptist divine services associated this singing with the long history of Eastern Christianity. For instance, in 1983 L. Semlek approvingly quoted many sentences from the Eastern church fathers regarding liturgical singing.[129] E. Goncharenko was another author who stressed the tradition from which the AUCECB drew, and as well as the Eastern church he pointed out the influence of distinctive Molokan singing on some liturgical melodies used in Russian Baptist churches.[130] The links with wider Russian musical tradition meant that some Baptist choir directors were open to the introduction of new music, if it came from Orthodox sources. There was some cooperation with contemporary Orthodox composers. For example, the wonderful choir hymns written by the Baptist poetry writer Victoria Mazharova (from Moscow), "Cherubs in Heaven" (unofficially called the "Baptist *Cherubikon*", the comparison being with the famous Orthodox liturgical "Cherubic Hymn" or "Song of the Angels"), and "Nailed to the Cross", were set to the music of the Orthodox composer Father Jonathan.[131] In the 1970s, N.D. Babich, the choir director of Alma-Ata Baptist Church, was corresponding with the Orthodox composer from Belorussia, N.V. Butomo, who sent him several musical compositions for church choirs. Some of Butomo's hymns were used in Baptist church services not only in Central Asia but also in other regions of the Soviet Union.[132]

The singing was often accompanied by various musical instruments. In the Soviet period Russian Baptists usually considered that only certain instruments could be used in "a manner worthy of the saints". These were

---

128. V. Volchansky, "*O Sluzhenii Orkestrov*" [On the Orchestra's Service], *BV*, no. 3 (1982), p. 55.

129. L. Semlek, "*Zhanry Khristianskikh Pesnopeny*" [The Genres of Christian Songs], *BV*, no. 3 (1983), pp. 68-71.

130. E. Goncharenko, "*Zhanry Pesnopeny ECB*" [The Singing Genres of the ECB], *BV*, no. 4 (1982), p. 65.

131. Testimony of V. Mazharova (e-mail, 04.04.07). See also: *Notny Sbornik*, vol. III, part II, pp. 188-90; vol. III, part I, pp. 189-90.

132. Testimony of N.D. Babich (INT, Castro Valley, California, USA, 2006). See also *Notny Sbornik*, vol. III, part II, pp. 190-1.

the harmonium, the piano, the mandolin, and, to some extent, the violin. In some large congregations there were also brass bands (in Russian: *dukhovoy* or "spiritual" orchestras), although in many places these did not exist. Other instruments were routinely rated as "worldly". Even the use of a microphone in church was sometimes condemned.[133] It was always stressed by preachers that the important aspect of the music was not its professional quality, although there were inevitably clashes between the musical professionalism that choir directors sought (especially in larger churches) and the desire by congregations to experience what was sometimes called singing "in the Spirit". There was a widespread awareness of the need for the singing and accompaniment with musical instruments to touch people's souls. One church member spoke of the experience of listening to a hymn which "gives you the shivers, and the Lord is near".[134] Despite the tensions that could be found over issues connected with musical excellence, both choir members and members of the congregation who were not in the choir shared this spiritual vision. Choir members devoted themselves to serving the church through singing in the choir, to a certain degree becoming similar to a zealous monastic "brotherhood" or even a "heavenly host" with their "angelic voices".[135]

The singing of hymns was also seen as a means of instruction. Many Baptist believers spoke of the songbook *Sbornik Dukhovnykh Pesen* as an effective sermon about Christ, a kind of prayer book. Indeed they usually memorized the "prayer" hymns first. It is significant that Russian Baptists often brought to the church meetings the hymnbook rather than the Bible, suggesting that the hymnbooks, in part, fulfilled for them the role of Orthodox prayer books. Hymnbooks were seen as "the first theological textbook" for Baptists during the Soviet period.[136] Singing was, like

---

133. See Ya. Tervits, "*Muzyka i Dukhovnoe Vozrastanie Veruyushchikh*" [Music and Spiritual Growth in Believers], *BV*, no. 3 (1981), p. 58; Khrapov, *Dom Bozhy*, <http://www.blagovestnik.org/books/00280.htm#60>

134. Expression of a Baptist church member from Kazakhstan.

135. Among Russian Baptists, harmonious singing by the choir was often compared with the singing of angels. See *SDP*, no. 296, p. 201; *PV*, no. 1056 (complemented edition). On the "brotherhood" aspect, the choir was also a place of fellowship.

136. E. Goncharenko, *Muzyka i Dukhovnoe Vozrastanie Tserkvi* [Music and the Spiritual Growth of the Church] (M.: Logos, 2002), p. 4.

preaching and other parts of worship, a "holy ordinance",[137] or "theology in melody",[138] and singing by the choirs was never compared by congregations to a "spiritual concert".[139] The aim was communication with God. Analysis of the words of the Russian Baptist hymns shows that in them the worshippers were considered to be communicating with God, expressed by the use of the lexical forms of the first and second persons, and that God was also speaking, as indicated by exclamatory intonations and an inclination towards Russian folk "epic" syntax.[140] The importance of the divine dimension was underlined by the fact that in many cases the names of the authors of the hymns were not usually stated. This also reflected the fact that in some respects many Russian Baptist songs were like folklore poetry, with a great number of versions of some popular hymns being used, especially in rural areas.[141] But because of the desire to have uniformity of teaching, in the 1950s and 1960s, in early editions of the hymnbook *Sbornik Dukhovnykh Pesen*, AUCECB leaders called on congregations to reject independent liturgical creations.[142] *Bratsky Vestnik* even asked readers "to send new hymns to Moscow for fraternal control".[143] The AUCECB was concerned to avoid theological, as well as musical discord. At the end of 1970s and in the early 1980s the first Baptist songbooks with printed music were published. In 1984, as part of the commemoration of the founding of the Baptist Union in Russian in 1884, Alexei Bychkov described how "a fundamental work, *Sbornik Dukhovnykh Pesen s*

---

137. See A. Karev, *"Svyashchennodeystviya Tserkvi"* [The Holy Ordinances of the Church], *BV*, no. 1 (1963), p. 36.

138. V. Popov, *"Prokhanov – Propovednik i Poet"* [Prokhanov as a Preacher and Poet], *BV*, no. 4 (1990), p. 47.

139. Testimony of E.S. Goncharenko, the leader of the Musical Department of the Russian Union of the ECB (INT, Omsk, Russia, 2006).

140. See Z. Tarlanov, *"Zametki o Sintaksise Gimnov Russkikh Baptistov"* [Short Commentary on the Syntax of Russian Baptist Hymns] in Z. Tarlanov, *Izbrannye Raboty po Yazykoznaniyu i Filologii* [Selected Works on Linguistics and Philology] (Petrozavodsk: Izd-vo PetrGU, 2005), p. 616.

141. Ibid., pp. 617-8.

142. See *Sbornik Dukhovnykh Pesen Evangel'skikh Khristian Baptistov* [The Songbook of the Evangelical Christians-Baptists] (M.: AUCECB, 1968), p. 6.

143. Words by Ya.I. Zhidkov. Cited in L. Kharlov, *"Iz Istorii Muzykal'no-pevcheskogo Sluzheniya Nashego Bratstva"* [From the History of the Musical and Singing Ministry of our Brotherhood], *BV*, no. 1 (1982), p. 57.

Notami [The Musical Christian Songbook], came out... [which] includes 580 hymns that showed the 100-year way of the united brotherhood."[144] The songs of the Evangelical Christians-Baptists over that period were seen as approximating to sound Christian preaching and teaching.

Ceremonial objects and acts

The dedication of Russian Baptist places of worship has already been considered. In early Russian Baptist communities the prayer houses, as they were often called, tended to be small wooden buildings. They were very simple, both inside and outside. However, during Brezhnev's time, at the end of the 1970s and the beginning of the 1980s, Soviet Baptists started to build unusually large church buildings, more or less successfully combining European and Byzantine architectural styles,[145] and moving away from the Baptist prayer houses which were still standard in Stalin's epoch. With the new buildings, issues concerning the erection of a cross and introducing wall paintings were discussed. The comments made were typically to the effect that "something should be done with these [huge] bare walls and ceilings".[146] Such a perspective would have been inconceivable before, since the issue of significant areas of wall and ceiling did not apply in small prayer houses: the only adornment was biblical texts. Reports like this began to appear in *Bratsky Vestnik* in the 1980s.

> From the life of the local churches, the city of Kuibyshev...
> The walls of the new prayer house are painted with pictures of
> biblical stories. There are [pictures of] Mount Calvary and the
> Jordan River, flowing from the hills, on the front wall. There
> is the text, 'Seek ye the Lord...' (Isa 55:6), against the back-
> ground of clouds... In his speech, the brother... gave a short

---

144. A. Bychkov, "*Otchetny Doklad S"ezdu ECB*" [Summary Report to the Council of the ECB], *BV*, no. 3 (1985), p. 25.

145. For instance, the testimony of a minister of the ECB from Bryansk, V.A. Serpikov (INT, Seattle, Washington, USA, 2006).

146. I heard this from several presbyters during *perestroika*.

review of the history of Kuibyshev Church; the Lord led the way from a small room… to such a noble edifice.[147]

The door of the [new] prayer house was hospitably opened, for all people to come for the holiday of the consecration. The words, 'God is love', are inscribed on the central wall. The believers, with loving care, decorated the house with fresh flowers. There are large bouquets of pink and white asters on the window sills, baskets of carnations and other flowers on the raised area near the pulpit. The participants in the holiday filled the sanctuary, galleries, staircases.[148]

The place of the aesthetic was being stressed in new ways. The report from Kuibyshev mentioned the wall paintings before the biblical text. The progression is highly significant: from "small room" to "noble edifice". The second report, which is from Kiev, similarly gives attention to the decorations in the large church building.

From the 1980s, with greater religious and political freedom, Soviet Baptists turned their attention to building impressive "temples". These were intended to give a signal to people outside in the community regarding the Baptist presence. More and more congregations placed crosses to the top of their churches.[149] An AUCECB article in 1990 made this statement:

Regarding the exaltation of the cross over prayer houses of Evangelical Christians-Baptists, we should accept the estimation of Ya.K. Dukhonchenko from his report to the Council of the representatives of Ukrainian Baptist churches, 'Let not anyone who sees fit to place the cross on the top of a prayer

---

147. *BV*, no. 4 (1981), p. 66. See also *BV*, no. 5 (1983), p. 71.

148. V. Kadaeva, "*Osvyashchenie Doma Molitvy v Svyatoshinskoy Tserkvi Kieva*" [The Consecration of the Prayer House of the Svyatoshinskaya Church in Kiev], *BV*, no. 6 (1989), p. 73.

149. See, for instance: G. Edelstein, *Vospominaniya* [Memories], <http://www.krotov.info/history/20/1960/ 1965edels.htm> accessed 5 November 2010.

house regard with contempt anyone who has a different opinion, and let not the latter judge the former.'[150]

This trend towards public Christianity had characterized the church in different countries at previous times in history, for example the church of the
fourth century, under Constantine the Great, or the nineteenth-century
Nonconformists in Britain. The Russian Baptist buildings that began to be
built from the 1980s onwards were sometimes even larger than Orthodox
or Catholic churches.[151] Baptist presbyters and choir members also started
wearing special service vestments. Some of these trends, not surprisingly,
were opposed by those who feared that long-accepted aspects of Baptist
tradition were being compromised. Tensions were evident in some Baptist
communities in Brezhnev's time. Later, in the Irkutsk Region for example
(and perhaps in some other places), a movement developed which came
to the point of complete rejection of any artwork portraying Christ. This
highly conservative element in Baptist life even refused (referring to the
commandment in Exod 20:4) to use illustrated children's Bibles for teaching children.[152]

It might be thought that the acceptance of more ceremonial objects
and acts would have been opposed by those within the CCECB, since they
criticized the AUCECB as unfaithful to the truth. However, this was not
necessarily the case. M.A. Vasiliev, a member of the Krasnodar congregation of the CCECB in the 1960s and 1970s, recalled that "our brethren
started to preach more about prisoners [for Christ]... than to proclaim the
Gospel. Then I found that our young people were wearing small portraits
of famous brother-prisoners." Vasiliev discovered that these small photos
were being revered and were functioning almost like icons. He continued

---

150. Cited in V. Kadaeva, "*44 Vsesoyuzny S'ezd ECB*" [The 44th All-Union Council of
the ECB], *BV*, no. 2 (1990), p. 54. This was a considerable change from early Stundist
and Baptist attitudes in Russia, in which Orthodox Christians were condemned for their
use of the cross. Baptists considered it an implement of execution. See, for instance,
Rozhdestvensky, *Yuzhnorussky Shtundizm*, pp. 184-5.

151. See, for instance, on a Baptist website, how the ECB church "House of the Gospel"
(Vinnitsa, Ukraine) looks – the outside and inside views: <http://baptist.vn.ua/photos/
church/index.shtml> accessed 5 November 2010.

152. Testimony of Baptist presbyter from Irkutsk, I.S. Tolmachev (Irkutsk, Russia, 2004).

his account: "I said to the brethren, 'What have you done! All you have to do now is to paint the portraits in oils and hang them on the wall in order to pray before them.'"[153] In the case of the dispute in Irkutsk, the majority of the local Baptists, although certainly conservative in their thinking, opposed the "iconoclastic" movement, using, whether knowingly or not, the famous arguments of St. John of Damascus against the iconoclasts, emphasizing the reality of the physical incarnation of the Savior, which affords proper grounds to depict him.[154] Baptists who favored paintings of Christ did not, of course, argue for adopting the theology behind Orthodox icons, but their perspective had similarities to some of the arguments used in favor of icons as "books for the illiterate" and "reminders about God".[155]

Many ritual acts of the Orthodox Christians with respect to icons have well-defined parallels in the attitude of Russian Baptists to the Bible. I will deal with this in more detail below, but the significance of the Bible as a ceremonial object deserves notice here. In accordance with Orthodox tradition, icons are consecrated, decorated in beautiful settings, and given a place of honor. Orthodox believers pray before them, kiss them, take the holy images with them on journeys, and consider that they receive divine grace through them, whether in church or in any other place. The belief is that the Lord reveals himself in this way and also that miraculous results – for example cures – are to be expected. Some icons that were badly injured by atheists often became the most venerated and were seen as the source of particular power.[156] For instance, Archbishop Mefody of Harbin and Manchuria, writing in 1925, talked about the renewal of icons which

---

153. Testimony of M.A. Vasiliev (INT, Everett, Washington, USA, 2006). There is also some information about repeated "holy" kissing of A.F. Prokofiev's photo (he was one of the leaders of the Initiative Group of Soviet Baptists in the 1960s) by a sister in Christ (testimony of B.M. Zdorovets, INT, Spokane, Washington, USA, 2006), as well as about the placing of a portrait of a deceased Baptist minister, as a mark of special respect to him, above the entrance door of a prayer house during the funeral. See *BL*, no. 5 (2007), pp. 1-3.
154. See St. John of Damascus, *Tri Zashchititel'nykh Slova* [On Holy Images] (SPb.: Izdanie I. Tuzova, 1893), pp. 6-7.
155. See Ibid., p. 95; A. Kartashev, *Vselenskie Sobory* [Ecumenical Councils] (M.: Respublika, 1994), pp. 475, 500-1, 533.
156. See, for instance, Archbishop Mefody, *O Znamenii Obnovleniya Svyatykh Ikon* [On the Sign of Renewal of the Holy Icons] [1925], (M.: Palomnik, 1999); S. Soshinsky, "*Chudo Obnovleniya*" [The Miracle of Renewal], *Novy Mir*, no. 6 (1992), pp. 231-7.

occurred in Russia in that period, when the Communists especially cruelly mocked the faith.

> When they took the icon, a Bolshevik woman started to mock it... Immediately, she fell into a fit of frenzy: she frothed at the mouth, her eyes hid under her brows... The icon of the Savior, surrounded by 12 apostles, made of paper, without glass, within a plain and simple framework [which was] already torn to pieces, has become as if brand-new... A godless man made stabs at it and snipped it, but these wounds... have healed... The divine grace was not revealed in the bejewelled icons... but in the cheapest ones which... are affordable for the village poor.[157]

Similarly, some old prints of the Holy Scriptures were closely associated among Russian Baptists with stories that can be categorized as "wonder-working" narratives. Here is one of the many traditional Baptist testimonies on that subject, also dating back to the 1920s, published in 1987:

> It was in the 1920s, when I was still a boy. Collectivization was in full swing... [The Communists] came to our house and took all our property. There was a large Bible lying on the table. It was about 20 kilograms in weight. The rural activists were carting the Bible and, along the way, decided to shoot at it... The first was aiming his gun but then moved away. The same happened with the second and the third activists... Atheist Sukhanov ran up and said boldly, 'I will shoot it!' He circled round the Bible for a long time and finally gave up... This Bible has been lying on the table of our prayer house and is there now. All of our believers know the story of this book.[158]

---

157. Archbishop Mefody, *O Znamenii Obnovleniya*, pp. 22-34.
158. *Kniga Zhizni* [The Book of Life] (editorial article), *VestI*, no. 1 (1987), pp. 27-8.

Reading these and similar stories told by Russian Christians (both Orthodox and Baptist), the impression gained is that the words "icon" and "Bible" could almost be interchangeable; a holy object is at the centre of the striking testimonies.

Other objects and ceremonies found among Russian Baptists show similarities to Orthodoxy. Although Russian Baptists did not cross themselves and did not usually wear crucifixes on their necks, there were other gestures where resemblances were apparent. Thus on coming to a church building, an Orthodox person bares his head (a man) or sets a head-scarf straight (a woman) and prayerfully signs himself/herself with the cross,[159] while a Russian Baptist, approaching a prayer house, would also bare his head (a man) or adjust her head-scarf (a woman) and pray for God's blessing during the forthcoming church service.[160] In church Russian Baptists prayerfully clasped their hands and bowed the heads.[161] These rituals, and also the postures of standing or kneeling during parts of church worship,[162] can all be attributed to some extent to adoption and adaptation of Orthodox practices by Russian Baptists. Some Russian Baptists have been insistent that they adopted these ceremonies not from the Orthodox Church but directly from the Bible, but the Bible has been used selectively. Why did Russian Baptists use, for instance, such "biblical practices" as kneeling to pray and "holy kissing", yet a practice such as foot washing which is clearly found in the New Testament has not been considered as being acceptable.[163] At least part of the answer appears to be that in the Orthodox Church in Russia the first two of these practices were normal, while the third was not practiced.

Among other Russian Baptist ceremonial service acts which can be seen as resembling Orthodox ways, there were a number associated with the role of presbyters. Baptist presbyters would stretch out and lift up their hands

---

159. See Men', *Tainstvo, Slovo i Obraz*, p. 199; M. Dobuzhinsky, ed., *Zakon Bozhy*, vol. I, pp. 13-14.

160. Head covering will be considered at greater length in chapter 7.

161. Those are ritual Christian acts, parallel with the sign of the cross.

162. See Kolesnikov, *Khristianin, znaesh' li ty*, vol. I, p. 34; Khrapov, *Dom Bozhy*, <http://www.blagovestnik.org/ books/00280.htm#77>

163. See [Anon], "*Voprosy Biblii, Trebuyushchie Raz"yasneniya*" [The Issues of the Bible which should be Explained], *BV*, no. 2 (1963), pp. 57-61; Kolesnikov, *Khristianin, znaesh' li ty*, vol. III, pp. 85-7.

before a baptism and during the consecration of prayer houses; there was laying-on of hands by presbyters after a baptism, during a wedding, and at an ordination; there was ritual washing or cleansing by presbyters of their hands before serving of the Lord's Supper (usually by wiping their hands on a wet towel); and there was anointing with oil for the cure of the sick, all displaying similarities to Orthodox practice.[164] It is true that a number of these ceremonial acts can be found in Baptist communities in other countries, but the way in which Russian Baptist presbyters have carried them out bears the imprint of Orthodox influence. The work of presbyters has also been closely associated with preaching, and in Russian Baptist churches the pulpit for preaching the Word of God had a function similar to that of the Orthodox Church *ambon*, the raised platform from which the Scriptures are read and the homily delivered.[165] Russian Baptist churches have never had the formal equivalent of the "opening of the Royal doors" of the Orthodox Church iconostasis, as a ceremonial act symbolizing the opening of the "gates of the Kingdom of God" for all people,[166] but the Table on which the Lord's Supper was placed has been seen as functioning like a holy altar, with the way to this being opened through the invitation of the presbyters. Soviet Baptists took the "altar" very seriously.[167]

The theology that governed worship in Russian Baptist churches has already been examined. The theological approach affected ceremonies. In the light of the sacramental view of the Lord's Supper it is not surprising that on the Saturday night before a celebration of the Lord's Supper, the altar table (a parallel to the Orthodox *credence table*) was carefully covered with a special tablecloth, which in large churches could be embroidered with images of the Cup, the Eucharistic Bread, angels, and Gospel texts. The biblical words embroidered there sometimes used lettering that was close to the "Church Slavonic" (Orthodox) lettering, the so-called *izhitsa*.[168]

---

164. See Krasovitskaya, *Liturgika*, p. 290; Kolesnikov, *Khristianin, znaesh' li ty*, vol. I, pp. 41-65.

165. I have heard the word "ambon" used in Baptist churches to describe the place where the pulpit is located.

166. See Krasovitskaya, *Liturgika*, p. 294; Dobuzhinsky, ed., *Zakon Bozhy*, vol. II, p. 119.

167. See Kolesnikov, *Khristianin, znaesh' li ty*, vol. I, pp. 72-3.

168. See, for instance: *VestI*, no. 4 (1997), p. 45; no. 3 (2000), p. 10.

As long as the tablecloth was used solely for liturgical purposes, it was a kind of *antimension* – the Orthodox consecrated linen or silk cloth kept in the altar – for Baptist presbyters. The Cups used at the Lord's Supper were usually filled with "church Cahors wine". (The Orthodox tradition of using "Cahors" developed as a result of a legendary choice of this wine made by Peter the Great). There was also in Russian Baptist churches a special church plate that was used for the Bread. In the Orthodox Church this (usually metal) plate was called the *diskos*. The Bread for a Baptist Communion service was baked with an accompanying prayer in the home of a church member.[169] On the Table, the Bread was usually covered with a white piece of linen. The task of covering, carried out on a Saturday night and often associated with the "mystery of the faith" (cf. 1 Tim 3:9), was usually in the hands of the oldest of the deacons of the church.[170]

The final aspect to be considered here is the place not only of sight but also of touch and of other senses in worship. Although Russian Baptists stressed the hearing of the Word, it is clear that much was invested in the visual. In addition, there was the reverential touching of church objects, the sensation of taste (for instance, during the Communion), and also the sense of smell. Although the incense found in Orthodox worship was never used among Russian Baptists liturgically, the theme was taken up to some extent by preachers, who made a point of contrasting the "sweet savour of Christ" (2 Cor 2:14-16) or the "incense with the prayers of the saints" (Rev 8:4) with the "stink" of human sins before God (Isa 3:16-24).[171] While this was figurative, and did not refer to actual smells, there was a link made with some characteristic smells at church. Part of the beauty of the experience of worship at the Lord's Supper was the scent of freshly baked Eucharistic Bread and the Cup with its red wine. There were fragrant flowers which decorated the prayer houses, especially on feast days. The richness of the earth was represented in selected vegetables and fruits (on the

---

169. Usually widowed deaconesses, known for their pious life, do this.

170. Detailed testimony of Omsk Baptist church deacon, A.N. Krivorotov (Omsk, Russia, 2009).

171. See, for instance: Khrapov, *Dom Bozhy*, <http://www.blagovestnik.org/books/00280.htm#57>; A. Vlasov, *Ot Izbytka Serdtsa* [Out of That Fills the Heart] (Idar-Oberstein, Germany: Titel Verlag, 2000), pp. 179-80.

Harvest Feast), fir branches (on the New Year and Christmas celebrations), or aromatic oil (used for anointing of the sick). Though every Baptist prayer house had its own atmosphere, there was some commonality, just as there was in Orthodox churches, especially through the use of incense. As Alexander Pushkin said in his famous *Ruslan and Ludmila*, "There's a Russian spirit... a Russian scent!"[172] Traditional Baptist worship drew from a wider Orthodox spirit.

The Bible: "This is God's Book"

The Bible, in Russian Baptist tradition, is very important for the content of Scripture, but also for the book itself. As a rule, a Bible of considerable dimensions lay on the pulpit of Soviet Baptist churches. This Bible was rarely used, and was there primarily for ceremonial, liturgical purposes, like the altar table Gospel in the Orthodox Church.[173] Russian Baptists purchased high quality covers for their church Bibles, and these were carefully decorated (especially by women) with various ornamental patterns – often flowers – or Christian symbols. In addition to the Bible in the pulpit, many church members made efforts to have their own Bibles. In Baptist homes there were often biblical texts on the walls or even at times on the ceilings.[174] What might be termed a sacramental attitude to the Bible (and not only to an old Bible) was apparent, for example, in the fact that it was considered as impious to put it on the floor,[175] to put anything on it,[176] to throw it,[177] or to lie on a bed if a Bible was underneath it.[178] There was a

---

172. A.S. Pushkin, *Sochineniya* [Works], 2 vols. (M.: Khudozhestvennaya Literatura, 1982), vol. I, p. 215.

173. See Dobuzhinsky, ed., *Zakon Bozhy*, vol. II, pp. 115-7.

174. For example, testimonies of church members from Krasnodar Territory, M.A. Vasiliev and O.E. Avdeeva (INT, Everett, Washington, USA, 2006).

175. Testimony of Baptist church member from Kishinev, P.P. Cherny (INT, Sacramento, California, USA, 2006).

176. "When I was a young Christian... I once put a newspaper on the Bible. An elder brother corrected me... The Bible must always be above all." – G. Kryuchkov, "*Otreshit'sya ot Vsego*" [To Renounce the World], *VestI*, no. 1 (2004), p. 4.

177. See Kolesnikov, *Khristianin, znaesh' li ty*, vol. I, p. 71.

178. See M. Khorev, "*Raznye Ucheniki*" [Different Disciples], *VestI*, no. 3 (1990), p. 5.

tradition of washing or wiping one's hands before taking the Scriptures.[179] Some underground church printers in Brezhnev's time could not bring themselves to destroy even obviously defective copies of the Scripture.[180] Often people prayed for blessing before they read the Bible.[181] There are some testimonies that *evangel'skie khristiane sovershennye* (Evangelical Perfect Christians) in the Ukraine, in Stalin's and Khrushchev's eras, had a rule that in seeking to read the Holy Scripture prayerfully, they should read on bended knees.[182] Russian Baptists were taught to keep the Bible *open* during prayer.[183] Sometimes Soviet Baptists also kissed their Bibles, for example when thanking God for saving Bibles that were not found during searches by the Communists.[184]

The experiences of Russian Baptists during periods of persecution produced many dramatic stories, including a number about the Bible. In 2002 *Vestnik Istiny* published the following recollections:

> The boy named Vanya ran into the courtyard... and informed
> [the believers] that the police were coming to make a search.
> The only treasure for the believers was their big, old Gospel,
> in a leather cover... There was no time for quiet reflection.
> They promptly coated the Gospel with dough, made it into
> the shape of a loaf, and put it into the burning hot stove. Then

---

179. "The sister... thoroughly washes her hands before she takes the Bible. No wonder, because this is the Word of God himself..." – V. Zhuravlev, *Sila v Nemoshchi: Svidetel'stva iz Zhizni* [Strength in Weakness: Life Testimonies] (Steinhagen, Germany: Samenkorn, 2008), v. II, p. 68. A known Baptist poem from Soviet times has the following lines, "Oh, grant me to look into the Bible!... She wiped her hands and opened the holy pages..." – *Stikhotvoreniya. Gde Dostat' Bibliyu?* [Poems. Where can you get the Bible?], <http://www.blagovestnik.org/books/00430/db/v4442325.html> accessed 5 January 2010.

180. See Yu. Kryuchkov, *Podpol'naya Pechat' CCECB v Sovetskom Soyuze* [The Underground Press of the CCECB in the Soviet Union] (Sacramento, CA: n.p., 2002), p. 124. I had occasion to meet with some Russian Baptists who would not throw out even any old Christian newspaper or magazine because the name of God was mentioned there.

181. Testimony of Baptist evangelist from Dushanbe, P.A. Semeryuk (INT, Sacramento, California, USA, 2006).

182. Testimony of B.M. Zdorovets (INT, Spokane, Washington, USA, 2006).

183. See, for instance: *"Lyubite Bibliyu!"* [Love the Bible!], *VS*, no. 3 (1965), p. 35; *VestI*, no. 3 (2003), p. 47.

184. Testimony of church member from Homel (Belarus), N.F. Mazhnaya (INT, Fresno, California, USA, 2006).

the police officers came. They made a complete search of the premises, but went away empty-handed... The agitated sisters took the precious loaf of spiritual bread baked in dough, and thanked the Lord heartily for the miraculous preservation of His living and saving Word... She [one of the sisters] gave the Gospel, with slightly deformed leather cover edges because of the high temperature, to the church. The congregation found great blessing in that Gospel for a long time. And to this day, it is a graphic evidence of God's mercy.[185]

This Gospel, seen as miraculously preserved by God, since it was not burned inside the burning hot stove during the comprehensive police search, testifies to Russian Baptist beliefs about the Bible. The edges of the old Gospel, somewhat charred, emphasized the reality of the miracle, and became a memorable detail, often rehearsed. Analyzing the testimony in *Vestnik Istiny*, it is clear that what was in view was not so much the content of the Bible as the Book itself, which in an ordinary Russian Baptist's eyes bore the imprint of special divine grace. The author of the report draws his readers' attention to the Gospel's distinctive features: that it was the "only treasure" of these believers; that it was "big", "old", and "in a leather cover"; and that its edges were damaged through fire. The reverent attitude to the sacred object mirrors the Orthodox attitude to their icons.

The Russian Orthodox perception of icons explicitly includes the belief that an icon can survive many attacks. In one Orthodox story, an anti-Christian attacker shot an arrow at an icon, but he did not damage it, only wounding himself, and he then came to believe.[186] In particular, icons could survive even the most concentrated fire, through the prayers of pious Christians. Such happenings were claimed as miracles of God. For example, there is a report about an Orthodox icon called "The Burning Bush", which

---

185. [Anon], "*Zhelaem Sokhranit' Vernost' Khristu*" [We want to Remain Faithful to Christ], *VestI*, no. 3 (2002), p. 31.

186. See *Chudesa Sv. Velikomuchenika Georgiya* [The Miracles of the Great Martyr St George] in *Zhitiya Svyatykh, Na Russkom Yazyke Izlozhennye po Rukovodstvu Chet'ikh-Miney Sv. Dimitriya Rostovskogo* [Lives of Saints, in the Russian Language, Retold According to the Menology by St. Dimitry Rostovsky], 12 vols. (M.: Sinodal'naya Tipografiya, 1903-1911), vol. VIII, pp. 377-9.

was in a house that burned down. The icon escaped destruction: a part of the wall where the icon was located miraculously survived.[187] In another case, during a serious fire which destroyed an ancient Russian Orthodox church in Kurgan Region, a miracle-working icon survived:

> The church had burnt to the ground... Next day... a child came to the site of fire... He moved apart some ashes and suddenly saw the eyes of the Most Holy Mother of God – so familiar, so dear. The icon! Alive! Not burnt! Just with a slightly darkened image because of the fire and smoke... The people prayed reverently, with tears, thanking the Lord and the Queen of Heaven for the miracle of the icon's survival.[188]

Although I am not arguing that Russian Baptists themselves would ever have talked about the Bible as an icon, I suggest there are some striking similarities between the Baptist story of the Bible and this Orthodox story. There is an outward resemblance (both the Gospel and the icon suffered a little), but of more significance is the spiritual affinity of the narrators, or participants in the events, from the Baptist congregation and the Russian Orthodox Church. Therefore, the usual Russian Baptist rejection, in what they said, of icons (as well as other holy images) did not mean in practice the rejection of the *idea* of an icon. The Bible was much more than a scriptural text for them: it was a *holy* Book. Thus N.A. Kolesnikov, whose name the older generation of ECB members often connect with the concept of "the clear and pure" (*chistoe i nezamutnennoe*) teaching of Russian Baptists,[189] spoke of any irreverent handling of the Bible as a "sacrilege towards the holy", and insisted that anyone who neglected this Book

---

187. See E. Rybalkina, *Ikona "Neopalimaya Kupina" Pomogaet Pozharnym* [The Icon "The Burning Bush" Helps Fire Fighters], *Komsomol'skaya Pravda*, 16 September 2009.

188. *Iz Istorii Monastyrya* [From the Monastery History], The Official Website of the Svyato-Kazansky Chimeevo Monastery, <http://www.chimeevo.ru/node/137?page=0,3> accessed 20 January 2010. Cf.: O. Tarasov, *Ikona i Blagochestie: Ocherki Ikonnogo Dela v Imperatorskoy Rossii* [Icon and Piety: Essays on Iconography in Imperial Russia] (M.: Progress-Kultura, 1995), p. 57.

189. For example, testimony of former senior presbyter, P.A. Chumakin (INT, Kent, Washington, USA, 2006), as well as many other ministers from Central Asia.

neglected its Author, i.e. God.[190] In this connection, it is important to note that Kolesnikov actually replicates one of the most famous and ancient "Orthodox" arguments against iconoclasts.[191]

The *Lives of the Saints*, a very popular work among Russian people, includes many touching examples of people suffering for the icon of the Savior, and this is portrayed as being the same as suffering for Christ himself.[192] To address a holy image in one's hour of need is the same as a direct appeal to the person depicted on it.[193] In one story a courageous Christian was tortured and his torturers attempted to force him to trample on an image of Christ. But he fearlessly said he had been mentally kissing this icon and was ready to die for it.[194] Again, there are strong parallels in Russian Baptists stories about heroes of faith and their attitude to the Bible.

> The more we love the Holy Scriptures the more we love… our Lord and Savior Jesus Christ… Love the Bible!… Pray in front of the opened Book; this bears much fruit… The Word of God (the Bible) is the light from heaven, which all the powers of darkness aim to extinguish… Therefore we have to act with fortitude for the Word of God. The history of the church is the chronicle of heroic struggles for the Holy Scriptures, and this path is blazing with the bonfires of martyrs.[195]

---

190. See Kolesnikov, *Khristianin, znaesh' li ty*, vol. I, pp. 71-2.

191. A martyr in the period of iconoclasm, St. Stephen the Younger (8th C.), according to the story from the *Lives of the Saints*, when standing before Emperor Constantine V, trampled on a coin bearing the imperial image. Stephen explained that if trampling on the imperial image was a crime, so was flouting the images of Christ in icons, because it was an outrage against the person depicted. See Kartashev, *Vselenskie Sobory*, p. 478. It is notable that this story was retold with sympathy in the official textbook of the ECB. See A. Karev, K. Somov, *Istoriya Khristianstva* [History of Christianity] (M.: AUCECB, 1990), p. 160.

192. See *"Pamyat' Prepodobnogo Iakova Ispovednika"* [The Life of St. James the Confessor] in *ZhSDR*, vol. VII, p. 454.

193. See *"Zhitie Prep. Zosimy, Igumena Solovetskogo"* [The Life of St. Zosima, Hegumen of Solovki] in *ZhSDR*, vol. VIII, pp. 266-7.

194. See *"Pamyat' Prep. Faddeya Ispovednika"* [The Life of St. Thaddaeus the Confessor] in *ZhSDR*, vol. IV, p. 834.

195. *"Lyubite Bibliyu!"* [Love the Bible!], *VS*, no. 3 (1965), pp. 34-5; *VestI*, no. 3 (2003), p. 47.

In this connection, there were a number of reports about the Bible from the prison camps, for example the martyrdom of a Baptist in a labor camp in the Stalinist era because he refused to tear up the New Testament and throw it in the fire,[196] and about the sufferings of young men from Baptist families during their military service in Khrushchev's and Brezhnev's times, who hid their Bibles and were determined not to give them to the camp commanders.[197] In 1979, shortly before the deportation of G.P. Vins from the USSR,[198] his warders intended to take his pocket Gospel away and throw it out into a garbage can:

> I... held the Gospel tightly in my hands and shouted loudly, 'I won't give it! This is God's Book!' Both soldiers became absolutely furious... One of them said hoarsely, 'I'll force you to tear up the holy book yourself now! I'll force you to eat it!' Both of them fell upon me, twisting my arms, but I tightly held the small Gospel, which was so dear to me and seemed to be so defenceless. 'This Book is my life. I believe in this Book. You can shoot at me, but I would not let you tear it off!' Extremely agitated, I shouted...[199]

Fortunately, the sudden help of a senior officer saved Vins from suffering major violence. The precious Gospel was not damaged.[200] These examples display well the spirit of Russian Baptists. The Bible was not just useful because of its teaching, but was *holy*. It is significant that Vins did not speak so much of his faith in God as of his faith in the physical Bible he held ("I believe in this Book") and he was prepared to die for a Bible. In Orthodox understanding, God's mysterious presence is communicated through specially

---

196. Testimony of a minister of the ECB from Kiev, L.E. Kovalenko (INT, Sacramento, California, USA, 2006).

197. For example, testimony of the presbyter V.N. Khot'ko (Petropavlovsk, Kazakhstan, 1999).

198. Vins was one of five Soviet prisoners of conscience exchanged for two Russian spies caught in the West. See, for instance: *Religion in Communist Dominated Areas*, vol. XVIII: 7, 8, and 9 (1979), pp. 115-6.

199. Vins, *Evangelie v Uzakh*, p. 218.

200. Ibid., p. 219.

venerated images (the icon itself is just a wood boarded and oil paints), and there is a similar perception of the Bible among Russian Baptists. Indeed the care put into painting icons, which were often selflessly painted over a long period of time and often under unfavorable external circumstances,[201] could be compared with the process of producing sizeable handwritten Bibles by Russian Baptists, which took place during Communist persecutions. The Scriptures, in full or in part, were reverently copied by hand.[202]

In the Russian Orthodox tradition, stories about appearances of the saints (usually in a dream), who gave directions about finding icons, were always popular. Following these appearances, Orthodox Christians often found old holy images, sometimes that had been lost, and received consolation and perhaps healing. Here are typical testimonies:

A peasant woman from the Bronnitsky district, Evdokiya Andrianova, heard a mysterious voice, in a dream, which commanded her to find the big and black [with age] icon in the village of Kolomenskoe, to wash it… and to pray before it.[203]

Prokhor was a servant in the boyar's [Russian aristocrat's] house… He dreamed that God's Mother spoke three times, commanding him to pray before… the icon for recovery from his illness. Prokhor did this… and felt healthy.[204]

---

201. See, for instance, L. Uspensky, *Bogoslovie Ikony Pravoslavnoy Tserkvi* [Theology of the Orthodox Icon] (Izd-vo bratstva Sv. Alexandra Nevskogo, 1997), pp. 495-558.

202. For instance, at the beginning of the 1980s, a Baptist woman from Donetsk Region, A.I. Musiets, copied by hand in block letters the whole Bible. – Testimonies of V.Ya. Sedykh, E.I. Sedykh, and A.I. Musiets (INT, Sacramento, California, USA, 2006). I have photos of the handwritten Bible. See also Ryzhenko, *Stranniki My Na Zemle*, pp. 132, 228-9.

203. *Ikona Bozhiey Materi, Imenuemaya "Derzhavnaya"* [The Icon of God's Mother Named the Sovereign] [website], <http://hram-vlad-butovo.ru/kalendar/bmater/03/03.15_1. htm> accessed 6 November 2010. See also "*Skazanie o Yavlenii Derzhavnoy Ikony Bozhiey Materi*" [The Story of the Creation of the Icon of God's Mother Named the Sovereign], *ZhMP*, no. 3 (1996), pp. 37-8.

204. *Ikona Presvyatoy Bogoroditsy, Imenuemaya "Kaluzhskaya"* [The Icon of the Most Holy Virgin Named the Kaluzhskaya] [website], <http://www.hram.ru/index.php/library-bogorodica-51> accessed 6 November 2010. See also Tarasov, *Ikona i Blagochestie*, p. 49.

Similar kinds of mystical experiences, but involving the Holy Scriptures instead of the icon, were typical of Soviet Baptists. In the period from the 1950s to the 1970s, there were a number of instances in which Soviet Baptists, in apparently miraculous ways, found old copies of the Bible which had been hidden in odd corners by believers during Stalin's terror of the 1930s, and which were, as a rule, well-preserved.[205] Such events produced expressions of thanksgiving among Baptist church members, similar to the Orthodox celebrations on the occasion of any discovery of old holy icons. Soviet Baptists certainly discerned a work of God's providence in such incidents. For example, one person recalled that it was in Khrushchev's and Brezhnev's times, when believers had few Bibles, that these old Bibles were found.[206]

During the 1960s and 1970s in particular, to buy a Bible was very difficult and was also very expensive. Rural Baptists, many of whom had no Bible, were known to be selling poods of wheat,[207] or even a whole cow in order to buy one.[208] In 1979 *Vestnik Istiny*, which was being published by the Council of Churches of the ECB in that period in difficult underground conditions, described prayer offered by Baptists who had just received recently published Bibles in this way:

>...We bent the knee before the Giver of all good things, and took the Bibles in our hands. Some clasped [the Bibles] to their bosoms... as the dearest treasure, some excitedly held them in their trembling hands, others raised them up with care. And our exalted prayers, with deep appreciation for the

205. For instance: testimonies of a Baptist evangelist from Dushanbe, P.A. Semeryuk (Sacramento, California, USA, 2007), and the pastor of Tallinn Baptist church, M. Remmel (Prague, Czech Republic, 2007).

206. Testimony of P.A. Semeryuk (Sacramento, California, USA, 2007).

207. A unit of weight used in Russia, equal to 16.38 kilograms.

208. Testimonies of Baptist minister from Donetsk Region, M.M. Kolivayko (INT, Sacramento, California, USA, 2006) and former senior presbyter from South Kazakhstan P.A. Chumakin (INT, Kent, Washington, USA, 2006). See also: *VestI*, nos. 4-5 (2006), p. 51; A. de Chalandeau, "The Theology of the Evangelical Christians-Baptists in the USSR", p. 92.

unspeakable gift from the Lord, were going up to the throne
of the Most High.[209]

Although great excitement was felt by everyone, there were Russian Baptist
members in the rural areas who could not read. Some church members felt
certain that those who were unable to read could learn reading by using the
Gospel, that is by opening the Bible and praying to God about their problem.[210] Even among those who could read, but were in some measure "un-
schooled", there was a tendency to turn to familiar, "commonly known"
biblical texts only. Certain pages in the Bible were often opened. The rest
of "the depths of the wisdom of God", i.e. the greater part of the Bible, remained largely unread. It is also well known that Russian Baptist ministers
often divided biblical passages into those "acceptable for divine services"
(for example for preaching) and so-called "pages for personal study", which
usually included "unclear" or "difficult" verses of the Scripture.[211] In many
instances, however, the hoped-for "personal study" of these difficult passages probably did not take place. I had occasion to hear comments of
this kind about the Bible from "unlearned" members of a Baptist community: "Such a thick book... and written in such small letters... you
know I cannot manage this...!" On the other hand, there were Baptists
who read and re-read the Bible from cover to cover dozens of times.[212]
What united Russian Baptists, whether they read the Bible carefully or
not, was a mystical attitude to the Holy Scriptures. A.M. Bychkov wrote in
Bratsky Vestnik in 1979 about the consolation afforded to a Russian Baptist
woman through a dream:

---

209. [Anon], *"Bozhy Dar"* [God's Gift], *VestI*, no. 4 (1979), p. 2.

210. For example, testimony of presbyter from Bryansk, V.A. Serpikov (INT, Seattle,
Washington, USA, 2006). The well known *Life of Saint Sergius of Radonezh* includes
a similar miraculous story. See M.A. Pis'menny, ed., *Zhitie prepodobnogo Sergiya
Radonezhskogo* [Life of Saint Sergius of Radonezh] (M.: RIPOL KLASSIC, 2003), pp. 14-
18.

211. For instance, testimonies of former senior presbyter of Krasnodar Territory, V.D.
Erisov (Sacramento, California, USA, 2008), and presbyter from Alma-Ata, A.T.
Evstratenko (INT, San Diego, USA, 2006).

212. For instance, testimony of Baptist minister from Krasnodar, V.Ya. Bgatov (INT, San
Diego, California, USA, 2006). See also: *BV*, no. 2 (1990), p. 91.

A sister felt deep sorrow at the death of her father, who was a church minister. However, on one occasion she dreamed about the father, who said to her, 'Do not worry about me! Read more of the Bible...'[213]

It is important to note that these words about the dream were written not by an ordinary Baptist church member but by the General Secretary of the AUCECB. The dream which Bychkov described was about the reading of the Bible but also about the appearance of the church minister, delivering his message. A parallel is Orthodox Christians' dreams which encouraged prayer before the famous icons. The spirit of the Eastern Christian tradition, which is inseparable from mysticism and which valued sacred objects, was one that had an impact on many Soviet Baptists, both the ordinary people and their presbyters.

Conclusion

An analysis has been undertaken in this chapter of the organization of the church year, the liturgical order, church music and singing, major ceremonial acts, and the place of the Bible among the Russian Baptists in the Soviet era. The examination has focused on the way in which what was done among the Russian Baptists suggests parallels with Russian Orthodoxy. There were certainly external liturgical distinctions between the Orthodox Church and Russian Baptists in a number of these areas. But this is not entirely dissimilar to the situation among autocephalous Orthodox churches, where it has been permissible to have some liturgical variety.[214] What is striking is that behind the external Orthodox-Baptist differences in the areas examined there were many points of similarity, and behind these similarities was the power of historical and spiritual affinity.

---

213. A. Bychkov, "*Obzor Poslaniya k Evreyam*" [Review of the Epistle to the Hebrews], *BV*, no. 5 (1979), p. 20.

214. See, for instance: Archimandrite Alipy (Kastal'sky), Archimandrite Isaiya (Belov), *Dogmaticheskoe Bogoslovie: Kurs Lektsiy* [Dogmatic Theology: A Course of Lectures] (M.: Svyato-Troitskaya Sergieva Lavra, 2007), p. 21.

Though a number of the elements that can be observed in Soviet Baptist liturgy can be found in other Baptist communities outside Russia, taken as a whole the evidence presented in this chapter indicates that Soviet Baptist practices in worship constituted a unique phenomenon. Looking at the common church feasts, for example, testifies to the amazing closeness of Russian Baptist thinking to Orthodoxy. The "rigidity" of the order (rite) of the Baptist divine service, and a strict adherence to numerous traditions, underlines the likeness. Although Orthodox icons were rejected, there was significant development in the Soviet period as Baptists introduced wall-paintings into their churches. The sacramental attitude to the Bible examined here also closely parallels Orthodox ceremonial acts and the reverence for icons. Historically the icon was not infrequently seen as a kind of Bible, "the Bible for those who were ignorant".[215] The converse was also true. Russian Baptist piety created its own icon: the Bible. Orthodox liturgy helped to shape the "spirit" of Russian Baptist worship, and the latter followed many of the attitudes and aspects to be found in the Orthodox tradition.

---

215. See, for instance, Tarasov, *Ikona i Blagochestie*, p. 47.

CHAPTER 6

Communal Spiritual Traditions

The distinctive features of Russian Baptist theology, ecclesiology and liturgy in the period being studied in this work inevitably helped to shape spiritual traditions within the Russian Baptist communities. These had to do with their everyday life, and affected cultural-religious, ethical and ecumenical dimensions. This chapter explores a number of specific components of this "life-world" (*Lebenswelt*),[1] in particular what I have termed a monastic spirituality; the place of saints and also of "holy fools"; ethical issues related to pacifism; the formation of a spiritual identity; and ecumenical relationships between Soviet Baptists and the Orthodox Church. Elements of monastic thinking can be found among Russian evangelicals as far back as the early twentieth century. In the 1920s, I.S. Prokhanov planned to build "The City of the Sun" (*Evangelsk*) in the Siberian backwoods, and this vision, if it had been enacted, might have taken the form of a large "evangelical monastery".[2] However, Russian Baptist links with Orthodox spirituality became more explicit from the 1960s. This chapter will seek to evaluate the extent to which all these aspects of spirituality, as they were made concrete in Baptist communal spiritual traditions and ways of living out the Baptist faith, had connections with the Orthodox tradition.

---

1. See, for this, E. Husserl, *The Crisis of European Sciences and Transcendental Phenomenology* (Evanston, IL: Northwestern University Press, 1970).

2. "The City of the Sun will be great // The habit of drunkenness or the power of money // Will not reign there // But people will glorify God by their life…" – *Khristianin*, no. 1 (1928), pp. 15-16. Some monastic motifs are apparent.

The "Monastic Way" of Russian Baptists

I have already argued, in chapter 4, that the preparation for baptism in Russian Baptist communities can be compared with the Orthodox order for monastic profession. The Russian Baptist way of living can be seen as mirroring the Orthodox concept of "monasticism in the world", or "white monasticism", which was developed by many Orthodox authors. Orthodox Christians seeking to live out their faith in a serious way in the context of militant atheism were encouraged to raise "a kind of monastery wall between one's soul and the [evil] world."[3] For example, Archbishop John (Shakhovskoy) wrote in the 1930s:

> Anyone can be a monk – in his heart… King David had several wives but was a monk … he became the favored teacher of the hermits, the great elder of all monks… The 'white monasticism' has begun again… This is the first apostolic, martyr Christianity, the genuine discipleship of Christ… If you want to burn with love for the Lord, choose any way: of the white or black monastic life… The Apostles were already pure white monks, both Peter with his wife and Paul without a wife… There are many covert monks and nuns in Russia now.[4]

It is significant that Russian Baptists often spoke appreciatively of the monastic ("narrow") way, and compared themselves, whether realizing the full implications of this or not, with those who had taken "angelic habit". *Bratsky Vestnik* published some observations in the mid-1980s which offered an interpretation of Russian Orthodox monasticism as a kind of forerunner of the evangelical movement in Russia:

---

3. Deacon L. Kalinin, *Predislovie* [Preface], in Archpriest Valentin Sventsitsky, *Dialogi* [Dialogues] (M.: Pravoslavny Svyato-Tikhonovsky Bogoslovsky Institut, 1995), p. 10.
4. Archbishop Ioann (Shakhovskoy), *Beloe inochestvo* [White Monasticism] [1932], in Archbishop Ioann (Shakhovskoy), *Izbrannoe* [Selected Works] (Petrozavodsk: Svyatoy ostrov, 1992), p. 119.

Orthodoxy gave rise to the great seeking for God among the Russian people... Infinite numbers of cloisters and hermit-ages ...churches and chapels testify to this... There was one thing that Orthodoxy did not bring to the Russian people – a knowledge of the Bible.[5]

The Russian monks... also wakened the spiritual thirst ... [and] contributed to the strivings for spirituality in Russia.[6]

The first quotation, from Alexander Karev, illustrates a common percep-tion among Russian Baptists about a lack of biblical knowledge in the Orthodox Church, while at the same time monasteries come first in his list of Orthodox elements associated with seeking for God. Nor is it the case that the Orthodox relationship to the Bible was always seen nega-tively by Russian Baptists. In 1988, as 1,000 years of Christianity were celebrated in Russia, gratitude was expressed in *Bratsky Vestnik* for the Synodal translation of the Holy Scripture: "We appreciate the services of the Russian Orthodox Church, she provided... the Scripture: first in the church Slavonic language, and then also... in Russian."[7]

Among the elements in monasticism which Russian Baptists applaud-ed were its contribution to pastoral care in the monastic elders' ministry (*starchestvo*), its charitable works and its sense of mission. The first two of these features were stressed in articles in *Bratsky Vestnik* in 1988. One spoke of:

5. Words by A. Karev. Cited in A. Bychkov, "*100-letie Ob"edinitel'nykh S"ezdov*" [The Centenary of the Uniting Councils], *BV*, no. 6 (1984), pp. 44-5.

6. I. Gnida, "*Dukhovno-Patrioticheskoe Sluzhenie*" [Spiritual and Patriotic Ministry], *BV*, no. 6 (1984), p. 51. See also V. Popov, "*Isikhazm Kak Chayanie Dukhovnosti: Opyt Istoricheskogo Analiza*" [Hesychasm as Aspiration of Spirituality: An Attempt at Historical Analysis], *Al'manakh "Bogomyslie"*, no. 2 (1991), pp. 127-31.

7. "*Poslanie Tserkvam*" *ECB* [Epistle to the Churches of the ECB], *BV*, no. 3 (1988), p. 71.

The special service started in the monasteries... which consisted in the spiritual care and guidance for souls seeking salvation... Many people... followed the elders' admonitions.[8]

In another article, "I Was Sick and You Visited Me", words from a Russian
Orthodox priest were quoted with approval.

'Faith without works is dead'. The works of charity were an
integral part of the life of the church in the Old Russia. The
first hospitals and nursing homes originated in monasteries.[9]

Russian Baptist writers did not hesitate to positively speak of "The
Missionary Works of the Old Russian Monks".[10] The way in which they
cherished warm feelings for the best manifestations of the monastic way of
life is aptly summed up in this statement:

From the beginning of the Christianization of Russia, domestic monks did not lose contact with the life of the common
people. The sufferings of their neighbors, and the needs of
their native land were causes for concern for Christian ascetics. This is evident, for example, in the life of Sergius of
Radonezh, who had a humble monk's heart... Deep medita-
tion on Divine truths, and heavenly flights of spirit did not
isolate him from the surrounding world.[11]

These examples illustrate the thinking of AUCECB leaders, but it is
significant that the underground publications of the CCECB contained
very similar sentiments in their references to monastic spirituality. Thus

8. M. Chernopyatov, A. Vasiliev, "*Pravoslavnaya Tserkov*" [The Orthodox Church], *BV*,
no. 3 (1988), p. 50.
9. V. Mazharova, "*Byl Bolen, i Vy Posetili Menya*" [I was Sick, and you Visited Me], *BV*, no.
6 (1988), p. 69.
10. See I. Raymer, *Missionerskaya Deyatel'nost' Drevnerusskogo Monashestva* [The
Missionary Works of the Old Russian Monks] (n.p.: Izd-vo "Logos", 1996).
11. Popov, *Isikhazm Kak Chayanie Dukhovnosti*, p. 125.

one of the influential founders of the CCECB, Yu.K. Kryuchkov, who was the brother of the major CCECB leader, G.K. Kryuchkov, wrote in 2001 about earlier Russian Baptist communal spiritual traditions:

> We involuntarily adopted the mentality from the Russian Orthodox environment. In turn, that religious environment was based on the patterns of the Lives of Saints, various ascetics, monks and anchorites...[12]

Indeed it could be argued that the sympathies of the "unregistered" Soviet Baptists for aspects of monastic asceticism were stronger than those in the AUCECB, which was wary of "extremism". For instance, the service book produced by N.P. Khrapov contained instructions about very strict ascetic Christian duties, such as public confession of sin before the community and extended fasting, which would not have been found in many monasteries.[13] The following is a typical quotation from an article related to Eastern church history, published in *Vestnik Istiny*, the CCECB periodical, in 1977:

> The monks read the Holy Scripture in their cells, and worked to earn their daily bread. All of their property was common... They gathered for prayer and singing of psalms at midnight... In the desert [John Chrysostom] strengthened his spirit, in silence contemplating God, and at the same time, as a deacon, he served people... He gave his own silver to the poor.[14]

---

12. Yu. Kryuchkov, *Vnutritserkovnoe Dvizhenie ECB v Byvshem Sovetskom Soyuze* [Within the Church Movement of the ECB in the Former Soviet Union] (Sacramento, CA: n.p., 2001), p. 57.

13. Among the practices and duties were the "closed" mode of Communion, preceded by strict fasting and confession of sins before the congregation; continuous ministry, i.e. no "vacations" for presbyters; obligatory regular visiting of all church members; the absence of payment for ministries in the community; and even sometimes fasts "for 10, 15, 30 days" with total abstinence from food. All of these indicate the spirit of these communities. See Khrapov, *Dom Bozhy*, <http://www.blagovestnik.org/books/00280.htm#76>

14. *"John Chrysostom"* (editorial article), *VestI*, no. 4 (1977), p. 30.

Nor was this interest restricted to far-distant history. A minister of the Kiev Baptist community which was linked to the CCECB (and which afterwards became "autonomous"), P.F. Kunda, speaks of long and positive contacts which the Kiev church members had with a Russian Orthodox monk in the 1970s.[15] The idea of "desert solitude", or "living in retreat", like monks, was not alien to the spirituality of these Russian Baptists. For example, Boris M. Zdorovets, from Kharkov (the Ukraine), recalled how the first leader of the Initiative Group, A.F. Prokofiev, as he considered taking the step of publically protesting against the AUCECB, asked Zdorovets to find for him a "secluded room" in Kharkov (Ukraine) for fasting and prayer, and Prokofiev added, "I will not leave that place till either I receive what I ask [from God] or I die."[16]

Although the stress on monastic life highlights the way in which monks acted as spiritual examples, there was also the example of nuns. A church member in an ECB church in Gomel (Belarus), Nina Mazhnaya, spoke of how she was converted to evangelical faith in the 1950s, and sympathetically recalled the various responses of her unbelieving neighbors. When she started to attend the Baptist church regularly, they called her both a "Stundist" and a "Nun".[17] Boris Zdorovets often used the imagery and vocabulary of monks and nuns in his description of aspects of Russian Baptist life in the Khrushchev and Brezhnev eras. For example, he spoke of how he felt sorry for young women who sincerely turned to God and joined Baptist churches, at which point they realized they had come into a "Baptist convent", since women in the congregations as a rule heavily outnumbered men. Young unmarried women were traditionally bound by the following public words – a kind of vow. The question was, "Would you accept, if an unbeliever makes an offer of marriage to you?" The answer

15. Testimony of P.F. Kunda (INT, Sacramento, California, USA, 2006).

16. Testimony of B.M. Zdorovets (INT, Spokane, Washington, USA, 2006). B.M. Zdorovets was the inventor of the "blue" (hectographic) printing in the CCECB. When I interviewed him he spoke of his adoption of the hectograph from a cult Young Communist book, entitled *Mal'chik iz Urzhuma*, about underground workers-revolutionaries. See, for instance, the following edition: A. Golubeva, *Mal'chik iz Urzhuma: Povest' o Detstve i Yunosti S.M. Kirova* [A Boy from Urzhum: The Story of the Childhood and Youth of S.M. Kirov] (M.: Detgiz, 1949), pp. 162-3, where there is a detailed description of an elementary hectograph and its operation.

17. Testimony of N.F. Mazhnaya (INT, Fresno, California, USA, 2006).

was, "No, I have fallen in love with Jesus!"[18] In this way, Russian Baptists actually promoted a convent-like community. If the issue is looked at from a different standpoint, communities of monks and nuns constituted a kind of sectarian movement within Orthodoxy, whose mode of life often shocked the common laity of the Russian church. Relatives often mourned those family members who entered Orthodox monastic communities, much as they would have done for people who had "gone into a sect".[19] From this perspective, it is no wonder that there was sympathy for monasticism among "genuine sectarians" – the Evangelical Christians-Baptists.

It is significant, also, how readily Soviet Baptists (both in the AUCECB and the CCECB) used some words and special terms drawn from monastic life, for instance: *obitel'* (cloister, spiritual or holy abode),[20] *kel'ya* (monastic cell) and *podvizhnichestvo* (asceticism, selfless devotion). These terms are seen in the hymns sung in Russian Baptist worship. Hymns which speak of the spiritual or holy "abode" include the following lines:

> He will raise a holy abode for us,
> He will give us a golden crown...[21]

> The time is passing; you and I are called
> To another abode...[22]

Other hymns refer to the "cell":

> Knocking, I stand against your door.
> Admit me into your cell![23]

---

18. Testimony of B.M. Zdorovets (INT, Spokane, Washington, USA, 2006).

19. See, for instance: D. Yusupova, "*Okhota na Ved'm*" [A Witch-hunt], *Ogonek*, no. 40 (1998); N. Petrovskaya, "*Ya Ushel v Monastyr', Chtoby Byt' Schastlivym Chelovekom*" [I went into the Monastery to be a Happy Man], *Pravoslavnaya Gazeta (Yekaterinburg eparchy)*, no. 1 (1996); Podberezsky, *Protestanty i Drugie*, p. 89.

20. Both *Sbornik Dukhovnykh Pesen* and *Pesn' Vozrozhdeniya* have whole sections named *Nebesnye Obiteli* [Heavenly Abodes]. See *SDP*, pp. 344-72; *PV*, p. 325-52.

21. *SDP*, no. 106, p. 78. See also no. 130, p. 93; no. 285, p. 194; no. 464, p. 309.

22. *PV*, no. 296, p. 192. See also no. 92, p. 60; no. 200, p. 130; no. 312, p. 203.

23. *SDP*, no. 140, p. 99; *PV*, no. 332, p. 215.

In the innermost cell of the heart...[24]

Similar themes appeared in articles in Russian Baptist periodicals:

> We have to reach the following spiritual [mountain] peaks: ...
> purity of heart, prayer, asceticism...[25]

> We have to follow the example of spiritual leaders who
> gave their lives for the Lord... and to continue their selfless
> devotion.[26]

> To strive to do [good] deeds for God's sake, to give self-sacri-
> ficing devotion... the asceticism of the narrow way...[27]

Some specific monastic motifs also struck a deep chord within the hearts
of Russian Baptists, for instance the mystical tradition of the "spiritual ladder", most famously associated with St. John Climacus (7th century),[28] in
which the picture is of gradual, submissive climbing of a "ladder" up to
God in heaven. The preface to the monastic *The Ladder of Divine Ascent*,
portraying the thinking of St. John Climacus, states:

> This book... presents to us a firmly-based ladder leading us up
> from the earthly to the holy of holies, at the summit of which
> is the God of love. Jacob saw... this ladder also... when he
> slept on his ascetic couch. Let us ascend... with diligence and

---

24. *SDP*, no. 122, p. 88; *PV*, no. 351, p. 226. See also this reference: "Where you are
now: in the secluded cell or on the working place..." – *"Nasha Bran"* [Our Battle]
(editorial article), *VestI*, no. 1 (1977), p. 9.

25. *"Semidesyatiletie Generalnogo Secretarya VSECB A. V. Kareva"* [The Seventieth Birthday
of the Secretary-General of the AUCECB, A.V. Karev], *BV*, no. 1 (1965), p. 76.

26. V. Zinchenko, *"Prodolzhenie Podviga"* [Continuity with the Exploit], *VestI*, no. 2
(1986), p. 10.

27. *"Veroyu Prines Bogu Zhertvu Luchshuyu"* [He Offered to God a Better Sacrifice]
(editorial article), *VestI*, no. 2 (2001), p. 36.

28. See St. John Climacus, *Lestvitsa* [The Ladder of Divine Ascent] (Svyato-Uspensky
Pskovsko-Pechersky Monastyr', 1994); *Monasheskaya Zhizn' (Vypusk 1)* [Monastic Life,
Issue 1] [1885] (Svyato-Uspensky Pskovo-Pechersky monastyr', 1994).

faith... The saintly Father, arranging the ascent for us, wisely decided... to depict a ladder that included 30 rungs of spiritual perfection...[29]

Russian Baptist authors such as Ya. Zhidkov, Karev and Kolesnikov referred on many occasions to this favorite theme of Orthodox spirituality, with the meaning of the rungs of the ladder being commented upon on some occasions, while on other occasions the whole ladder was seen as the cross of Christ or as the church:

> As with the ladder which Jacob saw in his dream, with the angels of God descending and ascending to heaven, we also have both descents and ascents in our spiritual life... The first rung... is forgiveness and justification... The second rung... is the receiving of the gift of the Holy Spirit...[30]

> The words of the Scripture about the ladder, which Jacob saw in a dream, also light up the Cross of Christ on Calvary... Jacob's ladder joined the earth with heaven. The Cross of Calvary has the image of reconciliation of heaven and the earth... Millions of sinners climbed this blessed ladder... to heaven.[31]

> The church is the ladder joining the earth with heaven ('because the church is the threshold of heaven') – Genesis 28:12.[32]

Although in the first quotation (from Ya. Zhidkov) the rungs were associated with stages marked out in Protestant spiritual experience,

---

29. St. John Climacus, *Lestvitsa*, p. 5.

30. Ya. Zhidkov, "*Preobrazhenie Gospodne*" [Transfiguration of the Lord], *BV*, nos. 5-6 (1962), p. 40; See also I. Tatarchenko, "*Dukhovnaya Lestnitsa*" [Spiritual Ladder], *BV*, no. 6 (1969), pp. 47-8; S. Fadyukhin, "*Bog Vsemogushchiy Blagoslovil Menya*" [God Almighty has Blessed me], *BV*, no. 5 (1982), p. 18.

31. A. Karev, "*Golgofa*" [Calvary], *BV*, no. 3 (1964), p. 24. See also A. Karev, "*Golgofa*" [Calvary], *BV*, no. 2 (1974), p. 25.

32. Kolesnikov, *V Pomoshch' Propovedniku*, vol. II, p. 295.

the Orthodox idea of the *long* daily spiritual transfiguration and theosis (θείωσις) was also clearly expressed.[33] An anonymous author in *Bratsky Vestnik* in 1972 was evidently influenced by depictions of *The Ladder* in two famous icons, one from the twelfth century and one from the sixteenth century.[34]

> *The Ladder* from the cloister of St. Catherine on Mount Sinai is a unique icon created in the 12th century... The ladder is going up to heaven, where Jesus Christ meets those who struggled through every hardship... The monks are climbing the ladder; some of them break down and fall ... into the hands of demons, who are on the watch for their victims, using cords and pincers, and shooting arrows from their bows... The way of ascetic righteousness opens before us, the way of the Christian's ascent to eternal life.[35]

> There is a ladder from earth to heaven. People dressed in monastic clothes are climbing it. The Lord is holding out His hands... This is an Old Russian icon of the 16th century. In the middle of the image, there is a church as the representation of the threshold of Paradise... There are many temptations on the way to things above – the demons, by their hooks and pincers, pull the monks off the ladder of salvation into the pit of hell...[36]

---

33. See, for instance: Lossky, *In the Image and Likeness of God*, pp. 97-110; N. Russell, *The Doctrine of Deification in the Greek Patristic Tradition* (N.Y.: Oxford University Press, 2004); Archbishop Georgy, *Obozhenie Kak Smysl Chelovecheskoy Zhizni* [Theosis as the Meaning of Human Life] (Izdanie Vladimirskoy Eparkhii, 2000).

34. There are two main versions of the icon *The Ladder*, narratively bearing a strong likeness to one another: the Byzantine (12th C.) and the Russian (16th C.) ones. Their images can be seen, for instance, on the official Russian Orthodox website *Pravoslavie.Ru*, <http://days.pravoslavie.ru/Images/ii986&1327.htm> accessed 7 November 2010.

35. O. Popova, *Vizantiyskie Ikony VI-XV Vekov* [The Byzantine Icons of the 6th – 15th Centuries], in *Istoriya Ikonopisi: Istoki, Traditsii, Sovremennost'. VI-XX Veka* [History of Icon Painting: Origin, Traditions, the Present. The 6th – 20th Centuries] (M.: ART-BMB, 2002), pp. 64-5. See also P. Rak, *Priblizheniya k Afonu* [Approaches to Mount Athos] (SPb.: Satis, 1995), p. 10.

36. E. Stepanova, *Za Tri Shaga do Nimba* [Three Strokes off the Nimbus]. *Neskuchny Sad*

The following is the description of the "spiritual ladder" in *Bratsky Vestnik*, which warned against taking a false step that could lead to a fall.

> This idea is well expressed by... a painting depicting some people climbing a ladder to heaven. The angels of Satan are shown flying near the ladder. They hold in their hands steel hooks, which are being used to push the people off the ladder. One man is already falling from the bottom rung of the ladder. There are some who are stumbling, even among those who have climbed high... God holds out His hands... but a man is falling... This painting alerts all believers to the danger of a lapse at any time.[37]

Although in the *Bratsky Vestnik* article the word "icon" was replaced by the neutral term "a painting", the editorial board of *Bratsky Vestnik* made an unambiguous identification of Soviet Baptists with Russian Orthodox monks, in their highly demanding divine ascent, as well as in their spiritual struggle against the powers of darkness. Soviet Baptists spoke about the ladder in church services,[38] described dreams about it,[39] and wrote poetry on the subject.[40] The monastic way, with its spiritual outlook, including the idea of a ladder from earth to heaven, fascinated Russian Baptists.

(The Orthodox Life's Periodical), no. 2 (2008), <http://www.nsad.ru/index.php?issue=45§ ion=10019&article=879> accessed 7 November 2010.

37. [Anon], "*Na Rasput'e*" [At the Crossroads], *BV*, no. 4 (1972), p. 66.

38. For example, the following was said during a church service of the Petropavlovsk Baptist community (Kazakhstan) at the end of the 1980s (I recorded the words), "Saving faith has three steps, like the rungs of a ladder... The first two of them are not able to save anybody, but the third one will save. However, it is impossible to rise to the third rung before having risen to the first two..."

39. See for instance, the chapter "Ladder to Heaven" (interview with A.T. Kharchenko) in the book *Podvig Very: Unikal'nye Svidetel'stva o Zhizni Khristian v SSSR* [Fight of Faith: Unique Testimonies about the Life of Christians in the USSR] (n.p.: Pacific Coast Slavic Baptist Association, 2009), pp. 371-7.

40. See, for instance, the poem *Lestnitsa Zhizni* [The Ladder of Life], <http://www. blagovestnik.org/books/ 00430/db/v6171177.html> accessed 7 November 2010.

Lives of Saints

The topic to be addressed here is the degree to which Russian Orthodox interpretations of holiness, which involved a focus on the "Lives of Saints", was echoed among Russian Baptists. The Orthodox classic, *Lives of the Saints*, seems to have been one influence, but there were others. It is important to note that the absence of official church canonization is not, by any means, an obstacle in the way of general public reverence for someone as a saint. In the Russian Orthodox Church, alongside universal canonization, there is also a local procedure, which involves the recognition within a certain diocese or even a monastery or a church, of the saintly life of someone known in that community.[41] It was this which provided the model that was taken up among the Russian Baptists.

For example, accounts of the holy lives of two Baptist ministers, Joseph A. Laptev and Ivan V. Ivolin, became widespread among the Baptist congregations of the Volga River region and the South of Russia. Several people recount stories about their lives with the same hagiographic features. They were both seen as "holy paupers" (*svyatye bessrebreniki*), giving their lives completely in the service of the Lord. In 1950s and 1960s, Joseph Laptev lived in the small town of Shakhuniya (Gorky Region) and served as a rural preacher. He was never married, and was seen as someone offering his whole life to God. According to eyewitness accounts, J.A. Laptev was a good, humble pastor, constantly fasting and praying. He never accepted any presents from members of the congregation, however much he was offered them. He refused even to eat meals in the villages where he served. When Laptev was invited to table in a house, the narratives state that he usually answered, "Thank you! There is nothing I want, I am fasting today." In the difficult post-war time, Joseph Laptev earned his daily bread by weaving wicker baskets and mending galoshes using old car tyres. He loved to copy instructive Christian books by hand, as well as texts of Holy Scripture (which decorated the whole room where he lived). It was also known that J.A. Laptev was on friendly terms with a local Orthodox priest and that they used to sit together for hours conversing with pleasure about

---

41. See, for instance, Fedotov, *Svyatye Drevney Rusi*, pp. 34-5.

spiritual things – both about what united all Christians and (delicately) about where Orthodox and Baptist ways had parted.[42]

Ivan V. Ivolin served in the 1960s as the pastor of Pyatigorsk Baptist Church (in the Northern Caucasus - Stavropol Territory). According to the testimonies, he (like Laptev) was a humble servant of God, a preacher of the Gospel, living a holy life almost in complete poverty. Brothers and sisters in the Baptist community wanted to help him. They often left gifts of food or clothes in his house without being noticed, but I.V. Ivolin immediately gave away all the gifts to the poor. When church members decided on a level of payment for the pastor, which was set at 90 roubles a month, he accepted only 30. Ivolin visited every church member seven times a year, encouraging them, consoling them and praying with them. In his way of preaching from the Bible – he was known as an outstanding preacher – Ivolin was a disciple of the biblical teacher of a previous generation, Ivan Kargel. Even visitors who came to Pyatigorsk from Moscow (Pyatigorsk is a spa town) said on many occasions that they had rarely heard sermons that were so simple and yet lodged themselves so deeply in their minds.[43] Even stylistically the stories of Laptev and Ivolin bear a strong resemblance to the Russian Orthodox "Lives of Saints".[44] The unmarried state of these holy Baptists also comes to the fore, which again mirrors the ancient monastic tradition.

It was not only unmarried ministers, however, who could be regarded as saints. A Baptist woman who died in the 1980s acquired such a reputation not only in her own Baptist community but also among Orthodox believers. This lady, who had four adopted children, barely survived the terrible famine and the persecutions of Christians in the 1930s. At the beginning of the World War II, when the area was occupied by the Nazis, all the

---

42. Testimonies of several church members of ECB from Gorky Region and Krasnodar Territory, for instance: M.A. Vasiliev and O.E. Avdeeva (INT, Everett, Washington, USA, 2006).

43. For example, testimonies of Baptist church members from Krasnodar, S.G. Odaryuk and N.M. Odaryuk (INT, Everett, Washington, USA, 2006). Some sermons of I.V. Ivolin were published. See for instance: I. Ivolin, *"Ogon' Svyatogo Dukha"* [The Fire of the Holy Spirit], *BV*, no. 3 (1969), pp. 45-6.

44. See, for instance, the life stories of Russian paupers for God: Sts. Feodor and Vasily – *ZhSDR*, vol. XII, pp. 160-72; St. Tikhon Lukhovsky – Ibid., vol. X, p. 389; St. Evstraty Pechersky – Ibid., vol. VII, pp. 573-7.

village activists and Communists were arrested. The German authorities compelled the peasants, who had been victims of the Soviet regime, to give evidence against the Communists. Many people willingly put their signatures to the charges against the Communists, but this Baptist woman refused and said that she had already forgiven her persecutors, as Christ taught. At this the Germans threatened her, and finally lashed her cruelly with a whip. However, she endured this suffering calmly. She did much simple, good Christian work over her long life and when she died in the 1980s many people in the area, both the Baptists and Russian Orthodox, gathered for the funeral. During the ceremony, according to some eyewitness accounts, despite the cloudless midday heat, raindrops started falling – "the heavens were weeping".[45]

The way in which saints suffered persecution was a recurring theme. There are many testimonies from older Russian Baptist church members about how Christians showed great courage both under Stalin's regime and during subsequent Communist years. In Soviet labor camps they were beaten and starved, and guard dogs were set on them. According to one commonly-accepted narration, on one occasion these dogs did not touch two Russian Baptists who were ready to die as martyrs.[46] The theme of the meekness of the most dangerous animals towards God's holy people echoes the Russian Orthodox *Lives of Saints*. For example, it is reported about St. Sergius of Radonezh that, when he lived in forest, ravenous wolves and bears did not touch him.[47] There are also some familiar hagiographical features, replete with pious interpretations, regarding the martyrdom for the faith of a Baptist, Nikolai Khmara (Altai Territory, 1964). Walter Sawatsky

---

45. Testimony from the website of the Russian Baptist Union, <http://old.baptist. org.ru> accessed 8 November 2010. The episode with the Germans has echoes of the hagiographical story about robbers who assaulted St. Seraphim of Sarov: he did not resist them and was beaten severely, but when the robbers were caught the Saint announced his forgiveness of them and interceded for mercy, which caused their repentance. See *"Zhitie prep. Serafima Sarovskogo"* [The Life of St. Seraphim of Sarov], in *ZhSDR*, vol. V, pp. 77-9.

46. For instance, testimonies of Baptist ministers: V.N. Khot'ko (Petropavlovsk, Kazakhstan, 2000), Ya. A. Meleshkevich (Bishkul, Kazakhstan, 2003). See also C. Prokhorov, *Sektantskie Rasskazy* [Sectarian Stories] (Idar-Oberstein, Germany: Titel Verlag, 2002), pp. 23-6.

47. *Zhitie prepodobnogo Sergiya Radonezhskogo* [Life of Saint Sergius of Radonezh], pp. 32-3. See also Cloistress Taisiya, *Russkoe Pravoslavnoe Zhenskoe Monashestvo*, pp. 15, 32, 245.

quotes words used about Khmara, which asserted that he had "talked about Christ till the end and therefore his captors had torn out his tongue".[48] The story of Khmara seems to have been shaped to some extent by the well-known narratives about the "Sufferings of St. Gordius the Martyr" and the "Life of St. Maximus the Confessor". The faithfulness of these saints, in the face of great evil, inspired vigour in Christians of all ages.[49]

A further marked feature of all of these saintly characters was a lack of concern about finance to provide for their own needs. A minister of a large Baptist church in Kazakhstan, who oversaw the distribution of substantial amounts of money donated for the poor, was recognizable by the threadbare clothes he wore. He was so self-neglectful in everyday life that he became a proverb among many people inside and outside the church.[50] This characteristic is seen in ministers, but also in lay members. Another account from Kazakhstan is about a Baptist congregation's treasurer, A.L. Manyakin, who in the 1960s, because he did not have any money of his own with him, walked a long way (rather than paying for transport) with the whole of the church's money in his possession to the place where it needed to be deposited. When the leaders in the congregation found out and asked the treasurer about this, he answered, "How could I have taken a penny from there [the bag], it is the Lord's money!"[51] The accounts do not suggest that any shortcomings were present in these saintly people.

Saints were recognized not only in and through their life, but in their death, and details were given about that final earthly event. In 1977 the General Secretary of the AUCECB, A.M. Bychkov, spoke about Orthodox people treating some pious Baptists with special respect at the time of their death:

---

48. Sawatsky, *Soviet Evangelicals Since World War II*, p. 143.

49. See *"Stradanie Sv. Muchenika Gordiya"* [The Sufferings of St. Gordius the Martyr], in *ZhSDR*, vol. V, pp. 146-7; *"Zhitie Prep. Maksima Ispovednika"* [The Life of St. Maximus the Confessor], in *ZhSDR*, vol. V, p. 715.

50. I am well acquainted with this remarkable minister. Since he is still alive, I do not mention his name here, knowing he would not approve of that.

51. Testimony of Baptist church members I.M. Kaplenkov and A.M. Kaplenkov (Petropavlovsk, Kazakhstan, 1997).

Recently, there was a funeral of an old Baptist presbyter in
a small town in Central Russia. When the procession approached the local Orthodox Church, the priest commanded
that the bells be sounded in honor of the deceased minister of
Christ...[52]

In certain cases eminent saints might predict their own deaths. A.I.
Mitskevich, Assistant General Secretary of the AUCECB, reproduced a
story about Ivan Kargel, who in his advanced years had a vision about
the time of his death, which was exactly fulfilled (Kargel died in 1937), a
spiritual phenomenon which impressed Mitskevitch.[53] Nor did this belong
only to earlier evangelical history in Russia. There was a report about a former Baptist prisoner's exact prediction of his date of death in Zhitomir in
1964. The account stated: "He had a special sensitivity to the voice of God,
but for this he had first to do ten years in Solovki prison for his Christian
faith."[54] Similar visions are to be found in Russian Orthodox monastic
communities.[55]

Analyzing the narratives of the Baptist "saints", although in a number
of the cases cited names are mentioned, many Baptist hagiographies, like
the Orthodox Lives of Saints, omit certain crucial details: it is not always
clear where and when the events were taking place. The moral example
and the spiritual edification come first, not the historical context. Here, for
example, is a characteristic note that many Soviet Baptists of the 1950s to
the 1970s struck in their intimate diaries, "The address of the Christian:
the Spiritual Homeland, the Gospel Region, Zion District, the Heavenly
City, Narrow Way Street, the Thorny Lane, the House of the Tabernacle.

---

52. A. Bychkov, "110-letie Russko-Ukrainskogo Bratstva ECB" [The 110th Anniversary
of the Russian-Ukrainian Brotherhood of the ECB], BV, no. 5 (1977), p. 70. For the
Orthodox tradition of sounding the bells to give the last honors to deceased Christians,
see, for instance, S. Bulgakov, Nastol'naya Kniga Dlya Svyashchenno-Tserkovno-Sluzhiteley
[Handbook for Church Servers] [1913] (M.: Izdatel'sky Otdel Moskovskogo Patriarkhata,
1993), pp. 1329-30.

53. Mitskevich, Istoriya Evangel'skikh Khristian-Baptistov, p. 116.

54. Testimony of Baptist church member from Zhitomir, N.O. Sobchenko (INT,
Sacramento, California, USA, 2006).

55. For a range of examples, see Cloistress Taisiya, Russkoe Pravoslavnoe Zhenskoe
Monashestvo, pp. 52, 53, 139, 140, 142, 149, 155, 162, 200, 218, 219.

The guide leading there is the Holy Spirit; to find the way, ask for the Watchman of Conscience."[56]

The style is somewhat reminiscent of John Bunyan, but a closer connection is with Orthodoxy, as indicated by these words by a Russian Orthodox hagiographical author about a particular saint: "But from what town or hamlet and from what family such a leading light was descended we did not find in the writings, God knows this; for us it is enough to know that he was a citizen of the heavenly Jerusalem, God was his Father and the Holy Church was his Mother, his close relations were all-night many-tearful prayers and unceasing groanings, and his neighbors were vigilant desert works."[57] The tendency to emphasize sainthood, to dwell on spiritual events, meant that often very little was said about actual historical data. To a considerable degree, the narratives of the saints in Russian Orthodox and Soviet Baptist hagiography contain similar features.

God's Fools

In the Russian context, the spiritual phenomenon of foolishness for Christ's sake has been closely related to the theme of holiness. In the Eastern Christian tradition, Christ himself, who taught that his Kingdom is "not from this world", was often interpreted as the first of "God's fools".[58] Although the place of the fool is ambiguous, many Russian Orthodox people consider God's fools as the most honored saints.[59] Their unconventional life style, even their "insanity", seems to many to demonstrate sincerity of religious feeling, child-like trust in God, and extreme forms of Christian asceticism. Hundreds of fools for Christ's sake became famous in Orthodox Russia, and a number were canonized.[60] In such an atmosphere, it is not surprising

---

56. From the personal files of a church member of Omsk Central Baptist Church, G.E. Kuchma.

57. Cited in V. Klyuchevsky, *Sochineniya*, vol. VII, pp. 74-5.

58. See, for instance, Yu. Ryabinin, *Russkoe Yurodstvo* [Russian Foolishness for Christ] (M.: RIPOL klassik, 2007), p. 5.

59. See, for instance, S. Ivanov, *Vizantiyskoe Yurodstvo* [Byzantine Foolishness for Christ] (M.: Mezhdunarodnye Otnosheniya, 1994), pp. 4-5.

60. See, for instance: S. Yurkov, *Pod Znakom Groteska: Antipovedenie v Russkoy Kulture,*

that Russian Baptists also had many fools for Christ. According to a curious legend going back to the nineteenth century, Ivan G. Ryaboshapka, one of the pioneers of the evangelical movement in the South of Russia, "played the fool" at fairgrounds. He liked to shout loudly, "He has stolen it! He has stolen it!" The people gathered around him and asked what had been stolen. Ryaboshapka answered them, "Satan stole the people's salvation!"… After a while he shouted again, "I have found it! I have found it!" The onlookers gathered again, "What you have found?" Ryaboshapka answered joyfully, "I have found my eternal salvation!" And then, having gathered large crowds, he started his unusual "popular preaching".[61]

In the period from the 1960s to the 1980s, dozens of "fools for Christ" became known among Soviet Baptists. The most famous of them was probably Vanya Moiseev. He came from the Moldavian village of Volontirovka, where his church was associated with the CCECB. In 1972, while in military service in the Soviet Army (in his second year of service) in the Crimean city of Kerch, Vanya suffered the death of a martyr for his Christian faith. There was a "holy simplicity" about him, an evident foolishness for Christ's sake, and also he was associated with miracles, all of which distinguished him from many other Baptist sufferers of the Communist times. The official sources of the CCECB reported that Vanya Moiseev saw visions of the heavenly Jerusalem, of Old Testament saints, and of apostles of Christ. It was said that he communed with the angels.[62] During his military service, Vanya prayed many hours a day, as he had done previously at home. In a simple way he told other soldiers and commanders (Communists) about

11 – *Nachalo 20 vv.* [Under the Sign of the Grotesque: Anti-behaviour in the Russian Culture, 11th – the Beginning of 20th C.] (SPb.: Letny sad, 2003), pp. 52-3; *Khristianstvo: Entsiklopedichesky Slovar'*, v. III, pp. 286-7.

61. *Ryaboshapka* (typescript), from personal files of Russian Baptist historian S.N. Savinsky (Salt Lake City, Utah, USA, 2006). See also, V. Koval'kov, E. Sokolov, "*I.G. Ryaboshapka*", *BV*, no. 6 (1981), p. 60. Being peasant by birth, I.G. Ryaboshapka used the language of common people. For example, there is a testimony about the following expression from his "baptismal rite", "You make a vow… to serve God faithfully to the grave". Cited in Savinsky, *Istoriya (1867-1917)*, p. 323. His appearance also often agreed with the status of a fool for Christ: for instance, there is a report about a visit to St. Petersburg by Ryaboshapka who traveled there for a meeting of brethren dressed in a red shirt and wide trousers – one of the trouser legs was tucked into his shabby boot, and the second one was "rolled high up". See *BV*, no. 6 (1981), p. 57.

62. See *Podrazhayte Vere Ikh*, pp. 350, 355-6.

Jesus Christ, enduring many mockeries and beatings because of this. Once he publicly prophesied that an unbelieving sergeant would get home leave. Vanya said: "I prayed with my spirit, and the Lord revealed it to me". Although this sergeant was someone who, it seemed, had no chance to visit his home in the foreseeable future, the leave was granted. Vanya miraculously recovered after a severe injury without any doctors; he could survive without food for several days; in the freezing winter weather he walked for entire nights outside in only a summer uniform, without detriment to his health; and he took all the punishments from his commanders without grumbling and even joyfully, happily scrubbing the floor of the barracks with brush and soap, which was always considered especially humiliating work for second-year soldiers. Finally he became a martyr for Christ.[63]

Comparing the exploits of Vanya Moiseev with the lives of well-known Russian fools for Christ's sake, there are many similar features: meekness of spirit and love for the people around them, including their oppressors; "strange" public conduct; great zeal in prayer; visions of the spiritual, angelic realm; gifts of miracle-working and prophecy; and an ascetic mode of life. Thus St. Procopius of Ustyug suffered with humility many "vexations, reproaches, and beatings" for his foolishness for Christ;[64] St. Michael Klopsky was known for his special asceticism, as well as indefatigable praying and also miracles;[65] St. Simon of Yuryevets walked in the winter in a flaxen shirt and without any footwear;[66] and St. Vasily the Blessed was considered worthy of angelic visions and had a powerful prophetic gift.[67] Similar things can be said about Procopius of Vyatka, Nikolai of Pskov, and

---

63. See *Inye Zhe Zamucheny Byli* [The Others were Tortured] (booklet of the CCECB, 1970s), pp. 1-32; *Podrazhayte Vere Ikh*, pp. 340-61; Testimony of a church member of the ECB from the Crimea, V.P. Litovchenko, who was personally acquainted with Vanya Moiseev (INT, Los Angeles, California, USA, 2006).

64. See Fedotov, *Svyatye Drevney Rusi*, pp. 202-3.

65. Ibid., pp. 203-4.

66. See A. Panchenko, "Smekh Kak Zrelishche" [Laughter as a Spectacle], in D. Likhachev, A. Panchenko, N. Ponyrko, *Smekh v Drevney Rusi* [Laughter in the Old Russia] (Leningrad: Nauka, 1984), p. 119.

67. See A. Panchenko, "Yurodivye na Rusi" [Fools for Christ in Russia], in A. Panchenko, *Russkaya Istoriya i Kultura* [Russian History and Culture] (SPb.: Yuna, 1999), p. 397; *Khristianstvo: Entsiklopedichesky Slovar'*, vol. I, pp. 338-9.

many other fools for Christ's sake in the Orthodox spiritual tradition.[68] The tradition continued in Orthodoxy, and (for instance) Baptist church members spoke well of a Russian Orthodox "fool for Christ" in the 1950s and 1960s who walked barefoot and prayed in winter as well as summer around the city of Mariupol.[69]

Boris Zdorovets from the Ukraine was another famous Soviet Baptist who can be seen as a fool for Christ. In December 1961, during his first arrest (because of his many activities among Christian youth), Boris "played the fool" with agents of the KGB and the militia for about three hours, not opening the door of his house despite their commands to do so. The militiamen had arrived at 5.00 a.m., and Zdorovets lectured them from inside the house, with the humor so characteristic of him, telling them that only bandits make a living at that time. They should, he said, come at 8 o'clock. The militiamen waited in the cold for a time and then began to break the door down. Boris, who was, like many Soviet Baptists, a pacifist, shouted at them through the door, "Hey, woman! Bring me the axe; some bandits are forcing the hut!"[70] When Zdorovets was imprisoned, he fasted for 15 days and nights (only drinking water) each time he was put into the punishment cell, where he ended up quite often because of his "misbehavior". When the policy of the CCECB towards its own "dissidents" became harsh, and excommunications even of reputable ministers became common practice, Zdorovets once challenged a CCECB leader who was handing out excommunications. In the midst of a church service Zdorovets gave this minister a rope and bar of soap, announcing "That is enough of tormenting God's people!"[71] Zdorovets had many visions in his life, prophesied ("to talk with the Lord through the Bible is the same as to communicate with your father by letters; that is not enough"), and in prayer in the labor camp in the

---

68. See, for instance: Hieromonk Alexey (Kuznetsov), *Yurodstvo i Stolpnichestvo* [Foolishness for Christ and Pillar Asceticism] [1913] (M.: Izd-vo Moskovskogo Podvoria Svyato-Troitskoy Sergievoy Lavry, 2000), pp. 202-4.

69. See V. Vivsik, *Vernye do Kontsa v Stalinskuyu Epokhu* [Faithful until Death in Stalin's Epoch] (Sacramento, CA: n.p., 2004), pp. 73-7.

70. Testimony of B.M. Zdorovets (INT, Spokane, Washington, USA, 2006).

71. The rope and soap may have been a picture of the dismal end of Judas Iscariot. See B. Zdorovets, *Kakim Sudom Sudite* [In the Way You Judge], <http://www.praize.com/denominations/group650/index.shtml> accessed 28 July 2009.

1960s he used homemade prayer beads with 33 apricot stones.[72] Some Baptists denounced such unusual conduct, but others saw this as genuine foolishness for Christ's sake.[73]

In the life of Zdorovets another important facet of traditional Russian foolishness for Christ was exemplified: courageous denunciation of the "powers that be", whether in church or state. Although well read and highly gifted, he often put on the "mask of foolishness",[74] which he used to condemn both representatives of the state atheistic authorities and some Baptist leaders. Such actions, unthinkable for common people and even for those from the Russian nobility, were often permitted to fools for Christ, through whom, according to a pious belief, God had spoken.[75] For example, in the sixteenth century when St. John of Moscow (known as John Big-Cap because he wore a heavy iron cap) met Tsar Boris Godunov, he openly warned the Tsar about the consequences of his unrighteous government.[76] Another sixteenth-century Russian saint, also a fool for Christ, Blessed Nicholai of Pskov, according to legend once offered the Tsar Ivan the Terrible a piece of raw meat during Lent. "I am a Christian and do not eat meat during Lent!" the Tsar responded, turning pale. "But you drink Christian blood!" said the saint.[77] Against such a historical background, Boris Zdorovets' denunciation of a "Baptist tsar", with a rope and soap in his hands, can be more readily understood.[78]

---

72. Testimony of B.M. Zdorovets (INT, Spokane, Washington, USA, 2006). Beads are mandatory for Orthodox monks, and 33 beads symbolize the years of the earthly life of Jesus Christ. See, for instance S. Trofimov, *Chetki* [The Beads] (M.: AST, 2001), pp. 16-25; *Pravoslavnaya Entsiklopediya* [Russian Orthodox Encyclopaedia], ed. by O. Markicheva (M.: AST, 2007), p. 373.

73. For instance, a Kharkov town newspaper *Sobytie* [Event] once published an extended article about Boris Zdorovets' life. In this article, written with evident sympathy, he was called a fool for Christ. – S. Rudenko, *"Vashe Vremya Konchilos"* [Your Time is Up], *Sobytie*, 29 Aug. 1992.

74. For the foolishness for Christ of sane Orthodox people in Russian history, see for instance A. Panchenko, "Yurodivye na Rusi", pp. 392-3.

75. See, for instance, *Svyatyni Drevney Moskvy* [Sacred Places of Ancient Moscow] (M.: Nikos, Kontakt, 1993), p. 7.

76. See Hieromonk Alexey, *Yurodstvo i Stolpnichestvo*, p. 187.

77. See, for instance, Fedotov, *Svyatye Drevney Rusi*, pp. 207-8.

78. There were also symbolic presents given to Baptist fools for Christ. Two handkerchiefs were presented to the newly elected presbyter of the Chernovtsy community, K.S. Sedletsky, at the end of the 1950s/beginning of the 1960s. It was prophetically said

Another case of "Christian foolishness" in Soviet Baptist life happened in Karaganda, Kazakhstan, in 1986. A Baptist who was well known in the region, N.N., had what he believed was a supernatural message to visit a local high-ranking officer of the KGB. Having presented himself at the KGB office, a short meeting, without any previous agreement, took place. During the meeting, there was the following remarkable dialogue.

> NN: The Lord himself has sent me to you to say that you should repent and believe in the Gospel.
> KGB officer: What is your business with me?
> NN: There is just one problem: the salvation of your soul.
> Officer: If this is the problem, I do not want to talk with you.
> NN: … I directed my steps to the [office] door, stooping down and saying, 'Shake off the dust from your feet' (Luke 9:5)… 'I do not know when your soul will pass into eternity – tomorrow or the day after tomorrow. I had occasion to talk with Volodya in the coalmine. 'I have enough time', he said, but he did not have enough time, he departed into eternity early…'
> Officer: You know, there is a penal code article on in-timidation. I can inform the right people, and you will be punished.
> NN: I stand ready for any punishment, so long as you are saved… I will continue to pray for you. God bless you… O Lord! … I beg of you: help him not to perish.[79]

In this story there are echoes of another version of the "sacred plot" of meetings of a "holy fool" with a "Tsar". There is divine revelation, a feel-ing of being an instrument in God's hands, an unexpected meeting but

---

regarding his "many tears" that the big hanky was for crying privately before God, and the small one for weeping in public. – Sedletsky, "Vospominaniya", p. 92.

79. V. Zhuravlev, *Velika Vernost' Tvoya, Gospodi: Svidetel'stva iz Zhizni* [Great is Your Faithfulness, My Lord: Life Testimonies] (Steinhagen, Germany: Samenkorn, 2006), v. I, pp. 309-10.

one that is at a "pre-ordained" time, forthright speech, and a hint about the death of a man who did not listen to God's word. Finally, "God's fool" concludes his speech by praying for the soul of the "Tsar". A similar picture can be seen in the description by Archpriest Avvakum of his famous meeting with the Greek Patriarchs, Paisy and Makary, during the Russian Orthodox Moscow Council in 1667. "God's fool" did not act on his own, but at God's bidding. "I was brought to the Eastern Patriarchs... God opened my sinful mouth, and Christ disgraced them by my mouth..."[80] Avvakum exhorted the newly arrived Patriarchs and also frightened them: "I said much to the Patriarchs from the Scripture... Rome fell long ago and is still lying down, and the Poles perished with it." He then criticized their Orthodoxy.[81] When words were unavailing, Avvakum moved to symbolic acts: "I have a clear conscience, and I shake off the dust adhering to my feet before you, as it is written... They started to push me and beat me, and the Patriarchs themselves ran at me... I retreated to the door and lay down on my side, and told them, 'You can sit, but I will lie for a while'..."[82] Finally, Avvakum told them, 'We are fools for Christ' sake! You are honorable, but we are despised! You are strong, but we are weak!'"[83] Such dramatic accounts helped to shape Russian Orthodox and Baptist "foolishness".

In response to even the most insignificant events, Russian Baptists sometimes involuntarily reacted in ways that had echoes of godly "foolishness". Once, during a Baptist church service, an insect alighted on presbyter N.N. and started to bite him. The presbyter firstly drove the insect away, but when it settled on him again, he decided to accept the painful bites, thinking how Christ endured sufferings, "As I might have driven the insect away, Christ might also have stopped his torments. But he decided... not to come down from the cross."[84] This kind of foolishness for Christ in miniature recalls Orthodox holy men such as St. Simeon Stylites, who according to his life story had open wounds where worms were feeding, and when some worms fell off he put them back, saying: "Eat what God has given

---

80. Avvakum, *Zhitie Avvakuma i Drugie Ego Sochineniya*, p. 60.
81. Ibid.
82. Ibid., pp. 60-1.
83. Ibid., p. 61.
84. Zhuravlev, *Sila v Nemoshchi: Svidetel'stva iz Zhizni*, vol. II, p. 90.

you."[85] Nikita of Pereyaslavl voluntarily left his naked body for the bites of mosquitos and midges which swarmed over him.[86] There are similar stories regarding other Russian saints, such as Seraphim of Sarov, Theodosius of the Cave, Nicander of Pskov and Sabbas of Vishera.[87] Although Russian Baptists often criticized "monastic extremes",[88] in practice it is much more difficult to distinguish fundamentally between the behavior and, more importantly, the motivation, of holy Orthodox monks-ascetics on the one hand and the remarkable Baptist presbyter, N.N., on the other. There is the same radical religious spirit.

The following Baptist examples can also be attributed, at least in part, to the influence of the unusual conduct of Russian Orthodox "God's fools". In the mid-1980s, an elderly preacher, I.A., from Alma-Ata, when preaching a lengthy sermon about the second coming of Christ, realized that some listeners had started to doze. He took a trumpet and blew loudly, causing a noisy commotion. The man explained his unusual behavior by referring to the scriptural text that believers ought to watch, because God's angel will sound his trumpet soon.[89] A parallel case, at approximately the same time, took place in the Baptist community in Divnogorsk (Krasnoyarsk Territory), where a preacher, calling his hearers to genuine Christian love, beat on an empty metal bucket, announcing that anyone without love was like "sounding brass" and a "tinkling cymbal" (1 Cor 13:1).[90] To be patient with such "foolishness" was sometimes a hard task, but one of the distinguishing marks of the true church in the Eastern Christian tradition has been kindly treatment of "God's fools".[91] Communities which spurned them were regarded as displaying a serious lack of charity "under their own

85. "Zhitie prep. Simeona Stolpnika" [The Life of St. Simeon Stylites], in ZhSDR, vol. I, p. 26.

86. Hieromonk Alexey (Kuznetsov), Yurodstvo i Stolpnichestvo, p. 320.

87. See their life stories: St. Seraphim of Sarov – ZhSDR, vol. V, p. 69; St. Theodosius of the Cave – Ibid., vol. IX, p. 133; St. Nicander of Pskov – Ibid., vol. I, p. 486; St. Sabbas of Vishera – Ibid., vol. II, p. 26.

88. See, for instance, Karev, Somov, Istoriya Khristianstva, pp. 88-92.

89. Testimony of Baptist church member from Alma-Ata, V.D. Pikalov (Omsk, Russia, 2007).

90. Testimony of Baptist church member from Krasnoyarsk Territory, D. Dyachenko (Omsk, Russia, 2007).

91. See, for instance, Panchenko, "Smekh Kak Zrelishche", pp. 72-3.

roofs".[92] For example, an old Baptist man, M.P., from Omsk, denounced the presbyter of his community many times for a number of reasons. The presbyter attempted humbly to endure this, recognizing that M.P. was a serious Christian. M.P. carried the Synodal Bible with him everywhere, and re-read it dozens of times. At the same time as uttering severe judgments in the area of spirituality, M.P.'s practical ministry was as the church area cleaner. While sweeping the area around the church, which he did very thoroughly, he often said to his pastor, "Here – I am a slave. Punish me, as you want. But at the church – I am your brother; and when you deserve it, do not beg for mercy, I will speak to you straight out!"[93]

The deliberate "playing the fool" that took place during some Soviet trials of Baptists was also notable, not least because of the very serious background to the "playing". This is illustrated in some passages from the full transcripts of "Baptists' trials" in Semipalatinsk in 1962 and in Fergana in 1971.

> *Judge*: 'Who is the leader of your illegal community?'
> *Accused Baptist*: 'I have already told you – Christ and the Holy Ghost.'[94]

> (Those accused declined any assistance from the state advocates and announced their wish to use the New Testament for their own defence. This was not allowed them).

> *Question*: 'One of your psalms has the following words, "It is worth working, it is worth struggling"… Tell us: to work – with whom, to struggle – against whom?'

---

92. For instance, the Senior Presbyter of Baptist churches of Kazakhstan, F.G. Tissen, once talked in a remarkable way about this question in the Soviet Baptist tradition (Saran, Kazakhstan, 1999).

93. Testimony of presbyter A.A. Rozenov (Omsk, Russia, 2006). The identity of M.P. was not to be disclosed.

94. *Zhapis' Sudebnogo Protsessa nad Baptistami g. Semipalatinska, 1962 g.* [Records of Baptists' Trial in Semipalatinsk, 1962], IEDE-4.

Answer: 'We wrestle not against flesh and blood, but against spiritual wickedness in high places.'

Question: 'You must have an official certificate confirming that you are a presbyter.'

Answer: 'A presbyter should work not by certificate, but by inspiration.'

Question to a Baptist witness: 'What do you know about the accused?'

Answer: 'I know that their names are written in the Book of life, that theirs is the Kingdom of Heaven, and that their reward in heaven is great!'

Question: 'Show us... this book, we need documents!'

Answer: 'This book is in heaven.'[95]

These atheistic judges had immense judicial power, backed up as they were by the Communist state, but they found themselves in an awkward situation during these trials. They could not understand what was being said to them, and they ended up sentencing believers to long terms of imprisonment for their "religious fantasies" (as the Communists said) rather than for criminal offences. Such sentences did not enhance the reputation of the judges. There was a saying in the Russian public consciousness: you cannot offend God's fool, or the Lord will punish you...[96] It is also notable that in Soviet labor camps (where prisoners were not divided into groups on the basis of their religion) there were instances of joint "playing the fool" by Russian Orthodox and Baptist prisoners. The famous former leaders of

---

95. "*Sud Nepravedny: Stenogramma Sudebnogo Protsessa*" [Unfair Trial: Full Trial Transcript], *VS*, no. 1 (1973), pp. 22-6.

96. See, for instance, O. Nadporozhskaya, ed., *Nebesnye Pokroviteli Sankt-Peterburga* [The Patron Saints of St. Petersburg] (SPb.: Izdatel'sky Dom "Neva", 2003), p. 87.

the CCECB, Joseph Bondarenko and Zdorovets, speak about this in their memoirs.[97] There was a shared "foolish" spirituality.

The way of peace

A monastic orientation within the spirituality of the Russian Baptist movement can also be seen in the traditional political indifference and pacifism of Russian Baptists. Many of them refused to participate in Soviet public life: they did not take part in elections, would not accept any jobs in "Communist" organizations, avoided Communist events, objected to military service and would not accept any Communist certificates, including passports.[98] Some believed it was wrong to seek medical assistance during illness, and some communities living in remote villages, whose way of life was connected with the land, even tried to do without Soviet money.[99] Many of these features were very similar to the way of life of those known as the True Orthodox Christians, who sought to live in the world as monks.[100] There is a report of the Communist Central Committee of Kazakhstan at the end of the 1950s about a True Orthodox Christians' village near Temirtau. The report noted: "They do not read any newspapers and books... nor take part in elections; they refuse military service."[101] In an earlier period some Russian Old Believers had also rejected passports,

---

97. Bondarenko, *Tri Prigovora*, pp. 122-3; testimony of B.M. Zdorovets (INT, Spokane, Washington, USA, 2006). At the "religious" prison camp in Mordovia, where the latter was imprisoned in the 1960s, there was even a Russian Orthodox "stylite", who sat, praying his rosary, on the upper plank bed for several years, ignoring any work calls and roll calls. He and Zdorovets were on friendly terms.

98. See *BSRUECB*, no. 21 (1975), p. 46; Kuksenko, *Nashi Besedy*, p. 113; Vlasov, *Ot Izbytka Serdtsa*, p. 10.

99. Testimony of B.M. Zdorovets about the *"evangel'skie khristiane sovershennye"* (Evangelical Perfect Christians) (INT, Spokane, Washington, USA, 2006).

100. See, for instance, I. Brazhnik, *Sotsial'naya Sushchnost' Sektantskogo Ekstremizma* [The Social Essence of Sectarian Extremism] (M.: Znanie, 1974), pp. 21-3. Many of the True Orthodox Christians were former monks. The Communists destroyed their last large secret cloister in the 1950s. See Shkarovsky, *Russkaya Pravoslavnaya Tserkov pri Staline i Khrushcheve*, pp. 252-4.

101. Cited in Shkarovsky, *Russkaya Pravoslavnaya Tserkov pri Staline i Khrushcheve*, p. 259. See also: Pospielovsky, *Russkaya Pravoslavnaya Tserkov v 20 veke*, pp. 317-20.

military service, and the use of money.[102] As an example of Soviet Baptist socio-political indifference, in 1967 a young Baptist woman who was on trial in Novosibirsk for illegal printing of literature for the CCECB was asked who had managed the process of printing at her home, and she answered simply, "Christ". The judges obtained nothing more from her.[103] There was a somewhat similar incident with a member of the Tambov Region community of the True Orthodox Christians. He burnt his identity card and refused to serve in the army. Standing trial, he was asked his name and answered, "God knows it". When he was asked, "Who are you?" he replied, "God's servant". The judge tried to arouse his public spirit, "But are you also a citizen of the USSR?" The answer was, "No, I belong to God".[104] The sense of being disconnected from society was similar in these Orthodox and Baptist instances.

In analyzing the pacifism of many within the Russian Baptist community, I would argue that the wider influences included the way of withdrawal espoused by the Orthodox monastic tradition and also the example of the early Russian sects preceding the Russian Baptists, the Dukhobors and Molokans, who held anti-militarist positions.[105] In addition Baptists drew to a certain extent from German Mennonite thinking on this issue.[106] There is, however, no univocal position on the military issue in the official statements of Russian Baptists and Evangelical Christians. The first confessions of both groups (in 1906 and 1910), undoubtedly influenced by the position of German Baptists, proclaimed "unconditional submission to the laws" of the land, including the necessity to "do military service when… the government demands",[107] and considered it was right to accept "mili-

---

102. See, for instance, S. Zenkovsky, *Russkoe Staroobryadchestvo*, pp. 497-9.

103. A. Pakina, *Raskol Evangel'skikh Khristian-Baptistov 1961 g. i Ego Vliyanie na Obshchiny Novosibirskoy Oblasti* [The 1961 Split of the Evangelical Christians-Baptists and its Influence on the Communities of the Novosibirsk Region] (diploma thesis), Novosibirsk State University, 2000, p. 33. This author makes reference to records of the local Religious Affairs officer, which she found in the State Archives of Novosibirsk Region.

104. N. Struve, *Christians in Contemporary Russia* (New York: Charles Scribner's Sons, 1967), pp. 247-8.

105. See, for example: Savinsky, *Istoriya (1867-1917)*, pp. 45, 49-51.

106. See Sawatsky, *Soviet Evangelicals Since World War II*, pp. 106, 115-120.

107. From the Baptist confession issued in 1906 (a translation of the Hamburg

tary obligation".[108] At the same time, the early confessions of faith had some important reservations in favor of Christian pacifism.[109] In 1920, during the Council of Evangelical Christians and Baptists held in Moscow that year, an absolutely pacifist resolution was *unanimously* adopted. This was a period when the Soviet power still saw Russian sectarians as allies rather than enemies.[110] Later, under government pressure, both the Evangelical Christians and Baptists made official decisions about acceptance of military service for their church members, but such resolutions split a great number of local congregations.[111]

From World War II onwards, the AUCECB dissociated itself on many occasions from pacifism.[112] In 1982 there was a typical statement in *Bratsky Vestnik* complaining: "It is sad… that some believers refuse their military duty."[113] Anti-militarist feelings, however, were prevalent especially in provincial churches.[114] Although most men from Russian Baptist congrega-

Confession of German Baptists). See Savinsky, *Istoriya (1917-1967)*, p. 27; Savinsky, *Istoriya (1867-1917)*, p. 314. See also *Istoriya Baptizma*, p. 433.

108. *Verouchenie Evangel'skich Khhristian, 1910 g.* [Creed of Evangelical Christians, 1910], in *Istoriya Baptizma*, p. 455.

109. See *Istoriya Baptizma*, pp. 433, 455.

110. See *Otchet Vserossiyskogo S"ezda Evangel'kich Khhristian Baptistov* [Report of All-Russian Council of Evangelical Christians Baptists] (Moscow, 27 May – 6 June, 1920), ARSECB, F. 1, op. 11de, d. 16, l. 24.

111. See Sawatsky, *Soviet Evangelicals Since World War II*, pp. 116-7; Savinsky, *Istoriya (1917-1967)*, p. 32; A. Savin, ed., *Sovetskoe Gosudarstvo i Evangel'skie Tserkvi Sibiri v 1920-1941 gg.* [The Soviet State and Evangelical Churches of Siberia in 1920-1941: Documents and materials] (Novosibirsk: Posokh, 2004), pp. 136, 155.

112. See, for instance: Pis'mo Prezidiuma VSECB Vsem Presviteram Obshchin ECB v SSSR (1953) [Letter of the Presidium of the AUCECB to All Presbyters of Baptist Communities of the USSR, 1953], ARSECB, F. 1, op. 1d1, d. 64, ll. 1-2; I. Motorin, *Otdavayte Kesarevo Kesaryu, a Bozhie Bogu* [Give to Caesar what is Caesar's, and to God what is God's], *BV*, no. 2 (1968), pp. 49-53; A. Mitskevich, "*Kak Osveshchaet Slovo Bozhie Vopros o Voennoy Sluzhbe*" [What the Word of God Says about Military Service], *BV*, no. 3 (1971), pp. 66-71; *Nastol'naya Kniga Presvitera*, pp. 197-203.

113. See, for example, "*Obrashchenie Plenuma VSECB*" [Appeal of the Plenum of the AUCECB], *BV*, no. 6 (1982), p. 54.

114. See Sawatsky, *Soviet Evangelicals Since World War II*, pp. 119-20, 129. The majority of my interviewees, the ministers and church members of the ECB, confirm this, for instance: M.M. Kolivayko (INT, Sacramento, California, USA, 2006), A.S. Shevchuk (INT, Los Angeles, California, USA, 2006), V.P. Zinchenko (INT, Seattle, Washington, USA, 2006), Ya.D. Diordienko (INT, Sacramento, California, USA, 2006), and many others.

tions were forced to serve time in the Soviet army, and held weapons in their hands,[115] many of them found it completely alien to their religious and moral convictions.[116] That is why those hundreds of conscientious objectors from Russian Baptist communities normally inspired respect even from those Russian Baptists who were most loyal to the Soviet power.[117] Those who would not participate in war endured long sentences in jail and in some cases were shot.[118] In the 1980s Baptist thinking began to change. The draft version of the new Russian Baptist confession, produced in 1980, stated in the section "Relations with the State", the following unsurprising words: "As citizens of our country, we feel obliged to 'render to all what is due them', including to serve in the army" (Bible references follow).[119] But when the actual confession was produced in 1985 the wording was much less definite, and the pacifist option was no longer condemned. The section read: "As citizens of their country, Christians are called to 'render to all what is due them', i.e. to keep the State laws" (the same Bible references follow).[120]

This very equivocation on the part of Russian Baptists might appear to set them at odds with Orthodox Church leaders, since the usual stance of the Russian Orthodox Church was to support the engagement of a

---

115. See, for example, Savinsky, *Istoriya (1917-1967)*, pp. 145, 154. *Bratsky Vestnik* even mentions a Baptist who was a hero of the Soviet Union. See *BV*, no. 4 (1985), pp. 76, 78.

116. In connection with this, there is a typical testimony of a famous minister from Kiev L.E. Kovalenko, "My constant prayer in the battlefield was, 'Lord, I ask you that I wouldn't be killed and that I wouldn't kill anybody!'…" (INT, Sacramento, California, USA, 2006).

117. In traditional congregations of the ECB, the following typical statement was widespread: "[A brother] who has much will-power, courage and patience, will not go to fight, but he who has little of these will take a weapon in his hands." See, for instance, *Sovetskoe Gosudarstvo i Evangel'skie Tserkvi Sibiri*, p. 232.

118. See I. Plett, *Istoriya Evangel'skich Khhristian-Baptistov s 1905 po 1944 gg.* [History of Evangelical Christians-Baptists, 1905-1944], <http://www.blagovestnik.org/books/00360. htm#8> accessed 8 November 2010. Also testimony of Baptist minister from Donetsk Region, M.M. Kolivayko (INT, Sacramento, California, USA, 2006); Cf. Sawatsky, *Soviet Evangelicals Since World War II*, p. 116.

119. *"Proekt Veroucheniya ECB"* [Project of the Creed of ECB], *BV*, no. 4 (1980), p. 52.

120. *Verouchenie Evangel'skikh Khristian – Baptistov, Prinyatoe na 43 S"ezde ECB v Moskve* [The Creed of the Evangelical Christians-Baptists Adopted at the 43th Council of the ECB in Moscow], *BV*, no. 4 (1985), p. 49.

Christian in war "for the Faith, the Tsar and the Fatherland"?[121] However, as is often the case, it is not possible to sum up the long and varied story of Orthodoxy in such a simple way. The resistant pacifism of the early church was never entirely lost in the Eastern Church. As noted above, it was to be found among monks and also priests.

The following Apostolic Canons, directly or indirectly, address the issue of priests and monks involving themselves in affairs of state. According to Canon 6, priests are forbidden to carry responsibility for "worldly things";[122] Canon 81, referring to Matthew 6:24 and speaking in strong terms, rules out state affairs for any bishops and priests;[123] and Canon 83, quoting Matthew 22:21, solemnly cautions any clergyman against serving in the army.[124] In addition, the 7th Canon of the Fourth Ecumenical Council forbade priests and monks, under the threat of excommunication, from engaging in any military service.[125] In the Canons of St. Basil the Great, there is a three-year ban on participation in Holy Communion for warriors who spill blood even in a "just war" (Canon 13),[126] as well as a strict prohibition of vengeance (Canon 43),[127] and excommunication of those who kill robbers (Canon 55), since although robbers should be punished, they should not be murdered.[128]

Based on this pious tradition, many Russian Orthodox books and "Lives of Holy Fathers" contained instructive tales about holy people who did not resist evildoers physically but defeated them morally: monastic elders washed the feet of criminals who had come to murder them; monks willingly helped robbers to load mules with the monk's own belongings; and holy monks defended brigands who had robbed them from the revenge that might have been carried out by other monks.[129] In the Russian

---

121. See, for instance, Shkarovsky, *Russkaya Pravoslavnaya Tserkov pri Staline i Khrushcheve*, pp. 119-37.
122. *Pravila Pravoslavnoy Tserkvi*, vol. I, p. 64.
123. Ibid., p. 165.
124. Ibid., p. 168.
125. Ibid., p. 345.
126. Ibid., vol. II, p. 394.
127. Ibid., p. 426.
128. Ibid., p. 436.
129. See, for instance, the section "Humility" in Hegumen Mark (Lozinsky), *Otechnik*

evangelical tradition, such Christian "testimonies" were narrated, and they inspired Baptists to act, in desperate straits, in the same way. In the middle of the 1970s, for example, one large Baptist family moved from Kirgizia to the Russian city of Syzran, where they had obtained a house. Their neighbors gave them a hostile reception: as soon as the Baptist family unloaded their belongings from a truck, entered the house and began to lay the table, rocks were thrown through the windows and all the glass was broken. When the new family went outside, they saw that logs and rubbish from the street side were blocking up their gates. There was no one in the street, but neighbors were secretly watching from their houses to see how the Baptists would respond. The family, having prayed and cleared away the rubbish, went to the nearest houses and started to invite guests to their house, saying that the table was laid for such good people. Nobody came to them on that day, but the family soon gained the respect of the whole street.[130]

But there was sometimes failure within the Baptist community – and an awareness of failure – to live up to these high standards. Many Soviet Baptists knew the tragic episode in the life of D.I. Mazaev, one of the most famous leaders of the Baptist Union in Russia before the Bolshevik Revolution. This story served as a warning about failure to follow the way of peace and as a challenge to churches dealing with such failure. In 1917, Mazaev's estate in the Caucasus suffered an armed attack by criminals. Defending himself, Mazaev shot through the door, which was being broken open. One of the intruders was killed on the spot, while others fled.[131] Under civil law, D.I. Mazaev, having acted in self-defence, was innocent. Also, he could have argued that the Baptist confession of 1906 was on his side, since it upheld the ordinance of "the sword" for punishing

Propovednika: 1221 Primer iz Prologa i Paterikov [The Book of the Lives of the Fathers, for Preachers: 1221 Illustrations from the Prologue and Paterikons] (Izd-vo Svyato-Troitskoy Sergievoy Lavry, 1997). See also an amazing story in N. Leskov, *Legenda o Sovestnom Danile* [The Legend of Contrite Danila], in N. Leskov, *Sobranie Sochineniy*, 12 vols., vol. X, pp. 82-98.

130. Testimony of church members of the ECB, A.S. Shevchuk, Ya.S. Shevchuk, and V.Ya. Virkh (INT, Los Angeles, California, USA, 2006).

131. See *Istoriya Evangel'skikh Khristian-Baptistov v SSSR*, p. 180; Savinsky, *Istoriya (1917-1967)*, p. 35; Kovalenko, *Oblako Svideteley Khristovykh*, p. 90.

"evil-doers".[132] But the congregation in which Mazaev was a member made the hard decision to excommunicate him. He himself "sincerely bewailed" what he had done at "every service", and this repentance was the reason why he was later restored to the church.[133]

The repudiation of pacifism by the AUCECB's leadership meant that Mazaev's sorrow about his deadly deed was not mentioned when *Bratsky Vestnik* carried an article by Levindanto stating that "Tolstoy's non-resistance... was foreign to D.I. Mazaev, and he did not hesitate to use a weapon against the terrible robbers threatening his life."[134] But many Russian Baptists were closer to the spirit of St. Basil the Great, who (as noted) called for the excommunication of those who killed a robber. Among Soviet Baptists, Levindanto represented the view from "above", while the pacifist position traditionally dominated thinking from "below", among ordinary believers.

The promotion of an agenda for peace from "above" (that is from the leadership of the AUCECB) did, however, take place when the AUCECB supported what were seen as the peace-loving policies of the Soviet Union. The language in *Bratsky Vestnik* echoed what was said in *Zhurnal Moskovskoy Patriarkhii* [Journal of the Moscow Patriarchate]. The first quotation that follows is from the Moscow Patriarchate's publication, in 1977, and the second from *Bratsky Vestnik*, four years later.

The household of the church, as well as our entire nation, cordially approve the consistent, truly peace-loving policy of the Soviet Union. The situation in Europe... has become quieter mainly simply through the efforts of our country.[135]

We are grateful to God that, in spite of the escalation of the international situation by the aggressive forces of the West, the

132. *Istoriya Baptizma*, p. 433.
133. See Kovalenko, *Oblako Svideteley Khristovykh*, p. 90.
134. N. Levindanto, *"Pamyati Deya Ivanovicha Mazaeva"* [In Memory of Dey Ivanovich Mazaev], *BV*, nos. 2-3 (1953), p. 96.
135. Patriarch Pimen, *"Rech' na Zasedanii Sovetskogo Komiteta Zashchity Mira"* [Soviet Peace Committee Meeting Speech], *ZhMP*, no. 11 (1977), pp. 36-7.

government of our country takes a line over peace... Many
international conferences... are grateful to our country for the
way of peace.[136]

The polemic here against the "aggressive" course of the countries of the
West, and at the same time the support of the "way of peace" that was
being set out and implemented in Russian foreign policy, certainly owed
something to Communist propaganda and the need for Baptists to be seen
to be loyal to the state, but there is also an indebtedness in such statements
to the traditional Russian Orthodox world-view, in which wrong thinking
is found in the West, while God's truth is known in the East.

The leaders of the Russian Orthodox Church and the AUCECB went
so far as to associate their own histories with that of the Soviet State.

The sixtieth anniversary of the Soviet State is in some way
also a jubilee of the Russian Orthodox Church... May the
humane, just and peace-loving national and foreign policy of
the Soviet State be triumphant![137]

...Our warmest congratulations on the sixtieth anniversary
of the Great October Socialist Revolution. This year, the
Evangelical Christians-Baptists observe their 110th anniversary [in Russia]; and the greater part of the brotherhood history
falls in the period when our country, for the first time in the
history of mankind, chose the road of building the Socialist
society.[138]

The first quotation, which is from the Journal of the Moscow Patriarchate
in 1977, somehow sought to associate the sixty years of the Communist

---

136. A. Bychkov, "*Doklad Plenumu VSECB*" [Report to the Plenum of the AUCECB],
BV, no. 5 (1981), p. 53.

137. N. Zabolotsky, "*K Shestidesyatiletiyu Sotsialisticheskoy Otchizny*" [In Commemoration
of the Sixtieth Anniversary of the Socialist Homeland], *ZhMP*, no. 11 (1977), pp. 38-41.

138. "*Predsedatelyu Prezidiuma Verkhovnogo Soveta SSSR Leonidu Il'ichu Brezhnevu*"
[To the Chairman of the Presidium of the Supreme Soviet of the USSR, Leonid Ilyich
Brezhnev], *BV*, no. 6 (1977), p. 8.

regime in Russia with the 1,000 years of Russian Orthodox history. The Russian Baptists had a mere 110 years to celebrate, which allowed them to make the claim, ostensibly with pride, that "the greater part of the brotherhood history" fell in the Soviet era. It is not easy to interpret such statements. Pride was being expressed in an atheistic regime. However, what was genuine was an attachment to the *Russian* State, an attachment felt by many Russian Christians, both Orthodox and Baptists. It was the Russian people who ultimately were "humane, just and peace-loving".

The theme of peace was taken up again in 1979 by Patriarch Pimen, the Patriarch of Moscow and All Russia. Addressing a group of activists belonging to Soviet Public Organizations he stated:

> The Russian Orthodox Church is showing concern over the alarming news about the Western European rearmament programme... In spite of the healthy and long-awaited process of 'East – West' policies of détente... the antagonism between good and evil continues.[139]

The ancient Russian Orthodox paradigm is evident: the confrontation of the East and the West is neither more nor less than the "antagonism between good and evil".[140] More specifically, the Russian Orthodox Church, while not apparently concerned about Soviet arms, found much to worry about in the West. A parallel might be the way in which the majority of White Guard emigrants, for all their anti-communism, fervently desired the victory of the USSR over Nazi Germany, as General A.I. Denikin put it: "We felt a pain during the days of defeat of the Army, even though it is called the 'Red' [Army] and not the 'Russian', and – joy during the days of its victories...".[141] Seeing everything through the lens of the support

139. Patriarch Pimen, "*Rech' na Sobranii Aktiva Sovetskikh Obshchestvennykh Organizatsy*" [Soviet Public Organizations Activists' Meeting Speech], *ZhMP*, no. 10 (1979), pp. 41-2.

140. It is interesting to compare this statement with the politico-religious thesis by the President of the United States, Ronald Reagan, about the Soviet Union as the "evil empire" (1983). See Ronald Reagan, "The 'Evil Empire' Speech", in J.M. Waller, ed., *The Public Diplomacy Reader* (Washington, DC: Institute of World Politics Press, 2007), pp. 137-43.

141. "*Obrashchenie Generala A. Denikina k Dobrovol'tsam*" [The Appeal of General A.

among Russian Christians for the East and suspicion about the West also
helps to explain this statement in *Bratsky Vestnik* in 1983, one that follows
the Orthodox line:

> In these days, when the cry arises in the West in support of
> the arms race, the words of Christ come back to our memory,
> 'All they that take the sword shall perish with the sword' (Matt
> 26:52).[142]

Orthodox and Baptist authors saw no possibility of peaceful initiatives
coming from the Western countries. Even the Soviet military campaign in
Afghanistan did not make any difference to Russian Orthodox and Baptist
rhetoric about the "peace-loving" Soviet state. In December 1979, when
the political decision to send Soviet troops to Afghanistan had already been
made, those present at the 42nd Convention of AUCECB in Moscow wrote
in a telegram to L.I. Brezhnev, "We unanimously entertain your peace-
loving proposals, directed at peace and disarmament, and are asking for
this in our prayers to Almighty God."[143] During the first half of the 1980s,
assurances that the AUCECB "prayerfully supported" the "wise policy" of
the USSR continued as before.[144] The nationalism of Orthodoxy also per-
meated Russian Baptist life, although the deepest Baptist instinct was "the
way of peace".

Denikin to the Volunteers] [1944], *Rodina*, nos. 6-7 (1991), p. 105.

142. "From the Life of the Local Churches" (editorial article), *BV*, no. 2 (1983), p. 76.

143. "*Telegramma Predsedatelyu Prezidiuma Verkhovnogo Soveta SSSR*" [Telegram to the
Chairman of the Presidium of the Supreme Soviet of the USSR], *BV*, nos. 1-2 (1980),
pp. 52-3. Though the AUCECB probably did not know at that point about the active
preparation for the military campaign, their telegram was published in *Bratsky Vestnik* in
1980 when everyone was talking about the war in Afghanistan.

144. See, for instance: *BV*, no. 4 (1981), p. 58; no. 2 (1983), pp. 76, 78; no. 1 (1985),
p. 37.

A Russian spiritual identity

This raises the issue of the extent to which, particularly in the period being examined in this study, Russian Baptists sought to promote the idea that their spiritual identity was distinctively Russian. In the eyes of the majority of the population of the Soviet Union, Orthodoxy seemed a much more traditionally "Russian" faith by comparison with the Baptist form of Christianity. Indeed there were those who strongly denied that the latter had any "Russian-ness" at all. It is notable that some Russian Orthodox and Communist commentators used the same vocabulary in condemning Soviet Baptists for choosing "alien" beliefs.[145] On occasions the response within the AUCECB was to agree with this charge.[146] However, as was discussed in chapter 2, the general body of Russian Baptist authors opposed such an approach to the issue of their identity.[147] Some apologists of the Russian Baptists pointed out to the representatives of the Orthodox the Greek origins of their beliefs,[148] and to the Soviet propagandists of the Communist Party the German roots of Marxism.[149] There was, however, a strong tendency among the Orthodox and the Baptists to consider their beliefs to be either "native Russian" or simply "the faith given by God".[150] The *Pochvenniki* [lit. return to the soil] of nineteenth-century Orthodoxy had their followers among Russian Baptists who found only indirect relationships between their community and the West. Some saw their beliefs as "a mixing of the [Russian] Orthodox and Molokan doctrines", so that they were not considered as bearers of Western teaching.[151]

---

145. See a review of the theme: Mitrokhin, *Baptizm: Istoriya i Sovremennost'*, pp. 21-9, 57-8.

146. See, for instance, A. Karev, "Russkoe Evangel'sko-Baptistskoe Dvizhenie" [The Russian Evangelical-Baptist Movement], in *Nastol'naya Kniga Presvitera*, pp. 155-75.

147. See, for instance, A. Bychkov, "*Stoletie Ob"edinitel'nykh S"ezdov*" [The Centenary of the Unifying Councils], *BV*, no. 6 (1984), pp. 44-7; Karetnikova, *Russkoe Bogoiskatel'stvo*, pp. 3-84; Savinsky, *Istoriya (1867-1917)*, pp. 160-8.

148. This argument was used by Russian Baptists before the Bolshevik Revolution. See, for instance, Mazaev, *Vospominaniya*, pp. 71-2.

149. See, for instance, Vlasov, *Ot Izbytka Serdtsa*, p. 157.

150. See, for instance, Savinsky, *Istoriya (1867-1917)*, pp. 26-53; Mazaev, *Vospominaniya*, p. 71.

151. See Kuksenko, *Nashi Besedy*, pp. 144-5.

In parallel with the discussions about spiritual identity which took place in publications, ideas about the self-sufficiency of the Russian Baptists and the independence of their way of life from the West were common among many ministers within Russian Baptist congregations in the Soviet period.[152] The following story told by the former senior presbyter of the Kazakhstan Union of Baptist churches, V.V. Gorelov, illustrates this theme well and reproduces his context and the spirit of his time. In the mid-1970s, a group of Baptists from Austria came to Alma-Ata, Kazakhstan. There was a warm meeting with local Baptist pastors and the visitors took part in a church service in the Central Baptist Church in Alma-Ata. However, shortly after their departure, the leading ministers of the church were required to meet with a regional Soviet Religious Affairs officer who started to lecture them for allowing foreigners to preach at the church. V.V. Gorelov replied to the charge with words that indicated his ability in diplomacy, "You know that all frontier posts, customs, the whole Soviet Army are in your power. So, please, do not let any foreigners into this country at all! We will get by somehow without them. But if you let foreigners into the country, we should entertain them freely, so that later they do not speak badly of us... We have received the visitors as our brothers in faith... If we were wrong, please, do not let foreigners in at all!"[153]

The use by Gorelov of a Slavophile motif that was traditional for Russia ("we will get by somehow without foreigners") disarmed the Religious Affairs officer. Nor was this an isolated incident. When the Communists portrayed Soviet Baptists as German or American "spies",[154] as they often did, the genuine Russian-ness of the Soviet Baptists was the strongest counter-evidence. This was particularly evident during the 1960s and 1970s when it was often alleged, "these people are political suspects, related to the West, especially to America". The response of one ordinary Baptist believer, who responded to this accusation at his works meeting, became

---

152. It is also true that a considerable part of them have emigrated to the economically prosperous Western countries, especially the USA, and live there now. A good many Russian Orthodox people have also emigrated to the West.

153. Testimony of former senior presbyter, V.V. Gorelov (INT, Los Angeles, California, USA, 2006).

154. See, for instance, Mitrokhin, *Baptizm: Istoriya i Sovremennost'*, pp. 57-8.

well known among Russian Baptist congregations. He stated: "You know me. I am a Baptist. Now, then, I tell you that I have never laid eyes on an American in my life!"[155] This elicited smiles and laughter and produced a positive attitude on the part of the officials. At local level it was recognized that Russian Baptists were "our people". Baptists did not become "ours" through agreement with Communist ideas: as a rule none were Komsomol or Party members. But they were seen to share in general anti-Western feelings.[156] It is notable in this connection that those among the CCECB who appealed to Western public opinion for help did not enjoy the support of the majority of their brotherhood.[157] When deported from the Soviet Union, Georgi Vins began his famous press campaign in the USA in defence of persecuted Baptists in the USSR and in 1982 was even received by the President of the USA, Ronald Reagan, the leader of the CCECB, G.K. Kryuchkov, gave Vins a lecture, and in particular forbade him "going to presidents".[158]

In line with their somewhat emotional anti-Western feelings, Soviet Baptists often preferred to welcome Orthodox people and sometimes even Communists rather than Western evangelicals. A.T. Kharchenko, who was for many years a member of the Sukhumi community of CCECB and took an active part in "underground" printing of evangelical literature, later said, "The Communist morality, in spite of its godlessness, was in a way higher than the Western, individualistic style of living, with its insensitivity to the life of the neighbor."[159] This kind of statement is not untypical, although other Baptists would not have gone so far. Those who categorized "Western" life in this way were normally dealing in stereotypes: usually they had little or no first-hand knowledge. What they did have, however, was a feeling for "*sobornost*", for the "communalism" of the Russian Baptists. Because of

---

155. Testimony of Baptist presbyter from Maikop, N.G. Man'ko (INT, Everett, Washington, USA, 2006).

156. The exceptions to the rule were perhaps ethnic German Soviet Baptists, who usually sympathized with their historical motherland, and a minor part of the CCECB which occasionally appealed to public opinion in the West in order to draw attention to the religious persecutions in the USSR.

157. See, for instance, Kuksenko, *Nashi Besedy*, pp. 71-2, 140.

158. Ibid., pp. 68-72.

159. Testimony of A.T. Kharchenko (INT, Sacramento, California, USA, 2006).

their encouragement of the collective spirit, Communists (despite being oppressors of religion) were sometimes "more native" to the Baptist brotherhood and sisterhood, which was traditionally lived out in community. Russian Baptists certainly hoped for the religious liberty that was found in the West, yet at the same time the way this was expressed in the West was somewhat "alien", owing to its individualistic basis.[160] A.V. Karev, the General Secretary of the AUCECB, who was torn between sympathy for the West and the East, nonetheless made his deepest feelings evident in 1957 in *Bratsky Vestnik*:

> ...The inner, spiritual resources [of our brotherhood]... should arouse the utmost praise and gratitude to God within the whole of Christendom, as the Russian Evangelical movement is a bearer of Apostolic Christianity. But we cannot say as much for Christian churches of the West, unfortunately. The most grievous fact in contemporary Western Christianity, including among Baptists, is their lack of the spirit of Apostolic Christianity, ... of their first love to Christ... testimony ... the priesthood of all believers, and... simplicity. Therefore, anyone who would like to find the country in the world where there is a church... with all the attributes of Apostolic Christianity should be pointed to the Soviet Union... We can say without any pride and conceit that the Evangelical-Baptist Church in the USSR is the Apostolic Church of the twentieth century.[161]

---

160. The kernel of the problem is elucidated well by the Orthodox theologian N.M. Zernov, "The West, starting from the individual, sees the community as the outcome of a collective desire to live and act together. For the East the community comes first and the individual is seen as a part of the whole". – N. Zernov, *Eastern Christendom* (N.Y.: G.P. Putnam's Sons, 1961), p. 229. And A.S. Khomyakov wrote, "When anyone falls, he falls alone; but no one is saved alone." – Khomyakov, *Tserkov' Odna*, p. 37. See also: P. Parushev, "Walking in the Dawn of the Light: On the Salvation Ethics of the Ecclesial Communities in the Orthodox Tradition from a Radical Reformation Perspective", PhD thesis, Fuller Theological Seminary, 2006, pp. 204-23.

161. A. Karev, "*Russkoe Evangel'sko-Baptistskoe Dvizhenie*" [The Russian Evangelical-Baptist Movement], *BV*, no. 4 (1957), pp. 37-8. Such ideas were found much earlier, in I.S. Prokanov's time. See, for instance, *Utrennyaya Zvezda*, nos. 6-8 (1922), pp. 6-14.

This passage, though written by a Baptist, is a piece of Slavophilism of the purest hue, exhibiting the spirit of Russian messianism. Even Russian Orthodox Slavophile authors would not all have ventured to assert so openly that the church in Russia was a "bearer of Apostolic Christianity" but that "we cannot say as much for Christian churches of the West, unfortunately", and to declare that the church in the USSR "is the Apostolic Church of the twentieth century".

Though such ideas, expressed in the official periodical of the AUCECB, might well arouse the suspicion that they were said for the benefit of (or under instructions from) the Soviet censors, there is evidence that Karev was neither acting against his conscience nor simply carrying out Communist commands. Karev's personal diary for 1959-62, published in 1999, reflects his clear perception of the anti-Christian nature of Soviet power, and yet at the same time conveys his belief in Russia's special historical role. Russia was passing through the crucible of sufferings, like the Apostolic Church, and was keeping the "true faith" not only for herself but also for other countries and nations, including the Western world, where, from the point of view of Karev, authentic Christianity had been lost. He wrote:

> We are the successors of those who were burnt to death in Nero's gardens and torn to pieces by lions in circus arenas!... [That is] the 'messianism of Russia'!

> The Christian West is Christianity without Christ ([quoting] F.M. Martsinkovsky).

> The sacred mission of the Russian evangelical movement is to uphold Apostolic Christianity![162]

Thus, in a way that echoes Orthodox Slavophilism, Karev refers sympathetically in his diary to the 'messianism of Russia'. For a Baptist even to mention the term is symptomatic of his sympathies.

---

162. For these and other similar thoughts see *"Dnevnik A. V. Kareva"* [A.V. Karev's Diary], *BV*, no. 1 (1999), pp. 44-51; nos. 2-3 (1999), pp. 53-7.

The specific character of some of the material written by foreign authors and published in *Bratsky Vestnik* is also significant. The editorial board chiefly selected for publication comments by Western Baptists who, having visited the USSR, praised the Soviet way of life and also – there was a special thrill in this – spoke of the superiority of the Christian life of Russian Baptists by comparison with Baptists in the English-speaking world. Slavophile tendencies were being reinforced. In 1962 *Bratsky Vestnik* reported about a visit to the Soviet Union by a delegation of African-American Baptist pastors.

> In Moscow, the guests visited the Kremlin, Red Square and V.I. Lenin's Mausoleum. They also admired the great success of our country at the Exhibition of Achievements of the National Economy... They were impressed by all that they saw and heard in the Soviet Union: the clean streets, the vast scale of building, free medical service, sincere warm-hearted Christians devoted to God... And they said, 'Yes, truly the light will come from the East!'[163]

The correspondent representing the AUCECB put the standard praise of socialism in the American pastors' mouths, but a sense of real conviction is present in his final, Eastern Christian proclamation, "Yes, truly the light will come from the East!" In the Russian Orthodox tradition the East (in contrast to the West) was always associated with the Kingdom of God and the Divine Light.[164] And Baptist *Bratsky Vestnik* stood solidly in that Russian tradition.

---

163. K. Pilipyuk, "*Prebyvanie v Sovetskom Soyuze Gruppy Negrityanskikh Baptistskikh Pastorov iz Ameriki*" [Visit of the Soviet Union by Black Baptist Pastors' Group from the USA], *BV*, nos. 5-6 (1962), pp. 32-4.

164. For example, the famous Orthodox theologian A. Schmemann wrote about this (in connection with the Orthodox understanding of Baptismal symbolism): "If facing the West... means facing Satan and his darkness, turning to the East signifies the conversion of man to the Paradise which was planted in the East, his conversion to Christ, the light of the world". – A. Schmemann, *Of Water and the Spirit*, p. 30. See also: I. Vorontsova, *Pravoslavnye Tainstva i Obryady* [The Orthodox Sacraments and Rites] (M.: Veche, 2006), pp. 51-2.

Similar sentiments were carried in *Bratsky Vestnik* in the 1970s. In 1972 reflections by Andrew MacRae, who was General Secretary of the Baptist Union of Scotland and who was then President of the European Baptist Federation, were featured. The editorial board of *Bratsky Vestnik* published an article by MacRae under the unusual (for Soviet people) title "Christian Life in the Soviet Union: Freedom of Faith". Having no doubt been briefed by his Russian Baptist hosts, he wrote:

> It is said that Russian Baptists are not allowed to have Sunday schools. In fact Sunday schools have never been a part of Russian tradition... The Russians always thought that sharing their faith with a younger generation was a mission of the Christian family. The number of young people admitted to church membership offers reliable evidence of the impact of the Christian family. We can learn from them... In a Communist society, the Baptist witness... has reached its present considerable magnitude in Russia. Over the same period, we Christians of Western Europe... fell into decay.[165]

The idea that the spiritual life of Russian Baptists was somehow deeper and more complete than that found in the West was being purveyed in a way that was consistent with self-perceptions found within the Russian Christian tradition. It was useful if foreigners were willing to affirm this interpretation. However, the foreigners, like MacRae, were not necessarily acting merely as mouth-pieces for their Russian hosts. A certain mystical "religious spirit" was genuinely felt by some foreigners who visited Russia. Thus *Bratsky Vestnik* was happy to publish some words in 1974 from one of the leaders of the Christian Peace Conference, Pastor N. Vikromasing.

> I was moved to the very bottom of my soul by the people's devotion at your church. Their prayers and singing are still ringing in my ears... Such religious piety, as that which I saw

---

165. A. MacRae, *"Khristianskaya Zhizn' v Sovetskom Soyuze: Religioznaya Svoboda"* [Christian Life in the Soviet Union: Freedom of Faith], *BV*, no. 5 (1972), pp. 13-14.

in the Soviet Union among both the Baptists and Russian
Orthodox people, is uncommon in the world of today.[166]

It seems that in this period in their history, Russian Baptist leaders, whether
in *Bratsky Vestnik* or elsewhere, actively dissociated themselves from the
West and went out of their way to emphasize the historical affinity between
Russian Baptist communal spiritual experience and the Russian Orthodox
spiritual tradition.

Orthodox-Baptist relationships

This period also saw good relationships increasingly fostered between
many representatives of the Russian Orthodox Church and Evangelical
Christians-Baptists in the USSR. *Bratsky Vestnik* regularly published Easter
and Christmas greetings from Russian Orthodox Church leaders, as well
as favorable messages in response on behalf of the AUCECB. There is no
evidence to suggest that this was being done only formally; the greetings
conveyed sincere mutual liking. The words of welcome, articles and commentaries included in *Bratsky Vestnik* from Baptists outside the USSR de-
creased markedly, while the Russian Orthodox presence in *Bratsky Vestnik*
increased. In part this was due to the influence of the Soviet power, which
pressurized Orthodox and Baptists to "struggle for peace" together on the
world stage.[167] In 1971, Patriarch-elect Pimen was addressed by leaders of
the AUCECB as "beloved brother":

> To Pimen, the Patriarch of Moscow and All Russia: 'Dear and
> beloved brother in our Lord Jesus Christ and minister of his
> church, …not wishing to be apart from the historical event in
> the life of the Russian Orthodox Church – the election of her
> Primate, the Patriarch of Moscow and All Russia – we express

---

166. "*Nam Pishut*" [Our Letters], *BV*, no. 4 (1974), pp. 79-80.
167. See, for instance, Shkarovsky, *Russkaya Pravoslavnaya Tserkov pri Staline i
Khrushcheve*, pp. 314-31; "*Golos Khristian v Zashchitu Mira*" [Voice of Christians in
Defence of Peace] (editorial article), *BV*, no. 2 (1976), pp. 5-8.

our unalloyed joy that this great decision has fallen to Your lot
and congratulate You… from the bottom of our heart on the
assumption of this high-holy and highly important ministry.
We are praying to our One Lord and Savior that he will give
You heavenly wisdom and the fullness of physical and spiritual
strength for leading the great Russian Orthodox Church…
Love in Christ… from the Presidium of the AUCECB.'[168]

The way in which Pimen subsequently fostered the relationship with the
Baptists (as noted in chapter 1) probably contributed to the Soviet Baptist
tendency to give prominence to the Patriarch; this tendency certainly became more pronounced throughout the 1970s and 1980s. It is particularly
noteworthy that the affirmation of the Russian Orthodox leadership continued in the period of perestroika, when religious freedom came to the
Soviet Union.

The greetings sent to the AUCECB at the major Christian festivals that
were published in *Bratsky Vestnik* in the later 1970s and the 1980s followed
a certain order: primacy was usually given to greetings from the Patriarch
of All Russia,[169] then some Orthodox Metropolitans followed,[170] next
some Russian Baptist ministers conveyed good wishes, and finally greetings from Western Christians were included. In 1989, for example, *Bratsky
Vestnik* carried extended compliments from Patriarch Pimen of Moscow
and All Russia, and then briefer greetings from Metropolitan Filaret of
Minsk and Belorussia, Metropolitan Alexey of Leningrad and Novgorod,
and Metropolitan Yuvenaly of Krutitsy and Kolomna. It was only at this
point that Russian Baptist leaders featured: Ya.K. Dukhonchenko, G.I.
Komendant, V.S. Glukhovsky and M.V. Melnik. Then, after brief words
from the Orthodox Archbishop Makary, there was a final list: "In addition, the [AUCECB] was sent holiday greetings from: the Baptist World

---

168. *"Patriarkhu Moskovskomu i Vseya Rusi Pimenu"* [To Pimen, the Patriarch of Moscow
and All Russia], *BV*, no. 4 (1971), pp. 14-15.

169. See, for instance, *BV*, no. 2 (1975), p. 13; no. 3 (1975), p. 11; no. 3 (1979), p. 40;
no. 3 (1988), p. 24.

170. See, for instance, *BV*, no. 3 (1982), pp. 40-2; no. 3 (1976), pp. 9-10; no. 3 (1987),
pp. 37-8; no. 3 (1988), pp. 24-5.

Alliance, the Estonian Evangelical Lutheran Church, the Christian Peace Conference, the European Baptist Federation, Dr. J. Akers, the Billy Graham Association, Pastor S. Park, Presbyterian Church of South Korea, the Society of Friends (Quakers) in the United States of America, the Ecumenical Forum of European Christian Women, and others."[171]

This example from 1989, by which time *Bratsky Vestnik* did not need to take into account what the Communists thought about the Baptist period-ical including (or not including) greetings from the West, indicated some-thing of the genuine priorities of AUCECB leaders. Despite the lack of Communist anti-Western pressure in this period, the letters and telegrams from outside Russia, including greetings from the Baptist World Alliance and the European Baptist Federation, were mentioned in *Bratsky Vestnik* but were not quoted.[172] By contrast, the words of the Russian Orthodox leaders were quoted in full. Moreover, in publishing Russian Orthodox messages, the editorial board of *Bratsky Vestnik* quite often closed their eyes in the 1970s and 1980s to some statements, that from the point of view *of* traditional Baptist beliefs, were highly controversial. In 1978, for example, this Christmas greeting was published:

> To the president of the AUCECB, A.E. Klimenko, '…May our great God, incarnate of the Holy Spirit and Mary Ever-Virgin, give you unbounded Christmas joy, abundant grace, bless you with a long life and grant much success in your min-istry. Brotherly love from the rector of Leningrad Theological Academy and Seminary, Cyril, the Archbishop of Vyborg.'[173]

Calling Mary by the name of the "Ever-Virgin" was never a practice in Russian Baptist churches, but the editorial staff of *Bratsky Vestnik* readily included in full the message of the Russian Orthodox Archbishop. Similar

---

171. *"Paskhal'nye Privetstviya i Pozdravleniya, Prislannye v Adres VSEHB"* [Easter Greetings and Compliments Sent to the AUCECB], *BV*, no. 3 (1989), pp. 36-8.

172. *Bratsky Vestnik* did publish greetings from Western Baptists from time to time, but from about the mid-1970s the emphasis was on the representatives of the Russian Orthodox Church.

173. *BV*, no. 1 (1978), p. 18.

trends can be found in the underground periodicals of the CCECB. For instance, an editorial of *Bratsky Listok* mentioned what it called an "ancient heresy" in the early church, which was that Mary was called "not by the name of the *Theotokos* [the one who gives birth to God] but by the name of the *Christotokos* [the one who gives birth to Christ]".[174] The Baptist editor undoubtedly gave priority here to Orthodox sources.

Another example of Russian Baptist recognition of the riches of the Orthodox tradition is the way, from the beginning of the 1980s, that *Bratsky Vestnik* published Russian "classical religious" (that is Russian Orthodox) poetry. In the period leading up to the celebration of 1,000 years of Christianity in Russia it is apparent that fewer poems by Baptist authors were being published in *Bratsky Vestnik*, while the number of Russian Orthodox poets whose work was included was increasing considerably. It must not be forgotten that *Bratsky Vestnik* was designed to be a periodical for the members of the Russian Baptist community, not to be a literary magazine. The number of literary pieces featured was, therefore, all the more remarkable.

The following are examples of much-acclaimed pieces of classical Russian Orthodox poetry that were published by *Bratsky Vestnik* in the period from 1980 to 1988: G.R. Derzhavin's *Bog* [God],[175] I.S. Nikitin's *Molenie o Chashe* [Praying for the Cup],[176] K.M. Fofanov's *Otrechenie Petra* [Peter's Denial],[177] A.M. Zhemchuzhnikov's *Pritcha o Seyatele i Semenakh* [The Parable of the Sower and the Seed],[178] D.S. Merezhkovsky's *O, Bozhe Moy* [Oh, My God],[179] V.S. Soloviev's *Emmanuil* [Immanuel][180] and *Prizvanie Avraama v Zemlyu Obetovannuyu* [The Call of Abraham to the Promised Land],[181] I.I. Kozlov's *Moya Molitva* [My Prayer],[182] and S.Ya. Nadson's

---

174. *BL*, no. 2 (1991), p. 1.
175. See *BV*, no. 3 (1980), pp. 54-6.
176. See *BV*, no. 4 (1980), pp. 63-6.
177. See *BV*, no. 5 (1985), pp. 66-7.
178. See *BV*, no. 3 (1987), p. 66.
179. See *BV*, no. 5 (1987), p. 52.
180. See *BV*, no. 6 (1987), p. 51.
181. See *BV*, no. 6 (1988), p. 46.
182. See *BV*, no. 2 (1988), p. 64.

Khristianka [A Christian Woman].[183] In this period *Bratsky Vestnik* also published some printed music by famous Orthodox composers, for example: A.A. Kopylov,[184] A.A. Arkhangelsky[185] and G.F. Lvovsky.[186]

Russian Orthodox authors were also increasingly commended or featured in *Bratsky Vestnik* in the 1980s. Thus in 1988 the General Secretary of the AUCECB, A.M. Bychkov, wrote an appreciation in *Bratsky Vestnik* of A.P. Lopukhin,[187] the pre-revolutionary Russian Orthodox theologian and publisher, and V.S. Soloviev, the famous Russian philosopher.[188] Bychkov said that in his view "Lopukhin was a [Russian] Orthodox theologian but his works are characterized by the purity of the Gospel, toleration and a desire to enlighten the masses".[189] A theological (Christological) article by A.P. Lopukhin was published in 1990 in *Bratsky Vestnik*.[190] The years 1989 and 1990 saw *Bratsky Vestnik* reprinting (probably from old Russian Orthodox miscellanies) a remarkable number of works by famous Russian Orthodox authors, including the following: F.M. Pestryakov's *Vera* [The Faith],[191] I.S. Nikitin's *Novy Zavet* [The New Testament],[192] S.Ya. Nadson's *Drug Moy, Brat Moy!* [My Friend, My Brother!],[193] V.A. Zhukovsky's *Savl na Doroge v Damask* [Saul on the Way to Damascus],[194] F.M. Dostoevsky's *Rozhdestvo Khristovo* [Christmas],[195] A.I. Sulotsky's *Golgofa* [Calvary],[196] S.F. Ryskin's *Pogrebenie Khrista* [The Burial of Christ],[197] A.N. Maykov's

183. See *BV*, no. 5 (1988), pp. 62-3.
184. See *BV*, no. 3 (1986), p. 37.
185. See *BV*, no. 3 (1987), pp. 64-5; no. 2 (1989), pp. 54-5.
186. See *BV*, no. 5 (1987), pp. 48-51.
187. See *BV*, no. 2 (1988), pp. 60-2.
188. See *BV*, no. 1 (1990), pp. 52-4.
189. See *BV*, no. 2 (1988), p. 62.
190. See A. Lopukhin, "*Yavleniya Voskresshego Khrista*" [The Appearances of the Risen Christ], *BV*, no. 1 (1990), pp. 5-9.
191. See *BV*, no. 2 (1989), p. 56.
192. See *BV*, no. 2 (1989), p. 65.
193. See *BV*, no. 3 (1989), p. 69.
194. See *BV*, no. 4 (1989), p. 51.
195. See *BV*, no. 6 (1990), pp. 68-70.
196. See *BV*, no. 1 (1991), p. 56.
197. Ibid., p. 57.

Khristos Voskres! [Christ is Risen!],[198] A.K. Tolstoy's *Greshnitsa* [A Sinful Woman],[199] L.N. Afanasiev's *Te Zvezdy v Nebe ne Pogasli* [Those Stars in the Sky have not Become Dim],[200] I.I. Kozlov's *O Drug, Pover'!* [Oh, Friend, Believe!],[201] K.K. Romanov's *Ne Govori, Chto k Nebesam* [Do not Say that the Heavens],[202] A.N. Pleshcheev's *On Shel Bezropotno* [He Humbly Walked],[203] and A.S. Khomyakov's *Voskreshenie Lazarya* [The Raising of Lazarus].[204]

The works chosen deal with central Christian beliefs that were held by Orthodox and Baptist writers alike. It should be noted, however, that the authors chosen were not only the kind of classical Russian Orthodox poets and writers that might have been expected. The great F.M. Dostoevsky, for instance, was known for the scornful language he used when writing about the forerunners of the Russian Baptists – the Stundists and Radstockists.[205] Grand Duke K.K. Romanov was a member of the Russian Imperial House and was a powerful advocate of Slavophilism.[206] A.S. Khomyakov, an influential nineteenth-century figure, considered socialism and capitalism to be products of the decadent west. He criticized the Roman Catholic Church for stressing freedom at the expense of unity, and Protestants for maintaining freedom but losing unity.[207]

Given this openness to Orthodoxy by Russian Baptists in the 1980s, it is little wonder that Russian Orthodox leaders were ready to reciprocate. In 1988, for example, Archpriest Viktor took part in a service at Kustanay

---

198. Ibid.

199. See *BV*, no. 2 (1991), pp. 57-8.

200. See *BV*, no. 6 (1991), p. 74.

201. See *BV*, no. 2 (1992), p. 43.

202. Ibid.

203. See *BV*, no. 3 (1992), pp. 50-1.

204. See *BV*, no. 4 (1992), p. 70.

205. See, for instance, F. Dostoevsky, *Mirages: Stundism and Radstockists*, in F. Dostoevsky, *A Writer's Diary*, Vol. 2, 1877-1881, trans. by K. Lantz (Evanston, IL: Northwestern University Press, 1994), pp. 816-20.

206. See, for instance: *Velikiy Knyaz' Konstantin Konstantinovich Romanov* [Grand Duke Konstantin Konstantinovich Romanov], ed. by S. Mironenko *et al.* (SPb.: ART-Palas, 2000).

207. See, for instance: A. Khomyakov, *Sochineniya Bogoslovskie* [Theological Works] (SPb.: Nauka, 1995). One of the most popular Russian Baptist hymns – *SDP*, no. 17; *PV*, no. 125 – is written by A.S. Khomyakov.

Baptist Church and stated: "We have a great opportunity to be together: as Baptists, as Orthodox people... We want our churches to be in accord in the future... for we have one Lord, one baptism, one native country, one land."[208]

It is also clear that these good relationships were found not only at the highest levels in the Orthodox Church and in Baptist life, but at all levels and in varied sections of the communities. There were enthusiastic Orthodox readers of *Bratsky Vestnik*, such as a head of a monastery, who wrote:

> Thank you very much for the periodical... It has rich contents and it meets the manifold demands of believers... God help you in such a difficult ministry! With thanks, Hegumen Eleazar.[209]

The same issue of *Bratsky Vestnik*, in 1980, contained this letter:

> When I received some issues of the periodical, I was pleasantly surprised to know how many people loving the Lord live in all parts of our country... I wish you much success, welfare, and divine help in your highly demanding work. Archpriest Konstantin.[210]

This kind of warmth was also reflected in some services of worship in Baptist churches to which Russian Orthodox representatives were invited. *Bratsky Vestnik* reported on this event in 1976:

> [At Leningrad Baptist Church], after congregational singing ...Metropolitan Nikodim said, 'Beloved brothers and sisters!

208. "From the Life of the Local Churches", *BV*, no. 5 (1988), p. 82.
209. "*Bratskomy Vestniku – 35 Let*" [The 35th Anniversary of Bratsky Vestnik], *BV*, no. 5 (1980), p. 62.
210. Ibid.

Your brother in Christ, a Russian Orthodox bishop, is now
before you... I feel as a Christian among Christians here'.[211]

In addition, there are many accounts from Russian Baptists (ministers and
church members) of good relationships in their local communities in the
1970s. A Russian Orthodox priest preached at Odessa Central Baptist
Church (Ukraine).[212] At a local Orthodox priest's invitation, the Taldy-
Kurgan (Kazakhstan) Baptist choir sang at the Orthodox Church, and in
turn Orthodox clergy sang at a Baptist church service.[213] There are testimonies about similar friendly contacts between Orthodox priests and
Baptists, for example, in Donetsk (Ukraine) and Sochi,[214] as well as in
the Kemerovo Region in Russia.[215] Certain individuals were recalled ap-
preciatively by Baptists, such as a Russian Orthodox seminary student in
Moscow,[216] and an Orthodox monk who visited Kiev Baptist Church.[217]
The erudition of Russian Orthodox clergy was held up as an example for
Baptist ministers.[218] "Some priests", who had a good knowledge of the
Holy Scripture, were highlighted.[219] Russian Baptists approved also of the
Orthodox custom of head covering, which was obligatory for Orthodox

---

211. *BV*, no. 2 (1976), p. 20. See a description of another divine service with a Russian
Orthodox bishop at Leningrad Baptist Church: "From the Life of the Local Churches",
BV, no. 5 (1988), pp. 88-90.

212. Testimony of Baptist church member from Odessa, N.N. Gavelovsky (INT,
Sacramento, California, USA, 2006).

213. Testimony of former senior presbyter from the South Kazakhstan, P.A. Chumakin
(INT, Kent, Washington, USA, 2006).

214. Testimony of Baptist church member from Donetsk, I.G. Panchenko (INT, Castro
Valley, California, USA, 2006).

215. Testimony of minister of ECB from Krasnodar, V.Ya. Bgatov (INT, San Diego,
California, USA, 2006).

216. Testimony of presbyter of ECB from Rostov, M.P. Zakharov (INT, Sacramento,
California, USA, 2006).

217. Testimony of Baptist presbyter from Kiev, P.F. Kunda (INT, Sacramento, California,
USA, 2006).

218. Testimony of minister of ECB from Bryansk, V.A. Serpikov (INT, Seattle,
Washington, USA, 2006).

219. Testimonies of Baptist church members: from Petropavlovsk (Kazakhstan), V.E.
Sagan (INT, Minneapolis, Minnesota, USA, 2006) and from Kyzyl (Russia), P.M.
Abankin (INT, Sacramento, California, USA, 2006).

Christian women,[220] prayers on bended knees in Orthodox worship,[221] and parishioners' respect for their priests.[222] Russian Orthodox sacred music and psalms,[223] and sometimes even Russian Orthodox theology as a whole, were welcomed by local Baptists, although Orthodox ceremonial rites were rejected.[224]

In the 1980s *Bratsky Vestnik* was keen to inform its readers about joint divine services in various Russian Baptist churches involving the participation of Russian Orthodox priests and also about Baptist presbyters taking part in services at Orthodox churches. *Bratsky Vestnik* repeatedly informed readers about this. For example, in 1985 a Baptist senior presbyter preached in an Orthodox Cathedral:

> On Russian Orthodox Bishop Anthony's invitation, [Baptist] senior presbyter V.N. Vlasenko... took part in the grand divine service... at Stavropol Cathedral of St. Andrew. Brother V.N. Vlasenko spoke there...[225]

The stress on the "grand" divine service suggests that Baptists were particularly proud of their involvement in the Cathedral worship. In 1989 *Bratsky Vestnik* carried a report from Gorky.

> From the life of the local churches: the city of Gorky. ...The grand meeting dedicated to the celebration of the Millennium of the Baptism of Russia took place... A sister recited the poem *Russia*... Hieromonk [a priest and monk] Makary,

---

220. Testimony of a church member of "pure" Baptists in Donetsk Region, V.Ya. Sedykh (INT, Sacramento, California, USA, 2006).

221. Testimony of minister of ECB from Kiev, L.E. Kovalenko (INT, Sacramento, California, USA, 2006).

222. Testimony of Baptist presbyter from Odessa, Ya.D. Shevchuk (INT, Portland, Oregon, USA, 2006).

223. Testimonies of: church member V.Ya. Sedykh (INT, Sacramento, California, USA, 2006), presbyter of ECB from Odessa, Ya.D. Shevchuk (INT, Portland, Oregon, USA, 2006).

224. Testimony of Baptist minister from Odessa, Ya.D. Diordienko (INT, Sacramento, California, USA, 2006).

225. *From the Life of the Local Churches*, BV, no. 5 (1985), pp. 79-80.

representing the Orthodox Church, addressed himself to the audience with a word of greeting… The holiday meeting was ended with the choral singing of Derzhavin's ode *God* and with prayers of thanksgiving.[226]

The evidence suggests that the fostering of closer ties with the Russian Orthodox Church reflected the mainstream of Soviet Baptist orientation from the 1960s to the 1980s. This is not to argue that the relationship between the Orthodox Church and Baptists was ideal in this period. For instance, at the end of the 1980s there was a conflict between the local Russian Orthodox parish and the Baptist community in a town in Stavropol Territory. Written invitations to Baptist church meetings were torn down from public notice boards and there was much talk among the Orthodox about the dangers of the spread of "sectarianism". However, a face-to-face meeting between the Baptist presbyter and the Orthodox priest, and their mutual desire to address the problem, contributed to the improvement of Christian relationships in the town.[227]

An important factor continually drawing Orthodox and Baptist closer together was the shared experience of persecution. A.M. Bychkov wrote in his memoirs about the

> … persecution of all [Soviet] citizens professing their faith in God: the Orthodox, the Protestants… This brought together all of us, the believers… we [the AUCECB and the Orthodox Church] sent messages with Christmas and Easter greetings to each other, at the level of the Patriarch and the members of the Holy Synod. Our senior presbyters of the ECB did the same at the level of the regional and the local churches.[228]

---

226. *BV*, no. 1 (1989), p. 74. The ode is a famous poem by the Russian (Orthodox) poet, Gavrila Derzhavin, in the 18th century.

227. Testimony of minister of ECB from Stavropol Territory, V.N. Savinsky (INT, Spokane, Washington, USA, 2006).

228. Bychkov, *Moy Zhiznenny Put'*, pp. 47-8.

As they faced atheistic opposition together, friendly relations developed even further, not only between the Orthodox and the Baptists within the "top circles", but to some extent at the "lower strata" also. Baptists who were active in the 1960s and 1970s remember with gratitude difficult situations they faced in the former USSR when Russian Orthodox people helped them. For example, a devout old Orthodox woman interceded with the Soviet militia on behalf of Baptist believers during a service of baptism in Alma-Ata in 1980.[229] In another instance an Orthodox man, also elderly, extended hospitality to two young Baptists when they were under pressure.[230] There are some testimonies about Russian Orthodox assistance to Baptist church members in their distribution of Bibles in Moldavia, which was a dangerous enterprise,[231] about joint moral resistance to state atheism in Kazakhstan,[232] and about mutual aid between Russian Orthodox priests and Baptist ministers in Soviet labor camps.[233] Baptists sought to help an Orthodox priest exiled in the Tuva Autonomous Soviet Socialist Republic (Siberia) in the 1970s,[234] and also an Orthodox priest persecuted by the Communists in Kirovograd Region (Ukraine).[235]

It should be noted, finally, that the various contacts between the Russian Orthodox Church and Baptist congregations in the Soviet Union

---

229. Testimony of Baptist presbyter from Alma-Ata, A.T. Evstratenko (INT, San Diego, California, USA, 2006).

230. Testimony of minister of ECB from Kiev, L.E. Kovalenko (INT, Sacramento, California, USA, 2006).

231. Testimony of Baptist presbyter from Moscow, V.P. Zinchenko (INT, Seattle, Washington, USA, 2006).

232. Testimony of former senior presbyter from Kazakhstan, V.V. Gorelov (INT, Los Angeles, California, USA, 2006).

233. Testimony of church member of ECB from the Crimea, V.P. Litovchenko (INT, Los Angeles, California, USA, 2006). See also: G. Vins, *Tropoyu Vernosti* [The Path of Faithfulness] (SPb.: Bibliya Dlya Vsekh, 1998), pp. 68-9. In his unpublished memoirs, B.M. Zdorovets writes, "Nikolai Petrovich [probably Khrapov] told us that finding himself alone at the [prison] camp he asked God over the course of a year to send a brother there, and finally cried out in his prayer, 'Send at least a priest... even if a rather poor priest!' God heard that prayer, and he had fellowship with the [Orthodox] priest many months and prayed with him." (Spokane, Washington, USA, 2010).

234. Testimony of Baptist church member from Kyzyl, P.M. Abankin (INT, Sacramento, California, USA, 2006).

235. Testimony of Baptist minister from Kirovograd, V.D. Bondarenko (INT, Los Angeles, California, USA, 2006).

sometimes led not only to the recognition of certain values in the spiritual experience of each other but to the conversion of some Orthodox people to Baptist beliefs, and of some Baptists to Orthodoxy. There are quite a number of accounts of events of this nature.[236] In earlier periods of Baptist life in Russia the movement tended to be out of Orthodoxy into evangelical communities, but from the 1960s there were Russian or Ukrainian Baptists who converted to Orthodoxy, with even some Soviet Germans with a Mennonite-Baptist family background doing so. The most famous of these were probably Heinrich Fast, who later became an archpriest, the rural dean of the churches of the Yenisei Region, and Alexander Klassen, who became a priest in Tomsk. Prior to the mid-1970s, Fast was an active member of the Mennonite Brethren community in Karaganda (Kazakhstan). Then he moved to Siberia and under influence of an Orthodox missionary, I. Lapkin (in Barnaul), and a local priest, A. Pivovarov (in Novosibirsk), he adopted Russian Orthodoxy. In the first half of the 1980s, Klassen, who was a Baptist church member in Karaganda, took the same route.[237] A number of Soviet Baptists converted to Orthodoxy through these gifted Mennonites. Another, wider consequence was that Siberian Orthodoxy felt a certain "Baptist influence" from the 1980s. This was expressed, for example, in recommendations to the Orthodox laity to read the Bible regularly,[238] in sermons that expounded the Bible being preached in Orthodox churches, in some attempts to set up church communities which were amazingly akin to the Russian Baptist model, and in using some songs, poems and sketches on biblical themes written by Baptist authors (as a rule, their names

---

236. For instance, testimonies of ministers of Baptist churches: V.Ya. Bgatov from Krasnodar (INT, San Diego, California, USA, 2006), Ya.D. Diordienko from Odessa (INT, Sacramento, California, USA, 2006), V.N. Savinsky from Stavropol Territory (INT, Spokane, Washington, USA, 2006).

237. Testimony of historian Viktor Fast, member of the Mennonite Brethren community of Karaganda (INT, Frankenthal, Germany, 2008).

238. I heard this assertion from an Orthodox priest, expressed as if in jest, "The Bible is a Protestant book, and so Russian Orthodox people should not overdo reading it." Father A. Borisov writes of an opinion in certain Orthodox circles that reading Scripture may be "harmful": Father A. Borisov, *Pobelevshie Nivy* [White Fields] (M.: Liga – Foliant, 1994), p. 69. There is the popular belief: "He who reads the Bible till its end will go mad". See, for instance: V. Leshchenko, *Russkaya Sem'ya, XI – XIX vv.* [Russian Family, 11th – 19th Centuries] (SPb.: SPGUTD, 2004), p. 483.

were not mentioned) at Orthodox children's camps and Sunday schools.[239]
Although the primary influence in the period being studied here was that
of Orthodoxy on Baptist life, a reverse influence was also present.

Conclusion

This chapter has examined the way in which Russian Baptists absorbed a
number of elements from Orthodox spiritual traditions. Many congregations of Evangelical Christians-Baptists in the Soviet Union, as they lived
in ways that were marginal to society, chose what can be seen as a "monastic" approach to serving God, albeit "monasticism in the world". They
were also fascinated by the "ladder", with its many rungs on the way to
spiritual perfection, depicting the gradual ascent to heaven. The traditional
Eastern Christian interpretation and expression of holiness which involved
saints and even "holy fools", was also in a measure characteristic of local
Russian Baptist communities. In addition, the political indifference and
pacifism of many Soviet Baptists intensified their likeness to some Russian
Orthodox radical groups. When a political stance was taken by Baptists,
it was articulated in ways that mirrored the Russian Orthodox Church.
There were numerous public censures by Baptists of the "hostile" Western
countries, with simultaneous support given to the "peacemaking" policy of
the USSR. Such a line of conduct was determined not only by Communist
pressure or the Soviet way of life, but also by the long shaping of Baptists
within the Russian Orthodox, "Slavophile" and anti-Western context. As
Russian Orthodox people and Baptists in the Soviet Union lived together
in isolation from the West, there was mutual interaction, with considerable
Orthodox influence being felt, but also real elements of impact of Baptist
beliefs and practical experience upon Russian Orthodoxy. The joint meetings which took place in the period and the warm expressions that were

---

239. Testimony of historian Viktor Fast (INT, Frankenthal, Germany, 2008). Also, a
Baptist presbyter from Odessa (Ukraine), Ya.D. Shevchuk, testifies about a certain positive
impact of Soviet Baptists on Russian Orthodoxy, emphasizing love for the Holy Scripture
and the church preaching in clear language for common people (INT, Portland, Oregon,
USA, 2006).

shared do not indicate a formal relationship but rather indicate that many Baptists felt an affinity with Orthodox Christians. Many Orthodox figures, such as I. Shakhovskoy, A. Men', D. Dudko and A. Borisov, testified that contrary to official and popular beliefs, there was "sectarianism in [Russian] Orthodoxy" and "[Russian] Orthodoxy in sectarianism".[240]

240. See Archbishop Ioann (Shakhovskoy), *"Sektantstvo v Pravoslavii i Pravoslavie v Sektantstve"* [Sectarianism in Orthodoxy and Orthodoxy in Sectarianism], *Pravoslavnaya Obshchina*, no. 4 (1992), pp. 71-7.

CHAPTER 7

Bible, Beliefs and Behavior

Issues related to theology, ecclesiology, liturgy and spiritual traditions among Russian Baptists have been examined in the previous chapters. The argument has been advanced that there were significant areas in the period 1960-1990 in which Baptist beliefs and practices resembled those of Orthodoxy. Yet in this period there was an inherited belief among many Russian Baptists that non-biblical customs and traditions characterized only Orthodox people, while Baptists did not have them: Baptists lived and did everything "according to the Bible".[1] However, as has already begun to be explored, within the worship and life of Baptist congregations of the late Soviet period there were many unwritten rules, customs and statutes, quite often not related directly to the Scriptures.[2] It is not that these were necessarily enforced from a rule-book: there was the power of unwritten tradition within Baptist communities in Russia. This attitude in itself had similarities to Orthodox approaches. N.S. Leskov in his work on "Little Things from the Lives of Bishops" (1878), spoke of things in the Orthodox Church that were "nowhere written as a law", but rather were observed as a tradition "in a dignified way and without any debates."[3] In this chapter the way in which this outlook worked out in Russian Baptist life is further explored. The focus here is on the unusual ways in which

---

1. See, for instance: Rogozin, *Otkuda vse eto poyavilos'*, pp. 5-17; *Osnovnye Printsipy Very Evangel'skikh Khristian – Baptistov*, pp. 59-60, 92-95.
2. Cf.: A. Tsyrulnikov, "*Predanie*" [The Tradition], *Put' Bogopoznaniya*, vol. 8 (2002), pp. 69-70.
3. N. Leskov, *Melochi Arkhiereyskoy Zhizni* [Little Things from the Lives of Bishops], in N. Leskov, *Sobranie Sochineniy*, 12 vols., vol. VI, p. 302.

biblical material was utilized, the poetic imagination, the ethos of community life, the area of dreams and unusual happenings, and prejudices and superstitions. Baptists wished to live "according to the Bible", but they also mirrored Orthodox ways.[4]

Reading the Bible

The approach to the reading of the Bible that characterized many Soviet Baptists can be described as "folk hermeneutics". One factor which shaped reading of the Scripture was the translation of the Bible that was used, which (as noted earlier) was normally the Synodal Bible. There was little desire, and little opportunity, at least at local level, to consult "scholars' books" that might have helped to explain the text. There was an undisguised preference shown for the chiefly oral *brotherly* (or "rustic") theology. One preacher attempted to express this when he said, rather enigmatically: "What do you choose, dear soul: the Lower or Upper Jerusalem?"[5] (The "lower" was earthly, based on "the wisdom of men", while the "upper" was heavenly, spiritual knowledge). There was also a legendary saying: "Read as it is written!"[6] The problem was that "as it is written" was often according to a specific national-language translation. Thus, for example, the word *vzyatka* ("bribe") occurs in the Russian Synodal Bible only four

---

4. Alexander Popov, "The Evangelical Christians-Baptists in the Soviet Union as a hermeneutical community: Examining the identity of the All-Union Council of the ECB (AUCECB) through the way the Bible was used in its publications" (PhD thesis, International Baptist Theological Seminary, University of Wales, 2010), explores specific aspects of the use of the Bible by Soviet Baptists. However, he looks mainly at *Bratsky Vestnik*. I am looking at a wider range of sources, including interviews, and I include the CCECB as well as the AUCECB.

5. This rhetorical question, from a "very simple" sermon, could be compared to the famous words by Tertullian, "What has Athens to do with Jerusalem? What has the Academy to do with the Church? What have heretics to do with Christians?" – Tertullian, *The Prescription Against Heretics*, in *The Ante-Nicene Fathers*, ed. by A. Roberts and J. Donaldson, 10 vols. (Grand Rapids: Eerdmans, 1978), vol. III, p. 246.

6. According to one of the "non-canonical parables" of the ECB, even the Apostle Paul, when asked why and under what circumstances a certain text in the Epistles appeared, insisted: "Read as it is written!"

times,[7] while the word *bribe* is used in the New American Standard Bible 26 times.[8] The Synodal Bible often substitutes the words "gifts", or "donations" for bribes. This had an effect on thinking about such "gifts". Any editions of the Bible that included commentaries and appendixes (which became available in the USSR in the 1980s) were not infrequently rejected, because: "In Revelation 22:18, on the last page of Scripture, it is written what punishment God will inflict on those who want to *add* something to Holy Writ, but today we see supplements (*"additions"*) by all kinds of theologians immediately after the words of warning from God."[9]

A common feature found among Russian Baptist interpreters was the reading of contemporary life directly back into the Bible in an anachronistic way. For example, they sometimes emphasized words from Isaiah 1:13, "incense is an abomination unto me", to censure tobacco smoking.[10] In response to some who mentioned that every biblical passage should be considered in its context, and so Isaiah could not have been saying anything about smoking, these interpreters sometimes replied: "Brothers, I do not find the word *context* in the Bible."[11] In debates with Pentecostals, in spite of the Baptist tendency to criticize Pentecostal views, some Baptist elders considered that Pentecostals should be taken seriously because they were mentioned in the Bible. The reference was not to issues like healing or speaking in tongues, but to Old Testament passages such as 1 Samuel 8:12 about "commanders of fifties" or "captains of fifties". The Russian word *pyatidesyatnik*, in the Synodal Bible, can refer both to a "commander of fifties" and a Pentecostal. The following dialogue allegedly once took place between a Russian Pentecostal and a Baptist leader.

---

7. See *Polnaya Simfoniya na Kanonicheskie Knigi Svyashchennogo Pisaniya* [The Exhaustive Concordance of the Canonical Books of the Holy Scripture] (SPb.: Biblia dlya Vsekh, 1996), p. 99.

8. See *New American Standard Exhaustive Concordance of the Bible* (Nashville, TN: Holman Bible Publishers, 1981), pp. 173-4.

9. Many such examples from old Russian Baptist practice were published in "*Mezhdunarodnaya Khristianskaya Gazeta*" in 2002-2005.

10. For instance, testimony of presbyter V.N. Khot'ko (Petropavlovsk, Kazakhstan, 1998). In the Russian Bible, the word in Isa 1:13 is *kurenie*, which means both "incense" and "tobacco smoking". Hence the confusion among some Baptists.

11. Testimony of Baptist presbyter from Kishinev, D. Sevastiyan (Prague, Czech Republic, 2009).

Pentecostal (*animatedly*): Our church is ancient, inseparable from Pentecost, described in the Acts of the Apostles! That is why we are called Pentecostals...

Baptist: Yes, I agree. You are younger than we Baptists are, as our church originates with John the Baptist.

Pentecostal: Is that [the church] from whom 'John's baptism' began, without the Holy Ghost?

Baptist: That is the very John the Baptist by whom our Lord Jesus Christ was baptized (and therefore became a Baptist, too)...

Pentecostal (*smiling*): Even Christ became a Baptist? All right then, but in addition, the Old Testament also confirms the antiquity of Pentecostals, being written long before the Nativity of Christ. As it says in 2 Kings, 'Then the king sent unto him a captain of fifty with his fifty...'[12]

Baptist: But let us read a bit further, 'And there came down fire from heaven, and consumed him [the captain] and his fifty'.[13] So, whose faith is true, if the Lord consumed the captain and his fifty [the Pentecostals]?[14]

This kind of interpretation of Scripture is reminiscent of Russian Orthodox popular use of the Bible. The Old Slavonic translation of the New Testament called the chief priests of the Jews *archiereuses*, the word used for modern Russian Orthodox bishops, and this led to the belief among some that it was bishops who crucified Christ.[15] As another example of

---

12. 2 Kings 1:9. In Russian literally: a Pentecostal with his fifty...
13. 2 Kings 1:10.
14. The authorship of this folk "Baptist parable" is unknown.
15. See Leskov, *Melochi Arkhiereyskoy Zhizni*, p. 192.

Russian Orthodox anachronism, an Orthodox priest, referring to John 12:13, explained to his parishioners the origin of the name Pussy Willow Sunday (the Russian name for Palm Sunday): "During the Entrance of the Lord into Jerusalem, the Jews by their tradition held branches of palm trees in their hands, while the Orthodox Christians [who were there] held branches of pussy willows."[16] This was not infrequently said quite seriously, and is an indication of a cultural phenomenon embedded in Christian life, Orthodox and Baptist, in the Soviet Union.[17]

Another dimension of Russian Baptist reading of the Bible was the "political" interpretations offered. The name of V.I. Lenin (VIL in abbreviated form – Soviet students usually abbreviated his name in this way in lecture notes) was associated by some Russian Baptists, who were seen as having studied the Bible "in depth", with the Babylonian god Bel. In the Russian Bible, the god Bel (see Jer 51:44 and the apocryphal story "Bel and the Dragon", in the extended book of Daniel, chapter 14) is spelled as Vil.[18] It is significant that Russian Baptists referred in these discussions to the Apocrypha: many were using the Russian Orthodox edition of the Bible. By contrast with Lenin, major Russian evangelical leaders of the past, such as I.S. Prokhanov, were seen as comparable to biblical heroes.[19]

L.I. Brezhnev, General Secretary of the Central Committee of the Communist Party, could be lauded by AUCECB leaders, as noted in chapter 3, but there were many ordinary Russian Baptists who saw him in a quite different light. In the aftermath of Brezhnev's death, at least one sermon, which became famous and was re-told, was preached by a CCECB minister on the rich man and Lazarus (Luke 16:19-26) in which the preacher spoke of a "striking resemblance" between this gospel story and some events from the recent past in the USSR. A parallel was drawn between the death of Brezhnev and that of the "impious rich man" in Jesus'

---

16. *Mezhdunarodnaya Khristianskaya Gazeta*, no. 7 (2004), p. 17.

17. In the Russian Orthodox context, this theme was analyzed in a profound way by A. Borisov. See Father A. Borisov, *Pobelevshie Nivy* [White Fields] (M.: Liga – Foliant, 1994).

18. For instance, testimony of Baptist church members from Vinnitsa, V. Vuzy and V. Karpenko (Odessa, Ukraine, 1994).

19. While I.S. Prokhanov, a hero for Evangelical Christians, was compared to King David, D.I. Mazaev, the early Baptist leader, was compared by some Evangelical Christians to Saul: *Pis'ma k Brat'yam Evangel'skim Khristianam-Baptistam*, pp. 53-4.

parable.[20] In this kind of interpretation of biblical narratives a contrast was often drawn between the power of the political world on the one hand and the "persecuted brotherhood" of Baptists on the other. Thus preachers took note, when speaking of Brezhnev's death, of the death at almost the same time of the well-known minister of the CCECB, N.P. Khrapov. The text in Luke 16 reads: "And it came to pass, that the beggar died, and was carried by the angels into Abraham's bosom." The application was: N.P. Khrapov died on 6 November 1982, a prisoner in a labor camp in Kazakhstan's Mangyshlak peninsula.[21] The text continues: "The rich man also died, and was buried." Four days after Khrapov's death, Brezhnev died.[22] Khrapov personified those believers who had nothing, while Brezhnev personified those who would not share with believers even the "crumbs" which fell from the "Soviet table" (Luke 16:21). The lesson was that there was punishment for worldly "rich men". There were echoes here of a speech which was much quoted among the Orthodox: St. Theodore of Studium, on the death of the Byzantine iconoclastic Emperor Leo V, compared him to "Pharaoh" and pronounced, "The foe fell down. Our torturer is overwhelmed."[23]

The Bible was also used by Russian Baptists in efforts they made to gain direct guidance from God. For example, basing their thinking on the biblical story from Genesis 24:12-14, in which Isaac met Rebekah after she came to the well to draw water, some Baptist young men proposed marriage to the first young unmarried woman to enter the prayer house on a certain day.[24] They prayed about what would happen and saw their approach as justified by Scripture. Others who were seeking a partner in life

---

20. There are different versions of this sermon. The version I have used is the earliest one, as far as I am aware, according to the retelling of it by presbyter V.N. Khot'ko (Petropavlovsk, Kazakhstan, 2001).

21. See *Podrazhayte Vere Ikh*, pp. 287-8; Savinsky, *Istoriya (1917-1967)*, p. 389.

22. See, for instance: Yu. Aksyutin, ed., *L.I. Brezhnev: Materialy k Biografii* [L.I. Brezhnev: Materials for the Biography] (M.: Politizdat, 1991), p. 8; *Sovetsky Entsiklopedichesky Slovar'*, p. 167.

23. The speech continued: "The hard-hearted Pharaoh perished. It was incumbent on the apostate to die exactly this way. The son of darkness had to face his death at night. He, who denuded God's churches, had to see bared swords against him at the house of the Lord." Cited in Kartashev, *Vselenskie Sobory*, p. 518.

24. For instance, testimony of Baptist church member from Kishinev, P.P. Cherny (INT, Sacramento, California, USA, 2006); Sedletsky, "Vospominaniya", pp. 77-85.

were impressed by the way individuals in the Bible were guided by dreams.
Some Baptists took the view that if a young man and a young woman had
a similar dream on the same night, God was indicating that he would bless
their marriage.[25] Another common way of using the Bible was the following: "Let the biblical passage that the preacher reads from the pulpit today
be God's message to me in my particular need."[26] There was a similar phenomenon in Russian Orthodoxy. Also, some Orthodox people would open
their Bibles and randomly choose a passage from Scripture. This was then
interpreted as God's answer for their situation.[27] This practice was not uncommon among Soviet Baptist members, but it was definitely condemned
by the leaders of the AUCECB churches.[28]

A common custom, which was promoted by Baptist elders, was the creation of biblical *riddles* and *puzzlers* (so-called *sukhariki* – "dried crusts").
It was almost impossible to arrive at the right answers to these riddles.
Usually the questions were addressed to young people, since the traditional
view was that elders should give young people difficult tasks to accomplish.
The problem for the young people was not so much their lack of biblical knowledge, though sometimes that was the issue, but the deliberately
obscure nature of the questions. Two examples give the flavour of these
biblical riddles. "When did a prophet of God die because of the patter of
feet?" and "In what story did a coffin sail the seas and the deceased call
upon God?" The answer to the first was the death of John the Baptist (Matt
14:6-11), the patter of feet being the dance of Heroidias' daughter. The
second riddle was about the Prophet Jonah, who prayed from a great fish's
belly (Jonah 2).[29] When these puzzles could not be solved, the elders asked:

---

25. For instance, testimony of Baptist church member from Chernovtsy, A.F. Bernik
(INT, Fresno, California, USA, 2006).

26. Testimony of former senior presbyter from Kuybyshev, V.F. Serpevsky (INT,
Vancouver, Washington, USA, 2006).

27. See, for instance, Cloistress Taisiya, *Russkoe Pravoslavnoe Zhenskoe Monashestvo*, p. 163.
Russian classical literature describes a similar practice. For instance: A.K. Tolstoy, *Sobranie
Sochineniy* [Collected Works], 4 vols. (M.: Khudozhestvennaya literatura, 1964), vol. III,
p. 18.

28. See, for instance, C. Prokhorov, "*O Vere Suetnoy i Istinnoy*" [On False and True Faith],
Mezhdunarodnaya Khristianskaya Gazeta, no. 9 (2002), p. 4.

29. Testimonies of Baptist ministers: V.N. Khot'ko (Petropavlovsk, Kazakhstan, 1997),
Ya.A. Meleshkevich (Bishkul', Kazakhstan, 1997). The "patter of feet" apparently

"What are you learning at school these days?" The whole attitude was in line with the ancient Eastern Christian way of dealing with those who might have a high opinion of themselves. Baptist young people were tested, rather as certain difficult and sometimes bizarre tests were set for novices in Orthodox monasteries, to cultivate humility.[30] Older Russian Baptist preachers liked to refer in their sermons to 1 Peter 4:12, often interpreting it in this way: the Lord teaches Christians not to avoid testing (trials) "as if some strange thing happened to you".[31] The riddles were one way of setting rigorous tests as to someone's knowledge of the Scripture, but the assessment of knowledge was less important than the testing of spirituality.[32]

The association of the Bible with spirituality was seen, too, in the traditional Russian Baptist advice that believers should not start reading the Holy Scripture without a special prayer. Otherwise, they would not be given a divine blessing and the *true* understanding of the text – Ephesians 1:17-18. The advice continued: it was wrong for anyone to read the Bible hastily and inattentively; no-one should misquote the Bible, by adding or missing out some words intentionally; there should be correction if someone inadvertently made a mistake when reading the Bible aloud; and it was sinful to laugh when someone made a mistake while reading the Bible. Other advice was connected with the view of the Bible (as considered earlier) as a kind of icon. No one should bend the corners of a Bible's pages, make notes on its pages with a pen (pencil was allowed) or read the Scripture and have a meal at the same time, in case pages were stained.[33] Baptist concern about reading the Bible can be compared to the Orthodox concern about prayer. Indeed the two were connected. Neither prayer nor personal Bible reading should be interrupted. B.M. Zdorovets encouraged

---

described the "worldly" activity of dancing.

30. See, for instance, in, Bishop Petr (Ekaterinovsky), *Ukazanie Puti k Spaseniyu, Opyt Asketiki* [Showing the Way to Salvation, the Ascetic Practice] [1885] (M.: Izd-vo Sretenskogo monastyrya, 2001). See also Cloistress Taisiya, *Russkoe Pravoslavnoe Zhenskoe Monashestvo*, pp. 55-7.

31. See, for instance: *BL*, no. 8 (1970), p. 2; *VestI*, no. 1 (2005), pp. 30-1.

32. For instance, testimony of Baptist presbyter from Frunze, A.K. Sipko, about his first Bible (INT, Spokane, Washington, USA, 2006).

33. Such advice was mentioned, for instance, in the testimonies of evangelist P.A. Semeryuk (INT, Sacramento, California, USA, 2006) and presbyter V.N. Khot'ko (Petropavlovsk, Kazakhstan, 1999).

this view by telling a story from the beginning of the 1960s about some visitors to a Baptist elder who lived near Kharkov, who found him reading the Bible. The elder did not answer the door, but they entered and joined him in silent study. After an hour the elder closed his Bible and "cordially greeted the guests".[34] Russian Baptists believed that a prayer should not be brought to an end abruptly for any reason – people calling, the telephone, or the needs of domestic animals.[35] The priority was speaking to God. However, many Baptists considered reading of the Bible more important since in that "God speaks".[36] Whether in reading the Bible or prayer, the spirit at work was a monastic one. One Russian Orthodox account spoke of "Mother Mavrikiya [who had] dedicated herself so fully to the spiritual life that all worldly things became alien to her... One day at church, Mother Mavrikiya was told that her monastic cell was on fire. 'Please let me know when the fire stops', she replied, continuing her prayer."[37]

In some cases the guidance about Bible reading among Russian Baptists was passed on informally, while in other cases rules were written down. Among the latter were regulations stating that Baptist members should read the Holy Scripture every day.[38] Often the rules applied to the use of the Bible in public. But besides the official church services, and personal study, there were meetings that took place in homes – meetings that were sometimes described, using the words of one hymn, as "delightful and marvellous".[39] Sometimes unbelievers visited these "spiritual fellowships" where, in an informal way, they found faith, perhaps more readily than in church.[40] One description shows the way in which Scripture governed the thinking about these meetings, despite study of the Bible not being mentioned:

---

34. Testimony of B.M. Zdorovets (INT, Spokane, Washington, USA, 2006).

35. For examples, testimonies of Baptist presbyters, V.N. Khot'ko (Petropavlovsk, Kazakhstan, 1999) and I.P. Fast (Shchuchinsk, Kazakhstan, 1999).

36. For instance, testimony of B.M. Zdorovets (INT, Spokane, Washington, USA, 2006).

37. Cloistress Taisiya, *Russkoe Pravoslavnoe Zhenskoe Monashestvo*, p. 46.

38. *The Church Regulations* of Petropavlovsk community of ECB (Kazakhstan) from the 1980s, which was typical of regulations in many Russian Baptist churches.

39. See *SDP*, no. 573, p. 382.

40. Zhuravlev, *Velika Vernost' Tvoya, Gospodi*, vol. I, p. 317.

> The warm feelings of contentment, joy and peace are too deep
> for words... That was the case in this memorable evening. It
> was a Tuesday. Some brothers and sisters gathered... and had
> a heart-to-heart talk... We sang, recited poetry, drank tea...
> Nobody wanted to part. O Lord... if we are so happy to be
> with You on earth, what is in store for us in eternity?! Truly,
> things which eye has not seen, ear has not heard, and which
> have not entered the heart of man, all these You prepared for
> those who love You!.. Thanks be to You for the indescribable
> gift of Your peace![41]

The expression "joy and peace... too deep for words" and the biblical
quotation "eye has not seen, ear has not heard..." (1 Cor 2:9) suggest an
attachment to *apophatic* language. What is conveyed here is the inner experience of Russian Baptists. These meetings were not for the formal purpose of "Bible study", although all involved would have seen themselves as
carrying out the commands of Scripture. Such meetings were frequently
characterized by spontaneity rather than preparation. What mattered was
the sense of the presence of the Lord.[42] Knowledge of the Bible was not
the final objective: such knowledge was a means of attaining to the Eastern
Christian feeling of being in touch with what was "indescribable".

Poetry, imagination and language

The description in the quotation above of how the "brothers and sisters"
who gathered on a Tuesday evening "sang, recited poetry, drank tea" highlights the place of poetry in Russian Baptist spirituality. There was also
"heart-to-heart talk". An analysis of the language of poetry that was written by Baptist authors of the late Soviet period, which was widely read in
churches and in smaller groups, offers crucial insights into areas already

---

41. Ibid.

42. As Russian Baptists sing often during such meetings, "Everything is prepared for the
feast. Jesus invites you." – *SDP*, no. 165, pp. 115-6.

examined in this study. Indeed investigation of the content and the place
of Russian Baptist poetry can be used to assess some of the arguments put
forward in previous chapters of this study regarding the way Baptist theology, ecclesiology, liturgy, and spiritual traditions resembled those found in
Orthodoxy. Russian Baptist preachers would at times have been reluctant
(in part because they were constrained by official doctrinal formulae) to
articulate all that they felt in these areas, and what was written and said by
imaginative, artistic and perhaps emotional members of the community,
who were moved not by the letter but by the *spirit* of Russian Baptist beliefs, is therefore of particular significance. The kind of theology expressed
in hymns has been studied, but the poetry that was written and recited had
its own particular flavour.

The majority of Russian Baptist poetic texts were written by hand, were
never officially published, and were anonymous. Many church members
(mainly women) copied the poems with loving care from one generation to
the next and preserved them in special notebooks (so-called *tetradki*).[43] The
specific character of these sources needs to be noted. The obvious limitation is that the role of the authors in their churches is often unknown. But
on the other hand the anonymity suggests that the poems which became
widely accepted did so because of their intrinsic power, not the name of the
author. Although many of the poems I have read could be quoted, I have
attempted to use those which appear to have been both authoritative and
popular among Baptist communities, and in addition whose authorship
can be authenticated today (though this is not the case in all instances).
On the whole I will quote extracts from those poems which were evidently
known across the Russian Baptist world. These have been copied and con-
served, with many finding their way on to reputable Christian (first of
all, Baptist) Russian-language websites. There were also poems that never
reached beyond a narrow circle. However, even if other poems – in the private notebooks of Baptists in certain communities, or perhaps in a certain

---

43. I am indebted here to a number of Baptist church members: the Karpenko and the
Gavelovskie families (Odessa, Ukraine, 1995), the Kaplenkov and Romanyuk families
(Petropavlovsk, Kazakhstan, 1998), N.S. Andrianova (Omsk, Russia, 2003), G.E.
Kuchma (Omsk, 2005), D.G. Savchenko and N.R. Savchenko (Omsk, 2011), and many
others. I was greatly helped by being able to read their manuscript notebooks.

part of Russia or in other republics of the former Soviet Union – were not of the same quality, overall the poetic material has remarkably similar features.

The argument (presented in chapter 4) that baptism and the Lord's Supper were thought of in sacramental terms among many Russian Baptists is confirmed by a range of poetical examples. In poetry the deepest feelings about these rites were expressed. This is a typical poem about "holy water baptism".

> Holy water baptism
> Is evidently showing this:
> God gives you His salvation,
> And you receive grace.
> Old habits are removed by the water,
> The Blood of Christ washed away sins.[44]

This poem, although it is not intended to be a statement of theological belief, conveys the sense of the close relationship between *holy* baptism and receiving God's *grace*. The person who is baptized receives salvation and is washed by both the *blood* of Christ and the baptismal *water*. Such an approach to baptism by no means does away with the necessity of saving faith. Baptism, as many Russian Baptists understood it, could be simultaneously an outward sign of salvation (the poem continues: "Holy water baptism is a visible sign of the Covenant") and also a means of salvation. Following the Russian Orthodox approach, sacramental reality was not to be reduced to any "merely symbolic" theological statement.

Poetry also took the Lord's Supper as a theme. One poet, Vera Kushnir, who was well known among Russian Baptists, wrote some amazing lines about Holy Communion, seeking to express in her poetry the essence of this sacrament.

> And simple bread was broken before them,

---

44. *Stikhotvoreniya. Kreshchenie* [Poems. The Baptism], <http://www.blagovestnik.org/books/00430/db/ v6195044.html> accessed 22 August 2010.

That all could eat, remembering His flesh,
The innocent and the broken, for all people...
For He became our food and drink,
Transforming into our blood and flesh,
That He would be in us, and we – in Him.[45]

The ideas embodied in this poem correspond in part with a symbolic understanding of the breaking of bread ("remembering" by breaking "simple" bread), but at the same time other strands are present. The Baptist poet uses words that would have been problematic for a Baptist theologian, "For He [Christ] became our food and drink // Transforming into our blood and flesh..." Probably the "transforming" here does not equate fully to the transformation found in the doctrine of *transubstantiation*, but the words have strong echoes of sacramental language. For comparison, the following is the traditional Orthodox Eucharistic theology as described by the Archpriest Alexander Men', "When the sacrament of the Eucharist is being celebrated... God's power – not invisibly, not only spiritually, but in reality – enters the elements that will become a part of our being. This feeds us; we partake of the Body and Blood, the bread and wine... And Christ himself enters our body and blood."[46]

Another theme taken up in Russian Baptist poetry was the significance of the building in which worship took place. This is a typical poem:

And everyone receives Christ's grace here –
In the prayer house, the gate of heaven is near...

Here is the house of God, holy ground!
Let us ask for blessing on this church building...
Everyone, stretching out his hands to the church,

---

45. V. Kushnir, *Khleb i Vino* [Bread and Wine], <http://kopilochka.net.ru/POEMS/poem05.php> accessed 22 August 2010.

46. *Otets A. Men' Otvechaet na Voprosy Slushateley* [Father A. Men' Answers the Questions of his Listeners], ed. A. Andreeva (M.: Fond im. A. Menya, 1999), p. 234. Cf.: A. Men', *Evkharistiya* [The Eucharist], <http://www.alexandrmen.ru/besedy/evharist.html> accessed 14 November 2010. See also: *Nastol'naya Kniga Svyashchennosluzhitelya*, vol. I, p. 429; Uspensky, *Anafora, Opyt historiko-liturgicheskogo analisa*, 125-8.

Will be heard by You.[47]

The reverent attitude to the church building in the Russian Baptist tradition, noted before, is seen in the expressions "gate of heaven" and "holy ground". It is in this special space that people receive God's grace. Thus it was necessary to ask for blessings on every prayer house, as was done in the act of consecration. The way that the poem speaks of prayer that involved stretching out hands to the church is an especially significant point. Though it is probably an allusion to certain biblical texts (for example, 2 Chr 6:29), the statement by this author that it is those who perform this ritual who will be "heard", breathes a "sacramental" spirit.

In another (well-known) Baptist poem, by Ya. Buzinny, there are the following noteworthy lines reflecting the traditional Eastern Christian understanding of the kind of prayer and worship that is pleasing to God:

> Two men were praying in God's house.
> One man stood on his feet. The other knelt down…
> I thought then of a field of ripe rye:
> A proud spike was towering over there,
> The nearest ear was bent down to the ground.
> The first spike was without corn, void;
> The other ear prepared grains for harvest.[48]

In this poem the story, reminiscent of the parable of the Pharisee and the tax-collector, is presented in a new way. The poem takes the reader far away from the original setting into Russian fields and into kneeling prayers in Orthodox and Russian Baptist practice. It is not surprising that some selections of the poems of Buzinny, an evangelical poet, were published by Russian Orthodox periodicals.[49] Poems also spoke about the way in which offerings of money should be brought during worship.

---

47. T. Kuzmina, *O Tserkvi* [On the Church] [1986], in T. Kuzmina, *V Luche Sveta* [In the Beam of Light] (SPb.: Bibliya Dly Vsekh, 2009), pp. 77-80.

48. Ya. Buzinny, *Molilis' Bogu Dvoe* [Two Men Prayed to God], <http://www.blagovestnik. org/books/ 00430/db/v889989.html> accessed 14 November 2010.

49. See, for instance, *Ofitsial'ny Sayt Shar'inskogo Blagochiniya* [The Official Website of

…Will two mites from a widow
Be pleasing to God?
How they could be of use to the church?
Let any noble one submit himself to the Lord;
Everyone, going to church with offerings,
Should bring two mites with deep humility.[50]

As with other stories from the Gospels, the famous incident of the "widow's mite" was applied in a specific way. In Russian Baptist tradition the offerings were not just money but were sacred objects.[51] In the Eastern Christian sacramental mind the church "pennies" (or two mites), brought to God with humility, bear the imprint of God's blessing.[52] There was a parallel with money given to monasteries.[53] Stealing from the church treasury was considered as a dreadful sin, because it was robbing God.[54]

A kind of Christian elegy was another widespread genre found in Russian Baptist poetry. In spite of the undoubted belief of Baptist poets in eternal life, nevertheless they wrote about the death of someone within their family or among their friends with profound sadness and tears. These poems also employed vivid metaphors, in the style of classical Russian poetry:

the Deanery of Shar'ya], <http://neophyt.narod.ru/Newspaper/N10.htm> accessed 14 November 2010. On kneeling prayers – see also the poem "Ne Ostavlyayte Sobrany Vashikh" [Do not Give up Meeting Together] by an anonymous Baptist author in *BV*, no. 4 (1981), p. 53.

50. *Stikhotvoreniya. Dve Lepty* [Poems. Two Mites], <http://days4god.com/publ/21-1-0-98> accessed 14 November 2010.

51. See, for instance, Kolesnikov, *Khristianin, znaesh' li ty*, vol. I, pp. 150-1.

52. Ibid., pp. 142-4.

53. A former senior presbyter from the South Kazakhstan, P.A. Chumakin (INT, Kent, Washington, USA, 2006), spoke of an "apostate" who placed a demand on the church board that his contributions to the church during his membership be returned. "The brethren adjudicated this extraordinary dispute in this way: let him bring a notarized copy of a certificate showing all his contributions, and then we will pay him back…" – Cf. the analogous Orthodox monastic practice: N. Sinitsyna, *Tipy Monastyrey i Russky Asketichesky Ideal* [The Types of Monasteries and the Russian Ascetic Ideal], in N. Sinitsyna, ed., *Monashestvo i Monastyri v Rossii* [Monks and Monasteries in Russia] (M.: Nauka, 2002), p. 123-4.

54. I remember an incident at Petropavlovsk Baptist church, when a man proved guilty of this sin was excommunicated. The thief was charged not so much with stealing but with mystically "robbing God". The thief himself said that during the theft he prayed and asked "a loan from God", promising God to "to pay back some day".

> Don't fear to die! Is wheat afraid
> Of the reapers' voices in harvest time,
> When their sickles glitter in the field?
> Don't fear to die! Is a wanderer afraid
> Of the father's home, he sees from far away?[55]

In many of these poems, as in Baptist obituaries, statements addressed directly to the dead are to be found. One of them spoke of the pain of the death of a "brother", probably another believer. It continued:

> But I still talk to you, as you are alive to me,
> And I love you, as well as call you brother.[56]

There was particular sorrow if the person died early in life. Here are examples from two different poems:

> You passed away so early…
> Thank God, there is heavenly peace
> Where the door is opened for you.[57]

> You left the church walls early…
> Farewell, raptured dweller!
> See you in the glory of heaven![58]

The living conversation with the brother in Christ, the heavenly peace prepared for the believing soul, the church walls within which the deceased

---

55. *Ne Boysya Umeret'* [Don't fear to die!], in *Vernost': Sbornik Khristianskikh Stikhov* [Faithfulness: Book of Christian Poems], Izdanie CCECB, 1984, p. 181. See its electronic version: <http://horoshoe.info/system/ files/Sbornik_stihov__Vernost_.pdf> accessed 14 November 2010.

56. M. Burchak, *Pamyati Geny* [In Memory of Gena], <http://www.blagovestnik.org/books/00430/db/v648527. html> accessed 22 August 2010.

57. *V Nebesny Pokoy* [To the Heavenly Peace], in *Vernost': Sbornik Khristianskikh Stikhov*, p. 167, <http:// horoshoe.info/system/files/Sbornik_stihov__Vernost_.pdf> accessed 14 November 2010.

58. *Voskhishchenny Zhitel'* [The Raptured Dweller], in *Vernost': Sbornik Khristianskikh Stikhov*, p. 168.

Christian is no longer present – all of these images illuminate the spiritual world of Russian Evangelical Christians-Baptists. The themes closely follow the perception of life and death held by Russian Orthodox Christians, with their prayers for the dead, their hope that the dead person has been received into the Kingdom of Heaven, and their warm feelings towards the sacred church building.

Finally, there were poems which had an epic quality. The forces of nature were linked with spiritual forces, as in this poem.

> It's not black clouds fallen from the sky;
> It's not a tempest raging in the field;
> But it is combined forces of untruth
> that fight against Christ's disciples.[59]

Such lines, by their feeling, style, and message, are close to traditional Russian folklore, to heroic epic, for instance. The sense of foreboding and of evil is reminiscent of some sorrowful poetry and songs of Old Believers who mourned the pious Russian Orthodoxy of bygone days, and spoke of similar "forces of untruth" fighting against the faith, "Go there, to the blue sea // to the worthy Solovki Monastery // and destroy the old and true Belief // and dictate to them new and untrue beliefs."[60] Poetry enabled these images to be brought to life among Baptist communities and to add to the general colourful palette of Russian spirituality.

In addition to and alongside poetic language, Russian Baptist congregations in the Soviet Union had a certain spoken language which those who were not in the community found it hard (often impossible) to understand. This was "heart-to-heart talk" (as in the informal groups), in a language that sometimes needed quite literally to be "interpreted" outside the community. The "Baptist dialect" had, however, many parallels with Church Slavonic, including numerous archaisms, biblical allusions and euphemisms. Among these were the following:

---

59. [Anon. of ECB], *VS*, no. 1 (1964); *VestI*, no. 2 (2003), p. 38.
60. Cited in S. Soloviev, *Istoriya Rossii s Drevneyshikh Vremen*, part 7, vols. XIII-XIV, p. 157.

Privetstvuyu vas! (Greetings to you!) – This was a form of traditional Baptist salutation, rather than the common Russian
"worldly" *zdravstvuyte* (how do you do?).[61]

Mir vashemu domu! (Peace be to your house!) – This was the
Orthodox greeting when a believing guest entered the house.
The reply of the hosts (Orthodox and Baptist) was *s mirom
prinimaem!* (We receive you with peace!).[62]

Serdechno blagodaryu! (I thank you from the bottom of my
heart!). This was much more common than the usual *spasibo*
(thank you).

Zhelayu obil'nykh blagosloveny! (I wish you great blessings!) – This was one of the traditional wishes at the end of
Baptist conversations.

Zasvidetel'stvovat', evangelizirovat', pokayat' (to testify, to
evangelize, to impel to repentance) – These words were used
about witness to unbelievers.

Priblizhenny, obrashchenny, kreshchaemy (novice, convert,
baptismal candidate) – These were stages in bringing people
to the status of "church member".

Brat'ya i sestry (brothers and sisters) – This was the traditional
way to address members of a community (because of endless
repetitions, often reduced to *brat'-sestry*).

---

61. N.P. Khrapov even writes, "To say a salutation equivalent to the worldly *zdravstvuyte* is
a sin". See Khrapov, *Dom Bozhy*, <http://www.blagovestnik.org/books/00280.htm#60>
62. Soviet Baptists adopted this form of Christian salutation, word for word, from Russian
Orthodox etiquette. See, for instance: *Povedenie v Khrame*, p. 174.

Sluzhitely'a, presviter'a, diakon'a, regent'a, etc. (ministers, presbyters, deacons, choir directors, etc.) The pronunciation was formally wrong because of the stress on the last syllable.

Posluzhit' slovom/peniem/"stikhom", etc. (to serve by the word/singing/"rhyme", etc.) This was about church preaching, Christian hymns, poetry, etc.

Sovershit' molitvu (to accomplish a prayer) – This was preferable to using "to pray".

Uchastvovat' v khleboprelomlenii (to participate in the breaking of bread) – This was the standard phrase.

Gospod' polozhil na serdtse (God put into one's heart) – This was an expression about divine leading.

Nashi levity (our Levites) – This was the solemn name for church choir singers.

Nashi sibirskie palestiny (our Siberian Palestine)[63] – Believers said this about their native land.

Pereyti v vechnost'/"pereyti chrez Iordan" (to go into eternity/"to cross the Jordan") – to die.

Chelovek iz naroda Bozh'ego (a man of the people of God) – a Jew.

Baptist Baptistovich (a Baptist and the son of a Baptist) – a believer (a Baptist) for generations.[64]

---

63. Any place name can be inserted here.
64. There were also widespread Baptist abbreviations: DVR (*deti veruyushchikh roditeley* – children from a Christian family), DSP (*deti starshikh presviterov* – children of Senior Presbyters), BMV (*bolee-menee veruyushchie* – more or less believers), all used as a rule in a

Navukhodonosor (Nebuchadnezzar) – This was used to describe an informer, a person "who informs in somebody's ear". This had to do with pronunciation, not with the biblical story.[65]

Khaldei (the Chaldeans) – atheists.

Deti faraona (children of pharaoh) – the bureaucracy (the authorities).

Zakonniki (legalists) – lawyers.

Bludnitsa Vavilonskaya (the whore of Babylon) – state atheism (in the USSR).

Khodyashchie v dlinnykh odezhdakh (those who are walking in long clothing) – about Russian Orthodox priests (usually with a negative meaning, cf.: Mark 12:38).

Deti Bozhii/deti Avraama (children of God/Abraham's children) – the believers. "Do Abraham's children live here?" was a question asked by Soviet Baptists.

Te, kto na Patmose (those who are on Patmos) – exiles (or prisoners) for their faith.

Those familiar with this "pious" dialect quickly distinguished the "ins" from the "outs".[66] A Baptist presbyter remarked that no atheist could properly pronounce the word "*Paralipomenon*" – the name of the books of

somewhat ironic manner.

65. The similarity is between the Russian syllabic pronunciation of Nebuchadnezzar and the phrase "who informs in somebody's ear".

66. For instance, testimonies of Baptist presbyter from Alma-Ata, A.T. Evstratenko (INT, San Diego, California, USA, 2006) and presbyter I.P. Fast (Shchuchinsk, Kazakhstan, 1999).

Chronicles in the Russian Synodal Bible.[67] Soviet Baptists might condemn Russian Orthodoxy for using Church Slavonic (liturgical) language that was hard to understand,[68] but they had their own language which was not understood by common people around them.[69]

In part this alternative world was sustained because most Russian Baptists had been brought up in the community. Indeed there was a saying that was widely-known: "Children imbibe the faith with their mother's milk." This idea was sometimes understood literally – with some Russian Baptists of an older generation who promulgated it referring particularly to the story of the young Moses (Exod 2:7-12). In his case, it was said, a short time breast-feeding from his mother was enough to mean that he was identified forever not as an Egyptian, but as a Hebrew. In the New Testament, a similar thought was taken from 2 Timothy 1:5, where Paul speaks about the sincere faith of Timothy, which "dwelt first" in his grandmother and mother.[70] Russian Baptists developed their poetry and pious "biblical-type" language in a largely closed and self-perpetuating community.

The saying about the "mother's milk" was one of several sayings that Russian Baptists knew and used: this was also part of their language. These sayings followed the steps of Christian experience. Thus "Christ was baptized at thirty, so we cannot be baptized before this age either" (Luke 3:23 was quoted).[71] It seems that such an understanding played into the

---

67. Testimony of presbyter V.N. Khot'ko (Petropavlovsk, Kazakhstan, 1999). Yu.K. Kryuchkov speaks of the following way of recognizing "false brothers" in Soviet times: the suspicious characters who appeared at church were simply asked to pray aloud... See Yu. Kryuchkov, *140-letnyaya Istoriya Tserkvi ECB na Rusi v Svete Bibleyskikh Istin* [140 Years of the History of the Church of the ECB in Russia in the Light of Biblical Truths] (Sacramento, CA: n.p., 2010), p. 358.

68. For instance, testimony of Baptist presbyter from Maikop, N.G. Man'ko (INT, Everett, Washington, USA, 2006); Rogozin, *Otkuda vse eto poyavilos'*, pp. 145-6.

69. A Soviet schoolmistress visited a church service in Petropavlovsk Baptist church in the late 1980s. When she was asked whether she had liked the sermon (preached by a local Baptist preacher known for being eloquent), she answered, "Was it really possible to understand anything? Was he not speaking *Old Church Slavonic*?" Baptist minister from Petropavlovsk, V.Ya Baranov, reminded me about this incident (INT, Minneapolis, Minnesota, USA, 2006).

70. Testimony of B.M. Zdorovets (INT, Spokane, Washington, USA, 2006).

71. For instance, testimonies of Baptists from Donetsk Region: presbyter M.M. Kolivayko and V.Ya. Sedykh (INT, Sacramento, California, USA, 2006).

authorities' hands when they sought to limit baptisms.[72] One minister, A.T. Kharchenko, also noted that some Baptists in Kirgizia in the 1960s said, "If God wants that you be baptized, the Religious Affairs officer will allow it."[73] At the time of repentance it was expected that a person would weep: "There is no true repentance without tears", because "Christ wept too".[74] A related saying was, "Believers cannot laugh, because God will punish them for jesting". The text used was Ephesians 5:4, which in fact referred to "crude joking". Russian Baptists extended this: B.M. Zdorovets, for example, by his own account, did not laugh for five years after his conversion.[75]

Other sayings included "Believers should not eat sweets", based on a mis-reading of 1 Timothy 5:6 ("she that lives in pleasure is dead while she lives"),[76] and "If a believer is praised on the earth, he will lose his reward in heaven".[77] References were sometimes made to Matthew 6:1-2,5,16, with these sayings taken absolutely literally. Finally, "You love God too much, so probably you will die soon", was a common saying. At one level

---

72. See Sawatsky, *Soviet Evangelicals Since World War II*, pp. 134-5; *VestI*, no. 3 (2001), pp. 2-3.

73. Testimony of A.T. Kharchenko (INT, Sacramento, California, USA, 2006). During the Communist persecutions, many Baptists practiced baptisms at night, motivated by safety reasons. However, the "mysterious" nighttime atmosphere apparently led some of them to the opinion that "Christ himself was baptized in the Jordan at night". – Report (with critical appraisal) by a minister of the ECB from Kiev, L.E. Kovalenko (INT, Sacramento, California, USA, 2006). Probably, this was a paraphrase of an ancient Orthodox legend. See, for instance, I. Porfiriev, *Istoriya Russkoy Slovesnosty* [History of Russian Literature] (Kazan: Tipo-Litografiya Imperatorskogo Universiteta, 1909), vol. I, p. 411. See also Archimandrite Rafail (Karelin), *More Zhiteyskoe: Otvety Na Voprosy Chitateley* [The Sea of Life: Answers to Questions from Readers] (M.: Moskovskoe Podvor'e Sv.-Troitskoy Sergievoy Lavry, 2008), p. 42.

74. For instance, testimonies of: Baptist church member from Pechora, M.N. Kukushkina (Everett, Washington, USA, 2006), presbyter V.N. Khot'ko (Petropavlovsk, Kazakhstan, 2000).

75. Testimony of B.M. Zdorovets (INT, Spokane, Washington, USA, 2006).

76. The Russian word *slastolyubivy* [voluptuous] was mixed up with the Russian expression *lyubit' slasti* [to love sweets]. Hence the confusion. For instance, testimony of Baptist evangelist from Dushanbe, P.A. Semeryuk (INT, Sacramento, California, USA, 2006). See also Val'kevich, *Zapiska o Propagande Protestantskikh Sekt*, Supplement 2, p. 14. Similar prohibitions were typical for Russian Orthodoxy. For example: "Orthodox people should not wash themselves often". See a large selection on the website of Kiev Orthodox Brethren of Sts. Princes-Martyrs Boris and Gleb: *Okolotserkovnye Sueveriya* [Around Church Superstitions], <http://kyivbratstvo.narod.ru/news/archive/2005_07_01_index.html> accessed 15 November 2010.

77. For instance, testimony of P.A. Semeryuk (INT, Sacramento, California, USA, 2006).

this warned young people against an excessive zeal in their faith under conditions of State militant atheism. However, Russian Baptists were also taking an imaginative leap back to New Testament reports and especially to traditions about the death of Christ's Apostles.[78] They saw themselves as inhabiting the same world, connecting with the past and yet translating this into their own Russian way of thinking – which often meant a Russian Orthodox way. Poetry, imagination and language all contributed to this process.

Common customs and rules

For Russian Baptists, the Bible offered a way into spiritual experience. But this was not only an inner world: certain kinds of behavior flowed out of the beliefs held. In a number of ways the behavior was affected by the Russian Orthodox environment. The Eastern ascetic monastic tradition manifested itself among Baptists by strict church rules.[79] There was also, however, the influence of the Soviet state, imposing its rules.[80] Baptist churches could not be an "island of freedom" in a nation that restricted citizens' rights and freedoms. It is not surprising, therefore, that the freedom for individual believers expressed in the congregational form of church government, which was avowedly espoused by Russian Baptists,[81] existed in theory rather than in practice. The actual way of organizing Baptist life was through centralized episcopalian rule (through senior presbyters), reflecting "Soviet-Orthodox"

---

78. For instance, testimony of Baptist church member from Belorus, N.N. Tsvirin'ko (INT, Fresno, California, USA, 2006). The appendix to the authoritative Baptist edition of the Russian Synodal Bible published by Pastor B. Gotze (Warsaw, Poland, 1939) had information about the martyrdom of the Apostles according to Tradition.

79. Many Soviet communities of ECB had their own, more or less detailed internal regulations ("monastic charters") entitled, for instance: *What a Member of the Church of Evangelical Christians-Baptists Shall and Shall Not Do.*

80. At times Baptists fell in with the state, as in this declaration that "we will always strive to train all believers… in the spirit of ardent patriotism, true love for work and genuine respect for the leadership of our country… In the name of the AUCECB (signatures)". – *BV*, no. 6 (1967), p. 3.

81. See, for instance, *Osnovnye Printsipy Very Evangel'skikh Khristian – Baptistov*, pp. 69, 74, 116-21.

thinking.[82] This mode of government was clearly visible not only in the AUCECB, which operated under state control, but also in the "independent" CCECB. Indeed the latter could be more authoritarian than the former.[83] For many ordinary church members in the "independent" group, the words "Publication of CCECB" on the cover page of books and periodicals often meant that they saw what they were reading as almost "ultimate truth". The phrase could be compared only with the official Russian Orthodox publications honored with a Patriarch's benediction or other words of approval: with the blessing of the Holy Synod.[84]

A noteworthy feature of the customs and rules within Russian Baptist communities was the attention given to fasting and prayer. During shorter fasts, for example of up to three days, there was complete abstention from food and water.[85] During longer fasts water was drunk.[86] In 1968 *Bratsky Listok*, published by the CCECB, commented:

> The weekly fasts on Fridays and the recently finished three-day fast are not pharisaic customs... The Pharisees kept the fast twice a week. The Lord wants us to surpass the Pharisees in the ministry of fasts and prayers, not by the number of days

82. See Kuksenko, *Nashi Besedy*, pp. 48, 109; Savinsky, *Istoriya (1917-1967)*, p. 192. Also testimonies of: Baptist presbyter from Moscow, V.P. Zinchenko (INT, Seattle, Washington, USA, 2006), presbyter from Rostov, M.P. Zakharov (INT, Sacramento, California, USA, 2006).

83. See, for instance: M. Shaptala, *Kak Eto Bylo* [The Way it Was] (Izdanie Bratstva Nezavisimykh Tserkvey ECB, 1999), pp. 49-50,80-85; Savinsky, *Istoriya (1917-1967)*, pp. 220-1; Kuksenko, *Nashi Besedy*, pp. 32,42-3.

84. Testimony of Baptist presbyter from Rostov, M.P. Zakharov (INT, Sacramento, California, USA, 2006).

85. For instance, testimonies of: P.F. Kunda, N.S. Kramarenko, V.V. Zinchenko, Ya.A. Grinchenko (INT, Sacramento, California, USA, 2006), B.M. Zdorovets (INT, Spokane, Washington, USA, 2006), Sedletsky, "Vospominaniya", pp. 89-90, 169-171. See also [Anon], *"Ne Ostavlyu Tebya, Ne Pokinu Tebya"* ["I will Never Desert You"], *BV*, no. 2 (1976), p. 61; *"Proekt Veroucheniya ECB"* [Project of the Creed of the ECB], *BV*, no. 4 (1980), p. 45; P. Shatrov, *"Deyaniya Apostolov"* [The Acts of the Apostles], *BV*, no. 6 (1985), p. 18.

86. There is some information about fasts among CCECB members of up to 10-25 days and even more. See, for instance: M. Khorev, *"Paskhal'ny Den'"* [Easter Day], *VestI*, no. 3 (1985), p. 23; Kuksenko, *Nashi Besedy*, pp. 58-9; testimonies of: P.M. Abankin, P.D. Karavan (INT, Sacramento, California, USA, 2006), B.M. Zdorovets (INT, Spokane, Washington, USA, 2006).

we fast but by our deeper humility and reverence before God. Therefore our churches everywhere agreed that the three-day fast is God's will.[87]

This anonymous author, referring in the context of the remarks to Matthew 5:20, was evidently concerned about someone's accusations that the fasting of radical Baptists was a legalistic practice, and so he rejected the idea that Baptists might "surpass the Pharisees" by the number of days they fasted. However, he actually came to the conclusion that it would be better if Baptists kept a three-day fast, compared to the Pharisees' fasts on two days a week. The strict patterns of fasting among Soviet Baptists were not drawn so much from Scripture as from Orthodox customs. Compulsory weekly fasting in Orthodox monastic life and in the more radical Soviet Baptist communities had much in common.[88] Prayer was also central, with grace said before and after meals (standing).[89] Other prayers were usually made kneeling. Baptist authors wrote about such practices as being "according to the Scripture", that is "on bended knees. The prophets, the righteous men of God, the Apostles and Christ himself prayed like that."[90] Similar words are found in an Orthodox source: "The Old Testament believers used to pray... also on bended knees... This old custom was sanctified by the examples of Jesus Christ and the apostles".[91] The shared attitudes to and interpretations of these Orthodox and Russian Baptist pious practices are evident.[92]

Another custom, alongside fasting and prayer, was giving alms "for Christ's sake". Stories about alms-giving were often retold in Soviet Baptist

---

87. *BL*, no. 7 (1968), p. 1.

88. A presbyter of the Omsk community of the CCECB, N.R. Savchenko, when imprisoned for his faith in the 1970s, had his food taken away one Friday by criminals in the prison, but in response he only thanked them since they reminded him about the day of fasting. – Testimony of presbyter S.Yu. Sipko, Omsk, Russia, 2008.

89. See, for instance, Zhuravlev, *Velika Vernost' Tvoya, Gospodi*, vol. I, pp. 242-3.

90. See, for instance, Khrapov, *Dom Bozhy*, <http://www.blagovestnik.org/books/00280. htm#77>

91. Diachenko, *Simvolicheskie Deystviya. Svyashchennosluzhiteli* [Symbolic Acts. Priests] (Kiev: Prolog, 2005), pp. 57-9.

92. See also: *Khristianstvo: Entsiklopedichesky Slovar'*, vol. I, p. 785; G. Diachenko, *Simvolicheskie Deystviya*, pp. 57-62.

meetings.[93] An example was the testimony of A. Kaprova, first published in the periodical the *Baptist* in 1909. One day this woman had a dream that she died holding in her hand a five-kopeck coin, which she had previously refused to give to a hungry man who was begging. In spite of the fact that the gates of heaven were opened to her, she suddenly recognized that the coin would be "an eternal reproach to her, burning her hand". The story finished with the passionate plea, "Distribute! Give! Do it while you have time... in order that you will have no money as you enter eternity!" The dream echoes older Orthodox stories.[94] Before his death in 1922, the wealthy and generous Baptist minister, D.I. Mazaev, who lost his large fortune during the Revolution and civil war, was said to have "greatly regretted that he had not distributed all his property for God's work".[95] Giving was seen as a mystical caring for "Christ himself".[96] Thus in *Bratsky Listok* in 1967 there was this explanation:

> The Lord, in the person of many brothers and sisters, languishes in prison today... He reaches out His hand for your help in the person of little children whose fathers... are imprisoned. What do you think of this...? Will the Lord say about you one day, 'I was hungry, and you gave me no meat: I was thirsty, and you gave me no drink: I was a stranger, and you did not take me not in: naked, and you did not clothe me: sick, and in prison, and you did not visit' (Matt 25:42-43).[97]

Many Soviet Baptists regularly supported people in need, the sick, and prisoners for their faith and their families. Often Baptists assisted people in

---

93. For instance, a report of a minister of the ECB from Kiev, L.E. Kovalenko (INT, Sacramento, California, USA, 2006).

94. A. Kaprova, *"Son"* [A Dream], *Bapt.*, no. 5 (1909), pp. 4-5. There is an Orthodox legend about a monk who, despite his vow of poverty, had kept some money. He was buried with his savings, and "this incident inspired such fear... that since then monks considered it a grievous fault to have even one gold coin". – Bishop Ignaty (Bryanchaninov), *Otechnik*, p. 404.

95. A. Nagirnyak, *"Dey Ivanovich Mazaev"*, *BV*, no. 1 (2008), p. 39.

96. See Archpriest V. Guriev, *Prolog v Poucheniyakh* [The Church Calendar with Homilies] (M.: Tipo-Litografiya I. Efimova, 1912), pp. 66, 938.

97. *BL*, nos. 11-12 (1967), p. 2.

need who they did not know, to fulfil the commandments of Jesus Christ.[98] The Russian Baptist movement gained ground mainly among the working classes or lower social strata,[99] and in the Soviet period Baptists were far removed from "high society", so that when they spoke of those being blessed who distributed "all their property", this was usually not something they could do in a way that was visible to outside observers. Nevertheless, the parallel with Orthodox monastic ideals is striking. The words of Jesus were used, "If you would be perfect, go and sell what you have, and give to the poor…" (Matt 19:21). Some Russian Baptists saw themselves as following this way, a way which Orthodox writers pointed out had been followed by "Sts. Anthony, Macarius the Egyptian, Pachomius the Great, and their followers".[100]

Certain accepted conventions governed the appearance of Baptist church members, especially in relation to what was worn. In the case of women, especially when attending church, the tendency was towards what might be associated with convents: long dark skirts, high-necked formal blouses and head-scarves. Women did not wear make-up or jewellery.[101] Even wedding rings were considered unacceptable.[102] The men wore almost "bureaucratic", dark "Soviet style" suits. Following the Orthodox tradition,[103] Soviet Baptists took 1 Corinthians 11:4-16 to teach that there should be head covering for women. There was a difference between a married woman and a girl, which was indicated by the headscarf of the married

---

98. See, for instance: *Uchilishche Blagochestiya, ili Primery Christianskikh Dobrodeteley, Vybrannye iz Zhity Svyatykh* [The School of Piety, or the Examples of Christian Virtues Selected from the Saints' Lives] (SPb.: Sinodal'naya Tipografiya, 1903), pp. 237-9. See I. Prokhanov, *In the Cauldron of Russia*, pp. 30-1; *Sibirskie Nivy*, no. 5 (2001), p. 17; also testimonies of Baptist church members from Essentuki, S.N. Savinsky and L.V. Savinskaya (INT, Salt Lake City, Utah, USA, 2006).

99. See, for instance, W. Sawatsky, "Protestantism in the USSR", in S.P. Ramet, ed., *Protestantism and Politics in Eastern Europe and Russia: The Communist and Postcommunist Eras* (Durham: Duke University Press, 1992), pp. 254-5.

100. *Monasheskaya Zhizn'*, p. 7.

101. Cf. the rules for Russian Orthodox women at church: *Povedenie v Khrame*, pp. 63-5.

102. For instance, testimonies of former senior presbyter of Krasnodar Territory, Ya.A. Grinchenko (INT, Sacramento, California, USA, 2006), presbyter V.N. Khot'ko (Petropavlovsk, Kazakhstan, 2000), and others.

103. See, for instance, A. Lopukhin, ed., *Tolkovaya Bibliya*, vol. XI, pp. 76-81; *Povedenie v Khrame*, pp. 61-3.

one (1 Cor 11:10). For the unmarried, the hair could be regarded as the head covering. Men always took off their hats for worship.[104] During baptisms in Russian Baptist communities, even young unmarried girls (who were baptized) usually wore head-scarves.[105] A presbyter from Moscow, V.P. Zinchenko recollected:

> Once, a KGB officer said that it was easy to recognize our sisters in the street. All they needed to do was to look for a modestly dressed woman, without any make-up, wearing a headscarf, on a Sunday morning, and she immediately led them to a Christian meeting.[106]

Regarding the wearing of ties by men, this custom became widespread among Soviet Baptists only in the 1980s. Before this, Baptists usually condemned ties. Some spoke contemptuously of ties as "strangleholds" or "arrow signs pointing to hell". One Baptist woman recalled: "I remember our sisters reproached the brothers one day…. when the latter started to come to church meetings wearing ties. We consulted a dictionary and read the definition that a tie serves as a man's neck adorning… So it seemed the sisters were forbidden decorations, but the brothers were allowed. Then we all, sisters together, condemned the brothers for this novelty – wearing ties *as Communists did*."[107] Shirtsleeves had to be long, particularly for preachers, even in hot summers.[108] In all cases the devout Orthodox had similar traditions.

---

104. For these customs see testimonies of: Baptist church members from Donetsk Region, V.Ya. Sedykh, E.I. Sedykh and A.I. Musiets (INT, Sacramento, California, USA, 2006), minister of the ECB from Bryansk, V.A. Serpikov (INT, Seattle, Washington, USA, 2006), Baptist presbyter V.N. Khot'ko (Petropavlovsk, Kazakhstan, 2000), and many others.

105. Cf. Khrapov, *Dom Bozhy*, <http://www.blagovestnik.org/books/00280.htm#58>

106. Interview with V.P. Zinchenko (INT, Seattle, Washington, USA, 2006).

107. Testimony of Baptist church member from Donetsk Region, E.I. Sedykh (INT, Sacramento, California, USA, 2006). Italics mine.

108. "One day a preacher came to our meeting dressed in a short-sleeved shirt… Our ministers did not give him the floor… They asked him smiling, 'What happened, brother, to your sleeves? Why is so much shirt lacking?' " – Testimony of minister of ECB from Bryansk, V.A. Serpikov (INT, Seattle, Washington, USA, 2006). These words can be compared with analogous strict Russian Orthodox rules (see, for instance: *Povedenie v*

Seriousness also characterized Russian Baptist communities. The say-ing, "Believers do not tell jokes or anecdotes, but only parables", became a catchphrase in conservative Baptist circles.[109] As an elder expressed it, "Believers may smile, but should never do this broadly so that their teeth will not be shown".[110] However, there was humor. Ideally, every Baptist joke had to contain some sort of Christian edification or warning. For example, in the 1970s the popular, ironical phrase, "Bee-keepers shall not inherit the kingdom of God", was motivated to some extent by the concern of Baptist churches about some members whose activities (bee-keeping being one example) meant they did not participate adequately in church life.[111] In response to the common expression "Russian-Ukrainian Baptist broth-erhood", these words achieved fame among many Byelorussian Baptists: "Brothers, what about the Byelorussians? Well, you used a hyphen between the words 'Russian' and 'Ukrainian', and probably that is what we are". This was seen as teaching Christian humility.[112] Even persecution could elicit a kind of humor. For example, when K.S. Sedletsky (future senior presbyter of Moldavia) lost his work as a herdsman in a village because of his religious convictions, he dared to say to his chief, a Communist: "You are probably afraid that I will convert your cows to Baptist beliefs."[113] Another presbyter, N.G. Man'ko recalled that the old prayer house in Maikop was situated in the neighborhood of the local prison until the 1970s, and the believers repeatedly said the authorities needed only to build a small covered way from the meeting place to the prison to "solve the Baptist problem in the city".[114] These ironic responses contain echoes of (hagiographical) stories about ancient martyrs, immensely popular in Russia: when St. Kodratos of

Khrame, p. 61), as well as with reports about Old Believers who did not usually allow people dressed in short-sleeved shirts to come to their churches at all. See, for instance, Ryabinin, *Russkoe Yurodstvo*, pp. 51-2.

109. For instance, testimony of Baptist church members from Donetsk Region, V.Ya. Sedykh, E.I. Sedykh and A.I. Musiets (INT, Sacramento, California, USA, 2006).

110. For instance, testimony of Baptist church member V.N. Cherepanov (Omsk, Russia, 2010).

111. See, for instance, Kuksenko, *Nashi Besedy*, p. 42.

112. Testimony of presbyter L.I. Mikhovich (Minsk, Belarus, 2008).

113. Sedletsky, "Vospominaniya", p. 69.

114. Testimony of Baptist presbyter from Maikop, N.G. Man'ko (INT, Everett, Washington, USA, 2006).

Nicomedia was put on a red-hot iron grate, he said to the executioners he was tired after a long journey and would "rest in the soft bed";[115] and St. Vitus, forced to go into a boiling cauldron, according to legend said "there is a lack of soap in this bath".[116] Among Russian Orthodox books with examples of "holy humor" there are *Little Things from the Lives of Bishops* and *The Bishops' Tours* by N.S. Leskov, *Little Things from the Lives of Arch-, Proto-, and Just Hiereus' Life* by Father M. Ardov, and *Spiritual Mines* by Father I. Okhlobystin.[117]

In the case of specific Russian Baptist customs, there were conservative groups of evangelicals elsewhere, for example the Strict Baptists in England, or the Brethren movement,[118] who had similar attitudes. Thus parallels can be found to the way Russian Baptists worked in various ways for their community,[119] abstained from foul language,[120] did not take anyone else's property (in a country where this was common),[121] held to marital

---

115. See *Stradanie Sv. Muchenika Kodrata Nikomidiyskogo* [The Sufferings of St. Kodratos of Nicomedia, the Martyr], *ZhSDR*, vol. VII, p. 222.

116. See *Stradanie Sv. Muchenika Vita* [The Sufferings of St. Vitus, the Martyr], *ZhSDR*, vol. X, p. 358.

117. N. Leskov, *Sobranie Sochineniy*, 12 vols., vol. VI, pp. 191-335; M. Ardov, *Melochi Arkhi... Proto... i Prosto Iereyskoy Zhizni* [Little Things from the Lives of Arch-, Proto-, and Just Hiereus' Life] (M.: Izd-vo im. Sabashnikovykh, 1995); I. Okhlobystin, *Tam, Gde Vostok: Dukhovnye Kopi* [There, where the East is: Spiritual Mines] (M.: Lepta, 2009). On the inadmissibility of jokes and laughing in Russian Orthodox churches, see for instance, *Povedenie v Khrame*, pp. 62, 71.

118. See, for instance: I.M. Randall, *Evangelical Experiences* (Carlisle: Paternoster Press, 1999), pp. 142-67.

119. "The people of the town were talking of us, 'This is the only building work where everybody not only does not steal but helps to the full extent of his or her resources!' " – Testimony of Baptist church member, N.F. Mazhnaya about the building of the prayer house in Chernovtsy (INT, Fresno, California, USA, 2006).

120. In some conflict situations they even aspired to complete silence, in imitation of Christ at his trial. Testimony of church member from Kazakhstan, N.D. Chumakina (INT, Seattle, Washington, USA, 2006). See also Pakina, "Raskol Evangel'skikh Khristian-Baptistov", p. 33; N. Shalatovsky, *Molchanie* [Silence], <http://www. blagovestnik.org/books/00430/db/v7848793.html> accessed 4 November 2009.

121. "There were many cases of stealing at Soviet school... And when the teachers started a new investigation, they first of all let Baptist children go, because they were free of suspicion". – Testimony of church member from Zhitomir, T.N. Karavan (INT, Sacramento, California, USA, 2006).

fidelity,[122] worked hard,[123] turned down even highly paid jobs if bosses demanded Sunday work,[124] and refused to drink alcohol or smoke tobacco.[125] Some Baptist elders in Russia also condemned the following: any "worldly" songs (only hymns should be sung), dancing, going to the theatre or the cinema,[126] and having a television set or watching TV, which was sometimes called "the satanic eye" or "a refrigerator for the soul".[127] Much of this was found in strict Orthodox circles: a famous Russian Orthodox author compared television with a sewerage system and argued that Christians with TVs at home could not pray in a way that was pleasing to God.[128] Other prohibitions in some communities included playing sports or reading "secular" books.[129] If some books connected with work had to be kept at home, they should not be put on the same shelf as the "divine books". Russian Orthodox literature was often considered as "divine" writing and acceptable, at least "for personal use".[130] On the use of money, usually

122. *The Church Regulations*. Single people were taught not to have sexual relationships before marriage. Also, Baptist women under no circumstances could agree to have an abortion.

123. For instance, the profession of carpenter (and joiner) was very popular among Soviet Baptists because they wanted to be "like Christ". – Testimonies of: presbyter of Baptist church from Pavlodar, P.A. Chumakin (INT, Seattle, Washington, USA, 2006), church member from Krasnodar, S.G. Odaryuk (INT, Everett, Washington, USA, 2006).

124. For instance, testimony of deacon of Baptist church from Syzran, Ya.S. Shevchuk (INT, Los Angeles, California, USA, 2006).

125. *The Church Regulations*.

126. In the late 1950s, believers in some Soviet Baptist churches were offered tickets to theatres and cinemas immediately after services. Differences over issues like this contributed to the split in the AUCECB – Testimony of former senior presbyter from Kuybyshev, V.F. Serpevsky, and Z.I. Serpevskaya (INT, Vancouver, Washington, USA, 2006).

127. The strong censure of television was combined with a qualified welcome of radio. The reason was that short-wave receivers enabled Christians to listen to Christian broadcasts from abroad. However, the owners of such receivers "were tempted" to listen not only to Christian broadcasts. – For instance, testimonies of Baptist presbyters from Odessa, Ya.D. Shevchuk, and V.S. Shevchuk (INT, Portland, Oregon, USA, 2006), minister from Bryansk, V.A. Serpikov (INT, Seattle, Washington, USA, 2006). See also Nikolskaya, *Russky Protestantizm i Gosudarstvennaya Vlast' v 1905-1991 Godakh*, p. 165.

128. See Archimandrite Rafail (Karelin), *Dykhanie Zhizni: O Molitve* [The Breath of Life: On Prayer] (Saratov: Izd-vo Saratovskoy Eparkhii, 2007), p. 171.

129. Baptist elders especially condemned anti-religious books and love-stories.

130. For instance, testimony of Baptist minister, Ya.A. Meleshkevich (Bishkul, Kazakhstan, 2003).

Russian Baptists did not insure their property (for what is more reliable than God's protection?), and they did not gamble or take part in lotteries ("games of Satan").[131] It is noteworthy that almost all of these specific rules of piety existed in Russian Orthodox parishes.[132] This Orthodox context is of great significance in understanding the regulations accepted by Baptist church members in relation to their behavior.[133]

Given the condemnation of games of chance, it is perhaps surprising that a section of the Russian Baptist community, in common with some Russian Orthodox trends, considered the drawing of lots a way of discovering God's will. Baptists made a distinction between the Old Testament practice, as an "external" way of finding God's will, and the "internal" way of understanding how to please God, by the Holy Spirit.[134] As always, they sought biblical precedent for their customs, in this case from Acts 1:23-26. For example, when the All-Russian General Council of Evangelical Christians and Baptists was established in 1920, P.V. Pavlov, who became chairman (I.S. Prokhanov became his assistant), was elected by drawing lots.[135] Elections of presbyters took place by lot in several Baptist communities in Central Asia in the 1960s.[136] Leaders of the AUCECB noted the practice elsewhere in the Soviet Union.[137] *Bratsky Vestnik* sometimes

---

131. For instance, testimony of Baptist presbyter, V.N. Khot'ko (Petropavlovsk, Kazakhstan, 2000).

132. See, for instance, Archpriest V. Mordasov, *1380 Polezneyshikh Sovetov Batyushki Svoim Prikhozhanam* [1380 Most Helpful Tips from the Father for his Parishioners] (Edinetsko-Brichanskaya Eparkhiya, 2004); *Povedenie v Khrame*, pp. 68-76, 172-5.

133. Much of this is illustrated, for instance, in *The Church Regulations* of Petropavlovsk community of the ECB (Kazakhstan).

134. See, for instance, works of Baptist authors: A. Mitskevich, *"Khozhdenie pred Bogom"* [Walking with God], *BV*, no. 1 (1956), pp. 43-5; P. Shatrov, *"Deyaniya Apostolov"* [The Acts of the Apostles], *BV*, no. 3 (1979), p. 33; Kolesnikov, *Khristianin, znaesh' li ty*, vol. II, pp. 132, 185. See also Russian Orthodox sources: *Tolkovaya Bibliya*, ed. by A. Lopukhin, vol. X, p. 12; *Nastol'naya Kniga Svyashchennosluzhitelya*, vol. IV, pp. 334-5.

135. See *Istoriya Evangel'skikh Khristian-Baptistov v SSSR*, p. 193.

136. For instance, G.D. Semeryuk wrote about this in his memoirs (unpublished manuscript), pp. 72-3. – Personal files of G.D. Semeryuk (Sacramento, California, USA, 2006).

137. See P. Shatrov, *"Deyaniya Apostolov"* [The Acts of the Apostles], *BV*, no. 3 (1979), p. 33; K. Sedletsky, *"Izbranie i Rukopolozhenie Sluzhiteley"* [Election and Ordination of Ministers], *BV*, no. 6 (1988), p. 51; S. Fadyukhin, *"Vospominaniya o Perezhitom, chast' II"* [Memoirs about My Life, part II], *Al'manakh po Istorii Russkogo Baptizma*, vol. III (2004), p. 253.

mentioned the lot as a way of discerning God's will, and authors did not necessarily warn against it. For example, in 1977 an anonymous Baptist author, reflecting on the mysterious "Urim and Thummim", remarked, "Making a decision by lot in conjunction with zealous prayer was used by the Apostles of Christ."[138] In addition, readers of *Bratsky Vestnik* in 1988 were told about the election of the Apostle Matthias (Acts 1:23-26), and also the old church legend that the Apostles, after leaving Jerusalem, decided by lot to which country each of them should go to preach the Gospel.[139] It seems that Russian Baptists, following Orthodox authors, accepted this legend uncritically. They did not follow through the implications of their own theology, which suggested that the lot was something which God's people used only before the coming of the Holy Spirit on the Apostles at Pentecost.[140]

The lot was also used in a number of Baptist families. This procedure sometimes took place during discussions about moving to a new area, when difficult choices had to be made. Usually, the use of the lot was not mentioned outside the family. The accounts by family members speak of extended fasting and general family prayer, after which the youngest child ("as the most sinless") was entrusted with drawing the lot. The choice was between several small pieces of paper with the names of different towns and villages written on them.[141] The procedure mirrors aspects of an ancient Russian Orthodox ceremony sometimes used when electing a new bishop or other leader. One custom was that the names of the three most favored candidates were written on separate sheets of paper and given to the Metropolitan, who after private prayer approved one of them, but another was that the pieces of paper were left on the Credence table by the

138. [Anon], *"Razmyshleniya nad Slovom Zhizni"* [Reflections on the Word of Life], *BV*, no. 5 (1977), p. 54.

139. Eusebius of Ceasarea, *Ecclesiastical History*, III, 1. See V. Popov, *"Vozniknovenie Khristianstva na Rusi"* [The Beginnings of Christianity in Russia], *BV*, no. 1 (1988), p. 46.

140. A.I. Mitskevich wrote, "During the election, the lot fell to Matthias, who was numbered with the eleven apostles. This method was often used in Israel... At a later date, after Pentecost, the apostles never resorted to this mode of election". – A. Mitskevich, *Mysli iz Knigi Deyany Apostolov* [Some Thoughts from the Book of the Acts of the Apostles], *BV*, 3 (1960), p. 38. This theology was not always translated into practice.

141. For instance, testimony of Baptist church member from Chernovtsy, A.F. Bernik (INT, Fresno, California, USA, 2006).

church altar and a small boy was sent to choose two sheets of paper to take
to the Metropolitan, and the name remaining on the Credence table was
considered to be God's choice.[142]

A whole number of Russian Orthodox Patriarchs, bishops and monastic
superiors were elected by lot, for instance: Patriarch Joseph,[143] St. Patriarch
Tikhon,[144] and St. Bishop Tikhon of Zadonsk.[145] Thus Russian Baptists
seem to have adapted the belief that prayer in combination with zealous
fasting facilitated the discovery of God's will through the lot, and that an
innocent child could be used in this process. As with many of the customs,
there was a biblical basis, but the behavior resembled Orthodox tradition.

The way of tears

The life of Soviet Baptists was marked by suffering. This was due to various hardships that they faced and especially the context of persecution.
However, there was an inner feeling of sadness and suffering associated
with their spirituality. Very often, in Baptist communities, as in Orthodox
parishes, the genuineness of someone's faith was bound up with shedding many tears.[146] Within the Orthodox tradition, here are some words
from a well-known Russian Orthodox Paterikon (The Book of the Lives of
Fathers), "'Is it a true spiritual rule that a monk should always weep during
his prayers?'... 'Verily so, my son ...Man, overthrown in the Fall, is in need
of lamentation. Where there is no sin, there is no need of weeping'."[147]

142. See *Nastol'naya Kniga Svyashchennosluzhitelya*, vol. IV, p. 335.

143. See, for instance, A. Osipovich, *Znachenie Pomestnogo Sobora v Zhizni Russkoy Pravoslavnoy Tserkvi* [The Significance of the Local Council in the Life of the Russian Orthodox Church], *ZhMP*, no. 2 (1971), p. 71.

144. See, for instance, Pospielovsky, *Russkaya Pravoslavnaya Tserkov v 20 veke*, p. 40.

145. See *Nastol'naya Kniga Svyashchennosluzhitelya*, vol. III, p. 705. For other examples see, for instance: Karamzin, *Istoriya Gosudarstva Rossiyskogo*, pp. 350, 408, 489; Cloistress Taisiya, *Russkoe Pravoslavnoe Zhenskoe Monashestvo*, p. 60.

146. "It is time to repent only when you want to weep", member of the ECB church in Pechora, M.N. Kukushkina testifies about the significance of tears in the Russian Baptist tradition (Everett, Washington, USA, 2006). See also Sedletsky, "Vospominaniya", pp. 91-3; Mitskevich, *Istoriya Evangel'skikh Khristian-Baptistov*, pp. 416-7.

147. Bishop Ignaty (Bryanchaninov), *Otechnik* [The Book of the Lives of Fathers], in

Many Baptist authors and older members of congregations recall tears at church.[148] One of the most popular hymns among Russian Baptists was Mikhail Lermontov's *Prayer* (1839), combining Christian faith and tears: "I believe and weep, and feel so light and free..."[149] In the Life of St. Theodosious, Hegumen of the Kiev Caves Monastery, the holy elder came to the Grand Prince of Kiev, when a joyful feast was taking place in his palace. Theodosious, with downcast eyes, sat silent. The guests finally noticed his sadness and he asked them, "Will we, brethren, be so joyful in the kingdom to come?" The powerful Prince suddenly wept, and the revel stopped.[150] This kind of situation was repeatedly enacted in the homes of Russian Baptists: during a celebration of a festal occasion, an elder appeared and with tears in his eyes asked the young people, "Will we, brothers and sisters, be so joyful when we present ourselves before the Lord?"[151]

Another aspect of the inner suffering that characterized Russian Baptist communities was church discipline. For example, at the beginning of 1980s the board of Dushanbe Baptist Church dealt with the case of P.A. Semeruyk. He had fallen away from his Christian testimony when he was young and had expressed profound repentance. He now wished to be considered as a preacher. The board decreed that he should begin to serve as a preacher (without the opportunity to be ordained) *ten years* on from the time of his repentance.[152] Such a ban bears a strong resemblance to the *ten-year penance* that was imposed in similar situations in the strictest Orthodox tradition (for instance, according to the Canon 9 of the Council

---

Bishop Ignaty (Bryanchaninov), *Polnoe Sobranie Tvoreny* [Complete Works], 8 vols. (M.: Palomnik, 2004), vol. VI, p. 270. Russian classical poet V.A. Zhukovsky wrote these characteristic lines, "Ah! Tears... tears are for our joy." – *Chudnoe Mgnovenie* [Wondrous Moment], Part 1, ed. by L. Ozerova (M.: Khudozhestvennaya Literatura, 1988), p. 65.

148. See, for instance: *SDP*, no. 62, p. 48; no. 78, pp. 57-8; no. 103, pp. 75-6; *PV*, no. 86, p. 56; no. 114, pp. 74-5; no. 210, pp. 136-7. Also Baptist testimonies of: B.M. Zdorovets from Kharkov (INT, Spokane, Washington, USA, 2006), L.Ya. Sokolovsky and E.Ya. Sokolovskaya from Donetsk Region (INT, San Diego, California, USA, 2006); Zhuravlev, *Velika Vernost' Tvoya, Gospodi*, vol. I, p. 75.

149. *SDP*, no. 283, p. 193; *PV*, no. 221, p. 143.

150. See *Zhitie Prep. Feodosiya Pecherskogo* [The Life of St. Theodosious of the Caves], in *ZhSDR*, vol. IX, p. 157.

151. A Baptist presbyter, V.N. Khot'ko, strikingly testified about this (Petropavlovsk, Kazakhstan, 1999).

152. Testimony of P.A. Semeryuk (Sacramento, California, USA, 2007).

of Ancyra).[153] Excommunication could be imposed for a range of misdeeds, including "learned" thinking. One common saying was "if you want to be a learned man, watch out that you are not excommunicated".[154] The theme of disloyalty in Baptist churches was often addressed.[155] The minister of Rostov Baptist Church, M.P. Zakharov, recollected:

> In Kharkov Region, in a community of the Council of Churches [CCECB], there was a curious incident. The presbyter was tired of all the inside information immediately reaching those who were 'outside' [i.e. the KGB]. It was clear that somebody was reporting to them, but the brethren failed to identify him/her. Then the presbyter made an announcement during a church members' meeting, 'Brothers and sisters, do you agree that the traitor... cannot participate in the Lord's Supper? Do you agree that he has to be excommunicated until he shows his genuine repentance?' The church expressed agreement... 'Well, let us announce right now', continued the presbyter, 'Let this person know that he is under the ban from today, *a heathen man and a publican* going to hell, if he does not stop it...' Everybody voted for the judgement 'by default'. Finally, the story goes that the traitor was anxious, and soon

153. See *Pravila Pravoslavnoy Tserkvi*, vol. II, p. 11. At the same time, one can see in such a strict church ban an echo of the Anabaptist (Mennonite) disciplinary tradition, which was appropriated by part of the German Baptist community in the USSR. See Snyder, *Anabaptist History and Theology*, pp. 374-5; *Istoriya Evangel'skikh Khristian-Baptistov v SSSR*, pp. 418-31.

154. I had occasion also to hear the following, stylized Orthodox expression among Russian Baptists: "But our Batiushka (Padre) was from the learned men, and sometimes, if he took pains, he delivered for us at church a sermon which passed all understanding..."

155. There are many noteworthy testimonies on the subject: of deacon of Baptist church from Syzran, Ya.S. Shevchuk (INT, Los Angeles, California, USA, 2006), presbyter from Alma-Ata, A.T. Evstratenko (INT, San Diego, California, USA, 2006), church member from Batumi, P.D. Karavan (INT, Sacramento, California, USA, 2006). On the same problems in the Russian Orthodox Church, see, for instance: Archpriest V. Tsypin, *Istoriya Russkoy Pravoslavnoy Tserkvi, 1917-1990*, pp. 155-7; Shkarovsky, *Russkaya Pravoslavnaya Tserkov pri Staline i Khrushcheve*, pp. 370-1.

he truly, deeply repented of having informed on his brethren
to the authorities…[156]

The language of "traitor" was often linked with references to Judas. There
was a widespread view, especially among the CCECB churches suffering
persecutions in the Khrushchev and Brezhnev eras, which was grimly expressed this way: "If one of the Twelve Apostles of Christ turned traitor,
even more so can this happen today – at least each 12th person in a church is
a Judas."[157] Even the strange worries about wearing ties that existed among
the most conservative Soviet Baptists were linked by some to Judas. Similar
ideas could be found in Orthodoxy. The "logic" was: a tie "chokes" a man's
throat like a stranglehold, so anyone wearing one could be like Judas, "who
hanged himself".[158]

Another area of anxiety for Russian Baptists, also at times connected
with Judas, had to do with missing meetings of the church or leaving meetings early. It was believed that "God will punish those who miss church
meetings". This view was known even among those outside the church
community. In the 1970s, a preacher of the CCECB was fined for participation in illegal meetings of Christian youth but in fact it was a mistake:
the person who led the meeting was his brother. There was an attempt to
explain to the Religious Affairs officer the mix-up (the surname being the
same), but the officer suddenly pronounced: "Why were you not there?
Everyone else was there, but you were not. *That* is why you will pay the
fine!" Russian Baptists, commenting on this incident, said that through
their sufferings under Soviet power God was reminding them of the verse
saying they should not miss church meetings ("not forsaking the assem-
bling of ourselves together, as the manner of some is" Heb 10:25) and
they should note that anyone breaking the commandment would not go

---

156. Testimony of M.P. Zakharov (INT, Sacramento, California, USA, 2006).
Italics mine.

157. For instance, testimonies of: Baptist church member from Homel, N.F. Mazhnaya
(INT, Fresno, California, USA, 2006) and presbyter from Rostov, M.P. Zakharov (INT,
Sacramento, California, USA, 2006).

158. For instance, testimony of presbyter V.N. Khot'ko (Petropavlovsk, Kazakhstan,
1998). I heard this also from some Russian Orthodox women, and they added a
prohibition regarding wearing a scarf tied around the neck.

unpunished.[159] The specific link made between Judas and church meetings was that "Believers should not leave a church meeting before it ends, because Judas did this".[160] In Orthodox society, the story of Judas was widely used as a "deterrent". This was done in many ways, for instance in the warning "any piece of food shall not be dipped in an [open] salt-cellar, because Judas did this",[161] and in the prohibition: "Believers should not kiss straight after the Eucharist, because it will be a Judas kiss."[162] These examples also demonstrate the propinquity of Russian Orthodox and Russian Baptist experiences, including their superstitious manifestations.

Widespread suffering was certainly experienced in the form of psychological pressure and at times physical attack from the Soviet authorities. Almost all Baptists, summoned to local departments of the KGB, were offered the opportunity to sign a document and become informers.[163] During such conversations various material benefits from the Soviet State, such as money, an apartment, a car,[164] and in some cases even a Bible,[165] were promised to them. When a believing person refused to deal with the

---

159. Testimony of Baptist church member from Zhitomir, N.O. Sobchenko (INT, Sacramento, California, USA, 2006). Among many Russian Orthodox homilies on the subject, there are words by St. Ioann Olenevsky (died 1951): "Why did you not go to church? The Mother of God will punish you." – *Zhitie i Chudesa Svyatogo Pravednogo Ioanna, Ispovednika, Olenevskogo Chudotvortsa* [The Life and Miracles of the Saint and Righteous John, the Confessor, the Miracle-Worker from Olenevka], <http://pravoslavie58region.ru/index.php?loc=ioann-3.htm> accessed 15 November 2010.

160. Testimony of B.M. Zdorovets (INT, Spokane, Washington, USA, 2006). Cf. a traditional Russian Orthodox exhortation: "Satan… turns us out of the church and so leaving the divine service before its end is sin." – *Povedenie v Khrame*, pp. 67, 71. See also Canon 9 of the Apostolic Canons: *Pravila Pravoslavnoy Tserkvi*, vol. I, pp. 68-9.

161. *Okolotserkovnye Sueveriya*, <http://kyivbratstvo.narod.ru/news/archive/2005_07_01_index.html>

162. Father D. Svechnikov, *Okkul'tism i Sueveriya: Vzglyad Pravoslavnogo Svyashchennika* [Occultism and Superstitions: a View from a Russian Orthodox Priest], <http://suevere.net/kak-ograditsya-ot-sueveriy/okkultizm-i-sueveriya-vzglyad-pravoslavnogo-svyaschennika/stranitsa-2.html> accessed 15 November 2010.

163. For instance, testimonies of Baptist presbyter from Alma-Ata, A.T. Evstratenko (INT, San Diego, California, USA, 2006), and church members, N.O. Sobchenko from Zhitomir and P.D. Karavan from Batumi (INT, Sacramento, California, USA, 2006).

164. For instance, testimonies of former senior presbyter from the South Kazakhstan, P.A. Chumakin (INT, Kent, Washington, USA, 2006) and deacon of Baptist church from Syzran, Ya.S. Shevchuk (INT, Los Angeles, California, USA, 2006).

165. Testimony of Baptist church member from Pavlodar, N.D. Chumakina (INT, Seattle, Washington, USA, 2006).

KGB,[166] he or she was threatened in every possible way.[167] For example, one ECB presbyter was taken by KGB agents, put in prison and left there in a solitary cell "forever" (as he was told), but he was soon released and the officers respectfully shook his hand because of his courage.[168] KGB officers demanded that the subject of conversations should remain secret, and Baptists were asked to sign a record of interrogations, but there was a tendency among Baptists to refuse to sign any document and even to tell the officers that all details of the interrogation would be passed on the Baptist community. This infuriated the KGB.[169]

It was particularly terrifying to be arrested and "taken away". In 1966, for example, A.I. Kolomiytsev, from Rostov Region, was arrested by the KGB and was carried by forest roads for a long time. Those holding him captive hinted that he could be shot, and then the officer of the KGB, interrogating him, sang a Soviet song that suggested the worst: "We're peaceful people, but our armoured train waits in reserve."[170] To hold on through such pressure was possible only for people with determined faith. These stories of suffering were recorded in hagiographical form in the traditional memoirs about Baptists in the Soviet period.[171] Many unusual experiences were noted. Presbyter M.M. Kolivayko recalls how he *dreamed* he would be put in the Mariupol prison. He was driven there on foot for three days after his trial (his crime was refusal to take arms during military service), but for

---

166. For instance, a member of Petropavlovsk ECB church (Kazakhstan), V.E. Sagan, answered officers, "Our wonderful Soviet literature teaches us to stand against treachery". (INT, Minneapolis, Minnesota, USA, 2006).

167. For instance, testimonies of: minister of CC ECB from Rostov Region, A.I. Kolomiytsev (INT, Vancouver, Washington, USA, 2006), presbyter from Alma-Ata, A.T. Evstratenko (INT, San Diego, California, USA, 2006), and many others.

168. Testimony of Baptist church members from Krasnodar, S.G. Odaryuk and N.M. Odaryuk (INT, Everett, Washington, USA, 2006).

169. For instance, testimonies of: presbyter of Baptist church in Pavlodar, P.A. Chumakin (INT, Seattle, Washington, USA, 2006), church member from Donetsk Region E.Ya. Sokolovskaya (INT, San Diego, California, USA, 2006), Baptist presbyter from Frunze, A.K. Sipko (INT, Spokane, Washington, USA, 2006).

170. Testimony of CCECB minister, A.I. Kolomiytsev about his arrest in 1966 (INT, Vancouver, Washington, USA, 2006).

171. A striking example is the hagiographical collection: *Podrazhayte Vere Ikh: 40 Let Probuzhdennomu Bratstvu* [Imitate Their Faith: The 40th Anniversary of the Revival Brotherhood] (M.: Sovet Tserkvey ECB, 2001).

some reason the warden did not want to admit him. Finally the warden said that out of pity he would admit him.[172] Thus the dream was fulfilled. There could also be specific temptations in prison.[173] G.K. Kryuchkov, the main leader of the CCECB, wrote about his imprisonment in the second half of the 1960s:

> I remember, during my time in the labor camp for the Lord's name, someone asked me, 'Could you issue an appeal to your churches... Maybe just one line. By one word from you, give them to understand that they do not need to circulate petitions for the persecuted believers. They will obey you... And we will set you free immediately...' However, I replied to him with daring words, 'I would rather go to the stake[174] than write such a message to God's people!'[175]

Kryuchkov mentioned here the possibility that he would "go to the stake". That this was meant literally is seen in the following words by Kryuchkov, elaborating on his statement, on the same page:

> ...Christ ordered, 'Be faithful until death...' Be faithful not until the first penalty, nor until the first imprisonment, but – until death! ...When I said this ['I would rather go to the stake'], I clearly understood that I should be ready to keep this promise. Therefore, I began to talk prayerfully with God, 'O Lord, I will go, I will go into the fire without fail, if that is Your will. Only give me the strength of mind to face it. Like every man, I am very weak, and so, at the sight of the fire, I

---

172. Testimony of minister from Donetsk Region, M.M. Kolivayko (INT, Sacramento, California, USA, 2006).

173. The themes of temptation and spiritual deception were part of Baptist preaching, referring to the Fall (Gen 3:1-7; 2 Cor 11:3); the danger of worshipping a creature (Deut. 4:19), and Jesus' temptation (Matt 4:1-11).

174. In Russian literally: *vzoydu na koster* (I will offer myself as a sacrifice by burning).

175. G. Kryuchkov, *Buduchi Rodom Bozhiim* [Being the Offspring of God], *VestI*, no. 3 (2002), p. 7.

will probably be in a state of shock, or fear, or the like, but please strengthen me...'[176]

What spirit impelled Baptists to speak about going to the stake in the 1960s? The Communists did not practice burning at the stake. But Kryuchkov was, it seems, drawing from an older Eastern Christian and Russian tradition. Archpriest Avvakum, in the seventeenth century, wrote these rather mysterious words:

> In today's Russia, [people] still go into the fire, experiencing bitter grief, being zealous in their piety, as did the ancient Apostles. They do not spare themselves, but go to their death for Christ's sake and for the sake of the Mother of God. Yet they will be alive forever. Those who have given themselves to burning, out of piety, as well as those who have died from a fast, do good deeds. I knew a certain Domentian, a priest. This man was ordinary, but his faith was warm and firm. His end was good: escaping from apostates, he burned himself... Yes, they did so reasonably – they found warmth...[177]

Although the tradition of martyrdom goes back to the earliest days of the Christian church, the language "he burned himself" suggests self-inflicted death, self-immolation. There were instances of this taking place. Avvakum and the Old Believers had a strong spirit of martyrdom, which was also found in Kryuchkov.[178] Such an outlook made a deep impression both on the flock and on some persecutors. In this regard, there were echoes of the

---

176. Ibid.

177. Avvakum, *Zhitie Avvakuma i Drugie Ego Sochineniya*, p. 226. Many thousands of adherents of the Old Orthodoxy burned themselves in the 17th and 18th centuries. See, for instance: A. Prugavin, *Samoistreblenie: Proyavlenie Asketizma i Fanatizma v Raskole* [Self-destruction: Displays of Asceticism and Fanaticism in the Schism], *Russkaya mysl'*, 1885, vol. I, pp. 77-111; vol. II, pp. 129-55; Zenkovsky, *Russkoe Staroobryadchestvo*, pp. 283-5, 469-71.

178. A well-known Russian Baptist historian of an older generation writes with sincere respect about the self-immolations (by burning) of the Old Believers, and simultaneously considers the Old Believers as spiritual forerunners of the Russian Baptists. – See *Al'manakh po Istorii Russkogo Baptizma*, vol. I (1999), p. 45.

outlook of Father Lazar' (Avvakum's associate), who in 1666 stunned the Russian Church Council in Moscow by saying that he would choose to go to the stake in order to test the truth of the "Old Belief": if he died in the flames than the supporters of Patriarch Nikon (who opposed the Old Believers) were right, but if he survived this would mean that the "new beliefs" were unacceptable.[179] Finally, Avvakum and Lazar' were burned at the stake in 1682.

The most zealous Baptists within the CCECB, following their radical leaders, were only one step from self-immolation. In his memoirs, the former executive minister of the CCECB in the Central Asian region Yu.F. Kuksenko, a participant in a mass protest demonstration in Moscow in May 1966, near the building of the Central Committee of the Communist Party, states that the believers rejected completely the suggestion by the authorities that they disperse peacefully, and started to scream all together, "We will die!" Kuksenko connected such desperate behavior with self-immolation and, knowing the Baptist radicals from the inside, he added, "I think that some of our demonstrators would have done this, if the command had been given".[180] Some Soviet citizens, not connected with Baptist congregations but in contact with certain radical Baptist individuals and favorable to them to some extent, also observed their readiness to die, not only as a result of persecution by atheists but "in protest" by burning themselves or by immoderate fasting. For example, former political prisoner and dissident, V.E. Ronkin, who served time in the 1960s with the CCECB leader Boris Zdorovets, wrote in his memoirs that the threat of some radical Soviet Baptists to set themselves on fire in Red Square (in Moscow) if Zdorovets died in prison received publicity in their ("political") labor camp. Though Ronkin was cautious, stating that he did not know the real situation,[181] the fact that this possibility was under serious discussion displays the spirit of those times, as well as the reputation of Soviet Baptists in the eyes of the dissidents.[182] Although there is no known case of

---

179. Zenkovsky, *Russkoe Staroobryadchestvo*, p. 311.

180. Kuksenko, *Nashi Besedy*, pp. 55-6.

181. See V. Ronkin, *Na Smenu Dekabryam Prikhodyat Yanvari* [Decembers give way to Januaries] (M.: Zven'ya, 2003), p. 285.

182. On how near some radical Baptists were to self-immolation under Soviet power, see

Russian Baptists who went as far as self-immolation, Boris Zdorovets himself confirmed to me that talks about the willingness of certain Baptists to set themselves on fire took place. In an attempt to vindicate such attitudes within the CCECB in this period, Zdorovets referred to the words of the Gospel of John, "Greater love has no man than this, that a man lay down his life for his friends".[183]

Dreams, visions and healing

Presbyter M.M. Kolivayko's dream that he would be put in Mariupol prison was typical of many experiences of dreams and visions recorded by Russian Baptists. In any formal statement setting out the theology of the Russian Baptist community, divine revelation was located in the Bible. Yet in practice there was a willingness to recognize and accept divine revelations that were received in other ways, such as through dreams and visions. Certainly, if they were questioned about dreams and visions, a standard Baptist reply from ministers and preachers would have been that they were "very dangerous" phenomena, sometimes leading to spiritual deception.[184] Here they followed classical Russian Orthodox ascetic authors, who constantly warned against "imaginations" and "spiritual deception",[185] not infrequently teaching ordinary monks to distrust any dreams and visions.[186]

---

also a literary work (a story) entitled *Kondraty Savelievich*, published by the periodical of the ECB: *SV*, no. 3 (2005), pp. 48-51.

183. A phone conversation with B.M. Zdorovets (12 April 2010).

184. For instance, testimonies of Baptist presbyters from the former USSR: P.F. Kunda, N.S. Kramarenko, and V.V. Zinchenko (INT, Sacramento, California, USA, 2006).

185. See, for instance: Bishop Ignaty (Bryanchaninov), *Slovo o Chuvstvennom i Dukhovnom Videnii Dukhov* [Homily on the Perceptional and Spiritual Visions of Spirits], in Bishop Ignaty (Bryanchaninov), *Polnoe Sobranie Tvoreny*, vol. III, pp. 5-66; Bishop Petr (Ekaterinovsky), *Ukazanie Puti k Spaseniyu, Opyt Asketiki* [Showing the Way to Salvation, the Ascetic Practice] (M.: Izd-vo Sretenskogo monastyrya, 2001).

186. For instance, there is a typical statement, "...Anchorites, going into the wilderness, adopted a rule to reject emphatically any visions and, with humility, conscious of being unworthy and sinful, deny any appearances in the spiritual realm." – Archimandrite Lazar', *O Taynykh Nedugakh Dushi* [On Covert Illnesses of the Soul] (M.: Izd-vo Sretenskogo monastyrya, 2004), p. 266. Cf.: Bishop Ignaty (Bryanchaninov), vol. III, p. 45.

Other Baptists described dreams and vision as "not serious", with the advice being not to take much notice of them.[187] Still others would have wanted to test the dreams and visions to see if they "correspond to our doctrines" (distancing themselves, for example, from Pentecostal views), and then some could be accepted on "biblical grounds".[188] Outside the formal setting, Baptists described countless "miraculous" dreams and visions, many of which bore similarities to *tonkie sny* – "fine" or "subtle" dreams found in Russian Orthodox monastic life.[189] Great numbers of such stories were passed on in Baptist communities.

Dreams often had to do with deep spiritual experiences or with dramatic provisions at times of need. The dreams themselves were often the subject of interpretation by the community. In the late 1950s, in Zelenodolsk (Tatarstan), a young man visited a Baptist church and told some of the believers about a dream in which he had caught a dove. The Baptist community interpreted this as his imminent receiving of the Holy Spirit. Shortly after this the young man became a Baptist church member and later a minister.[190] In another case of conversion and calling, a teenager living in the Kirovograd Region had been reading the Gospel. He fell asleep and had a dream, subsequently seen as "from the Lord". In the dream many people stood on a dark street waiting for the Judgement of God. Suddenly, in radiant glory, Jesus Christ appeared and began to distribute potatoes to poor people. Those who took a potato found salvation. Christ gave a potato to the teenager. As in the Zelenodolsk story, the young man became a presbyter.[191] In the 1960s, a member of Alma-Ata Baptist Church had a vision: one day he woke up because a pigeon had flown into the house and landed

187. For instance, testimonies of minister of ECB from Kiev, L.E. Kovalenko and evangelist from Dushanbe, P.A. Semeryuk (INT, Sacramento, California, USA, 2006).
188. In such cases, they referred, for instance, to Joseph's dreams (Gen 37:5-11) and Paul's visions (Acts 16:9; 2 Cor 12:1-7).
189. See, for instance: Bishop Ignaty (Bryanchaninov), *Polnoe Sobranie Tvoreny*, vol. I, pp. 571-2. See also typical descriptions of numerous miracles, "subtle" dreams and visions in Russian Orthodox monastic life: Cloistress Taisiya, *Russkoe Pravoslavnoe Zhenskoe Monashestvo*, pp. 52, 53, 139, 140, 142, 149, 155, 162, 200, 218, 219.
190. Testimony of presbyter from Tatarstan, N.V. Sabursky and E.N. Saburskaya (INT, Minneapolis, Minnesota, USA, 2006).
191. Testimony of Baptist presbyter, A.A. Pikhay (INT, Los Angeles, California, USA, 2006).

on him. A voice told him to visit a large needy family and provide help for them.[192] It is significant that in the Russian Orthodox tradition if a pigeon (especially a white one) alights on a person, it indicates the receiving of the gift of the Holy Spirit.[193]

In other cases dreams and vision-like insights were seen as giving guidance or protection. In 1968, Pavlodar Baptist Church was engaged in a great deal of fasting and prayer, seeking a new presbyter. Two members of the church had dreams in which a young man dressed in a grey suit put their prayer house in order. Soon after this a young ordained minister moved to their city and came into the church wearing his only (grey) suit. Partly because of the dreams, he was elected as presbyter of the congregation that very day.[194] In 1971, a choir director in Frunze Baptist Church, seeing a postman in his street, felt an impulse to say to his wife that the postman was bringing a letter to them with an invitation to move to Kuybyshev for church ministry there. This proved to be the case. The family had never visited Kuybyshev and had no relatives or friends there, but on the basis of the prior insight about the letter, the family moved to Kuybyshev.[195] In another incident in the 1970s, in Odessa, a six-year-old boy from a Baptist family was lost. His relatives could not find him, despite searching for the whole day. However, a family friend (also a Baptist) fell asleep for a short time and saw a tram track, the lost boy, and his sandals close to a familiar door. On the basis of this dream the boy was found.[196] In an example of apparently miraculous protection, associated with a vision, in the 1970s in Homel Region some KGB officers drove round a village in search of a local

192. Testimony of Baptist minister from Alma-Ata, N.D. Babich (INT, Castro Valley, California, USA, 2006).

193. See, for instance, the Lives of the Saints: St. John Chrysostom – ZhSDR, vol. III, p. 319; St. Gregory of Acragant – Ibid., vol. III, p. 638; St. Andrew the Fool-for-Christ – Ibid., vol. II, p. 64; St. Ephrem the Sirian – Ibid., vol. V, p. 895; St. Theodore of Edessa – Ibid., vol. XI, p. 224; St. Theodore of Cyrene – Ibid., vol. XI, p. 83; St. Fabian – Ibid., vol. XII, p. 86.

194. Sedletsky, "Vospominaniya", pp. 169-71. His ministry was seen as a blessing for this church. – Testimony of Baptist presbyter from Pavlodar, P.A. Chumakin, and N.D. Chumakina (INT, Seattle, Washington, USA, 2006).

195. Testimony about their life: former senior presbyter from Kuybyshev, V.F. Serpevsky, and Z.I. Serpevskaya (INT, Vancouver, Washington, USA, 2006).

196. Testimony of Baptist presbyter from Odessa, Ya.D. Shevchuk, and V.S. Shevchuk (INT, Portland, Oregon, USA, 2006).

Baptist who was known because of his religious activity. The Baptist was on the street and saw a black motor car (the KGB "Volga"), which prompted him to pray, and although the car passed close by the KGB officers took no notice of him. What he saw in his vision were "spirits of wickedness" hovering over the car.[197] These kinds of narratives have many older (and more recent) counterparts in Russian Orthodoxy.[198]

Russian Baptists also passed on stories in which dreams proved to be false. In the 1950s, a Baptist whose priceless New Testament was stolen when he was in the Soviet Army, received a "prophetic dream" with clear directions about where the book was, but it was not there. He commented: "Then I understood that my dream was false, a demonic temptation."[199] Another member of a Baptist community (an elderly member), who claimed to receive many "heavenly revelations", refused to accept any critical comments about his revelations. He responded to any critic: "How dare you contradict me? I saw the Lord on two occasions, but you contradict me!"[200] There were also dramatic and alarming incidents. For example, a Soviet Baptist received a revelation "from above" which he believed meant that he should go "to meet the Bridegroom". He climbed up on the roof of his shed, "saw" Christ descending from heaven, and... took a step forward. He fell from the roof and became an invalid.[201] This bears some remarkable similarities to an Orthodox legend about a zealous ascetic who fell under demonic influence or spiritual deception through false visions, and climbed a high mountain where he saw a "heavenly chariot", supposedly sent by God to "take him to paradise like Elijah". When the joyful monk

---

197. Testimony of M.I. Petrenko and I.E. Petrenko, church members from Belorussia (INT, Fresno, California, USA, 2006).

198. See, for instance: *Pravoslanye Chudesa v 20 Veke: Svidetel'stva Ochevidtsev* [Orthodox Miracles in the 20th Century: Eyewitnesses' Accounts], ed. by V. Gubanov (M.: Trim, 1993).

199. Testimony of Baptist presbyter from Maikop, N.G. Man'ko (INT, Everett, Washington, USA, 2006).

200. Testimony about the elder by B.M. Zdorovets (INT, Spokane, Washington, USA, 2006).

201. Testimony of B.M. Zdorovets (INT, Spokane, Washington, USA, 2006).

began to try to get into the chariot, the vision disappeared and he fell down the mountain and died.[202]

Russian Orthodox devotional writings abound in alarming illustrations of extreme conduct within monastic settings. Bishop Ignaty Bryanchaninov in his *Asketicheskie Opyty* (Ascetic Experience) wrote about a monastic elder from a cloister in the Diocese of Orel. The elder fell under terrible demonic deception: displaying misguided religious zeal, he cut his hand off (in pursuance of Jesus' words from the Gospel) and thought that some godly people would venerate it as a "holy relic".[203] In the same way, in the 1950s, an evangelical woman in western Ukraine, following the same Scripture and also a special revelation, "fulfilled the commandment" of Christ (as she put it) and cut her hand off.[204] Russian Orthodox authors also refer to a Constantinopolitan monk named Polychronius, who had a vision that he could offer powerful proof of the truth of the Monothelite doctrine that Christ (despite the creed of the Sixth Ecumenical Council) has solely a divine will. Polychronius volunteered to raise a dead person publicly, but he was unsuccessful.[205] In the 1970s, several members of the Dzhetysay community of the CCECB, with fasting and prayers, tried to raise a dead child in public, but this also failed.[206] There were also some cases within the CCECB of extremely long fasts (lasting a month and more) when the participants almost died because of emaciation.[207] G.K. Kryuchkov himself repeatedly kept a fast during his three years in a labor camp, abstaining from food for up to 17 days.[208]

---

202. Hieromonk Alexey (Kuznetsov), *Yurodstvo i Stolpnichestvo*, p. 392. For illustrations of monks' spiritual deceptions by demons see also: Bishop Ignaty (Bryanchaninov), *Slovo o Smerti* [Homily on Death], in Bishop Ignaty (Bryanchaninov), *Polnoe Sobranie Tvoreny*, vol. III, pp. 5-294; Archimandrite Lazar', *O Taynykh Nedugakh Dushi* [On Covert Illnesses of the Soul] (M.: Izd-vo Sretenskogo monastyrya, 2004), pp. 176-414.

203. See Bishop Ignaty (Bryanchaninov), *Polnoe Sobranie Tvoreny*, vol. I, p. 221.

204. A. Mitskevich, *"Khozhdenie pred Bogom"* [Walking with God], *BV*, no. 1 (1956), p. 45.

205. See, for instance: Kartashev, *Vselenskie Sobory*, p. 439; Archimandrite Rafail (Karelin), *Dykhanie Zhizni*, pp. 147-8.

206. Kuksenko, *Nashi Besedy*, p. 66.

207. Testimony of B.M. Zdorovets (INT, Spokane, Washington, USA, 2006). Cf.: Khrapov, *Dom Bozhy*, <http://www.blagovestnik.org/books/00280.htm#76>

208. Testimony of his brother, Yu.K. Kryuchkov, who met the leader of the CCECB in Transbaikalia where the latter was set free in 1969 (INT, Sacramento, California,

Among Soviet Baptists there were also many legendary stories about the "great miracles" associated with Gennady Kryuchkov, just as there were in Orthodox communities in connection with revered Orthodox figures. Although he was caught and sentenced once, on many other occasions he escaped detection, despite the activities of the police, informers and even mediums.[209] For example, the story was often told about how one day a car with Kryuchkov inside was pursued by a black KGB "Volga" and suddenly Kryuchkov's car was taken by supernatural power from the road (perhaps by angels) and carried to a safe place.[210] There were other legends about how the best officers of the KGB unsuccessfully searched for Kryuchkov. Some Baptists even began to wonder if he existed.[211] Kryuchkov lived secretly, deep underground. His personal contacts with other leaders of the CCECB were rare; he contacted them more often through tape cassettes, delivered by several messengers.[212] As an example of his way of traveling, he secretly left one of the meetings of the CCECB by car, then changed to a motorcycle, which took him to a boat that ferried him across a river, and he was then carried further by another car.[213]

There were continuing tensions in Baptist communities, as in Orthodoxy, over visions and prophetic utterances. The "Baptist visions" sometimes had a pronounced legalistic character, for instance: at the time of resurrection of the dead, the Lord will not recognize sisters who used make-up or brethren

USA, 2006).

209. For instance, testimonies of Baptist church members, N.O. Sobchenko from Zhitomir, and P.D. Karavan from Batumi (INT, Sacramento, California, USA, 2006). For more about Kryuchkov's alleged activities: *Predsedatel' CC ECB, G.K. Kryuchkov, Nekrolog* [The Leader of the CCECB, G.K. Kryuchkov, Obituary Notice], <http://jesuschrist.ru/news/2007/7/16/13334> accessed 14 July 2009.

210. For example, an account (with critical appraisal of the miracles) by former minister of the CCECB, O. Korotky (Prague, Czech Republic, 2006): "That was the beginning of miracles..." (cf.: John 2:11).

211. For instance, testimony of Baptist church members from Donetsk Region, L.Ya. Sokolovsky and E.Ya. Sokolovskaya (INT, San Diego, California, USA, 2006).

212. Testimony of a minister of the CCECB from Sukhumi, D.I. Chueshkov (INT, Seattle, Washington, USA, 2006); Kuksenko, "Nashi Besedy", pp. 57-8, 99-101.

213. Testimony of Baptist presbyter from Rostov, M.P. Zakharov, who personally participated in G.K. Kryuchkov's "safety measures" (INT, Sacramento, California, USA, 2006).

who wore clothes "improper for the saints".[214] In these revelations the strict monastic spirit was evident. The concern to respond rightly was present in the classical question, "If Russians shave off their beards, where will they stand at the Last Judgment – among the bearded righteous or with the shaven heretics?"[215] But there was also, in Orthodoxy, a desire for moderation. The response to excessive fasting, for example, was not to applaud it as piety, but to see it as a display of pride or even an evidence of demonic possession.[216] Thus Bishop Ignaty Bryanchaninov wrote:

> Demons suggest to a monk that he bear a heavy load of immoderate fasting, immoderate vigil, a burdensome rule of prayer, excessive poverty of clothes, excessive zeal for physical labours – in order to bring him to arrogance, or to force him to expend energy and health and become unfit for deeds of devotion.[217]

In one of N.S. Leskov's stories, a Father Superior ordered that a monk, because of his love of foretelling the future, should be locked in with an icon, *The Blessed Silence,* "until the spirit of prophesy leaves him".[218] In one Russian Baptist service an unknown "prophet" visited the church and suddenly exclaimed, "The Spirit says..." The Baptist presbyter interrupted him by starting singing the hymn "Please, Hear the Prayer and the Sigh", and then read a text from Scripture.[219] Some types of "spiritual" behavior were affirmed; others were condemned.

---

214. For instance, B.M. Zdorovets spoke about such a "revelation" (INT, Spokane, Washington, USA, 2006).

215. S. Soloviev, *Istoriya Rossii s Drevneyshikh Vremen,* part 7, vol. XIII-XIV, p. 550. Judging by pictures of the Russian Baptist pioneers featured in the official history by the AUCECB, the majority of the men had beards. See the inset between pp. 128 and 129 in *Istoriya ECB v SSSR.*

216. See, for instance: Monk Merkury, *V Gorakh Kavkaza, Zapiski Sovremennogo Pustynnozhitelya* [In the Mountains of the Caucasus, Memoirs of a Contemporary Hermit] (M.: Palomnik, 1996), pp. 36-40; Zenkovsky, *Russkoe Staroobryadchestvo,* pp. 282-3.

217. Bishop Ignaty (Bryanchaninov), *Polnoe Sobranie Tvoreny,* vol. III, p. 32.

218. See N. Leskov, *Sobranie Sochineniy,* 12 vols., vol. II, p. 335.

219. I was present at this incident.

Visions and dreams were sometimes connected with healing. In the 1960s, a member of the Zhitomir Church of the CCECB, whose children had often been ill, had a dream about a remarkable cow that gave a great deal of milk, and in the dream the children drank the milk and made a quick recovery. In the morning, under the impression of the dream, the Baptist went to the bazaar, where he looked for the cow a long time and finally found it – "exactly her", as he reported. He immediately bought this "gift from the Lord", and his children were soon better.[220] In many Baptist communities any hasty visit to a doctor, or an attempt to deal with physical problems without a parallel cure of the spirit, was discouraged.[221] There were echoes here of the reluctance of Orthodox monks to seek medical help.[222] Soviet Baptist attitudes towards medicine varied. At one extreme there were those who denied the value of doctors and argued that using any drugs showed a "lack of faith". By contrast, there were those who pressed for Baptists to recognize the necessity of medical care,[223] placing emphasis on the New Testament report that the Evangelist Luke was a physician (Col 4:14).[224] Baptist church preaching often included the idea that Christians "in the day of adversity" have to "consider" (Eccl 7:14), with the application of this being that in a time of physical illness there might be spiritual benefit.[225]

Although the situation was complex, and certainly a desire for physical health was not an end in itself in the teaching of Soviet Baptists (their context was one of suffering), numerous recoveries from illnesses "by faith", i.e.

220. Testimony of Baptist church members from Zhitomir, N.O. Sobchenko and T.N. Karavan (INT, Sacramento, California, USA, 2006).
221. See, for instance, Khrapov, *Dom Bozhy*, <http://www.blagovestnik.org/books/00280.htm#98>
222. See, for instance, *Uchilishche Blagochestiya*, pp. 68-9, 206-7. Many Orthodox monks and nuns did not seek medical attention at all. See, for instance, Cloistress Taisiya, *Russkoe Pravoslavnoe Zhenskoe Monashestvo*, pp. 89, 116; Ryabinin, *Russkoe Yurodstvo*, p. 263.
223. See, for instance: Mitskevich, *Istoriya Evangel'skikh Khristian-Baptistov*, p. 263; V. Slobodyanik, *Voprosy Dukhovnoy Zhizni* [The Issues of Spiritual Life], *BV*, no. 2 (1965), pp. 58-9; A. Mitskevich, *O Vospitanii Veruyushchikh* [On the Upbringing of Believers], *BV*, no. 5 (1986), p. 61.
224. For example, testimony of the ex-president of the AUCECB, V.E. Logvinenko (Odessa, Ukraine, 1995).
225. See, for instance: Kolesnikov, *V Pomoshch' Propovedniku*, v. I, pp. 43, 55-6.

without medical intervention, apparently took place. Stories were told of remarkable recoveries in families, for example in the case of a mother who had severe asthma. After prayer she felt impelled to ask her little children to pick wild flowers in the meadow: she then infused these, drank the "herbal remedy" and was cured. This narrative came from the early 1960s.[226] In another case, in the 1970s, a child had a severe head injury. The doctors, it was said, gave up hope, but believers prayed passionately and the child recovered in a few days.[227] In these cases ministers were not involved, but in other cases, after fasting and prayer, presbyters heard the confession of the sick and anointed them with oil (following James 5:14-16). Accounts speak of recoveries from "a cancer",[228] from leukemia and "other incurable diseases",[229] and from "many diseases".[230] In traditional Baptist testimonies, the emphasis is not on "victorious struggle" against illness, but humble submission to receive "all that God sends". Thus in 1987 a minister who had stomach cancer prepared himself to die, but was healed.[231] After the death of the famous minister S.T. Golev, *Bratsky Listok* noted his striking gift of praying for the sick and the "possessed", with resultant healings, but added, "If he had been proud, God would not have granted him so amazing a gift in the last years of his life."[232] True visions, dreams and healing gifts were, it was believed, given to saintly people.

226. Testimony of ECB church member from Homel, N.F. Mazhnaya (INT, Fresno, California, USA, 2006).
227. Testimony of former senior presbyter from Kuybyshev, V.F. Serpevsky, and Z.I. Serpevskaya (INT, Vancouver, Washington, USA, 2006).
228. Testimony of former senior presbyter of Krasnodar Territory, Ya.A. Grinchenko (INT, Sacramento, California, USA, 2006).
229. Testimony of CCECB minister from Sukhumi, D.I. Chueshkov (INT, Seattle, Washington, USA, 2006).
230. Testimony of ECB church member from the Crimea, V.P. Litovchenko about the ministry of her father, presbyter of a church of the CCECB, P.M. Shokha (INT, Los Angeles, California, USA, 2006).
231. Testimony of Baptist minister from Kirovograd, V.D. Bondarenko (INT, Los Angeles, California, USA, 2006).
232. *BL*, no. 2 (1976), p. 2. See also *Podrazhayte Vere Ikh*, p. 24.

Common prejudices

Russian Baptists held to many prejudices and even superstitions. In common with some branches of the Orthodox Church, many saw the "coming of Antichrist" in the Communist regime and regarded the idea that Soviet power might be "ordained of God" as unthinkable.[233] The attitude to Lenin was mentioned above. Some Baptists composed the name "LENIN" from matches, and then the number 666 from the same quantity of matches.[234] There is a notable report about a portrait of Lenin, which was hung, under the pressure of the authorities, in a Baptist prayer house in Kazakhstan. This was what was done in buildings used by Soviet organizations. Shortly after this, however, someone defaced the picture, putting out Lenin's eyes.[235] This kind of action was not carried out only by radical sectarians. Nor was it part of the Baptist psyche to destroy images. Indeed N.S. Leskov, after citing several reports about damage done to icons by some radical Orthodox priests and laymen, said that in the nineteenth century Stundists removed icons from their homes but "avoided damaging them".[236] The damage done by the Orthodox to icons was connected with a tradition in Orthodoxy about preserving the purity of icons. For example, in 1654 the Patriarch Nikon put out the eyes of images which in his view did not satisfy the requirements for a "true" icon painting.[237] Thus Baptist actions were in line with an Orthodox understanding of great zeal for God.[238]

---

233. For instance, testimony of M.I. Petrenko and I.E. Petrenko, church members from Belorussia (INT, Fresno, California, USA, 2006).

234. Testimony of B.M. Zdorovets (INT, Spokane, Washington, USA, 2006). In Russian, both the name "Lenin" and the number "666" are composed from 15 matches each. Though the Soviet Baptist songbooks had hymns numbered 666 they were never sung.

235. See I. Shnayder, *Evangel'skie Obshchiny v Aktyubinskoy Stepi* [Evangelical Communities in the Aktyubinsk Steppe] (Steinhagen, Germany: Samenkorn, 2006), p. 273.

236. N. Leskov, *Eparkhial'ny Sud* [Diocesan Court] [1880], in N. Leskov, *Sobranie Sochineniy*, 12 vols., vol. VI, pp. 341-2. For evidence of destruction see, for instance, A. Vvedensky, *Bor'ba s Sektantstvom*, pp. 48-9.

237. See V. Klyuchevsky, *Sochineniya*, vol. III, p. 288.

238. Radicals quoted the scriptural words, "The zeal of your house has consumed me" (John 2:17). See also the destruction of Old Believers' icons by the official Russian Church: Tarasov, *Ikona i Blagochestie*, pp. 147-50.

Baptists were opposed not only to Lenin but to certain actions of the Soviet state which restricted their communal life. For some Baptists, however, it was necessary to do what the state required, while others were defiant. The split in the 1960s was over a number of issues, including registration of churches. Following the demands of the state, the AUCECB aspired to register officially as many as possible of the communities of Evangelical Christians-Baptists in the USSR. By the 1980s they were thanking God for the "blessings" of registration.[239] But the CCECB, in most cases, considered "so-called registration" as a sin which would lead to eternal death.[240] This prejudice was so strong that it led to ideas like the following being spread among CCECB members: "When Christ comes to take his church, if she has registered her marriage with the State... of course, He will repudiate such a church! Would you be pleased if your bride registered her marriage with another man?"[241] One young man from a family that supported the CCECB said to his former friend, who was in an AUCECB church: "Get out of here, Mr. Registration!"[242] The CCECB also condemned churches that remained independent of either of the two main groups of Baptists. They stated: "The Autonomous churches... are autonomous from Christ", "the Independent churches... are independent from the Christian narrow way", "the churches uniting with the AUCECB are not united with God", "sin reigns there... while our head is God; Jesus Christ is at the head of our church and his word is leading us."[243] The refusal to register officially was a

---

239. Here is a typical quotation from *Bratsky Vestnik*: "The church receives special blessings from God concerning official registration... The Children of God thank the Lord heartily for the opportunity to conduct their meetings freely." – "From The Life of the Local Churches", *BV*, no. 1 (1982), p. 72.

240. From an appeal of the Organizing Committee of ECB churches (1962): "For the sake of registration – to ruin union with God, to lose blessings, to lose eternal life... what is the use of doing it?" – Cited in G. Kryuchkov, *Velikoe Probuzhdenie XX Veka* [The Great Revival in the 20th Century] (n.p.: Izd-vo "Khristianin", 2008), p. 89. See also *Vopros Registratsii i Sud'ba Spaseniya* [The Question of Registration and the Fate of Salvation], *BL*, nos. 1-3 (1975), pp. 1-4.

241. See more details in Prokhorov, "The State and the Baptist Churches in the USSR (1960-1980)", pp. 49-51.

242. Testimony of Baptist church members from Donetsk Region, V.A. Sheremet and I.L. Sheremet (Sacramento, California, USA, 2009).

243. See, for instance: Kryuchkov, *Velikoe Probuzhdenie XX Veka*, pp. 279, 296-7, 343, 357. Cf. some tropes from the Russian Orthodox liturgy: "He, who is crowning the earth with flowers, was crowned with thorns", "the stretching out of the Lord's hands on the

phenomenon found not only among Russian Baptists, but also, for example, among the "catacomb" Orthodoxy (communities of the True Orthodox Church and the True Orthodox Christians).[244] The feeling of being the only true believers is also reminiscent of the famous words of Archpriest Avvakum about the Greeks coming to learn from the Russians.[245]

Linked with the anti-Soviet outlook that was to be found was an antipathy towards the colour red. Not surprisingly, churches did not want to have red flags. One old Baptist recalled: "When one day (on November 7th) our presbyter hung out a red flag from the roof of the prayer house... we knew at once that he served not only the church of God."[246] However, the thinking about red went much further. In some radical Baptist communities, church members were discouraged from wearing any red clothes. To attend church dressed in "scarlet" was considered as especially improper. There were references to the Old Testament Tabernacle,[247] to the colour of sin (Cf.: Isa 1:18), to Christ being mocked in a scarlet robe before his execution (Matt 27:28), and to the colour of the "scarlet beast" and "the whore of Babylon" (Rev 12:3; 17:3-4),[248] sometimes connecting the last two images with the Communist power. On one occasion in the 1960s an atheistic lecturer was seeking to prove that God did not exist by showing

---

cross healed... the one who stretched out his hands to the fruit of the tree of knowledge of good and evil", "by His sores the Lord is healing human sores"... Cited in Bishop V. Milov, *Chteniya po Liturgicheskomy Bogosloviyu* [The Liturgical Theology Reader] (Kiev: Obshchestvo Lyubiteley Pravoslavnoy Literatury, 2004), pp. 33-6. Cf. the following Russian Baptist preachers' traditional interpretation of Christ's being taking into custody: "Then they laid their hands on him and took him" (Mark 14:46)". – "And he, who himself laid his healing hands on children and the sick, made it possible for the guards to 'lay their hands on him'". – Unpublished memoirs by B.M. Zdorovets.

244. See, for instance: T. Beeson, *Discretion and Valour*, pp. 98-100; Shkarovsky, *Russkaya Pravoslavnaya Tserkov pri Staline i Khrushcheve*, pp. 242-61; Pospielovsky, *Russkaya Pravoslavnaya Tserkov v 20 veke*, pp. 314-30.

245. *Zhitie Avvakuma*, p. 60.

246. Testimony of deacon of Baptist church from Syzran, Ya.S. Shevchuk (INT, Los Angeles, California, USA, 2006).

247. For instance, testimony of Baptist presbyter, V.I. Mikhaylov (Omsk, Russia, 2009). Cf.: I. Kargel, *Svet Iz Teni Budushchikh Blag* [Light from the Shadows of Good Things to Come] [1908] (SPb.: Biblia dlya Vsekh, 1994), pp. 97-8, 116. Scarlet in the Tabernacle was understood as associated with sin.

248. For instance, testimony of presbyter V.N. Khot'ko (Petropavlovsk, Kazakhstan, 1999).

firstly that Satan did not exist. He argued that it was well known that people in different parts of the world imagined Satan variously: Europeans – with a black face; Africans – with a white face. The line of argument was that Satan did not exist at all. B.M. Zdorovets, who was in the audience, raised his hand and acting as a "simpleton" said that everybody knows what colour Satan is. The lecturer was surprised and asked for the answer. Zdorovets, with a serious look on his face, said, "Look around; what colour are our flags, all symbolic... everybody knows that *Satan is red*."[249] The incident disrupted the lecture. Many Russian Orthodox people had the same attitude towards red. Father D. Dudko wrote about the reluctance of children from Orthodox families to wear the Pioneers' [the Communist youth organization] red neckerchiefs, and if some were compelled to obey the Soviet school rules they consecrated the neckerchiefs with holy water.[250] The radical groups of True Orthodox Christians rejected red outright.[251]

Another area of prejudice had to do with certain words. The most "watchful" Orthodox Christians and Soviet Baptists were inclined to be suspicious of Russian words with the prefix *bes-* (un-, which in Russian is literally *demon*) as well as of the numerous "barbarisms" used in Russian language. Such words were not infrequently "tested" for their acceptability to a Christian. In opposing Soviet organizations, it was said that "believers must not go to so*BES*, which was the official abbreviation of the "social security department" in the former Soviet Union.[252] Some of the words used in common speech that were rejected by Orthodox and Baptist believers were *BESserdechny* (unfeeling), *BESsovestny* (unscrupulous), *BESsoznatelny* (unconscious), and *BESchelovechny* (inhuman).[253] It seems that only

249. Testimony of B.M. Zdorovets (INT, Spokane, Washington, USA, 2006).

250. See D. Dudko, *O Nashem Upovanii* [On our Hope] (Korntal: Svet na Vostoke, 1991), p. 96.

251. See, for instance, Shkarovsky, *Russkaya Pravoslavnaya Tserkov pri Staline i Khrushcheve*, p. 246.

252. In addition, the first part of the abbreviation (so-) literally means in Russian: "together with".

253. See, for instance, a remarkable Russian Orthodox source: I. Seleznev, *"K Chemu Privela Revolyutsiya v Russkoy Grammatike"* [How the Revolution Resulted in the Russian Grammar], *Svet Pravoslaviya*, 22 Feb. 2003. There are also Soviet Baptist reports on the subject: B.M. Zdorovets (INT, Spokane, Washington, USA, 2006); V.N. Khot'ko (Petropavlovsk, Kazakhstan, 1999).

BESpartiyny (non-party) and *BESplatny* (free of charge) were acceptable exceptions to the rule.[254] When English-language words began to be used more commonly in Russia in the 1980s, similar issues arose. Some Baptists opposed the university qualification and prefix *MAGistr* (Master), as a word "derived from *magic*". Even political *DEMOcracy* was opposed, as "the government of demons". There were also problems with *ADministration,* since *ad* in Russian is "hell". Some Russian Orthodox Christians did not recommend *limonad* (lemonade) – *limon* and *ad* (lemon and hell).[255] A Christian publishing house, which took the name *Triada* ("Trinity" in Greek), was held in suspicion among provincial Baptists since it sounded in Russian like *three hells*.[256]

Many of these prejudices were the product of limited education, mixed with some superstition. The lack of education, as noted previously, was inevitable given the discrimination against believers. This was exacerbated by a disdain for education within some Baptist communities, which expressed itself in anti-intellectual catchphrases (in Russian, they were expressed in verse) such as "to preserve the faith in purity, I'd take all books and burn them up."[257] Some Russian Baptists made a point of rejecting (and even burning) books by popular Protestant authors translated from English into Russian.[258] Within the Russian Orthodox Church, the burning of "imperfectly Orthodox" works (as they were viewed by some), also took place, with the destruction carried out by zealous priests and monks.[259] The attitude to authors and books was, however, a complex area.

---

254. Testimony of Baptist evangelist from Dushanbe P.A. Semeryuk (INT, Sacramento, California, USA, 2006).

255. See *Okolotserkovnye Sueveriya,* <http://kyivbratstvo.narod.ru/news/archive/2005_07_01_index. html>

256. For instance, testimonies of presbyter V.N. Khot'ko and church member A.M. Kaplenkov (Petropavlovsk, Kazakhstan, 1999).

257. Evidently, this is a paraphrase of Famusov's words from the famous comedy by A.S. Griboyedov *Woe From Wit* (1824).

258. See, for instance: B. Sysoev, *"Sobrat' Vse Knigi By Da Szhech'!"* [I'd Take all Books and Burn them Up!], *SV,* no. 2 (2002), pp. 15-17. Also testimonies of church ministers of the ECB: V.N. Khot'ko (Petropavlovsk, Kazakhstan, 1997) and I.P. Fast (Shchuchinsk, Kazakhstan, 1998).

259. See, for instance: O. Kleman, *"Trudnosti i Nedomoganiya Russkoy Tserkvi"* [The Hardships and Indispositions of the Russian Church], *Russkaya Mysl',* 18-24 June 1998; M. Shevchenko, *"Istoriya iz Zhizni Provintsial'noy Inkvizitsii"* [A Story of the Life of the

Another extreme was the way a "respected" author was quoted: there was little concern about quoting accurately or even giving credit to the author. This was demonstrated, for example, by the unsophisticated, unattributed paraphrases that were presented from famous sermons (sometimes even homilies of the great church fathers) by many Baptist preachers, and by widespread copying and using, without any agreement with the authors, of books, articles and poetry. And Russian Baptist authors themselves were often happy to have their writings used.[260] Where authors were known, this usage enhanced their authority.

The prejudice against education was a specific aspect of a wider distaste for organized ways of life. A kind of pseudo-biblical reaction, especially to new modes of organization, was common among Russian Baptists. Thus, for example, they did not tend to fasten their seat belts in cars. This was common among the majority of Soviet drivers, but some Russian Baptists, looking at the issue from a "spiritual point of view", considered that to fasten a seat belt was a sign of "lack of faith" or "distrust of the Lord".[261] Another example of opposition to organization was a lack of punctuality. This, however, was not new: it reflected the common "Soviet-Orthodox" style of life.[262] Soviet Germans-Baptists admitted that the first tradition they lost when they settled in Russia was the well-known German punctuality.[263] One of the "classical" announcements in Russian Baptist congregations was: "The assembly of our church members will be tomorrow at 7 o'clock... So everybody should gather by about eight."[264]

Provincial Inquisition], *Nezavisimaya gazeta*, 29 May 1998.

260. For example, N.A. Kolesnikov as a leader of the AUCECB, repeatedly said that young preachers could freely use any parts of his books and sermons without reference to him, "if this is done to the glory of God". – Testimony of N.A. Kolesnikov (Shchuchinsk, Kazakhstan, 1998).

261. There was perhaps a paradox: Calvinists who came to Russia used seat belts, but Russian Baptists, who did not accept the doctrine of absolute predestination, often ignored the belts (as well as other road regulations).

262. See, for instance, B. Achariya, *Politichesky Mentalitet Rossiyan Glazami Inostrannogo Uchenogo* [The Political Mentality of Russians in the Eyes of a Foreign Scientist], *Vestnik Rossiyskogo Universiteta Druzhby Narodov*, no. 1 (1999), pp. 107-11.

263. For instance, testimony of presbyter I.P. Fast (Shchuchinsk, Kazakhstan, 1999).

264. This was in fact very realistic, but gained ground in Soviet Baptist churches as a joke in the 1980s. If there was criticism of members for being asleep, and late for church, there was a popular "biblical reply" (quoted from Ps 127) "He gives His beloved sleep".

In part this attitude also reflected rural life, which was not as clock-defined as was the case in cities. Indeed many Russian Baptists disliked city life. "God founded the countryside, while Satan built the city!" they said, referring to Genesis 4:17, where it is recorded that the first town was built by Cain.[265] At one time most Baptist members were in rural congregations, but by the 1960s the congregations in industrial centres became the dominant Russian Baptist communities.[266] A similar state of affairs also pertained in Russian Orthodox parishes.[267] However, there was still a longing for the simpler, less structured life in the country. Many Russian Baptists walked tens of kilometers, in winter and summer, to visit remote places where Baptist meetings were held or a respected individual lived.[268] For example, B.M. Zdorovets had a "great desire" in his youth to visit God-fearing men, even if they lived a long way away.[269] There is a parallel with the motivation of Russian Orthodox pilgrims to visit "holy places".[270]

In Russian Baptist family life a number of prejudices and superstitions were also evident. Baptist congregations, as well as Russian Orthodox parishes, traditionally condemned birth control, and often proclaimed, in "patriarchal" manner (referring to Gen 1:28), that "God himself commanded people to be fruitful and multiply". Therefore large families were normal for Russian Baptist churches in the period under review. The categorical (and actually superstitious) statement was sometimes made: "If a believing family has less than three children, the spirituality of the parents is open to

---

265. For instance, testimony of Baptist church member, A.K. Sipko (Omsk, Russia, 2008).

266. See, for instance, Savinsky, *Istoriya (1917-1967)*, pp. 114-5.

267. Shkarovsky, *Russkaya Pravoslavnaya Tserkov pri Staline i Khrushcheve*, pp. 89-93, 116-8; Pospielovsky, *Russkaya Pravoslavnaya Tserkov v 20 veke*, pp. 181-2.

268. See, for instance, *Podrazhayte Vere Ikh*, p. 33. Also testimonies of ministers and church members from the former USSR: Ya.A. Grinchenko (INT, Sacramento, California, USA, 2006), A.S. Shevchuk, Ya.S. Shevchuk, V.Ya. Virkh (INT, Los Angeles, California, USA, 2006).

269. Testimony of B.M. Zdorovets (INT, Spokane, Washington, USA, 2006).

270. Cf.: "Love for the monasteries and holy places roused Russian people to the tradition of religious wayfaring and pilgrimage... With a prayer on their lips, they walked patiently from one cloister to another in all seasons of the year". – *Zakon Bozhy*, ed. by S. Slobodskoy, p. 696. "The overwhelming majority of Russian pilgrims belongs to commons..." – *Khristianstvo: Entsiklopedichesky Slovar'*, v. II, p. 280.

question."[271] In such a case, presbyters could ask quite embarrassing questions regarding the intimate relationships of married couples, a custom which also mirrored Russian Orthodox tradition.[272] When there were children, names had to be chosen. In traditional Russian Orthodox families names were not chosen randomly, but in close connection with the date of birth and using the church calendar with its saints' days.[273] This was not done in Russian Baptist families, but there was often a desire for "a sign from above" about a name. The choice of a name in Soviet Baptist families was not infrequently made "with a prayer, by the Gospel".[274] The name was therefore more likely to be a biblical name, and some names which were very strange in Soviet society were chosen, such as Avel' (Abel), Iosif (Joseph), Veniamin (Benjamin), Mark, Eva (Eve) and Ruf' (Ruth). Some reports suggest that a name was found by randomly opening the Bible, although there is no evidence that this was the usual practice.[275] The child was then blessed.[276] There was a terrible fear in some radical Baptist circles (mostly in large families) that if infants died before being blessed in church they would go to hell.[277] This echoes Orthodox thinking about the power of infant baptism.[278]

---

271. I heard this on several occasions. I will not include details for ethical reasons.

272. In Russian Orthodox tradition there was a tendency to ask very embarrassing, "personal" questions during church confession. See, for instance, the theme reviewed in B. Rybakov, *Strigolniki* [The Strigolniks] (M.: Nauka, 1993), pp. 94-7; Father A. Borisov, *Pobelevshie Nivy*, pp. 34-6.

273. See, for instance, *Khristianstvo: Entsiklopedichesky Slovar'*, vol. I, p. 604.

274. For instance, testimony of a minister of the ECB from Kiev, L.E. Kovalenko (INT, Sacramento, California, USA, 2006).

275. For instance, testimony of Baptist church member, G.A. Prokhorova (Odessa, Ukraine, 1995).

276. As discussed in chapter 3.

277. I heard about this belief among some Russian Baptist families, for instance, from presbyter of Omsk Central Baptist church, A.V. Zalesny (Omsk, Russia, 2008), as well as from members of several conservative Slavic Baptist communities (immigrants from the USSR) in Sacramento (California, USA, 2009). However, traditional hymns of the ECB clearly speak about paradise for all children who die young. See *SDP*, nos. 507 and 508 (the section "On burial").

278. The Orthodox source *Mytarstva Prepodobnoy Feodory* (The Spiritual Trials of St. Theodora) asserts that deceased unbaptized infants "do not see God's face". See *Zhitie Prepodobnogo Vasiliya Novogo i Videnie Grigoriya, Uchenika Ego, o Mytarstvakh Prepodobnoy Feodory* [Life of St. Basil the New and the Vision by Gregory, His Disciple, of the Spiritual Trials of St. Theodora] (M.: Tipo-Litografiya I. Efimova, 1893), p. 143.

Although families with children (often several children) were emphasized, single women, whether unmarried or widows, were often the largest
group in Soviet Baptist communities. The way in which "family values"
were addressed in churches was of little relevance to them.[279] Nevertheless,
encouraged to some extent by the single life of the Apostle Paul (1 Cor
7:7-8), they often became the most active and effective members of Baptist
congregations.[280] A traditional Russian saying, "What the eyes fear, the
hands do" ("you never know what you can do till you try"), was adapted
and applied to these dedicated single women. "At our church, what the eyes
fear, the sisters do!"[281]

The situation of Baptist women who were married to husbands who
were atheists or were Orthodox was more complicated. It was common
to speak about the problems of women whose husbands did not let their
wives go to the prayer house.[282] The relationship was compared to the wise
Abigail and the foolish Nabal, or to Esther and the despotic Ahasuerus.[283]
Often the members of a Baptist congregation had in their minds the hard
life of the Baptist woman in this situation. They gained the impression
that it would be dangerous to visit the home since the "terrible" spouse
might beat visitors. However, it was often the case that when presbyters of
a Baptist church did visit these homes they found husbands being ruled by
their wives. As a Baptist minister said, "If that husband is a priest in the
family, then his wife is definitely a high priest."[284]

---

279. See, for instance, L. Andronoviene, *"Svobodnye Ponevole: Odinokie Zhenshchiny v
Khristianskoy Srede"* [Involuntarily Free: Lonely Women in Christian Communities], *Vera
i Zhizn'*, no. 3 (2004), pp. 8-9.

280. For instance, testimonies of: former senior presbyter Ya.A. Grinchenko (INT,
Sacramento, California, USA, 2006), Baptist evangelist from Dushanbe, P.A. Semeryuk
(INT, Sacramento, California, USA, 2006).

281. For instance, testimony of Baptist church member S. Ryzhenko (Petropavlovsk,
Kazakstan, 2001).

282. No doubt there were Baptist women who had real difficulties. But the picture of
the "unbelieving husbands" was a stereotype. For instance, testimony on this theme by
the senior presbyter of the South Kazakhstan Baptist churches, H.A. Gavrilov (Alma-Ata,
Kazakhstan, 1999).

283. See 1 Kings 25, Esth. 4:11-16 and references among Soviet Baptists to godly women
of the Bible.

284. Testimony of the Senior Presbyter of Baptist churches of Kazakhstan, F.G. Tissen
(Saran, Kazakhstan, 1999).

Although single women gave so much to the churches, and although married women carried many responsibilities, their role in leadership in the Baptist congregations was limited. As a rule, women did not preach during Baptist church services. As far back as the 70th canon of the Sixth Ecumenical Council there was an edict, "Women are not permitted to speak at the time of the Divine Liturgy; but, according to the words of Paul the Apostle, let them be silent."[285] Russian Baptists did not quote this Orthodox source, but their practice was in line with it. What they did use to justify their policy was the famous statement of the Apostle Paul, quoted by the Orthodox and other Christian traditions, "let your women keep silence in the churches" (1 Cor 14:34).[286] *Bratsky Vestnik* formulated this idea more delicately, "Women prevail in the Union of Evangelical Christians-Baptists... That is natural enough, since from the beginning of Christianity it is known how much a woman's heart is able to love Jesus Christ. At the same time, men, dedicating their lives to Christ... [become] practiced preachers."[287] However, in communities where there was lack of ministers (for example, in rural areas), the "elder brothers" who had wider oversight for these communities overcame their prejudices and resorted to other texts, about "daughters who prophesy" (Acts 21:9), thus concluding that "on biblical grounds" it was permissible to allow sisters to preach publicly,[288] and even to be leaders in their congregations.[289] This kind of female leadership was present in Russian Orthodox convents but was never possible in Russian Orthodox parishes.[290]

---

285. *Pravila Pravoslavnoy Tserkvi*, vol. I, p. 559.

286. For instance, testimony of former senior presbyter of Krasnodar Territory, Ya.A. Grinchenko (INT, Sacramento, California, USA, 2006).

287. *"40-letie Velikogo Oktyabrya i Evangel'skie Khristiane-Baptisty"* [The 40th Anniversary of the Great October Revolution and Evangelical Christians-Baptists] (editorial article), *BV*, no. 6 (1957), IEDE-2.

288. For instance, testimony of Baptist church members from Donetsk Region, V.Ya. Sedykh, E.I. Sedykh and A.I. Musiets (INT, Sacramento, California, USA, 2006).

289. See, for instance: "From the Life of the Local Churches" (editorial article), *BV*, no. 3 (1986), p. 75; V. Kadaeva, *"Uchastie Sester v Zhizni i Sluzhenii Tserkvey"* [The Participation of Sisters in the Life and Ministry of Churches], *BV*, no. 1 (1988), pp. 71-2.

290. A comparison might be made between a Russian Orthodox convent headed by the Mother Superior (hegumene) and an all-female Russian Baptist congregation.

Conclusion

This chapter has offered an analysis of beliefs and behavior found in Russian Baptist communities. Although their emphasis was on the Bible, the study of the Bible was not undertaken in a systematic way. There was much more interest in the connection between the Bible and the imaginative world of Russian Baptists, a world expressed in poetry and in religious language known within the community. It has been argued in this chapter that the themes in the poetry reinforce theological and spiritual themes already examined in earlier chapters. In significant ways, aspects of Baptist spirituality parallel Orthodox experience. There were also many regulations and customs which were affirmed as biblical and evangelical by Baptists, for example regarding fasting, alms-giving and modes of dress, which were remarkably similar to Orthodox practices. Both Russian Baptists and the Orthodox were in a context from the 1960s to the 1980s of suffering for their faith, and for both of them there was an emphasis on "tears" and on martyrdom – even to the extent of justifying self-inflicted death. At the same time as being serious and cautious in some of their spiritual expressions, the Baptist communities were places where many dreams, visions and miraculous healings were claimed to have taken place. As with the Orthodox, Baptist leaders urged care in this area, but grass-roots spirituality was full of the "supernatural". In their commitment to their beliefs and ways of behaving, Russian Baptists were often strongly prejudiced against other ways of looking at the world. Family life was perceived from a certain perspective, with customs that had similarities with the Orthodox *Domostroy*.[291] In all these areas, the claim that life was governed solely by the Bible is a dubious one: the shape of Baptist belief and behavior bore many similarities to Orthodox tradition.

---

291. A famous Russian medieval book on Orthodox rules for family life.

CHAPTER 8

Popular Piety: An Alternative Culture

The way in which Russian Baptists operated in the later Soviet period means that in their community life they created an alternative culture. To some extent this was true from the beginning of the Baptist and evangelical movements in Russia in the nineteenth century. However, in the 1960s the specific features of the context – the Soviet policy on religion in particular – contributed to the Russian Baptist alternative culture being re-shaped. Important elements of theology and practice that were evident in the period have already been examined. This chapter probes more deeply into some of the popular piety that characterized the Russian Baptists from the 1960s to the 1980s. There were stories that sustained them and helped them, under pressure, to make their identity stronger. This process was also assisted by the moral markers which were established in their communities. With these markers in place, Russian Baptists were able to uphold their faith within schools, colleges and workplaces. The authorities attempted to suppress the Baptist (and wider Christian) witness, and this chapter examines how Baptists portrayed that interaction. There is also an analysis of popular thinking about the sacraments and about a "promised land". In looking at all of these areas, the relationship with Russian Orthodoxy will be considered in each case.

Stories that sustained the Community

As they looked for stories to sustain them, Soviet Baptists not infrequently turned to the works of Leo Tolstoy. He was regarded as one of the most authoritative of writers by many in the Baptist community.[1] His uneasy relationship with Russian Orthodoxy meant that his writings appealed to some educated Soviet Baptists. They were able, when it suited them, to quote aspects of the critique he offered of the Orthodox Church hierarchy. For example, a favorite illustration used in Russian Baptist preaching was the story by L.N. Tolstoy, *Three Hermits* (1886),[2] in which the piety of ordinary Russian Orthodox monks was contrasted with the ruling bishop's haughtiness. The latter expressed his dissatisfaction at the simple praying (which he pointed out was canonically wrong) of three elderly hermits, who lived on a small northern island. The bishop taught them a correct, formal prayer and then sailed away on a boat with a sense that he had done his duty. However the hermits, running on top of the water, caught up with the boat and said to the bishop, "We have forgotten your teaching!.. Please teach us again!" The bishop, realizing that they could "walk on water", replied: "Your own prayers will reach the Lord, men of God. It is not for me to teach you. Pray for us, sinners!" The lesson that Baptist preachers drew from this story – as they once again implicitly identified with Orthodox monks – was that even the simplest prayers and "irregular" (from the point of view of the official church) ways of praying to God, if they came from the heart, were more pleasing to God than the most formally "correct" ("hierarchically-authorized" or canonical Orthodox) prayers.[3]

One of the respected authors among Russian Baptists, I.V. Podberezsky, wrote that, "Leo Tolstoy once noticed that as soon as a Russian man (*muzhik*) begins to seek God seriously, the first thing he does is leave Orthodoxy.

---

1. See, for instance, Prokhanov, *In the Cauldron of Russia*, pp. 59,78-81. Also testimonies of the well-known minister of the CCECB from Rostov Region, A.I. Kolomiytsev (INT, Vancouver, Washington, USA, 2006), a Baptist minister from Odessa, Ya.D. Diordienko (INT, Sacramento, California, USA, 2006).

2. See, for instance, L.N. Tolstoy, *Sobranie Sochineniy* [Collected Works], 22 vols. (M.: Khudozhestvennaya literatura, 1982), vol. X, pp. 342-7.

3. For instance, the testimony of a well-known Baptist evangelist from Dushanbe, P.A. Semeryuk (INT, Sacramento, California, USA, 2006). The theme of the limited power of a bishop's prayers in comparison with the unskilful but living prayers of some ordinary people occurs repeatedly in Russian Christian literature. See, for instance, N.S. Leskov's *The Tale of the God-favored Woodcutter* (1890). Cf. Archpriest V. Guriev, *Prolog v Poucheniyakh*, p. 25.

He goes to Stundism, to the *Khlysty*, anywhere, as long as he leaves it."[4] The point to observe is not whether this judgment is true or not – it can certainly be challenged – but rather to note that even when Russians left Orthodoxy (as happened with Tolstoy himself[5]) it was still the case that Orthodoxy remained a pervasive influence on them, as Orthodox faith and practice touched all areas of traditional Russian life. That was shown clearly, for example, in the stories told by Tolstoy about righteous individuals to be found among the ordinary Orthodox population. Stylistically, the stories belonged to hagiography; they were instructive and were designed to have an appeal to even the most conservative Russian Orthodox people. Such popular stories by Tolstoy as, for instance, *Alesha Gorshok* (Alyosha the Pot), about Alyosha, a young village boy nicknamed "the Pot" because he broke a pot, *Svechka* (The Candle), *Dva Starika* (Two Old Men), *Chem Lyudi Zhivy* (What Men Live By) not only vividly described Russian life but were also seen by many well-known Russian authors as advocating the "Orthodox spirit".[6] For Russian Baptists, Tolstoy's "spirit" was one with which they could identify.

There were also stories (with several variations) recounted among Russian Baptists in the 1950s to the 1980s which related to figures in Russian evangelical and Baptist history. Thus Ivan Ryaboshapka, the famous peasant leader of the Russian evangelical movement in the second half of the nineteenth century, was allegedly once invited for a discourse on matters of faith in the presence of the Russian Tsar. A Russian Orthodox

---

4. I. Podberezsky, *Byt' Protestantom v Rossii* [To be a Protestant in Russia] (M.: Blagovestnik, 1996), p. 99.

5. Among many works on the excommunication of Leo Tolstoy and his attitude to this event, I would single out the following book: Archbishop Ioann (Shakhovskoy), *K Istorii Russkoy Intelligentsii, Revolyutsiya Tolstogo* [History of the Russian Intelligentsia, Tolstoy's Revolution] (M.: Lepta, 2003).

6. See, for instance: N.S. Leskov, *"Luchshy Bogomolets"* [The Best Devout Person], in N. Leskov, *Sobranie Sochineniy* [Collected Works], 11 vols. (M.: Gosizdat Khudozhestvennoy Literatury, 1958), vol. XI, pp. 100-12; N.S. Leskov, *"Graf L.N. Tolstoy i F.M. Dostoevsky kak Eresiarkhi"* [Count L.N. Tolstoy and F.M. Dostoevsky as Heresiarches], in Leskov, *Zerkalo Zhizni*, pp. 421-38; V. Nazarov, *"Metafory Neponimaniya: L.N. Tolstoy i Russkaya Tserkov' v Sovremennom Mire"* [Metaphors of Incomprehension: L.N. Tolstoy and the Russian Church in the Modern World], *Voprosy Filosofii*, no. 8 (1991), pp. 155-6; A. Tarasov, *Chto Est' Istina? Pravedniki L'va Tolstogo* [What is Truth? The Righteous Men of Leo Tolstoy] (M.: Yazyki Slavyaskoy Kul'tury, 2001).

leader – according to one version of the story, the Patriarch of All Russia – was supposedly also present.[7] When Ryaboshapka heard the latter being called *Vladyko* (Sovereign), he announced boldly that he knew only the Sovereign of heaven (God) and the ruler of this world (Satan), and he asked what kind of sovereign, heavenly or demonic, was in view. The Patriarch was very embarrassed and struggled to reply.[8] According to one account he fell dead.[9] There are evident absurdities in this legend. A provincial peasant preacher would not have been invited into the presence of the Tsar. Also, Ryaboshapka died long before 1917, when the patriarchate in Russia was restored.[10] However, the legend probably reflects actual discussions that early Russian Stundists-Baptists had with Orthodox clergy.[11] Despite the outwardly "anti-Orthodox" (to be more precise – anti-clerical) orientation of the story, it has Orthodox echoes. A holy man or woman, fearless in the face of the "powers that be", speaks the "truth of God", and powerful opponents become impotent. Their mouths are shut.[12] They might even be severely punished by God. As noted previously, in Eastern Christian tradition the death of Arius coincided with fearless witness and fervent prayer by a saint.[13] Popular legends also surrounded the martyr St. Catherine, famous for her wisdom in discussions with philosophers.[14]

---

7. See Pushkov, *Ne smushchyaysya!* <http://rusbaptist.stunda.org/dop/smu1.htm> accessed 15 May 2011.

8. Testimony of Baptist church members from Essentuki, S.N. Savinsky and L.V. Savinskaya (INT, Salt Lake City, Utah, USA, 2006). See also N. Khrapov, *Schast'e Poteryannoy Zhizni* [The Happiness of a Lost Life], 3 vols. (M.: Protestant, 1990), vol. I, pp. 103-5.

9. For instance, testimony of Baptist presbyter V.N. Khot'ko (Petropavlovsk, Kazakhstan, 1999). Cf. Khrapov, *Schast'e Poteryannoy Zhizni*, vol. I, pp. 103-5.

10. See *Istoriya Evangel'skikh Khristian-Baptistov v SSSR*, p. 546.

11. See, for instance, G. Mazaev, *Vospominaniya* [Memories] (Korntal: Svet na Vostoke, 1992), pp. 35-66; V. Popov, *Stopy Blagovestnika* [The Feet of the Evangelist] (M.: Blagovestnik, 1996), pp. 60-66.

12. Ps 31:18, for instance, was quoted: "Let the lying lips be put to silence".

13. St. Alexander of Constantinople was named. See, for instance: *Uchilishche Blagochestiya*, pp. 85-6; G. Orlov, *Tserkov' Khristova: Rasskazy iz Istorii Khristianskoy Tserkvi* [The Church of Christ: Stories from Church History], <http://ftp.kelia.ru/orlov/Main.htm> accessed 6 November 2009.

14. See, for instance, Archpriest V. Guriev, *Prolog v Poucheniyakh*, p. 213.

There is also a "plausible legend" (as Russian Baptist historian, S.N. Savinsky, puts it)[15] about Ryaboshapka visiting Dey Mazaev, one of early leaders of the Russian Baptist Union. Mazaev, according to the story, had heard a great deal about the exceptional gifts that Ryaboshapka had in preaching, and about his work in the South of Russia. On this basis, Mazaev sent an invitation to Ryaboshapka to visit an estate in the North Caucasus which Mazaev (a very wealthy farmer) owned. Many people gathered at Mazaev's house the night before the date that Ryaboshapka was due to arrive. None of them knew him by sight. Ryaboshapka arrived early, knocked at the door, and was met by a domestic servant who mistook him for an ordinary traveler because of his peasant clothes. The servant invited him to stay overnight in the house and he was fed and put to bed without anyone paying much attention to him. Only the next day, when a cook noticed that the wanderer was reading his large Bible for a long time, did the household become aware that the guest was Ryaboshapka. The confused Mazaev asked Ryaboshapka why he had not introduced himself and the latter replied that he wanted to know how ordinary wanderers would be received at this house.[16] This story, by both its plot and its spirit, is imbued with Eastern Christian ideas and with some changes of details could be a Russian Orthodox story about "the Fathers" (*Paterikon*). A typical example from Orthodox tradition would be St. Sergius of Radonezh, who was sometimes unrecognized by visitors to the cloister because of his modest attire and simple labor.[17]

Among other narratives recounted by Soviet Baptists were stories related to Lenin and Stalin, notably a supposed meeting of the leader of the Evangelical Christian Union, I.S. Prokhanov, with Lenin, during which the latter apparently expressed his support for Russian evangelicals (or "sectarianism").[18] However, Prokhanov himself, in his book *In the*

---

15. *Ryaboshapka* (typescript), from personal files of Russian Baptist historian S.N. Savinsky (Salt Lake City, Utah, USA, 2006).

16. Ibid.

17. See, for instance, *Uchilishche Blagochestiya*, pp. 110-2; *Zhitie prepodobnogo Sergiya Radonezhskogo*, pp. 64-7.

18. Testimonies of Baptist church members: V.V. Kitsen and N.I. Kitsen from Chernovtsy (INT, Fresno, California, USA, 2006), S.N. Savinsky and L.V. Savinskaya from Essentuki (INT, Salt Lake City, Utah, USA, 2006), presbyter V.N. Khot'ko (Petropavlovsk,

Cauldron of Russia, mentioned only a telegram he sent to Lenin. Prokhanov received no answer from the Bolshevik leader, but only from an assistant, V.D. Bonch-Bruevich. Indeed Prokhanov was sceptical about any idea that Lenin was sympathetic to believers.[19] Despite the complete absence of evidence about a meeting of Prokhanov with Lenin (and despite the "anti-Lenin" thinking of some Baptists, already noted), Soviet Baptists took hold of such stories as they were passed down. In the case of this particular story, there is an element in it of the traditional Russian belief in the good *Tsar-batyushka* (King-father) who takes care of the common people, and whose servants, not him, are "malicious".[20] Neither the Orthodox people nor Russian Baptists could fully avoid such illusions. One story relating to Stalin was that at the beginning of the Great Patriotic War (1941-45) Stalin sought help from the Pope for the war with Fascism and the Pope imposed a condition, which was that all churches in the USSR (including Baptist churches) should be opened. Stalin allowed this to take place.[21] Linked with this, is the story that the countries of the West made it a condition for opening their second front in Europe during WWII that there should be freedom for Evangelical Christians-Baptists in the USSR.[22] Some Orthodox authors similarly see a connection between the second front and the restoration of Orthodoxy.[23] But there is no firm evidence that Stalin changed his attitude to religion in Russia for the sake of receiving help from the Allies. It is more likely that he wanted to use the rich

---

Kazakhstan, 2000).

19. See Prokhanov, *In the Cauldron of Russia*, pp. 176-7.

20. These views were aphoristically expressed, for instance, in the well-known fable *Miron* by I.A. Krylov (1830). See, for instance, I. Krylov, *Basni* [Fables] (M.: Khudozhestvennaya Literatura, 1984), pp. 245-6.

21. This is a widely-believed legend among the "pure" Soviet Baptists. For instance, testimonies of church members from Donetsk Region, V.Ya. Sedykh, E.I. Sedykh, and A.I. Musiets (INT, Sacramento, California, USA, 2006). However, Stalin's scepticism about the Vatican is also well known: "The Pope! How many divisions has he got?" See, for example, W. Churchill's memoirs *The Second World War*, 6 vols. (Boston: Houghton Mifflin, 1975), vol. I, p. 135 ff.

22. This is another enduring legend of Russian Baptists. This was mentioned, for instance, by a presbyter from Alma-Ata, A.T. Evstratenko (INT, San Diego, California, USA, 2006), and by Baptist historian S.N. Savinsky (see Savinsky, *Istoriya (1917-1967)*, p. 150).

23. See, for instance, Pospielovsky, *Russkaya Pravoslavnaya Tserkov v 20 veke*, pp. 192-3. This author also refers to some other Orthodox sources on the theme.

historical experience of the church and the energy of patriotic Christians in the USSR (first of all the Orthodox, but Baptists too) to resist the German invasion.[24] Nonetheless, Orthodox and Baptist legends persisted.

Moral markers

As Russian Baptists marked out their identity, they did so not only by using "historical" narratives to sustain them, but also by the use of moral markers. The most distinctive "Baptist commandments", which quite often made a significant impression (positive and negative) on ordinary Soviet citizens, were the following: among Baptists there should be no drinking of alcohol, no smoking, no use of foul language, no adultery, no stealing and no telling of lies. On the issue of drinking alcohol, even small quantities were forbidden. The following typical statement of popular piety appeared in a traditional Russian Baptist poem and was often quoted from there: "A spoonful of wine for a good appetite caused much trouble for brother Titus."[25] It was said that the attitude of Soviet Baptists to alcohol was part of the reason they were persecuted. Stories were told about Soviet police officers who happened to let out the "secret": "If you drank vodka instead of praying, nobody would disturb you."[26] This made the issue a clearly "spiritual" one. However, there were Baptists who were probably not fully convinced about the policy. In the wine-producing Republics and regions of the USSR (for example Moldavia and Georgia) some "apocryphal" tales could be heard which suggested that the rules were not always implemented. For example,

---

24. See, for instance, Shkarovsky, *Russkaya Pravoslavnaya Tserkov pri Staline i Khrushcheve*, pp. 195-216; Archpriest V. Tsypin, *"Russkaya Pravoslavnaya Tserkov' v Velikuyu Otechestvennuyu Voynu"* [The Russian Orthodox Church in the Great Patriotic War], *ZhMP*, no. 5 (2005), pp. 66-71; *Istoriya Evangel'skikh Khristian-Baptistov v SSSR*, pp. 228-32.

25. The puzzling allusion to Titus might be related to an inaccurate reading of 1 Tim. 5:23.

26. For instance: "Otvet na Antireligioznuyu Stat'yu 'Ne Bud'te Trupom Sredi Zhivykh'" [Answer to the Antireligious Article 'Do not be Dead among the Living'] [1962], ARSECB, F. 1, op. 28d, d. 61, l. 2. Also testimonies of church members of ECB from Syzran Ya.S. Shevchuk, A.S. Shevchuk, V.Ya. Virkh (INT, Los Angeles, California, USA, 2006).

two Baptists met in a shop selling liquor and pretended not to recognize each other. In a variant story, they met in the doorway of the shop and one said, "There is no bread here". The other replied, "I know".[27] Both presumably knew the real reason they were in the shop.

The strict abstinence taught among Russian Baptists can be paralleled in some measure in Russian Orthodox monastic life.[28] However, there was not the same opposition to alcohol in Orthodoxy as there was among Baptists, and given the prevailing climate in Russia it was difficult for some younger Russian Baptists to hold to the strict line taken by their pastors and parents. On the issue of tobacco smoking, too, Russian Baptists were much stricter than was the case in popular Orthodox thinking. Sometimes Baptists even considered tobacco smoking to be "censing" or "burning incense" to the devil.[29] During discussions with smokers, Baptists often asked their favorite question: is it permissible to smoke cigarettes in God's temple? The Orthodox influence meant that the answer was a categorical "no" (no-one can smoke in church), and Baptists, referring to the Apostle Paul, then declared that the human body is a temple of God (of the Holy Spirit), and therefore smoking is not allowed.[30] When Baptists who had been brought up under strict teaching about their conduct failed to live up to the standards in these areas – drunkenness was a particular problem – there was acute embarrassment. Even worse, some of those converted to evangelical Christianity directly from unbelieving backgrounds at times seemed to fare better in resisting a "worldly life" than those from Baptist families. The response given to this problem was that the former knew sin

27. For instance, testimonies (with negative assessment of this legend): Baptist evangelist from Dushanbe P.A. Semeryuk (INT, Sacramento, California, USA, 2006), Baptist minister from Donetsk Region V.A. Sheremet (Sacramento, California, USA, 2009).

28. See, for instance: St. Nilus of Sora, *Ustav o Skitskoy Zhizni* [The Rule of Scete Life] (Yekaterinburg: Novo-Tikhvinsky Zhensky Monastyr', 2002); *Monasheskaya Zhizn'* [Monastic Life] (Svyato-Uspensky Pskovo-Pechersky monastyr', 1994); M. Kudryavtsev, *Istoriya Pravoslavnogo Monashestva* [History of the Orthodox Monasticism] (M.: Krutitskoe patriarshee podvor'e, 1999).

29. For example, testimony of Baptist presbyter V.N. Khot'ko (Petropavlovsk, Kazakhstan, 2000). As noted previously, the Russian word *kurenie* means both "incense" and "tobacco smoking".

30. See, for instance, [Anon], *"Vred Kureniya"* [Hazards of Smoking], *BV*, no. 5 (1946), IEDE-2. Also testimony of minister of ECB from Kiev, L.E. Kovalenko (INT, Sacramento, California, USA, 2006).

from experience and did not want to revert to it, while the latter were "attracted by unknown feelings".[31] From another perspective, the strictness of some rules did not mirror surrounding Orthodox life and perhaps because of that these rules were sometimes found to be unworkable.

Many incidents narrated in Baptist communities' legends had to do with the "purity" of Baptists. This was seen as a notable element in their alternative culture. On the question of pure speech, obscenities were termed a "prayer to Satan".[32] In one popular report, Soviet police officers wanted to detain a Baptist preacher and tried to do so the day after a Baptist wedding, but in the twilight they could not identify him immediately and instead caught an unbeliever who immediately started to use foul language. The police officer exclaimed disappointedly: "Release him! This is one of 'our' [Soviet] men. Baptists are not foul-mouthed."[33]

The theme of marital fidelity and the chastity of members of Baptist communities was also the subject of many stories. For example, the KGB allegedly sent women of easy virtue to known Baptist ministers to seduce and discredit them. In the vast majority of these tales, as they were told, the plans failed, but in reality moral lapses sometimes took place.[34] Acknowledgement of the possibility of failure led to other rules. Presbyters of Baptist churches, unless accompanied by their wives (or other ministers), were not allowed to visit any young unmarried women, even if these women were reckoned to be the most spiritual church members.[35] Other rules, for members as well as ministers, went further. In many communities

31. For instance, testimonies of Slavic Baptist presbyters V. Jerke and E. Prannik (Charlotte, North Carolina, USA, 2009).

32. For instance, testimony of Baptist evangelist from Dushanbe, P.A. Semeryuk (INT, Sacramento, California, USA, 2006).

33. Testimony of Baptist church members from Tashkent, V.T. Vasiliev and R.F. Vasilieva (INT, Sacramento, California, USA, 2006).

34. For instance, testimonies of Baptist presbyter from Alma-Ata A.T. Evstratenko and V.N. Evstratenko (INT, San Diego, California, USA, 2006), P.A. Semeryuk (INT, Sacramento, California, USA, 2006), B.M. Zdorovets (INT, Spokane, Washington, USA, 2006).

35. For instance, testimonies of Baptist presbyters I.P. Fast (Shchuchinsk, Kazakhstan, 1999) and V.N. Khot'ko (Petropavlovsk, Kazakhstan, 2000).

it was stated that until a couple were married they should not kiss each other, or perhaps should not even hold hands.[36]

While these moral markers were valued by Baptist leaders, and in some instances were admired by those outside the community, in many cases they were seen as extremely strange by the wider Russian population. The prohibition regarding stealing was an example of a rule that might have been admired in theory, but in practice was often despised. In one *kolkhoz* (collective farm), all the people stole grain, but a Baptist, who worked there did not do so, and this enraged the majority of the people around him. They threatened to drive him out of the collective and so he began to drag home heavy bags, as if taking home grain. Suddenly there was an inspection of the *kolkhoz*, and some workers gave evidence, with great pleasure, that they had seen the Baptist stealing. However, when the officers came to conduct a search of the believer's home, they found out that he had not carried home grain in his sacks, but some (useless) earth.[37] Although the use of "pious" methods to mislead others was not encouraged, stories abounded about how this method worked. There was an ancient saying, "Pious fraud is equal to truth".[38]

One story was of a young Stundist who was being pursued by policemen (before the Bolshevik Revolution) apparently ran past an elder in the church who was sitting in front of his house, and as the police pursued the fugitive they asked the elder what direction the Stundist had taken. The elder immediately rose to his feet and replied: "All the time I have been *standing* here, nobody has run by!"[39] In 1961 a Baptist who was about

---

36. For instance, testimonies of: P.A. Semeryuk (INT, Sacramento, California, USA, 2006), B.M. Zdorovets (INT, Spokane, Washington, USA, 2006).

37. For instance, testimony of Baptist church member from Omsk, P.K. Sedletsky (Omsk, Russia, 2010). See also the article *"Propoved' s Polichnym"* [Preaching... Bang to Rights], *SV*, no. 3 (2001), pp. 38-40.

38. *Tsarstvennoe Slovo* [The Royal Word], ed. by E. Okuntsova (M.: RIPOL klassik, 2009), p. 376. Incidents of holy fraud sometimes occur in *Lives of Saints* and *Prolog* [The Church Calendar]. See the life stories of St. Ephraem the Syrian – *ZhSDR*, vol. V, pp. 898-9; Sts. John, Sergius, and Patricius – Ibid., vol. VII, pp. 404-6; Archpriest V. Guriev, *Prolog v Poucheniyakh*, p. 659.

39. Testimony of Baptist presbyter V.N. Khot'ko (Petropavlovsk, Kazakhstan, 2000). A similar story from the 1960s was told by a minister of the CCECB from Rostov Region A.I. Kolomiytsev (Vancouver, Washington, USA, 2006). See also famous story by N.A. Vodnevsky "White Lie?" – N. Vodnevsky, *Litsom k Svety* [Face Turned to the Light] (M.:

to board a train and who was carrying a large quantity of paper for an underground Christian press saw a policeman on the platform. To avoid dangerous inquiries, he immediately asked the policeman if he would look after the papers while he found a man to assist him to carry them, explaining that he was moving the papers on the instructions of the *Komsomol* organization. And the ("unrighteous") policeman guarded them, while the ("holy") Baptist found an assistant.[40]

The Russian expression *lozh' vo spasenie* (pious fraud), probably originated in the Church Slavonic translation, *"Lozh' kon' vo spasenie..."*, of texts such as Psalm 33:17a. In Orthodoxy there was a spectrum of opinion on this subject.[41] In practice Baptists often followed the Orthodox in relishing the triumphs of the godly over the godless, but the usual Baptist teaching was that a believing person should not deceive anyone (including enemies) under any circumstances, even when facing death. The advice regarding what to do if the honest answer of a Christian to an interrogator's question might endanger the life of another person was that such a question should be answered by silence.[42] Many stories about Baptist encounters with state interrogators were calculated to promote the idea of the moral superiority of Christianity over Communism. Boobbyer speaks of the centrality of "moral and spiritual survival" for dissidents under interrogation.[43] Some Baptists emphasized the "philosophical poverty" of atheism,

---

Protestant, 1993), pp. 348-51.

40. Testimony of B.M. Zdorovets (INT, Spokane, Washington, USA, 2006). The couriers who delivered the books and periodicals of the CCECB throughout the country spoke about delivering the literature "at all costs" for the "revolutionary work" to continue. – Testimony of Baptist church members from Donetsk Region, L.Ya. Sokolovsky and E.Ya. Sokolovskaya (INT, San Diego, California, USA, 2006).

41. See, for instance, a "round table" of Orthodox priests. – "Byvaet li Lozh' vo Spasenie? Otvechayut Svyashchennosluzhiteli" [Does Pious Fraud Exist? The Clergy Answer], *Zhurnal "Foma"*, no. 2 (2008). See also: *"Slovo Svyateyshego Patriarkha Kirilla"* [Sermon of His Holiness the Patriarch Kirill], 17 Feb. 2010, The Russian Orthodox Church (the official website of the Moscow Patriarchate), <http://www.patriarchia.ru/db/text/1092502.html> accessed 9 December 2010.

42. For instance, testimonies of Baptist presbyters from North Kazakhstan L.V. Lauer and I.P. Fast. (Shchuchinsk, Kazakhstan, 1998).

43. P. Boobbyer, "Religious Experiences of the Soviet Dissidents", *Religion, State & Society*, Vol. 27, Nos. 3/4 (1999), p. 379. For more on moral aspects of resistance to the Communist regime in the USSR, see P. Boobbyer, *Conscience, Dissent and Reform in Soviet Russia* (Abingdon, UK: Routledge, 2005).

a theme which was typically "Orthodox".[44] Most attempts by Communists in the USSR to "re-educate" Christians as atheists ended in failure.[45] Even when Baptists lapsed from active Christian commitment, they very rarely became Communists. On the other hand, there were many reports in Baptist circles about the conversion of members of the Communist Party to Baptist beliefs.[46] One newly converted former Communist said: "When, in the past, I visited an unfamiliar town, I could not even imagine going to a house to ask where Communists live or to say to them, 'Dear comrades, please let me in to spend the night. I am a member of the Communist party, too!' I would be considered mentally ill. But now I have real brothers and sisters in almost every town in the country and I can expect their hospitality, and they mine."[47] A sense of the moral and spiritual superiority of Baptists, over Communists (but also often over Orthodox Christians), helped them to sustain their alternative culture.

Sacraments and superstitions

Russian Baptist communities, like Russian Orthodox communities, were also sustained through the sacraments. The Russian Baptist approach to the sacraments was examined in chapter 4. However, at the level of popular piety more features can be identified, some of which suggest superstitions.

---

44. See, for instance: I. Il'in, "Muchenichestvo: Tserkov' v Sovetskom Soyuze" [Martyrdom: the Church in the Soviet Union] [1937], in I. Il'in, *Sobranie Sochineniy* [Collected Works], 10 vols. (M.: Russkaya Kniga, 1998), vol. VII, pp. 223-320; N. Berdyaev, *The Origin of Russian Communism* (Ann Arbor, MI: The University of Michigan Press, 2004), pp. 158-88; Archbishop Ioann (Shakhovskoy), *Vremya Very* [The Age of Faith] (N.Y.: Izd-vo im. Chekhova, 1954), pp. 67-71; Archbishop Ioann (Shakhovskoy), *Moskovsky Razgovor o Bessmertii* [Moscow Conversation about Immortality] (N.Y.: Ichthys, 1972), pp. 139-42.

45. See, for instance: Sawatsky, *Soviet Evangelicals Since World War II*, pp. 131-53; Shkarovsky, *Russkaya Pravoslavnaya Tserkov pri Staline i Khrushcheve*, pp. 359-93.

46. See, for instance: C. de Grunwald, *The Churches and the Soviet Union* (New York: The Macmillan Company, 1962), p. 169; Nikolskaya, *Russky Protestantizm i Gosudarstvennaya Vlast' v 1905-1991 Godakh*, pp. 168-70. Also testimonies of Baptist ministers and church members: M.P. Zakharov from Rostov, P.A. Semeryuk from Dushanbe (INT, Sacramento, California, USA, 2006), V.E. Sagan from Petropavlovsk (INT, Minneapolis, Minnesota, USA, 2006).

47. See Prokhorov, "The State and the Baptist Churches in the USSR", p. 48.

After someone was baptized and joined a Baptist community, participating in the Lord's Supper became possible for them. This involved drinking from a common Cup, and debates took place about the problem of "social hygiene". In Baptist communities elsewhere, for example in England, this problem was solved by the introduction of individual cups.[48] But in Russia, as in much of Eastern Europe, the opposite view was taken by Baptist leaders. This kind of statement was often made: "If someone is squeamish about receiving communion with his or her brothers and sisters in Christ from one Cup, that person is sinning. The Holy Scripture teaches us – 'drink all of it'."[49] In some cases, the next step was adopting the rather superstitious idea that someone who seeks to receive Communion last has greater blessing. By that time the Cup was seen as "most-pure" because of being touched by the lips of many believers (though wiped from time to time by white napkins) and was specially blessed by God. A text referred to, without any interest in its context, was "the last shall be first and the first shall be last" – Luke. 13:30.[50] There are suggestions in Russian Orthodox circles of a similar attitude to the sequence in which lay people drink from the Cup.[51]

One notable difference between the participation of Baptist presbyters in the Lord's Supper and the practice among Orthodox priests was that Baptist ministers traditionally participated in the Lord's Supper last, i.e. after all the church members, whereas Orthodox priests communed first, before their flock.[52] For some Baptist members, there was the temptation to try to commune after the ministers had done so, and so, some believed, to maximize blessing. There is a report about a large Baptist congregation where it was not easy to keep order during the Lord's Supper. One church

---

48. See I.M. Randall, *English Baptists of the 20th Century* (Didcot: Baptist Historical Society, 2005), pp. 57-8.

49. Matt 26:27. This opinion was traditional among Baptist communities in Central Asia. I remember some of the strictest elders even disapproving of wiping lips dry with a handkerchief after communion.

50. For example, the testimony (with a critical appraisal of it) of Baptist presbyter V.N. Khot'ko (Petropavlovsk, Kazakhstan, 1999).

51. See *Okolotserkovnye Sueveriya*, <http://kyivbratstvo.narod.ru/news/archive/2005_07_01_index.html>

52. On the order of the Orthodox Communion see, for instance: Dobuzhinsky, ed., *Zakon Bozhy*, vol. II, pp. 206-8; Men', *Tainstvo, Slovo i Obraz*, p. 67.

member came several times to the presbyters after the service to say that the Cup had passed by, and so this person was able (until it became clear what was happening) to commune *after* the ministers.[53] Another example of popular belief about the power of the bread and wine is seen in the case of an elderly Baptist woman, NN from Omsk. One Sunday, towards the end of the 1980s, at the time of celebration of the Lord's Supper in her church, she noticed that a crumb of the Eucharistic bread had accidentally fallen to the floor. The presbyter, who had not seen this happen, had pressed the crumb under his shoe. This Baptist member picked up the "mutilated crumb", which emphasized to her the "broken body" of Christ, and added it to a piece of clean bread received from the hands of the presbyter. She ate with faith and prayer and, according to her, was almost immediately cured of a long-standing disease.[54]

Among many similar, very typical reports about the attitude to the consecrated bread and wine, there is one from a rural Baptist church in North Kazakhstan which illustrates a clash of cultures. At the end of the 1980s some Soviet Baptists began to use synthesizers in church worship. This rural congregation received an electronic musical instrument as a gift from abroad. Church elders disliked the synthesizer (because it was "unnatural" music), but their presbyter, referring to the experience of European Baptists, said that the synthesizer is acceptable for praising God. Soon, however, at the time of celebration of the Lord's Supper, this presbyter inadvertently spilt a few drops from the Cup on to the synthesizer. It stopped working and could not be repaired. "That is how the Lord settled the matter", said the elders with satisfaction.[55] This highly sacramental view of the Lord's Supper, tinged as it was by superstition, parallels the peculiarities of Orthodox notions of piety and, at least partly, Orthodox ideas about the mystical nature and the mysterious power of the sacraments, particularly in respect of the Eucharist and its spiritual efficacy.

---

53. Testimony of Baptist evangelist from Dushanbe, P.A. Semeryuk (INT, Sacramento, California, USA, 2006).

54. This report was given to me first hand on condition of anonymity (Omsk, Russia, 2007).

55. Testimony of Baptist presbyter V.N. Khot'ko (Petropavlovsk, Kazakhstan, 2001).

The argument was presented in chapter 4 that ordination to ministry was also, for Russian Baptists, sacramental. There were certain customs associated with the "proper way" to conduct elections for presbyters in Baptist churches. If a man was proposed for this position and his nomination was supported by all (or the majority) of the community, his own reaction was crucial. Men who tried to refuse, asserting that they were unworthy, were those who should be persuaded, or "forced" to submit to ordination. There was even the method of "frightening" such a person by threats of divine punishment if he did not fulfil God's will. By contrast, the person seen to be *seeking* to become a presbyter was the person who should be discouraged from any steps towards that calling. There was an awareness that Paul said "if a man desires the office of a bishop, he desires a good work", but this was discounted on the grounds that to "desire", was not the same as to "solicit".[56] The customs relating to ordination were mirrored in the rules about inviting visiting ministers (e.g. a minister or preacher from another Baptist church who happened to be present) to preach. The visitor was supposed to refuse at first, and then only to accept when the invitation was reiterated. Those ministers who did not observe these proprieties were looked at suspiciously.[57] Orthodoxy also thought in terms of humble self-deprecation as a virtue in priests, sometimes expressed in the traditional appeal of holy men "not to entrust a great voyage to a small boat".[58]

The way in which Baptist ministers operated together also had Orthodox overtones. "The most important thing in our brotherhood is to take counsel", asserted many Baptist presbyters.[59] From this would emerge what was "right". However, it often remained a mystery who made the "right decision" about a particular matter, and exactly how the decision was reached.

---

56. For instance, testimony of former senior presbyter from South Kazakhstan, P.A. Chumakin (INT, Kent, Washington, USA, 2006).

57. For instance, testimony of Baptist evangelist from Dushanbe, P.A. Semeryuk (INT, Sacramento, California, USA, 2006). He said that one preacher who sought every opportunity to preach (and for that very reason was not allowed to do so), complained that he left the church every time feeling like "an unmilked cow".

58. Cf.: *"Nad Knigoy Svyateyshego Alexy, Patriarkha Moskovskogo I Vseya Rusi 'Slova, Rechi, Poslaniya'"* [On the Book of His Holiness Alexis, the Patriarch of Moscow and All Russia, 'Sermons, Speeches, Pastoral Letters'], *ZhMP*, no. 1 (1949), p. 12.

59. For instance, testimonies of Baptist church ministers N.A. Kolesnikov (Shchuchinsk, Kazakhstan, 1998) and Ya.A. Meleshkevich (Bishkul, Kazakhstan, 2003).

The belief was that local ministers and senior presbyters, perhaps with the involvement of AUCECB leaders in Moscow, would be guided in the proper direction. This understanding about the *brotherhood* of Evangelical Christians-Baptists has strong similarities to the conciliar understanding of the *Church* in Russian Orthodoxy.[60] Even the idea of '*bratstvo*' (brotherhood) itself, or '*dukh bratstva*' (the spirit of the brotherhood), had to a certain extent a sacred meaning. A favorite biblical text in this connection was "Love the brotherhood", 1 Pet 2:17). Thus the ministers formed a kind of collective guard to maintain "gospel truth" and its interpretation. When they spoke of "the spirit of the brotherhood" they referred to the way in which they implemented (often unwritten) Russian Baptist customs. Thus alongside formal differences between the ecclesiology of Orthodoxy and Russian Baptist churches, there was a shared sense of the role of the "priestly" ministry.

There was also an understanding of ministers as spiritual mentors. The theme of spiritual discipleship in the brotherhood of Evangelical Christians-Baptists often echoed language used by Russian Orthodox writers when speaking about monastic obedience under the guidance of a "monastic elder". Although there was a focus on the training of young men, as noted previously the number of women in Russian Baptist churches meant that their role was of great importance. Examples of female commitment were available for them in the tales known among Orthodox believers, as in this typical Russian Orthodox report, "Mother Superior said frankly: ...this [nun] does not have the cloistral spirit and she will return to the world, but you have the cloistral spirit and will live here... and become a good nun."[61] The alternative culture of Russian Baptist churches fitted into this pattern. Those older Baptist men and women who sought to encourage younger church members saw this work as a major calling. One young man became

---

60. See, for instance: N. Uspensky, *"Sobornost' Tserkvi"* [The Conciliar Nature of the Church], *ZhMP*, no. 7 (1959), pp. 45-51; Archpriest Sergei (Bulgakov), *"Tserkov' kak Predanie"* [The Church as Tradition], *ZhMP*, no. 12 (1989), pp. 67-73; A. Khomyakov, *Sochineniya Bogoslovskie* [Theological Works] (SPb.: Nauka, 1995). There was also a certain Mennonite influence on the concept of *brotherhood* in Russian Baptist history. See, for instance: J. Dyck, "Fresh Skins for New Wine", *Theological reflections*, vol. 6 (2006), pp. 114-28; Davis, *Anabaptism and Asceticism*, pp. 192-3.

61. Cloistress Taisiya, *Russkoe Pravoslavnoe Zhenskoe Monashestvo*, pp. 161-2.

a believer after World War II through the testimony of a Baptist elder, and when the latter was dying he presented to the convert his New Testament, saying: "You are the only one I have led to God who is going to church meetings and has been baptized; so… do not draw back from the Christian faith! Otherwise I will be fruitless before God." These words so touched the young Baptist that at any moment of temptation he said to himself: "No! I will not do it. I do not want to distress the Lord and my dear elder."[62]

As well as sacraments associated with the life of the church, there were the sacraments of human life, and these, in some cases, had elements of superstition associated with them. It is not that Soviet Baptists held to the many superstitions that were typical of Russian life. They preached against everyday superstitions about a black cat running across their path, about not shaking hands across the threshold, about touching wood, and about spitting over a shoulder. "If you meet a woman with empty buckets", they said (an empty bucket was a bad sign), "it means only that she is going to fetch water."[63] But in some more serious matters – for instance, timing of the wedding day for their children – superstitious factors had an impact. On the question of the choice of the wedding day, they followed Russian Orthodox tradition and generally did not plan weddings in May, because "good people do not marry in May".[64] There was a Russian superstition that people marrying in May would languish (*mayat'sya*) for the rest of their lives.[65] Another Russian Orthodox custom regarding weddings, which had no association with superstition but was part of the Orthodox Church year, was that marriage did not take place in Lent.[66] Although Lent was

---

62. Testimony of an ECB minister from Kiev, L.E. Kovalenko (INT, Sacramento, California, USA, 2006).

63. Testimony of Baptist minister from Petropavlovsk, V.Ya. Baranov (INT, Minneapolis, Minnesota, USA, 2006).

64. In my own experience and to my knowledge very few Baptist weddings took place in May.

65. See, for instance, Father D. Svechnikov, *Okkul'tism i Sueveriya: Vzglyad Pravoslavnogo Svyashchennika* [Occultism and Superstitions: a View of Russian Orthodox Priest], <http://sueverie.net/kak-ograditsya-ot-sueveriy/okkultizm-i-sueveriya-vzglyad-pravoslavnogo-svyaschennika/stranitsa-2.html> accessed 15 November 2010.

66. See, for instance: *Khristianstvo: Entsiklopedichesky Slovar'*, vol. I, p. 351; P. Kuz'menko (ed.), *Russky Pravoslavny Obryad Venchaniya* [The Russian Orthodox Marriage Ceremony] (M.: Bukmen, 1996), p. 15.

not usually observed by Soviet Baptists (they usually observed only Holy Week), some communities followed the Orthodox lead and did not celebrate marriages in that period.[67]

A final area in which popular piety associated sacrament and superstition was in relation to death and burial. Many customs and signs among Soviet Baptists in this area were closely connected with Russian Orthodox beliefs. For example, in Orthodox and Baptist thinking, if someone's death came quickly and was "easy" that was an indirect confirmation of Christian righteousness, whereas if death was "prolonged" and "hard" it indicated "hidden sins".[68] There was also the ancient Orthodox popular belief, especially held among monks and partly maintained by some "Eastern-orientated" Russian Baptists that those who are holy do not suffer the same decay of their bodies.[69] Among some Baptists, for instance, it was said that if a dead person had a light-coloured face it was a sign that his or her soul had gone to paradise, but if the face was dark, it was a "bad sign".[70] Other Baptist traditions, each of which has a popular Russian or Orthodox counterpart, included the following: in the house where there was a dead body, mirrors were veiled; there was a service with Christian funeral songs near the coffin in the house; the deceased was usually buried after three days, no later than at lunchtime; the dead body was carried feet first; at the cemetery loud weeping was often considered to be a display of love to the deceased; and the coffin, put in the grave, was ritually strewn with handfuls of earth before burial. During the funeral meal, as a rule, besides the usual Russian dishes, a special *kut'ya* (boiled rice with raisins and honey) was cooked,

---

67. For instance, testimonies of presbyter from Tatarstan, N.V. Saburskiy, and E.N. Saburskaya (INT, Minneapolis, Minnesota, USA, 2006).

68. For instance, testimony of Baptist evangelist from Dushanbe, P.A. Semeryuk (INT, Sacramento, California, USA, 2006). For Russian Orthodox beliefs, see P. Kuz'menko, ed., *Russky Pravoslavny Obryad Pogrebeniya* [The Russian Orthodox Burial Ceremony] (M.: Bukmen, 1996), pp. 74-5.

69. See, for instance: Cloistress Taisiya, *Russkoe Pravoslavnoe Zhenskoe Monashestvo*, pp. 157, 169; Ryabinin, *Russkoe Yurodstvo*, p. 256; *Pravoslavnaya Entsiklopediya* [Russian Orthodox Encyclopaedia], ed. by O. Markicheva, p. 177.

70. For instance, testimony of Baptist presbyter, V.E. Shcherbakov (Omsk, Russia, 2007). This also echoes Orthodox beliefs. See Archbishop Veniamin, *Novaya Skrizhal'*, pp. 256-7.

with everyone eating it using spoons only (forks were not used) and all those invited were given handkerchiefs or towels as a keepsake.[71]

Among some Soviet Baptists in the 1960s and 1970s, there was a view that the Bible (or the New Testament) used by the deceased should be put into the coffin. This was associated with a blessed Christian parting. The position of the Bible might also be significant. In some churches when a minister was being buried the Bible was laid in the coffin to the right of the head of the deceased minister. In Orthodoxy, in the case of priests, the same position for the Gospel can be found.[72] There was some variation within Orthodoxy, and priests and lay people were treated differently. There was an ancient Russian Orthodox custom in which a deceased bishop or priest had the New Testament lying on top of them in the coffin. In the case of lay people an icon was put in one of their hands.[73] For Russian Baptists, as argued previously, their sacramental attitude to the Bible meant that in actuality it was often treated as a kind of icon. In general, Russian Baptist ministers adopted a similar approach to death and burial as to other church ordinances. Ministers asserted that Baptists "do not have any traditional observances", since "these are not found in the Bible", but then at a certain point the key phrase appeared, "we usually do the following" and an impressively long list of "evangelical" traditions might be announced.[74] These helped to shape the alternative communities.

---

71. For example, testimony of Baptist deacon, A.V. Afanakin, who conducted funeral services for many years (Omsk, Russia, 2008). For Orthodox traditions see Bulgakov, *Nastol'naya Kniga Dlya Svyashchenno-Tserkovno-Sluzhiteley*, pp. 1294-1314, 1360; Kuz'menko (ed.), *Russky Pravoslavny Obryad Pogrebeniya*, pp. 80-90.

72. Testimony (with critical appraisal of the practice) of former senior presbyter of Krasnodar Territory, V.D. Erisov (Sacramento, California, USA, 2008). See also a photo captioned "The Parting Service at the Prayer House" in *Vesti*, no. 2 (2001), p. 37. In this the Bible was laid in the coffin to the right of the head of the deceased Russian Baptist minister. The same position of the Gospel is seen in the case of a deceased Russian Orthodox bishop: Bourdeaux, *Opium of the People: The Christian Religion in the USSR*, the inset between pp. 128 and 129.

73. See *Khristianstvo: Entsiklopedichesky Slovar'*, vol. II, p. 356; Bulgakov, *Nastol'naya Kniga Dlya Svyashchenno-Tserkovno-Sluzhiteley*, pp. 1290-2; Kuz'menko, ed., *Russky Pravoslavny Obryad Pogrebeniya*, pp. 15, 80.

74. See, for instance, remarkable material on the subject: V. Leont'ev, "*Pokhoronit' po-Khristianski: Interv'yu s Presviterami Tsentral'noy Omskoy Tserkvi*" [To Bury in the Christian Way: Interview with Presbyters of Central Baptist Omsk Church], *SV*, no. 2 (2004), pp. 16-21.

Schools, colleges and work-places

Baptist communities had to interact with wider society. Confrontation frequently took place in the school setting, with teachers routinely unfairly marking down Baptist children.[75] Often Baptist children, with the connivance of their teachers, were beaten by hooligans.[76] However, when schools investigated incidents involving fights, stealing or smoking, Baptist children were usually above suspicion – their reputation was far better than the reputation of Young Pioneers and *Komsomol* members.[77] One Baptist challenged Soviet teachers in this way: "All the hooligans in our area are Pioneers, but please show me hooligans from a Baptist family!"[78] But this did not stop Baptist families being singled out, especially because they often refused to wear *oktyabryatskie zvezdochki* (October Children's badges) and *pionerskie galstuki* (Young Pioneer neckerchiefs), thus undermining the standard "uniformity" in schools in the USSR.[79] The kind of dialogue that frequently took place between Baptists and Soviet teachers was along these lines: Baptist: "Do you want your children to become Baptists?" Teacher: "Certainly not!" Baptist: "And I do not wish my children to become Communists".[80] Sometimes atheists were appointed to the same dormitory

---

75. For instance, testimonies of Baptist church members V.P. Gorelova from Alma-Ata (INT, Los Angeles, California, USA, 2006), T.N. Karavan from Zhitomir (INT, Sacramento, California, USA, 2006), N.S. Kramarenko from Sukhumi (INT, Sacramento, California, USA, 2006), V.S. Shevchuk from Odessa (INT, Portland, Oregon, USA, 2006).

76. For instance, testimonies of Baptist church members S.N. Savinsky and L.V. Savinskaya from Essentuki (INT, Salt Lake City, Utah, USA, 2006), E.D. Cherkasskikh from Donetsk Region (INT, Everett, Washington, USA, 2006), V.E. Sagan from Petropavlovsk (INT, Minneapolis, Minnesota, USA, 2006).

77. For instance, testimonies of Baptist church members T.N. Karavan from Zhitomir (INT, Sacramento, California, USA, 2006), V.Ya. Virkh from Syzran (INT, Los Angeles, California, USA, 2006).

78. Testimony of Baptist church member from Petropavlovsk (Kazakhstan), V.E. Sagan, about his conversations with Soviet teachers (INT, Minneapolis, Minnesota, USA, 2006).

79. Testimonies of Baptist church members T.N. Karavan from Zhitomir (INT, Sacramento, California, USA, 2006), E.I. Sedykh from Donetsk Region (INT, Sacramento, California, USA, 2006), V.Ya. Virkh from Syzran (INT, Los Angeles, California, USA, 2006), V.E. Sagan from Petropavlovsk (INT, Minneapolis, USA, 2006).

80. Testimony of A.T. Kharchenko from Sukhumi (INT, Sacramento, California, USA, 2006).

room as Baptist young people, to intensify antireligious pressure and (for example) prevent them from praying.[81] Stories circulated within Baptist communities about Communist teachers (or the school head) wanting to deprive some Baptists of parental rights, and preparing for this purpose all the necessary documents, while believing people prayed and asked protection from God. Then something dramatic happened – teachers becoming seriously ill, being dismissed, or even suddenly dying – and the school authorities left Baptist children alone.[82]

On leaving school, it was almost impossible for those professing Christian faith to graduate from university. In some cases they might be able to enter a university (perhaps by an oversight), but usually when their faith became clear some pretext was found under which they were expelled.[83] In some cases young men and women from Baptist families studied by correspondence and receive university degrees. Where they had to answer questions about scientific atheism and Marxist-Leninist philosophy, Baptists usually tried to separate knowledge from belief. They aimed to quote from sources rather than expressing any opinion of their own.[84] Those Soviet Baptists who managed to achieve a university-level education often became among the most difficult and inconvenient people for Soviet authorities to deal with, since their very existence conflicted with the thesis of atheists that believers were illiterate and ignorant people.[85] However,

81. For instance, testimonies of Baptist presbyter from Kiev, P.F. Kunda (INT, Sacramento, California, USA, 2006), and church member from Kazakhstan, N.D. Chumakina (INT, Seattle, Washington, USA, 2006).

82. Testimonies of: Baptist minister from Stavropol Territory, V.N. Savinsky (INT, Spokane, Washington, USA, 2006), church members from Donetsk Region, V.Ya. Sedykh, E.I. Sedykh and A.I. Musiets (INT, Sacramento, California, USA, 2006), from Belorussia, M.I. Petrenko and I.E. Petrenko (INT, Fresno, California, USA,2006).

83. See, for instance: BL, no. 3 (1968), p. 3; Bondarenko, Tri Prigovora, pp. 54-7; Sedletsky, "Vospominaniya", pp. 57-67. Also testimonies of Baptist church ministers: Ya.D. Diordienko from Odessa (INT, Sacramento, California, USA, 2006), V.V. Zinchenko from Alma-Ata (INT, Sacramento, California, USA, 2006), V.V. Gorelov from Alma-Ata (INT, Los Angeles, California, USA, 2006).

84. For instance, testimonies of Baptist ministers Ya.D. Diordienko from Odessa, L.E. Kovalenko from Kiev (INT, Sacramento, California, USA, 2006), member of the Mennonite Brethren community of Karaganda V. Fast (INT, Frankenthal, Germany, 2008).

85. For instance, testimonies of Baptist presbyters and church members K.S. Sedletsky from Chernovtsy ("Vospominaniya", p. 94), Ya.D. Shevchuk from Odessa (INT, Portland,

not only were better-educated Baptists an anomaly in Soviet society, they were also ill-fitting members of Baptist communities. Quite often the finger of suspicion was privately pointed at them, with church members wondering if they had secretly renounced the faith for the sake of university education.[86]

The attitude to Baptists in the work-place was very varied. In some cases their supervisors and colleagues highly appreciated them as good workers and as those who did not get drunk. Baptists spoke about bosses who pronounced that "all drunkards should be dismissed and only sectarians hired!"[87] On the other hand, Baptists were often dismissed from their employment "for no reason at all", or "for reasons of policy".[88] Some who had a promoted rank, "Shock worker of communist labor", had that taken away.[89] Within Baptist communities stories circulated about how Soviet Baptists were at first dismissed, but then all possible means were used to persuade them to return to their work-places because without them widespread looting was taking place.[90] These stories were usually not told in a way which would enable verification of the extent to which this happened or of the nature of the circumstances. More dramatic tales were told of Communist bosses who were most active in harassing Baptists coming to an untimely death, creating fear in those around them.[91]

Oregon, USA, 2006), N.N. Tsvirin'ko from Belorussia (INT, Fresno, California, USA, 2006), S.N. Savinsky from Essentuki (INT, Salt Lake City, Utah, USA, 2006), J. Dyck from Karaganda (INT, Oerlinghausen, Germany, 2007).

86. For instance, testimonies of Baptist minister from Kiev L.E. Kovalenko and evangelist from Dushanbe P.A. Semeryuk (INT, Sacramento, California, USA, 2006).

87. For instance, testimonies of Baptist church members V.P. Gorelova (INT, Los Angeles, California, USA, 2006) and N.O. Sobchenko (INT, Sacramento, California, USA, 2006).

88. Testimonies: of Baptist church members from Zhitomir, N.O. Sobchenko and T.N. Karavan; Baptist church ministers, N.S. Kramarenko from Sukhumi and Ya. D. Diordienko from Odessa (INT, Sacramento, California, USA, 2006); church minister from Bryansk V.A. Serpikov (INT, Seattle, Washington, USA, 2006).

89. Curious testimony of Baptist presbyter from Odessa, Ya.D. Shevchuk (INT, Portland, Oregon, USA, 2006).

90. For instance, testimonies of Baptist church members from Chernovtsy V.V. Kitsen and N.I. Kitsen (INT, Fresno, California, USA, 2006).

91. See, for instance: *"Vmeste Molimsya, Vmeste Raduemsya"* [We are Praying and Rejoicing Together] (Interview with Omsk Baptist Church Presbyter, I.A. Kabluchkin), *SV*, no. 4 (2003), pp. 12-13. Also testimonies of M.I. Petrenko and I.E. Petrenko, church members from Belorussia (INT, Fresno, California, USA, 2006).

Baptists also enjoyed relating incidents in which resourceful Baptists allegedly out-witted Communist Party organizers or atheistic lecturers. The plot was usually along these lines: the Communists created an intolerant atmosphere for a believing person in a factory and then called a meeting of the work collective at which the Party organizer made strident antireligious statements and suggested that the Baptist be disciplined and perhaps dismissed. At that moment a witty reply from the Baptist unexpectedly put the Communists in an awkward or ridiculous situation.[92] Other workers then supported the Baptist being victimized.[93] In some stories the Party organizer even lost his position in the factory,[94] or suddenly changed his mind, started to pray (privately) and soon became a member of a Baptist church.[95] When atheistic lecturers spoke, Baptists intervened with powerful points. At a certain stage, either then or later, the atheistic lecturer became silent (or even mysteriously lost his voice) and finally he left ignominiously.[96] Many of the listeners who attended the lecture, even if they were formally unbelievers, supported the lone Baptist.[97] These stories sustained the morale of the Baptist communities in the USSR.

A particular challenge for Baptists was military service. The pacifist influence among Russian Baptists commonly enough led to disagreements with the Soviet State "on the subject of weapons" (*"po oruzheynomu voprosu"*).[98] The majority of young men from Baptist families who were drafted into

---

92. Baptists were also stirred up by this: "I listen to the party organizer and begin to boil; such conversations always awake my zeal for God." Testimony of V.Ya. Sedykh from Donetsk Region (INT, Sacramento, California, USA, 2006).

93. For instance, testimonies of Baptist church member from Makeevka, L.V. Svetlov (INT, Spokane, Washington, USA, 2006), Baptist church ministers, N.S. Kramarenko from Sukhumi (INT, Sacramento, California, USA, 2006), N.G. Man'ko from Maikop (INT, Everett, Washington, USA, 2006).

94. For instance, testimony of Baptist church member from Makeevka, L.V. Svetlov (INT, Spokane, Washington, USA, 2006).

95. For instance, testimony of a presbyter of the ECB from Rostov, M.P. Zakharov (INT, Sacramento, California, USA, 2006).

96. For instance, testimonies of Baptist church members from Chernovtsy, V.V. Kitsen and N.I. Kitsen (INT, Fresno, California, USA, 2006).

97. For instance, testimonies of A.K. Sipko, B.M. Zdorovets (INT, Spokane, Washington, USA, 2006) and P.A. Chumakin (INT, Kent, Washington, USA, 2006).

98. The expression relayed by Yu.K. Kryuchkov (INT, Sacramento, California, USA, 2006).

the army, during their first visit to the military registration office simply informed the authorities about their religious beliefs but they did not refuse to serve. But some adamantly refused to take the oath, sometimes with great defiance.[99] This could provoke commanders into cruel treatment of them.[100] During Khruschev's time refusal to take the military oath meant imprisonment.[101] In Brezhnev's period, they were simply directed to a construction battalion, where their military service was not connected with use of weapons.[102] Sometimes atheists were placed in military barracks to discourage Baptist witness.[103] The narratives about military service, as with the work-place narratives, were varied. In some cases those who refused the oath or were open in other ways in expressing religious convictions received threats and punishment in the first months of the army service (usually from a deputy commander),[104] but then were apparently unexpectedly appointed by senior officers to the position of military clerk, storekeeper or checker.[105] Under alternative circumstances Baptists suffered and were even killed. Such a person was seen as an "army martyr".[106]

---

99. For example, the characteristic words of an elderly Baptist women from Donetsk Region: "I brought up my children in the fear of God. When my son was drafted into the army, he refused the oath and armed military service…" – Testimony of A.I. Musiets (INT, Sacramento, California, USA, 2006). Some defiance was couched in biblical terms: "If I forget you, O Jerusalem… let my tongue cleave to the roof of my mouth." (Ps 137:5-6).

100. For instance, testimony of Baptist presbyter from Frunze, A.K. Sipko (INT, Spokane, Washington, USA, 2006).

101. For instance, testimonies of Baptist minister from Odessa, Ya.D. Diordienko (INT, Sacramento, California, USA, 2006) and former senior presbyter from Kazakhstan, V.V. Gorelov (INT, Los Angeles, California, USA, 2006).

102. For instance, testimonies of Baptist presbyters from the former USSR: P.F. Kunda, N.S. Kramarenko, and V.V. Zinchenko (INT, Sacramento, California, USA, 2006).

103. For instance, testimony of Baptist presbyter from Kiev, P.F. Kunda (INT, Sacramento, California, USA, 2006).

104. For instance, testimonies of Baptist presbyter from Odessa, V.N. Gavelovsky (INT, Sacramento, California, USA, 2006), church member from Krasnodar Territory, M.A. Vasiliev (INT, Everett, Washington, USA, 2006).

105. For instance, testimonies of Baptist presbyters and church members from the former USSR: P.V. Sedykh (INT, Sacramento, California, USA, 2006), M.A. Vasiliev (INT, Everett, Washington, USA, 2006), V.P. Zinchenko and D.I. Chueshkov (INT, Seattle, Washington, USA, 2006).

106. See, for instance: *Podrazhayte Vere Ikh*, pp. 340-73; Sedletsky, "Vospominaniya", pp. 248-53. Also testimonies of former senior presbyter from South Kazakhstan, P.A. Chumakin (INT, Kent, Washington, USA, 2006), ECB church member from the Crimea,

Children from Baptist families at Soviet schools or in Soviet higher education, those at work and young men in the army, were all exposed to ridicule, opposition and discrimination. This was true for Orthodox as well as Baptist believers. In this context all believers found ways of resisting the authorities. Often they refused to wear any Communist symbols, avoided participating in secular youth events, and were known for entering boldly into arguments with atheists.[107] The Orthodox intelligentsia was active in organizing various underground Christian seminars, and producing unauthorized religious literature (*samizdat* – self-published work), which was produced on typewriters.[108] Often this literature, which was addressed to a more intellectual readership, was as much of a headache for the Soviet authorities as the activity of the illegal publications that reflected the popular evangelical piety of the Soviet Baptists.[109] Although in their conscientious witness in the areas of education and of work Soviet Baptists did not follow Orthodox ways of operating, there was a possibly subconscious "exchange of experience" as both found themselves in conflict with a hostile state. Some wider issues connected with this conflict now need to be examined.

"Public Enemies"

The theme of persecution and imprisonment "for the truth" was prominent in the oral and written tradition of Russian Baptists. The reasons for

V.P. Litovchenko (INT, Los Angeles, California, USA, 2006).

107. See, for instance, the following Orthodox testimonies on the theme: A. Danilova, *"Patriakh Kirill: Shtrikhi k Portretu"* [Patriarch Kirill: Some Traits of the Portrait], *Mgarsky Kolokol*, vol. 74 (March 2009); *"Interv'yu Arkhimandrita Evlogiya (Gutchenko)"* [Interview with Archimandrite Evlogy (Gutchenko)], *Andreevsky Vestnik*, vol. 15 (2007); Dudko, *O Nashem Upovanii*, p. 96.

108. See, for instance: L. Alekseeva, *Istoriya Inakomysliya v SSSR* [History of Dissidence in the USSR] (Benson, VT: Khronika Press, 1984), pp. 229-33; Shkarovsky, *Russkaya Pravoslavnaya Tserkov pri Staline i Khrushcheve*, pp. 261-83; J. Ellis, *The Russian Orthodox Church: A Contemporary History* (London: Croom Helm, 1986), pp. 294-5.

109. See, for instance, reports about the CCECB's own printing presses and their extensive use: Yu. Kryuchkov, *Podpol'naya Pechat' CCECB v Sovetskom Soyuze* [The Underground Press of the CCECB in the Soviet Union] (Sacramento, CA: n.p., 2002); G. Kryuchkov, *Velikoe Probuzhdenie XX Veka* [The Great Revival in the 20th Century] (n.p.: Izd-vo "Khristianin", 2008).

the persecution varied according to the historical epoch. In Tsarist times Baptists were usually deprived of liberty for their "seduction" of Orthodox people into sectarianism. In Lenin's time a crucial issue was their refusal to take arms, in Stalin's time they became "public enemies", and a later focus was on "infringement of Soviet legislation on religious cults".[110] By the 1960s many narratives had to do with encounters between Baptists and the KGB. On the one hand there was a fear of the KGB's almost unlimited powers, with Baptists believing that they were behind (for example) splits in Baptist communities and incidents in which church ministers met with accidents.[111] Worries about KGB control meant that some Soviet Baptists who emigrated to the USA in the 1980s continued to be afraid of the "long arm" of the KGB.[112] Yet alongside this were stories of Baptists who were fearless in their dealings with the KGB. In these tales, Baptists, as a rule, showed not only courage, but also keen wit and some subtle irony, as in the case of a Baptist presbyter accused of supporting informal courses for preachers. When being interrogated by a Religious Affairs officer, he defended the courses on the grounds that Baptists were criticized for their insufficient erudition.[113] Some resourceful Baptists also relied for their defence on the inadequate awareness within the KGB of theological issues and denominational distinctions. For example, one Baptist presbyter, charged

---

110. For instance, testimonies of Baptist ministers Ya.S. Shevchuk from Syzran (INT, Los Angeles, California, USA, 2006), A.I. Kolomiytsev from Rostov Region (INT, Vancouver, Washington, USA, 2006), Ya.D. Diordienko from Odessa (INT, Sacramento, California, USA, 2006).

111. For instance, testimonies of: former senior presbyter from Kuybyshev, V.F. Serpevsky, and Z.I. Serpevskaya (INT, Vancouver, Washington, USA, 2006), church members from Nizhny Novgorod, P.I. Runov and G.I. Runova (INT, Salt Lake City, Utah, USA, 2006), from Krasnodar, S.G. Odaryuk and N.M. Odaryuk (INT, Everett, Washington, USA, 2006), etc.

112. For instance, testimonies of P.P. Rytikov and A.S. Sheyko, ministers of Baptist churches from Lugansk Region (INT, Sacramento, California, USA, 2006), etc.

113. He stated: "Our brethren can retell at church, for instance, the love story of David and Bathsheba, but not fully chastely (2 Sam. 11:2-5), or they may not fully understand that Israel, elected by God in ancient times, is an aggressor today in the Arab-Israeli war. So we really need courses for preachers..." – Testimony of former senior presbyter of Baptist churches in Krasnodar Territory, V.D. Erisov (Sacramento, California, USA, 2008). Similar satirical moments in conversations with officers of KGB are recollected also by Baptist evangelist from Dushanbe P.A. Semeryuk (Sacramento, California, USA, 2006), church member from Odessa, L.M. Gavelovskaya (INT, Sacramento, California, USA, 2006), and others.

with the baptism of seventeen-year-olds, stated: "All citizens should be equal before our Soviet laws... Why can Russian Orthodox priests baptize children, while Baptists cannot? Is this just?" The argument was accepted and the presbyter was restored to his position.[114]

Officers of the KGB or Religious Affairs officers did not, however, want to be seen as those who were ignorant about religion. During interrogations of Baptists, the officers might refer to the Scriptures, saying to the accused, for example: "Does not the Bible say that followers of Christ will be insulted and that all kinds of evil will be said against them falsely? So, go and suffer."[115] On one occasion a Baptist who was under pressure to become an informer said: "Do you suggest I should become Judas?" The officer of the KGB replied: "What!? Absolutely not! But the Bible speaks of an observer (soglyadatay)."[116] Sometimes officers of the KGB made themselves aware of specific aspects of Baptist history in Russia. One presbyter recalled that "they showed me some pre-revolutionary magazines, which spoke about how Tsarist gendarmes watched Baptist meetings".[117] KGB officers also referred to the content of Baptist sermons, which had been relayed by informers.[118] In addition, the officers of the KGB had their own superstitions about religion. Some believed that "certain words discrediting the socialist way of life could be printed between the lines in foreign editions of the Bible".[119] Some security officers, after conversations with Baptists, came to a belief in God (although perhaps not the kind of commitment which Baptists wanted) and this resulted in them finding ways to help Baptists who were in trouble.[120]

---

114. Testimony of V.D. Erisov (Sacramento, California, USA, 2008).

115. Sedletsky, "Vospominaniya", p. 120.

116. Testimony of Baptist minister from Krasnodar Region, V.Ya. Bgatov (INT, San Diego, California, USA, 2006).

117. Testimony of former senior presbyter from Kazakhstan, V.V. Gorelov (INT, Los Angeles, California, USA, 2006).

118. For instance, testimony of minister of the CCECB, A.I. Kolomiytsev (INT, Vancouver, Washington, USA, 2006).

119. For instance, testimony of Baptist minister from Alma-Ata, V.V. Zinchenko (INT, Sacramento, California, USA, 2006).

120. For instance, testimonies of Baptist presbyters and church members: N.V. Sabursky from Tatarstan (INT, Minneapolis, Minnesota, USA, 2006); A.I. Kolomiytsev from Rostov Region (INT, Vancouver, Washington, USA, 2006), P.D. Karavan from Batumi

There was a tradition among Baptists to see God at work in the rise of evil powers, and this can be seen even in the attitude of Baptists to Stalin's terror.[121] This also mirrored the Russian Orthodox spirit. Orthodox and Baptists sometimes saw oppressive powers as a punishment "because of our sins and the sins of our fathers".[122] A sense of God's providence led to a tendency on the part of some Baptists to thank God for the KGB.[123] Persecuting powers operated under divine permission for the purification and final triumph of the church. One picture used was of "a pike that lives in the lake to keep all the fish awake".[124] The KGB were even seen as "pastors", in that "any serious fault of a Baptist did not pass unnoticed [by the KGB], and consequently all church members really tried to lead a life of sanctity".[125] But this did not mean that Baptists were necessarily passive in the face of opposition. In the cases mentioned above, in which an experienced atheistic propagandist was appointed to "look after" Baptist men or women, the story typically ended with the "Soviet adviser" either refusing the "impossible task" or (on occasions) becoming a believer.[126]

In a variety of situations Baptists spoke up against atheist propaganda, for example with "inconvenient questions", and they sometimes engaged in vigorous debates with learned atheists. Legendary plots of an ideological

(INT, Sacramento, California, USA, 2006), N.I. Kitsen from Chernovtsy (INT, Fresno, California, USA, 2006).

121. See, for instance, Mitskevich, *Istoriya Evangel'skikh Khristian-Baptistov*, p. 278.

122. Testimony of B.M. Zdorovets (INT, Spokane, Washington, USA, 2006).

123. On the providential reasons for the existence of the Soviet power see, for instance: N. Trubetskoy, *"My i Drugie"* [We and Others], in *Russkaya Ideya*, pp. 385-401; Archpriest G. Florovsky, *"Evraziysky Soblazn"* [The Eurasian Allurement], *Novy Mir*, no. 1 (1991), pp. 195-211. Cf. this approach with the traditional Russian Orthodox assessment of the Tartar invasion: "Because of our sins people unknown, the godless, have come… Because of the pride of Russian princes God has permitted such things." – From *Tverskaya Letopis'* [The Tver Chronicle], in *Izbornik: Povesti Drevney Rusi* [Manuscript with Collected Writings: Narratives of Ancient Russia], ed. by L. Dmitriev and N. Ponyrko (M.: Khudozhestvennaya Literatura, 1986), pp. 135-6.

124. Testimony of Baptist church member from Makeevka, L.V. Svetlov (INT, Spokane, Washington, USA, 2006).

125. For instance, testimony of Baptist presbyter from Tatarstan, N.V. Sabursky (INT, Minneapolis, Minnesota, USA, 2006).

126. For instance, testimonies of Baptist presbyter from Kiev, P.F. Kunda (INT, Sacramento, California, USA, 2006), church member from Kazakhstan, N.D. Chumakina (INT, Seattle, Washington, USA, 2006).

collision of a Baptist with narrow-minded Communists (party organizers, Religious Affairs officers, atheistic lecturers or officers of the KGB) were often patterned after the traditional motifs used in Russian Orthodox narratives. One of these is the famous story, told in several versions, about a certain anti-religious meeting in Russia in the 1930s. One Easter Day, in a small provincial Russian town, the Communists gathered many local people together and for a long time attacked the Christian faith. Then a fearless Orthodox priest asked to speak and simply said in a loud voice, "Christ is Risen!" And the people responded all together: "He is Risen Indeed!" The Communists had no way of dealing with this affirmation of faith.[127] This Easter example was repeatedly used in meetings of Russian Baptists, although they usually said "a brother" instead of "an Orthodox priest".[128] However, in practice Baptist and Orthodox Christians in the later Soviet period did not have such dramatic opportunities. It is true that in the way Baptist encounters were narrated (as in the Orthodox narratives, such as the *Lives of Saints*) the confrontation served to vindicate the believer.[129] But the Soviet authorities took their revenge and in classical tradition the faithful witnesses endured "blessed suffering" for Christ's sake.[130]

Their encounter with the authorities included, for a considerable number of believers, a great deal of physical suffering. In May 1966, when radical Baptists engaged in their protest near the building of the Central Committee of the Communist Party in defence of prisoners and freedom of conscience in the USSR, the participants in the demonstration were seeking a meeting with Brezhnev. All they received were beatings and arrests.[131]

---

127. See, for instance: N. Dozorov, "*Paskhal'noe Chudo v Tagile*" [Easter Miracle in Tagil], *Nash Put'*, no. 113 (1937), <http://rys-arhipelag.ucoz.ru/publ/voskresenie_khristovo_posle_bolshevistskoj_revoljucii/29-1-0-1660> accessed 6 December 2010.

128. For instance, testimonies of Baptist presbyter from Tatarstan, N.V. Saburgsky and E.N. Saburskaya (INT, Minneapolis, Minnesota, USA, 2006), church members from Sukhumi, L.A. Fayer and E.F. Fayer (INT, Sacramento, California, USA, 2006).

129. For instance, testimonies of Baptist presbyters and church members from the former USSR: V.N. Gavelovsky, P.F. Kunda (INT, Sacramento, California, USA, 2006), A.K. Sipko, B.M. Zdorovets (INT, Spokane, Washington, USA, 2006), Sedletsky, "Vospominaniya", pp. 119-32.

130. For instance, testimonies of B.M. Zdorovets (INT, Spokane, Washington, USA, 2006), V.V. Kitsen and N.I. Kitsen (INT, Fresno, California, USA, 2006), Sedletsky, "Vospominaniya", pp. 132-61.

131. See *BL*, no. 5 (1966), Supplement; *VestI*, no. 3 (2003), pp. 21-4; Kuksenko, *Nashi*

Some Russian Orthodox clergy and laity acted in the same spirit as the radical Baptists. In the 1960s protests by Archbishop Yermogen of Kaluga and two Moscow priests, Fathers Nikolai Eshliman and Gleb Yakunin led to their dismissal from their posts, and in the same period there was the well-publicized defence of the Uspensky Pochaevsky Monastery (in Ternopol Region) when the authorities employed threats, beat monks and pilgrims, and put some monks in mental institutions, all in an ultimately unsuccessful attempt to close down the monastery.[132] While some Baptists and Orthodox Christians engaged in direct resistance, others employed more subtle methods. Khrushchev's period saw an attempt by the authorities to close down the Orthodox theological academies in Moscow and Leningrad. In a masterstroke, Orthodox leaders quickly invited Christian students from African countries to study there, and given the way the Communist leaders praised the "national-liberation" movements of peoples in the Third World this move made it impossible for them to implement their closure plans.[133] These kinds of imaginative responses by the churches, rather than the response of open rebellion, met with the approval of many believers, both in Russian Orthodox parishes and in Baptist communities where "political" methods of struggle were opposed.[134]

Of the Baptists who were sentenced to hard labor in prison camps, a name which became very well known was "Alyoshka the Baptist", from *One Day in the Life of Ivan Denisovich* by Alexander Solzhenitsyn.[135] Here was a unique, positive image of a Baptist in public Soviet literature. The context was the collision of two important ideological tendencies in the USSR at that time: the attempt to show some of the truth about Stalin's terror and the simultaneous attempt to fight against religion. In the communities of

---

Besedy, pp. 55-6.

132. See, for instance: Shkarovsky, *Russkaya Pravoslavnaya Tserkov pri Staline i Khrushcheve*, pp. 380-1; V. Koval'sky, *"Pochaevskaya Lavra"* [The Pochaevsky Monastery], *Blagovest*, 23 Sept. 2005. The latter Orthodox author also enigmatically comments that the party chief in charge of the desecration of the monastery soon after had a family tragedy: his children died and his wife was put in a mental hospital.

133. See Shkarovsky, *Russkaya Pravoslavnaya Tserkov pri Staline i Khrushcheve*, p. 377.

134. For instance, testimony of former senior presbyter of Baptist churches in Krasnodar Territory, V.D. Erisov (Sacramento, California, USA, 2008).

135. A. Solzhenitsyn, *"Odin Den' Ivana Denisovicha"* [One Day in the Life of Ivan Denisovich], *Novy Mir*, no. 11 (1962), pp. 8-71.

the CCECB, members who were in labor camps were given special attention by the churches. Generous financial contributions were regularly made for those imprisoned and in particular their families. Church members sent letters of spiritual encouragement to the labor camps, posted parcels for the prisoners, and delivered to Soviet official organizations various petitions, which were incorporated in the "Baptist *samizdat*".[136]

The typical narratives about the spiritual fortitude of the Soviet Baptists condemned and imprisoned for their faith as enemies of the atheistic state, inevitably mirrored similar Orthodox stories.[137] The general "moderate" (as distinct from the "radical") view was that a true Christian should be humble and not provoke the authorities into any use of force, but if despite that Christians were arrested and had to endure the harsh conditions of a labor camp, they should be steadfast to the end, even if this meant martyrdom.[138] Also the "moderate" Christian ethics allowed believers to run from their persecutors. Deviations from this line, of course, were not uncommon. Some Christians had a desire for martyrdom, while others denied the faith. But both the Orthodox hierarchy and the majority of Baptist presbyters simply encouraged those who were suffering to see themselves as part of the cloud of Christian witnesses reaching as far back as the early church, with that witness also expressed in the experiences of believers within the

---

136. See, for instance: V. Ketler, *"Trud Nebol'shoy, No Delali"* [There Was Little Work, But We Did It], *Sibirskie Nivy*, no. 5 (2001), p. 17; Bondarenko, *Tri Prigovora*, pp. 155-8. Also testimonies of Baptist ministers and church members: S.N. Savinsky and L.V. Savinskaya from Essentuki (INT, Salt Lake City, Utah, USA, 2006), N.V. Sabursky and E.N. Saburskaya from Tatarstan (INT, Minneapolis, Minnesota, USA, 2006).

137. See, for instance, reports about the Orthodox sufferers for the faith in the period, e.g. B.V. Talantov (died during his imprisonment), Archbishop Ermogen, A. Levitin, Z. Krakhmalnikova. D. Pospielovsky, *The Russian Church under the Soviet Regime, 1917-1982*, 2 vols. (Crestwood, NY: St. Vladimir's Seminary Press, 1984), vol. II, p. 432; Archpriest V. Tsypin, *Istoriya Russkoy Pravoslavnoy Tserkvi, 1917-1990*, pp. 165-6; A. Levitin-Krasnov, *Po Moryam, Po Volnam* [Across the Seas, Across the Waves] (Paris: Poiski, 1986). See also: M. Bourdeaux, "Dissent in the Russian Orthodox Church", *Russian Review*, vol. 28, 4 (1969), pp. 416-27; Alekseeva, *Istoriya Inakomysliya v SSSR*, pp. 221-4; *Religious Prisoners in the USSR: A Study by Keston College* (Keston: Greenfire Books, 1987), p. 71.

138. Cf., for instance, the *Easter Message* of Father Sergi (Zheludkov) as a response to the radical *Lenten Letter* of A.I. Solzhenitsyn to Patriarch Pimen (1972). – *Documents*, in G. Simon, *Church, State and Opposition in the USSR* (London: C. Hurst & Company, 1974), pp. 206-8.

Orthodox Christian tradition, a tradition to which Russian Baptists were connected to no small degree as they experienced the same sufferings.[139]

In the labor camps, as elsewhere in Baptist life, there was an awareness that the authorities reacted in very different ways to the presence of Christians. In some cases, because of their honesty, Baptists in labor camps occupied special positions and had "white-collar jobs".[140] Other prisoners, as a rule, wished them well. State atheism was not held in high esteem behind the barbed wire. Baptists were quite often called – in the Orthodox manner – *batyushki* ("Fathers"), a designation many recollect with pleasure.[141] But in other cases there was harsh treatment of believers. In these instances the stories also contained examples of severe divine punishment falling upon the oppressors. These narratives parallel many Orthodox stories about Divine Judgment, which can be found, for example, in the Orthodox *Lives of Saints*,[142] in the works of Bishop Ignaty Bryanchaninov,[143] and in Archimandrite Lazar'.[144] In the famous story by dissident writer Yuli Daniel, *The Hands* (1963), just (divine) punishment is meted out to a former Cheka[145] member who participated in the shooting

139. Cf., for instance: V. Bolotov, *Lektsii po Istorii Drevney Tserkvi* [Lectures on the History of the Ancient Church], 4 vols. (M.: Izdanie Spaso-Preobrazhenskogo Valaamskogo Monastyrya, 1994), vol. II, pp. 130-40.

140. See, for instance: Mitskevich, *Istoriya Evangel'skikh Khristian-Baptistov*, p. 205. Also testimonies of Baptist ministers and church members: M.P. Zakharov from Rostov (INT, Sacramento, California, USA, 2006), A.I. Kolomiytsev from Rostov Region (INT, Vancouver, Washington, USA, 2006), L.V. Svetlov from Makeevka (INT, Spokane, Washington, USA, 2006). The latter, for example, said that during a difficult period of his term of imprisonment he received help from another Baptist prisoner, who was given considerable supervisory authority over some aspects of labor camp life, as was put "in Joseph's hands in Egypt".

141. For instance, testimony of Baptist minister from Odessa, Ya.D. Diordienko (INT, Sacramento, California, USA, 2006). See also: Bondarenko, *Tri Prigovora*, p. 283; G. Kostyuchenko, *"Svidetel'stvo o Gospode – Nasha Zashchita"* [Testimony about the Lord is Our Protection], *VestI*, no. 1 (1983), p. 36.

142. See, for instance, *Uchilishche Blagochestiya*, pp. 114-5, 248-50, 371.

143. See, for instance: Bishop Ignaty (Bryanchaninov), *"Asketicheskie Opyty"* [Ascetic Experiences], in Bishop Ignaty (Bryanchaninov), *Polnoe Sobranie Tvoreny*, vol. I, pp. 77-530; *"Slovo o Smerti"* [Homily on Death], in Bishop Ignaty (Bryanchaninov), *Polnoe Sobranie Tvoreny*, vol. III, pp. 5-294.

144. See Archimandrite Lazar', *O Taynykh Nedugakh Dushi* [On Covert Illnesses of the Soul] (M.: Izd-vo Sretenskogo monastyrya, 2004), pp. 176-414.

145. Cheka means *Extraordinary Commission* ("for combating Counter-revolution, Sabotage, and Speculation").

of Orthodox priests soon after the Bolshevik Revolution.[146] The domestic anti-Soviet authors of the Khrushchev-Brezhnev period often noted that many of the Communists who were especially involved in Stalin's atrocities were later, "by the highest justice", thrown into labor camps or shot.[147] It seems that there has been a prevalent Orthodox-Byzantine world-view in Russia which presents the Gospel message to a considerable degree in a rather "frightening" manner.[148] Orthodox writers, some "dissident" authors in the Soviet times, and Russian Baptists shared a similar mentality. The real enemies were not believers but were state-supported powers, and they would ultimately be judged.

Promised Land

In the context of suffering in which they found themselves, it is not surprising that in Russian Baptist popular piety there was the hope of a "promised land", of ultimate freedom from slavery. At times in the 1960s and 1970s this could be expressed in very surprising and contradictory ways. In a statement that was completely at odds with the views of other Baptists, one preacher from Kazakhstan compared Lenin with Moses, who "led the peoples of our country from slavery and oppression out into the kingdom of justice and happiness".[149] Even during the hearings of Baptist cases in Soviet courts, it was common for believers to refer to "Lenin's law of liberty of conscience for believers".[150] Perhaps less surprisingly, given the

---

146. See, for instance, N. Arzhak (Yu. Daniel), *"Ruki"* [The Hands], in *Tsena Metafory, Ili Prestuplenie i Nakazanie Sinyavskogo i Danielya* [The Price of Metaphor, or the Crime and Punishment of Sinyavsky and Daniel], ed. by E. Velikanova (M.: Yunona, 1990), pp. 89-92.

147. For instance, this idea is repeatedly present in Alexander Solzhenitsyn's writings (*The Gulag Archipelago, One Day in the Life of Ivan Denisovich*, etc).

148. See Russian Baptist and Orthodox "apocalyptic" letters of the Khrushchev period: V. Kozlov *et al.*, eds., *Kramola: Inakomyslie v SSSR pri Khrushcheve i Brezhneve, 1953-1982 gg.* [Sedition: Dissidence in the USSR under Khrushchev and Brezhnev, 1953-1982] (M.: Materik, 2005), pp. 160-7.

149. Cited in A. Nikiforov, F. Sim, *Podryazhayutsya Voyti Skvoz' Tesnye Vrata* [They Make Every Effort to Enter through the Narrow Door] (Petropavlovsk: n.p., 1985), p. 27.

150. *"Sud Nepravedny"* [Unfair Trial], *VS*, no. 1 (1973), pp. 24-5. See also *BSRUECB*, no. 17 (1974), p. 4.

need to affirm the Soviet system publically, *Bratsky Vestnik* wrote on the 100th anniversary of Lenin's birthday, "As Everest [is the highest] among all mountains of the world, there was our great sociologist-humanist Vladimir Il'ich Lenin… There is no exploitation in the Soviet State founded by the genius of Lenin."[151] But more commonly, hope was placed in movement to a "promised land" elsewhere, a place which God would provide, rather than Baptists seeking to prove to themselves that the Soviet State had provided all they wanted. Among Russian Baptists one of the most quoted texts was the words of Christ: "When they persecute you in this city, flee to another" (Matt 10:23). Families of believers did move on the basis of this instruction.[152]

As Baptists considered where they might move, they were influenced by rumours about certain wonderful places in the Soviet Union where there was freedom of worship and where Christians were not oppressed. Despite the absence of firm evidence, these stories regularly circulated in Baptist communities. Among the places often mentioned as "promised lands" were Western Ukraine, Central Asia, Abkhazia and the Baltic Republics. Various legends were associated with each of these places. In Western Ukraine "there is freedom, even the state flag is not completely red there!"[153] Central Asia was described in this way: "Can you imagine it? The Baptists in Alma-Ata [openly] ride motorcycles to church meetings!"[154] The reputation of Abkhazia was that "there are many churches there and they are not persecuted at all".[155] Soviet Byelorussian Baptists spoke about

151. *BV*, no. 2 (1970), pp. 6-7. *Journal of the Moscow Patriarchate* had similar statements at that time. See, for instance, *ZhMP*, no. 11 (1977), pp. 36-7.

152. For instance, testimonies of Baptist church members: N.S. Kolesnik and V.D. Kolesnik from Dnepropetrovsk Region (Vancouver, Washington, USA, 2006), M.A. Vasiliev and O.E. Avdeeva from Krasnodar Territory (INT, Everett, Washington, USA, 2006).

153. For instance, testimonies of Baptist church members: P.V. Ivanov from Chernovtsy (INT, Fresno, California, USA, 2006), M.A. Vasiliev from Krasnodar (INT, Everett, Washington, USA, 2006), A.A. Mikhaylov from Prokhladny (INT, Fresno, California, USA, 2006).

154. Testimony of Baptist minister from Alma-Ata, V.V. Zinchenko, about stories current in congregations of the ECB in Western Siberia at the beginning of the 1960s (INT, Sacramento, California, USA, 2006).

155. Testimony of Baptist presbyter from Sukhumi, N.S. Kramarenko, about some legends among Baptists in Byelorussia at the end of the 1950s (INT, Sacramento,

freedom of worship in the Baltic republics.[156] For their part, the members of Baptist churches who actually lived in these various regions of the USSR testified about the "far from happy life" of Baptists there as they lived under the Soviet power.[157] However, dreams of a "better life" helped to sustain Baptists who were struggling, and when the decision was made by some to move to a new town or area this decision was less likely to be influenced by awareness of actual reality and was more likely to be the result of prophetic dreams, miraculous visions and revelations, and the casting of lots.[158]

The logical development, for some Baptists (ultimately for many), of the search for the "promised land", was Baptist emigration abroad. With some softening of the Soviet regime's attitude regarding emigration, starting approximately in the mid-1970s, the desire to go abroad was increasingly evident among many Baptists. They found certain verses from the Bible (usually from the Old Testament) which they used to justify their decision. For example, Is. 13:14 was quoted: "Every man shall turn to his own people, and flee every one into his own land." Sometimes this might make sense, for example in the case of ethnic Germans moving from Russia to Germany, but it seems strange coming, for instance, from Russians and Ukrainians going to the USA.[159] Regardless of how texts were used, Russian Baptists began to assert that they must carry out the "will of God". Even the most determined defenders of free will among Soviet Baptists allowed overtones of fatalism to enter their thinking: "What can we do, if we are

---

California, USA, 2006). A.T. Kharchenko also spoke about the good reputation of Abkhazia among Baptist communities in Kirgizia (INT, Sacramento, California, USA, 2006).

156. For instance, testimonies of members of Baptist churches from Belorussia, M.I. Petrenko, I.E. Petrenko, and N.N. Tsvirin'ko (INT, Fresno, California, USA, 2006).

157. For instance: Sedletsky, "Vospominaniya", pp. 133-61; Bondarenko, *Tri Prigovora*, pp. 238-53. Also testimonies of Baptist church ministers A.T. Evstratenko (INT, San Diego, California, USA, 2006) and A.K. Sipko (INT, Spokane, Washington, USA, 2006).

158. For instances, testimonies of former senior presbyter from Kuybyshev, V.F. Serpevsky, and Z.I. Serpevskaya (INT, Vancouver, Washington, USA, 2006), Baptist church members from Belorussia, M.I. Petrenko and I.E. Petrenko (INT, Fresno, California, USA, 2006), A.F. Bernik from Chernovtsy (INT, Fresno, California, USA, 2006).

159. I heard this text used. Another text was Jer 16:15-16 (the "hunters and fishers", returning "the children of Israel from the land of the north"), which implicitly equated the Soviet Baptists to the Jews.

told from above to go there?"[160] However, many of them admitted in con-
fidential conversations that besides religious motives (freedom of worship) they had other aspirations. There was an "anti-Communist" spirit
among some Soviet Baptists, and some were also motivated by material
considerations.[161]

The search for a "promised land" can be linked to national Russian
historical consciousness. Slightly paraphrasing A.S. Pushkin's words, some
Baptists said about themselves: "We were slaves of a tenacious, restless
urge for a change of place."[162] This urge was seen in Orthodox experience.
Throughout the centuries, conscious of all the wretched injustices of Russian
life, many Orthodox peasants sought for the legendary Belovodie or the
miraculous town, Kitezh.[163] Such wanderings were especially characteristic
for the Old Believers, who did not wish to obey the "laws of Antichrist".[164]
There were even special sects of "Wanderers and Runners".[165] However,

160. For instance, testimony of Baptist evangelist from Dushanbe, P.A. Semeryuk (INT,
Sacramento, California, USA, 2006).

161. See, for instance, Kuksenko, *Nashi Besedy*, pp. 150-1.

162. Testimony of minister of the ECB from Kiev, L.E. Kovalenko (INT, Sacramento,
California, USA, 2006). Cf.: A. Pushkin, *Eugene Onegin*, VIII, 13. – A.S. Pushkin, *Eugene
Onegin*, transl. by C. Johnston (London: Penguin, 2003), p. 180.

163. See, for instance: A. Klibanov, *Narodnaya Sotsial'naya Utopiya v Rossii: Period
Feodalizma* [People's Social Utopia in Russia: the Feudal Period] (M.: Nauka, 1977), pp.
219-25; *"Legenda o Grade Kitezhe"* [The Legend of the City of Kitezh], in *Pamyatniki
Literatury Drevney Rusi, XIII v.* [Literary Monuments of the Early Rus, the 13th Century]
(M.: Khudozhestvennaya Literatura, 1978), pp. 210-27. In Russian evangelical history
there were "utopias" too: *Dukhoboria* [The Land of the Dukhobors], *Evangelsk* ["The
City of the Gospel", also named "The City of the Sun"], Baptist agricultural communes,
etc. See, for instance: A. Bezhentseva, *Strana Dukhoboria* [Dukhoboria Land] (Tbilisi:
Russky Klub, 2007), pp. 46-69; Mitrokhin, *Baptizm: Istoriya i Sovremennost'*, pp. 205-6;
Prokhanov, *In the Cauldron of Russia*, pp. 231-2; *"Ekspeditsiya po Izyskaniyu Zemel' dlya
Goroda Solntsa"* [Expedition Searching for the Lands of the City of the Sun], *Khristianin*,
no. 2 (1928), pp. 44-52. See also N. Breyfogle, "Heretics and Colonizers: Religious
Dissent and Russian Colonization of Transcaucasia, 1830-1890" (PhD thesis, University
of Pennsylvania, 1998), pp. 79-145.

164. See, for instance: E. Smorgunova, *"Iskhod Staroverov Vchera i Segodnya: Ukhod ot
Mira i Poiski Zemli Obetovannoy"* [Exodus of the Old Believers Yesterday and Today:
Escape from the World and Searching for the Promised Land], in *Istoriya Tserkvi:
Izuchenie i Prepodavanie* [Church History: Studying and Teaching] (Yekaterinburg: Izd-vo
Ural'skogo Gosuniversiteta, 1999), pp. 211-9.

165. See, for instance, V. Anderson, *Staroobryadchestvo i Sektantstvo* [Old Belief and
Sectarianism] (SPb.: Izdanie V.I. Gubinskogo, 1909), pp. 168-82; Zenkovsky, *Russkoe
Staroobryadchestvo*, pp. 497-9; Some Russian Baptists also testify about similar tendencies

while resettlement within Russia, despite all the troubles and burdens connected with this event, was common practice for many Orthodox people
and Russian Baptists (whether this happened under compulsion or voluntarily), and moral justification was given, emigration "to the other end of
the world" was usually considered in an entirely different way. Orthodox
authors wrote: "The ease with which these sectarians [Baptists] break off
their connection with Russia, testifies to the absence of any gravitational
pull within them towards the native land, a feeling that is so natural for
every Russian man."[166] Yet many Baptists saw moving abroad as "wrong"
and "bad". Hence the widespread "guilt complex" among many Baptists
emigrants, a phenomenon rooted in the feeling that they had changed the
"native soil" for a "hateful" foreign one. Ideally, according to archetypal
Russian spirituality, Russian Christians would be better to suffer martyrdom at the hands of Christ's enemies in Russia than to live safely abroad.
In his poem *The Execution*, written to 1927 and often quoted to this day,
including by some Russian Baptists emigrants,[167] Vladimir Nabokov expressed this deep feeling with great force.

On certain nights as soon as I lie down
my bed starts drifting into Russia,
and presently I'm led to a ravine,
to a ravine, led to be killed...

. . . .

But how you would have wished, my heart,
that *thus* it all had really been:
Russia, the stars, the night of execution
and full of racemosas the ravine![168]

---

in the brotherhood in Soviet times. See, for example, the chapter "Running man"
(interview with N.S. Kolesnik and V.D. Kolesnik) in the book: *Podvig Very: Unikal'nye
Svidetel'stva o Zhizni Khristian v SSSR* [Fight of Faith: Unique Testimonies about the
Life of Christians in the USSR] (n.p.: Pacific Coast Slavic Baptist Association, 2009),
pp. 23-30.

166. Val'kevich, *Zapiska o Propagande Protestantskikh Sekt v Rossii*, p. 222.

167. Incidentally, I heard this poem for the first time from Russians in Sacramento
(California, USA) in 2006.

168. V. Nabokov, *Poems and Problems* (London: Weidenfeld & Nicolson, 1971),

In the case of many of the hundreds of thousands of Russian Baptists who have gone to the USA, there has frequently been deep disappointment. These words are often heard: "We are not entrusted with any good work here; we still do not learn English, and at the same time we forget Russian."[169] Nostalgia has led many to idealize their former life in the Soviet Union. A few, after the Communist regime collapsed, returned to countries of the former USSR.[170] Many more simply expressed failure: "As soon as the possibilities for preaching the Gospel in the USSR were opened up, we ran away from there."[171] The alternative Baptist community in Russia was not as strongly shaped by its piety as might have seemed to be the case.

Conclusion

This chapter has undertaken an analysis of the diverse manifestations of Russian Baptist popular piety and has made connections with Orthodox spirituality. Russian Baptists drew strength from traditions and stories, from Leo Tolstoy as well as from their own community's history. Another way in which the Baptist community was given inner coherence was by the moral markers which marked out Baptist Christians from citizens of the USSR who were shaped by other prevailing perspectives. Inner life was also renewed by a range of sacraments, as was the case in Orthodoxy, and this chapter has argued that at the level of popular piety these sacraments had elements of superstition mixed into them, again mirroring Orthodox life. It was crucial that Russian Baptists had a strong sense of their identity as those converted to Christ, serving God, and part of full-blooded, congregational Christian life, since within society they did not belong. The challenges of living as an alternative community began at school and

---

p. 47. Padus racemosa (bird cherry tree) is a bush with white blossoms, reckoned to be indigenous to Russia.

169. A typical testimony of Baptist church member from Petropavlovsk, G.N. Mokey (INT, Minneapolis, Minnesota, USA, 2006).

170. Though such occurrences are comparatively rare (I personally know only a few cases), the story of such people is told by Russian Baptists.

171. These or similar words were repeated by elders I interviewed.

continued through into the work-place. There were many experiences of discrimination, although in numerous Baptist narratives, as in Orthodox stories, God vindicated his faithful witnesses. For some Baptists, suffering was intense. The outcome, for example for those in labor camps, could be that their faith was seen as praiseworthy, but it could also be "suffering unto death". Ultimate triumph, however, as in many traditional Orthodox tales, was to be expected: the wicked would experience divine judgment. Finally, there was a hope within Russian Baptist life, a hope that was also there in Orthodox movements, of a "promised land". This was never fully explained, and in part the vision is in line with the apophatic rather than the cataphatic approach to faith. The movement of so many Baptists out of Russia is at odds with much of the strongly Russian piety examined in this study. This movement was not to be explained rationally, as seen in the question that has been asked, "Could God really have made a mistake that I was born in Russia?"[172] Going to the West has not meant that Russian Baptists have found Kitezh and Belovodie. That search continues.

172. The grieving words of an aged Baptist, whom I interviewed. This person, although living in the USA for a long time, mentally still remains in Russia.

CHAPTER 9

Conclusion

This work has sought to analyze the experience of the Evangelical Christians-Baptists (ECB) in the USSR in the period 1960 to 1990, with the particular focus of the study being an examination of evidence regarding the ways in which Russian Orthodox thinking and practice were mirrored in the Russian Baptist movement. As noted in the introduction, recent studies have been undertaken which seek to examine the identity of the Evangelical Christians-Baptists in the Soviet period.[1] But relatively little attention has been paid in these and other studies to the possibility that elements within Russian Orthodoxy have played a significant role in the shaping of Russian Baptist identity. Also, the scholarly theses and some of the important books that have been produced have tended to concentrate on the All-Union Council of Evangelical Christians-Baptists (AUCECB), which was formed in 1944. This study has looked at the AUCECB and also the Council of Churches of Evangelical Christians-Baptists (CCECB), while was formed as a result of a group splitting from the AUCECB in the 1960s. This division has been analyzed, for example by Walter Sawatsky in *Soviet Evangelicals since World War II*,[2] but the tendency has been to see the two Baptist groups as standing in opposition to one another. This study suggests that if the dimension of the Orthodox tradition is used as a lens through which to look at Russian Baptists from the 1960s to the 1990s, the

---

1. See especially A. Puzynin, "The Tradition of the Gospel Christians" (2008), and Alexander Popov, "The Evangelical Christians-Baptists in the Soviet Union as a Hermeneutical Community" (2010).

2. W. Sawatsky, *Soviet Evangelicals since World War II* (Kitchener, Ontario: Herald Press, 1981).

two Baptist groups exhibit remarkable similarities. Both of them exhibited a range of features to be found in Russian Orthodoxy.

Areas of commonality

The emergence and development of Russian Evangelicals and Baptists in the nineteenth century, a phenomenon considered in chapter 2, was shaped by a number of influences. The considerable contribution of Protestants from outside Russia to this process cannot be denied. However, this Russian "choice of faith" was not something that began in the nineteenth century. When Orthodoxy was first embraced by the Russian rulers and then by the people, a choice was made. Later, Russian Old Believers and sectarians made their own choices. In none of these cases was something entirely new formed. The way in which strands of belief were woven together in an era of religious change has been investigated by S.I. Zhuk in his work on what he calls the 'Lost Reformation' of the period 1830 to 1917.[3] It is this kind of approach which has been pursued in this work. The growth of Evangelical and Baptist communities in the Orthodox setting, growth that took place increasingly because of the conversion of those with an Orthodox or a Molokan background, did not, I have argued, lead simply to a Russian Protestant movement. The Russian Baptist movement, as it assumed its own particular identity, developed its own unique and deeply national characteristics. In particular, although Baptists often distinguished them-selves from Orthodoxy, there were clear Orthodox-Baptist commonalities.

These commonalities were evident in the later Soviet period in the area of theology. Chapter 3 gave attention to an analysis of Russian Baptist thinking about the nature of God, which mirrored Orthodox "apophat-ic" approaches, and to soteriology, where I argued that Baptist statements which have seemed to suggest Arminian influence actually resonated with important Orthodox themes. In the area of anthropology, Russian Baptists placed great emphasis on holiness and on confession of sin, which echoed

---

3. S. Zhuk, *Russia's Lost Reformation: Peasants, Millennialism, and Radical Sects in Southern Russia and Ukraine, 1830-1917* (Washington, D.C.: Woodrow Wilson Center Press, 2004).

Orthodox spirituality. This chapter also explored the question of Scripture and tradition. It is true that Russian Baptists never gave their traditions the position that Orthodoxy accorded to Tradition. Officially Russian Baptists affirmed *Sola Scriptura*. However, they saw their tradition as having remarkable power. Thus A.K. Sipko argued for the Russian Baptist theological tradition in this way: "In Russia, there was and is the best theology – the living, pure, tested by experience, tried for firmness and purity in the extreme conditions."[4] This sense of being connected with the Russian past was fully in the spirit of Russian Orthodoxy. Nor were these similarities evident only in theory: they were found in practice. Thus as Russian Baptists dealt with the death of believers and their entry into the life to come, some of their customs resembled those developed in Orthodox tradition.

Russian Baptist thinking about church and sacraments was closely linked with their broader theological approach. On the basis of the evidence presented in chapter 4, I argued that Russian Baptists saw a mystical depth in the sacraments which echoed Orthodox tradition. Mark Elliott wrote in 1995 about how "Slavic Christianity, in both its Orthodox and Evangelical expressions, strongly emphasizes God's awesomeness, majesty, and holiness... Eastern Orthodox and Slavic Evangelicals have a more sacramental understanding of faith than is typical for Western Evangelicals."[5] This study has traced crucial ecclesiological and sacramental developments in detail. Thus whereas the traditional Russian Baptist view of the "ordinances" restricted them to baptism and the Lord's Supper, by the 1960s seven ordinances were being listed, in line with Orthodox tradition, and the language of sacrament was being commonly used by Baptists. Many of the ways in which Baptists operated in relation to the sacraments were shown, in chapter 4, to mirror monastic and wider Orthodox tradition. Although Russian Baptists officially denied that external church ceremonies had saving power and spoke in formal terms of the "symbolism" of church ordinances, at the level of daily church practice their approach to

---

4. A. Sipko, *Derzhis' Obraztsa Zdravogo Ucheniya: Sbornik Statey* [Keep the Pattern of Sound Teaching: Collection of Articles] (Spokane, WA: NCG Inc., 2010), p. 224.

5. M. Elliott, "Eastern Orthodox and Slavic Evangelicals: What Sets Them Both Apart From Western Evangelicals", *East-West Church & Ministry Report*, vol. 3, no. 4 (1995), p. 15.

baptism, entry into the church, the Lord's Supper, ministerial ordination, consecration of buildings, marriage, prayer for children and for the sick, and burial, all resembled aspects of Orthodox practice.

The analysis undertaken in chapter 5, of the Russian Baptist "church year", the liturgical order used in worship, church music and singing, the major ceremonial acts and the place of the Bible, all suggest significant correspondences with Russian Orthodoxy. For example, the common church feasts observed in Baptist communities follow the Orthodox pattern rather than that found in Western Christian tradition. To take another example, I argued that the sacramental attitude to the Bible – not only to the content of the Bible but to the book itself – closely paralleled Orthodox reverence for icons. The same kinds of resemblances were examined in chapter 6, which looked at Russian Baptist communal spiritual traditions. The influential American writer and philosopher Ayn Rand advocated the idea of civilization expressed in individualism, as opposed to the "barbarism" expressed in communal life.[6] But for Russian Orthodoxy and for Russian Baptists it was community, the feeling for *sobornost,* which gave meaning to the life of individuals. Some features of Russian Baptist communal spirituality which mirrored Orthodoxy were the "monastic way", including the spirituality of the Ladder, and the place of "saints" and "holy fools" in the community. All of this created a particular Russian Baptist identity. When A.V. Karev made the breathtaking statement in 1957, "We can say without any pride and conceit that the Evangelical-Baptist Church in the USSR is the Apostolic Church of the twentieth century",[7] he was articulating a strong sense of Baptist identity, but the decades that followed would increasingly show how that identity was shared with Orthodoxy, not least through the closer ties that were fostered between the two communities.

In chapters 7 and 8, I probed some of the beliefs, behavior and popular piety in the Russian Baptist communities more deeply. I argued that many of the common regulations and customs which were affirmed by Baptists as being biblical and evangelical, for instance in relation to fasting,

---

6. See A. Rand, *The Fountainhead* [1943] (N.Y.: Plume, 2005), p. 715.

7. A. Karev, *"Russkoe Evangel'sko-Baptistskoe Dvizhenie"* [The Russian Evangelical-Baptist Movement], *BV,* no. 4 (1957), p. 38. Such ideas were found much earlier, in I.S. Prokanov's time. See, for instance, *Utrennyaya Zvezda,* nos. 6-8 (1922), pp. 6-14.

alms-giving and modes of dress, were remarkably similar to Orthodox practices. The hostile atheistic surroundings meant that Orthodox believers and Baptists were facing the same pressures, resisting policies designed to stamp out Christian witness. In the case of Baptists, part of the response was to engage in especially strict disciplinary actions in order to preserve the purity of the community. *Bratsky Vestnik* noted this repeatedly, with regret, in the period from the 1960s to the 1980s.[8]

However, at the same time the inner life of Baptist communities was renewed by a range of sacraments, as was the case in Orthodoxy, and chapter 8 argued that at the level of popular piety these sacraments had elements of superstition mixed into them, again mirroring Orthodox life. The challenges for Baptists of living as an alternative community were many-faceted. For some Baptists, the suffering was great, especially for those in labor camps. But final victory, as in many well-known Orthodox narratives, would come. Areas of Orthodox-Baptist commonality abounded.

Seeking explanations

My contention that there are many ways in which Russian Baptist beliefs and practices resemble Orthodoxy is not the interpretation that has commonly been given of the relationship. The statements which have been common currency in Orthodox conversation have often been of this kind: "The Baptists are the most harmful sect", "Kat'ka[9] invited a German [to Russia] to plant potatoes, but instead he planted the *Stunda* for us."[10] It is also possible to find not a few nominally Orthodox theologians who demonstrate a markedly *sectarian* spirit, intolerant of any dissent.[11] On the other

---

8. See, for instance, A. Karev, "*Informatsiya o s"ezde ECB v Moskve*" [Information about the Baptist Council in Moscow], *BV*, no. 6 (1966), pp. 21-2; A. Bychkov, "*Otchetny Doklad S"ezdu ECB*" [Summary Report to the Council of the ECB], *BV*, no. 3 (1985), p. 22; "*Ocherednoy Plenum VSECB*" [Regular Plenum of the AUCECB] (editorial article), *BV*, no. 3 (1986), pp. 40-1.

9. They were speaking of the Russian Empress Catherine the Great.

10. My attention was drawn to this by Baptist historian S.N. Savinsky (INT, Salt Lake City, Utah, USA, 2006).

11. See Archbishop Ioann (Shakhovskoy), "*Sektantstvo v Pravoslavii i Pravoslavie v*"

hand, Russian Baptists have been quick to condemn any formal, external Orthodox practices observed among their church members, for example the possession of a small crucifix or icon. Some radical Baptists taught that there was salvation for "Baptists only".[12] At the same time, many Baptist presbyters could preach from the pulpit sermons that were suffused with the Orthodox essence and spirit. Nor was it the case by any means that inter-confessional hostility was typical. As has been shown in this work, the period being examined here was one in which many events indicated that a surprising Orthodox-Baptist rapprochement was taking place. Not only did Baptists accord more respect to Orthodox leaders, but the place of "sectarians" was affirmed, at least to some extent, within Orthodoxy.[13]

Perhaps this coming together was not, however, so surprising, although it has not been the subject of analysis. The religious boundaries were never rigid. There were always Christian believers in Russia who held, as some put it, that God's truth was too great for any one mind, or a church, or even a denomination, and that "in eternity" Christians would find out that none of them had the full truth. Thus in one of his books, Archpriest J. Meyendorff draws attention to the fact that Tertullian, even after associating himself with Montanism, wrote a number of important works which were marked by an "Orthodox spirit".[14] It is precisely this kind of interaction that I have been arguing took place as Russian Baptists lived in an Orthodox "territory". The Baptist community transformed the doctrines

Sektantstve" [Sectarianism in Orthodoxy and Orthodoxy in Sectarianism], *Pravoslavnaya Obshchina*, no. 4 (1992), pp. 71-7.

12. In the summer of 2006 in the USA, during my interviews with Baptist elders, immigrants from the former USSR, several representatives of the CCECB, and some "pure" Baptists expressed such an opinion.

13. For example, Archpriest O. Stenyaev interpreted the Gospel parable about the Good Samaritan in this way: a Russian Orthodox priest, in a hurry to conduct religious rites, passed by a suffering man, but a sectarian stopped on the street in order to help him and dress his wounds. See *Pravoslavie.Ru* (Internet-journal), 1 February 2005, <http://www.pravoslavie.ru/news/ print12544.htm> accessed 9 December 2010.

14. See J. Meyendorff, *Vvedenie v Svyatootecheskoe Bogoslovie* [Introduction to Patristic Theology] (N.Y.: RBR, 1985), pp. 52-3. And one of the most important works of Tertullian remains his *Prescription against Heretics*. See Tertullian, "The Prescription against Heretics", in A. Roberts and J. Donaldson, eds., *The Ante-Nicene Fathers*, 10 vols. (Grand Rapids: Eerdmans, 1978), vol. III, pp. 243-68.

and ideas that came to them from evangelicals outside Russia, until at times these became almost unrecognizable.

This process was assisted to a significant degree by the size of Russia. As N.V. Gogol memorably suggested in *The Government Inspector* (possibly looking at a map of Russia): "You could gallop from here for three years and not reach a foreign country!"[15] Very few Russian Baptists traveled outside their country to meet with and talk to Baptists from elsewhere. Their contacts were largely with other Russians, Baptists and Orthodox. The Communist leaders of the USSR also indirectly contributed to this process, for example in their post-World War II policy of strict isolationism. It was in this post-war period (and in particular from the 1960s onwards), I have argued, that Russian Baptists uniquely brought together some evangelical and Orthodox ideas and traditions. Archpriest Sergy (Savinykh), in answer to a question that I put to him, wrote in 2006: "The Russian Baptists, in their spiritual life and church practice, are much different from Western Baptists... In the past [few] decades, the native Baptist tradition took on 'Russian' features."[16]

This is not to suggest that what I have set out in this study proves that Russian Baptists were in all cases consciously absorbing Orthodox theology, liturgical patterns and spiritual traditions. With many of the features I have investigated, the process was taking place without Baptists making conscious decisions about their beliefs, liturgical practices and behavior. Indeed in the period being studied both Russian Orthodox and Baptist believers, it could be argued, were the inheritors of an older Russian way of believing in Christ, an approach that was not readily reduced to rational theological formulae. Orthodoxy certainly had the Ecumenical Creeds, while Baptists held to the Bible and also to their confessions of faith, but the more powerful currents which were at work were under the surface, in a largely undefined Russian tradition. I have suggested that to some extent this was linked with the thinking of the Slavophiles. A cultural and theological opposition to the West has been evident in Orthodoxy but was in

---

15. N.V. Gogol, *The Government Inspector*, transl. by D. Campbell (London: Sylvan Press, 1947), p. 29.

16. E-mail, Archpriest Sergy (Savinykh) to me, 15.02.2006.

part intrinsic also to Russian Baptists.[17] Some Russian Baptist "*Pochvenniks*" maintained the idea of the exceptional, indeed unique identity of "great Russia", which contributed to their defence of the concept of the independent origin and development of the native evangelical movement.[18]

It is also possible that a process was at work in the 1960s which was similar to that explored by E. Troeltsch and H.R. Niebuhr, who noted that second generation sectarians begin to gravitate toward church structures that replicate the ways of the historic churches.[19] This analysis does not apply in its strict form, since over several generations Russian Baptists and evangelicals had held largely to their traditional "sectarian" outlook. But the thesis is still helpful, since what was happening in the period looked at in this research was that a new phase was emerging in Russian Baptist life. As has been argued here, increasingly there were many aspects of liturgy and of communal practices that contain Orthodox echoes. Of course, this was not true of all Soviet Baptists, or of all the beliefs of Soviet Baptists. In each chapter of this study I have indicated ways in which Baptist and Orthodox beliefs differed. However, in this study as a whole I have sought to show the strong tendency that existed among Russian Baptists to mirror Orthodoxy ways, and in addition the evidence presented has to do as much, if not more, with local practices as with official statements by theologians.

Further possibilities for research

This study has not taken the analysis beyond 1990. One possible area of fruitful examination would be the diversity that has arisen among the

---

17. See a review of the theme: V. Solodovnikov, "*Sdelano v Amerike*" [Made in America], *Slovo Very*, no. 1 (2002), pp. 25-30.

18. See, for instance, A. Bychkov, "*Stoletie Ob"edinitel'nykh S"ezdov*" [The Centenary of the Unifying Councils], *BV*, no. 6 (1984), pp. 44-5.

19. See H.R. Niebuhr, *The Social Sources of Denominationalism* (Hamden, CT: Shoe String Press, 1954), pp. 19-20; E. Troeltsch, *The Social Teaching of the Christian Churches* (Louisville, KY: Westminster/ John Knox Press, 1992), v. I, pp. 331-43. See also S. Nesdoly, "Evangelical Sectarianism in Russia: A Study of the Stundists, Baptists, Pashkovites, and Evangelical Christians, 1855-1917"; S. Dunn, E. Dunn, "Some Comments on Sectarianism in the Soviet Union", *Soviet Studies*, Vol. 20, 3 (1969), pp. 410-2.

former Soviet Baptists since the 1990s. Some have moved decisively in an Orthodox-orientated direction. The Baptists of Georgia are notable in this regard. In the 1990s, the President of the Baptist Union of Georgia adopted a new approach and was officially robed with sumptuous church vestments and held a mitre and a crosier. Local Baptist churches were decorated with frescos and candles and a censer began to be used during church services.[20] Unlike the Baptists of Georgia, Russian Baptist churches have not adopted these practices. They have seen them as artificial, with their external "Orthodox form" considerably outstripping their "Baptist substance". With the ending of Communism and of the USSR, a great deal of American evangelical thinking has entered the Russian evangelical community. Meanwhile the hundreds of thousands of Russian Baptists who have emigrated to the USA have formed their own sub-cultures, a phenomenon which has been studied to some extent.[21] While some aspects of religion in the post-Soviet area are being investigated,[22] there is room for more detailed work on the effects on Orthodox, Baptist and other evangelical communities of the massive changes that took place when the USSR came to an end.

More research could also be undertaken into regional differences within the Soviet Baptist community. As Alexander Popov has suggested, the "modern national and denominational unions which replaced the single All-Union Council demonstrated the great diversity that was concealed in the previous structure".[23] Popov's own work, concentrating as it does on the publications of the AUCECB, tends to suggest a degree of uniformity. To some extent the diversity had to do with the particular balance of Western and Eastern Christian thinking held by those who wrote for *Bratsky Vestnik* in particular. But there were no doubt geographical features. The study

---

20. See W.B. Boswell, "Liturgy and Revolution Part II: Radical Christianity, Radical Democracy, and Revolution in Georgia", *Religion in Eastern Europe*, vol. XXVII, no. 3 (2007), pp. 15-31; *Mezhdunarodnaya Khristianskaya Gazeta*, no. 7 (2005), p. 6.

21. S.W. Hardwick, *Russian Refuge: Religion, Migration and Settlement on the North American Pacific Rim* (Chicago: Chicago University Press, 1993).

22. See, for example: P. Froese, *The Plot to Kill God: Findings from the Soviet Experiment in Secularization* (Berkeley, CA: University of California Press, 2008), pp. 142-64.

23. Popov, "The Evangelical Christians-Baptists in the Soviet Union as a hermeneutical community", p. 288.

that Irina Bondareva-Zuehlke produced for Moldova is an example of what could be done in respect of other regions.[24] In this work I have not attempted to make comparisons across the territory of the USSR, but there are indications that there were customs I have investigated within Russian Baptist life that were more typical of Baptists further East, who were often more cut off from Western thinking.

Finally, Bondareva-Zuehlke's study of the issue of "separation or co-operation" among Russian Baptists suggests that more could be explored regarding the two Baptist communities, the AUCECB and the CCECB, which after the split in the 1960s both claimed to represent authentic Russian Baptist life. To some extent the role of the AUCECB, as by far the larger Union, has claimed more of the attention of historians. Thus Ernest Payne's 1974 book on Soviet Baptists, *Out of Great Tribulation: Baptists in the USSR*, offered a useful introduction to the AUCECB as it was at that time.[25] Payne, who was a president of the World Council of Churches, had natural links with the "official" Baptists. Others have given attention to the split itself or to the sufferings of the underground Baptists, but in this study I have suggested that at the level of communal spiritual traditions the two groups shared much in common. Indeed in some (although not in all) areas, the CCECB, as the supposedly more radical and certainly anti-state Baptist group, may have also been more traditionally Russian. There is scope for further probing of this phenomenon.

Reconciling warring brothers

A Russian Baptist poem from the Soviet era has these words:

> …Reconcile warring brothers,
> and their Father will fold you in his arms.

---

24. I. Bondareva-Zuehlke, "Separation or Co-operation? Moldavian Baptists (1940-1965)", in K.G. Jones and I.M. Randall, eds., *Counter-Cultural Communities. Baptist Life in Twentieth-Century Europe* (Milton Keynes, UK: Paternoster, 2008), pp. 63-113.
25. E.A. Payne, *Out of Great Tribulation: Baptists in the USSR* (London: Baptist Union, 1974).

As this is read in the light of the research that has been undertaken here, it is difficult to avoid the impression that among Russian Orthodox and Baptist believers in the period examined there has been a trend towards drawing together as "brothers". This common inclination may often have been operating at the subconscious level. What has been explored in this study has been to a considerable extent Russian "popular belief" in Christ, in which strict systematization was an alien approach. The Orthodox and Baptist "brothers" were not united primarily by confessional statements, indeed they offered few if any rigorous theological expositions or rational theological formulae. It is true that there were different, distinct confessional identities – "Orthodoxy" and "Russian Baptists" – but whereas much attention has been given to external differences between these traditions, I have sought to show how many things closely corresponded *inside* the general Russian Christian tradition. Many examples have been used to substantiate this case. At the level of daily church practice, Russian Baptists could not, I have argued, be termed "classical Protestants". This has been apparent in such areas as Scripture and tradition, faith and good works, church sacraments, and many aspects of devotion.

The Baptist poem quoted above promises that when there is spiritual reconciliation God is at work and will "fold you in his arms". It is this mystical sense of God's presence which has been a marked feature within both Orthodox and Baptist traditions in Russia. Nor was this "enfolding" an individualistic experience. Whereas there has been a tendency towards individualism in some branches of Protestantism, the thinking and practice of Russian Baptists in the area of ecclesiology indicates that they held to a high view of the church as a visible community. There was much about the liturgy, about mystery, about the sacraments, and about the approach to church history within Russian Baptist communities that had strong echoes of Orthodoxy. Although American influence in recent years has drawn some Russian Baptists away from an interest in tradition, among other Russian evangelicals a love for the writings of the church fathers, who are often considered as "also our fathers", has been increasing. At the same time, many Russian Orthodox people are realizing more and more the importance of regular reading of the Bible, are appreciating the role of close-knit church communities, and are responding to preaching that is living and accessible. In my view these are good preconditions for further posi-tive and fruitful developments in interdenominational dialogue in Russia. I hope that this work can contribute to that process.

Conclusion

This study has not approached Russian Baptist life as if it was entirely separate from Russian Orthodoxy. V.S. Soloviev in his late book *Three Conversations* (1900), spoke of the three great Apostles of Christ as point-ing to three great Christian traditions: Peter to Roman Catholicism, John to Eastern Orthodoxy, and Paul to Protestantism. Soloviev sees these tra-ditions as in a measure mutually enriching and supplementing each oth-er.[26] More recently, H.A. Stammler, writing in 1979 in the *St. Vladimir's Theological Quarterly*, spoke of Orthodoxy and Protestantism as "two prov-inces of Christendom".[27] Russian Baptists in the period examined here did not generally engage in this kind of theological discourse. For them, the Russian Baptist way, with all its beliefs and customs, was simply the biblical way. They were often more concerned to highlight "unbiblical" Orthodox customs than to acknowledge the resemblances that have been the focus of this study. Those seeking salvation, Russian Baptists believed, should be-come members of their congregations. This was much "safer" for them than hoping for salvation in other Christian denominations, including Russian Orthodoxy.[28] On the other hand (for instance) one of the famous Russian Baptist hymns spoke about the church as the gathering of Christians "from all communities and flocks".[29] In the Russian context there was an implicit

---

26. See, for instance, an English publication of the book: V. Solovyov, *War, Progress, and the End of History: Three Conversations, Including a Short Story of the Anti-Christ* (Hudson, N.Y.: Lindisfarne Press, 1990).

27. H. Stammler, "Russian Orthodoxy in Recent Protestant Church History and Theology", *St. Vladimir's Theological Quarterly*, nos. 3-4 (1979), p. 215.

28. These are very typical views held by Baptist presbyters whom I know well from Kazakhstan. They have made statements such as these about salvation in other Christian denominations: "No one knows whether or not salvation will be possible for them", and "we are completely in the dark about this".

29. *SDP*, no. 293, p. 199; *PV*, no. 252, p. 162.

acceptance within this sentiment of Russian Orthodoxy as well as evangelical Christianity – these were the main "flocks" that were present. But to
what extent Russian Baptists were explicitly open to Orthodox ways or to
influences from Orthodox tradition in specific cases has not been the primary focus of this work. Rather the point that has been argued throughout,
using a wide range of evidence, has been that Russian Baptists had certain
ideas, certain ways of conducting worship and certain patterns of spiritual
behavior that were remarkably similar to those found in Orthodoxy, and
which therefore mirrored the pervasive religious context of Russia. As has
sometimes been said, scratch a Russian Baptist and you will find a monk.

Bibliography

1. Primary

1.1 Archival Documents

1.1.1. The Archives of the Russian Union of the Evangelical Christians-Baptists (Moscow, Russia)

"Vtoroy Vserossiysky S"ezd Evangel'skikh Khristian" [The Second All-Russian Council of the Evangelical Christians] [1911], ARSECB, F. 1, op. 11de, d. 25, ll. 13-21.

"Avtobiografiya M.K. Kalweita" [The Autobiography of M.K. Kalweit] [1913], ARSECB, F. 1, op. 5-8, d. 20.

"Otchet Vserossiyskogo S"ezda Evangel'kich Khhristian Baptistov" (Report of All-Russian Council of Evangelical Christians Baptists) [Moscow, 27 May-6 June, 1920], ARSECB, F. 1, op. 11de, d. 16.

"Polozhenie o Soyuze Evangel'skikh Khristian-Baptistov" [The Statutes of the Union of Evangelical Christians-Baptists] [1944], ARSECB, F. 1, op. 11da, d. 54.

"To all Senior Presbyters (On Ordination)" [1945], ARSECB, F. 1, op. 1d1, d. 1d1-139.

"Polozhenie o Soyuze Evangel'skikh Khristian-Baptistov" [The Statutes of the Union of Evangelical Christians-Baptists] [1948], ARSECB, F. 1, op. 1d1, d. 96.

"Pis'mo Prezidiuma VSECB Vsem Presviteram Obshchin ECB v SSSR" [Letter of the Presidium of the AUCECB to All Presbyters of Baptist Communities of the USSR] [1953], ARSECB, F. 1, op. 1d1, d. 64.

"V Sovet po Delam Religioznykh Kul'tov" [To the Council for the Affairs of Religious Cults] [1958], ARSECB, F. 1, op. 2pd, d. 15.

"Svedeniya o Kolichestve Obshchin Evangel'skikh Khristian-Baptistov i Chlenov Obshchin" [The Data on the Quantity of Communities of Evangelical Christians-Baptists and Church Members] [1958], ARSECB, F. 1, op. 2pd, d. 08.

"Statisticheskie Svedeniya po VSECB" [Statistical data of the AUCECB] [1959], ARSECB, F. 1, op. 2pd, d. 06.

"Polozhenie o Soyuze Evangel'skikh Khristian-Baptistov v SSSR" [The Statutes of the Union of Evangelical Christians-Baptists of the USSR] [1960], ARSECB, F. 1, op. 28d, d. 52.

"Instruktivnoe Pis'mo Starshim Presviteram VSECB" [Letter of Instructions for the Senior Presbyters of the AUCECB] [1960], ARSECB, F. 1, op. 22d.6, d. 4.

"Instruktivnoe Pis'mo Starshim Presviteram VSECB" [Letter of Instructions for the Senior Presbyters of the AUCECB] [1960], Novosibirsk Baptist Church Archives.

"Popravki A.F. Prokofieva i G.K. Kryuchkova k 'Polozheniyu o Soyuze ECB'", 1960 [Amendments of A.F. Prokofiev and G.K. Kryuchkov to the 'Statutes of the Union of ECB', 1960] [1961], ARSECB, F. 1, op. 28d.2, d. 5.

"Otvet na Antireligioznuyu Stat'yu 'Ne Bud'te Trupom Sredi Zhivykh'" [Answer to the Antireligious Article 'Do not be Dead among the Living'] [1962], ARSECB, F. 1, op. 28d, d. 61.

"Kratkie Sovety Molodezhi" [Short Advice to the Youth] (From *Vestnik Spaseniya*, 1965), ARSECB, F. 1, op. 28d5, d. 2, l. 32.

"Otchet o Vstreche Predstaviteley Soveta Tserkvey Evangel'skikh Khristian-Baptistov so VSECB" [Report on the Meeting of Representatives of the Council of Churches with the AUCECB], ARSECB, F. 1, op. 32.1, d. 32.1-23.

"Pis'mo A.V. Karevu ot Anonima" [Anonymous Letter to A.V. Karev], ARSECB, F. 1, op. 28d7a, d. 19.

"Pis'mo A.V. Karevu ot Chlena Tserkvi ECB Yu.M. Paydich" [Letter of Baptist church member Yu.M. Paydich to A.V. Karev] [1969], ARSECB, F. 1, op. 28d7a, d. 13.

"Osvyatis'!" [Be Holy!] [From *Vestnik Spaseniya*, 1973], ARSECB, F. 1, op. 28d, d. 18, ll. 1-3.

"Chastichny Analiz 'Bratskogo Listka' za 1975 g. v Svyazi s Desyatiletiem Ego Vypuska" [Partial Analysis of 'Fraternal Leaflet' of 1975 on the Occasion of the 10th Anniversary of its Issue] [1975], ARSECB, F. 1, op. 28d, d. 46.

1.1.2. Southern Baptist Historical Library and Archives (Nashville, USA)

The Autobiography of Jacob Delakoff, Independent Missionary in Russia, The European Harvest Field: March 1935, pp. 2-7; April 1935, pp. 4-6; May 1935, pp. 12-16; June 1935, pp. 8-11; September 1935, pp. 11-13,18; October 1935, pp. 12-14; November 1935, pp. 11-15; December 1935, pp. 14-16.

1.1.3. Copies of V.A. Pashkov Papers (the Library of International Baptist Theological Seminary, Prague, Czech Republic)

Letter of J. Delyakov to V.A. Pashkov, November 2, 1884. Copies of Pashkov Papers, 2/8/39.

"Razgovor Pravoslavnogo i Pashkovtsa o Svyashchennom Pisanii i Predaniyakh Tserkovnykh" [The Conversation of an Orthodox and a Pashkovite about Scripture and Church Tradition]. – Copies of Pashkov Papers, 1/9.

1.1.4. Personal files of S.N. Savinsky (Salt Lake City, Utah, USA, 2006)

"Ryaboshapka" (typescript).

1.1.5. Personal files of P.K. Sedletsky (Omsk, Russia)

K.S. Sedletsky, "Vospominaniya" [Memoirs], typescript (Omsk, Russia, 2007).

1.1.6. Personal files of G.E. Kuchma (Omsk, Russia)

Unpublished manuscripts.

1.1.7. Personal files of D.G. Savchenko and N.R. Savchenko (Omsk, Russia)

Unpublished manuscripts.

1.1.8. Audio-archives of V. Getman (Seattle, USA, 2006)

E.N. Pushkov, "On the hymnal 'Pesn' Vozrozhdeniya' (about the amendments for the edition of 2002)" [2005].

1.2. Documentary Publications and Memoirs

Alexis, Bishop, *Materialy Dlya Istorii Religiozno-Ratsionalisticheskogo Dvizheniya na Yuge Rossii vo Vtoroy Polovine XIX Stoletiya* [Materials for the History of the Religious-Rationalistic Movement in the South of Russia in the Second Half of the 19th Century] (Kazan: Tsentral'naya Tipografiya, 1908).

_____, *Vnutrennyaya Organizatsiya Obshchin Yuzno-Russkikh Neobaptistov* [Internal Structure of Communities of the South-Russian neo-Baptists] (Kazan: Tsentral'naya Tipografiya, 1908).

Avvakum, archpriest, *Zhitie Avvakuma i Drugie Ego Sochineniya* [The Life of Avvakum and his other Writings] (M.: Sovetskaya Rossiya, 1991).

Beznosova, O., ed., *Evangel'skoe Dvizhenie v Rossiyskoy Imperii, 1850-1917: Ekaterinoslavskaya Guberniya, Sbornik Dokumentov i Materialov* [The Evangelical Movement in the Russian Empire, 1850-1917: The Ekaterinoslav Province, Collection of Documents and Materials] (Dnepropetrovsk: Samencorn, 2006).

Bonch-Bruevich, V., ed., *Materialy k Istorii i Izucheniyu Russkogo Sektantstva i Raskola* [Materials for the History and Study of Russian Sectarianism and Old Believers], Part 1 (SPb.: Tip. B.M. Vol'fa, 1908).

_____, *Presledovanie Baptistov* [The Persecution of Baptists] (Izdanie "Svobodnogo Slova", 1902).

Bondarenko, I., *Tri Prigovora* [Three Verdicts] (Odessa: n.p., 2006).

Bychkov, A., *Moy Zhiznenny Put'* [My Life] (M.: Otrazhenie, 2009).

Claassen, W., ed., *Anabaptism in Outline (Selected Primary Sources)* (Kitchener: Herald Press, 1981).

Dmitriev, L., and Likhachev, D., eds., *Pamyatniki Literatury Drevney Rusi* [Literary Monuments of the Early Rus], ed. by L. Dmitriev and D. Likhachev, 12 vols. (M.: Khudozhestvennaya Literatura, 1978-1990).

Dogmatika: Zaochnye Bibleyskie Kursy [Dogmatics: Bible Correspondence Courses] (M.: AUCECB, 1970).

Dukhovnye Pesni (s Notami) [Songbook with Printed Music], 3 vols. (Leningrad: Izdanie I.S. Prokhanova i Ya.I. Zhidkova, 1927-1928).

Fast, A., ed., *Sovetskoe Gosudarstvo, Religiya i Tserkov', 1917-1990. Dokumenty i Materialy* [Soviet State, Religion and Church, 1917-1990. Documents and Materials] (Barnaul: IPP "Altai", 2009).

Friesen, P.M., *Die Alt-Evangelische Mennonitische Bruderschaft in Russland (1789-1910) im Rahmen der Mennonitischen Gesamtgeschichte* (Halbstadt, Taurien: Raduga, 1911).

Inye Zhe Zamucheny Byli [The Others were Tortured] (booklet of the CCECB, 1970s).

Ispovedanie Very Khristian-Baptistov [The Creed of the Christians – Baptists] (M.: Izdanie N.V. Odintsova, 1928).

Istoriya Evangel'skikh Khristian-Baptistov v SSSR [History of the Evangelical Christians – Baptists in the USSR] (M.: AUCECB, 1989).

Istoriya Evangel'sko-Baptistskogo Dvizheniya v Ukraine: Materialy i Dokumenty [History of the Evangelical-Baptist Movement in the Ukraine: Materials and Documents], ed. by S. Golovashchenko (Odessa: Bogomyslie, 1998).

Ivan IV Grozny, *Sochineniya* [Works] (SPb.: Asbuka, 2000).

Izbornik: Povesti Drevney Rusi [Manuscript with Collected Writings: Narratives of Ancient Russia], ed. by L. Dmitriev and N. Ponyrko (M.: Khudozhestvennaya Literatura, 1986).

Izlozhenie evangel'skoy very [Statement of the Evangelical Faith] in Sannikov, S., ed., *Istoriya Baptizma* [History of the Baptists] (Odessa: OBS, 1996), pp. 435-58.

Karev, A., *Dukhovnye Stat'i* [Theological Articles] (Korntal: Svet na Vostoke, 1974).

_____, *Izbrannye Stat'i* [Selected Articles] (M.: AUCECB, 1977).

Kargel, I., *Svet Iz Teni Budushchikh Blag* [Light from the Shadows of Good Things to Come] (SPb.: Biblia dlya Vsekh, 1994).

_____, *Sobranie Sochineniy* [Collected Works] (SPb.: Bibliya Dlya Vsekh, 1997).

Khristova Tserkov' Est' Sobranie Krestom Iskuplennykh Lyudey: 90-letie Petropavlovskoy Tserkvi ECB [Christ's Church is the Assembly of Atoned-for People: The 90th Anniversary of Petropavlovsk church of ECB] (Petropavlovsk: n.p., 1998).

Konstitutsiya (Osnovnoy Zakon) Soyuza Sovetskikh Sotsialisticheskikh Respublik [The Constitution of the USSR] (M.: Politizdat, 1978).

Liven, S., *Dukhovnoe probuzhdenie v Rossii* [Spiritual Revival in Russia] (Korntal: Svet na Vostoke, 1967).

Materialy XXII S"ezda Kommunisticheskoy Partii Sovetskogo Soyuza [The Materials of the 22nd Congress of the Communist Party of the Soviet Union] (M.: Gospolitizdat, 1961).

Materialy Vneocherednogo XXI S"ezda Kommunisticheskoy Partii Sovetskogo Soyuza [The Materials of the Extraordinary 21st Congress of the Communist Party of the Soviet Union] (M.: Gospolitizdat, 1959).

Mazaev, G., *Vospominaniya* [Memories] (Korntal: Svet na Vostoke, 1992).

Nastol'naya Kniga Presvitera [The Handbook for Presbyters], 2 vols. (M.: AUCECB, 1982-1987).

Notny Sbornik Dukhovnykh Pesen ECB [Musical Songbook of ECB], 3 vols. (M.: AUCECB, 1973-1988).

Ob Osvyashchenii [On Sanctification] (Sovet Tserkvey ECB, 1990).

O Religii i Tserkvi: Sbornik Dokumentov [On Religion and Church: Collected Documents] (M.: Politizdat, 1965).

O Religii i Tserkvi: Sbornik Dokumentov [On Religion and Church: Collected Documents] (M.: Politizdat, 1981).

Pesn' Vozrozhdeniya [Song of Revival] (Izdanie Soveta Tserkvey ECB, 1978).

Pis'ma k Brat'yam Evangel'skim Khristianam – Baptistam [Letters to the Brothers, the Evangelical Christians-Baptists] (Tiflis: 'Trud' F.E. Machkovskoy, 1916).

Podrazhayte Vere Ikh: 40 Let Probuzhdennomu Bratstvu [Imitate Their Faith: The 40th Anniversary of the Revival Brotherhood] (M.: Sovet Tserkvey ECB, 2001).

Podvig Very: Unikal'nye Svidetel'stva o Zhizni Khristian v SSSR [Fight of Faith: Unique Testimonies about the Life of Christians in the USSR] (n.p.: Pacific Coast Slavic Baptist Association, 2009).

Prokhanov, I., *In the Cauldron of Russia, 1869-1933* (N.Y.: All-Russian Evangelical Christian Union, 1933).

Rozhdestvensky, A., *Yuzhnorussky Shtundism* [South-Russian Stundism] (SPb.: Tipografiya Departamenta Udelov, 1889).

Sbornik Dukhovnykh Pesen Evangel'skikh Khristian Baptistov [The Songbook of the Evangelical Christians–Baptists] (M.: AUCECB, 1968).

Shaptala, M., *Kak Eto Bylo* [The Way it Was] (Izdanie Bratstva Nezavisimykh Tserkvey ECB, 1999).

Val'kevich, V., *Zapiska o Propagande Protestantskikh Sekt v Rossii i v Osobennosti na Kavkaze* [A Report on the Propaganda of Protestant Sects in Russia and in Particular in the Caucasus] (Tiflis: Tipografiya Kants. Glavnonachal'stvueshchego Grazhd. ch. na Kavkaze, 1900).

Vernost': Sbornik Khristianskikh Stikhov [Faithfulness: Book of Christian Poems] (Izdanie CCECB, 1984).

Verouchenie Russkikh Evangel'skikh Khristian-Baptistov [The Creed of the Russian Evangelical Christians-Baptists] (Rostov na Donu: Tipografiya F.P. Pavlova, 1906).

Vins, G., *Evangelie v Uzakh* [The Gospel in Bonds] (Elkhart, IN: Russian Gospel Ministries, 1991).

_____, *Tropoyu Vernosti* [The Path of Faithfulness] (SPb.: Bibliya Dlya Vsekh, 1998).

Yasevich-Borodaevskaya, V., *Bor'ba za Veru: Istoriko-Bytovye Ocherki i Obzor Zakonodatel'stva po Staroobryadchestvu i Sektantstvu* [Struggle for the Faith: Historical and Every-Day Essays and Legislation Review of Old Belief and Sectarianism] (SPb.: Gosudarstvennaya Tipografiya, 1912).

Zakony o Raskol'nikakh i Sektantakh [The Laws on the Old Believers and Sectarians] (M.: Izdanie A. Skorova, 1903).

1.3. Periodical Publications

1.3.1. Baptist
[Anon], *"Nazvanie 'Baptisty'"* [The Name 'the Baptists'], *Bapt.*, no. 1 (June 1907), pp. 2-4.

"Nashi Presvitery" [Our Presbyters], *Bapt.*, 1907: no. 1, pp. 20-1; no. 2, p. 10; no. 4, pp. 17-8; no. 5, p. 12.

Ivanov, V., *"Kniga Episkopa Alekseya"* [The Book by Bishop Alexis], *Bapt.*, no. 9 (1908), pp. 23-7.

Kaprova, A., *"Son"* [A Dream], *Bapt.*, no. 5 (1909), pp. 4-5.

Ivanov, V., *"O Postakh"* [On Fasts], *Bapt.*, no. 14 (1910), pp. 5-6.

_____, *"Tsar' Antiokh"* [King Antiochus], *Bapt.*, no. 27 (1910), pp. 4-5.

_____, *"Obshchiny i Presvitery"* [Communities and Presbyters], *Bapt.*, nos. 21-24 (1914), pp. 8-11.

_____, *"Privet s Novym Godom"* [New Year Greetings], *Bapt.*, nos. 21-24 (1914), pp. 20-2.

"Doklad P.V. Pavlova" [P.V. Pavlov's Report], *Bapt.*, no. 3 (1925), pp. 6-7.

Ivanov-Klyshnikov, P., *"Shestidesyatiletie: 1867-1927"* [The Sixty Years: 1867-1927], *Bapt.*, no. 5 (1927), pp. 13-14.

1.3.2. Utrennyaya Zvezda [The Morning Star]
"35-letny Yubiley [Sluzheniya] Ivana Stepanovicha Prokhanova" [The 35th Anniversary of (the Ministry of) Ivan Stepanovich Prokhanov], *Utrennyaya Zvezda*, nos. 6-8 (1922), pp. 1-14.

1.3.3. Khristianin [Christian]
"Konferentsii Kezikskie" [Keswick Conferences], BL, *Prilozhenie k Zhurnalu "Khristianin"*, no. 8 (1906), p. 8.

[Anon], *"Predvaryayushchaya Blagodat"* [Prevenient Grace], *Khristianin*, no. 10 (1926), pp. 17-18.

Prokhanov, I., *"Gorod Solntsa"* [The City of the Sun], *Khristianin*, no. 1 (1928), pp. 15-16.

"Ekspeditsiya po Izyskaniyu Zemel' dlya Goroda Solntsa" [Expedition Searching for the Lands of the City of the Sun], *Khristianin*, no. 2 (1928), pp. 44-53.

1.3.4. Bratsky Vestnik [Fraternal Bulletin]

"Sovmestnaya rezolyutsiya evangel'skikh khristian i baptistov po voprosu sliyaniya v odin soyuz" [The Joint Resolution of Evangelical Christians and Baptists on the Question of Amalgamation into the One Union], *BV*, no. 1 (1945), p. 33.

Karev, A., *"Eshche Odin Shag v Dele Edinstva"* [One More Step to Unity], *BV*, no. 3 (1945), pp. 7-8.

"Osnovopolozhniki Nashego Bratstva" [The Founders of our Brotherhood], *BV*, no. 5 (1947), pp. 33-9.

Zhidkov, Ya., *"Molokane – Nashi Predki"* [The Molokans are our Forefathers], *BV*, no. 1 (1953), pp. 50-1.

Levindanto, N., *"Pamyati Deya Ivanovicha Mazaeva"* [In Memory of Dey Ivanovich Mazaev], *BV*, nos. 2-3 (1953), pp. 95-8.

Mitskevich, A., *"Khozhdenie pred Bogom"* [Walking with God], *BV*, no. 1 (1956), pp. 39-47.

Karev, A., *"Russkoe Evangel'sko-Baptistskoe Dvizhenie"* [The Russian Evangelical-Baptist Movement], *BV*: no. 3 (1957), pp. 5-51; no. 4 (1957), pp. 5-38.

Mitskevich, A., *"Mysli iz Knigi Deyany Apostolov"* [Some Thoughts from the Book of the Acts of the Apostles], *BV*, 3 (1960), pp. 33-9.

[Anon], *"Ispovedanie Petra i Preobrazhenie Khrista"* [The Confession of Peter and the Transfiguration of Christ], *BV*, no. 4 (1960), pp. 41-9.

[Anon], *"Chto Takoe Blagodat'?"* [What does Grace Mean?], *BV*, nos. 5-6 (1960), pp. 114-6.

Molokanov, F., *"O Edinstve"* [On Unity], *BV*, nos. 5-6 (1961), pp. 78-80.

Pilipyuk, K., *"Prebyvanie v Sovetskom Soyuze Gruppy Negrityanskikh Baptistskikh Pastorov iz Ameriki"* [Visit of the Soviet Union by Black Baptist Pastors' Group from the USA], *BV*, nos. 5-6 (1962), pp. 32-8.

Zhidkov, Ya., *"Preobrazhenie Gospodne"* [Transfiguration of the Lord], *BV*, nos. 5-6 (1962), pp. 39-41.

Karev, A., *"Svyashchennodeystviya Tserkvi"* [The Holy Ordinances of the Church], *BV*, no. 1 (1963), pp. 36-48.

Somov, K., *"Vera i Dela"* [Faith and Works], *BV*, no. 2 (1963), pp. 43-53.

[Anon], *"Voprosy Biblii, Trebuyushchie Raz"yasneniya"* [The Issues of the Bible which should be Explained], *BV*, no. 2 (1963), pp. 54-61.

Fadyukhin, S., *"O Preobrazhenii Khrista"* [On the Transfiguration of Christ], *BV*, no. 5 (1963), pp. 33-7.

Motorin, I., "*Torzhestvo Edinstva Veruyushchikh*" [Triumph of the Believers' Unity], *BV*, no. 1 (1964), pp. 21-5.

Karev, A., "*Chto Govorit Bibliya o Predopredelenii*" [What does the Bible say on Predestination?], *BV*, no. 1 (1964), pp. 55-7.

———, "*Chto Govorit Bibliya ob Otstuplenii*" [What does the Bible say on Apostasy?], *BV*, no. 1 (1964), pp. 57-9.

Vanin, M., "*Osvyashchenie*" [Consecration], *BV*, no. 2 (1964), pp. 44-57.

Karev, A., "*Golgofa*" [Calvary], *BV*, no. 3 (1964), pp. 15-26.

Slobodyanik, V., "*Voprosy Dukhovnoy Zhizni*" [The Issues of Spiritual Life], *BV*, no. 5 (1964), pp. 22-30.

Mitskevich, A., "*O Sudakh Bozh'ikh*" [On God's Judgements], *BV*, no. 6 (1964), pp. 22-28.

Somov, K., "*Voprosy Very*" [The Issues of Faith], *BV*, no. 6 (1964), pp. 29-40.

"*Semidesyatiletie Generalnogo Secretarya VSECB A.V. Kareva*" [The Seventieth Birthday of the Secretary-General of the AUCECB, A.V. Karev], *BV*, no. 1 (1965), pp. 63-78.

Slobodyanik, V., "*Voprosy Dukhovnoy Zhizni*" [The Issues of Spiritual Life], *BV*: no. 2 (1965), pp. 53-60; no. 4 (1965), pp. 27-33.

Karev, A., "*Osanna*" [Hosanna], *BV*, no. 3 (1965), pp. 16-23.

Mitskevich, A. "*Vtoroe Prishestvie Khista*" [The Second Coming of Christ], *BV*, no. 5 (1965), pp. 51-3.

Karev, A., "*Voskresenie Iisusa Khrista*" [Resurrection of Jesus Christ], *BV*, no. 2 (1966), pp. 15-28.

Levindanto, N., "*Blagochinie Pomestnykh Tserkvey*" [Discipline of Local Churches], *BV*, no. 2 (1966), pp. 29-43.

Karev, A., "*Voprosy Veruyushchikh*" [Believers' Queries], *BV*, no. 3 (1966), pp. 17-29.

"*Verouchenie Evangel'skikh Khristian-Baptistov*" [The Creed of the Evangelical Christians–Baptists], *BV*, no. 4 (1966), pp. 15-8.

"*Doklad General'nogo Sekretarya VSECB A.V. Kareva*" [Report of the General Secretary of AUCECB, A.V. Karev], *BV*, no. 6 (1966), pp. 15-36.

"*Ustav Soyuza ECB v SSSR*" [The Regulations of the Union of the ECB in the USSR], *BV*, no. 6 (1966), pp. 50-3.

Motorin, I., "*Otdavayte Kesarevo Kesaryu, a Bozhie Bogu*" [Give to Caesar what is Caesar's, and to God what is God's], *BV*, no. 2 (1968), pp. 49-53.

Karev, A., "*Mysli o Dukhe Svyatom*" [Reflections on the Holy Spirit], *BV*, no. 4 (1968), pp. 28-48.

Mitskevich, A., *"Deystviya Svyatogo Dukha"* [Actions of the Holy Spirit], *BV*, no. 3 (1969), pp. 34-8.

Ivolin, I., *"Ogon' Svyatogo Dukha"* [The Fire of the Holy Spirit], *BV*, no. 3 (1969), pp. 45-6.

[Anon], *"Tolkovanie na Evangelie ot Luki"* [Interpretation of the Gospel According to Luke], *BV*, no. 5 (1969), pp. 59-62.

Tatarchenko, I., *"Dukhovnaya Lestnitsa"* [Spiritual Ladder], *BV*, no. 6 (1969), pp. 47-9.

"Vystupleniya po Voprosu Edinstva" [Speeches on the Theme of Unity] (Council of ECB, 1969), *BV*, no. 2 (1970), pp. 65-9.

Fadyukhin, S., *"Ispovedanie Nashey Very"* [Our Creed], *BV*, no. 5 (1970), pp. 45-50.

"K Konchine Patriarkha Moskovskogo i Vseya Rusi Aleksiya" [In Memory of Alexius, Patriarch of Moscow and All Russia], *BV*, no. 5 (1970), pp. 58-60.

[Anon], *"Evangelie ot Luki"* [The Gospel According to Luke], *BV*, no. 6 (1970), pp. 42-7.

Karev, A., *"Zloupotrebleniya Otlucheniyami"* [Abuse of Excommunication], *BV*, no. 1 (1971), pp. 66-9.

Tatarchenko, I., *"Sretenie Gospodne"* [The Meeting of the Lord], *BV*, no. 2 (1971), pp. 41-3.

Mitskevich, A., *"Kak Osveshchaet Slovo Bozhie Vopros o Voennoy Sluzhbe"* [What the Word of God Says about Military Service], *BV*, no. 3 (1971), pp. 66-71.

Bychkov, A., *"Pomestny Sobor Russkoy Pravoslavnoy Tserkvi"* [The Local Council of the Russian Orthodox Church], *BV*, no. 4 (1971), pp. 11-12.

"Obrashchenie Pomestnogo Sobora Russkoy Pravoslavnoy Tserkvi k Khristianam Vsego Mira" [The Appeal of the Local Council of the Russian Orthodox Church to Christians of the Whole World], *BV*, no. 4 (1971), pp. 12-14.

"Patriarkhu Moskovskomu i Vseya Rusi Pimenu" [To Pimen, the Patriarch of Moscow and All Russia], *BV*, no. 4 (1971), pp. 14-15.

"Obituaries": *BV*, no. 4 (1971), pp. 79-80; no. 1 (1979), pp. 68-9; no. 6 (1983), p. 74; no. 1 (1984), pp. 59-60; no. 3 (1985), p. 80; no. 5 (1985), pp. 68-71; no. 3 (1987), pp. 69-72; no. 4 (1990), pp. 58-63.

Karev, A., *"Grekh i Pobeda nad Nim"* [Victory over Sin], *BV*, no. 1 (1972), pp. 14-23.

Dukhonchenko, Ya., *"Khozhdenie pered Bogom"* [Walking with God], *BV*, no. 4 (1972), pp. 49-53.

[Anon], *"Uverennost' v Spasenii"* [Assurance of Salvation], *BV*, no. 4 (1972), pp. 56-9.

[Anon], "*Na Rasput'e*" [At the Crossroads], *BV*, no. 4 (1972), pp. 65-6.

[Anon], "*Osen'*" [The Autumn], *BV*, no. 4 (1972), pp. 68-9.

[Anon], "*O Biblii*" [On the Bible], *BV*, no. 4 (1972), pp. 69-73.

"*Khristianskaya Zhizn' v Sovetskom Soyuze: Religioznaya Svoboda*" [Christian Life in the Soviet Union: Freedom of Faith], *BV*, no. 5 (1972), pp. 13-14.

Karev, A., "*Mysli o Edinstve Tserkvi*" [Thoughts on Church Unity], *BV*, no. 5 (1973), pp. 24-9.

Mel'nikov, N., "*Obzor Evangel'skikh Povestvovany*" [Review of the Gospel Stories], *BV*, no. 5 (1973), pp. 60-4.

Karev, A., "*Golgofa*" [Calvary], *BV*, no. 2 (1974), pp. 22-8.

Tyark, O., "*Poslanie k Rimlyanam*" [Epistle to Romans], *BV*, no. 4 (1974), pp. 29-37.

"*Tserkov' – Nevesta Khrista*" [The Church is the Bride of Christ] (editorial article), *BV*, no. 4 (1974), pp. 37-43.

Fadyukhin, S., "*Dukh Svyatoy*" [The Holy Spirit], *BV*, no. 5 (1974), pp. 46-9.

Nikodim, Metropolitan, "*Iisus Khristos Osvobozhdaet i Ob"edinyaet*" [Jesus Christ Makes Free and Joins Together], *BV*, no. 6 (1974), pp. 15-19.

Iliya, metropolitan, "*Doklad na Obshchuyu Temu*" [Report on General Theme], *BV*, no. 6 (1974), pp. 23-5.

"*Otchetny Doklad General'nogo Sekretarya VSECB A.M. Bychkova*" [Summary Report of the Secretary-General of AUCECB, A.M. Bychkov], *BV*, no. 1 (1975), pp. 21-57.

Zhidkov, M., "*Vodnoe kreshchenie i vecherya Gospodnya*" [Water Baptism and the Lord's Supper], *BV*, no. 2 (1975), pp. 52-60.

"*Vstrecha v Leningrade*" [Meeting in Leningrad] (editorial article), *BV*, no. 4 (1975), pp. 13-27.

"*Iz Zhizni Pomestnykh Tserkvey*" [From the life of the local churches]: *BV*, no. 5 (1975), pp. 74-9; no. 6 (1979), pp. 66-74; no. 4 (1981), pp. 66-79; no. 5 (1983), pp. 65-78; no. 2 (1986), pp. 68-80; no. 5 (1986), pp. 62-80; no. 6 (1986), pp. 53-76; no. 1 (1987), pp. 61-80; no. 5 (1987), pp. 56-80; no. 2 (1992), pp. 79-94.

"*Tserkovnye Prazdniki ECB na 1976 God*" [Church Feasts of the ECB for 1976], *BV*, no. 6 (1975), p. 75.

Tyark, O., "*Evangelie ot Marka*" [The Gospel according to Mark], *BV*, no. 1 (1976), pp. 30-8.

"*Golos Khristian v Zashchitu Mira*" [Voice of Christians in Defence of Peace] (editorial article), *BV*, no. 2 (1976), pp. 4-8.

[Anon], *"Ne Ostavlyu Tebya, Ne Pokinu Tebya"* ["I will Never Desert You"], *BV*, no. 2 (1976), pp. 58-64.

Bychkov, A., Fadyukhin, S., *"Istoriya Perevoda Biblii na Russky Yazyk"* [The History of Translation of the Bible into Russian], *BV*, no. 3 (1976), pp. 61-6.

"Sobesedovanie VSECB s Predstavitelyami Bratskikh Mennonitov" [Negotiations of the AUCECB with Representatives of the Mennonite Brethren] (editorial article), *BV*, no. 3 (1976), pp. 67-74.

[Anon], *"Putniki v Nebesny Khanaan"* [Travellers to the Heavenly Canaan], *BV*, no. 6 (1976), pp. 52-4.

[Anon], *"Razmyshleniya nad Slovom Zhizni"* [Reflections on the Word of Life], *BV*, no. 5 (1977), pp. 47-57.

Bychkov, A., *"110-letie Russko-Ukrainskogo Bratstva ECB"* [The 110th Anniversary of the Russian-Ukrainian Brotherhood of the ECB], *BV*, no. 5 (1977), pp. 67-71.

"Predsedatelyu Prezidiuma Verkhovnogo Soveta SSSR Leonidu Il'ichu Brezhnevu" [To the Chairman of the Presidium of the Supreme Soviet of the USSR, Leonid Ilyich Brezhnev], *BV*, no. 6 (1977), p. 8.

Meshcheryakov, V., *"Spasenie Po Blagodati"* [Salvation by Grace], *BV*, no. 6 (1977), pp. 38-41.

Fadyukhin, S., *"Ob Osoboy Bozh'ey Lyubvi k Izbrannym"* [On God's Special Love for the Elect], *BV*, no. 5 (1978), pp. 17-19.

Vysotsky, N., *"Znachenie i Sila Dukhovnoy Muzyki"* [The Meaning and Power of Religious Music], *BV*, no. 5 (1978), pp. 57-66.

Mitskevich, A., *"Pastyrskoe Sluzhenie"* [The Shepherd's Ministry], *BV*, no. 2 (1979), pp. 25-32.

Kolesnikov, N., *"Pospeshim k sovershenstvu"* [Let us go on to Maturity], *BV*, no. 2 (1979), pp. 34-9.

Chekalov, I., *"O Evangelii ot Ioanna"* [On the Gospel according to John], *BV*, no. 2 (1979), pp. 45-50.

Shatrov, P., *"Deyaniya Apostolov"* [The Acts of the Apostles], *BV*, no. 3 (1979), pp. 25-34.

Kharlov, L., *"Istoriya Tserkovnoy Muzyki i Peniya"* [The History of Church Music and Singing], *BV*, no. 4 (1979), pp. 53-66.

Bychkov, A., *"Obzor Poslaniya k Evreyam"* [Review of the Epistle to the Hebrews], *BV*, no. 5 (1979), pp. 19-21.

Kharlov, L., *"Istoriya Razvitiya Khristianskogo Peniya na Rusi"* [The History of the Development of Christian Singing in Russia], *BV*, no. 6 (1979), pp. 50-6.

"*Telegramma Predsedatelyu Prezidiuma Verkhovnogo Soveta SSSR*" [Telegram to the Chairman of the Presidium of the Supreme Soviet of the USSR], *BV*, nos. 1-2 (1980), pp. 52-3.

"*Ustav Soyuza ECB v SSSR*" [The Regulations of the Union of the ECB in the USSR], *BV*, nos. 1-2 (1980), pp. 58-65.

Derzhavin, G.R., *Bog* [God] (ode), *BV*, no. 3 (1980), pp. 54-6.

"*Proekt Veroucheniya ECB*" [Project of the Creed of ECB], *BV*, no. 4 (1980), pp. 32-52.

Kreyman, V., "*Nekotorye Voprosy Dukhovnogo Muzykal'nogo Tvorchestva*" [Some Issues in Sacred Musical Creativity], *BV*, no. 4 (1980), pp. 57-61.

Nikitin, I.S., "*Molenie o Chashe*" [Praying for the Cup] (poem), *BV*, no. 4 (1980), pp. 63-6.

Tyark, O., "*Evangelie ot Marka*" [The Gospel according to Mark], *BV*, no. 5 (1980), pp. 14-26.

"*Bratskomy Vestniku – 35 Let*" [The 35th Anniversary of 'Bratsky Vestnik'], *BV*, no. 5 (1980), pp. 61-6.

Tervits, Ya., "*Muzyka i Dukhovnoe Vozrastanie Veruyushchikh*" [Music and Spiritual Growth in Believers], *BV*, no. 3 (1981), pp. 58-63.

"*Ne Ostavlyayte Sobrany Vashikh*" [Do not Give up Meeting Together] (poem), *BV*, no. 4 (1981), pp. 53-4.

Mitskevich, A., "*Desyatiletie Pervogo Vypuska Uchashchikhsya ZBK VSEKhB*" [The 10th Anniversary of the First Graduates of the Bible Correspondence Courses of the AUCECB], *BV*, no. 4 (1981), pp. 61-2.

Keshe, A., "*Iz Praktiki Regentskogo Sluzheniya*" [From Practical Experience of Choir Ministry], *BV*, no. 5 (1981), pp. 43-50.

"*Materialy Plenuma AUCECB, Iyun' 1981 Goda*" [Materials of Plenum of the AUCECB, June 1981], *BV*, no. 5 (1981), pp. 52-66.

Kharlov, L., "*Iz Istorii Muzykal'no-pevcheskogo Sluzheniya Nashego Bratstva*" [From the History of the Musical and Singing Ministry of our Brotherhood], *BV*, no. 6 (1981), pp. 46-52.

Koval'kov, V., Sokolov, E., "*I.G. Ryaboshapka*", *BV*, no. 6 (1981), pp. 57-65.

Kharlov, L., "*Iz Istorii Muzykal'no-pevcheskogo Sluzheniya Nashego Bratstva*" [From the History of the Musical and Singing Ministry of our Brotherhood], *BV*, no. 1 (1982), pp. 53-9.

Vyzu, R., "*Nagornaya propoved'*" [The Sermon on the Mount], *BV*, no. 2 (1982), pp. 5-17.

Volchansky, V., "*O Sluzhenii Orkestrov*" [On the Orchestra's Service], *BV*, no. 3 (1982), pp. 54-6.

Shatrov, P., *"Deyaniya Apostolov"* [The Acts of the Apostles], *BV*, no. 4 (1982), pp. 14-19.

Pimen, Patriarch, *"Spasenie Svyashchennogo Dara Zhizni"* [Saving the Sacred Gift of Life], *BV*, no. 4 (1982), pp. 40-50.

Goncharenko, E., *"Zhanry Pesnopeny ECB"* [The Singing Genres of the ECB], *BV*, no. 4 (1982), pp. 65-70.

Fadyukhin, S., *"Bog Vsemogushchiy Blagoslovil Menya"* [God Almighty has Blessed me], *BV*, no. 5 (1982), pp. 17-22.

"Telegramma Presidiumu Verkhovnogo Soveta SSSR" [Telegram to the Presidium of the Supreme Soviet of the USSR], *BV*, no. 6 (1982), pp. 51.

"Obrashchenie Plenuma VSECB" [Appeal of the Plenum of the AUCECB], *BV*, no. 6 (1982), p. 54.

Semlek, L., *"Zhanry Khristianskikh Pesnopeny"* [The Genres of Christian Songs], *BV*, no. 3 (1983), pp. 67-71.

[Anon], *"Istoriya Kanona Novogo Zaveta"* [The History of the Canon of the New Testament], *BV*, no. 6 (1983), pp. 32-41.

Nikolaev, S., *"Reformatskaya Tserkov'"* [The Reformed Church], *BV*, no. 1 (1984), pp. 44-52.

Shatrov, P., *"Deyaniya Apostolov"* [The Acts of the Apostles], *BV*, no. 4 (1984), pp. 23-7.

"Bratskomy Vestniky – 40 Let" ['Bratsky Vestnik' is Aged 40] (editorial article), *BV*, no. 5 (1984), pp. 45-50.

Bychkov, A., *"Stoletie Ob"edinitel'nykh S"ezdov"* [The Centenary of the Unifying Councils], *BV*, no. 6 (1984), pp. 44-7.

Gnida, I., *"Dukhovno-Patrioticheskoe Sluzhenie"* [Spiritual and Patriotic Ministry], *BV*, no. 6 (1984), pp. 51-6.

[Anon], *"My Sozdany vo Khriste Iisuse na Dobrye Dela"* [We are Created in Christ Jesus for Good Works], *BV*, no. 1 (1985), pp. 15-6.

Shatrov, P., *"Deyaniya Apostolov"* [The Acts of the Apostles], *BV*, no. 1 (1985), pp. 18-21.

Vyzu, R., *"Vy hram Bozhy, i Dukh Bozhy zhivet v vas"* [You are God's Temple and God's Spirit Lives in You], *BV*, no. 2 (1985), pp. 20-3.

Shatrov, P., *"Deyaniya Apostolov"* [The Acts of the Apostles], *BV*, no. 2 (1985), pp. 24-30.

Bychkov, A. *"Otchetny Doklad S"ezdu ECB"* [Summary Report to the Council of the ECB], *BV*, no. 3 (1985), pp. 15-34.

Verouchenie Evangel'skikh Khristian – Baptistov, Prinyatoe na 43 S"ezde ECB v Moskve [The Creed of the Evangelical Christians-Baptists Adopted at the 43rd Council of the ECB in Moscow], *BV*, no. 4 (1985), pp. 33-49.

[Anon], "*Velika Vasha Nagrada na Nebesakh*" [Your Reward in Heaven is Great], *BV*, no. 5 (1985), pp. 12-15.

Mitskevich,V., "*Apostol'sky Simvol Very*" [The Apostles' Creed], *BV*, no. 5 (1985), pp. 20-35.

Fofanov, K.M., "*Otrechenie Petra*" [Peter's Denial] (poem), *BV*, no. 5 (1985), pp. 66-7.

Shatrov, P., "*Deyaniya Apostolov*" [The Acts of the Apostles], *BV*, no. 6 (1985), pp. 12-20.

"*Bogosluzhenie v MOECB*" [Divine Service at Moscow Church] (editorial article), *BV*, no. 6 (1985), pp. 59-62.

Bychkov, A., "*Iisus Khristos – Spasitel'*" [Jesus Christ is the Saviour], *BV*, no. 1 (1986), pp. 14-16.

[Anon], "*Kniga Proroka Daniila*" [The Book of Daniel], *BV*, no. 2 (1986), pp. 26-30.

"*Ocherednoy Plenum VSECB*" [Regular Plenum of the AUCECB] (editorial article), *BV*, no. 3 (1986), pp. 39-55.

Dukhonchenko, Ya., "*Bud' Obraztsom Dlya Vernykh*" [Be a Good Example for the Faithful], *BV*, no. 5 (1986), pp. 20-5.

Mitskevich, A., "*O Vospitanii Veruyushchikh*" [On the Upbringing of Believers], *BV*, no. 5 (1986), pp. 58-62.

"*Mysli o Molitve*" [Thoughts on Prayer], *BV*, no. 6 (1986), pp. 30-1.

Savchenko, P., "*Lyuteranskaya Tserkov'*" [The Lutheran Church], *BV*, no. 3 (1987), pp. 47-53.

Zhemchuzhnikov, A.M., "*Pritcha o Seyatele i Semenakh*" [The Parable of the Sower and the Seed] (poem), *BV*, no. 3 (1987), p. 66.

"*Mysli o Khristianskom Mirolyubii*" [Thoughts on Christian Peacefulness], *BV*, no. 5 (1987), p. 47.

Merezhkovsky, D.S., "*O, Bozhe Moy*" [Oh, My God] (poem), *BV*, no. 5 (1987), p. 52.

Kulikov, V., "*Nadlezhit nam ispolnit' vsyakuyu pravdu*" [It is Proper for us to do this to Fulfill all Righteousness], *BV*, no. 6 (1987), pp. 9-12.

"*Mysli o Cheloveke*" [Thoughts on Man], *BV*, no. 6 (1987), p. 48.

Soloviev, V.S., "*Emmanuil*" [Immanuel] (poem), *BV*, no. 6 (1987), p. 51.

Popov, V., "*Vozniknovenie Khristianstva na Rusi*" [The Beginnings of Christianity in Russia], *BV*, no. 1 (1988), pp. 46-50.

Kadaeva, V., *"Uchastie Sester v Zhizni i Sluzhenii Tserkvey"* [The Participation of Sisters in the Life and Ministry of Churches], *BV*, no. 1 (1988), pp. 70-3.

Bychkov, A., *"A.P. Lopukhin"*, *BV*, no. 2 (1988), pp. 60-2.

Kozlov, I.I., *"Moya Molitva"* [My Prayer] (poem), *BV*, no. 2 (1988), p. 64.

Chernopyatov, M., Vasiliev, A., *"Pravoslavnaya Tserkov'"* [The Orthodox Church], *BV*, no. 3 (1988), pp. 47-55.

"Poslanie Tserkvam ECB" [Epistle to the churches of ECB], *BV*, no. 3 (1988), pp. 70-2.

Gnida, I., *"Tserkovnye ustanovleniya"* [The Church Institutions], *BV*, no. 4 (1988), pp. 71-80.

Sergienko, G., *"Edinenie i Preemstvennost' v Sluzhenii"* [Unity and Continuity of Ministry], *BV*, no. 4 (1988), pp. 80-3.

Shatrov P., *"Deyaniya Svyatykh Apostolov"* [The Acts of the Saint Apostles], *BV*, no. 5 (1988), pp. 33-44.

Nadson, S., *"Khristianka"* [A Christian] (poem), *BV*, no. 5 (1988), pp. 62-3.

Soloviev, V.S., *"Prizvanie Avraama v Zemlyu Obetovannuyu"* [The Call of Abraham to the Promised Land] (poem), *BV*, no. 6 (1988), p. 46.

Sedletsky, K., *"Izbranie i Rukopolozhenie Sluzhiteley"* [Election and Ordination of Ministers], *BV*, no. 6 (1988), pp. 50-4.

Mazharova, V., *"Byl Bolen, i Vy Posetili Menya"* [I was Sick, and you Visited Me], *BV*, no. 6 (1988), pp. 69-71.

Mad'yugin, E., *"Blagodat' Bozhiya"* [The Grace of God], *BV*, no. 1 (1989), pp. 18-23.

Gladkov, B., *"Podlinnost' Evangely"* [The Authenticity of the Gospels], *BV*, no. 1 (1989), pp. 25-35.

"Prazdnovanie Tysyacheletiya Kreshcheniya Rusi v Moskovskoy Tserkvi" [The Celebration of the Millennium of the Baptism of Russia in the Moscow Church] (editorial article), *BV*, no. 1 (1989), pp. 68-73.

"Evangel'skie Poucheniya" [The Gospel's Homilies], *BV*, no. 2 (1989), p. 33.

Kokhanets, S., *"Khristianskaya Pesn"* [Christian Song], *BV*, no. 2 (1989), pp. 52-3.

Pestryakov, F.M., *"Vera"* [The Faith] (poem), *BV*, no. 2 (1989), p. 56.

"Prazdnovanie Tysyacheletiya Kreshcheniya Rusi v Moskve" [The Celebration of the Millennium of the Baptism of Russia in Moscow] (editorial article), *BV*, no. 2 (1989), pp. 61-7.

Nikitin, I.S., *"Novy Zavet"* [The New Testament] (poem), *BV*, no. 2 (1989), p. 65.

"*Paskhal'nye Privetstviya i Pozdravleniya, Prislannye v Adres VSEHB*" [Easter
Greetings and Compliments Sent to the AUCECB], *BV*, no. 3 (1989), pp.
36-8.

Nadson, S.Ya., "*Drug Moy, Brat Moy!*" [My Friend, My Brother!] (poem), *BV*, no.
3 (1989), p. 69.

Zhukovsky, V.A., "*Savl na Doroge v Damask*" [Saul on the Way to Damascus]
(poem), *BV*, no. 4 (1989), p. 51.

Kadaeva, V., "*Osvyashchenie Doma Molitvy v Svyatoshinskoy Tserkvi Kieva*" [The
Consecration of the Prayer House of the Svyatoshinskaya Church in Kiev],
BV, no. 6 (1989), pp. 73-80.

Lopukhin, A., "*Yavleniya Voskresshego Khrista*" [The Appearances of the Risen
Christ], *BV*, no. 1 (1990), pp. 5-9.

Bychkov, A., "*Vladimir Sergeevich Soloviev*", *BV*, no. 1 (1990), pp. 52-4.

Kadaeva, V., "*44 Vsesoyuzny S"ezd ECB*" [The 44th All-Union Council of the
ECB], *BV*, no. 2 (1990), pp. 34-46.

Kadaev, A., "*Vecherya Gospodnya – Khleboprelomlenie*" [The Lord's Supper –
Breaking of Bread], *BV*, no. 3 (1990), pp. 10-15.

"*Ustav Soyuza ECB*" [The Regulations of the Union of ECB], *BV*, no. 3 (1990),
pp. 82-94.

Popov, V., "*Prokhanov – Propovednik i Poet*" [Prokhanov as a Preacher and Poet],
BV, no. 4 (1990), pp. 43-50.

Dostoevsky, F.M., "*Rozhdestvo Khristovo (Christmas). Mal'chik u Khrista na Elke*"
[A Boy at Christ's Christmas Party], *BV*, no. 6 (1990), pp. 68-70.

Sulotsky, A.I., "*Golgofa*" [Calvary] (poem), *BV*, no. 1 (1991), p. 56.

Ryskin, S.F., "*Pogrebenie Khrista*" [The Burial of Christ] (poem), *BV*, no. 1
(1991), p. 57.

Maykov, A.N., "*Khristos Voskres!*" [Christ is Risen!] (poem), *BV*, no. 1 (1991), p.
57.

Kulikov, V., "*Raduytes', Chto Imena Vashi v Knige Zhizni*" [Rejoice that your
Names are in the Book of Life], *BV*, no. 2 (1991), pp. 12-13.

Tolstoy, A.K., "*Greshnitsa*" [A Sinful Woman] (poem), *BV*, no. 2 (1991), pp.
57-8.

Sergey, I., "*Uverennost' v Spasenii*" [Assurance of Salvation], *BV*, no. 4 (1991), pp.
16-17.

Afanasiev, L.N., "*Te Zvezdy v Nebe ne Pogasli*" [Those Stars in the Sky have not
Become Dim] (poem), *BV*, no. 6 (1991), p. 74.

Kozlov, I.I., "*O Drug, Pover'!*" [Oh, Friend, Believe!] (poem), *BV*, no. 2 (1992),
p. 43.

Romanov, K.K., *"Ne Govori, Chto k Nebesam"* [Do not Say that the Heavens]
(poem), *BV*, no. 2 (1992), p. 43.

Pleshcheev, A.N., *"On Shel Bezropotno"* [He Humbly Walked] (poem), *BV*, no. 3
(1992), pp. 50-1.

Khomyakov, A.S., *"Voskreshenie Lazarya"* [The Raising of Lazarus] (poem), *BV*,
no. 4 (1992), p. 70.

"Dnevnik A. V. Kareva" [A.V. Karev's Diary], *BV*, no. 1 (1999), pp. 44-51; nos.
2-3 (1999), pp. 53-7.

Nagirnyak, A., *"Dey Ivanovich Mazaev"*, *BV*, no. 1 (2008), pp. 31-42.

1.3.5. Bratsky Listok [Fraternal Leaflet]

"Ustav Soveta Tserkvey ECB" [Regulations of the Council of Churches of ECB],
BL, no. 11 (1965), supplement.

"Vsem Tserkvam ECB" [To All Churches of ECB], *BL*, no. 5 (1966), supplement.

"I Narekut Imya Emu" ["And They Shall Call His Name"], *BL*, nos. 11-12
(1967), pp. 1-2.

"Soobshchenie o Khodataystvakh Soveta Tserkvey ECB" [A Report on the Petitions
of the CCECB], *BL*, no. 3 (1968), pp. 1-8.

"Izbrannym Bozh'im" [To God's Elect] (editorial article), *BL*, no. 7 (1968), pp.
1-2.

"Veliki Dela Gospodni" ["Great are the Works of the Lord"], *BL*, no. 8 (1970),
pp. 1-2.

"Iz Zhizni Khartsyzskoy Obshchiny" [From the Life of the Khartsyzsk
Community], *BL*, no. 1 (1973), pp. 1-2.

"Vopros Registratsii i Sud'ba Spaseniya" [The Question of Registration and the Fate
of Salvation], *BL*, nos. 1-3 (1975), pp. 1-4.

"Golev Sergey Terent'evich" (Obituary), *BL*, no. 2 (1976), p. 2.

Kryuchkov, G., *"20 Let po Puti Vozrozhdeniya"* [20 Years on the Way of Revival],
BL, no. 4 (1981), pp. 1-4.

"Svyataya Troitsa" [The Holy Trinity] (editorial article), *BL*, no. 2 (1991), pp. 1-2.

"On Lyubil Gospoda i Tserkov'" [He Loved the Lord and the Church], *BL*, no. 5
(2007), pp. 1-4.

1.3.6. Byulleten' Soveta Rodstvennikov Uznikov Evangel'skikh Khris-tian-Baptistov v SSSR [Bulletin of the Council of Prisoners' Relatives of the Evangelical Christians-Baptists of the USSR]:

No. 17 (1974); no. 21 (1975); no. 23 (1975); no. 24 (1975).

1.3.7. Vestnik Istiny [Bulletin of the Truth]

"Nasha Bran" [Our Battle] (editorial article), VestI, no. 1 (1977), pp. 8-10.

"John Chrysostom" (editorial article), VestI, no. 4 (1977), pp. 30-2.

Martsinkovsky, V., "V.S. Soloviev", VestI, no. 1 (1979), pp. 34-41; no. 2 (1979), pp. 31-8.

[Anon], "Bozhy Dar" [God's Gift], VestI, no. 4 (1979), pp. 2-3.

"Ioann Zlatoust o Slove Bozhiem" [John Chrysostom on God's Word], VestI, no. 4 (1979), p. 33.

"Kak Bog Razgovarivaet s Lyud'mi" [How God Speaks with People] (editorial article), VestI, no. 2 (1980), pp. 15-20.

Shmidt, B., "Khristos – Istinny Bog" [Christ is the True God], VestI, no. 1 (1982), pp. 4-12.

Peters, P., "Vse Sie Preodolevaem" [In all these Things we are more than Conquerors], VestI, no. 2 (1982), pp. 27-31.

Minyakov, D., "O Vechere Gospodney" [On the Lord's Supper], VestI, no. 1 (1983), pp. 8-10.

Khorev, M., "Pishu Vam, Deti" [I Write You, My Children], VestI, no. 1 (1983), pp. 27-33.

Kostyuchenko, G., "Svidetel'stvo o Gospode – Nasha Zashchita" [Testimony about the Lord is Our Protection], VestI, no. 1 (1983), pp. 34-6.

"Luchshaya Uchast" [The Best Lot] (editorial article), VestI, no. 2 (1983), pp. 36-9.

Germanyuk, S., "Pribliz'tes' k Bogu" [Draw near to God], VestI, no. 1 (1984), pp. 18-20.

Khorev, M., "Pishu Vam, Deti" [I Write You, My Children], VestI, no. 1 (1984), pp. 34-44.

Redin, A., "Rodilis' li Vy Svyshe?" [Are You Born Again?], VestI, nos. 2-3 (1984), pp. 26-8.

Khorev, M., "Paskhal'ny Den'" [Easter Day], VestI, no. 3 (1985), pp. 21-3.

Artyushchenko, B., "Pobednaya Pesn" [The Victorious Song], VestI, no. 3 (1985), pp. 30-3.

Zinchenko, V., "Prodolzhenie Podviga" [Continuity with the Exploit], VestI, no. 2 (1986), pp. 10-11.

Rodoslavov, E., "Udivitel'ny Podvig" [Amazing Exploit], VestI, nos. 3-4 (1986), pp. 12-20.

"Kniga Zhizni" [The Book of Life] (editorial article), VestI, no. 1 (1987), pp. 26-9.

John Chrysostom, *"O Molitve"* [On Prayer], *VestI*, no. 2 (1987), pp. 17-20.

_____, *"Slovo o Pokayanii"* [Homily on Repentance], *VestI*, no. 1 (1990), pp. 11-13.

Khorev, M., *"Raznye Ucheniki"* [Different Disciples], *VestI*, no. 3 (1990), pp. 4-5.

Kryuchkov, G., *"Ya s Vami, Govorit Gospod"* [The Lord says, "I am with you"], *VestI*, nos. 3-4 (1991), pp. 6-19.

Baturin, N., *"Da Budet Svet…"* ["Let There Be Light…"], *VestI*, no. 2 (1992), pp. 4-9.

Misiruk, S., *"Uzkiy Put'"* [The Narrow Way], *VestI*, no. 2 (1996), supplement, pp. 18-45.

[Anon], *"Poydem s Maloletnimi Nashimi…"* ["We will go with our Young…"], *BV*, no. 1 (2001), pp. 38-40.

"Spisok Uznikov, Osuzhdennykh za Slovo Bozh'e v SSSR" [The List of the Prisoners for the Word of God in the USSR], *VestI*, no. 2 (2001), pp. 22-3.

"Veroyu Prines Bogu Zhertvu Luchshuyu" [He Offered to God a Better Sacrifice] (editorial article), *VestI*, no. 2 (2001), pp. 36-7.

"Zakon Tvoy Razorili" ["They Have Broken Thy Law"] (editorial article), *VestI*, no. 3 (2001), pp. 2-3.

"Uzniki za Imya Khrista" [Prisoners for Christ's Name] (editorial article), *VestI*, no. 3 (2001), p. 36.

Kryuchkov, G., *"Buduchi Rodom Bozhiim"* [Being the Offspring of God], *VestI*, no. 3 (2002), pp. 3-7.

[Anon], *"Zhelaem Sokhranit' Vernost' Khristu"* [We want to Remain Faithful to Christ], *VestI*, no. 3 (2002), pp. 30-5.

"Slovo Uznika" [Prisoner's Word] (editorial article), *VestI*, no. 2 (2003), pp. 37-8.

"V Te Pamyatnye Dni" [In Those Memorable Days] (editorial article), *VestI*, no. 3 (2003), pp. 21-4.

"Lyubite Bibliyu!" [Love the Bible!] (editorial article), *VestI*, no. 3 (2003), pp. 46-7.

Kryuchkov, G., *"Otreshit'sya ot Vsego"* [To Renounce the World], *VestI*, no. 1 (2004), pp. 2-5.

Ivanov, N., *"Ne Budem Chuzhdat'sya Stradaniy"* [Let Us not Avoid Sufferings], *VestI*, no. 1 (2005), pp. 30-1.

Kryuchkov, G., *"Prorochesky Golos"* [The Prophetic Voice], *VestI*, nos. 4-5 (2007), pp. 16-22.

"Kievskoe Ob''edinenie Mezhdunarodnogo CCECB" [Kiev Association of International CCECB] (editorial article), *VestI*, no. 2 (2009), pp. 18-19.

1.3.8. Vestnik Spaseniya [Bulletin of Salvation]

"Obrashchenie ko Vsey Molodezhi" [Appeal to All the Youth] (editorial article), *VS*, no. 3 (1965), pp. 2-3.

"Kratkie Sovety Molodezhi" [Short Advice to the Youth] (editorial article), *VS*, no. 3 (1965), p. 32.

"Lyubite Bibliyu!" [Love the Bible!] (editorial article), *VS*, no. 3 (1965), pp. 32-5.

"Sud Nepravedny: Stenogramma Sudebnogo Protsessa" [Unfair Trial: Full Trial Transcript], *VS*, no. 1 (1973), pp. 20-7.

1.3.9. Zhurnal Moskovskoy Patriarkhii [Journal of the Moscow Patriarchate]

"Nad Knigoy Svyateyshego Alexy, Patriarkha Moskovskogo I Vseya Rusi 'Slova, Rechi, Poslaniya'" [On the Book of His Holiness Alexis, the Patriarch of Moscow and All Russia, 'Sermons, Speeches, Pastoral Letters'] (editorial article), *ZhMP*, no. 1 (1949), pp. 12-22.

Uspensky, N., *"Sobornost' Tserkvi"* [The Conciliar Nature of the Church], *ZhMP*, no. 7 (1959), pp. 45-51.

"Vypiska iz Postanovleniya Svyateyshego Patriarkha i Svyashchennogo Sinoda" [Excerpt from the Decision of His Holiness the Patriarch and the Holy Synod] (editorial article), *ZhMP*, no. 2 (1960), p. 27.

"Vechnaya Pamyat' Pochivshim" [Imperishable Memory of the Deceased] (editorials), *ZhMP*, no. 1 (1971), pp. 32-3; no. 2 (1971), pp. 32-5; no. 3 (1971), pp. 19-23; no. 1 (1972), pp. 27-9; no. 3 (1972), pp. 29-32; no. 4 (1972), pp. 29-30.

Osipovich, A., *"Znachenie Pomestnogo Sobora v Zhizni Russkoy Pravoslavnoy Tserkvi"* [The Significance of the Local Council in the Life of the Russian Orthodox Church], *ZhMP*, no. 2 (1971), pp. 64-71.

"Obituaries": no. ZhMP, 4 (1971), pp. 22-4; no. 2 (1972), pp. 26-7; no. 4 (1972), p. 28; no. 12 (1972), pp. 21-2.

"Pomestny Sobor Russkoy Pravoslavnoy Tserkvi" [Local Council of the Russian Orthodox Church] (editorial article), *ZhMP*, no. 7 (1971), pp. 4-73.

Feodosy, bishop, *"O Blagoslovenii Plodov"* [On the Blessing of Fruits], *ZhMP*, no. 9 (1971), pp. 41-3.

Filaret, archbishop, *"O Filiokve"* [On Filioque], *ZhMP*, no. 1 (1972), pp. 62-75.

Nikodim, metropolitan, *"Predanie i Sovremennost"* [Tradition and Modernity], *ZhMP*, no. 12 (1972), pp. 54-9.

St. Gregory of Nyssa, *"O Blazhenstvakh, Slovo 7"* [On the Beatitudes, the Homily 7], *ZhMP*, no. 7 (1977), pp. 25-7.

Pimen, Patriarch, *"Rech' na Zasedanii Sovetskogo Komiteta Zashchity Mira"* [Soviet Peace Committee Meeting Speech], *ZhMP*, no. 11 (1977), pp. 36-7.

Zabolotsky, N., *"K Shestidesyatiletiyu Sotsialisticheskoy Otchizny"* [In Commemoration of the Sixtieth Anniversary of the Socialist Homeland], *ZhMP*, no. 11 (1977), pp. 38-41.

Pimen, Patriarch, *"Rech' na Sobranii Aktiva Sovetskikh Obshchestvennykh Organizatsy"* [Soviet Social Organizations Activists' Meeting Speech], *ZhMP*, no. 10 (1979), pp. 41-2.

_____, *"Slovo Pri Vruchenii Arkhiereyskogo Zhezla Episkopu Podol'skomu Vladimiru"* [The Word on the Investiture with Bishop's Staff to Vladimir, the Bishop of Podolsk], *ZhMP*, no. 9 (1985), pp. 7-8.

Bulgakov, S., archpriest, *"Tserkov' kak Predanie"* [The Church as Tradition], *ZhMP*, no. 12 (1989), pp. 67-73.

"Skazanie o Yavlenii Derzhavnoy Ikony Bozhiey Materi" [The Story of the Creation of the Icon of God's Mother Named the Sovereign] (editorial article), *ZhMP*, no. 3 (1996), pp. 37-8.

Tsypin, V., archpriest, *"Russkaya Pravoslavnaya Tserkov' v Velikuyu Otechestvennuyu Voynu"* [The Russian Orthodox Church in the Great Patriotic War], *ZhMP*, no. 5 (2005), pp. 66-71.

1.4. Author's Interviews with and testimonies of Baptist ministers and church members from the USSR

Abankin, P.M. (Sacramento, California, USA, 2006).

Afanakin, A.V. (Omsk, Russia, 2008).

Agafonov, L.F., Panchenko I.G., Yurkevich I.R., Deryabin N.V., Babich N.D., and Gavelovsky N.N. (Castro Valley, California, USA, 2006).

Baranov, V.Ya (Minneapolis, Minnesota, USA, 2006).

Bgatov, V.Ya. (San Diego, California, USA, 2006).

Bondarenko, V.D. (Los Angeles, California, USA, 2006).

Cherepanov, V.N. (Omsk, Russia, 2010).

Cherkasskikh, E.D., Vasiliev, M.A., and Avdeeva, O.E. (Everett, Washington, USA, 2006).

Cherny, P.P. (Sacramento, California, USA, 2006).

Chueshkov, D.I. (Seattle, Washington, USA, 2006).

Chumakin, P.A. (Kent, Washington, USA, 2006).

Chumakin, P.A., and Chumakina, N.D. (Seattle, Washington, USA, 2006).

Diordienko, Ya.D. (Sacramento, California, USA, 2006).

Dyck, J.P. (Oerlinghausen, Germany, 2007).

Erisov, V.D. (Sacramento, California, USA, 2008).

Evstratenko, A.T., and Evstratenko, V.N. (San Diego, California, USA, 2006).

Fast, I.P. (Shchuchinsk, Kazakhstan, 1999).

Fast, V. (Frankenthal, Germany, 2008).

Fayer, L.A., and Fayer, E.F. (Sacramento, California, USA, 2006).

Gavelovsky, V.N., and Gavelovskaya, L.M. (Sacramento, California, USA, 2006).

Goncharenko, E.S. (Omsk, Russia, 2006).

Gorelov, V.V., and Gorelova, V.P. (Los Angeles, California, USA, 2006).

Grinchenko, Ya.A. (Sacramento, California, USA, 2006).

Ivanov, V.V., Ivanova, A.F., Ivanov, P.V., Artemova, V.N., Kitsen, N.I., and
    Kitsen, V.V. (Fresno, California, USA, 2006).

Jerke, V., and Prannik, E. (Charlotte, North Carolina, USA, 2009).

Kabluchkin, I.A. (Omsk, Russia, 2009).

Kaplenkov, I.M., and Kaplenkov, A.M. (Petropavlovsk, Kazakhstan, 1997).

Kharchenko, A.T. (Sacramento, California, USA, 2006).

Khot'ko, V.N. (Petropavlovsk, Kazakhstan, 1997-2001).

Kolesnik, N.S., and Kolesnik, V.D. (Vancouver, Washington, USA, 2006).

Kolesnikov, N.A. (Shchuchinsk, Kazakhstan, 1998).

Kolivayko, M.M., and Sedykh, P.V. (Sacramento, California, USA, 2006).

Kolomiytsev, A.I. (Vancouver, Washington, USA, 2006).

Kovalenko, L.E. (Sacramento, California, USA, 2006).

Krivorotov, A.N. (Omsk, Russia, 2008).

Kryuchkov, Yu.K. (Sacramento, California, USA, 2006).

Kukushkina, M.N. (Everett, Washington, USA, 2006).

Kunda, P.F., Kramarenko, N.S., and Zinchenko, V.V. (Sacramento, California,
    USA, 2006).

Litovchenko, V.P. (Los Angeles, California, USA, 2006).

Logvinenko, V.E. (Odessa, Ukraine, 1995).

Man'ko, N.G. (Everett, Washington, USA, 2006).

Mazhnaya, N.F., Petrenko, M.I., and Petrenko, I.E. (Fresno, California, USA,
    2006).

Meleshkevich, Ya.A. (Bishkul', Kazakhstan, 1997-2003).

Mikhaylov, A.A., Mikhaylova, N.I., and Bernik, A.F. (Fresno, California, USA,
    2006).

Mikhaylov, V.I. (Omsk, Russia, 2009).

Mokey, V.N. (Minneapolis, Minnesota, USA, 2006).

Odaryuk, S.G., and Odaryuk, N.M. (Everett, Washington, USA, 2006).

Pikhay, A.A. (Los Angeles, California, USA, 2006).

Rozenov, A.A. (Omsk, Russia, 2006).

Rudnev, A.S., Savinsky, V.N., and Tishchenko, Yu.P. (Spokane, Washington, USA, 2006).

Runov, P.I., and Runova, G.I. (Salt Lake City, Utah, USA, 2006).

Sabursky, N.V., and Saburskaya, E.N. (Minneapolis, Minnesota, USA, 2006).

Sagan, V.E. (Minneapolis, Minnesota, USA, 2006).

Savchenko, D.G, and Savchenko, N.R. (Omsk, Russia, 2011).

Savinsky, S.N., and Savinskaya, L.V. (Salt Lake City, Utah, USA, 2006).

Sedykh, V.Ya., Sedykh, E.I., and Musiets A.I. (Sacramento, California, USA, 2006).

Semeryuk, P.A. (Sacramento, California, USA, 2006).

Serpevsky, V.F., and Serpevskaya, Z.I. (Vancouver, Washington, USA, 2006).

Serpikov, V.A. (Seattle, Washington, USA, 2006).

Shcherbakov, V.E. (Omsk, Russia, 2007).

Sheremet, V.A., and Sheremet, I.L. (Sacramento, California, USA, 2009).

Shevchuk, Ya.D., and Shevchuk, V.S. (Portland, Oregon, USA, 2006).

Shevchuk, Ya.S., Shevchuk, A.S., and Virkh, V.Ya. (Los Angeles, California, USA, 2006).

Sipko, A.K. (Spokane, Washington, USA, 2006).

Sobchenko, N.O., Karavan, P.D., and Karavan, T.N. (Sacramento, California, USA, 2006).

Sokolovsky, L.Ya., and Sokolovskaya, E.Ya. (San Diego, California, USA, 2006).

Svetlov, L.V. (Spokane, Washington, USA, 2006).

Sysoeva, T. (Syracuse, NY, USA, 2007).

Tsvirin'ko, V.M., and Tsvirin'ko, N.N. (Fresno, California, USA, 2006).

Vasiliev, V.T., and Vasilieva, R.F. (Sacramento, California, USA, 2006).

Vivsik, V.O. (Sacramento, California, USA, 2006).

Zakharov, M.P. (Sacramento, California, USA, 2006).

Zalesny, A.V. (Omsk, Russia, 2008).

Zdorovets, B.M. (Spokane, Washington, USA, 2006).

Zinchenko, V.P. (Seattle, Washington, USA, 2006).

1.5. Unpublished

"80-letniy Yubiley Pervoy Alma-atinskoy Tserkvi ECB 'Golgofa'" [The 80th Anniversary of the First Almaty Church of ECB 'Calvary'], Almaty Baptist Church Archives (1997).

Apatova, I., "Germenevtika Sinodal'nogo perevoda" [Hermeneutics of the Synodal Translation] (diploma thesis), Moscow Theological Seminary of ECB, 2006.

Kuksenko, Yu., "Nashi Besedy" [Our Conversations] (typescript), Kazakhstan's Baptist Union Archives (2002).

Nikolaev, O., "Protestantskie Ob"edineniya Orenburzh'ya: Istoriya, Sovremennoe Sostoyanie, Vzaimootnosheniya s Gosudarstvom" [The Protestant Associations of the Orenburg Region: History, the Present, and their Relationship with the State], Russian Academy of Public Service under the President of the Russian Federation, 1999.

Pakina, A., "Raskol Evangel'skikh Khristian-Baptistov 1961 g. i Ego Vliyanie na Obshchiny Novosibirskoy Oblasti" [The 1961 Year Split of the Evangelical Christians-Baptists and Its Influence on the Communities of the Novosibirsk Region] (diploma thesis), Novosibirsk State University, 2000.

Semeryuk, G.D., "Memoirs" [typescript]. Sacramento, California, USA, 2006.

Sysoev B., "Istoriya Evangel'skogo Dvizheniya v Karagande i Karagandinskoy Oblasti" [The History of the Evangelical Movement in Karaganda and Karaganda Region], Kazakhstan's Baptist Union Archives (2001).

Zdorovets, B., "Neposlushnye Deti ili Neputevye Ottsy" [Disobedient Children or Good-for-nothing Fathers] (typescript). Spokane, Washington, USA, 2010.

2. Dissertations

Beznosova, O., "*Pozdnee Protestantskoe Sektantstvo Yuga Ukrainy, 1850-1905*" [Late Protestant Sectarianism in the South of Ukraine, 1850-1905] (PhD thesis, Dnepropetrovsk State University, 1997).

Blane, A., "The Relations between the Russian Protestant Sects and the State, 1900-1921" (PhD thesis, Duke University, 1964).

Bondareva, I., "Separation or Cooperation? Moldavian Baptists, 1940-1965" (MTh dissertation, International Baptist Theological Seminary, University of Wales, 2004).

Breyfogle, N., "Heretics and Colonizers: Religious Dissent and Russian Colonization of Transcaucasia, 1830-1890" (PhD thesis, University of Pennsylvania, 1998).

Coleman, H., "The Most Dangerous Sect: Baptists in Tsarist and Soviet Russia, 1905-1929" (PhD thesis, University of Illinois, 1998).

Corrado, S., "The Philosophy of Ministry of Colonel Vasily Pashkov" (MA thesis, Wheaton College, 2000).

De Chalandeau, A., "The Theology of the Evangelical Christians-Baptists in the USSR, as Reflected in the Bratskii Vestnik" (PhD thesis, Strasbourg: Universite des Sciences Humaines, 1978).

Dyck, J., "Moulding the Brotherhood: Johann Wieler (1839-1889) and the Communities of the Early Evangelicals in Russia" (MTh Dissertation, International Baptist Theological Seminary, University of Wales, 2007).

Greenfeld, L., "Eastern Orthodox Influence on Russian Evangelical Ecclesiology" (MTh Dissertation, University of South Africa, 2002).

Il'inskaya, T., "*Fenomen 'Raznoveriya' v Tvorchestve N.S. Leskova*" [The Phenomenon of 'Raznoverie' in N.S. Leskov's Writings] (Doctor of Philology degree thesis, St. Petersburg State University, 2010).

Klippenstein, L., "Mennonite Pacifism and State Service in Russia: A Case Study in Church–State Relations, 1789-1936" (PhD thesis, University of Minnesota, 1984).

Kuznetsova, M., "Early Russian Evangelicals (1874-1929): Historical Background and Hermeneutical Tendencies Based on I.V. Kargel's Written Heritage" (PhD thesis, University of Pretoria, 2009).

Makeev, A., "*Analiz Filosofsko-Teologicheskikh Osnov Trudovoy Etiki Anglo-Shotlandskikh Puritan i Rossiyskikh Protestantov: Na Primere Baptistov i Evangel'skikh Khristian*" [An Analysis of the Philosophical and Theological Foundations of the Work Ethics of the English-Scottish Puritans and Russian Protestants: By Way of the Baptists' and Evangelical Christians' Example] (Candidate of Philosophy degree thesis, Russian Academy of Public Service under the President of the Russian Federation, 2002).

Nesdoly, S., "Evangelical Sectarianism in Russia: A Study of the Stundists, Baptists, Pashkovites, and Evangelical Christians, 1855-1917" (PhD thesis, Queen's University, 1971).

Nichols, G., "Ivan V. Kargel (1849-1937) and the Development of Russian Evangelical Spirituality" (PhD thesis, International Baptist Theological Seminary, University of Wales, 2009).

Pilli, T., "Evangelical Christians-Baptists of Estonia: The Shaping of Identity, 1945-1991" (PhD thesis, International Baptist Theological Seminary, University of Wales, 2007).

Parushev, P., "Walking in the Dawn of the Light: On the Salvation Ethics of the Ecclesial Communities in the Orthodox Tradition from a Radical Reformation Perspective" (PhD thesis, Fuller Theological Seminary, 2006).

Popov, A., "The Evangelical Christians-Baptists in the Soviet Union as a Hermeneutical Community: Examining the Identity of the All-Union

Council of the ECB (AUCECB) through the Way the Bible Was Used in Its Publications" (PhD thesis, International Baptist Theological Seminary, University of Wales, 2010).

Puzynin, A., "The Tradition of the Gospel Christians: A Study of their Identity and Theology during the Russian, Soviet, and Post-Soviet Periods" (PhD thesis, University of Wales, 2008).

Reshetnikov, Yu., "Stanovlennya ta Diferentsiatsiya Evangel'skogo Rukhu v Ukraini" [Formation and Differentiation of the Evangelical Movement in the Ukraine] (Candidate of Philosophy degree thesis, G.S. Skovoroda Philosophy Institute of National Academy of Sciences of Ukraine, 2000).

Rybarczyk, E., "Beyond Salvation: An Analysis of the Doctrine of Christian Transformation Comparing Eastern Orthodoxy With Classical Pentecostalism" (PhD thesis, Fuller Theological Seminary, 1999).

Sanders, T., "The Kingdom of God Belongs to Such as These: Exploring the Conversion Experiences of Baptist Children" (PhD thesis, Dallas Baptist University, 2009).

Sawatsky, W., "Prince Alexander N. Golitsyn (1773-1844): Tsarist Minister of Piety" (PhD thesis, University of Minnesota, 1976).

Steeves, P., "The Russian Baptist Union, 1917-1935: Evangelical Awakening in Russia" (PhD thesis, University of Kansas, 1976).

3. Reference

Averintsev, S., ed., *Khristianstvo: Entsiklopedichesky Slovar'* [Christianity: Encyclopedia], 3 vols. (M.: Bolshaya Rossiyskaya Entsiklopediya, 1993-1995).

Barr, L., ed., *Southern Baptist Handbook* (Nashville: Sunday School of the Southern Baptist Convention, 1994).

Bulgakov, S., *Nastol'naya Kniga Dlya Svyashchenno-Tserkovno-Sluzhiteley* [Handbook for Church Servers] (M.: Izdatel'sky Otdel Moskovskogo Patriarkhata, 1993).

Elwell, W., ed., *Evangelical Dictionary of Theology* (Grand Rapids: Baker Book House, 1991).

Hillerbrand, H., ed., *The Encyclopedia of Protestantism*, 4 vols. (New York: Routledge, 2004).

_____, *The Oxford Encyclopedia of the Reformation*, 4 vols. (New York: Oxford University Press, 1996).

Lopukhin, A., ed., *Tolkovaya Bibliya* [Study Bible], 12 vols. (SPb.: Strannik, 1904-1913).

Markicheva, O., ed., *Pravoslavnaya Entsiklopediya* [Russian Orthodox Encyclopaedia] (M.: AST, 2007).

Marthaler, B., ed., *New Catholic Encyclopedia*, 2nd ed., 15 vols., (Detroit: Gale, 2003).

Melton, J., ed., *Encyclopedia of Protestantism* (New York: Facts On File, 2005).

Mennonite Encyclopaedia, 4 vols. (Scottdale, PA: Mennonite Publishing House, 1955-1959).

Nastol'naya Kniga Svyashchennosluzhitelya [The Handbook for Priests], 7 vols. (M.: Izdanie Moskovskoy Patriarkhii, 1977-1994).

New American Standard Exhaustive Concordance of the Bible (Nashville, TN: Holman Bible Publishers, 1981).

Polnaya Simfoniya na Kanonicheskie Knigi Svyashchennogo Pisaniya [The Exhaustive Concordance of the Canonical Books of the Holy Scripture] (SPb.: Biblia dlya Vsekh, 1996).

Prokhorov, A.M., ed., *Bol'shaya Sovetskaya Entsiklopediya* [The Great Soviet Encyclopedia], 3rd ed., 30 vols. (M.: Sovetskaya Entsiklopediya, 1969-1978).

_____, *Sovetsky Entsiklopedichesky Slovar'* [The Soviet Encyclopedia] (M.: Sovetskaya Entsiklopediya, 1982).

Veniamin, archbishop, *Novaya Skrizhal', ili Ob"yasnenie o Tserkvi i Vsekh Sluzhbakh i Utvaryakh Tserkovnykh* [The New Tablet, or An Explanation for the Church, Liturgy and All Church Services and Utensils] (M.: Izd-vo Pravoslavnogo Bratstva Sv. Filareta, 1999).

Wardin, A.W., Jr., ed., *Baptists Around the World* (Nashville, Tennessee: Broadman and Holman, 1995).

_____, *Evangelical Sectarianism in the Russian Empire and the USSR.* ATLA Bibliography Series, 36 (Lanham, MD: Scarecrow, 1995).

4. Patristics and Ascetic Writings

Bryanchaninov, I., bishop, *Polnoe Sobranie Tvoreny* [Complete Works], 8 vols. (M.: Palomnik, 2002-2007).

Dobrotolyubie [The Philokalia], 5 vols. (M.: Tipo-Litografiya I. Efimova, 1895-1900).

Drevny Paterik ili Dostopamyatnye Skazaniya o Podvizhnichestve Svyatykh i Blazhennykh Ottsov [The Ancient Paterikon or Memorable Legends about the Asceticism of the Holy and Blessed Fathers] (M.: Blagovest, 2002).

Ekaterinovsky, P., bishop, *Ukazanie Puti k Spaseniyu, Opyt Asketiki* [Showing the Way to Salvation, the Ascetic Practice] (M.: Izd-vo Sretenskogo monastyrya, 2001).

Guriev, V., archpriest, *Prolog v Poucheniyakh* [The Church Calendar with Homilies] (M.: Tipo-Litografiya I. Efimova, 1912).

John Climacus, St., *Lestvitsa* [The Ladder of Divine Ascent] (Svyato-Uspensky Pskovsko-Pechersky Monastyr', 1994).

John of Damascus, St., *Tochnoe Izlozhenie Pravoslavnoy Very* [Exact Exposition of the Orthodox Faith] (M.: Lod'ya, 1998).

_____, *Tri Zashchititel'nykh Slova* [On Holy Images] (SPb.: Izdanie I. Tuzova, 1893).

Lozinsky, M., hegumen, *Otechnik Propovednika: 1221 Primer iz Prologa i Paterikov* [The Book of the Lives of the Fathers, for Preachers: 1221 Illustrations from the Prologue and Paterikons] (Izd-vo Svyato-Troitskoy Sergievoy Lavry, 1997).

Nilus of Sora, St., *Ustav o Skitskoy Zhizni* [The Rule of Scete Life] (Yekaterinburg: Novo-Tikhvinsky Zhensky Monastyr', 2002).

Pravila Pravoslavnoy Tserkvi [The Canons of the Orthodox Church], ed. by Bishop Nikodim, 2 vols. (M.: Otchiy Dom, 2001).

Svyatootecheskie Nastavleniya o Molitve i Trezvenii [The Patristic Writings on Prayer and Abstinence] (M.: RIPOL klassik, 2008).

Tertullian, *The Writings*, in *The Ante-Nicene Fathers*, ed. by A. Roberts and J. Donaldson, 10 vols. (Grand Rapids: Eerdmans, 1978), v. III.

Tvoreniya Svyatogo Ottsa Nashego Ioanna Zlatousta, Arkhiepiskopa Konstantinopol'skogo, v Russkom Perevode [The Writings of St. John Chrysostom, Our Father, the Archbishop of Constantinople, a Russian Translation] (SPb.: Izdanie S.-Peterburgskoy Dukhovnoy Akademii, 1895-1906).

Uchilishche Blagochestiya, ili Primery Christianskikh Dobrodeteley, Vybrannye iz Zhity Svyatykh [The School of Piety, or the Examples of Christian Virtues Selected from the Saints' Lives] (SPb.: Sinodal'naya Tipografiya, 1903).

Zhitiya Svyatykh, Na Russkom Yazyke Izlozhennye po Rukovodstvu Chet'ikh-Miney Sv. Dimitriya Rostovskogo [Lives of Saints, in the Russian Language, Retold According to the Menology by St. Dimitry Rostovsky], 12 vols. (M.: Sinodal'naya Tipografiya, 1903-1911).

5. Secondary (books and collected articles)

Afanasiev, Yu., ed., *Sovetskoe Obshchestvo: Vozniknovenie, Razvitie, Istorichesky Final* [Soviet Society: Origins, Development, and Historical Finale], 2 vols. (M.: RGGU, 1997).

Aksyutin, Yu. (ed.), *L.I. Brezhnev: Materialy k Biografii* [L.I. Brezhnev: Materials for the Biography] (M.: Politizdat, 1991).

Alekseeva, L., *Istoriya Inakomysliya v SSSR* [History of Dissidence in the USSR] (Benson, VT: Khronika Press, 1984).

Alipy (Kastal'sky), archimandrite, and Isaiya (Belov), archimandrite, *Dogmaticheskoe Bogoslovie: Kurs Lektsiy* [Dogmatic Theology: A Course of Lectures] (M.: Svyato-Troitskaya Sergieva Lavra, 2007).

Anderson, V., *Staroobryadchestvo i Sektantstvo* [Old Belief and Sectarianism] (SPb.: Izdanie V.I. Gubinskogo, 1909).

Andreeva, A., ed., *Otets A. Men' Otvechaet na Voprosy Slushateley* [Father A. Men' Answers the Questions of his Listeners] (M.: Fond im. A. Menya, 1999).

Andronoviene, L., *Involuntarily Free or Voluntarily Bound: Singleness in the Baptistic Communities of Post-communist Europe* (Prague: IBTS, 2003).

Arabadzhi, D., *Ocherki Khristianskogo Simvolizma* [Essays on Christian Symbolism] (Odessa: Druk, 2008).

Ardov, M., *Melochi Arkhi... Proto... i Prosto Iereyskoy Zhizni* [Little Things from the Lives of Arch-, Proto-, and Just Hiereus' Life] (M.: Izd-vo im. Sabashnikovykh, 1995.

Arseniev, N., *Mysticism and the Eastern Church* (Crestwood, NY: St. Vladimir's Seminary Press, 1979).

Athanasius (Sakharov), bishop, *O Pominovenii Usopshikh po Ustavu Pravoslavnoy Terkvi* [On Remembrance of the Dead according to the Statutes of the Orthodox Church] (SPb.: Satis", 1999).

Bach, M., *God and the Soviets* (New York: Thomas Y. Crowell Company, 1958).

Bachinin, V., *Vizantizm i Evangelizm: Genealogiya Russkogo Protestantizma* [Byzantinism and Evangelism: The Genealogy of Russian Protestantism] (SPb.: Izd-vo S.-Peterburgskogo Universiteta, 2003).

Baker, A., *Religion in Russia Today* (Nashville: Southern Publishing Association, 1967).

Baptist Hymnal (Nashville, TN: Convention Press, 1991).

Bartos, E., "Salvation in the Orthodox Church: An Evangelical Perspective", in *Baptists and the Orthodox Church: On the Way to Understanding*, ed. by I. Randall (Prague: IBTS, 2003), pp. 46-63.

Bebbington, D.W., *Evangelicalism in Modern Britain: A History from the 1730s to the 1980s* (London: Unwin Hyman, 1989).

Beeson, T., *Discretion and Valour: Religious Conditions in Russia and Eastern Europe* (Philadelphia: Fortress Press, 1982).

Belov, A., *Sekty, Sektantstvo, Sektanty* [Sects, Sectarianism, and Sectarians] (M.: Nauka, 1978).

Berdyaev, N., *The Origin of Russian Communism* (Ann Arbor, MI: The University of Michigan Press, 2004).

Berdyaev, N., *Tsarstvo Dukha i Tsarstvo Kesarya* [The Kingdom of the Spirit and the Kingdom of Caesar] (M.: Respublika, 1995).

Berkhof, L., *Systematic Theology* (Grand Rapids: Eerdmans Publishing Co., 1981).

Bezhentseva, A., *Strana Dukhoboria* [Dukhoboria Land] (Tbilisi: Russky Klub, 2007).

Bobrishchev-Pushkin, A., *Sud i Raskol'niki-Sektanty* [The Court and Dissenters-Sectarians] (SPb.: Senatskaya Tipografiya, 1902).

Bobyleva, S., ed., *Nemtsy Ukrainy i Rossii v Konfliktakh i Kompromissakh XIX – XX Stoletiy* [The Germans of the Ukraine and Russia in the Conflicts and Compromises in the 19th-20th Centuries] (Dnepropetrovsk: RVV DNU, 2007).

Bockmuehl, K., "Sanctification", in *New Dictionary of Theology*, ed. by S. Ferguson (Downers Grove, IL: InterVarsity Press, 1988), pp. 613-615.

Bolshakoff S., *Russian Nonconformity* (Philadelphia: The Westminster Press, 1950).

Bolotov, V., *Lektsii po Istorii Drevney Tserkvi* [Lectures on the History of the Ancient Church], 4 vols. (M.: Izdanie Spaso-Preobrazhenskogo Valaamskogo Monastyrya, 1994).

Bonch-Bruevich, V., *Izbrannye Sochineniya* [Selected Works], 3 vols. (M.: Izd-vo AN SSSR, 1959), v. I.

Bondareva-Zuehlke, I., "Separation or Co-operation? Moldavian Baptists (1940-1965)", in K.G. Jones and I.M. Randall, eds., *Counter-Cultural Communities. Baptist Life in Twentieth-Century Europe* (Milton Keynes, UK: Paternoster, 2008), pp. 63-113.

Boobbyer, P., *Conscience, Dissent and Reform in Soviet Russia* (Abingdon, UK: Routledge, 2005).

Borisov, A., *Pobelevshie Nivy* [White Fields] (M.: Liga – Foliant, 1994).

Bourdeaux, M., *Faith on Trial in Russia* (New York: Harper & Row, 1971).

_____, M., *Opium of the People: The Christian Religion in the USSR* (Indianapolis: The Bobbs-Merrill Company, 1966).

_____, *Religious Ferment in Russia: Protestant Opposition to Soviet Religious Policy* (London: Macmillan, 1968).

Brandenburg, H., *The Meek and the Mighty. The Emergence of the Evangelical Movement in Russia* (London: Mowbrays, 1976).

Brazhnik, I., *Sotsial'naya Sushchnost' Sektantskogo Ekstremizma* [The Social Essence of Sectarian Extremism] (M.: Znanie, 1974).

Budur, N., ed., *Pravoslanaya Vera* [The Orthodox Faith] (M.: OLMA-PRESS, 2002).

Bukhshtab, B., *Russkie Poety* [Russian Poets] (Leningrad: Khudozhestvennaya Literatura, 1970).

Bulgakov, S., *Ocherki Ucheniya Pravoslavnoy Tserkvi* [Essays on the Doctrines of the Russian Orthodox Church] (Paris: YMCA-Press, 1989).

_____, *The Orthodox Church*, rev. trans. by Lydia Kesich (Crestwood, N.Y.: St. Vladimir's Seminary Press, 1988).

Burenin, S., ed., *Povedenie v Khrame* [Church Behaviour] (Rostov-na-Donu: Feniks, 2007).

Cairns, E., *Christianity through the Centuries: A History of the Christian Church*, 3rd ed. (Grand Rapids: Zondervan, 1996).

Chekalov, I., *Nravstvennoe Bogoslovie: Khristianskaya Etika* [Moral Theology: Christian Ethics] (M.: FS ECB, 1993).

Churchill, W., *The Second World War*, 6 vols. (Boston: Houghton Mifflin, 1948-1953).

Clancy, M., *Sacred Christmas Music: The Stories Behind the Most Beloved Songs of Devotion* (N.Y.: Sterling Publishing, 2008).

Coffey, J., *John Goodwin and the Puritan Revolution: Religion and Intellectual Change in Seventeenth-Century England* (Woodbridge: The Boydell Press, 2006).

Coleman, H., *Russian Baptists and Spiritual Revolution, 1905-1929* (Bloomington, IN: Indiana University Press, 2005).

Colwell, J., *Promise and Presence: An Exploration of Sacramental Theology* (Milton Keynes, UK: Paternoster, 2005).

_____, *The Rhythm of Doctrine: A Liturgical Sketch of Christian Faith and Faithfulness* (Milton Keynes: Paternoster, 2007).

Conant, R., *The Political Poetry and Ideology of F.I. Tiutchev* (Ann Arbor, MI: Ardis, 1983).

Corrado, S., *Filosofiya Sluzheniya Polkovnika Pashkova* [The Philosophy of Ministry of Colonel Vasily Pashkov] (SPb.: Bibliya Dlya Vsekh, 2005).

Cross, A., and Thompson, P., eds., *Baptist Sacramentalism* (Carlisle: Paternoster Press, 2003).

Davis, K., *Anabaptism and Asceticism: A Study in Intellectual Origins* (Kitchener, Ontario: Herald Press, 1974).

De Grunwald, C., *God and the Soviets* (London: Hutchinson, 1961).

_____, *The Churches and the Soviet Union* (New York: The Macmillan Company, 1962).

Diachenko, G., *Simvolicheskie Deystviya. Svyashchennosluzhiteli* [Symbolic Acts. Priests] (Kiev: Prolog, 2005).

Dobuzhinsky, M., ed., *Zakon Bozhy* [God's Law], 5 vols. (M.: Terra, 1991).

Dostoevsky, F., *A Writer's Diary*, trans. by K. Lantz, 2 vols. (Evanston, IL: Northwestern University Press, 1994).

_____, *Polnoe Sobranie Sochineniy* [The Complete Works], 30 vols. (Leningrad: Nauka, 1984).

Dudarev, P., ed., *Sbornik propovednicheskikh obraztsov* [Collection of Preaching Samples] (SPb.: Izdanie I. Tuzova, 1912).

Dudko, D., *O Nashem Upovanii* [On Our Hope] (Korntal: Svet na Vostoke, 1991).

Dunning, H.R., *Grace, Faith and Holiness. A Wesleyan Systematic Theology* (Kansas City: Beacon Hill Press, 1988).

Dunstan, J., "Soviet Schools, Atheism and Religion", in Ramet, S., ed, *Religious Policy in the Soviet Union* (Cambridge, UK: Cambridge University Press, 1993), pp. 158-186.

Durasoff, S., *The Russian Protestants, Evangelicals in the Soviet Union: 1944-1964* (Rutherford: Farleigh Dickinson University Press, 1969).

Dyck, C.J., ed., *A Legacy of Faith: The Heritage of Menno Simons* (Newton, Kans.: Faith and Life Press, 1962).

Ellis, C.J., *Gathering: A Theology and Spirituality of Worship in the Free Church Tradition* (London: SCM Press, 2004).

Ellis, J., *The Russian Orthodox Church: A Contemporary History* (London: Croom Helm, 1986).

Elliott, M., Deyneka, A., "Protestant Missionaries in the former Soviet Union", in Witte, J., and Bordeaux, M., eds., *Proselytism and Orthodoxy in Russia: The New War for Souls* (Maryknoll, N.Y.: Orbis Books, 1999), pp. 197-227.

Epp, P., *100 Let pod Krovom Vsevyshnego* [100 Years in the Shelter of the Most High] (Omsk – Steinhagen: Samenkorn, 2007).

Erickson, M., *Christian Theology*, 2nd ed. (Grand Rapids: Baker Book House, 1998).

Fairbairn, D., *Eastern Orthodoxy through Western Eyes* (Louisville, Ken.: Westminster John Knox Press, 2002).

Fast, V., *Ya s Vami vo Vse Dni do Skonchaniya Veka* [I Am with You Always to the End of the Age] (Karaganda – Steinhagen: Aquila, 2001).

Fedotov, G., *Svyatye Drevney Rusi* [The Saints of Old Russia] (M.: Moskovsky Rabochy, 1990).

_____, *The Russian Religious Mind* (N.Y.: Harper & Row, 1965).

Fletcher, W., *The Russian Orthodox Church Underground, 1917-1970* (London: Oxford University Press, 1971).

Fletcher, W., *Religion and Soviet Foreign Policy, 1945-1970* (London: Oxford University Press, 1973).

Fountain, D., *Lord Radstock and the Russian Awakening* (Southampton: Mayflower Christian Books, 1988).

Fowler, S., *More Than A Symbol: The British Baptist Recovery of Baptismal Sacramentalism* (Carlisle: Paternoster Press, 2002).

Friedman, R., *The Theology of Anabaptism* (Eugene, OR: Wipf and Stock Publishers, 1998).

Friesen, P., *The Mennonite Brotherhood in Russia (1789-1910)* (Fresno, CA: General Conference of Mennonite Brethren Churches, 1978).

Froese, P., *The Plot to Kill God: Findings from the Soviet Experiment in Secularization* (Berkeley, CA: University of California Press, 2008).

Furman, D., ed., *Na Puti k Svobode Sovesti* [On the Way to Liberty of Conscience] (M.: Progress, 1989).

Georgy, archbishop, *Obozhenie Kak Smysl Chelovecheskoy Zhizni* [Theosis as the Meaning of Human Life] (Izdanie Vladimirskoy Eparkhii, 2000).

Gogol, N.V., *Polnoe Sobranie Sochineniy* [The Complete Works], 14 vols. (M.: Izd-vo AN SSSR, 1937-1952).

_____, *The Government Inspector*, transl. by D. Campbell (London: Sylvan Press, 1947).

Golubeva, A., *Mal'chik iz Urzhuma: Povest' o Detstve i Yunosti S.M. Kirova* [A Boy from Urzhum: The Story of the Childhood and Youth of S.M. Kirov] (M. – L.: Detgiz, 1949).

Golubinsky, E., *Istoriya Russkoy Tserkvi* [The History of the Russian Church], 2 vols. (M.: Universitetskaya Tipografiya, 1901-1911).

Golubovich, V., ed., *My Byli Baptistami* [We were Baptists] (M.: Gospolitizdat, 1960).

Goncharenko, E., ed., *Alliluiya* [Hallelujah] (Spiritual Songs) (M.: Kinoob"edinenie "Moskva", 1991).

_____, *Muzyka i Dukhovnoe Vozrastanie Tserkvi* [Music and the Spiritual Growth of the Church] (M.: Logos, 2002).

Gordienko, N., *Osnovy Nauchnogo Ateizma* [Principles of Scientific Atheism] (M.: Prosveshchenie, 1988).

Gorokhov, M., *Kniga Nasushchnykh Voprosov o Pravoslavnoy Vere* [Book of Vital Issues concerning the Orthodox Faith] (M.: Arbor, 1998).

Grushevsky, M., *Z Istorii Religiynoy Dumki na Ukraini* [From the History of Religious Thought in the Ukraine] (Kyiv: Osvita, 1992).

Gubanov, V., ed., *Pravoslanye Chudesa v 20 Veke: Svidetel'stva Ochevidtsev* [Orthodox Miracles in the 20th Century: Eyewitnesses' Accounts] (M.: Trim, 1993).

Gusev-Orenburgsky, S., *Glukhoy Prikhod i Drugie Rasskazy* [A Remote Parish and Other Stories] (N.Y.: Izd-vo im. Chekhova, 1952).

Gutsche, W., *Westliche Quellen des russischen Stundismus* [Western Sources of Russian Stundism], 2nd ed. (Kassel: J.G. Oncken, 1957).

Hardwick, S., *Russian Refuge: Religion, Migration and Settlement on the North American Pacific Rim* (Chicago: Chicago University Press, 1993).

Hebly, J., *Protestants in Russia* (Belfast: Christian Journals Ltd, 1976).

Heier, E., *Religious Schism in the Russian Aristocracy, 1860-1900. Radstockism and Pashkovism* (The Hague: Martinus Nijhoff, 1970).

Hilborn, D., ed., *Evangelicalism and the Orthodox Church* (London: ACUTE, 2001).

Hulse, E., *An Introduction to the Baptists* (Haywards Heath, UK: Carey Publications Ltd., 1973).

Husserl, E., *The Crisis of European Sciences and Transcendental Phenomenology* (Evanston, IL: Northwestern University Press, 1970).

Hutten, K., *Iron Curtain Christians: The Church in Communist Countries Today* (Minneapolis: Augsburg Publishing House, 1967).

Illarion, archimandrite, *Svyashchennoe Pisanie i Tserkov'* [The Holy Scripture and the Church] (M.: Pechatnya A. Snegirevoy, 1914).

Il'in, I., "Muchenichestvo: Tserkov' v Sovetskom Soyuze" [Martyrdom: the Church in the Soviet Union], in I. Il'in, *Sobranie Sochineny* [Collected Works], 10 vols. (M.: Russkaya Kniga, 1998), v. VII, pp. 223-320.

Ivanov, M., and Sinichkin, A., eds., *Evangel'skie Khristiane-Baptisty: 140 Let v Rossii* [The Evangelical Christians-Baptists: During 140 Years in Russia] (M.: RS ECB, 2007).

Ivanov, S., *Vizantiyskoe Yurodstvo* [Byzantine Foolishness for Christ] (M.: Mezhdunarodnye Otnosheniya, 1994).

Jones, K., and Randall, I., eds., *Counter-Cultural Communities: Baptistic Life in Twentieth-Century Europe* (Milton Keynes, UK: Paternoster, 2008).

Kahle, W., *Evangelische Christen in Russland und der Sovetunion* [Evangelical Christians in Russia under the Soviet Union] (Wuppertal und Kassel: Onken Verlag, 1978).

Karamzin, N., *Istoriya Gosudarstva Rossiyskogo* [History of the Russian Empire] (M.: Eksmo, 2009).

Karev, A., Somov, K., *Istoriya Khristianstva* [History of Christianity] (M.: AUCECB, 1990).

Kartashev, A., *Ocherki po Istorii Russkoy Tserkvi* [Essays on the History of the Russian Church], 2 vols. (Paris: YMCA-PRESS, 1991).

_____, *Vselenskie Sobory* [Ecumenical Councils] (M.: Respublika, 1994).

Keener, C., *The IVP Bible Background Commentary: New Testament* (Downers Grove, IL: IVP, 1993).

Khomyakov, A., *Sochineniya Bogoslovskie* [Theological Works] (SPb.: Nauka, 1995).

_____, *Tserkov' Odna* [The Church is One] (M.: Dar", 2005).

Khrapov, N., *Schast'e Poteryannoy Zhizni* [The Happiness of a Lost Life], 3 vols. (M.: Protestant, 1990).

Klibanov, A., *History of Religious Sectarianism in Russia (1860s-1917)* (Oxford: Pergamon Press, 1982).

_____, *Narodnaya Sotsial'naya Utopiya v Rossii: Period Feodalizma* [People's Social Utopia in Russia: the Feudal Period] (M.: Nauka, 1977).

_____, *Religioznoe Sektantstvo i Sovremennost'* [Religious Sectarianism Today] (M.: Nauka, 1969).

_____, ed., *Russkoe Pravoslavie: Vekhi Istorii* [Russian Orthodoxy: Milestones of the History] (M.: Politizdat, 1989).

Klyuchevsky, V., *Sochineniya* [Works], 9 vols. (M.: Mysl, 1987-1990).

Kolarz, W., *Religion in the Soviet Union* (London: Macmillian & Co Ltd, 1961).

Kolesnikov, N., *Khristianin, znaesh' li ty, kak dolzhno postupat' v dome Bozh'em?* [Christian, do you know how People ought to Conduct themselves in God's Household?], 3 vols. (M.: Druzhba i Blagaya Vest', 1998-2001).

_____, *V Pomoshch' Propovedniku: Sbornik Konspektov* [Assistance to the Preacher: A Collection of Sermons], 2 vols. (M.: Zlatoust, 1995-1996).

Koni, A., *Na Zhiznennom Puti: Iz Zapisok Sudebnogo Deyatelya* [On Life's Path: From the Notes of a Lawyer], 2 vols. (M.: T-vo I.D. Sytina, 1914).

Kovalenko, L., *Oblako Svideteley Khristovykh* [Cloud of Witnesses for Christ] (Kiev: Tsentr Khristianskogo Sotrudnichestva, 1997).

Kozlov, V., *et al.*, eds., *Kramola: Inakomyslie v SSSR pri Khrushcheve i Brezhneve, 1953-1982 gg.* [Sedition: Dissidence in the USSR under Khrushchev and Brezhnev, 1953-1982] (M.: Materik, 2005).

K.P. Pobedonostsev i Ego Korrespondenty: Pis'ma i Zapiski [K.P. Pobedonostsev and his Correspondents: Letters and Memoranda] (Moscow – Petrograd: Gos. Izd-vo, 1923).

Krasnikov, N., ed., *Voprosy Preodoleniya Religioznykh Perezhitkov v SSSR* [The Issues of Overcoming Religious Carry-overs in the USSR] (M.: Nauka, 1966).

Krasovitskaya, M., *Liturgika* [Study of Liturgy] (M.: Izd-vo Pravoslavnogo Svyato-Tikhonovskogo Bogoslovskogo Instituta, 2000).

Kryuchkov, G., *Velikoe Probuzhdenie XX Veka* [The Great Revival in the 20th Century] (n.p.: Izd-vo "Khristianin", 2008).

Kryuchkov, Yu., *140-letnyaya Istoriya Tserkvi ECB na Rusi v Svete Bibleyskikh Istin* [140 Years of the History of the Church of the ECB in Russia in the Light of Biblical Truths] (Sacramento, CA: n.p., 2010).

_____, *Podpol'naya Pechat' CC ECB v Sovetskom Soyuze* [The Underground Press of the CCECB in the Soviet Union] (Sacramento, CA: n.p., 2002).

_____, *Vnutritserkovnoe Dvizhenie ECB v Byvshem Sovetskom Soyuze* [Within the Church Movement of the ECB in the Former Soviet Union] (Sacramento, CA: n.p., 2001).

Kudryavtsev, M., *Istoriya Pravoslavnogo Monashestva* [History of Orthodox Monasticism] (M.: Krutitskoe patriarshee podvor'e, 1999).

Kuroedov, V., *Religiya i Tserkov' v Sovetskom Obshchestve* [Religion and Church in the Soviet Society] (M.: Politizdat, 1984).

Kuznetsov, A., hieromonk, *Yurodstvo i Stolpnichestvo* [Foolishness for Christ and Pillar Asceticism] (M.: Izd-vo Moskovskogo Podvoria Svyato-Troitskoy Sergievoy Lavry, 2000).

Kuz'menko, P., ed., *Russky Pravoslavny Obryad Pogrebeniya* [The Russian Orthodox Burial Ceremony] (M.: Bukmen, 1996).

_____, *Russky Pravoslavny Obryad Venchaniya* [The Russian Orthodox Marriage Ceremony] (M.: Bukmen, 1996).

Kuzmina, T., *V Luche Sveta* [In the Beam of Light] (SPb.: Bibliya Dly Vsekh, 2009).

Lane, C., *Christian Religion in the Soviet Union: A Sociological Study* (Albany, NY: State University of New York Press, 1978).

Latimer, R., *Dr. Baedeker and His Apostolic Work in Russia* (London: Morgan & Scott, 1908).

_____, *Under Three Tsars: Liberty of Conscience in Russia* (N.Y.: F. H. Revell, 1909).

Lawrence, J., *Russians Observed* (London: Hodder and Stoughton, 1969).

Lazar', archimandrite, *O Taynykh Nedugakh Dushi* [On Covert Illnesses of the Soul] (M.: Izd-vo Sretenskogo monastyrya, 2004).

Leontiev, K., "O Vsemirnoy Lyubvi" [On Universal Love], in Vasiliev, E., ed., *Russkaya Ideya* [The Russian Idea] (M.: Ayris Press, 2004), 190-226.

Leshchenko, V., *Russkaya Sem'ya, XI – XIX vv.* [Russian Family, 11th – 19th Centuries] (SPb.: SPGUTD, 2004).

Leshchuk I., *Labirinty Dukhovnosti* [Labyrinths of Spirituality] (Odessa: Khristianskoe Prosveshchenie, 2001).

Leskov, N.S., *Sobranie Sochineniy* [Collected Works], 11 vols. (M.: Gosizdat Khudozhestvennoy Literatury, 1956-1958).

_____, *Sobranie Sochineniy* [Collected Works], 12 vols. (M.: Pravda, 1989).

_____, "Velikosvetsky Raskol" [Schism in High Society], in N.S. Leskov, *Zerkalo Zhizni* [The Mirror of Life] (SPb.: Biblia dlya Vsekh, 1999), pp. 32-147.

Levitin-Krasnov, A., *Po Moryam, Po Volnam* [Across the Seas, Across the Waves] (Paris: Poiski, 1986).

Lidov, A., ed., *Ierotopiya: Issledovanie Sakral'nykh Prostranstv* [Hierotopy: Study of Sacral Spaces] (M.: Radunitsa, 2004).

Likhachev, D., *et al.*, *Smekh v Drevney Rusi* [Laughter in the Old Russia] (Leningrad: Nauka, 1984).

Lossky, V., *In the Image and Likeness of God* (Crestwood, NY: St. Vladimir's Seminary Press, 1974).

_____, *Orthodox Theology: An Introduction* (Crestwood, NY: St. Vladimir's Seminary Press, 1978).

_____, *The Mystical Theology of the Eastern Church* (Crestwood, NY: St. Vladimir's Seminary Press, 1976).

Lyalina, G., *Baptizm: Illyuzii i Real'nost'* [Baptists: Illusions and Reality] (M.: Politizdat, 1977).

Lyubashchenko, V., *Istoriya Protestantizmu v Ukraini: Kurs Lektsiy* [History of Protestantism in the Ukraine: A Course of Lectures], 2nd ed. (Kyiv: Polis, 1995).

MacDonald, W., *Bibleyskie Kommentarii dlya Khristian, Novy Zavet* [Believer's Bible Commentary, New Testament] (Bielefeld, Germany: CLV, 2000).

Maddox, R., *Responsible Grace: John Wesley's Practical Theology* (Nashville, TN: Kingswood Books, 1994).

Makary (Bulgakov), metropolitan, *Istoriya Russkoy Tserkvi* [History of the Russian Church], 9 vols. (M.: Izd-vo Spaso-Preobrazhenskogo Valaamskogo Monastyrya, 1994-1997).

_____, *Pravoslavno-dogmaticheskoe bogoslovie* [The Orthodox-Dogmatic Theology], 2 vols. (M.: Palomnik, 1999).

Malkov, P., *Vvedenie v Liturgicheskoe Predanie* [Introduction to Liturgical Tradition] (M.: Izd-vo PSTGU, 2006).

Mamsik, T., "Sibirskie Raskol'niki-Nemolyaki: Radikal'ny Protestantizm na Vostoke Rossii" [Siberian Dissenters, the Nemolyaks: The Radical Protestantism in the East of Russia], in L. Dmitrieva, *et al.*, eds., *Protestantizm v Sibiri: Istoriya i Sovremennost'* [Protestantism in Siberia: The History and the Present] (Omsk: TOO "Poligraf", 1998), pp. 76-81.

Marshall, M., *Common Hymnsense* (Chicago: GIA Publications, 1995).

Martsinkovsky, V., *Smysl Zhizni: Sbornik Statey* [Meaning of Life: Collected Articles] (Novosibirsk: Posokh, 1996).

Masaryk, T., *Rossiya i Evropa* [Russia and Europe: Essays on Spiritual Currents in Russia], 3 vols. (SPb.: RHGI, 2004).

McBeth, H., *The Baptist Heritage* (Nashville, TN: Broadman Press, 1987).

McGrath, A., *Reformation Thought: An Introduction*, 3rd ed. (Oxford: Blackwell Publishers, 2001).

Mefody, archbishop, *O Znamenii Obnovleniya Svyatykh Ikon* [On the Sign of Renewal of the Holy Icons] (M.: Palomnik, 1999).

Melgunov, S., *Tserkov' i Gosudarstvo v Rossii: K Voprosy o Svobode Sovesti* [Church and State in Russia: On the Issue of Freedom of Conscience] (M.: T-vo I.D. Sytina, 1907).

Melnikov, F., *Kratkaya Istoriya Drevlepravoslavnoy Tserkvi* [A Short History of the Old Orthodox Church] (Barnaul: Izd-vo BGPU, 1999).

Melnikov, P., "Zapiska o Russkom Raskole" [A Report on the Russian Schism], in V. Kelsiev, ed., *Sbornik Pravitel'stvennykh Svedeny o Raskol'nikakh* [Collection of Government Data on Schismatics], Part 1 (London: Trubner & Co., Paternoster Row, 1860), pp. 169-98.

Mel'nikova, E., and Odintsov, M., eds., *Svoboda Sovesti v Rossii: Istorichesky i Sovremenny Aspekty* [Freedom of Conscience in Russia: Historical and Modern Aspects] (M.: Rossiyskoe Ob"edinenie Issledovateley Religii, 2007).

Men', A., *Tainstvo, Slovo i Obraz: Pravoslavnoe Bogosluzhenie* [Sacrament, Word and Image: The Orthodox Divine Service] (M.: Fond imeni A. Menya, 2001).

Merkury, monk, *V Gorakh Kavkaza, Zapiski Sovremennogo Pustynnozhitelya* [In the Mountains of the Caucasus, Memoirs of a Contemporary Hermit] (M.: Palomnik, 1996).

Meyendorff, J., archpriest, *Byzantine Theology: Historical Trends and Doctrinal Themes* (N.Y.: Fordham University Press, 1983).

_____, *Pravoslavie i sovremenny mir* [Orthodoxy and the Contemporary World] (Minsk: Luchi Sofii, 1995).

_____, *Vvedenie v Svyatootecheskoe Bogoslovie* [Introduction to Patristic Theology] (N.Y.: RBR, 1985).

Milov, V., bishop, *Chteniya po Liturgicheskomy Bogosloviyu* [The Liturgical Theology Reader] (Kiev: Obshchestvo Lyubiteley Pravoslavnoy Literatury, 2004).

Mironenko, S., *et al*, eds., *Velikiy Knyaz' Konstantin Konstantinovich Romanov (Grand Duke Konstantin Konstantinovich Romanov)* (SPb.: ART-Palas, 2000).

Mitrokhin, L., *Baptizm* [The Baptists] (M.: Politizdat, 1966).

_____, *Baptizm: Istoriya i Sovremennost'* [The Baptists: The History and the Present] (SPb.: Russky Khristiansky Gumanitarny Institut, 1997).

Mitskevich, A., *Istoriya Evangel'skikh Khristian-Baptistov* [History of the Evangelical Christians-Baptists] (M.: Rossiysky Soyuz ECB, 2007).

Monasheskaya Zhizn' (Vypusk 1) [Monastic Life, Issue 1] (Svyato-Uspensky Pskovo-Pechersky monastyr', 1994).

Mordasov, V., archpriest, *1380 Polezneyshikh Sovetov Batyushki Svoim Prikhozhanam* [1380 Most Helpful Tips from the Father for his Parishioners] (Edinetsko-Brichanskaya Eparkhiya, 2004).

Mysticheskoe Bogoslovie [Mystical Theology] (Kiev: Put' k Istine, 1991).

Nabokov, V., *Poems and Problems* (London: Weidenfeld & Nicolson, 1971).

Nadporozhskaya, O., ed., *Nebesnye Pokroviteli Sankt-Peterburga* [The Patron Saints of St. Petersburg] (SPb.: Izdatel'sky Dom "Neva", 2003).

Nemtsev, V., *Soyuz Lyubvi* [The Love Union] (Minsk: "Probuzhdenie", 2002).

Nesdoly, S., *Among the Soviet Evangelicals* (Edinburgh: The Banner of Truth Trust, 1986).

Nichols, G., "Ivan Kargel and the Pietistic Community of Late Imperial Russia", in Corrado, S., and Pilli, T., eds., *Eastern European Baptist History: New Perspectives* (Prague: IBTS, 2007), pp. 71-87.

Nichols, G., *The Development of Russian Evangelical Spirituality: A Study of Ivan V. Kargel (1849-1937)*, (Eugene, OR: Wipf and Stock, 2011).

Niebuhr, H.R., *The Social Sources of Denominationalism* (Hamden, Conn: Shoe String Press, 1954).

Nikiforov, A., Sim, F., *Podryazhayutsya Voyti Skvoz' Tesnye Vrata* [They Make Every Effort to Enter Through the Narrow Door] (Petropavlovsk: n.p., 1985).

Nikolin, A., *Tserkov' i Gosudarstvo* [Church and State] (M.: Izd-vo Sretenskogo monastyrya, 1997).

Nikolskaya, T., *Russky Protestantizm i Gosudarstvennaya Vlast' v 1905-1991 Godakh* [Russian Protestantism and State Authority, 1905-1991] (SPb.: Izd-vo Evropeyskogo Universiteta, 2009).

Novitsky, O., *Dukhobortsy: Ikh Istoriya i Verouchenie* [The Doukhobors: Their History and Beliefs] (Kiev: Universitetskaya Tipografiya, 1882).

Odle, J.T., ed., *Why I am a Baptist* (Nashville, TN: Broadman Press, 1972).

Odintsov, M., *Put' Dlinoyu v Sem' Desyatilety* [The Way Lasted Seventy Years], in Furman, D., ed., *Na Puti k Svobode Sovesti* [On the Way to Liberty of Conscience] (M.: Progress, 1989), pp. 29-71.

Okhlobystin, I., *Tam, Gde Vostok: Dukhovnye Kopi* [There, where the East is: Spiritual Mines] (M.: Lepta, 2009).

Okuntsova, E., ed., *Tsarstvennoe Slovo* [The Royal Word] (M.: RIPOL klassik, 2009).

Osnovnye Printsipy Very Evangel'skikh Khristian – Baptistov [The Basic Principles of Belief of the Evangelical Christians–Baptists] (Sbornik Publikatsy) (Odessa: Russian Gospel Ministries, 1992).

Ouspensky, L., *Theology of the Icon*, 2 vols. (Crestwood, N.Y.: St. Vladimir's Seminary Press, 1992).

Ozerova, L., ed., *Chudnoe Mgnovenie* [Wondrous Moment], Part 1 (M.: Khudozhestvennaya Literatura, 1988).

Panchenko, A., *Russkaya Istoriya i Kultura* [Russian History and Culture] (SPb.: Yuna, 1999).

Panchenko, A., "Smekh Kak Zrelishche" [Laughter as a Spectacle], in Likhachev, D., *et al.*, *Smekh v Drevney Rusi* [Laughter in the Old Russia] (Leningrad: Nauka, 1984), pp. 72-153.

Pantskhava, I., ed., *Konkretno-Sotsiologicheskoe Izuchenie Sostoyaniya Religioznosti i Opyta Ateisticheskogo Vospitaniya* [Specific-Sociological Study of the State of Religiosity and the Experience of Atheistic Education] (M.: Izd-vo Moskovskogo Universiteta, 1969).

Parushev, P., "Towards Convictional Theological Education: Facing challenges of contextualisation, credibility and relevance", in Penner, P., ed., *Theological Education as Mission* (Erlangen, Germany: Neufeld Verlag Schwartzenfeld, 2005), pp. 185-208.

Pascal, P., *The Religion of the Russian People* (London: Mowbrays, 1976).

Payne, E., *Out of Great Tribulation: Baptists in the USSR* (London: Baptist Union of Great Britain and Ireland, 1974).

Pestov, N., *Sovremennaya Praktika Pravoslavnogo Blagochestiya* [The Contemporary Practice of Orthodox Piety], 4 vols. (SPb.: Satis, 1994-1996).

Pilli, T., *Dance or Die: The Shaping of Estonian Baptist Identity under Communism* (Milton Keynes: Paternoster, 2008).

Pis'menny, M., ed., *Zhitie prepodobnogo Sergiya Radonezhskogo* [Life of Saint Sergius of Radonezh] (M.: RIPOL KLASSIC, 2003).

Plett, I., *Zarozhdenie Tserkvey ECB* [The Origin of Churches of the ECB] (Izd-vo CC ECB "Khristianin", 1994).

Podberezsky, I., *Byt' Protestantom v Rossii* [To be a Protestant in Russia] (M.: Blagovestnik, 1996).

_____, *Protestanty i Drugie* [Protestants and Others] (SPb.: Mirt, 2000).

Poems and Political Letters of F.I. Tyutchev, trans. by J. Zeldin (Knoxville: University of Tennessee Press, 1973).

Pollock, J., *The Faith of the Russian Evangelicals* (N.Y.: McGray - Hill Book Company, 1964).

Popov, V., *Stopy Blagovestnika* [The Feet of the Evangelist] (M.: Blagovestnik, 1996).

Popova, O., "Vizantiyskie Ikony VI-XV Vekov" [The Byzantine Icons of the 6th – 15th Centuries], in *Istoriya Ikonopisi: Istoki, Traditsii, Sovremennost'. VI-XX Veka* [History of Icon Painting: Origin, Traditions, the Present. The 6th – 20th Centuries] (M.: ART-BMB, 2002), pp. 41-94.

Porfiriev, I., *Istoriya Russkoy Slovesnosty* [History of Russian Literature] (Kazan: Tipo-Litografiya Imperatorskogo Universiteta, 1909).

Pospielovsky, D., *Pravoslavnaya Tserkov' v Istorii Rusi, Rossii i SSSR* [The Orthodox Church in the History of Old Russia, Russia and the USSR] (M.: BBI, 1996).

_____, *Russkaya Pravoslavnaya Tserkov' v 20 veke* [The Russian Orthodox Church in the 20th Century] (M.: Respublika, 1995).

_____, *The Russian Church under the Soviet Regime, 1917-1982*, 2 vols. (Crestwood, NY: St. Vladimir's Seminary Press, 1984).

_____, *Totalitarizm i Veroispovedanie* [Totalitarianism and Confession] (M.: BBI, 2003).

Prava Cheloveka: Osnovnye Mezhdunarodnye Dokumenty [Human Rights: the Fundamental International Documents] (M.: Mezhdunarodnye Otnosheniya, 1989).

Pritzkau, J., *Geschichte der Baptisten in Sudrussland* [History of the Baptists in South Russia] (Lage: Logos Verlag, 1999).

Prokhorov, C., *Opyt Otechestvennogo Evangel'skogo Bogosloviya* [An Introduction to Russian Evangelical Theology] (SPb.: Mezhdunarodnoe Khristianskoe Izdatel'stvo "Titul", 2009).

_____, *Sektantskie Rasskazy* [Sectarian Stories] (Idar-Oberstein, Germany: Titel Verlag, 2002).

_____, "The State and the Baptist Churches in the USSR (1960-1980)", in K.G. Jones and I.M. Randall, eds., *Counter-Cultural Communities. Baptist Life in Twentieth-Century Europe* (Milton Keynes, UK: Paternoster, 2008), pp. 1-62.

Prugavin, A., *Monastyrskie Tyur'my v Bor'be s Sektantstvom: K Voprosu o Veroterpimosti* [Monastery Prisons in the Struggle against Sectarianism: On the Issue of Toleration] (M.: Posrednik, 1905).

_____, *Raskol i Sektantstvo v Russkoy Narodnoy Zhizni* [Schism and Sectarianism in Russian National Life] (M.: T-vo I.D. Sytina, 1905).

Pushkin, A.S., *Eugene Oneguine*, trans. by H. Spalding (Charleston, SC: BiblioLife, 2009).

_____, *Polnoe Sobranie Sochineniy* [The Complete Works], 10 vols. (Leningrad: Nauka, 1977-1979).

Pushkov, E., *Ne smushchyaysya!* [Do not be Confused!] (SPb.: Bibliya Dlya Vsekh, 2010).

Puzynin, A., *The Tradition of the Gospel Christians: A Study of their Identity and Theology during the Russian, Soviet, and Post-Soviet Periods* (Eugene, OR; Wipf and Stock, 2010).

Puzynin, A., *Traditsiya Evangel'skikh Khristian* [The Tradition of the Gospel Christians] (M.: BBI, 2010).

Rafail (Karelin), archimandrite, *Dykhanie Zhizni: O Molitve* [The Breath of Life: On Prayer] (Saratov: Izd-vo Saratovskoy Eparkhii, 2007).

_____, *Eshche Raz o Ereticheskich Zabluzhdeniyach Professora MDA, A.I. Osipova* [More on the Heretical Errors of Professor MDA, A.I. Osipov] (M.: Krest sv. Niny, 2003).

_____, *More Zhiteyskoe: Otvety Na Voprosy Chitateley* [The Sea of Life: Answers to Questions from Readers] (M.: Moskovskoe Podvor'e Sv.-Troitskoy Sergievoy Lavry, 2008).

Rak, P., *Priblizheniya k Afonu* [Approaches to Mount Athos] (SPb.: Satis, 1995).

Ramet, S.P., ed., *Protestantism and Politics in Eastern Europe and Russia: The Communist and Postcommunist Eras* (Durham: Duke University Press, 1992).

_____, *Religious Policy in the Soviet Union* (Cambridge, UK: Cambridge University Press, 1993).

Rand, A., *The Fountainhead* (N.Y.: Plume, 2005).

Randall, I.M., ed., *Baptists and the Orthodox Church: On the Way to Understanding* (Prague: IBTS, 2003).

_____, *Communities of Conviction: Baptist Beginnings in Europe* (Prague: EBF, 2009).

_____, "Eastern European Baptists and the Evangelical Alliance, 1846-1896", in Corrado, S., and Pilli, T., eds., *Eastern European Baptist History: New Perspectives* (Prague: IBTS, 2007), pp. 14-33.

_____, *Evangelical Experiences* (Carlisle: Paternoster Press, 1999).

_____, *The English Baptists of the Twentieth Century* (Didcot: Baptist Historical Society, 2005).

Raymer, I., *Missionerskaya Deyatel'nost' Drevnerusskogo Monashestva* [The Missionary Works of the Old Russian Monks] (n.p.: Izd-vo "Logos", 1996).

Reagan, R., "The 'Evil Empire' Speech", in Waller, J.M, ed., *The Public Diplomacy Reader* (Washington, DC: Institute of World Politics Press, 2007), pp. 137-143.

Religious Prisoners in the USSR: A Study by Keston College (Keston: Greenfire Books, 1987).

Reshetnikov, Yu., and Sannikov, S., *Obzor Istorii Evangel'sko-Baptistskogo Btatstva na Ukraine* [A Review of the History of the Evangelical–Baptist Brotherhood in the Ukraine] (Odessa: Bogomyslie, 2000).

Rimsky, S., *Rossiyskaya Tserkov' v Epokhu Velikikh Reform* [The Russian Church in the Age of the Great Reforms] (M.: Krutitskoe Patriarshee Podvor'e, 1999).

Rogozin, P., *Otkuda vse eto poyavilos?* [From whence do all these come?] (Rostov-na-Donu: Missiya "Probuzhdenie, 1993).

Ronkin, V., *Na Smenu Dekabryam Prikhodyat Yanvari* [Decembers Give Way to Januaries] (M.: Zven'ya, 2003).

Rowe, M., *Russian Resurrection: Strength in Suffering. A History of Russia's Evangelical Church* (London: Marshall Pickering, 1994).

Rudenko, A., "Evangel'skie Khristiane-Baptisty i Perestroyka v SSSR" [The Evangelical Christians–Baptists and Perestroika in the USSR] in Furman, D., ed., *Na Puti k Svobode Sovesti* [On the Way to Liberty of Conscience] (M.: Progress, 1989), pp. 341-57.

Russell, N., *The Doctrine of Deification in the Greek Patristic Tradition* (N.Y.: Oxford University Press, 2004).

Ryabinin, Yu., *Russkoe Yurodstvo* [Russian Foolishness for Christ] (M.: RIPOL klassik, 2007).

Rybakov, B., *Strigol'niki* [The Strigolniks] (M.: Nauka, 1993).

_____, *Yazychestvo Drevney Rusi* [Paganism of Ancient Russia] (M.: Nauka, 1988).

Rybarczyk, E., *Beyond Salvation: Eastern Orthodoxy and Classical Pentecostalism on Becoming Like Christ* (Milton Keynes: Paternoster, 2004).

Ryrie, Ch., *Basic Theology* (Wheaton, IL: Victor Books, 1986).

Ryzhenko, S., *Stranniki My Na Zemle. Istoriya Petropavlovskoy Obshchiny ECB, 1908-1988* [We are Strangers on the Earth. Chronicle of Petropavlovsk Community of the ECB, 1908-1988] (Petropavlovsk – Steinhagen: Samenkorn, 2008).

Sannikov, S., *Dvadtsat' Vekov Khristianstva (Twenty Centuries of Christianity)*, 2 vols. (Odessa: Bogomyslie, 2001), v. II.

_____, ed., *Istoriya Baptizma* [History of the Baptists] (Odessa: OBS, 1996).

_____, ed., *Nashe kredo: Odesskaya bogoslovskaya seminariya ECB* [Our Creed: Odessa Baptist Theological Seminary] (Odessa: Bogomyslie, 1993).

_____, ed., *Podgotovka k kreshcheniyu* [Preparation for Baptism] (Odessa: OBS, 2005).

_____, *Vecherya Gospodnya* [The Lord's Supper] (M.: Protestant, 1990).

Savchenko, P., *Sravnitel'noe Bogoslovie* [Comparative Theology] (M.: AUCECB, 1991).

Savin, A., ed., *Sovetskoe Gosudarstvo i Evangel'skie Tserkvi Sibiri v 1920-1941 gg.* [The Soviet State and Evangelical Churches of Siberia in 1920-1941: Documents and materials] (Novosibirsk: Posokh, 2004).

Savinsky, S., "Baptisty v Rossii v XIX Veke" [The Baptists in Russia in the 19th Century], in Sannikov S., ed., *Istoriya Baptizma* [History of the Baptists] (Odessa: OBS, 1996).

_____, *Istoriya evangel'skikh khristian-baptistov Ukraini, Rossii, Belorussii* [History of the Evangelical Christians-Baptists of the Ukraine, Russia, and Belorussia] (1867-1917) (SPb.: Biblia dlya Vsekh, 1999).

_____, *Istoriya evangel'skikh khristian-baptistov Ukraini, Rossii, Belorussii* [History of the Evangelical Christians-Baptists of the Ukraine, Russia, and Belorussia] (1917-1967) (SPb.: Biblia dlya Vsekh, 2001).

Sawatsky, W., "Protestantism in the USSR", in Ramet, S.P., ed., *Protestantism and Politics in Eastern Europe and Russia: The Communist and Postcommunist Eras* (Durham: Duke University Press, 1992), pp. 237-75.

_____, "Russian Mennonites and Baptists (1930-1990)", in Toews, P., ed., *Mennonites and Baptists, A Continuing Conversation* (Winnipeg: Kindred Press, 1993), pp. 113-31.

_____, *Soviet Evangelicals Since World War II* (Kitchener, Ontario: Herald Press, 1981).

Schmemann, A., "Moment of Truth for Orthodoxy", in Bridston, K., and Wagoner, W., eds., *Unity in Mid-Career: an Ecumenical Critique* (N.Y.: Macmillan, 1963), pp. 47-56.

_____, *Of Water and the Spirit: A Liturgical Study of Baptism* (Crestwood, NY: St. Vladimir's Seminary Press, 1974).

Sergy (Stragorodsky), archbishop, *Pravoslavnoe uchenie o spasenii* [The Orthodox Doctrine of Salvation] (M.: Izdatel'sky otdel Moskovskogo Patriarkhata, 1991).

Shakhovskoy, I., archbishop, *Izbrannoe* [Selected Works] (Petrozavodsk: Svyatoy ostrov, 1992).

_____, *K Istorii Russkoy Intelligentsii, Revolyutsiya Tolstogo* [History of the Russian Intelligentsia, Tolstoy's Revolution] (M.: Lepta, 2003).

_____, *Moskovsky Razgovor o Bessmertii* [Moscow Conversation about Immortality] (N.Y.: Ichthys, 1972).

_____, *Vremya Very* [The Age of Faith] (N.Y.: Izd-vo im. Chekhova, 1954).

Shchapov, A., *Sochineniya* [Works], 3 vols. (SPb.: Izdanie M.V. Pirozhkova, 1906-1908).

Shtrikker, G., ed., *Russkaya Pravoslavnaya Tserkov' v Sovetskoe Vremya, 1971-1991* [The Russian Orthodox Church at the Soviet Times, 1971-1991], 2 vols. (M.: Propilei, 1995).

Shenderovsky, L., *Evangel'skie Khristiane* [The Evangelical Christians] (Toronto: Izdanie Kanadskogo Soyuza Evangel'skikh Khristian, 1980).

Shevchenko, T., *Zibrannya Tvoriv* [Collected Works] (Kyiv: Naukova Dumka, 2003).

Shkarovsky, M., "Poslednyaya Ataka na Russkuyu Pravoslavnuyu Tserkov'" [The Last Attack against the Russian Orthodox Church], in Afanasiev, Yu., ed., *Sovetskoe Obshchestvo: Vozniknovenie, Razvitie, Istorichesky Final* [Soviet

Society: Origins, Development, and Historical Finale], 2 vols. (M.: RGGU, 1997), v. II, pp. 328-99.

_____, *Russkaya Pravoslavnaya Tserkov' pri Staline i Khrushcheve* [The Russian Orthodox Church under Stalin and Khrushchev] (M.: Krutitskoe Patriarshee Podvor'e, 1999).

Shnayder, I., *Evangel'skie Obshchiny v Aktyubinskoy Stepi* [Evangelical Communities in the Aktyubinsk Steppe] (Steinhagen, Germany: Samenkorn, 2006).

Simon, G., *Church, State and Opposition in the USSR* (London: C. Hurst & Company, 1974).

Sinitsyna, N., "*Tipy Monastyrey i Russky Asketichesky Ideal*" [The Types of Monasteries and the Russian Ascetic Ideal], in Sinitsyna, N., ed., *Monashestvo i Monastyri v Rossii* [Monks and Monasteries in Russia] (M.: Nauka, 2002), pp. 116-49.

Sipko, A., *Derzhis' Obraztsa Zdravogo Ucheniya: Sbornik Statey* [Keep the Pattern of Sound Teaching: Collection of Articles] (Spokane, WA: NCG Inc., 2010).

Skazkin, S., ed., *Nastol'naya Kniga Ateista* [The Handbook of Atheists] (M.: Politizdat, 1983).

Slobodskoy, S., ed., *Zakon Bozhy* [God's Law] (Omsk: Omich, 1995).

Smirnov, P., *Istoriya Khristianskoy Pravoslavnoy Tserkvi* [History of the Christian Orthodox Church] (M.: Krutitskoe Patriarshee Podvorie, 1998).

Smorgunova, E., "*Iskhod Staroverov Vchera i Segodnya: Ukhod ot Mira i Poiski Zemli Obetovannoy*" [Exodus of the Old Believers Yesterday and Today: Escape from the World and Searching for the Promised Land], in *Istoriya Tserkvi: Izuchenie i Prepodavanie* [Church History: Studying and Teaching] (Yekaterinburg: Izd-vo Ural'skogo Gosuniversiteta, 1999), pp. 211-9.

Snyder, A., *Anabaptist History and Theology: An Introduction* (Kitchener, Ontario: Pandora Press, 1995).

Soloviev, A., Archpriest, *Starchestvo po Ucheniyu Svyatykh Ottsov i Asketov* [The Eldership According to the Teaching of the Holy Fathers and Ascetics] (M.: Blagovest, 1995).

Soloviev, S.M., *Sochineniya* [Works], 18 vols. (M.: Mysl', 1988-1996).

Soloviev, V., *Freedom, Faith, and Dogma: Essays by V.S. Soloviev on Christianity and Judaism*, trans. by V. Wozniuk (Albany, NY: State University of New York Press, 2008).

_____, *Sobranie Sochineniy* [Collected Works], 9 vols. (SPb.: Obshchestvennaya Pol'za, 1901-1903).

_____, *War, Progress, and the End of History: Three Conversations, Including a Short Story of the Anti-Christ* (Hudson, N.Y.: Lindisfarne Press, 1990).

Spurgeon, C.H., *12 Sermons on the Lord's Supper* (Grand Rapids, MI: Baker Book House, 1994).

Stanley, C., *When the Enemy Strikes* (Nashville, TN: Thomas Nelson, 2004).

Staton C.P., Jr., ed., *Why I am a Baptist: Reflections on Being Baptist in the 21ˢᵗ Century* (Macon, GA: Smyth & Helwys Publishing, Inc., 1999).

Stepnyak-Kravchinsky, S., *Shtundist Pavel Rudenko* [Stundist Pavel Rudenko] (SPb.: Bibliya dlya Vsekh, 1997).

_____, *Sochineniya* [Works], 2 vols. (M.: GIHL, 1958).

Struve, N., *Christians in Contemporary Russia* (New York: Charles Scribner's Sons, 1967).

Suri, J., *Power and Protest: Global Revolution and the Rise of Détente* (Cambridge, MA: Harvard University Press, 2003).

Sventsitskaya, I., *Ot Obshchiny k Tserkvi: o Formirovanii Khristianskoy Tserkvi* [From Community to Church: On the Forming of the Christian Church] (M.: Politizdat, 1985).

Sventsitsky, V., archpriest, *Dialogi* [Dialogues] (M.: Pravoslavny Svyato-Tikhonovsky Bogoslovsky Institut, 1995).

_____, *Monastyr' v Miru* [Monastery in the World] (M.: Lestvitsa, 1999).

Svyatyni Drevney Moskvy [Sacred Places of Ancient Moscow] (M.: Nikos, Kontakt, 1993).

Taisiya, cloistress, *Russkoe Pravoslavnoe Zhenskoe Monashestvo* [Russian Orthodox Women's Monasticism] (Minsk: Izd-vo Belorusskogo ekzarkhata, 2006).

Talberg, N., *Istoriya Russkoy Tserkvi* [The History of the Russian Church] (M.: Izd-vo Sretenskogo Monastyrya, 2004).

Tarasov, A., *Chto Est' Istina? Pravedniki L'va Tolstogo* [What is Truth? The Righteous Men of Leo Tolstoy] (M.: Yazyki Slavyaskoy Kul'tury, 2001).

Tarasov, O., *Ikona i Blagochestie: Ocherki Ikonnogo Dela v Imperatorskoy Rossii* [Icon and Piety: Essays on Iconography in Imperial Russia] (M.: Progress-Kultura, 1995).

Tarlanov, Z., *Izbrannye Raboty po Yazykoznaniyu i Filologii* [Selected Works on Linguistics and Philology] (Petrozavodsk: Izd-vo PetrGU, 2005).

Thrower, J., *Marxist-Leninist 'Scientific Atheism' and the Study of Religion and Atheism in the USSR* (Berlin: Mouton Publisher, 1983).

Toews, P., ed., *Mennonites and Baptists, A Continuing Conversation* (Winnipeg: Kindred Press, 1993).

Tolstoy, A.K., *Sobranie Sochineniy* [Collected Works], 4 vols. (M.: Khudozhestvennaya literatura, 1963-1964).

Tolstoy, L.N., *Polnoe Sobranie Sochineniy* [The Complete Works], 90 vols. (M.: GIHL, 1935-1958).

_____, *Resurrection* (Charleston, SC: Forgotten Books, 2008).

_____, *The Novels and Other Works of Lyof N. Tolstoi*, 24 vols. (N.Y.: Charles Scribner's Sons, 1911), v. XXI.

Toporov, V., *Svyatost' i Svyatye v Russkoy Dukhovnoy Kul'ture* [Holiness and the Saints in the Russian Spiritual Culture], 2 vols. (M.: Yazyki Russkoy Kul'tury, 1995-1998).

Troeltsch, E., *The Social Teaching of the Christian Churches*, 2 vols. (Louisville, Ken.: Westminster / John Knox Press, 1992).

Trofimov, S., *Chetki* [The Beads] (M.: AST, 2001).

Trotter E., *Lord Radstock: An Interpretation and A Record* (London: Hodder and Stoughton, 1914).

Trubchik, V., *Vera i Traditsiya* [Faith and Tradition] (Kobrin: Soyuz ECB v Resp. Belarus, 2007).

Tsvetaev, D., *Protestantstvo i Protestanty v Rossii do Epokhi Preobrazovany* [Protestantism and Protestants in Russia before the Age of the Reforms] (M.: Universitetskaya Tipografiya, 1890).

Tsypin, V., archpriest, *Istoriya Russkoy Pravoslavnoy Tserkvi, 1917-1990* [History of the Russian Orthodox Church, 1917-1990] (M.: Izdatel'sky Dom "Khronika", 1994).

Tuck, W.P., *Our Baptist Tradition* (Macon, GA: Smyth & Helwys Publishing, Inc., 1993).

Tyutchev, F., *Stikhotvoreniya* [Poetry] (M.: Pravda, 1978).

Ushinsky, A., *O Prichinakh Poyavleniya Ratsionalisticheskikh Ucheniy Shtundy i Nekotorykh Drugikh Podobnykh Sekt v Sel'skom Pravoslavnom Naselenii* [On the Causes of the Appearance of the Rationalistic Teachings of the Stunda and Some Other Similar Sects in the Rural Orthodox Population] (Kiev, 1884).

Uspensky, L., *Bogoslovie Ikony Pravoslavnoy Tserkvi* [Theology of the Orthodox Icon] (Izd-vo bratstva Sv. Alexandra Nevskogo, 1997).

Van Ness, I.J., Nowlin, W.D., *The Baptist Spirit and Fundamentals of the Faith* (Whitefish, MT: Kessinger Publishing, 2008).

Vasiliev, E., ed., *Russkaya Ideya* [The Russian Idea] (M.: Ayris Press, 2004).

Velikanova, E., ed., *Tsena Metafory, Ili Prestuplenie i Nakazanie Sinyavskogo i Danielya* [The Price of Metaphor, or the Crime and Punishment of Sinyavsky and Daniel] (M.: Yunona, 1990).

Vivsik, V., *Vernye do Kontsa v Stalinskuyu Epokhu* [Faithful until Death in Stalin's Epoch] (Sacramento, CA: n.p., 2004).

Vlasov, A., *Ot Izbytka Serdtsa* [Out of That Fills the Heart] (Idar-Oberstein, Germany: Titel Verlag, 2000).

Vvedensky, A., *Bor'ba s Sektantstvom* [Struggle against Sectarianism] (Odessa: Tipografiya Eparkhial'nogo Doma, 1914).

Vodnevsky, N., *Litsom k Svety* [Face Turned to the Light] (M.: Protestant, 1993).

Vogel, F., Motulsky, A., *Human Genetics: Problems and Approaches* (Heidelberg, Germany: Springer, 1997).

Vorontsova, I., *Pravoslavnye Tainstva i Obryady* [The Orthodox Sacraments and Rites] (M.: Veche, 2006).

Voslensky, M., *Nomenklatura: Gospodstvuyushchy Klass Sovetskogo Soyuza* ["Nomenklatura": The Soviet Ruling Class] (M.: Sovetskaya Rossiya, 1991).

Walters, P., "A Survey of Soviet Religious Policy", in Ramet, S., ed., *Religious Policy in the Soviet Union* (Cambridge, UK: Cambridge University Press, 1993), pp. 3-30.

_____, ed., *World Christianity: Eastern Europe* (Monrovia, CA: Missions Advanced Research & Communication Center, 1988).

Walvoord, J., and Zuck, R., *The Bible Knowledge Commentary: New Testament* (Wheaton, IL: Victor Books, 1983).

Wardin, A., "Mennonite Brethren and German Baptists: Affinities and Dissimilarities", in Toews, P., ed., *Mennonites and Baptists, A Continuing Conversation* (Winnipeg: Kindred Press, 1993), pp. 97-112.

Ware, T. (Bishop Kallistos of Diokleia), *The Orthodox Church* (London: Penguin Books, 1997).

Weber, M., *The Protestant Ethic and The Spirit of Capitalism* (London: Routledge, 1992).

Yablokov, I., *Sotsiologiya Religii* [Sociology of Religion] (M.: Mysl', 1979).

Yurkov, S., *Pod Znakom Groteska: Antipovedenie v Russkoy Kulture, 11 – Nachalo 20 vv.* [Under the Sign of the Grotesque: Anti-behaviour in the Russian Culture, 11th – the Beginning of 20th C.] (SPb.: Letny sad, 2003).

Yuzov, I., *Russkie Dissidenty: Starovery i Dukhovnye Khristiane* [Russian Dissidents: the Old Believers and Spiritual Christians] (SPb.: Tipografiya A.M. Kotomina, 1881).

Zander, L., *Vision and Action* (London: Gollancz, 1952).

Zenkovsky, S., *Russkoe Staroobryadchestvo* [The Russian Old Believers] (Minsk: Belorussky Ekzarkhat, 2007).

Zernov, N., *Eastern Christendom* (N.Y.: G.P. Putnam's Sons, 1961).

Zernov, N., *Moscow the Third Rome* (N.Y.: AMS Press, 1971).

Zernov, N., *The Russians and Their Church* (Crestwood, NY: St. Vladimir's Seminary Press, 1978).

Zhitie Prepodobnogo Vasiliya Novogo i Videnie Grigoriya, Uchenika Ego, o Mytarstvakh Prepodobnoy Feodory [Life of St. Basil the New and the Vision by Gregory, His Disciple, of the Spiritual Trials of St. Theodora] (M.: Tipo-Litografiya I. Efimova, 1893).

Zhuk, S., *Russia's Lost Reformation: Peasants, Millenialism, and Radical Sects in Southern Russia and Ukraine, 1830-1917* (Washington, D.C.: Woodrow Wilson Center Press, 2004).

Zhukov, A., ed., *Istoriya Yaponii* [The History of Japan], 2 vols. (M.: Institut vostokovedeniya RAN, 1998).

Zhuravlev, V., Part. I: *Velika Vernost' Tvoya, Gospodi: Svidetel'stva iz Zhizni* [Great is Your Faithfulness, My Lord: Life Testimonies] (Steinhagen, Germany: Samenkorn, 2006).

Zhuravlev, V., Part. II: *Sila v Nemoshchi: Svidetel'stva iz Zhizni* [Strength in Weakness: Life Testimonies] (Steinhagen, Germany: Samenkorn, 2008).

Zosimovsky, Z., *Est' li u Russkikh Religiya?* [Do the Russians have a Religion?] (SPb.: "Stroitel", 1911).

6. Periodicals

Achariya, B., *"Politichesky Mentalitet Rossiyan Glazami Inostrannogo Uchenogo"* [The Political Mentality of Russians in the Eyes of a Foreign Scientist], *Vestnik Rossiyskogo Universiteta Druzhby Narodov*, no. 1 (1999), pp. 107-11.

Akhalmosulishvili, L., *"Reforma po-Gruzinski, ili Priblizhenie k Natsional'noy Kul'ture"* [A Reform in the Georgian Way, or an Approaching to the National Culture], *Mezhdunarodnaya Khristianskaya Gazeta*, no. 7 (2005), p. 6.

Al'manakh po Istorii Russkogo Baptizma [Almanac of the History of Russian Baptists], vols. 1-4 (SPb.: Bibliya Dlya Vsekh, 1999-2009).

Amnesty International Report 1980 (London: Amnesty International Publications, 1980).

_____ *1982* (London: Amnesty International Publications, 1982).

Andronoviene, L., *"Svobodnye Ponevole: Odinokie Zhenshchiny v Khristianskoy Srede"* [Involuntarily Free: Lonely Women in Christian Communities], *Vera i Zhizn'*, no. 3 (2004), pp. 8-9.

Beermann, R., "The Baptists and Soviet Society", *Soviet Studies*, vol. 20, 1 (1968), pp. 67-80.

Besnosova, O., *"Deutsche Siedler und Mennoniten und die Verbreitung der evangelistischen Bewegung in der Ukraine im 19. Jh"* [German Settlers and Mennonites and the Spread of the Evangelistic Movement in the Ukraine in the 19th C.], *Aquila*, no. 4 (1999), S. 16-19.

_____, *Die Mission der Mennonitenbruder unter Orthodoxen Sud-Ukrainas 1860-1890* [The Mission of the Mennonite Brethren among Orthodox People in South of the Ukraine in 1860-1890], *Aquila*, no. 3 (1999), S. 18-23.

Boobbyer, P., "Religious Experience of the Soviet Dissidents", *Religion, State and Society*, vol. 27, nos. 3/4 (1999), pp. 373-90.

Boswell, W.B., "Liturgy and Revolution Part I: Georgian Baptists and the Non-violent Struggle for Democracy", *Religion in Eastern Europe*, vol. 27, no. 2 (2007), pp. 48-71.

Boswell, W.B., "Liturgy and Revolution Part II: Radical Christianity, Radical Democracy, and Revolution in Georgia", *Religion in Eastern Europe*, vol. 27, no. 3 (2007), pp. 15-31.

Bourdeaux, M., "Dissent in the Russian Orthodox Church", *Russian Reviev*, vol. 28, 4 (1969), pp. 416-27.

"Byvaet li Lozh' vo Spasenie? Otvechayut Svyashchennosluzhiteli" [Does Pious Fraud Exist? The Clergy Answer], *Zhurnal "Foma"*, no. 2 (2008).

Coleman, H., "Becoming a Russian Baptist: Conversion Narratives and Social Experience", *Russian Review*, vol. 61, 1 (2002), pp. 94-112.

Cox, J., "What I Have Learned About Missions from Writing 'The British Missionary Enterprise Since 1700'", *International Bulletin of Missionary Research*, vol. 32, 2 (2008), pp. 86-7.

Danilova, A., *"Patriakh Kirill: Shtrikhi k Portretu"* [Patriarch Kirill: Some Traits of the Portrait], *Mgarsky Kolokol*, vol. 74 (March 2009).

Denikin, A., *"Obrashchenie Generala A. Denikina k Dobrovol'tsam"* [The Appeal of General A. Denikin to the Volunteers] (1944), *Rodina*, nos. 6-7 (1991), p. 105.

Dunn S., Dunn E., "Some Comments on Sectarianism in the Soviet Union", *Soviet Studies*, vol. 20, 3 (1969), pp. 410-2.

Dyck, J., "Fresh Skins for New Wine", *Theological reflections*, vol. 6 (2006), pp. 114-28.

Elliott, M., "Eastern Orthodox and Slavic Evangelicals: What Sets Them Both Apart From Western Evangelicals", *East-West Church & Ministry Report*, vol. 3, no. 4 (1995), pp. 15-16.

Emelianov, G., *"Ratsionalizm na Yuge Rossii"* [Rationalism in South Russia], *Otechestvennye Zapiski*, no. 3 (1878), pp. 203-24; no. 5 (1878), pp. 199-230.

Fadyukhin, S., *"Vospominaniya o Perezhitom, chast' II"* [Memoirs about My Life, part II], *Al'manakh po Istorii Russkogo Baptizma*, vol. III (2004), pp. 111-319.

Florovsky, G., archpriest, *"Evraziysky Soblazn"* [The Eurasian Allurement], *Novy Mir*, no. 1 (1991), pp. 195-211.

"Interview with Archimandrite Evlogy (Gutchenko)", *Andreevsky Vestnik*, vol. 15 (2007).

Kalnev, M., *"Pochemu Pravoslavnye Otpadayut v Sektantstvo?"* [Why do Orthodox People go over to Sectarianism?], *Missionerskoe Obozrenie*, nos. 7-8 (1906), pp. 62-73.

Karaev, N., *"V Trudakh Blagovestiya"* [In Labours in Evangelism], *Dukhovny Khristianin*, no. 3 (1914), pp. 72-4.

Karetnikova, M., *"Russkoe Bogoiskatel'stvo"* [Russian God-seeking], *Al'manakh po Istorii Russkogo Baptizma*, vol. I (1999), pp. 3-84.

Kartashev, A., *"Byl li Apostol Andrey na Rusi?"* [Did the Apostle Andrew Visit Russia?], *Khristianskoe Chtenie*, no. 7 (1907), pp. 83-95.

_____, "Spirit of the Old Believers' Schism", *St. Vladimir's Theological Quarterly*, nos. 2-3 (1974), pp. 138-45.

Ketler, V., *"Trud Nebol'shoy, No Delali"* [There Was Little Work, But We Did It], *Sibirskie Nivy*, no. 5 (2001), p. 17.

Kleman, O., *"Trudnosti i Nedomoganiya Russkoy Tserkvi"* [The Hardships and Indispositions of the Russian Church], *Russkaya Mysl'*, 18-24 June 1998.

Klippenstein, L., "Johann Wieler (1839-1889) Among Russian Evangelicals: A New Source of Mennonites and Evangelicalism in Imperial Russia", *Jornal of Mennonite Studies*, no. 5 (1987), pp. 44-60.

Kohan, J., "Interview with Georgi Vins", *Religion in Communist Dominated Areas*, vol. 18: 7, 8, and 9 (1979), pp. 115-7.

Koval'sky, V., *"Pochaevskaya Lavra"* [The Pochaevsky Monastery], *Blagovest*, 23 September 2005.

Lane, C., "Russian Piety among Contemporary Russian Orthodox", *Journal for Scientific Study of Religion*, no. 14 (1975), pp. 139-58.

Leont'ev, V., *"Pokhoronit' po-Khristianski: Interv'yu s Presviterami Tsentral'noy Omskoy Tserkvi"* [To Bury in the Christian Way: Interview with Presbyters of Central Baptist Omsk Church], *Slovo Very*, no. 2 (2004), pp. 16-21.

Leven, Ya., *"Kreshchenie – Istselenie"* [Baptism as Healing], *Mezhdunarodnaya Khristianskaya Gazeta*, no. 8 (2005), p. 2.

Melgunov, S., *"Shtundisty ili Baptisty? Po Povodu Sudebnogo Presledovaniya Sektantov po 29 st. Ustava o Nakazaniyakh"* [Stundists or Baptists? On the Subject of Prosecution of Sectarians According to Article 29 of the Penal Code], *Russkaya Mysl'*, vol. 11 (1903), pp. 159-66.

Mileant, A., Bishop, "Thoughts about the Kingdom of God, or the Church", *Missionary Leaflet*, no. 83 (1999).

Nazarov, V., *"Metafory Neponimaniya: L.N. Tolstoy i Russkaya Tserkov' v Sovremennom Mire"* [Metaphors of Incomprehension: L.N. Tolstoy and the Russian Church in the Modern World], *Voprosy Filosofii*, no. 8 (1991), pp. 155-6.

Negrov, A., "Hermeneutics in Tradition", *Theological Reflections*, vol. 4 (2004), pp. 33-55.

Pilli, T., "Christians as Citizens of a Persecuting State", *Theological reflections*, vol. 6 (2006), pp. 146-61.

Pavlov, V., *"Pravda o Baptistakh"* [The Truth about the Baptists], *Al'manakh po Istorii Russkogo Baptizma*, vol. I (1999), pp. 220-72.

_____, *"Vospominaniya Ssyl'nogo"* [Memoirs of an Exile], *Al'manakh po Istorii Russkogo Baptizma*, vol. I (1999), pp. 194-219.

Petrovskaya, N., *"Ya Ushel v Monastyr', Chtoby Byt' Schastlivym Chelovekom"* [I went into the Monastery to be a Happy Man], *Pravoslavnaya Gazeta (Yekaterinburg eparchy)*, no. 1 (1996).

Popov, V., *"Isikhazm Kak Chayanie Dukhovnosti: Opyt Istoricheskogo Analiza"* [Hesychasm as Spiritual Aspiration: An Attempt at Historical Analysis], *Al'manakh "Bogomyslie*, vol. 2 (1991), pp. 115-34.

_____, *"Protestanty Zemli Russkoy"* [The Protestants of the Russian Land], *NG–Religii*, 19 September 2007.

Prokhorov, C., "Apophaticism and Cataphaticism in Protestantism", *Theological reflections*, vol. 6 (2006), pp. 58-68.

_____, "On Several Peculiarities of the Understanding of Baptism in the Russian Baptist Church", *Theological reflections*, vol. 8 (2007), pp. 89-105.

Prugavin, A., *"Samoistreblenie: Proyavlenie Asketizma i Fanatizma v Raskole"* [Self-destruction: Displays of Asceticism and Fanaticism in the Schism], *Russkaya mysl'*, 1885, vol. I, pp. 77-111; vol. II, pp. 129-55.

Rowe, M., "Soviet Baptists Engage in Perestroika", Religion in Communist Lands, vol. 18.2 (1990), pp. 184-7.

Rozanov, V., *"Russkaya Tserkov'"* [The Russian Church], *Polyarnay Zvezda*, vol. 8 (1906), pp. 524-40.

Rudenko, S., *"Vashe Vremya Konchilos"* [Your Time is Up], *Sobytie*, 29 August 1992.

Rybalkina, E., *"Ikona 'Neopalimaya Kupina' Pomogaet Pozharnym"* [The Icon "The Burning Bush" Helps Fire Fighters], *Komsomol'skaya Pravda*, 16 September 2009.

Sannikov, S., *"Razmyshleniya Redaktora"* [Editor's Thoughts], *Almanach "Bogomyslie"*, vol. 1 (1990), pp. 3-6.

_____, *"Vecherya Gospodnya"* [The Lord's Supper], *Almanach "Bogomyslie"*, vol. 1 (1990), pp. 65-116.

Sapiets, M., "Monasticism in the Soviet Union", Religion in Communist Lands, vol. 4.1 (1976), pp. 28-34.

Savinsky, S., *"Strigol'niki"* [The Strigolniks], *Al'manakh "Bogomyslie"*, vol. 1 (1990), pp. 183-90.

Sedletsky, P., *"Propoved' s Polichnym"* [Preaching… Bang to Rights], *Slovo Very*, no. 3 (2001), pp. 38-40.

Seleznev, I., *"K Chemu Privela Revolyutsiya v Russkoy Grammatike"* [How the Revolution Resulted in the Russian Grammar], *Svet Pravoslaviya*, 22 February 2003.

Shakhovskoy, I., archbishop, *"Sektantstvo v Pravoslavii i Pravoslavie v Sektantstve"* [Sectarianism in Orthodoxy and Orthodoxy in Sectarianism], *Pravoslavnaya Obshchina*, no. 4 (1992), pp. 71-7.

Shevchenko, M., *"Istoriya iz Zhizni Provintsial'noy Inkvizitsii"* [A Story of the Life of the Provincial Inquisition], *Nezavisimaya gazeta*, 29 May 1998.

Sipko, S., *"Vmeste Molimsya, Vmeste Raduemsya"* [We Are Praying and Rejoicing Together] (Interview with Omsk Baptist Church presbyter, I.A. Kabluchkin), *Slovo Very*, no. 4 (2003), pp. 10-14.

Solodovnikov, V., *"Sdelano v Amerike"* [Made in America], *Slovo Very*, no. 1 (2002), pp. 25-30.

Solzhenitsyn, A., *"Odin Den' Ivana Denisovicha"* [One Day in the Life of Ivan Denisovich], *Novy Mir*, no. 11 (1962), pp. 8-71.

Soshinsky, S., *"Chudo Obnovleniya"* [The Miracle of Renewal], *Novy Mir*, no. 6 (1992), pp. 231-7.

Stammler, H., "Russian Orthodoxy in Recent Protestant Church History and Theology", *St. Vladimir's Theological Quarterly*, nos. 3-4 (1979), pp. 207-16.

Sukhanov, A., *"Preniya o Vere"* [Debate on the Faith], *Chteniya v Obshchestve Istorii i Drevnostey Rossiyskikh*, no. 2 (1894).

Sysoev, B., *"Sobrat' Vse Knigi By Da Szhech'!"* [I'd Take all Books and Burn them Up!], *Slovo Very*, no. 2 (2002), pp. 15-17.

"The Question of Registration and the Fate of Salvation" [From: *Bratsky Listok*, no. 1-3, 1975], *Religion in Communist Dominated Areas*, vol. 14: 7, 8, and 9 (1975), pp. 114-7.

Timchenko, I., *"Muzykal'naya Osnova Bogosluzheniya ECB"* [The Musical Basis of Church Service of the ECB], *Put' Bogopoznaniya*, no. 1 (1996), pp. 61-73.

Tsyrulnikov, A., *"Predanie"* [The Tradition], *Put' Bogopoznaniya*, vol. 8 (2002), pp. 18-73.

Urry, J., "John Melville and the Mennonites: A British Evangelist in South Russia, 1837 – ca. 1875", *Mennonite Quarterly Review*, no. 4 (1980), pp. 305-22.

_____, "The Mennonite Commonwealth in Imperial Russia Revisited", *The Mennonite Quarterly Review*, no. 2 (2010), pp. 229-47.

Uspensky, N., *"Anafora, Opyt istoriko-liturgicheskogo analisa"* [Anaphora, An Attempt of The Historical-Liturgical Analysis], *Bogoslovskie trudy*, vol. 13 (1975), pp. 40-147.

Vibe, P., Sennikova, L., *"Postradavshie za Veru: O Sud'be Nemetskikh Religioznykh Obshchin Omskoy Oblasti v 1950 – 1980 gg."* [Aggrieved People: Their Faith: On the Life of German Religious Communities of the Omsk Region, 1950-1980], *Kul'tura dlya Rossiyskikh Nemtsev Omskoy Oblasti*, no. 4 (2003), pp. 10-15.

Wardin, A., "Baptist Immersions in the Russian Empire: Difficult Beginnings", *Journal of European Baptist Studies*, no. 3 (2010), pp. 37-44.

_____, "How Indigenous was the Baptist Movement in the Russian Empire?", *Journal of European Baptist Studies*, vol. 9, 2 (2009), pp. 29-37.

Yusupova, D., *"Okhota na Ved'm"* [A Witch-hunt], *Ogonek*, no. 40 (1998).

Zacek, J., "The Russian Bible Society and the Russian Orthodox Church", *Church History*, vol. 35 (1966), 411-37.

Znamenski, A., "Shamanism and Christianity on the Russian Siberian Borderland: Altaian Responses to Russian Orthodox Missionaries (1830-1917)", *Itinerario*, no. 1 (1998), pp. 107-30.

7. Electronic Sources

7.1. Compact disks

Istoriya Evangel'skogo Dvizheniya v Evrazii [History of the Evangelical Movement in Eurasia] *1.0 – 5.0* (Odessa: EAAA, 2001-2006).

Istoriya Evangel'skogo Dvizheniya v Evrazii 2.0 (Odessa: EAAA, 2002):

[Anon], *"Vred Kureniya"* [Hazards of Smoking], *BV*, no. 5 (1946).

"Vecherya Gospodnya" [The Lord's Supper] (editorial article), *BV*, no. 3 (1947).

Orlov, M. and Karpov, A., *"Vodnye Kreshcheniya po Vere"* [Water Baptism by Faith], *BV*, no. 1 (1953).

Mitskevich, A., *"Iz Evangel'sko-Baptistskoy Dogmatiki"* [Extracts from Evangelical-Baptist Theology], *BV*, no. 5 (1956).

Motorin, I., *"O Bogosluzhenii"* [On the Divine Service], *BV*, no. 1 (1957).

"40-letie Velikogo Oktyabrya i Evangel'skie Khristiane-Baptisty" [The 40th Anniversary of the Great October Revolution and Evangelical Christians-Baptists] (editorial article), *BV*, no. 6 (1957).

Motorin, I., *"Uchenie Biblii o Boge"* [The Biblical Doctrine of God], *BV*, no. 1 (1960).

Franchuk, V., *Prosila Rossiya Dozhdya u Gospoda* [Russia has asked the Lord for Rain] (2001).

Istoriya Evangel'skogo Dvizheniya v Evrazii 4.0 (Odessa: EAAA, 2005):

Zhapis' Sudebnogo Protsessa nad Baptistami g. Semipalatinska [Records of Baptists' Trial in Semipalatinsk] (1962).

Ustav Soyuza Tserkvey ECB: Izdanie Soveta Tserkvey ECB [The Regulations of the Union of the ECB: Publication of the Council of Churches of the ECB] (1965, 1974).

7.2. Internet

Buzinny, Ya., *Molilis' Bogu Dvoe* [Two Men Prayed to God] (poem), <http://www.blagovestnik.org/books/00430/db/v889989.html> accessed 14 November 2010.

Dozorov, N., *"Paskhal'noe Chudo v Tagile"* [Easter Miracle in Tagil], *Nash Put'*, no. 113 (1937), <http://rys-arhipelag.ucoz.ru/publ/voskresenie_khristovo_posle_bolshevistskoj_revoljucii/29-1-0-1660> accessed 6 December 2010.

Edelstein, G., *Vospominaniya* [Memories], <http://www.krotov.info/history/20/1960/1965edels.htm> accessed 5 November 2010.

Gololob, G., *Evangel'skie Vozrazheniya Pravoslavnym* [The Evangelical Answer to Orthodox People], <http://rusbaptist.stunda.org/dop/antipr2.htm> accessed 16 September 2010.

'House of the Gospel' Vinnitsa Baptist Church (Ukraine), <http://baptist.vn.ua/photos/church/index.shtml> accessed 5 November 2010.

Ikona Bozhiey Materi, Imenuemaya "Derzhavnaya" [The Icon of God's Mother Named the Sovereign] (website), <http://hram-vlad-butovo.ru/kalendar/bmater/03/03.15_1.htm> accessed 6 November 2010.

Ikona Presvyatoy Bogoroditsy, Imenuemaya "Kaluzhskaya" " [The Icon of the Most Holy Virgin Named the Kaluzhskaya] (website), <http://www.hram.ru/index.php/library-bogorodica-51> accessed 6 November 2010.

Iz Istorii Monastyrya [From the Monastery History], The Official Website of the Svyato-Kazansky Chimeevo Monastery, <http://www.chimeevo.ru/node/137?page=0,3> accessed 20 January 2010.

Kargel, I., *Lektsii o Vtorom Prishestvii Gospoda Iisusa Khrista* [Lectures on the Second Coming of the Lord Jesus Christ], <http://www.blagovestnik.org/books/00417.htm> accessed 11 May 2010.

Khrapov, N.P., ed., *Dom Bozhy i Sluzhenie v Nem (Sovet Tserkvey Evangel'skikh Khristian-Baptistov)* [God's House and its Service (The Council of Churches of the Evangelical Christians–Baptists)] (1972-1974), <http://www.blagovestnik.org/books/00280.htm> accessed 20 November 2009.

Kushnir, V., *Khleb i Vino* [Bread and Wine], <http://kopilochka.net.ru/POEMS/poem05.php> accessed 22 August 2010.

Men', A., *Evkharistiya* [The Eucharist], <http://www.alexandrmen.ru/besedy/evharist.html> accessed 14 November 2010.

Milne, G., *Australian Baptist Ministries*, <http://www.baptist.org.au/index.php?option=com_content&task=view&id=48&Itemid=8> accessed 17 November 2007.

Missionerov Prizyvayut k Bolee Aktivnomy Sluzheniyu [Missionaries are Called to the More Active Ministry], Pravoslavie.Ru (Internet-journal), 1 February 2005, <http://www.pravoslavie.ru/news/print12544.htm> accessed 9 December 2010.

Okolotserkovnye Sueveriya [Around Church Superstitions], <http://kyivbratstvo.narod.ru/news/ archive/2005_07_01_index.html> accessed 15 November 2010.

Orlov, G., *Tserkov' Khristova: Rasskazy iz Istorii Khristianskoy Tserkvi* [The Church of Christ: Stories from Church History], <http://ftp.kelia.ru/orlov/Main.htm> accessed 6 November 2009.

Osipov, A., *Evkharistiya i Svyashchenstvo* [The Eucharist and Priesthood], <http://orthtexts.narod.ru/17_Evhar_svyasch.htm> accessed 30 November 2010.

O Trekh Obetakh Monashestva [On the Three Monastic Vows], <http://www.wco.ru/biblio/books/triobeta/Main.htm> accessed 21 April 2010.

Plett, I., *Istoriya Evangel'skich Khhristian-Baptistov s 1905 po 1944 gg.* [History of Evangelical Christians-Baptists, 1905-1944], <http://www.blagovestnik.org/books/00360.htm#8> accessed 8 November 2010.

Popov, V., *Khristiane Baptisty v Rossii: Istoriya i Sovremennost'* [Christians-Baptists in Russia: History and the Present], <http://baptist.org.ru/go/history> accessed 4 September 2009.

Predsedatel' CCECB, G.K. Kryuchkov, Nekrolog [The Leader of the CCECB, G.K. Kryuchkov, Obituary Notice], <http://jesuschrist.ru/news/2007/7/16/13334> accessed 14 July 2009.

Roman, hieromonk, *Stikhi* [Poems], <http://tropinka.orthodoxy.ru/zal/poezija/roman/index.htm> accessed 18 December 2009.

Shalatovsky, N., *Molchanie* [Silence], <http://www.blagovestnik.org/books/00430/db/v7848793.html> accessed 4 November 2009.

Sidwell, M., *The Russian Baptists*, <http://www.bju.edu/library/collections/fund_file/russianbap.html#russ65>

Skornyakov, Ya., *Slovo k Knizhnikam Poslednego Vremeni* [A Word to the Scribes of the Last Times], <http://www.rushhohol.com/sermons/Book/Skornyakov/Slovo_knizhnikam.doc> accessed 13 June 2008.

Slovo Svyateyshego Patriarkha Kirilla [Sermon of His Holiness the Patriarch Kirill], 17 February 2010, The Russian Orthodox Church (the official website of the Moscow Patriarchate), <http://www.patriarchia.ru/db/text/1092502.html> accessed 9 December 2010.

Stepanova, E., *Za Tri Shaga do Nimba* [Three Strokes off the Nimbus]. *Neskuchny Sad* [The Orthodox Life's Periodical], no. 2 (2008), <http://www.nsad.ru/index.php?issue=45§ion= 10019&article=879> accessed 7 November 2010.

Stikhotvoreniya. Dve Lepty [Poems. Two Mites], <http://days4god.com/publ/21-1-0-98> accessed 14 November 2010.

Stikhotvoreniya. Gde Dostat' Bibliyu? [Poems. Where can you get the Bible?], <http://www.blagovestnik.org/books/00430/db/v4442325.html> accessed 5 January 2010.

Stikhotvoreniya. Kreshchenie [Poems. The Baptism], <http://www.blagovestnik.org/books/00430/db/v6195044.html> accessed 22 August 2010.

Stikhotvoreniya. Lestnitsa Zhizni [Poems.The Ladder of Life], <http://www. blagovestnik.org/books/00430/db/v6171177.html> accessed 7 November 2010.

Stikhotvoreniya o Molitve [Poems about Prayer], Vserossiyskoe Ioanno- Predtechenskoe Pravoslavnoe Bratstvo "Trezvenie", <http://trezvenie.org/ dobr/stih/full/&id=738#_Toc249208258> accessed 28 October 2010.

Svechnikov, D., *Okkul'tism i Sueveriya: Vzglyad Pravoslavnogo Svyashchennika* [Occultism and Superstitions: a View from a Russian Orthodox Priest], <http://sueverie.net/kak-ograditsya-ot-sueveriy/okkultizm-i-sueveriya- vzglyad-pravoslavnogo-svyaschennika/stranitsa-2.html> accessed 15 November 2010.

Vins, G., *Pora Domoy* [It is Time to Go Home], <http://www.blagovestnik.org/ books/00430/db/v6059350.html> accessed 25 April 2010.

Zdorovets, B., *Kakim Sudom Sudite* [In the Way You Judge], <http://www.praize. com/denominations/group650/index.shtml> accessed 28 July 2009.

Zhitie i Chudesa Svyatogo Pravednogo Ioanna, Ispovednika, Olenevskogo Chudotvortsa Chudotvortsa [The Life and Miracles of the Saint and Righteous John, the Confessor, the Miracle-Worker from Olenevka], <http://pravoslavie58region.ru/index.php?loc=ioann-3.htm> accessed 15 November 2010.

Some Unacknowledged Quotations in *Bratsky Vestnik* (Fraternal Bulletin)

Compared with Dobrotolyubie ('The Philokalia')

Bratsky Vestnik	*Philokalia*
1.	**1.**
Russian text:	**Russian text:**
««Ты же, когда молишься, войди в комнату твою и, затворив двери твои, помолись Отцу твоему, Который втайне» – Мф. 6, 6. Горница души есть тело; двери суть пять чувств телесных. Душа входит в горницу, когда ум не блуждает туда и сюда. «И Отец твой, видящий тайное, воздаст тебе явно». Видит Ведающий все сокровенное... и воздает явно дарами великими». – Мысли о молитве. Братский Вестник, №6' 1986. С. 30-31.	«Ты же, егда молишися, вниди в клеть твою, и затворив двери твоя, помолися Отцу твоему, Иже втайне (Мф. 6, 6). Клеть души есть тело; двери наши суть пять чувств телесных. Душа входит в клеть свою, когда ум не блуждает туда и сюда... И Отец твой, видяй втайне воздаст тебе яве... Видит, ведающий все сокровенное... и воздает явными дарами великими». – Из Жития св. Григория Паламы, архиепископа Солунского. – Добротолюбие. В 5-ти тт. М.: Типо-Литография И. Ефимова, 1900. Т. 5. С. 480-481.

English translation:	English translation:
"'But thou, when thou prayest, enter into thy closet, and when thou hast shut thy door, pray to thy Father which is in secret' (Matt 6:6, KJV). The chamber of the soul is the body; our doors are the five bodily senses. The soul enters its chamber when the mind does not wander hither and thither. 'And thy Father which seeth in secret shall reward thee openly.' God who knows all secret things sees mental prayer and rewards it openly with great gifts." – *Mysli o Molitve* [Thoughts on Prayer], *Bratsky Vestnik*, no. 6 (1986), pp. 30-1.	"'But thou, when thou prayest, enter into thy closet, and when thou hast shut thy door, pray to thy Father which is in secret' (Matt 6:6, KJV). The closet of the soul is the body; our doors are the five bodily senses. The soul enters its closet when the mind does not wander hither and thither... 'And thy Father which seeth in secret shall reward thee openly'... God who knows all secret things sees mental prayer and rewards it openly with great gifts. – *From 'The Life of Saint Gregory Palamas, the Archbishop of Thessalonica'*, in: *Dobrotolyubie* [The Philokalia], 5 vols. (M.: Tipo-Litografiya I. Efimova, 1900), vol. V, pp. 480-1.

2.

Russian text:

«Молясь, просил я часто себе того, что мне казалось хорошим, не предоставляя Господу устроить то, что Сам Он признает полезным. Но, получив просимое, впоследствии крайне скорбел: зачем просил, чтобы исполнилась моя воля? – потому что дело оказывалось для меня не таким, как я думал». – Мысли о молитве. Братский Вестник, №6' 1986. С. 31.

English translation:

"While I was at prayer, I would often keep asking for what seemed good to me. I would not leave it up to the Lord to arrange what He knew would turn out for my profit. But, when I obtained my request I became greatly ashamed at having been so stubborn about getting my own way; for in the end the matter did not turn out to be what I had imagined it would." – *Mysli o Molitve* [Thoughts on Prayer], *Bratsky Vestnik*, no. 6 (1986), p. 31.

2.

Russian text:

«Много раз, молясь, просил я, да будет мне, что казалось благом для меня, …а не Богу предавая устроить лучше то, что Он ведает полезным для меня. Но получив (просимое), бывал потом в великой скорби, и именно за то, что не просил, – да будет лучше по воле Божией; ибо дело оказывалось для меня не таким, как я думал». – Аскетические наставления преподобного Нила Синайского. – Добротолюбие. М., 1895. Т. 2. С. 211.

English translation:

"Many times while I was at prayer, I would keep asking for what seemed good to me… I would not leave it up to God to arrange what He knew would turn out for my profit. But, when I obtained (my request) I became greatly ashamed at having been so stubborn about getting my own way; for in the end the matter did not turn out to be what I had imagined it would." – "The Ascetic Homilies by St. Nilus of Sinai", in *The Dobrotolyubie* (M.: Tipo-Litografiya I. Efimova, 1895), vol. II, p. 211.

3. **Russian text:** «Высоко достоинство человека. Смотри, каковы небо, земля, солнце и луна: и не в них благоволил успокоиться Господь, а в человеке. Человек драгоценнее всех тварей. В Слове Божием написано: «Ангел Господень ополчается вокруг боящихся Его»». – Мысли о человеке. Братский Вестник, №6' 1987. С. 48. **English translation:** "The dignity of man is high. Look at the heavens, how great they are, and at the earth, the sun, and the moon; nevertheless man is more precious than all creatures, for the Lord's goodness has been reserved for him. It is written in God's Word, *'The Angel of the Lord encampeth round about them that fear him'*." – *Mysli o Cheloveke* [Thoughts on Man], *Bratsky Vestnik*, no. 6 (1987), p. 48.	**3.** **Russian text:** «Высоко достоинство человека. Смотри, каковы небо, земля, солнце и луна: и не в них благоволил упокоиться Господь, а только в человеке. Поэтому человек драгоценнее всех тварей… Написано: Ангельския ополчения окрест боящихся Его (Псал. 33, 8)». – Наставления св. Макария Великого о христианской жизни. – Добротолюбие. М., 1895. Т. 1. С. 156. **English translation:** "The dignity of man is high. Look at the heavens, how great they are, and at the earth, the sun, and the moon; nevertheless man is more precious than all creatures, for the Lord's goodness has been reserved for him alone… It is written, *'The Angel of the Lord encampeth round about them that fear him'* (Ps 34:7)." – "The Homilies by St. Macarius the Elder on Christian Life", in *The Dobrotolyubie* (M.: Tipo-Litografiya I. Efimova, 1895), vol. I, p. 156.

4.	4.
Russian text:	**Russian text:**
«Не будем откладывать покаяние и исправление на завтра, потому что завтрашний день не в наших руках». – Евангельские поучения. Братский Вестник, №2' 1989. С. 33.	«Каждодневно думай, что ныне имеем мы потрудиться в мире сем, а завтра – не знаю». – Преподобный авва Исаия о подвижничестве и безмолвии. – Добротолюбие. М., 1895. Т. 1. С. 464-465.
English translation:	**English translation:**
"Do not postpone your repentance and improvement for tomorrow, because tomorrow is not in our hands." – *Evangel'skie Poucheniya* [The Gospel's Homilies], *Bratsky Vestnik*, no. 2 (1989), p. 33.	"Think every day that we have an opportunity today to do good in this world, but tomorrow – I do not know." – "St. Isaiah on Asceticism and Silence", in *The Dobrotolyubie* (M.: Tipo-Litografiya I. Efimova, 1895), vol. I, pp. 464-5.

APPENDIX 2
Some Unacknowledged Quotations in *Bratsky Vestnik*

Compared with other Orthodox sources

Bratsky Vestnik	Orthodox Sources
1.	**1.**
Russian text:	**Russian text:**
«Не в словах одних молитва, а более в душевном расположении. Молиться надобно всегда. Да не прекращается память о Господе. Облекаешься в одежду – возблагодари Господа, даровавшего нам одеяния. Прошел ли день – благодари Подателя всех благ. Таким образом непрестанно будешь молиться, не в словах заключая молитву, но через всю жизнь приближаясь к Богу, тогда жизнь твоя будет непрерывной и непрестанной молитвой». – Мысли о молитве. Братский Вестник, №6' 1986. С. 30.	«...Надобно не в словах одних поставлять молитву, а паче в душевном расположении молитвенном. И молиться надобно всегда, при всяком случае... Облекаешься в одежду – усугуби любовь к Богу, даровавшему нам покровы... Прошёл ли день – благодари Даровавшего нам солнце... Таким образом непрестанно будешь молиться, не в словах заключая молитву, но чрез все течение жизни приближаясь к Богу, чтобы жизнь твоя была непрерывною и непрестанною молитвою». – Св. Василия Великого наставления о молитве и трезвении. – Святоотеческие наставления о молитве и трезвении. М.: РИПОЛ классик, 2008. С. 7-8.

English translation:

"Prayer is not merely in syllables, but the power of prayer should be expressed in the moral attitude of the soul. That extends throughout our life in remembrance of the Lord. As you put on a cloak, intensify your love for the Lord, who provided us with the apparel... When the day has passed, thank the Lord, who gave us all blessings... This is how you pray continually – not by offering prayer in words, but by joining yourself to God through your whole way of life, so that your life becomes one continuous and uninterrupted prayer." – *Mysli o Molitve* [Thoughts on Prayer], *Bratsky Vestnik*, no. 6 (1986), p. 30.

English translation:

"We should not express our prayer merely in syllables, but the power of prayer should be expressed in the moral attitude of our soul and in the virtuous actions that extend throughout our life... As you put on a cloak, intensify your love for God, who provided us with essential apparel... When the day has passed, thank the Lord, who gave us the sun... This is how you pray continually – not by offering prayer in words, but by joining yourself to God through your whole way of life, so that your life becomes one continuous and uninterrupted prayer." – "St. Basil the Great on Prayer and Abstinence", in *Svyatootecheskie Nastavleniya o Molitve i Trezvenii* [The Patristic Writings on Prayer and Abstinence] (M.: RIPOL klassik, 2008), pp. 7-8.

2.

Russian text:

«Ты говоришь: много раз просил и не получил просимого. Без сомнения, не получил ты потому, что просил с неверием и рассеяно или просил неполезного тебе. А если полезного просил, то не имел постоянства. Ибо написано: «Много может усиленная молитва праведного» – Иак. 5, 16». – Мысли о молитве. Братский Вестник, №6' 1986. С. 31.

English translation:

"You say: I have asked many times and not received. No doubt you did not receive because you asked without believing, and absent-mindedly, or you asked something useless for yourself. And even if you asked for something useful, you had no constancy. Because it is written, 'The effectual fervent prayer of a righteous man availeth much' (James 5:16 KJV)."[1] – *Mysli o Molitve* [Thoughts on Prayer], *Bratsky Vestnik*, no. 6 (1986), p. 31.

2.

Russian text:

«Но говоришь: много раз просил я и не получил просимого. Без сомнения, не получил ты потому, что просил худо, – с неверием и рассеяно, или просил неполезного тебе. А если и полезного просил, то не имел постоянства. Ибо написано: в терпении вашем стяжите души ваша (Лк. 21, 19)». – Св. Василия Великого наставления о молитве и трезвении. С. 16-17.

English translation:

"But you say: I have asked many times and not received. No doubt you did not receive because you asked with wrong motives – without believing, and absent-mindedly, or you asked something useless for yourself. And even if you asked something useful, you had no constancy. Because it is written, 'In your patience possess ye your souls' (Luke 21:19 KJV)." – "St. Basil the Great on Prayer and Abstinence", pp. 16-17.

---

1. It is strange that Baptist editor replaced the biblical text, to which St. Basil the Great referred here.

3.

Russian text:

«Для того медлит Господь даровать нам просимое, чтобы побудить нас неотлучнее пребывать перед Ним в молитве, и чтобы мы со страхом хранили полученное от Него, ибо все, что приобретаем со многим трудом, стараемся сохранить». – Мысли о молитве. Братский Вестник, №6' 1986. С. 31.

English translation:

"The Lord delays in giving us what we are asking, in order to impel us to pray to Him all the time, and in order that we keep His gifts in fear; for whatever we obtain with a great deal of work, we do our best to keep it…" – *Mysli o Molitve* [Thoughts on Prayer], *Bratsky Vestnik*, no. 6 (1986), p. 31.

3.

Russian text:

«…Для того медлит Он даровать тебе просимое, чтобы заставить тебя неотлучнее пребывать пред Ним и чтобы ты, узнав, что такое дар Божий… со страхом хранил его. Ибо все, что приобретает кто со многим трудом, старается он сохранить…» – Св. Василия Великого наставления о молитве и трезвении. С. 17.

English translation:

"He delays in giving you what you are asking, in order to make you to walk with Him all the time, and in order that you learn what the gift of God is… and will keep it in fear. For whatever someone obtains with a great deal of work, he does his best to keep it…" – "St. Basil the Great on Prayer and Abstinence", p. 17.

4.

Russian text:

«Есть ли что сладостнее мирной жизни? Пусть будет все, что ценится в жизни: богатство, здоровье, очаг, родные, друзья, но не будет мира, что пользы в том?» – Мысли о христианском миролюбии. Братский Вестник, №5' 1987. С. 47.

English translation:

"Out of all things, what is sweeter to enjoy than peace?.. If someone had all the things which are valued in life: wealth, health, house, relatives, friends, but lacked the benefit of peace, what use would that be?" – *Mysli o Khristianskom Mirolyubii* [Thoughts on the Christian Peacefulness], *Bratsky Vestnik*, no. 5 (1987), p. 47.

4.

Russian text:

«Что сладостнее для людей мирной жизни? …Если будет всё, что ценится в этом мире: богатство, здоровье, жена, дети, дом, … друзья, …но не будет при этом блага – мира, какая польза от всех благ?..» – Св. Григорий Нисский. О блаженствах, Слово 7. – Творения св. Григория Нисского. М.: Типография В. Готье, 1861. Ч. 2. С. 455.

English translation:

"Out of all the things sought in this life, what is sweeter for human beings to enjoy than peace?.. If one had all the things which are valued in life: wealth, health, wife, children, house… friends… but lacked the benefit of peace, what would you gain from those?.." – St. Gregory of Nyssa, "On the Beatitudes, Homily 7", in *Tvoreniya sv. Grigoriya Nisskogo* [The Writings of St. Gregory of Nyssa] (M.: Tipografiya V. Got'e, 1861), part II, p. 455.

5.

Russian text:

«Рассуди: что за жизнь тех, которые враждуют между собой и подозревают друг друга? Они смотрят угрюмо и гнушаются друг другом. Господь хочет, чтобы мы умножали благодать мира и чтобы наша жизнь служила врачевством для других. Кто так поступает, тот справедливо может называться блаженным – Мф. 5, 9». – Мысли о христианском миролюбии. Братский Вестник, №5' 1987. С. 47.

English translation:

"Each one of you is capable of working out what life is like for those who hold each other in suspicion and hatred. They find everything about each other horrible, their meetings are disagreeable... The Lord wants us to multiply the grace of peace, in order that our own lives may become a cure for other people. He who follows this way may rightly be called a blessed – Matt 5:9." – *Mysli o Khristianskom Mirolyubii* [Thoughts on the Christian Peacefulness], *Bratsky Vestnik*, no. 5 (1987), p. 47.

5.

Russian text:

«Рассуди сам с собою, какова жизнь взаимно друг друга подозревающих и ненавидящих? Встречи их неприятны, все одному в другом отвратительно... Господу угодно в обилии приумножить для тебя благодать мира, чтобы жизнь твоя была врачевством чужой болезни... И таковые в подлинном смысле называются сынами Божиими, соделавшись блаженными». – Св. Григорий Нисский. О блаженствах, Слово 7. С. 458-459, 467.

English translation:

"Each one of you is capable of working out for himself what life is like for those who hold each other in suspicion and hatred, whose meetings with each other are disagreeable, who find everything about each other horrible... The Lord intends the grace of peace to be abundantly multiplied among you, in order that your own lives may become a cure for other people's sickness... And such persons are rightly called sons of God, being blessed..." – St. Gregory of Nyssa, "On the Beatitudes, Homily 7", pp. 458-9, 467.

6.	6.
Russian text: «Кто оправдывает себя, тот удаляет себя от покаяния». – Евангельские поучения. Братский вестник, №2' 1989. С. 33.	**Russian text:** «Кто оправдывает себя, тот отчуждает себя от покаяния». – Преподобный авва Исаия. – Настольная книга священнослужителя. М.: Издание Московской Патриархии, 1988. Т. 6. С. 731.
English translation: "The one who justifies himself moves away from repentance". – *Evangel'skie Poucheniya* [The Gospel's Homilies], *Bratsky Vestnik*, no. 2 (1989), p. 33.	**English translation:** "He who justices himself is estranging himself from repentance". – "St. Abba Isaiah", in *Nastol'naya Kniga Svyashchennosluzhitelya* [The Handbook for Priest] (M.: Moskovskaya Patriarkhiya, 1988), v. VI, p. 731.

7.

Russian text:

«Два великих дела принадлежат
пастырю церкви: дело
спасения собственной души и
неотделимое от него – спасение
душ, вверенных его попечению.
Внимайте себе и всему стаду, в
нем же вас Дух Святой поставил
епископами – Деян. 20.28...»
– Евангельские поучения.
Братский вестник, №2' 1989. С.
33.

English translation:

"A shepherd of the church should
accomplish two great works: the
work of the salvation of his own soul
and - inseparable from that – the
salvation of Christ's flock entrusted
to his care. Take heed therefore
unto yourselves, and to all the flock,
over the which the Holy Ghost
hath made you overseers Acts 20:28
(KJV)" – *Evangel'skie Poucheniya*
[The Gospel's Homilies], *Bratsky
Vestnik*, no. 2 (1989), p. 33.

7.

Russian text:

«...Дабы исполнить два основных
великих дела: спасение своей души
и спасение вверенного твоему
водительству стада Христова. В
этом назидает нас апостол Павел:
Внимайте убо себе и всему стаду,
в нем же вас Дух Святый постави
епископы... (Деян. 20,28)». –
Слово Патриарха Пимена. Журнал
Московской Патриархии, №9' 1985.
С. 7.

English translation:

"...In order to accomplish two main
great works, the salvation of your own
soul and the salvation of Christ's flock
entrusted to your guidance, the Apostle
Paul teaches us: 'Take heed therefore
unto yourselves, and to all the flock,
over the which the Holy Ghost hath
made you overseers...' (Acts 20:28
KJV)." – "Slovo Patriarkha Pimena"
[Sermon of the Patriarch Pimen],
Zhurnal Moskovskoy Patriarkhii, no. 9
(1985), p. 7.

Comparison of Versions of the Poem "An Old Legend"[1.]

Cloistress Valeriya (Makeeva)	Russian Baptist version
An Old Legend *(According to: Pravoslavny Vestnik* [Orthodox Herald], No. 4, 1999)	**The Penny** *(Handwritten in a notebook belonging to the Savchenko family in Omsk, the late 1940s)*
This took place in the olden times. On a dark night by a forest path A priest came walking to the village From a call to a sick-bed in a distant parish.	This took place in the olden times. Late at night by a forest path A presbyter walked unhurriedly From a call to a sick-bed in a distant parish.
He walks along and prays to God For the sick and for unhappy people, Suddenly they block his way: – Halt! – and out steps a fierce bandit.	He walks along and prays to God For all the poor and sick people… Suddenly they blocked his way. "Halt!" – and out steps a fierce bandit.

1. Translated by M. Raber.

– Stop, don't make a move! –
         they seized the priest,
They took him deep into the woods,
There the bandits were noisily carousing,
There a fire blazed in the clearing.

They brought the elder to the ataman:
– Give us your money! – he cried, –
Turn out the pockets of your cassock,
Share out the offerings with the flock!

– I haven't a penny, believe me, brothers!
I pledged myself to poverty long ago.
– Search him! – they rifled through his
clothes,
They searched – but there really was
nothing!

– And what riches do you have at home?
If you don't tell the truth – it'll be too bad
                 for you!
Don't you really have a single penny
                to your name?
And he answered them: – I never have!

"Stop! Don't make a move!" –
         they seized the presbyter,
They took him deep into the woods,
There the bandits were noisily carousing,
There a fire blazed in the clearing.

They brought the elder to the ataman.
"Money!" – he barked, laughing. –
"Come on, turn out your pockets,
Share out the offerings with the flock!"

"I haven't a penny. Believe me, brothers!
I pledged myself to poverty long ago."
"Search him!" – they rifled through his
clothes,
They searched: but there really was
nothing.

"And what riches do you have at home?
If you don't tell the truth – it'll be too bad
                 for you!
Don't you really have a single penny
                to your name?"
And he answered them: "Not a penny."

"Very well, we'll believe you this time.
We've already done well today –
                    you're a lucky old man!
We've no use for a chewed up old beast
like you.
But next time – you won't be left alive."

"Brothers! I'll tell you about God!" –
"Get out of here, old man, don't make us
angry! –
They took him back to the road.
– Beat it! Get out of here!"

The old priest returned home,	The old presbyter returned home,
He started to undress for bed,	He started to undress for bed.
When suddenly, something round went rolling,	Suddenly… something round went rolling,
Metal rang faintly as it hit the floor.	Metal rang faintly as it hit the floor.
The priest was frightened: – What was that?	The elder was disturbed: What was that?
Did I really tell a lie?	Did I really tell a lie?
He began to search around and saw a coin,	He began to search around and saw it: a coin.
Yes, a coin – a stray penny!	Yes, a coin – a stray penny!

And the elder wept: "O God!
I have served you without fault,
I served eternal righteousness, and
                    what happened?
I have sinned before You, I have sinned!"

The elder dressed hurriedly,
And went to the killers in the forest,
The night received him in silence,
The gloomy sky hung over him.

Soon he turned into the clearing
And gasping, shouted: – Hey!
Take me to the ataman,
Take me to him right away!

Here they come, the bushes rustled...
– Is that you, old man? Get out of here!
– Take me, it's an important matter.
– Well, get going, but don't expect
              anything good!...

The bandits' shadows flicker,
Singing, dancing, and oceans of wine...
The old priest fell to his knees,
The feast suddenly went quiet, silence...

Opening his arms to the bandits,
The elder sobbed uncontrollably:
– I am guilty before you, brothers,
I lied, I lied to you!

The elder dressed hurriedly,
And went to the killers in the forest,
The night received him in silence,
The gloomy sky hung over him.

And here is the turn to the clearing
Gasping, he shouts: – Hey!
Take me to the ataman,
Take me to him right away!"

Ssh, they're coming! The bushes rustle,
"Is that you, old man? Get out of here!
"Take me, it's an important matter...
"Well, get going, but don't expect
              anything good!"

Here are campfires and the bandits'
shadows,
Singing, dancing and oceans of wine.
The old presbyter fell to his knees,
The feast suddenly went quiet. Silence...

Opening his arms to the bandits,
The elder sobbed uncontrollably:
"I am guilty before you, brothers.
I lied, I lied to you!"

I – a servant of the great God,
A slave of Eternal Truth – I have sinned.
I taught others to choose the straight road
To eternal righteousness.

Unwittingly I sullied myself with a lie,
I hid money from you; here is the penny,
It's only a little, but the truth of God
Isn't destroyed by the coin's worth,
                                    but by the lie!

And now I have sullied myself with a lie,
I hid money from you – here is the penny!
It's only a little, but the truth of God
Isn't destroyed by the coin's worth,
                                    but by the lie!

A lie, no matter whether it seems
Tiny or enormous,
Will rule over the soul
Once it has crept into the heart.

Truth sternly demands truth,
Never cease to tremble
Before even the millionth part of an
offense,
Before every single particle of a lie.

O, forgive me, forgive me for this,
Give peace to my tormented soul!"
All are silent, all gaze at the coin,
As though it were enchanted.

The night passed, it was already morning.
The forest brightened, became clearer
                                    and then,
The grace-filled miracle occurred,
The company bowed before the elder.

The night passed, it was already morning.
The forest cleared; it came to life…
                                    and then
The grace-filled miracle occurred:
The company bowed before the elder.

All the bandits fell sobbing,
– Good pastor, forgive us, forgive!
Holy righteousness has dawned upon us,
Teach us to follow after it!

All the bandits fell sobbing:
"Good pastor, forgive us, forgive!
Holy righteousness has dawned upon us,
Teach us to follow after it!"

The rays of sunrise flamed
And the darkness disappeared forever.
This took place in the olden times…
It can always happen again!

The rays of sunrise flamed
And the darkness disappeared forever.
This took place in the olden times…
It can always happen again!

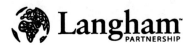

Langham Literature and its imprints are a ministry of Langham Partnership.

Langham Partnership is a global fellowship working in pursuit of the vision God entrusted to its founder John Stott –

to facilitate the growth of the church in maturity and Christ-likeness through raising the standards of biblical preaching and teaching.

Our vision is to see churches equipped for mission and growing to maturity in Christ through the ministry of pastors and leaders who believe, teach and live by the Word of God.

Our mission is to strengthen the ministry of the Word of God through:
- nurturing national movements for training in biblical preaching
- multiplying the creation and distribution of evangelical literature
- strengthening the theological training of pastors and leaders by qualified evangelical teachers

Our ministry

Langham Preaching partners with national leaders to nurture indigenous biblical preaching movements for pastors and lay preachers all around the world. With the support of a team of trainers from many countries, a multi-level programme of seminars provides practical training, and is followed by a programme for training local facilitators. Local preachers' groups and national and regional networks ensure continuity and ongoing development, seeking to build vigorous movements committed to Bible exposition.

Langham Literature provides majority world pastors, scholars and seminary libraries with evangelical books and electronic resources through grants, discounts and distribution. The programme also fosters the creation of indigenous evangelical books for pastors in many languages, through training workshops for writers and editors, sponsored writing, translation, strengthening local evangelical publishing houses, and investment in major regional literature projects, such as one volume Bible commentaries like *The Africa Bible Commentary.*

Langham Scholars provides financial support for evangelical doctoral students from the majority world so that, when they return home, they may train pastors and other Christian leaders with sound, biblical and theological teaching. This programme equips those who equip others. Langham Scholars also works in partnership with majority world seminaries in strengthening evangelical theological education. A growing number of Langham Scholars study in high quality doctoral programmes in the majority world itself. As well as teaching the next generation of pastors, graduated Langham Scholars exercise significant influence through their writing and leadership.

To learn more about Langham Partnership and the work we do visit **langham.org**

Russian Baptists and Orthodoxy,

320030101445329

CPSIA information can be obtained at www.ICGtesting.com
Printed in the USA
LVOW12s0825260214

375238LV00005BA/397/P